Braga

Bragança

NORTHERN PORTUGAL

Vila Real

0 kilometres   50

0 miles   25

**DOURO AND
TRÁS-OS-MONTES**
Pages 234–263

Viseu

Guarda

CENTRAL
PORTUGAL

Coimbra

Castelo
Branco

**ESTREMADURA
AND RIBATEJO**
Pages 172–195

THE BEIRAS
Pages 196–223

Portalegre

Évora

Beja

SOUTHERN
PORTUGAL

Faro

ALENTEJO
Pages 292–315

ALGARVE
Pages 316–333

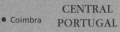

EYEWITNESS TRAVEL
PORTUGAL

EYEWITNESS TRAVEL

PORTUGAL

Main consultant: MARTIN SYMINGTON

LONDON, NEW YORK,
MELBOURNE, MUNICH AND DELHI
www.dk.com

PROJECT EDITOR Ferdie McDonald
ART EDITOR Vanessa Hamilton
EDITORS Caroline Ball, Francesca Machiavelli
DESIGNERS Anthea Forlee, Carolyn Hewitson,
Nicola Rodway, Dutjapun Williams

MAIN CONTRIBUTORS
Susie Boulton, Christopher Catling, Clive Gilbert, Marion Kaplan, Sarah
McAlister, Alice Peebles, Carol Rankin, Norman Renouf,
Joe Staines, Robert Strauss, Nigel Tisdall,
Tomas Tranæus, Edite Vieira

PHOTOGRAPHERS
Joe Cornish, Paul Harris, Robert Reichenfeld,
Linda Whitwam, Peter Wilson, Francesca Yorke

ILLUSTRATORS
Richard Draper, Paul Guest, Stephen Gyapay,
Claire Littlejohn, Maltings Partnership, Isidoro González-Adalid
Cabezas/Acanto Arquitectura y Urbanismo S.L., Paul Weston,
John Woodcock, Martin Woodward

Reproduced by Colourscan (Singapore)
Printed and bound by South China Printing Co. Ltd., China

First American Edition, 1997
10 11 12 13 10 9 8 7 6 5 4 3 2 1

Published in the United States
by DK Publishing, 375 Hudson Street,
New York, New York 10014

**Reprinted with revisions 1999, 2000,
2001, 2002, 2003, 2004, 2006, 2008, 2010**

Copyright © 1997, 2010 Dorling Kindersley Limited, London

ISSN 1542-1554

ISBN 978-0-7566-6160-1

FLOORS ARE REFERRED TO THROUGHOUT IN ACCORDANCE WITH EUROPEAN USAGE,
I.E., THE "FIRST FLOOR" IS ONE FLIGHT UP

*Front cover main image: Bom Jesus do Monte, Staircase of
the Five Senses, Minho*

MIX
From responsible
sources
FSC™C018179

**The information in this
DK Eyewitness Travel Guide is checked regularly.**
Every effort has been made to ensure that this book is as up-to-date
as possible at the time of going to press. Some details, however,
such as telephone numbers, opening hours, prices, gallery hanging
arrangements and travel information, are liable to change. The
publishers cannot accept responsibility for any consequences arising
from the use of this book, nor for any material on third-party
websites, and cannot guarantee that any website address in this
book will be a suitable source of travel information. We value the
views and suggestions of our readers very highly. Please write to:
Publisher, DK Eyewitness Travel Guides,
Dorling Kindersley, 80 Strand, London Great Britain WC2R 0RL.

◁ Palácio da Pena rising above the wooded Parque da Pena, Sintra

CONTENTS

HOW TO USE
THIS GUIDE **6**

Equestrian statue of José I
in Praça do Comércio, Lisbon

INTRODUCING
PORTUGAL

LISBON

Typical blue-trim house near Beja in the Alentejo

Entrance to the chapterhouse at
Alcobaça monastery, Estremadura

17th-century tile decoration
on Palácio Frontelra, Lisbon

The great Gothic
monastery of Batalha

HOW TO USE THIS GUIDE

This guide helps you get the most from a visit to Portugal, providing expert recommendations as well as detailed practical information. The opening chapter *Introducing Portugal* maps the country and sets it in its historical and cultural context. Each of the nine regional chapters, plus *Lisbon*, describe important sights, using maps, pictures and illustrations. Features cover topics ranging from architecture and festivals to beaches and food. Hotel and restaurant recommendations can be found in *Travellers' Needs*. The *Survival Guide* contains practical information on everything from transport to personal safety.

LISBON

Lisbon has been divided into five main sightseeing areas. Each of these areas has its own chapter, which opens with a list of the major sights described. All sights are numbered and plotted on an *Area Map*. Information on the sights is easy to locate as the order in which they appear in the chapter follows the numerical order used on the map.

Sights at a Glance
lists the chapter's sights by category: Churches, Museums and Galleries, Historic Buildings, Parks and Gardens.

1 Area Map
For easy reference, the sights covered in the chapter are numbered and located on a map. The sights are also marked on the Street Finder maps on pages 128–41.

A locator map shows clearly where the area is in relation to other parts of the city.

All the pages relating to Lisbon have red thumb tabs.

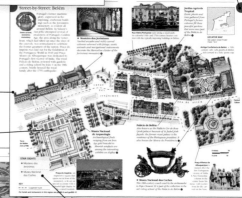

2 Street-by-Street Map
This gives a bird's-eye view of the heart of each of the sightseeing areas.

A suggested route for a walk is shown in red.

Stars indicate the sights that no visitor should miss.

3 Detailed Information
All the sights in Lisbon are described individually. Addresses and practical information are provided. The key to the symbols used in the information block is shown on the back flap.

1 Introduction

A general account of the landscape, history and character of each region is given here, explaining both how the area has developed over the centuries and what attractions it has to offer the visitor today.

PORTUGAL REGION BY REGION

Outside Lisbon, the rest of Portugal has been divided into nine regions, each of which has a separate chapter. The most interesting cities, towns and sights to visit are located and numbered on a *Regional Map*.

2 Regional Map

This shows the main road network and gives an illustrated overview of the region. All entries are numbered and there are also useful tips on getting around the region.

Each area of Portugal can be identified quickly by its colour coding, shown on the inside front cover.

3 Detailed Information

All the important towns and other places to visit are described individually. They are listed in order, following the numbering given on the Regional Map. Within each entry, there is further detailed information on important buildings and other sights.

Story boxes explore specific subjects further.

For all the top sights, a Visitors' Checklist provides the practical information you need to plan your visit.

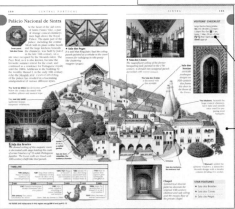

4 The Top Sights

These are given two or more full pages. Historic buildings are dissected to reveal their interiors; museums and galleries have colour-coded floorplans to help you locate the most interesting exhibits.

INTRODUCING
PORTUGAL

DISCOVERING PORTUGAL

Portugal offers a remarkable variety of landscapes and experiences for all visitors. Within a short distance, the scenery can change completely. It is possible to go from high northern pastures to rolling southern plains in a day and visitors will never be more than a

Madeira dahlia flower

couple of hours from sun-soaked shores on the mainland. Madeira and the Azores are subtropical paradise islands for lovers of nature and tranquillity. These pages give a quick taste of each region, with descriptions, highlights and pointers on how to get the most out of a visit.

A view across the tiled roofs of the historic Alfama district

LISBON

- **Historic *bairros***
- **Magnificent Manueline architecture in Belém**
- **Traditional *fado* music**
- **Electric nightlife**

Portugal's capital offers an irresistible combination of ancient and modern sights. Lisbon extends from Belém with its exuberant 16th-century Manueline architecture, including the grand **Mosteiro dos Jerónimos** *(see pp104–5)*, to the 21st-century urban landscape of **Parque das Nações** *(see p119)*. In between, the city extends across a series of hills characterized by different districts. The historic *bairros* of Castelo and Alfama have been peopled since Phoenician times. Traditional *fado* music originated in the back-street cafés here and can still be enjoyed in several venues *(see pp64–5)*. The Bairro Alto district is home to Lisbon's thriving nightlife scene.

THE LISBON COAST

- **Cosmopolitan coast resorts**
- **Fairy-tale Sintra**
- **Ostentatious palace at Mafra**
- **Caparica beaches and Arrábida scenery**

Estoril *(see pp164–5)* and Cascais *(see p164)*, on the coastline to the west of Lisbon, were built as resorts for the wealthy a century ago and are now dynamic suburban centres that retain a relaxed holiday atmosphere. Beyond Cascais, the dramatic rocky coastal landscape of Europe's western-most point climbs to the fairytale woods of the Sintra hills and to the historic town of **Sintra** *(see pp158–63)*, with architectural highlights such as the **Palácio da Pena** *(see pp162–3)*. Further north lies the enormous 18th-century **Palácio da Mafra** *(see p154)*, testament to the ostentation of King João V and containing an exquisite,

rococo-style library. The beach at **Ericeira** *(see p155)* is good for surfing, as are several other beaches along the Sintra coast. The best beaches, though, are on the other side of the Tejo. The Caparica coast is one long beach that stretches from **Costa da Caparica** *(see p165)* to the hills of the **Serra da Arrábida** *(see p169)*, passing some of Portugal's most beautiful coastal scenery as well as some of the most protected beaches on the west coast.

ESTREMADURA AND RIBATEJO

- **Magnificent medieval monasteries**
- **Sweeping Lezíria plain**
- **Enchanting Óbidos**
- **Fine Ribatejan wines**

Estremadura is a rolling landscape of vineyards, wheatfields, woodland, industries and busy small towns. Scattered across this region are some of the

The extravagant façade of the Palácio da Pena, Sintra

country's greatest monuments: the abbey at **Batalha** *(see pp184–5)*; the sumptuous Cistercian church at **Alcobaça** *(see pp180–81)*; and Tomar's **Convento de Cristo** *(see pp188–9)*, a feast of architectural styles. Along the coast, the fishing ports of **Peniche** *(see p176)* and **Nazaré** *(see p182)* are full of character. The 14th-century walled town of **Óbidos** *(see pp176–7)* is incredibly picturesque. Across the Tejo, the Lezíria plain of the Ribatejo region includes some of Europe's most important wetlands for migrating birds. This landscape is well suited to breeding horses, and the town of **Golegã** *(see p192)* hosts a colourful horse fair in November. Portuguese bullfighting has deep roots in Ribatejo; **Vila Franca de Xira** *(see p194)* and **Santarém** *(see p193)* are both good places to catch a bullfight. The wines of both regions are very good, particularly the Ribatejan reds from around Almeirim.

The imposing Convento de Cristo in Tomar, Estremadura

Brightly-painted *moliceiro* boats in Aveiro, Beira Litoral

THE BEIRAS

- **Remote fortified towns**
- **Soaring granite peaks of the Serra da Estrela**
- **Charming Coimbra**

The three Beiras – Litoral, Alta and Baixa – offer a wide variety of rewarding sights and activities. The interior, Beira Baixa, is famous for the historic, now idyllic villages of **Monsanto** *(see*

pp222–3) and **Idanha-a-Velha** *(see p223)*. Remote fortified towns such as **Almeida** *(see p217)* and **Sabugal** *(see p222)* are also worth seeking out. In Beira Alta, the granite peaks of **Serra da Estrela** *(see pp220–21)*, the country's highest mountain range is great walking country and winter snowfall attracts skiers to the slopes. **Coimbra** *(see pp204–9)*, Portugal's third largest city, is full of charm and historic importance. North of Coimbra is the forest reserve of **Buçaco** *(see pp212–13)*. Partly planted by monks, it is now the site of a unique hotel, the **Palace Hotel Bussaco** *(see p391)*, housed in an extravagant palace built for Portugal's second last king. Nearby is the relaxed spa town of **Luso** *(see p211)*. Also in Beira Litoral, the coastal town of **Aveiro** *(see pp202–3)* has an impressive maritime heritage which is most clearly visible in the colourful *moliceiro* boats that sail on its lagoon.

DOURO AND TRÁS-OS-MONTES

- **Scenic Douro valley vineyards**
- **Historic Oporto**
- **Isolated Serra do Barroso**
- **Medieval Bragança**

The Douro valley is famous as the birthplace of port and now deserves recognition for its very distinctive table wines, too. The steep river

valley, particularly in the upper reaches beyond **Peso da Régua** *(see p252)*, has been shaped by the cultivation of the vine, and is an area of breathtaking natural beauty. **Oporto** *(see pp238–49)*, at the mouth of the Douro, is an old city of immense character. Portugal's second city boasts two of the country's foremost cultural institutions: the Serralves Museum of Modern Art and the Casa da Música concert hall. Trás-os-Montes is a remote region of extreme climates, little development, and much untamed beauty. Highlights include the wild, boulder-strewn landscapes of **Serra do Barroso** *(see p258)*, the attractive spa town of **Chaves** *(see p258–9)*, the medieval outpost of the region's capital **Bragança** *(see pp260–61)*, and the serene and spectacular scenery and walks of the **Parque Natural de Montesinho** *(see p262)*.

Vine-clad hills, typical of the Douro valley

MINHO

- **Verdant landscapes**
- **Remarkable Parque Nacional da Peneda-Gerês**
- **Splendid Baroque Bom Jesus do Monte**

The Minho region is Portugal's greenest thanks to high rainfall. The name for the local wine, *vinho verde* (green wine), reflects this. The intensely cultivated and densely populated Minho countryside offers dramatic landscapes. To the east lies the rocky terrain of the Serra do Gerês and the spectacular scenery of the **Parque Nacional da Peneda-Gerês** (*see pp272–3*). **Braga** (*see pp278–9*) is the region's main city. Nearby is the magnificent religious sanctuary of **Bom Jesus do**

Endless lavender fields in the Alentejo region

Monte (*see pp280–81*). On the coast, **Viana do Castelo** (*see pp276–7*) is an elegant 13th-century town. The centre of **Guimarães** (*see pp282–3*) is similarly attractive, and any of the smaller towns along the Cávado, Lima and Minho rivers are worth stopping in.

ALENTEJO

- **Vast, rolling plains**
- **Delicious wine and olives**
- **The elegant, ancient city of Évora**

This is Portugal's biggest region, taking up most of

The Minho's spectacular religious sanctuary of Bom Jesus do Monte

the country south of Lisbon save for the strip of southern coastline that is the Algarve. It is also among the least densely populated, making it a region of wide open spaces. The idyllic landscape of olive groves, cork trees and wheatfields create an impression of unlimited space. The region also produces some of the country's best red wines as well as a surprising number of excellent whites which are usually very good value. Vineyards are located around **Vidigueira** (*see p312*). This tranquil landscape is irregularly dotted with picturesque medieval towns on hilltops, often clustered around a castle, such as at **Marvão** (*see p296*) and **Monsaraz** (*see p309*). The capital, **Évora** (*see pp304–7*), is a captivating walled city. The northern towns of **Portalegre** (*see pp296–7*), **Castelo de Vide** (*see pp297*), **Elvas** (*see pp298–9*), **Estremoz** (*see pp302–3*) and **Vila Viçosa** (*see pp300–301*) are also well worth a visit. Southern Alentejo is flatter and hotter than the north, but the eastern towns of **Moura** (*see p312*), **Serpa** (*see p312*) and **Mértola** (*see p315*), along the Guadiana river, offer plenty of interest. On the west side is the attractive Alentejo coastline, whose rougher seas and cooler temperatures have prevented it from developing to the extent of the Algarve. This is popular surfing territory, with small cove beaches surrounded by cliffs.

ALGARVE

- **Gorgeous beaches**
- **Luxury resorts**
- **World-class golf courses**
- **Picturesque port towns**
- **Unspoilt interior**

The Algarve is perfect for holidaymakers, with a coastline of stunning beaches and temperate seas, ample sunshine throughout the year, and a gently hilly hinterland perfect for golf courses (*see pp442–3*). Although these ideal conditions have been over-exploited in some areas, and get overcrowded at some points during the year, there are still many places along this leisure coast that are not dominated by resorts. The short west coast, from Odeceixe to **Cabo de São Vicente** (*see p321*), is wilder and less accessible than the south

A stretch of golden beach in the Algarve

coast. The south coastline has beautiful beaches at **Lagos** (*see pp322–3*), **Portimão** (*see p324*) and **Albufeira** (*see p325*). These areas are also where much of the best golf is to be found. **Faro** (*see pp328–30*), the capital, is a pleasant town and its old citadel and pedestrianized shopping streets are well worth exploring. The coastline to the east of Faro is characterised by the wide lagoon and marshes of the **Parque Natural da Ria Formosa** (*see p331*), which extend to the picturesque hamlet of **Cacela Velha** (*see p332*). The beaches beyond this protected area are long, narrow sand dunes with limited construction. **Tavira** (*see p332*), the main town in this area, is one of the most attractive in the region. The charming and secluded towns of **Monchique** (*see pp320–21*), **Silves** (*see pp324–5*) or **Loulé** (*see pp326–7*) prove that much of the interior of the Algarve retains a peaceful atmosphere and is largely unaffected and unaltered by tourism.

MADEIRA

- **Breathtaking landscapes**
- **Sophisticated Funchal**
- *Levada* **walks**
- **Porto Santo's golden beach**

Verdant Madeira's deeply-cleft valleys, dramatic cliffs, canyons and rust-coloured volcanic peaks are simply awe-inspiring. The island's dense vegetation seems almost miraculous when compared to the nearby dry and barren islands in this small archipelago off the west coast of Africa. Famous for the variety and vibrancy of its flora and the beauty of its gardens, Madeira's reputation as paradise is well deserved. **Funchal** (*see pp346–9*) is a busy and pretty city whose oldest parts have been untouched by tourism. Visitors with an urge for nature should rent a car,

A view of southern Madeira's dramatic cliffs

catch a bus, or simply discover the area's natural beauty on foot. Beyond Funchal and the southeast coast, Madeira is rural. The extensive network of *levadas*, or irrigation channels, allows walkers easy access to every part of the island. Among the most striking landscapes are those around the jagged central peaks and ravines of **Pico Ruivo** (*see p356*) and **Pico do Arieiro** (*see p353*). Here, it is possible to study the astonishing rock formations left over from the violent volcanic unheavals that led to the creation of the island. The high plateau of **Paúl da Serra** (*see p356*) and the sheer cliffs of the north coast that plunge into the sea with waterfalls that cascade for hundreds of feet are also magnificent. The long stretch of unspoilt golden sand on the neighbouring island of **Porto Santo** (*see p359*) attracts sunlovers.

THE AZORES

- **Volcanic lakes and springs**
- **Whale-watching**
- **Wild coastal scenery**

A vast archipelago of nine islands in the mid-Atlantic, the Azores remain relatively undeveloped for tourism, particularly on the small and far-flung islands of **Flores** (*see p373*) and **Corvo** (*see p373*). The climate is similar to that on Madeira, albeit slightly wetter and cooler. This makes for misty peaks and green expanses, criss-crossed by thick hedges of hydrangea. The central group of islands – **Faial** (*see p372*), **Pico** (*see pp370–71*), **São Jorge** (*see p369*), **Terceira** (*see pp366–7*) and **Graciosa** (*see p369*) – is perhaps the most rewarding for visitors who are seeking to immerse themselves in nature. Pico is a centre for whale-watching, while Faial is a popular port of call for sailing boats crossing the Atlantic. São Jorge is famous for a cheddar-like cheese made from the milk of cows who graze its lush pastures. **São Miguel** (*see pp364–5*), the archipelago's main island, is also the biggest, most developed and most varied. It is famous for its *lagoas*, volcanic crater lakes that offer spectacular scenery. **Santa Maria** (*see p366*), the other island in the eastern group, has a slightly warmer climate than the others as well as sandy beaches.

The turquoise waters of a crater lake on the Azores island of São Miguel

Putting Portugal on the Map

Situated in the extreme southwest corner of Europe, Portugal occupies roughly one-sixth of the Iberian Peninsula with a population of just over 10 million. To the north and east, a border measuring approximately 1,300 km (800 miles) separates Portugal from its only neighbouring country, Spain, and to the south and west, 830 km (500 miles) of coastline meets the Atlantic Ocean. The Atlantic archipelagos of Madeira and the Azores are included in Portugal's territory.

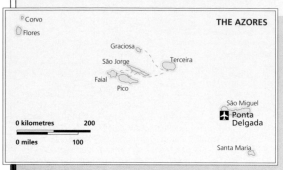

The Azores

The Azores lie 1,300 km (800 miles) to the west of Lisbon in the Atlantic Ocean. Of volcanic origin, the islands are scattered over a distance of 650 km (400 miles).

Madeira

Lying 965 km (600 miles) southwest of Lisbon in the Atlantic Ocean, the Madeiran archipelago has two inhabited islands, Madeira and Porto Santo.

KEY

✈	International airport
🚢	Ferry port
▬	Motorway
▬	Major road
▬	Minor road
—	Main railway line
–•–	International boundary

ATLANTIC

OCEAN

0 kilometres   100

0 miles   50

EUROPE

NORWAY
SWEDEN
ESTONIA
LATVIA
LITHUANIA
DENMARK
POLAND
UNITED
KINGDOM
GERMANY
REPUBLIC
OF
IRELAND
NETHERLANDS
CZECH
REPUBLIC
SLOVAKIA
BELGIUM
LUXEMBOURG
AUSTRIA
HUNGARY
SWITZERLAND
SLOVENIA
FRANCE
ITALY
PORTUGAL
SPAIN
Lisbon
TUNISIA
Azores
ALGERIA
LIBYA
MOROCCO
Madeira

SPAIN

GREATER LISBON

Odivelas
Sacavém
N119
A9 (CREL)
IC17 (CRIL)
A1 – IP1 (E1)
Queluz
Amadora
A12 – IP1
IC3
A5
N6
LISBON
Belém
Tejo
Montijo
Cacilhas
Almada
Barreiro
Trafaria
Moita
Costa de
Caparica
Seixal
N11
A2 – IP7 (E1)
N10
IC21
Coina

0 kilometres		10
0 miles		5

Greater Lisbon
The capital of Portugal is a hilly city on the Tagus estuary. The country's main port and business centre, Greater Lisbon has a population of around two million.

N120
Sil
A6
Chaves
Bragança
N122 (E82)
IP4 (E82)
Duero
N2
la Real
A52
N102 (E802)
N620 (E80)
Guarda
Alagón
Tormes
N110
N405
MADRID
NIV (E5)
NII (E90)
NV (E90)
NIII (E901)
N401
A23
SPAIN
UGAL
Castelo
Branco
Plasencia
N630 (E803)
Tajo
Portalegre
N521
Cáceres
N521
N430
Mérida
Guadiana
A6 (E90)
Badajoz
N4
NV (E90)
N256
EX112
Ardila
N432
N630 (E803)
Guadiana
N260
N423
N433
A49 (E1)
Sevilla
Genil
Huelva
A92
A92
A92
Granada
N323 (E902)
A359
Jerez de
la Frontera
A4 (E5)
N331
N340 (E15)
Málaga

A PORTRAIT OF PORTUGAL

ost visitors to Portugal head for the sandy coves, rocky coastline and manicured golf links of the Algarve. But beyond the south coast resorts lies the least explored corner of Western Europe: a country of rugged landscapes, sophisticated cities, rural backwaters and sharply contrasting traditions.

Portugal appears to have no obvious geographical claim to nationhood, yet this western extremity of the Iberian Peninsula has existed within borders virtually unchanged for nearly 800 years. Its ten million people speak their own language, follow their own unique cultural traditions, and have a centuries-old history of proud independence from, and distrust of neighbouring Spain.

Horseman at festival in Vila Franca de Xira, Ribatejo

For a small country, the regions of Portugal are immensely varied. The rural Minho and Trás-os-Montes in the north are the most traditional – some would say backward. Over the last few decades many inhabitants of these neglected regions have been forced to emigrate in search of work.

The south of the country could not be more different. The Algarve, blessed with beautiful sandy beaches and a wonderful, warm Mediterranean climate all year round, has been transformed into a holiday playground for North Europeans.

Two great rivers, the Tagus and the Douro, rise in Spain and then flow westwards across Portugal to the Atlantic Ocean. From the wild upper reaches of the Douro valley, comes Portugal's most famous product – port wine, from steeply terraced vineyards hewn out of the mountainsides. The Tagus, by contrast, is wide and languid, often spilling out over the flat, fertile, Ribatejo flood plain where fine horses and fighting bulls graze.

Crowded beach at high season at Albufeira in the Algarve

◁ Traditional agriculture on smallholdings near Ponte de Lima in the Minho

Rolling grassland of the Alentejo with village and medieval castle of Terena

At the mouths of the Tagus and Douro stand Portugal's two major cities, Lisbon and Oporto respectively. Lisbon, the capital, is a cosmopolitan metropolis with a rich cultural life and many national museums and art galleries. Oporto is a serious rival to Lisbon, especially in terms of commerce and industry. Most centres of population, however, are very much smaller: from the fishing communities on the Atlantic coast to the tiny medieval villages in the vast sun-baked plains of the Alentejo and the mountainous interior of the Beiras.

Woman stripping osiers for wickerwork in Madeira

Far out in the Atlantic Ocean lie two remote archipelagos that are self-governing regions of the Portuguese state: warm, luxuriant Madeira off the coast of Morocco, and the nine rainy, green, volcano tips that make up the Azores, about one third of the way across the Atlantic between Lisbon and New York.

POLITICS AND ECONOMICS

In the final quarter of the 20th century, a new era of Portuguese history began. From the late 1920s, under the long dictatorship of António Salazar, the country was a virtual recluse in the world community. The principal concern of foreign policy was the ultimately futile defence of Portugal's African and Asian colonies. Domestic industry and commerce were dominated by a few wealthy families, in an economic framework of extreme fiscal tightness.

The Carnation Revolution of 1974 brought this era to an end. At first the re-establishment of democracy was a painful process, but since the 1980s Portugal has assumed an increasingly confident Western European demeanour. Entry into the European Community in 1986 was welcomed at all levels of society, and led to an explosion of new construction,

Barredo quarter of Oporto, Portugal's second city

the like of which Portugal had never seen. Traditional exports, such as cork, resin, textiles, tinned sardines and wine, have been joined by new, heavier industries such as vehicle construction and cement manufacturing.

Grants and loans from the EU have funded the building of new roads, bridges and hospitals, and brought significant improvements in agriculture. Oporto was the European Capital of Culture in 2001 and in July 2002 the euro became Portugal's currency.

Luxury yachts in the harbour at Vilamoura in the Algarve

THE PORTUGUESE WAY OF LIFE

A mild-mannered and easy-going people, the Portuguese have an innate sense of politeness, a quality they also respect in others. They tend to use formal modes of address, calling new acquaintances by their Christian names, prefixed by Senhor, Senhora or Dona. In spite of this, they are gregarious folk, often to be seen eating, drinking and making merry in large groups – at a *festa*,

Collecting seaweed for fertilizer in the Ria de Aveiro lagoon

or in a restaurant celebrating a birthday or a first communion. Except for the older sectors of the population, most Portuguese have some knowledge of English and will be eager to speak it. There is a special weakness for children who are cherished, indulged and welcomed everywhere. Visitors who bring their youngsters with them will discover an immediate point of contact with their hosts. Nevertheless, behind the smiles and the good humour, there is a deep-rooted aspect of the national psyche which the Portuguese themselves call

View from the mountaintop village of Monsanto near the border with Spain

Farmworkers breaking for a picnic lunch in the fields of the Alentejo

The family is the bosom of Portuguese daily life. Although old customs are gradually changing, especially in the cities, it is quite common for three generations to live under one roof, and it is normal for both men and women to stay living in the family home until they marry. One thing that has changed dramatically is family size. A generation ago, families of ten or more children were commonplace – especially in remote, rural areas. Nowadays, one or two children constitute an average-sized family, often looked after by a grandmother while both parents go out to work.

saudade, a sort of ethereal, aching melancholy that seems to yearn for something lost or unattainable.

In so far as these generalizations hold true, so too do a couple of Portuguese characteristics which can prove irritating. The first is a relaxed attitude to time: no visitor should interpret lack of punctuality as a personal slight. The second is the fact that many Portuguese men tend to discard their native courtesy completely when they are behind the wheel of a car. Reckless driving, particularly high-speed tailgating, is a national pastime.

Catholicism is at the heart of Portuguese life, especially in the north, where you will see a crucifix or the image of a saint watching over most homes, cafés and

Tiled housefront in Alcochete, a small town on the Tagus estuary

barbers' shops. Weddings and first communion services are deeply religious occasions. Although church attendance is in decline, particularly in the cities, national devotion to Our Lady of Fátima remains steadfast, as does delight in festivals *(romarias)* honouring local saints, another tradition that is strongest in the north.

LANGUAGE AND CULTURE

There are few faux pas more injurious to national esteem, than to suggest that Portuguese is a mere dialect of Spanish. Great pride is taken in the language and literature. *Os Lusìadas*, the national epic by 16th-century poet Camões, is studied reverentially, while many Portuguese also delight in the

Town gate of Óbidos with shrine of Nossa Senhora da Piedade, lined with 18th-century tiles

Religious procession in the village of Vidigueira in the Algarve

detached, ironic portrait of themselves in the 19th-century novels of Eça de Queirós. Pride too, is taken in *fado*, the native musical tradition which expresses the notion of *saudade*. In rural areas, especially the Minho, there is still an enthusiastic following for folk dancing.

There are several excellent newspapers, but the country's best-selling daily is *A Bola*, which is devoted exclusively to sport, football being a national obsession. Bullfighting too has its adherents, although with nothing like the passion found in Spain.

Transport in the remote Beira Alta

The Portuguese have long been avid watchers of television and are now producing many home-grown soap operas, films and documentaries. Up until just a few years ago, virtually all of these were imported from abroad.

The country has become more forward-looking in recent years, but most aspects of heritage hark back to the Discoveries. The best-loved monuments are those built in the one uniquely Portuguese style of architecture, the Manueline, which dates from this period. Many *azulejo* tile paintings, another cherished tradition, also glory in Portugal's great maritime past.

When the Portuguese joined the European Community in 1986, Commission President Jacques Delors solemnly warned them that they should think of themselves as "Portuguese first, and European second". Typically, the Portuguese were too polite to laugh out loud. How could anyone have imagined that this little country was in danger of suddenly throwing overboard centuries of culture nurtured in staunch independence?

Open-air café in Praça da Figueira in Lisbon's Baixa

Vernacular Architecture

Traditionally, Portugal's rural architecture varied with climatic conditions and locally available building materials. Although lightweight bricks are now ubiquitous, many older houses still stand. There are the thick-walled granite houses of the north designed to keep out the cold and rain. The Beiras' milder climate means their houses are made of brick or limestone. In the Alentejo and the Ribatejo, the clay houses are long and low, to suit hot summers and chilly winters. The Algarve's gentler Mediterranean climate has led to houses of clay or stone.

Window in Marvão *(see p296)*

Yellow-trimmed houses below walls of Óbidos *(see pp176–7)*

Chimneys are small or nonexistent. Instead, smoke escapes through openings in the roof.

Roofs are constructed of slate or schist tiles, or occasionally thatch.

Village houses *in the Minho (see p265) and Trás-os-Montes regions (see p235) are twostoreyed and usually built with the staircase on the outside. The veranda is used for extra living space.*

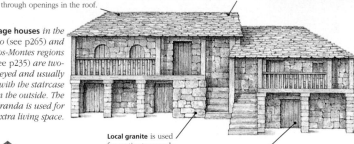

Local granite is used for rustic stonework.

The ground floor is used to keep animals and for storage.

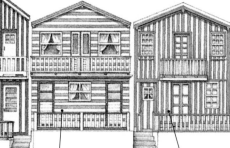

Fishermen's houses *found in the Costa Nova region south of Aveiro (see p203) are painted in brightly coloured stripes. Forests planted to prevent the sand dunes from encroaching on the land provide the raw material.*

Raised platforms guard against flooding.

Modern examples use tiles or painted façades to continue the tradition of striped houses.

Different coloured stripes painted onto the wood allowed the fishermen to identify their houses through the region's frequent mists.

Rooftops of Castelo de Vide in the Alentejo *(see p297)*

TILED ROOFS

Throughout Portugal, red clay roof tiles give towns and villages a memorable skyline. The most traditional and widely used type of roof tile is the *telha de canudo* or tubular tile. Originating from the Moors, these half-cylindrical tiles are placed in two layers: the first is placed with the concave side facing up and the second with the concave side facing down, covering the joints of the first.

Telhados de quatro águas, the distinctive tiled roofs found in Tavira, the Algarve *(see p332)*

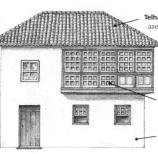

Telhas de canudo are used to cover the roof.

Verandas are glassed in and so can be used all year round.

Limestone used for the walls is usually stuccoed and whitewashed.

Houses in the Beiras (see pp196–223) *often have verandas, usually on the first floor. These are built to face the sun, at the same time affording protection from the cold north winds.*

Thatched houses *in the Sado Estuary (see p167) are now rare. Surviving examples have walls that consist of a wooden frame supporting woven sections made of straw and reed. The simple houses use only local materials.*

Wooden beams

PORTUGAL'S WINDMILLS

Windmills are thought to have existed in Portugal since the 11th century. Many pristine examples still dot the hillsides, particularly in coastal regions.

Most windmills *have a cylindrical brick or stone base. The upper section revolves to catch the wind in its canvas sails. Estremadura (see pp172–95) has good examples.*

Azorean windmills, *such as this example on Faial (see p372), are fairly similar to the Portuguese model, but show the clear influence of early Dutch and Flemish settlers in their sail design.*

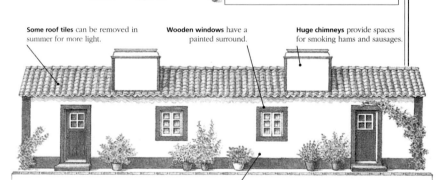

Some roof tiles can be removed in summer for more light.

Wooden windows have a painted surround.

Huge chimneys provide spaces for smoking hams and sausages.

Colour-trimmed houses *of the Alentejo and Ribatejo regions are mainly constructed of clay. Long and oblong in shape, they have few openings, to ensure that the heat is trapped in winter and kept out in summer.*

Whitewashing protects the walls, deflects the hot summer sun and acts as a deterrent for pests and vermin. Many householders consider it a point of honour ro renew their whitewash each year.

CHIMNEYS OF THE ALGARVE

These are an important decorative feature of houses in the Algarve (see pp316–33). The Moorish influence can be seen in their cylindrical or prismatic shapes and the geometric designs perforating the clay. The chimneys are whitewashed and many have details picked out in colour to accentuate their ornamentation.

Manueline Architecture

The style of architecture that flourished in the reign of Manuel I *(see pp 46–9)* and continued after his death is essentially a Portuguese variant of Late Gothic. It is typified by maritime motifs inspired by Portugal's Age of Discovery, and by elaborate "all-over" decoration. The artists behind it include João de Castilho and Diogo Boitac, renowned for the cloister of the Mosteiro dos Jerónimos *(see pp104–5)*, and Francisco and Diogo de Arruda, designers of the Torre de Belém *(see p108)*.

Twisted Manueline pillory in Chaves *(see pp258–9)*

The portal *of the church of Conceição Velha in Lisbon* (see p85) *was commissioned by Manuel in the early 16th century. The king himself appears in the carved relief in the tympanum.*

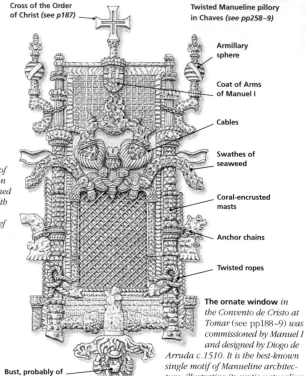

Cross of the Order of Christ *(see p187)*

Armillary sphere

Coat of Arms of Manuel I

Cables

Swathes of seaweed

Coral-encrusted masts

Anchor chains

Twisted ropes

Bust, probably of the designer Diogo de Arruda

The ornate window *in the Convento de Cristo at Tomar* (see pp188–9) *was commissioned by Manuel I and designed by Diogo de Arruda c.1510. It is the best-known single motif of Manueline architecture, illustrating its exotic naturalism and complex use of maritime detail.*

Gil Vicente *created the Belém Monstrance (1506) from the first gold brought back from India. Made for Santa Maria de Belém (see p105), its superstructure echoes the south portal.*

DECORATIVE DETAILS

The most important motifs in Manueline architecture are the armillary sphere, the Cross of the Order of Christ and twisted rope. Naturalistic and fantastic forms are often used, as well as flatter, finely crafted designs similar to those found on contemporary Spanish silverware. Later Manueline schemes sometimes incorporate Italian Renaissance ornamentation.

The armillary sphere was a navigational device that became the emblem of Manuel I himself.

The Cross of the Order of Christ was the emblem of a military order that helped to finance early voyages. It also emblazoned sails and flags.

REBUILDING THE MANUELINE PORTAL OF MADRE DE DEUS

Portal of Madre de Deus church today

The Manueline portal of the church of Madre de Deus in Lisbon *(see p121)* was destroyed in the 1755 earthquake, but it was not until 1872 that João Maria Nepomuceno was commissioned to rebuild it. For accuracy, he referred to an early 16th-century painting by an unknown artist, *The Arrival of the Relics of Santa Auta at the Church of Madre de Deus*, now in the Museu Nacional de Arte Antiga *(see pp94–7)*. The splendid procession in the picture is shown heading towards the Manueline portal of the church, which is clearly depicted. Like others of that period, it stands proud of the building and dominates the façade. The Manueline style favoured rounded rather than pointed arches and this one has an interesting trefoil shape.

The painting of *The Arrival of the Relics* showing the original 16th-century portal

---

Curving branches and crinkled exotic foliage recall Indian sculptural motifs.

Cross of the Order of Christ

In the Royal Cloister of Batalha (see pp184–5), *early 15th-century pointed Gothic arches incorporate exquisite Manueline screens on colonnettes, probably by Diogo Boitac, whose two designs alternate.*

Soft limestone allowed complex patterns to be carved in the tracery.

Armillary sphere

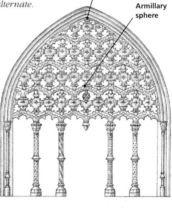

The colonnettes have all-over ornamentation, with repeated patterns of pearls, shells and coil motifs.

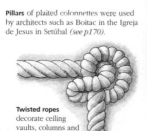

Pillars of plaited colonnettes were used by architects such as Boitac in the Igreja de Jesus in Setúbal *(see p170)*.

Twisted ropes decorate ceiling vaults, columns and arches, and girdle entire buildings inside and out.

The Palace Hotel do Bussaco, *today a luxury hotel (see p212), was originally built as a royal hunting lodge about the end of the 19th century. An extraordinary building, the palace incorporates every conceivable element of Manueline architecture and decoration, illustrating the persistence of the style in Portuguese design, which continues to this day.*

Azulejos – Painted Ceramic Tiles

The idea of covering walls, floors and even ceilings
with tiles was introduced to Spain and Portugal by
the Moors. From the 16th century onwards, Portugal
started producing its own decorative tiles. By the 18th
century, no other European country was producing as
many tiles, for such a variety of purposes and in so
many different designs; the blue and white tiles of the
Baroque era are considered by many to be the finest.
Azulejos became and still remain a very important addition to the interior and
exterior architecture of
Portuguese buildings.

**1716 *Detail from Panel of
Christ Teaching in the Temple***
Around 1690 blue and white story-
telling tiles began to be produced.
These figures are from a typical
scheme by António de Oliveira
Bernardes (c.1660–1732),
the greatest master of the
genre. The central panels
are surrounded by a com-
plex architectural border
*(Igreja Da Misericórdia,
Évora, see p305).*

c.1520 *Frieze of Spanish-made Tiles*
These Moorish-style tiles were produced
by compartmental techniques using
raised and depressed areas to prevent the
tin-glaze colours from running *(Palácio
Nacional de Sintra, see pp160–61).*

c.1680 Hunting Cat
Naturalistic panels of
this period were often
naively drawn, but used
a wide range of colours
*(Museu Nacional do
Azulejo, see pp120–21).*

1500	1600	1700
RENAISSANCE	MANNERIST	BAROQUE
1500	1600	1700

c.1650 *Carpet Tiles*
So-called because
they imitated the
patterns of Moorish
rugs, these were
produced mainly in
blue, yellow and
white. They often
covered whole walls
*(Museu Nacional do
Azulejo, see pp120–21).*

1565 *Susannah and the Elders*
The mid-16th century saw the introduction
of the maiolica technique. This allowed
artists to paint directly onto prepared flat
tiles using several colours, as these did
not run in the firing process. This panel
of a biblical episode is one of the earliest
produced in Portugal. The decorative
details are typical of the Renaissance
(Quinta da Bacalhoa, see p169).

1736 *Capela de São Filipe*
The small chapel inside Setúbal's castle is
a fine example of a complete decorative
scheme using blue and white tiles. The
panels, illustrating the life of St Philip,
are signed by Policarpo de Oliveira
Bernardes, son of the great António
(Castelo de São Filipe, see p170).

c.1670 *Tiled Altar Frontal*
The exuberant scheme incorporates
Hindu motifs and other exotic themes
inspired by the printed calicoes and
chintzes brought back from India *(Museu
Nacional do Azulejo, see pp120–21).*

1865 Viúva Lamego Tile Factory, Lisbon
For the first half of the 19th century, relatively few tiles were produced The fashion then returned for covering whole surfaces with tiles, and simple stylized designs were used to decorate shop fronts and residential areas. This naive, chinoiserie figure is part of a scheme dating from 1865 that covers the entire façade of the factory.

c.1770–84 Corredor das Mangas
The Rococo period saw the reintroduction of polychromatic azulejos. This antechamber in the royal palace at Queluz has tiled panels showing hunting scenes, the seasons and the continents *(Palácio de Queluz, see pp166–7)*.

c.1970 Tile Pattern
The original design for this strikingly modern scheme by architect Raúl Lino dates from about 1910. Many of Portugal's leading modern artists have worked with *azulejos (Museu Nacional do Azulejo, see pp120–21).*

1927 Battle of Ourique
The early years of the 20th century saw a revival of large-scale historical scenes in traditional blue and white. This panel is by Jorge Colaço *(Carlos Lopes Pavilion, Parque Eduardo VII, Lisbon, see p113).*

1800	1900	
NEO-CLASSICAL	**ART NOUVEAU**	**MODERN**
1800	1900	

c.1800 The Story of António Joaquim Carneiro, Hatmaker
Delicate Neo-Classical ornamentation surrounds the blue and white central subject matter in this charming tale of a shepherd boy who makes his fortune as a hatmaker in the big city. Sophisticated designs of this kind disappeared during the upheavals of the Peninsular War (see p54) at the beginning of the 19th century *(Museu Nacional do Azulejo, see pp120–21).*

c.1770 Gatekeeper
"Cut out" figures like this musketeer are an amusing feature of tile schemes in many palaces and mansions from the 18th century onwards. They stand guard at the entrance, on landings or on staircases *(Museu Nacional do Azulejo, see pp120–21).*

TILES IN DOMESTIC ARCHITECTURE

Art Nouveau friezes and decorations in deep colours enliven the façade of this early 20th-century house in Aveiro. To this day, tiles are used to cover façades of houses. They are relatively cheap to produce, long-lasting and need little maintenance. Tiled houses brighten up many Portuguese towns and villages. The town of Ovar *(see pp200–201)* is particularly striking.

Vila Africana, Aveiro (see p202)

The Wines of Portugal

Although still overshadowed by the excellence and fame of port, Portuguese table wine deserves to be taken seriously. After years of investment in the industry, many of the reds, such as the full-bodied wines from the Douro (made with some of the same grapes as port), have established an attractive style all their own. Great whites are fewer, but most regions have some. And of course there is *vinho verde*, the usually white, light, slightly carbonated wine from the north.

Sparkling rosés, *such as Mateus and Lancers, have been Portugal's great export success. But the country now has many excellent wines that reach beyond the easy-drinking charms of these.*

WINE REGIONS

Many of Portugal's wine regions maintain their individual style by specializing in particular Portuguese grape varieties. The introduction of modern wine-making techniques has improved overall quality, and as yet the increasing use of imported grape varieties seems no threat to Portuguese individuality.

OPORTO

LISBON

KEY

- ☐ Vinhos Verdes
- ☐ Douro
- ☐ Dão
- ☐ Bairrada
- ☐ Estremadura
- ☐ Ribatejo
- ☐ Setúbal
- ☐ Alentejo

```
0 kilometres      50
0 miles       25
```

***Vinho verde* vineyards in the village of Lapela, near Monção in the Minho**

Cellar of the Palace Hotel do Bussaco, *(see p212),* famous for its red wine

HOW TO READ A WINE LABEL

Tinto is red, *branco* is white, *seco* is dry and *doce* is sweet. Other essential information is the name of the producer, the region and the year. Wines made to at least 80 per cent from a single grape variety may give the name of that grape on the label. *Denominação de Origem Controlada* (DOC) indicates that the wine has been made according to the strictest regulations of a given region, but, as elsewhere, this need not mean higher quality than the nominally simpler *Vinho Regional* appellation. The back label often describes grape varieties and wine-making techniques used.

This wine is from the Douro and is made according to DOC regulations for the region.

The name of this wine means "banks of the River Tua", further specifying its geographical origin.

Reserva **means** that the wine has been aged, probably in oak casks. It also implies that the wine is of higher quality than non-reserva wine from the same producer.

The Sociedade Agricola e Comercial dos Vinhos Vale da Corça, Lda, produced and bottled this wine.

Vinho verde, *"green wine"* *from the Minho region, can be either red or white, but the fizzy, dry reds are generally consumed locally. Typical white* vinho verde *is bone dry, slightly fizzy, low in alcohol and high in acidity. A weightier style of white* vinho verde *is made from the Alvarinho grape, near the Spanish border. Among the best brands are Soalheiro and Palácio da Brejoeira.*

Bairrada *is a region where the small and thick-skinned Baga grape dominates. It makes big, tannic wines, sometimes with smoky or pine-needle overtones and like the older Dão wines, they need time to soften. Modern winemaking and occasional disregard for regional regulations have meant more approachable reds (often classified as Vinho Regional das Beiras) and crisper whites. Quality producers include Luís Pato and Caves Aliança.*

Ribatejo *is the fertile valley of the Tagus to the north and east of Lisbon. After Estremadura, it is Portugal's biggest wine region measured by volume, but its potential for quality wines has only just begun to be realized. As in Estremadura, Vinho Regional bottlings are frequently better than DOC ones. Producers to look for include Quinta da Alorna, Casa Branco and Fiuza and Bright.*

The Douro *region is best known as the source of port wine, but in most years about half of the wine produced is fermented dry to make table wine, and these wines are now at the forefront of Portuguese wine-making. The pioneer, Barca Velha, was launched half a century ago and is both highly regarded and among the most expensive. Other quality producers include Calheiros Cruz, Domingos Alves de Sousa, Quinta do Crasto, Niepoort and Ramos-Pinto.*

Picking grapes for vinho verde

Setúbal, *to the south of Lisbon, is best known for its sweet, fortified Muscat wine, Moscatel de Setúbal. In addition, the region also produces excellent, mostly red, table wine. Two big quality producers dominate the region: José Maria da Fonseca (see p169) and J.P. Vinhos. The co-operative at Santo Isidro de Pegões makes good-value wines, while interesting smaller producers include Venâncio Costa Lima, Hero do Castanheiro and Ermelinda Freitas.*

The Dão region *now offers some of Portugal's best wines. Small producers, such as Quinta dos Roques, Quinta da Pellada and Quinta de Cabriz, and the large Sogrape company make fruity reds for younger drinking, fresh, dry whites and deeper, richer reds which retain their fruit with age – a far cry from the heavy, hard-edged, and often oxidized wines of the past.*

Estremadura *is Portugal's westernmost wine area and has only recently emerged as a region in its own right. Several producers now make modern Vinho Regional wines with character, look for wines by DFJ, Casa Santos Lima, Quinta de Pancas and Quinta do Monte d'Oiro. The most interesting DOC is Alenquer. Bucelas, to the south of the region, produces characterful white wines.*

Alentejo *produced wine has possibly made the biggest leap in quality in the last decade. Long dismissed by experts as a region of easy-drinking house reds for restaurants, this area now produces some of Portugal's most serious red wines and a surprising number of excellent whites. Among the best producers are Herdade do Esporão, Herdade dos Coelheiros, Cortes de Cima and João Portugal Ramos.*

PORTUGAL THROUGH THE YEAR

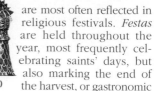

Monção's Festa da Coca (June)

While July and August are the most popular months for visiting, spring and autumn can be more rewarding if you want to tour and experience local culture. Free of excessive heat and crowds, the country is more relaxed. There is deep-rooted respect throughout the country for ancient traditions, which are most often reflected in religious festivals. *Festas* are held throughout the year, most frequently celebrating saints' days, but also marking the end of the harvest, or gastronomic and even sporting events. *Festas* call for prayers, processions, fireworks, eating and drinking, traditional folk dances and general merrymaking.

SPRING

From the Algarve to Trás-os-Montes, the country erupts in wild flowers as warmer days set in. This is the time to see the countryside at its most beautiful, although rain can be expected until the end of May.

Easter is a time of great religious celebration, with Holy Week processions taking place all over the country.

Fátima on 13 May, when 100,000 pilgrims gather every year

MARCH

Madeira Islands Golf Open *(Mar)*. Venue changes from year to year.
International Chocolate Festival *(Mar)*, Óbidos. This popular event attracts people from all over the world.

Funchal Flower Festival (April)

APRIL

Holy Week *(week before Easter)*, Braga. Events in the country's religious capital are particularly traditional and solemn. Torchlit processions are led by church authorities.

Easter Sunday is also the beginning of the bullfighting season throughout Portugal.
Mãe Soberana *(second Sun after Easter)*, Loulé, Algarve. Pilgrimage to Nossa Senhora da Piedade *(see p326)*.
FIAPE *(end Apr)* Estremoz. An international agricultural, cattle and handicrafts fair.
Algarve Music Festival *(Apr–May)*, throughout the region. Concerts and performances by the Gulbenkian Ballet.
Flower Festival *(late Apr)*, Funchal, Madeira. Shops and houses are decorated with flowers. Ends with a parade of flower-covered floats.

MAY

Festas das Cruzes *(early May)*, Barcelos. The Festival of the Crosses celebrates the day the shape of a cross appeared in the earth in 1504.
Pilgrimage to Fátima *(12–13 May)*. Huge crowds make the pilgrimage to the place where the Virgin appeared to three children in 1917 *(see p186)*.

Queima das Fitas *(mid-May)*, Coimbra. Lively celebrations mark end of the university's academic year *(see p209)*.
Festa do Senhor Santo Cristo dos Milagres *(fifth Sun after Easter)*, Ponta Delgada, São Miguel, Azores. The largest religious festival in the Azores.
Festa do Espírito Santo *(Pentecost)*, Azores. High point of the festival of the Holy Spirit *(see p367)*.
Pilgrimage to Bom Jesus *(Pentecost)*, Braga. Penitents climb the spectacular staircase on their knees *(see pp278–9)*.

Children carrying a cross at the Festas das Cruzes, Barcelos (May)

SUMMER

Most visitors choose the summer months to visit Portugal. Since many businesses shut down in August, it is holiday time for locals too. Many families spend the entire summer by the seaside.

Summer is a good time to visit the cooler Minho, when the north is busy with saints' day festivals *(see pp228–9)*.

The famed horsemen of the Ribatejo, Vila Franca de Xira (July)

JUNE

Festa de São Gonçalo *(first weekend)*, Amarante. Young, unmarried men and women in the town swap phallus-shaped cakes as tokens of love.
Feira Nacional da Agricultura *(early Jun)*, Santarém. A combination of agricultural fairs, bullfighting and displays of folk dancing.
Sintra Festival *(Jun–Jul)*, Sintra. Classical music concerts and ballet programme.
Santo António *(12–13 Jun)*, Lisbon. Celebrated in the Alfama district with singing and dancing, food and drink. Locals put up lanterns and streamers and bring out chairs for the thousands who arrive.
Festa da Coca *(Thu after Trinity Sun)*, Monção. Part of the Corpus Christi Day celebrations, the festival features scenes of St George in comic battle with the dragon.
São João *(23–24 Jun)*, Oporto. Mid-summer festivities include making wishes while jumping over small fires, and the *barcos rabelos* boat race *(see pp228–9)*.
São Pedro *(29 Jun)*, Lisbon. More street celebrations with eating, dancing and singing.

JULY

Festa do Colete Encarnado *(first weekend)*, Vila Franca de Xira. Named after the red waistcoats of the Ribatejo horsemen, the festival consists of bullfights and bull running.
Festa dos Tabuleiros *(mid-Jul 2011, then every four years)*, Tomar. Music, dancing, fireworks and a bullfight *(see pp186–7)*. Four hundred women carry trays of decorated loaves on their heads.
Festa da Ria *(mid-late Jul)*, Aveiro. Folk dances, boat races and a best-decorated boat competition *(see p203)*.
Festival da Cerveja *(late Jul)*, Fábrica do Inglês, Silves. This is a lively beer festival with folk dancing.

AUGUST

Festas Gualterianas *(first weekend)*, Guimarães. Three-day festival dating back to 1452. Torchlight procession, dancing, and medieval parade.
Madeira Wine Rally *(first weekend)*, Funchal, Madeira. Car enthusiasts flock to this challenging car rally, one of the stages of the European championships.
Festa da Nossa Senhora da Boa Viagem *(early Aug)*, Peniche. A crowd gathers at the harbour with lighted candles to greet a statue of the Virgin that

Festa dos Tabuleiros, Tomar

arrives by boat. Fireworks and dancing in the evening.
Jazz em Agosto *(early Aug)* Lisbon. Popular jazz festival with music in the gardens of the Gulbenkian Centre.
Semana do Mar *(1 week in Aug)*, Horta, Faial, Azores. Food, music, crafts, water sports and lively competitions in this sea festival.
Festival do Marisco *(mid-Aug)*, Olhão. A seafood festival, hosted by one of the big fishing ports in the Algarve.
Romaria de Nossa Senhora da Agonia *(weekend nearest to 20 Aug)*, Viana do Castelo. Religious procession, followed by display of floats, drinking, folk dancing, fireworks and bands. There is also a Saturday afternoon bullfight, and a ceremonial blessing of the town's fishing boats.

Girl in traditional dress, Viana do Castelo

The sun-drenched Algarve, a major attraction for summer visitors

Procession at the Romaria de Nossa Senhora da Nazaré

AUTUMN

In many ways, this is the best season for touring and sightseeing. From mid-September temperatures cool sharply, and autumn is usually drier than spring. This is a mellow, fruitful time of year with the countryside a collage of brown, gold and red.

September is also the start of the *vindima* (the vintage) season. Grapes are harvested and crushed to wine in a spirit of festivity, especially in the port-growing Douro region.

SEPTEMBER

Wine Festival *(early Sep)*, Funchal and Estreito de Câmara de Lobos, Madeira. The Funchal festival is a lively, popular event, but the one in Estreito de Câmara de Lobos is more authentic.
Romaria da Nossa Senhora dos Remédios *(6–9 Sep)*, Lamego. The annual pilgrimage to this famous Baroque shrine is the main feature of three days of celebration. Activities include a torchlit procession and live bands.
Romaria da Nossa Senhora da Nazaré *(8 Sep and following weekend)*, Nazaré. Includes processions, folk dancing, and bullfights.
Feiras Novas *(mid-Sep)*, Ponte de Lima. A huge market with fairground,

fireworks, carnival costumes and a brass band competition.
Festa da Senhora da Consolação *(throughout Sep)*, Sintra. A celebration of Portugal's patron saint with a month of parties, music and food in the Assafora area.
National Folklore Festival *(mid-Sep)*, the Algarve. Colourful music and dance groups converge on the region's towns.
Feira de São Mateus *(last week)*, Elvas. Festival offering a mixture of religious, cultural and agricultural events.

Musicians in regional costume at the National Folklore Festival in September

Open de Portugal de Golfe *(Oct)*, venue changes from year to year.
Portuguese Grand Prix, *(Oct)*, Estoril. Motorcycling Grand Prix held annually.
Pilgrimage to Fátima *(12–13 Oct)*. Final pilgrimage of the year, on the date of the Virgin's last appearance.
Festa das Latas *(late Oct)*, Coimbra. A celebration to welcome new students.
Festival de Gastronomia *(last two weeks)*, Santarém. Sample the best of regional cooking at this food festival.

NOVEMBER

All Saints' Day *(1 Nov)*. Candles are lit in churches and homes, and flowers placed on graves to honour the dead.
Feira Nacional do Cavalo *(first 2 weeks)*, Golegã. Horse parades and races. Included are celebrations for St Martin's Day *(11 Nov)* with a grand parade and running of bulls.
Casinos do Algarve Rally *(mid-Nov)*, Algarve. Car rally.

Damon Hill winning the Grand Prix at Estoril in 1995

OCTOBER

Feira de Outubro *(first or second week)*, Vila Franca de Xira. Bulls are run through the streets and bullfights staged.

Horsemen at the Feira Nacional do Cavalo, Golegã

Wintry snow scene in the Serra de Montemuro, south of Cinfães (see p249)

WINTER

Seekers of mild, sunny climes fly south to the Algarve where many of the resorts remain alive in winter. For golfers too, the coolest months of the year are the most appealing. January and February also see the spectacular blossoming of almond trees right across southern Portugal.

Bolo rei, a cake enjoyed over the Christmas period

Other visitors migrate even further south to sub-tropical Madeira where winter, in particular Christmas and the New Year, is high season.

PUBLIC HOLIDAYS

New Year's Day (1 Jan)
Carnaval (Feb)
Good Friday (Mar or Apr)
Dia 25 de Abril, *commemorating 1974 Revolution (25 Apr)*
Dia do Trabalhador, *Labour Day* (1 May)
Corpus Christi (variable)
Camões Day (10 Jun)
Assumption Day (15 Aug)
Republic Day (5 Oct)
All Saints' Day (1 Nov)
Dia da Restauracção, *commemorating independence from Spain, 1640* (1 Dec)
Immaculate Conception (8 Dec)
Christmas Day (25 Dec)

DECEMBER

Christmas (*25 Dec*). Everywhere churches and shops display cribs. On Christmas Eve *bacalhau* (salted dried cod) is eaten. Presents are opened, and people go to midnight mass.
In Madeira traditional *bolo de mel* (honey cake) is made, and children plant wheat, maize or barley in pots. The pots are placed around the crib to symbolize renewal and plenty.

JANUARY

New Year. Celebrations all over Portugal with spectacular firework displays welcoming in the New Year.
Festa dos Rapazes (*25 Dec – 6 Jan*), around Bragança. Boys dress up in masks and rampage through their villages in an ancient pagan rite of passage. (*see p229*).
Epiphany (*6 Jan*). The traditional crown-shaped cake for

Men in Carnaval costume, Ovar

Epiphany, *bolo rei* (king's cake), is made with a lucky charm and a bean inside. The person who gets the bean must buy the next cake. *Bolo rei* is also made at Christmas.
Festa de São Gonçalinho (*2nd week*), Aveiro. Festival in which loaves of bread are thrown to the crowds from the top of a chapel in thanks for the safe return of a fisherman, or for finding a husband.

Almond trees in blossom in February, the Algarve

FEBRUARY

Fantasporto (*2 weeks in Feb*), Oporto. An important international film festival, showing many films by new directors, including science fiction films.
Carnaval (*varies according to Easter*). Celebrated all over Portugal with spectacular costumes and floats; particularly colourful parades take place in Ovar, Sesimbra, Torres Vedras, Funchal and Loulé. Loulé's festivities are connected with the annual Almond Gatherers' Fair.

The Climate of Portugal

Mainland Portugal has a pleasant climate with long, hot summers and mild winters. In the north winters are cool and wet; heading further south temperatures increase and rainfall decreases all the way down to the Algarve, where the climate is Mediterranean. Further inland a more Continental climate prevails with hotter summers and colder winters than on the coast. Madeira is rainy in the north, warmer and drier in the south, and the Azores are mild with year-round rainfall and strong winds.

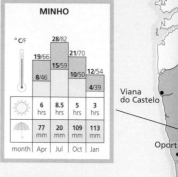

MINHO

°C/F

		28/82		
	19/66		21/70	
		15/59		12/54
8/46			10/50	
				4/39

☀	6 hrs	8.5 hrs	5 hrs	3 hrs
☂	77 mm	20 mm	109 mm	113 mm
month	Apr	Jul	Oct	Jan

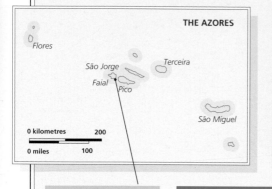

THE AZORES

Flores
São Jorge — Terceira
Faial — Pico
São Miguel

0 kilometres 200
0 miles 100

ESTREMADURA AND RIBATEJO

°C/F

	21/70	20/68	
17/63	16/61	15/59	14/57
12/54			9/48

☀	8 hrs	11 hrs	6.5 hrs	4.5 hrs
☂	55 mm	2.5 mm	60 mm	92.5 mm
month	Apr	Jul	Oct	Jan

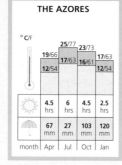

THE AZORES

°C/F

	25/77	23/73	
19/66	17/63	16/61	17/63
12/54			12/54

☀	4.5 hrs	6 hrs	4.5 hrs	2.5 hrs
☂	67 mm	27 mm	103 mm	120 mm
month	Apr	Jul	Oct	Jan

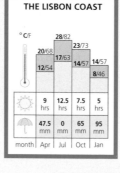

THE LISBON COAST

°C/F

	28/82		
20/68		23/73	
	17/63	14/57	14/57
12/54			8/46

☀	9 hrs	12.5 hrs	7.5 hrs	5 hrs
☂	47.5 mm	0 mm	65 mm	95 mm
month	Apr	Jul	Oct	Jan

MADEIRA

Porto Santo

Madeira

0 kilometres 20
0 miles 10

Funchal

MADEIRA

°C/F

	25/77	24/75	
19/66	18/64	18/64	19/66
14/57			13/55

☀	6 hrs	7.5 hrs	6 hrs	4.5 hrs
☂	39 mm	2.5 mm	75 mm	103 mm
month	Apr	Jul	Oct	Jan

Viana do Castelo
Oporto
Aveiro
BEIRA LITORAL
Leiria
Santarém
LISBON
Setúbal
Sines
Lagos

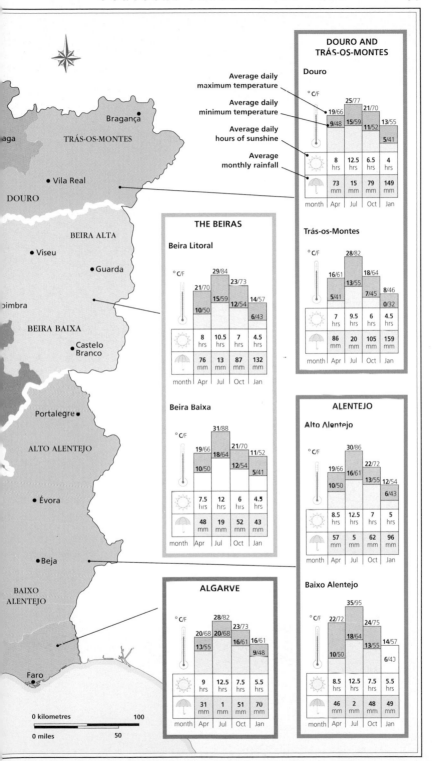

DOURO AND TRÁS-OS-MONTES

Average daily maximum temperature
Average daily minimum temperature
Average daily hours of sunshine
Average monthly rainfall

Douro

°C/F

	19/66	25/77	21/70	
	9/48	15/59	11/52	13/55
				5/41

	8 hrs	12.5 hrs	6.5 hrs	4 hrs
	73 mm	15 mm	79 mm	149 mm
month	Apr	Jul	Oct	Jan

Trás-os-Montes

°C/F

	16/61	28/82	18/64	
	5/41	13/55	7/45	8/46
				0/32

	7 hrs	9.5 hrs	6 hrs	4.5 hrs
	86 mm	20 mm	105 mm	159 mm
month	Apr	Jul	Oct	Jan

THE BEIRAS

Beira Litoral

°C/F

	21/70	29/84	23/73	
	10/50	15/59	12/54	14/57
				6/43

	8 hrs	10.5 hrs	7 hrs	4.5 hrs
	76 mm	13 mm	87 mm	132 mm
month	Apr	Jul	Oct	Jan

Beira Baixa

°C/F

	19/66	31/88	21/70	
	10/50	18/64	12/54	11/52
				5/41

	7.5 hrs	12 hrs	6 hrs	4.5 hrs
	48 mm	19 mm	52 mm	43 mm
month	Apr	Jul	Oct	Jan

ALENTEJO

Alto Alentejo

°C/F

	19/66	30/86	22/72	
	10/50	16/61	13/55	12/54
				6/43

	8.5 hrs	12.5 hrs	7 hrs	5 hrs
	57 mm	5 mm	62 mm	96 mm
month	Apr	Jul	Oct	Jan

Baixo Alentejo

°C/F

	22/72	35/95	24/75	
	10/50	18/64	13/55	14/57
				6/43

	8.5 hrs	12.5 hrs	7.5 hrs	5.5 hrs
	46 mm	2 mm	48 mm	49 mm
month	Apr	Jul	Oct	Jan

ALGARVE

°C/F

	20/68	28/82	23/73	
	13/55	20/68	16/61	16/61
				9/48

	9 hrs	12.5 hrs	7.5 hrs	5.5 hrs
	31 mm	1 mm	51 mm	70 mm
month	Apr	Jul	Oct	Jan

Bragança

TRÁS-OS-MONTES

aga

• Vila Real

DOURO

BEIRA ALTA

• Viseu

• Guarda

oimbra

BEIRA BAIXA

• Castelo Branco

Portalegre •

ALTO ALENTEJO

• Évora

• Beja

BAIXO ALENTEJO

Faro

0 kilometres   100

0 miles   50

OM MANVEL

per graça de ds̄. Rey de portugall z dos
algaruee. daquem z dalē mar
em africa. señor de guinee z da cōquista nauegaçam z cō
merçio dethiopia arabia persia. z da jndia zc̄. ꝯ
quantoe. esto aperpetua memoria feito buem fazemo
saber que assi como oproprio z p̄ñçipall cuydado dos̄. q̄
tem alguū cargo deue ser trabalhar como as cousas q̄
lhes sam emcarregadas. sciam postas. no maie. prosper
z melhorado estado que ser possa. assy tanto maie cab
a esto nos. reie. z p̄ñçepe. fazello. quanto coin maie. ex
cellente preminencia sam per ds̄. postos. na terra peça
bem della z de seue. bassallos. z pa toda execuçam z exē
plo de virtude. ꝯ por que esta obrigaçam tam deuida

THE HISTORY OF PORTUGAL

Portugal is one of the oldest nation states in Europe: its foundation in 1139 predates that of its neighbour, Spain, by nearly 350 years. The Romans, who arrived in 218 BC, called the whole peninsula Hispania, but the region between the Douro and Tagus rivers was named Lusitania after the Celtiberian tribe that lived there. When the Roman Empire collapsed in the 5th century, Hispania was overrun first by Germanic tribes, then by Moors from North Africa in 711. Military reconquest by the Christian kingdoms of the north began in earnest in the 11th century and it was during this long process that Portucale, a small county of the kingdom of León and Castile, was declared independent by its first king, Afonso Henriques.

The new kingdom expanded southwards to the Algarve and Portuguese sailors began to explore the African coast and the Atlantic. Portugal's golden age reached its zenith in the reign of Manuel I with Vasco da Gama's voyage to India in 1498 and the discovery of Brazil in 1500. Eastern trade brought incredible wealth, but

Portuguese ship (c.1500)

military defeat in Morocco meant that the prosperity was short-lived. Spain invaded in 1580 and Spanish kings ruled Portugal for the next 60 years.

After Portugal regained independence, her fortunes were restored by the discovery of gold in Brazil. In the second half of the 18th century, the chief minister, the Marquês de Pombal, began to modernize the country and to limit the reactionary influence of the church. However, Napoleon's invasion in 1807 and the loss of Brazil in 1825 left Portugal impoverished and divided. Power struggles between Absolutists and Constitutionalists further weakened the country, and despite a period of stability from the 1850s, the debt crisis worsened. In 1910, a republican revolution overthrew the monarchy.

The economy deteriorated until a military coup in 1926 led to the long dictatorship of António Salazar, who held power from 1928 to 1968. The Carnation Revolution ended his rule in 1974 and democracy was restored in 1976. Portugal's depleted economy was gradually revived by an influx of funds through joining the EU in 1986.

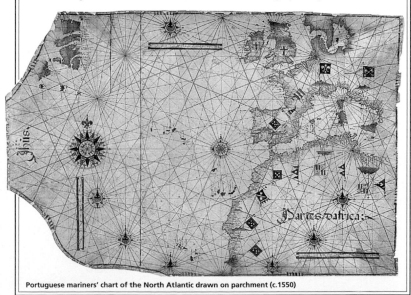

Portuguese mariners' chart of the North Atlantic drawn on parchment (c.1550)

◁ Illuminated frontispiece of the *Leitura Nova*, showing Portugal's coat of arms and portrait of Manuel I (c.1520)

The Rulers of Portugal

Afonso Henriques declared himself Portugal's first
king in 1139, but his descendants' ties of marriage
to various Spanish kingdoms led to dynastic disputes.
João I's defeat of the Castilians in 1385 established the
House of Avis which presided over the golden age of
Portuguese imperialism. Then in 1580, in the absence
of a direct heir, Portugal was ruled by Spanish kings for
60 years before the Duke of Bragança became João IV.
A Republican uprising ended the monarchy in 1910.
However, in the first 16 years of the
Republic there were 40 different
governments, and in 1926 Portugal
became a dictatorship under the
eventual leadership of Salazar.
Democracy was restored by the
"Carnation" Revolution of 1974.

1481–95 João II

1248–79 Afonso III

1211–23 Afonso II

1185–1211 Sancho I

1438–81 Afonso V

1279–1325 Dinis

1100	1200	1300	1400	1500
HOUSE OF BURGUNDY			AVIS	
1100	1200	1300	1400	1500

1325–57 Afonso IV

1357–67 Pedro I

1223–48 Sancho II

1367–83 Fernando I

1139–85 Afonso Henriques (Afonso I)

1433–8 Duarte

1521–57 João III

1385–1433 João I

1495–1521 Manuel I

1828–53 Maria II

1557–78 Sebastião

1932–68 António
Salazar (prime minister)

1621–40 Felipe III
(Philip IV of Spain)

1750–77 José I

1976–8 & 1983–5
Mário Soares
(prime minister)

1640–56 João IV

1853–61
Pedro V

1656–83 Afonso VI

1816–26
João VI
(regent from
1792)

2002–04
José Manuel
Durão
Barroso
(prime
minister)

1683–1706
Pedro II (regent
from 1668)

1861–89
Luís I

| 1600 | 1700 | 1800 | 1900 | 2000 |

HAPSBURG BRAGANÇA REPUBLIC

| 1600 | 1700 | 1800 | 1900 | 2000 |

1598–1621 Felipe II
(Philip III of Spain)

2004 05
Pedro
Miguel de
Santana
Lopes
(prime
minister)

1985–95
Aníbal
Cavaco Silva
(prime
minister)

1580–98 Felipe I
(Philip II of Spain)

2005–06
José
Sócrates
Carvalho
Pinto de
Sousa
(prime
minister)

1578–80 Henrique

1995–2002
António Guterres
(prime minister)

2006–
Aníbal
Cavaco Silva
(prime
minister)

1777–1816
Maria I and Pedro III

1908–10
Manuel II

1826–28 Pedro IV

1706–50 João V

1889–1908 Carlos I

Prehistoric and Roman Portugal

Gold solidus (c.400 AD)

From about 2000 BC Portugal's Stone Age communities were supplanted by foreign invaders, most notably the Iberians and the Celts. When Rome defeated the Carthaginians in 216 BC and took over all their territories in eastern Spain, she still had to subdue Celtiberian tribes living in the west. One of these, the Lusitani, put up fierce resistance. After their defeat in 139 BC, their name was preserved in Lusitania, a province of Roman Hispania, corresponding roughly to present-day Portugal. Romanization led to four centuries of stability and prosperity, but as the Roman Empire collapsed, Lusitania was overrun by Germanic tribes, first the Suevi and then the Visigoths.

IBERIAN PENINSULA IN 27 BC
▢ *Roman provinces*

The amphitheatre probably dated from the building boom of the 1st century AD.

The forum and principal temple

Dolmen of Comenda
Dolmens such as this one near Évora were communal burial chambers. Many were built by the Neolithic peoples who lived in the Iberian Peninsula in the third millennium BC.

The main road led north to Aeminium (Coimbra).

Porca of Murça
Trás-os-Montes has preserved 16 statues of animals like this granite pig (see p259), probably used in Celtic fertility rituals.

Palestra (exercise area of the baths)

The Baths of Trajan had a spectacular view of the ravine below the city walls.

TIMELINE

c.2000 BC Iberian tribes arrive in the peninsula, probably from Africa

Iberian Gold gorget

139 BC Celtiberian resistance to Roman rule ends with the death of Viriatus, leader of the Lusitani tribe

3000 BC	2000 BC	1000 BC

2500 BC Portugal inhabited by late Stone Age people. Many megalithic tombs date from this time

Celtic stone warrior, 1st millennium BC

1000 BC Phoenicians set up trading stations and settlements along the southern coast

218 BC The Romans invade the Iberian Peninsula

c.700 BC Celtic invaders settle in Portugal

Floor Mosaic

Under Roman rule, the wealthy built lavishly decorated villas. This mosaic of a triton (1st century AD) comes from the House of the Fountains just outside the walls of Conimbriga.

WHERE TO SEE PREHISTORIC AND ROMAN PORTUGAL

The Alentejo is rich in Stone Age megaliths *(see p308)*, while the north has the two best examples of Celtiberian settlements at Sanfins *(p246)* and Briteiros *(p283)*. Many traces of the Roman period, including roads and bridges, are found throughout Portugal. Apart from Conimbriga, major sites, such as the villas at Pisões *(p313)* and Milreu *(p327)*, are mainly in the south. Faro's Museu Municipal *(p329)* has a good collection of local finds.

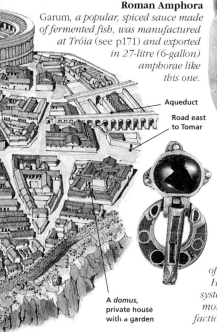

Roman Amphora

Garum, a popular, spiced sauce made of fermented fish, was manufactured at Tróia (see p171) and exported in 27-litre (6-gallon) amphorae like this one.

Aqueduct

Road east to Tomar

A domus, private house with a garden

Visigothic Buckle

The Visigoths were warlike yet cultured people who strengthened the position of Christianity. However, their system of elective monarchy led to factional disputes.

Citânia de Briteiros, *a hilltop settlement founded around the 5th century AD, survived until well into the Roman period. It was discovered in 1874 (p283).*

RECONSTRUCTION OF CONIMBRIGA

The extensive remains of Conimbriga *(see p210)* give a vivid picture of how thoroughly Romanized Portugal became under the empire. The town expanded rapidly in the 1st century AD, when it achieved the self-governing status of a *municipium*. It fell to the Suevi in AD 468.

Évora's temple dates *from the 2nd century AD (see p304). It is almost all that remains of an important Roman city.*

AD 73 Emperor Vespasian grants towns in the Iberian Peninsula same rights as Latin towns in Italy	**415** Visigoths invade the peninsula and drive out the Vandals and the Alani	**585** Visigoths take over the Suevian kingdom, fixing their capital at Toledo in Spain
	AD 200 Christianity becomes established in the peninsula	

AD 1	AD 200	AD 400	AD 600

27 BC During the rule of the Emperor Augustus the Iberian Peninsula is divided into three; Lusitania is the name given to the central province south of the River Douro	**409** Invasion by "barbarian" tribes from central Europe: the Vandals, the Alani and the Suevi	
	411 Suevian kingdom established in Galicia and northern Portugal	*Visigothic chapel at São Frutuoso (see p275)*

Moorish Domination and Christian Reconquest

Bronze Moorish oil lamp in the shape of a bird

When Muslims from North Africa defeated the Visigoths in 711, the Iberian Peninsula became a province of the Caliphate of Damascus. Then, in 756, Abd al Rahman established the independent kingdom of Al Andalus, his capital Córdoba becoming one of the world's great centres of culture. Moorish control of the peninsula remained virtually undisputed for the next 300 years until the small Christian kingdoms in the north began the Reconquest. In the 11th century, as Moorish power waned, "Portucale" was just a small county of the Kingdom of León and Castile, centred on the Douro. It became independent after Afonso Henriques defeated the Moors at Ourique in 1139.

IBERIAN PENINSULA IN 1100
- County of Portucale
- Kingdom of León and Castile
- Moorish kingdoms

Without the Virgin to watch over them, the Faro fishermen's nets are empty.

Moorish Plate
Vivid depictions of a hunting dog, a falcon and a gazelle decorate this 11th-century plate found at Mértola, a river port on the Guadiana used by eastern traders.

The fishermen set off with new hope.

Coexistence
Under Moorish rule, co-operation between the faiths was common. This miniature from the 13th century shows the friendly meeting of two knights, one a Christian, the other a Moor.

TIMELINE

10th-century Hispano-Moorish ivory casket

711 Large Muslim army of Berbers and Arabs (the Moors) conquers Iberian Peninsula following dispute over Visigothic succession			
722 Christian victory at Covadonga in Asturias marks start of gradual reconquest	**868** Vímara Peres takes Oporto from the Moors	**878** Christian forces recapture Coimbra	

AD 700	AD 800	AD 900	AD 1000

756 Battle of Al Musara; Abd al Rahman defeats governor of Córdoba and founds kingdom of Al Andalus		**955** Moorish leader Al Mansur retakes Coimbra, then forces Christian frontier back to the River Douro	**1008–31** Civil war; Al Andalus divided into small kingdoms known as *taifas*
	Nora, *a bucket wheel for raising water introduced by the Moors*		

Stone Relief of São Tiago
In wars against the Moors, the apostle St James (São Tiago) assumed a special role. At Ourique in 1139, soldiers claimed to have seen him leading the Christian forces into battle.

WHERE TO SEE MOORISH PORTUGAL

The influence of the Moors is strongest in the south, in towns like Lagos (*see p322*), Faro (*p328*) and Silves, where they ruled for longer and the architecture (*p23*) retains many Arab features. In Mértola (*p315*), the church preserves much of the old mosque. Further north, the Castelo dos Mouros, in Sintra (*p159*), and many other fortresses were taken over and rebuilt by the Christians.

12th-century Silver Dirham
This coin was minted at Beja by the Almohads, a Muslim sect even stricter than their forerunners, the Almoravids.

This cistern well was found on the site of the archaeological museum at Silves, a Moorish centre in the Algarve (p325).

The lost statue of the Virgin is recovered from the sea and restored to its rightful place on the walls.

Out at sea the fishermen's nets are full once more.

Capture of Lisbon
The Reconquest was given the status of a crusade by the pope. Lisbon was taken in 1147 with the aid of English troops bound for the Holy Land.

FARO UNDER MOORISH RULE

Christians who lived under Moorish rule were called Mozarabs. At Faro they placed a statue of the Virgin on the walls of the city, but resentful Muslims took the statue down. These four scenes from the Cantigas de Santa Maria tell the story of the miracle that followed.

1097 Alfonso VI of León and Castile entrusts Portucale to his son-in-law Henry of Burgundy	**1139** Battle of Ourique; Afonso Henriques declares himself King of Portugal	**1143** Treaty of Zamora establishes Portugal's independence	**1165–9** Geraldo sem Pavor captures a number of cities from the Almohads, including Évora and Badajoz
1086 Invasion of the Almoravids			

1050	**1100**	**1150**

1064 Christians regain Coimbra	**1128** Battle of São Mamede; Afonso Henriques defeats his mother Teresa to win control of county of Portucale	**1153** Founding of Cistercian Abbey at Alcobaça
Henry of Burgundy		**1147** Fall of Lisbon to Crusader army; Almoravid empire falls to the Almohads

Henry of Burgundy

The New Kingdom

The Portuguese Reconquest was completed in 1249 when Afonso III captured Faro in the Algarve. His successor, King Dinis, encouraged agriculture and commerce, earning the nickname of the "farmer king". He also built castles to defend the border from Castilian attack and expanded the navy. Territorial disputes with Castile came to a head in 1383 when King Fernando died and his son-in-law, Juan I of Castile, claimed the Portuguese throne for his wife Beatriz. Juan's opponents favoured Pedro I's illegitimate son, João of Avis, elected king by the *cortes* (parliament) in Coimbra in 1385.

14th-century statue of armed knight

IBERIAN PENINSULA IN 1200

- Kingdom of Portugal
- Spanish kingdoms
- Territory under Moorish rule

Cancioneiro da Ajuda
King Dinis was a fine musician and poet. This illumination is from a collection of troubadour songs, many by the king himself.

Coat of arms of Portugal

The frieze shows scenes from the life of Pedro and Inês.

The aedicules contain finely carved scenes from the life of St Bartholomew, Dom Pedro's patron saint.

The faithful dog at the feet of the deceased was a common feature of Gothic tombs.

Fortifications of Serpa
King Dinis had a chain of fortified towns and castles built along the borders with Castile and Moorish Spain. This 16th-century drawing shows the medieval walls and towers of Serpa (see p312).

TIMELINE

Leiria Castle

1185 Sancho I becomes king; his victories in the Algarve are reversed by Al-Mansur, the Almohad caliph

1211 First *cortes* (parliament) held at Coimbra

1254 The *cortes* held at Leiria includes representatives of the towns

1200

1250

1173 Remains of St Vincent brought from Cabo de São Vicente to Lisbon

1179 Portugal recognized as kingdom by the pope

Afonso III

1248 Anarchic reign of Sancho II ends in his deposition by his brother Afonso III

1249 Afonso III completes reconquest of the Algarve, but his claim to sovereignty is challenged by Castile

1256 Lisbon becomes capital of Portugal in place of Coimbra

St Isabel (1271–1336)
King Dinis did not approve of his wife's acts of charity. A legend tells how the bread Queen Isabel was about to distribute to the poor turned into roses when she was challenged by her husband.

Six angels support the recumbent king.

Cross of Sancho I
Sancho's reign (1185–1211) saw royal power and wealth increase despite disputes between the king and his bishops over papal authority.

TOMB OF PEDRO I

The Gothic carvings on the royal tomb at Alcobaça *(see pp180–81)* are the finest of their kind in Portugal. The forthright Pedro, who ruled from 1357–67, is remembered chiefly for the tragic tale of his murdered mistress, Inês de Castro, whose matching tomb stands facing Pedro's.

St Bartholomew is martyred by being flayed alive.

WHERE TO SEE MEDIEVAL PORTUGAL

Of the many castles built or rebuilt in this period, the most picturesque are at Almourol *(see p191)* and Óbidos. In the citadel of Bragança *(pp260–61)* stands the Domus Municipalis, a medieval meeting hall. Most surviving Romanesque buildings, however, are religious: the cathedrals in Oporto, Lisbon *(p72)* and Coimbra *(p202)* and many smaller churches in the north, such as those at Rates *(p274)*, Roriz *(p250)* and Bravães *(p269)*.

Óbidos Castle, *now a pousada, was rebuilt by King Dinis when he gave this fairy-tale town to his wife Isabel as a wedding present in 1282 (p174).*

Oporto's Sé *(p242) has been much altered but the twin-towered west front retains its original 13th-century character.*

1279–1325 King Dinis consolidates Portugal's independence

1288 Portugal's first university founded in Lisbon

1297 Castile recognizes Portugal's sovereignty over the Algarve

Knight of the Order of Christ

1300

1355 After murder of Inês de Castro, Pedro takes up arms against his father Afonso IV

1319 Foundation of the Order of Christ *(see p187)*

1336 Death of St Isabel of Portugal

1349 Following Black Death, a law is passed enforcing compulsory rural labour

1350

1357 Accession of Pedro I, who has murderers of Inês de Castro brutally executed

1372 Fernando I's unpopular marriage to Leonor Teles leads to riots

1383 João of Avis ends regency of Leonor Teles and proclaims himself defender of the realm

1384 Juan I of Castile invades Portugal

The House of Avis

After João of Avis had defeated the Castilians in 1385 to become João I of Portugal, he strengthened his position through an important alliance with England. His long reign saw the start of Portuguese imperialism and the beginning of maritime expeditions promoted by his son, Henry the Navigator *(see pp48–9)*. Further voyages of discovery in the reign of Manuel I "the Fortunate", led to trade with India and the East and, following Afonso de Albuquerque's capture of Goa, initially brought great wealth. So, too, did the colonization of Brazil. However, the lure of overseas adventure weakened mainland Portugal, which suffered serious depopulation. The age of expansion ended when a foolhardy military expedition to Morocco, led by King Sebastião, was soundly defeated in 1578.

IBERIAN PENINSULA IN 1500

▪ Portugal

☐ Spain (Castile and Aragon)

16th-century Porcelain Plate
In 1557 the Portuguese were granted Macao as a trading post in China. This Chinese plate bears the arms of Matias de Albuquerque, a descendant of the great Afonso, conqueror of Goa.

Arms of English royal family

John of Gaunt used the alliance with Portugal to pursue his own claim to the throne of Castile.

Troops Landing at Arzila
The kings of the Avis dynasty constantly sought to extend their domains to Morocco, where they established a small colony around Tangier. This Flemish tapestry celebrates Afonso V's capture of Arzila in 1471.

Luís de Camões
After serving in India and Morocco, where he lost an eye, the poet wrote Os Lusíadas (see p190), an epic on the Discoveries.

TIMELINE

1400	1425	1450	1475

1385 João I defeats Castilian army at Battle of Aljubarrota

1415 Capture of Ceuta in Morocco

1386 Alliance with England formalized by Treaty of Windsor

c.1425 *Leal Conselheiro*, a treatise on courtly behaviour written by King Duarte

1418 Henry the Navigator made governor of the Algarve

1441 Lagos is site of first slave market in modern Europe

King Duarte

1471 Conquest of Moroccan fortresses of Arzila and Tangier

1482–3 João II successfully resists the Conspiracy of the Nobles

1496 Jews expelled from the country or forcibly converted

1495–1521 Reign of Manuel I and great period of discoveries

1494 Spain and Portugal divide the Atlantic region by Treaty of Tordesillas

Wedding of Manuel I

Manuel's reign marked the highest point in Portugal's golden age of discovery and conquest. His marriages were made to reinforce ties with Spain. Shown here is his third: to Leonor, sister of Carlos I of Spain, in 1518.

João I drew support from the merchants of Lisbon and Oporto rather than the nobles, many of whom sided with Castile.

Archbishop of Braga

Portugal's bishops took João's side after the pope had refused to legitimize the children of Inês de Castro *(see pp44–5).*

WHERE TO SEE GOTHIC PORTUGAL

Many churches include Gothic elements, such as the cloister of the Sé in Oporto *(see p242)* and the richly sculpted portal of the Sé in Évora *(p306).* Tomar's Convento de Cristo *(pp188–9)* is predominantly Gothic, as is the church at Alcobaça *(pp180–81).* The finest church, however, is at Batalha, built in thanks for João I's victory at the Battle of Aljubarrota. It also contains major examples of Manueline architecture *(see pp24–5).*

Batalha (pp184–5) *incorporates a wide range of Gothic styles. The plain, lofty nave contrasts with the ornamented exterior.*

Battle of Alcácer-Quibir (1578)

King Sebastião saw his African expedition as a crusade against Islam. After Alcácer-Quibir, he and 8,000 of his troops lay dead, 15,000 captives were sold into slavery and the House of Avis dynasty was doomed.

JOÃO I AND THE ENGLISH

João's alliance with England against Castile led to his marriage in 1387 to Philippa of Lancaster, daughter of John of Gaunt, son of Edward III. This illustration from the chronicle of Jean de Wavrin shows the new king entertaining his father-in-law.

Belém Monstrance (see p24)

1531 Inquisition introduced into Portugal

1510 Beginning of Portuguese empire in Asia; Goa conquered by Afonso de Albuquerque

1536 Death of Gil Vicente, Portugal's greatest dramatist

1572 Publication of *Os Lusíadas*, a verse epic celebrating Portugal's history by Luís de Camões

1500	1525	1550	1575

c.1502 Work starts on the Jerónimos monastery in Belém *(see pp104–5)*

1498 Vasco da Gama reaches India

1521–57 Reign of João III, known as "the Pious"

Gil Vicente

1559 Jesuit University established at Évora *(see p306)*

1578 King Sebastião's expedition to Morocco ends in his death and total defeat at the Battle of Alcácer-Quibir

The Age of Discovery

Portugal's astonishing period of conquest and exploration began in 1415 with the capture of the North African city of Ceuta. Maritime expeditions into the Atlantic and along the West African coast followed, motivated by traditional Christian hostility towards Islam and desire for commercial gain. Great riches were made from the gold and slaves taken from the Guinea coast, but the real breakthrough for Portuguese imperialism occurred in 1498 when Vasco da Gama *(see p106)* reached India. Portugal soon controlled the Indian Ocean and the spice trade, and established an eastern capital at Goa. With Pedro Álvares Cabral's "discovery" of Brazil, Portugal became a mercantile super-power rivalled only by Spain.

Portuguese padrão

Armillary Sphere
This celestial globe with the earth in its centre was used by navigators for measuring the position of the stars. It became the personal emblem of Manuel I.

Magellan (c.1480–1521)
With Spanish funding, Portuguese sailor Fernão de Magalhães, known as Magellan, led the first circumnavigation of the globe (1519–22). He was killed in the Philippines before the voyage's end.

1500–1501 Gaspar Corte Real reaches Newfoundland.

1427 Diogo de Silves discovers the Azores.

1434 Gil Eanes rounds Cape Bojador (Western Sahara).

1460 Diogo Gomes discovers the Cape Verde archipelago.

1470s Discovery of island of São Tomé.

1482 Diogo Cão reaches the mouth of the Congo.

1500 Pedro Álvares Cabral reaches Brazil.

1485 On his third voyage Diogo Cão reaches Cape Cross (Namibia).

1488 Bartolomeu Dias rounds Cape of Good Hope.

The Adoration of the Magi
Painted for Viseu Cathedral shortly after Cabral returned from Brazil in 1500, this panel is attributed to Grão Vasco (see p215). The second king, Baltazar, is depicted as a Tupi Indian.

African Ivory Salt Cellar
This 16th-century ivory carving shows Portuguese warriors supporting a globe and a ship. A sailor peers out from the crow's nest at the top.

Japanese Screen (c.1600)
This screen shows traders unloading a nau, or great ship. Between 1575 and their expulsion in 1638, the Portuguese monopolized the carrying trade between China and Japan.

HENRY THE NAVIGATOR

Although he did not sail himself, Henry (1394–1460), the third son of João I, laid the foundations for Portugal's maritime expansion that were later built upon by João II and consolidated by Manuel I. As Master of the wealthy Order of Christ and Governor of the Algarve, Henry was able to finance expeditions along the African coast. By the time he died he had a monopoly on all trade south of Cape Bojador. Legend tells that he founded a great school of navigation either at Sagres *(see p322)* or Lagos.

KEY

— — Discoverers' routes

1543 Portuguese arrive in Japan.

1513 Trading posts set up in China at Macau and Canton.

1510 Capture of Goa.

1498 Vasco da Gama reaches Calicut in India.

1518 Fortress built in Colombo (Sri Lanka).

1512 Portuguese reach Ternate in the Moluccas (Spice Islands).

Cloves

Pepper

Nutmeg

Cinnamon

The Spice Trade
Exotic spices were a great source of wealth for Portugal. The much-disputed Moluccas, or Spice Islands, were purchased from Spain in 1528.

PORTUGUESE DISCOVERIES

The systematic attempt to find a sea route to India, which led to a monopoly of the spice trade, began in 1482 with the first voyage of Diogo Cão, who planted a *padrão* (stone cross) on the shores where he landed.

Lateen-rigged Caravel
These ships with three triangular sails were favoured by the first Portuguese explorers who sailed close to the African coast. For later journeys across the open ocean, square sails were found more effective.

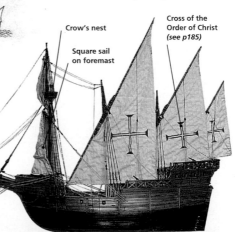

Crow's nest

Square sail on foremast

Cross of the Order of Christ *(see p185)*

Spanish Rule

Philip II of Spain

When Henrique, the Cardinal-King, died without an heir in 1580, Philip II of Spain successfully claimed the Portuguese throne through his mother, a daughter of Manuel I. Under Spanish rule, influential positions were held by Portuguese nobles, but a common foreign policy led to a steady loss of colonies to the Dutch. In 1640 a Portuguese revolt took place in Lisbon and the Duke of Bragança was chosen to become King João IV. Spain retaliated and the ensuing war continued until 1668. Meanwhile Portugal was forced to rely economically on her overseas territories.

Restoration of João IV
Two weeks after his supporters had ousted the Spanish in 1640, João was crowned on a platform outside the Royal Palace in Lisbon.

Spanish Armada
In 1588 Philip II of Spain hoped to invade England with his great fleet. It sailed from Lisbon where it had been equipped and provisioned.

The Graça fort was held by the Spanish.

António Vieira
Vieira (1606–97) was a Jesuit priest, writer and orator. He was sent on many diplomatic missions and clashed with the Inquisition over his support for Christianized Jews.

WAR OF INDEPENDENCE
Portugal's long war against Spain (1640–68) was fought mostly in the Alentejo. This *azulejo* panel from Palácio Fronteira in Lisbon *(see p123)* shows the Battle of Linhas de Elvas (1658). A Portuguese army besieged in Elvas *(see pp298–9)* was relieved by fresh troops from Estremoz, who soundly defeated the Spanish.

TIMELINE

1580 Battle of Alcântara; Spanish invade and Philip II of Spain becomes King of Portugal

1588 Spanish Armada sets sail from Lisbon to invade England

1614 Publication of the *Peregrinação* by Fernão Mendes Pinto, an account of his travels in Asia in the mid-16th century

1624 Dutch capture Portuguese colony of Bahia in Brazil

1631 Birth of painter Josefa de Óbidos

1580 | **1600** | **1620**

1583 Philip returns to Spain leaving his nephew, Cardinal-Archduke Albert of Austria, as viceroy

1581 The king invites Italian architect Filippo Terzi to Lisbon to remodel the Royal Palace and to build many churches

Church of São Vicente de Fora (see p72) by Filippo Terzi and Baltasar Álvares, completed in 1627

1626 Jesuit missionary António de Andrade crosses the Himalayas into Tibet

Indo-Portuguese Contador

Luxury cabinets, known as contadores, were made from teak and ebony in Portugal's overseas colonies. Many came from Goa. This fine 17th century example is from the Museu Nacional de Arte Antiga (see pp94–7).

The besieged Portuguese army at Elvas was retreating from a previous unsuccessful campaign in Spain.

Stout bastions deflected the attackers' cannon fire.

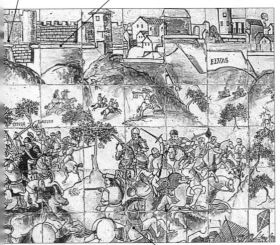

WHERE TO SEE 17TH-CENTURY PORTUGAL

Under Spanish rule an austere style of architecture prevailed, typified by São Vicente de Fora *(see p70)* in Lisbon, the Sé Nova in Coimbra *(p206)* and Santarém's Jesuit church *(p193)*. At Vila Viçosa the style is evident in the long, plain façade of the palace of the Dukes of Bragança *(pp300–301)*. Colourful *azulejos* from the period can be seen at Palácio Fronteira *(p123)* and the Museu Nacio-nal do Azulejo *(pp120–21)*.

Palácio dos Biscainhos *in Braga (p279) was built by rich emigrants returning from Brazil. Enlarged in later centuries, it retains its 17th-century core.*

The relieving army from Estremoz surprised and routed the Spanish.

Josefa de Óbidos

Born in Spain, Josefa (1631–84) came to Óbidos (see pp176–7) when young. Trained by her father, she painted religious subjects and realistic still lifes.

The Inquisition

In the 16th and 17th centuries, the Inquisition, set up by the Catholic church, burned heretics in Lisbon's Terreiro do Paço to ensure religious conformity.

1639 Portuguese vessels barred from Japanese ports

1654 Fall of Pernambuco; Dutch driven from Brazil

1656 Death of João IV; his widow, Luisa de Guzman, is regent for young King Afonso VI

1665 Spanish defeated at Battle of Montes Claros

1668 Spain recognizes Portuguese independence

1683 Pedro II becomes King

Pedro II

1640

Catherine of Bragança

1640 The Restoration: 4th Duke of Bragança crowned King João IV after uprising against Spanish rule

1660

1662 Catherine of Bragança marries Charles II of England

1667 Degenerate Afonso VI is deposed by his brother Pedro, who marries Afonso's French wife and becomes regent

1680

1697 Gold discovered in Minas Gerais region of Brazil

1698 Last meeting of Portuguese *cortes*

The Age of Absolutism

**Gold coin
of João V**

The 18th century was a period of mixed fortune for Portugal. Despite vast revenues from Brazilian gold and diamonds, João V almost bankrupted the country with his extravagance. In contrast, Pombal, chief minister of João's successor José I, applied the ideas of the Enlightenment, reforming government, commerce and education. When Maria I succeeded in 1777, she reversed many of Pombal's decrees. The French invasion of 1807 forced Maria, by then mad, and the royal family into exile in Brazil.

Tightrope Walker
This device, used at Coimbra University in the later 18th century, shows the centre of gravity when an object is in balance.

The library contains richly carved Baroque bookcases and more than 40,000 volumes.

Marquês de Pombal (1699–1782)
After the 1755 earthquake (see pp62–3), Pombal insisted that Lisbon be rebuilt on strictly rational lines. Here he proudly presents the new city.

Queen's apartments

João V
This miniature (1720) by Castriotto shows João V drinking chocolate, a fashionable drink of the nobility, served to him by the Infante Miguel.

The basilica contains many marble status made by Italian masters set amid a stunning scheme of yellow, pink, red and blue marble.

TIMELINE

1703 Methuen Treaty with Britain secures market for Portuguese wines in Britain, and for British woollen goods in Portugal

1723 Building of Baroque staircase of Bom Jesus near Braga *(see pp280–81)*

1755 Earthquake devastates Lisbon and much of southern Portugal

1730 Consecration of basilica at monastery-palace at Mafra

1700	1720	1740

1706–50 Reign of João V "the Magnanimous", a period of great artistic extravagance

Bom Jesus do Monte

1733 First Portuguese opera, *The Patience of Socrates* by António de Almeida, performed at Royal Palace in Lisbon

1748 First water flows along Águas Livres aqueduct in Lisbon

1750 José I succeeds João V

Águas Livres Aqueduct

Opened in 1748, the aqueduct was paid for by the citizens of Lisbon. João V had it built across the Alcântara valley against the advice of his engineers.

18th-Century Dressing Chair

This richly gilded walnut chair has sturdy cabriole legs, showing the influence of the English Queen Anne style.

The belltowers contain a carillon of 114 bells.

MONASTERY AT MAFRA

Begun in 1717, this vast monument to João V incorporates a royal palace, a church and a monastery *(see p154)*. It took 38 years to complete and contains some 880 rooms and 300 monks' cells.

The King's apartments are separated from the Queen's by a long gallery.

WHERE TO SEE 18TH-CENTURY PORTUGAL

Baroque churches are found throughout Portugal, many with ornate interiors of gilded wood *(talha dourada)* such as São Francisco *(see p243)* and Santa Clara *(p241)* in Oporto. Tiled interiors are also very common *(pp22–3)*. Coimbra University houses the glittering Capela de São Miguel and a fine Baroque library. As well as the palaces at Mafra and Queluz, many elegant country houses, notably the Casa de Mateus, date from this era *(pp256–7)*.

Queluz Palace (pp166–7), *residence of Maria I, was begun in 1747. It is the finest example of Rococo architecture in Portugal.*

The Capela de São Miguel *at Coimbra University (pp208–9) was redecorated in Baroque style in the reign of João V.*

1756 Douro valley becomes world's first demarcated wine region

1759 Pombal expels Jesuits from Portugal

1762 Spain declares war on Portugal

Statue of José I

1772 Pombal reorganizes Coimbra University, adding mathematics and natural sciences to the syllabus

1777 Accession of Maria I, who dismisses Pombal

1775 Machado de Castro's statue of José I unveiled as centrepiece of reconstructed Lisbon

Maria I

1760 **1780** **1800**

1789 Portuguese suppress Brazilian independence movement in Minas Gerais

1807 The French, under Junot, invade Portugal; royal family flees to Brazil

1808 French forced to retreat by Anglo-Portuguese force under Sir Arthur Wellesley; Treaty of Sintra

1792 Maria I's son João named Regent

Reform and Revolution

Portugal suffered many depredations during the upheavals of the Peninsular War, and after the loss of Brazil. A period of chaos culminated, in 1832, in civil war between the Liberal Pedro IV and the Absolutist Miguel: the War of the Two Brothers. Though the Liberals won, later governments were often reactionary. The second half of the century saw a period of stability and industrial growth, but attempts at expansion in Africa failed. By 1910, discontent with the constitutional monarchy was such that a Republican uprising forced King Manuel II into exile.

1820 Revolution
The revolution led to the royal family's return from Brazil and a new Liberal constitution. This proved unworkable and was revoked following an army coup in 1823.

Zé Povinho
This long-suffering, Everyman figure first appeared in 1875, created by artist and potter Rafael Bordalo Pinheiro. He expressed the concerns of the average Portuguese working man.

Republican ships shell the king's palace in Lisbon.

Personification of Portuguese Republic

Priests are led away by Republican soldiers.

Peninsular War (1808–14)
Napoleon tried twice to invade Portugal but was repulsed by an Anglo-Portuguese force led by Wellington. A key victory for the allies came at Buçaco (see pp212–13) in 1810.

THE BIRTH OF THE REPUBLIC

Republicanism spread among the middle classes and the army via a secret society called the Carbonária. The revolution took place in Lisbon in October 1910 and lasted less than five days. This contemporary poster celebrates the main events.

TIMELINE

1809–20 Regency dominated by Charles Stuart, British minister at Lisbon

1822 Radical new constitution. Brazil becomes independent under João VI's son Pedro

Teatro Nacional Dona Maria II

1853 First Portuguese postage stamps issued

1856 Opening of first railway from Lisbon to Carregado

1810

1826 Moderate charter introduced by Pedro IV, who then abdicates in favour of his young daughter Maria

1810 Battle of Buçaco

1828 Miguel, who is betrothed to his niece Maria, is crowned king

1830

1842 Founding of National Theatre

1834 Monasteries dissolved

1832–4 War of the Two Brothers; defeat of Absolutist Miguel

1851–80 The Regeneration: period of industrial development

1850

5 Reis stamp

The Drunkards by José Malhôa
Malhôa (1855–1933) created a virtual social history of the period in genre paintings like this one, showing a group of peasants sampling new wine.

King Manuel II flees to England from Ericeira aboard the royal yacht.

Portugal and Africa
Captain Serpa Pinto's crossing of southern Africa in 1879 led to a plan to form a Portuguese colony from coast to coast.

Republican troops set up barricades at key points in Lisbon. They meet with little opposition.

Leading figures of the Republican party

Eça de Queirós
The great novelist (1845–1900) painted a scathing picture of the Portuguese bourgeoisie. He spent many years abroad as a diplomat.

WHERE TO SEE 19TH–CENTURY PORTUGAL

Neo-Classicism, which dominated the early part of the century, can be seen in Lisbon's Palácio da Ajuda *(see p109)*. More Romantic historical styles emerged later in the century, ranging from the fantastical Neo-Gothic of the Palácio da Pena *(pp162–3)* in Sintra to the subtle Orientalism of Monserrate *(p157)*. Notable stations associated with the spread of Portugal's railways include Lisbon's Rossio and São Bento in Oporto *(p241)*.

Rossio station *(p80)* in Lisbon has a striking façade in Neo-Manueline style by José Luís Monteiro. Completed in 1887, the station contains one of the first iron vaults in Portugal.

Ponte de Dom Luís I *(p244)* in Oporto dates from 1886. Its two-tier design by Teófilo Seyrig was inspired by the nearby railway bridge built by Gustave Eiffel.

1865–8 Coalition of two main parties

1869 Slave trade abolished in all Portuguese territories

1888 Publication of *Os Maias* by Eça de Queirós, a satirical examination of Portuguese lethargy

Manuel II

1910 Revolution: Manuel II abdicates and flees into exile

1870	1890	1910

1861–89 Reign of moderate Luís I

1877 Serpa Pinto sets out from Benguela in Angola to cross southern Africa

1886 Building of Ponte de Dom Luís I in Oporto

1908 Carlos I and his heir, Luís, assassinated by Republicans

1890 Plan to link African colonies of Mozambique and Angola is thwarted by ultimatum from the British

Modern Portugal

Modern tiles decorating a Lisbon metro station

The early years of the new Republic were marked by political and economic crisis, until a military coup in 1926 paved the way for the New State of 1933. Under the oppressive regime of prime minister António Salazar, the country was freed of its debts, but suffered poverty and unemployment. Portugal's reliance on its African colonies led to costly wars, unrest in the army and the overthrow of the government in 1974. The painful return to democracy was rewarded by admission to the European Community in 1986.

1949 Portugal signs the North Atlantic Treaty and becomes a founder member of NATO

1966 Opening of Ponte Salazar (now Ponte 25 de Abril) across the Tagus (see p112)

1922 First flight across the South Atlantic by Gago Coutinho and Sacadura Cabral

1911 Women given the vote

1933 Founding of the *Estado Novo* (New State), harsh dictatorship led by Salazar. Government bans all strikes and censors the press, crushing opposition through brutal secret police force, the PIDE

1935 Death of poet Fernando Pessoa who wrote under four different names, in four distinct styles. This portrait by José de Almada Negreiros is in Lisbon's Centro de Arte Moderna (see p118)

1966 National football team with brilliant Eusébio *(centre, kneeling)* reach quarter-finals of World Cup

1955 Armenian oil magnate Calouste Gulbenkian dies leaving 2,355 million escudos (£55 million) to set upa foundation for the arts and education

1910	1920	1930	1940	1950	1960

1910	1920	1930	1940	1950	1960

1916 Portugal enters World War I on side of the British and French

1918 Assassination of President Sidónio Pais; postwar years are period of social unrest with frequent strikes and changes of government

1928 António Salazar made finance minister; he imposes austerity measures, balancing the budget by 1929. In 1932 he becomes prime minister

1949 Neurosurgeon António Egas Moniz wins Nobel Prize for Medicine for his work developing the prefrontal lobotomy

1958 In the presidential elections, the opposition candidate General Delgado wins so much support that the result is rigged against him. He is later assassinated

1917 Three peasant children in Fátima claim to see Virgin Mary; site of vision becomes focus of major pilgrimage

1942 Salazar meets Spanish dictator Franco to confirm mutual policy of non-aggression

1961 India annexes Portuguese colonies of Goa, Damão and Diu

1926 Coup puts military in charge of Republic; General Carmona is new president, holding office until his death in 1951

1939–45 In World War II Portugal is theoretically neutral but, after threats to her shipping, is forced to sell minerals to Germany. From 1943 Portugal permits British and American bases in the Azores. Here Salazar *(centre)* talks to troops stationed there

1986 Portugal joins European Community. Soares becomes the first civilian president of Portugal in 60 years

1998 Lisbon hosts Expo '98; the mascot Gil embodies the theme of water and the oceans

1985 Social Democrats, under Aníbal Cavaco Silva, come to power

1974 Carnation Revolution: in a near bloodless coup, Marcelo Caetano's regime is overthrown by the MFA (Armed Forces Movement), a group of discontented left-wing army officers

2004 Portugal hosts the Euro 2004 football tournament

1995 António Guterres of the Socialist Party elected prime minister

2006 Aníbal Cavaco Silva comes to power

1970	1980	1990	2000	2010	2020
1970	1980	1990	2000	2010	2020

1976 In the first free elections for nearly 50 years, the Socialist Mário Soares becomes prime minister

1988 Rosa Mota *(centre)* wins women's marathon at the Olympic Games in Seoul

1975 All of Portugal's remaining colonies except Macao are granted independence, putting an end to long, unwinnable wars in Africa. Troops, such as these on patrol in the Angolan bush, are hastily brought home

THE CARNATION REVOLUTION

The revolution of 25 April 1974 gained its popular name when people began placing red carnations in the barrels of soldiers' guns. Led by army officers disaffected by the colonial wars in Africa, the revolution heralded a period of great celebration, as Portugal emerged from decades of insularity. The political situation, however, was chaotic: the new government pushed through a controversial programme of nationalization and land reform in favour of the peasants, but in November 1975 the left-wing radicals were ousted by a short-lived counter-coup.

GOLPE MILITAR
"MOVIMENTO DAS FORÇAS ARMADAS" DESENCADEIA ACÇÃO DE MADRUGADA

Newspaper headline announcing revolution

LISBON

Lisbon at a Glance

Portugal's capital sits on the north bank of the Tagus estuary, 17 km (10 miles) from the Atlantic. The city has a population of about 550,000, but the conurbation of "Grande Lisboa", which has engulfed many surrounding villages, has nearly two million people. Razed to the ground by the earthquake of 1755 *(see pp62–3)*, the city centre is essentially 18th century, with carefully planned, elegant streets in the Baixa. On the hills on either side of the centre, the narrow streets of the Alfama and Bairro Alto make it a personal, approachable city. Since its days of glory during the Age of Discovery, when the city was at the forefront of world trade, Lisbon has been an important port. Today the docks have moved; however, the great monuments in Belém still bear witness to the city's maritime past.

The Museu Nacional de Arte Antiga *houses paintings, decorative art and sculpture. Of particular interest are the Flemish-influenced Portuguese painting such as this* Apparition of Christ to the Virgin *by Jorge Afonso (see pp94–5).*

The Mosteiro dos Jerónimos *is a magnificent 16th-century monastery. Commissioned by Manuel I, much of it is built in the peculiarly Portuguese style of architecture, known as Manueline. The extravagantly sculpted south portal of the church, designed by João de Castilho in 1516, is one of the finest expressions of the style (see pp104–5).*

BELÉM
(see pp98 –109)

The Torre de Belém *was a beacon for navigators returning from the Indies and the New World, and a symbol of Portuguese naval power (see p108).*

◁ Twin Romanesque towers of the Sé rising over the rooftops of the Baixa

The Elevador de Santa Justa, *built at the turn of the century, is a wrought-iron lift decorated with filigree that links the Baixa quarter with the Largo do Carmo (see p84).*

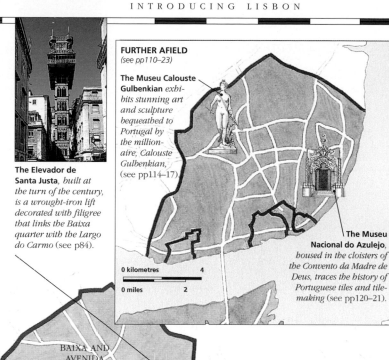

FURTHER AFIELD
(see pp110–23)

The Museu Calouste Gulbenkian *exhibits stunning art and sculpture bequeathed to Portugal by the millionaire, Calouste Gulbenkian, (see pp114–17).*

The Museu Nacional do Azulejo, *housed in the cloisters of the Convento da Madre de Deus, traces the history of Portuguese tiles and tile-making (see pp120–21).*

0 kilometres   4

0 miles   2

BAIXA AND AVENIDA
(See pp78–85)

BAIRRO ALTO AND ESTRELA
(See pp86–97)

ALFAMA
(See pp66–77)

The Castelo de São Jorge, *once a Moorish castle and then the abode of the Portuguese kings, was transformed in the 1930s into tranquil public gardens. The battlements afford spectacular views of the city (see pp76–7).*

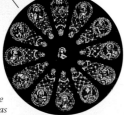

The Sé, *Lisbon's greatly restored cathedral, is a sturdy Romanesque building noted for its beautiful rose window. Ecclesiastical robes and silver are among the many religious objects on display in the treasury (see p72).*

0 metres   500

0 yards   500

The 1755 Lisbon Earthquake

The first tremor of the devastating earthquake was felt at 9:30am on 1 November. A few minutes later there was a second, far more violent shock, reducing over half the city to rubble. Although the epicentre was close to the Algarve, Lisbon, as the most populated area, bore the worst. Over 20 churches collapsed, crushing the crowds who had assembled for All Saints' Day. A third shock was followed by fires which quickly

Ex-voto tile panel offered by survivors

This anonymous painting *of the arrival of a papal ambassador at court in 1693 shows how Terreiro do Paço looked before the earthquake.*

spread. An hour later, huge waves came rolling in from the Tagus and flooded the lower part of the city. Most of Portugal suffered damage and the shock was felt as far away as Italy. Perhaps 15,000 people lost their lives in Lisbon alone.

Some buildings that might have survived an earthquake alone were destroyed by the fire that followed.

The old royal palace, the 16th-century Paço da Ribeira, was utterly ruined by the earthquake and ensuing flood.

The royal family *was staying at the palace in Belém, a place far less affected than Lisbon, and survived the disaster unscathed. Here the king surveys the city's devastation.*

Ships crammed full of people fleeing the fire were wrecked and anchors thrown up to water level.

This detail is *from an ex-voto painting dedicated to Nossa Senhora da Estrela, given by a grateful father in thanks for the sparing of his daughter's life in the earthquake. The girl was found miraculously alive after being buried under rubble for seven hours.*

THE RECONSTRUCTION OF LISBON

Marquês de Pombal (1699–1782)

No sooner had the tremors abated than Sebastião José de Carvalho e Melo, chief minister to José I and later to become Marquês de Pombal, was outlining ideas for rebuilding the city. While philosophers moralized, Pombal's initial response is said to have been, "bury the dead and feed the living". He restored order, then began a progressive town-planning scheme. His efficient handling of the crisis gained him almost total political control.

REACTIONS TO THE DISASTER

French author, Voltaire

The earthquake had a profound effect on European thought. Eye-witness accounts appeared in the papers, many written by foreigners living in Lisbon. A heated debate arose as to whether the earthquake was a natural phenomenon or an act of divine wrath. Lisbon had been a flourishing city, famed for its wealth – also for its Inquisition and idolatry. Interpreting the quake as punishment, many preachers prophesied further catastrophes. Leading literary figures debated the significance of the event, among them Voltaire, who wrote a poem about the disaster, propounding his views that evil exists and man is weak and powerless, doomed to an unhappy fate on earth.

The ancient castle walls succumbed to the reverberating shock waves.

Flames erupted as the candles lit for All Saints' Day ignited the city's churches. The fire raged for seven days.

Some of Lisbon's finest buildings were destroyed, along with gold, jewellery, priceless furniture, archives, books and paintings.

At 11am, tidal waves rolled into Terreiro do Paço. The Alcântara docks, to the west, bore the brunt of the impact.

Churches, homes *and public buildings all suffered in the disaster. The Royal Opera House, here shown in ruins, was only completed in March the same year.*

A CONTEMPORARY VIEW OF THE EARTHQUAKE

This anonymous German engraving of 1775 gives a vivid picture of the scale of the disaster. Many who fled the flames made for the Tagus, but were washed away in the huge waves which struck the Terreiro do Paço. The human and material losses were incalculable.

The reconstruction *of the centre of Lisbon took place rapidly. By the end of November the Marquês de Pombal had devised a strikingly modern scheme for a grid of parallel streets running from the waterfront to Rossio. The new buildings are shown in yellow.*

Modern-day Lisbon *holds many reminders of the earthquake. Pombal's innovative grid system is clearly visible in this aerial view of the Baixa (see pp70–85). The scheme took many years to complete, and the triumphal arch spanning Rua Augusta was not finished until over a century later, in 1873.*

Fado: the Music of Lisbon

A graphic depiction of the music's low-life associations from the 1920s

Like the blues, *fado* is an expression of longing and sorrow. Literally meaning "fate", the term may be applied to an individual song as well as the genre itself. The music owes much to the concept known as *saudade*, meaning a longing both for what has been lost, and for what has never been attained, which perhaps accounts for its emotional power. The people of Lisbon have nurtured this poignant music in back-street cafés and restaurants for over 150 years, and it has altered little in that time. It is sung as often by women as men, always accompanied by the *guitarra* and *viola* (acoustic Spanish guitar). *Fado* from Coimbra has developed its own lighter-hearted style.

A guitarra accompanist

All female *fadistas* wear a black shawl in memory of Maria Severa.

The *guitarrista* plays the melody and will occasionally perform a solo instrumental piece.

Maria Severa *(1810–36) was the first great* fadista *and the subject of the first Portuguese sound film in 1931. Her scandalous life and early death are pivotal to* fado *history, and her spiritual influence has been enormous, inspiring* fados, *poems, novels and plays.*

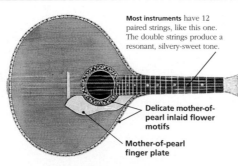

Most instruments have 12 paired strings, like this one. The double strings produce a resonant, silvery-sweet tone.

Delicate mother-of-pearl inlaid flower motifs

Mother-of-pearl finger plate

THE GUITARRA

Peculiar to Portuguese culture, the *guitarra* is a flat-backed instrument shaped like a mandolin, with eight, ten or twelve strings, arranged in pairs. It has evolved from a simple 19th-century design into a finely decorated piece, sometimes inlaid with mother-of-pearl. The sound of the *guitarra* is an essential ingredient of a good *fado*, echoing and enhancing the singer's melody line.

All kinds of themes *may occur in fado. This song of 1910, for example, celebrates the dawning of the liberal republic. Such songsheets remained a favoured means of dissemination, even after the first records were made in 1904.*

Alfredo Duarte *(1891–1982) was a renowned writer of fado lyrics dealing with love, death, longing, tragedy and triumph. Affectionately known as O Marceneiro (the master carpenter) because of his skill as a joiner, he is still revered and his work widely performed.*

A cultural icon *for the Portuguese, Amália Rodrigues (1921–99) was the leading exponent of fado for over 50 years. She crystallized the music's style in the postwar years, and made it known around the world.*

The *viola* provides rhythm accompaniment, but the player will never take a solo.

The music has long inspired *great writers and painters. O Fado (1910) by José Malhôa (see p55) shows it in an intimate setting with the fadista captivating his listener. The air of abandonment underlines the earthiness of many of the songs.*

THE FADO HOUSE

Lisbon's best *fado* houses are those run by *fadistas* themselves. Based on a love of the music and on relationships with other performers, such houses usually offer a truer *fado* experience than the larger, tourist-oriented houses. A good example is the **Parreirinha de Alfama**, owned by Argentina Santos (shown above). Less slick, but more emotionally charged, are performances of *fado vadio*, "itinerant" fado, in humbler restaurants and bars such as **Tasca do Chico** in Bairro Alto.

WHERE TO ENJOY FADO IN LISBON

Any of these fado houses will offer you good food, wine and music – or visit the Casa do Fado for a fascinating exhibition on the history of fado.

Casa de Linhares
Beco dos Armazens do Linho 2.
Map 8 E4. **Tel** *218 865 088.*

Casa do Fado
Largo do Chafariz de Dentro 1.
Tel *218 823 470.* 🚌 *28, 35.*
🕙 *10am–6pm Tue–Sun.*

Clube de Fado
Rua S João de Praça 92.
Map 8 D4. **Tel** *218 852 704.*

O Faia
Rua da Barroca 54–6.
Map 4 F2. **Tel** *213 426 742.*

Parreirinha de Alfama
Beco do Espírito Santo 1.
Map 7 E4. **Tel** *218 868 209.*

Senhor Vinho
Rua do Meio à Lapa 18.
Map 4 D3.
Tel *213 977 456.*

ALFAMA

It is difficult to believe that this humble neighbourhood was once the most desirable quarter of Lisbon. For the Moors, the tightly packed alleyways around the fortified castle comprised the whole city. The seeds of decline were sown in the Middle Ages when wealthy residents moved west for fear of earthquakes, leaving the quarter to fishermen and paupers. The buildings survived the 1755 earthquake *(see pp62–3)* and, although there are no Moorish houses still standing, the quarter retains its kasbah-like layout. Compact houses line steep streets and stairways, their façades strung with washing.

Portugal's coat of arms in the treasury of the Sé

Long-overdue restoration is under way in the most dilapidated areas, but daily life still revolves around local grocery stores and small, cellar-like tavernas.

Above the Alfama, the imposing Castelo de São Jorge crowns Lisbon's eastern hill. This natural vantage point, a defensive stronghold and royal palace until the 16th century, is today a popular promenade, with spectacular views from its reconstructed ramparts.

West of the Alfama stand the proud twin towers of the Sé. To the northeast, the domed church of Santa Engrácia and the white façade of São Vicente de Fora dominate the skyline.

SIGHTS AT A GLANCE

Museums and Galleries
Museu de Artes
  Decorativas **2**
Museu Militar **6**

Churches
Santa Engrácia **5**
Santo António à Sé **9**
São Vicente de Fora **3**
Sé **8**

Historic Buildings
Casa dos Bicos **7**
Castelo de São Jorge pp76–7 **10**

Belvederes
Miradouro da Graça **11**
Miradouro de Santa Luzia **1**

Markets
Feira da Ladra **4**

GETTING THERE
The 12 and 28 trams rattle up the narrow streets of the Alfama from the Baixa. Bus 37 does a circuit from the Castle to Rossio. Many buses run east along Avenida Dom Infante Henrique to Santa Apolónia station, and west to Belém.

KEY

▨	Street-by-Street: Alfama *pp68–9*
▤	Railway station
ℹ	Tourist information
Ⓜ	Metro station
—	Castle walls

0 metres 250
0 yards 250

◁ Ironwork balconies on a house in Rua dos Bacalhoeiros, beside the Casa dos Bicos

Street-by-Street: Alfama

A fascinating quarter at any time of day, the
Alfama comes to life in the late afternoon
and early evening when the locals emerge at their
doorways and the small tavernas start to fill. A
new generation of younger residents has resulted
in a small number of trendy shops and bars.
Given the steep streets and steps of the quarter,
the least strenuous approach is to start at the
top and work your way down. A walk
around the maze of winding alleyways will reveal picturesque
corners and crumbling churches
as well as panoramic views from
the shady terraces, such as the
Miradouro de Santa Luzia.

On Largo das Portas do Sol, café
tables look out over the Alfama towards
the Tagus estuary. Portas do Sol was one
of the entrance gates to the old city.

Statue of St. Vincent

Largo das Portas do Sol has its
own terrace viewpoint on a
converted rooftop on the east
side of the Santa Luzia church.

The church of Santa Luzia
has 18th-century blue and
white *azulejo* panels
on its south wall.

Castelo
de São
Jorge

★ Museu de Artes Decorativas
*Set up as a museum by the banker
Ricardo do Espírito Santo Silva, the
17th-century Palácio Azurara houses
fine 17th- and 18th-century Portuguese furniture and decorative arts* ❷

KEY

– – – Suggested route

0 metres	25
0 yards	25

STAR SIGHTS

★ Miradouro de
Santa Luzia

★ Museu de Artes
Decorativas

**★ Miradouro
de Santa Luzia**
*The view from this
bougainvillea-clad
terrace spans the tiled
roofs of the Alfama
toward the Tagus.
This is a pleasant
place to rest after
a walk around the
area's steep streets* ❶

Beco dos Cruzes, like most of the alleyways *(becos)* that snake their way through the Alfama, is a steep cobbled street. Locals often hang washing between the tightly packed houses.

LOCATOR MAP
See Lisbon Street Finder map 8

Rua de São Pedro is the scene of a lively early-morning fish market where the *varinas* sell the catch of the day. *Peixe espada* (scabbard fish) is one of the fish sold here.

Largo do Chafariz de Dentro is named after the 17th-century fountain *(chafariz)* that was originally placed within *(dentro)* rather than outside the 14th-century walls.

BECO DAS CRUZES

BECO DO MEXIAS

RUA DE SÃO MIGUEL

BECO DA CARDOSA

LAGO DO CHAFARIZ DE DENTRO

BECO DO POCINHO

RUA DE SÃO PEDRO

The church of Nossa Senhora dos Remédios was rebuilt after the 1755 earthquake *(see pp62–3)*. The pinnacled Manueline portal is all that remains of the original building.

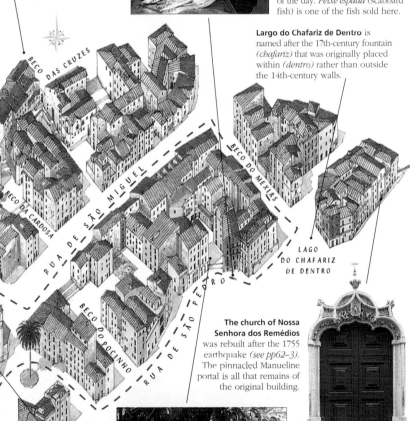

São Miguel was rebuilt after it was damaged in the 1755 earthquake. It retains a few earlier features, including a fine ceiling of Brazilian jacaranda wood.

Popular restaurants hidden in the labyrinth of alleyways spill out onto open-air patios. The Lautasco *(see p408)*, in Beco do Azinhal, serves excellent Portuguese food.

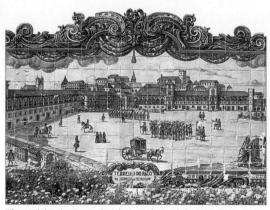

Tile panel showing pre-earthquake Praça do Comércio, Santa Luzia

Miradouro de Santa Luzia ❶

Rua do Limoeiro. **Map** 8 D4. 🚌 *28.*

The terrace by the church of Santa Luzia provides a sweeping view over the Alfama and the River Tagus. Distinctive landmarks, from left to right, are the cupola of Santa Engrácia, the church of Santo Estêvão and the two startling white towers of São Miguel. While tourists admire the views, old men play cards under the bougainvillea-clad pergola. The south wall of Santa Luzia has two modern tiled panels, one of Praça do Comércio before it was flattened by the earthquake, the other showing the Christians attacking the Castelo de São Jorge *(see pp76–7)* in 1147.

Museu de Artes Decorativas ❷

Largo das Portas do Sol 2. **Map** 8 D3. **Tel** *218 881 991.* 🚌 *37.* 🚋 *12, 28.* ⭕ *10am–5pm Wed–Mon.* ⚫ *1 Jan, Easter, 1 May, 25 Dec.* 🎨 ♿ **www.**fress.pt

Also known as the Ricardo do Espìrito Santo Silva Foundation, the museum was set up in 1953 to preserve the traditions and increase public awareness of the Portuguese decorative arts. The foundation was named after a banker who bought the 17th-century Palácio Azurara in 1947 to house his fine collection of

furniture, textiles, silver and ceramics. Among the 17th- and 18th-century antiques displayed in this handsome mansion are many fine pieces in exotic woods, including an 18th-century rosewood backgammon and chess table. Also of note are the collections of 18th-century silver and Chinese porcelain, and the Arraiolos carpets *(see p303).* The spacious rooms still retain some original ceilings and *azulejo* panels.

18th-century china cutlery case, Museu de Artes Decorativas

In the adjoining building are workshops where artisans preserve the techniques of cabinet-making, bookbinding, gilding and other traditional crafts. Temporary exhibitions, lectures and concerts are also held in the palace.

Stone figure of a woman praying by the tomb of Carlos I in São Vicente de Fora

São Vicente de Fora ❸

Largo de São Vicente. **Map** 8 E3. **Tel** *218 824 400.* 🚌 *12, 34.* 🚋 *28.* **Church** ⚫ *for renovation.* **Monastery** ⭕ *10am–5pm Tue–Sun.* 🚹 📷 🎨 *to cloisters.*

St Vincent was proclaimed Lisbon's patron saint in 1173, when his relics were transferred from the Algarve *(see p321)* to a church on this site outside *(fora)* the city walls. Designed by Italian architect Filippo Terzi, and completed in 1627, the off-white façade is sober and symmetrical, in Italian Renaissance style, with statues of saints Vincent, Augustine and Sebastian over the entrance. Inside, one is drawn immediately to Machado de Castro's Baroque canopy over the altar, flanked by life-size wooden statues.

The church is currently closed for restoration, but the adjoining former Augustinian monastery, with its 16th-century cistern and vestiges of the former cloister, can still be visited. The monastery is famous for its 18th-century *azulejos.* Among the panels in the entrance hall off the first cloister there are lively, though historically inaccurate, tile scenes of Afonso Henriques attacking Lisbon and Santarém. Around the cloisters the tiled rural scenes, surrounded by floral designs and cherubs, illustrate the fables of La Fontaine. A passageway leads to the old refectory, transformed into the Bragança Pantheon in 1885. The stone sarcophagi of almost every king and queen are here, from João IV, who died in 1656, to Manuel II, last king of Portugal. Only Maria I and Pedro IV are not buried here. A stone mourner kneels at the tomb of Carlos I and his son Luís Felipe, assassinated in Praça do Comércio in 1908.

Feira da Ladra 4

Campo de Santa Clara. **Map** 8 F2. ◐
7:30am–1pm Tue & Sat. ▦ 12. ▤ 28.

The stalls of the so-called
"Thieves' Market" have
occupied this site on the edge
of the Alfama for over a century, laid out under the shade
of trees or canopies. As the
fame of this flea market has
grown, bargains are increasingly hard to find amongst the
mass of bric-a-brac, but a few
of the vendors have interesting
wrought-iron work, prints and
tiles, as well as second-hand
clothes. Evidence of Portugal's
colonial past is reflected in
the stalls selling African
statuary, masks and jewellery.
Fish, vegetables and herbs are
sold in the central wrought-
iron marketplace.

Bric-a-brac for sale in the Feira da Ladra

Santa Engrácia 5

Campo de Santa Clara. **Map** 8 F2.
Tel 218 854 820. ▦ 12. ▤ 28.
◐ 10am–5pm Tue–Sun. ◉ public
hols. ▨ ♿

One of Lisbon's most striking
landmarks, the soaring
dome of Santa Engrcia punc-
tuates the skyline in the east
of the city. The original church
collapsed in a storm in 1681.
The first stone of the Baroque
monument, laid in 1682,
marked the beginning of a
284-year saga which led to
the invention of a saying that
a Santa Engrácia job was
never done. The church was
not completed until 1966.
    The interior is paved with
coloured marble and crowned
by a giant cupola. As the
National Pantheon, it houses
cenotaphs of Portuguese
heroes, such as Vasco da
Gama (see p106) and Afonso

de Albuquerque, Viceroy of
India (1502–15) on the left,
and on the right Henry the
Navigator (see p49). More
contemporary tombs include
that of the fadista Amália
Rodrigues (see p65). A lift
up to the dome offers a 360-
degree panorama of the city.

Museu Militar 6

Largo do Museu de Artilharia.
Map 8 F3. **Tel** 218 842 569. ▦ 9,
25, 28, 39, 746. ▤ 28. ◐ 10am–
5pm Tue–Fri, 10am–12:30pm &
1:30–5pm Sat & Sun. ◉ public hols.
▨ www.geira.pt/mmilitar

Located on the site of a 16th-
century cannon foundry and
arms depot, the military
museum contains an extensive
display of arms, uniforms and
historical documents.
Visits begin in the Vasco
da Gama room with a
collection of cannons
and modern murals
depicting the discovery
of the sea route to India.
The Salas da Grande
Guerra display exhibits
related to World War I
Other rooms focus on
the evolution of wea-
pons in Portugal, from
primitive flints to spears
to rifles. The large courtyard, flanked by cannons, tells
the story of Portugal in tiled
panels, from the Christian Reconquest to World War I. The
Portuguese artillery section in
the oldest part of the museum
displays the wagon used to
transport the triumphal arch
to Rua Augusta (see p85).

**The multicoloured marble interior
beneath Santa Engrácia's dome**

Casa dos Bicos 7

Rua dos Bacalhoeiros. **Map** 8 D4.
▦ 9, 28, 746, 759. ▤ 18, 25.
◉ to the public.

This conspicuous house,
faced with diamond-shaped
stones (bicos), was built in
1523 for Brás de
Albuquerque, illegitimate son
of Afonso, Viceroy of India
and conqueror of Goa and
Malacca. The façade is an
adaptation of a style popular
in Europe during the 16th
century. The two top storeys,
ruined in the earthquake of
1755, were restored in the
1980s, recreating the original
from old views of Lisbon in
tile panels and engravings.
In the interim the building
was used for salting fish
(Rua dos Bacalhoeiros means
street of the cod fishermen).
Once home to exhibitions,
the Casa dos Bicos is now
closed to the public.

The curiously faceted Casa dos Bicos, and surrounding buildings

The façade of the Sé, the city's cathedral

Sé ⑧

Largo da Sé. **Map** 8 D4. **Tel** 218 866 752. ▦ 37. ▦ 12, 28. **Sé** ◯ 9am–7pm daily. **Cloister** ◯ 10am–6pm daily (to 5pm in winter). 🚪 📷 ▨ to Gothic cloister and treasury.

In 1150, three years after Afonso Henriques recaptured Lisbon from the Moors, he built a cathedral for the first bishop of Lisbon, the English crusader Gilbert of Hastings, on the site of the old mosque. Sé is short for Sedes Episcopalis, the seat (or see) of a bishop. Devasted by three earth tremors in the 14th century, as well as the earthquake of 1755, and

renovated over the centuries, the cathedral you see today blends a variety of architectural styles. The façade, with twin castellated belltowers and a splendid rose window, retains its solid Romanesque aspect. The gloomy interior, for the most part, is simple and austere, and hardly anything remains of the embellishment lavished upon it by King João V in the first half of the 18th century. Beyond the renovated Romanesque nave the ambulatory has nine Gothic chapels. The Capela de Santo Ildefonso contains the 14th-century sarcophagi of Lopo Fernandes Pacheco, companion in arms to King Afonso IV, and his wife, Maria Vilalobos. The bearded figure of the nobleman, sword in

Carved tomb of the 14th-century nobleman Lopo Fernandes Pacheco in chapel in the ambulatory

Detail of the Baroque nativity scene by Joaquim Machado de Castro

hand, and his wife, clutching a prayer book, are carved onto the tombs with their dogs sitting faithfully at their feet. In the adjacent chancel are the tombs of Afonso IV and his wife Dona Beatriz.

The Gothic **cloister**, reached via the third chapel in the ambulatory, has elegant double arches with some finely carved capitals. One of the chapels is still fitted with its 13th-century wrought-iron gate. Archaeological excavations in the cloister have unearthed various Roman and other remains.

To the left of the cathedral entrance the Franciscan chapel contains the font where the saint was baptized in 1195 and is decorated with a charming tiled scene of St Antony preaching to the fishes. The adjacent chapel contains a Baroque nativity scene made of cork, wood and terracotta by Machado de Castro (1766).

The **treasury** is at the top of the staircase on the right. It houses silver, ecclesiastical robes, statuary, illustrated manuscripts and a few relics associated with St Vincent, which were transferred to Lisbon from Cabo de São Vicente in 1173 (see p321). Legend has it that two sacred ravens kept a permanent vigil over the boat that transported the relics. The ravens and the boat became a symbol of the city of Lisbon, still very much in use today. It is also said that the descendants of the two ravens used to live in the cloisters of the cathedral.

SANTO ANTÓNIO (c.1195–1231)

The best-loved saint of the Lisboetas is St Antony of Padua. Although born and brought up in Lisbon, he spent the last months of his life in Padua, Italy. St Antony joined the Franciscan Order in 1220, impressed by some crusading friars he had met at Coimbra, where he was studying. The friar was a learned and passionate preacher, renowned for his devotion to the poor and his ability to convert heretics. Many statues and paintings of St Antony depict him carrying the Infant Jesus on a book, while others show him preaching to the fishes, as St Francis preached to the birds.

In 1934 Pope Pius XI declared St Antony a patron saint of Portugal. The year 1995 saw the 800th anniversary of his birth – a cause for major celebrations throughout the city. Lisbon celebrates St Antony on 13 June, the day of the saint's death (see p31).

Santo António à Sé ⑨

Largo Santo António à Sé, 24.
Map 7 C4. *Tel* 218 869 145.
🚌 37. 🚋 12, 28. ⬜ *8am–7pm daily.* 🏛 **Museu Antoniano**
Tel 218 860 447. ⬜ *10am–1pm, 2–6pm Tue–Sun.* 📷

The popular little church of Santo António allegedly stands on the site of the house in which St Antony was born. The crypt, reached via the tiled sacristy on the left of the church, is all that remains of the original church destroyed by the earthquake of 1755. Work began on the new church in 1757 headed by Mateus Vicente, architect of the Basílica da Estrela *(see p93)* and was partially funded by donations collected by local children with the cry "a small coin for St Antony". Even today the floor of the tiny chapel in the crypt is strewn with escudos and the walls are scrawled with devotional messages from worshippers.

The church's façade blends the undulating curves of the Baroque style with Neo-Classical Ionic columns on either side of the main portal. Inside, on the way down to the crypt, a modern *azulejo* panel commemorates the visit of Pope John Paul II in 1982. In 1995 the church was given a facelift for the saint's eighth centenary. It is traditional for young couples to visit the

The Miradouro and Igreja da Graça seen from the Castelo de São Jorge

church on their wedding day and leave flowers for St Antony who is believed to bring good luck to new marriages.

Next door the small **Museu Antoniano** houses artefacts, relating to St Antony, as well as gold and silverware which used to decorate the church. The most charming exhibit is a 17th-century tiled panel of St Antony preaching to the fishes.

Castelo de São Jorge ⑩

See pp76–7.

Tiled panel recording Pope John Paul II's visit to Santo António à Sé

Miradouro da Graça ⑪

Map 8 D2. 🚌 37. 🚋 12, 28.

The working-class quarter of Graça developed at the end of the 19th century. Today, it is visited chiefly for the views from its *miradouro* (belvedere). The panorama of rooftops and skyscrapers is less spectacular than the view from the castle, but it is a popular spot, particularly in the early evenings when couples sit at café tables under the pines. Behind the *miradouro* stands an Augustinian monastery, founded in 1271 and rebuilt after the earthquake. Once a flourishing complex, the huge building is now used as barracks but the church, the **Igreja da Graça**, can still be visited. Inside, in the right transept, is the *Senhor dos Passos*, a representation of Christ carrying the cross on the way to Calvary. This figure, clad in brilliant purple clothes, is carried on a procession through Graça on the second Sunday in Lent. The *azulejos* on the altar front, dating from the 17th century, imitate the brocaded textiles usually draped over the altar.

Castelo de São Jorge ⑩

**Stone head
of Martim
Moniz**

Following the recapture of
Lisbon from the Moors in
1147, King Afonso Henriques
transformed their hilltop
citadel into the residence
of the Portuguese kings. In
1511 Manuel I built a more lavish
palace in what is now the Praça do
Comércio and the castle was used
variously as a theatre, prison and arms depot.
After the 1755 earthquake the ramparts remained
in ruins until 1938 when Salazar *(see pp56–7)*
began a complete renovation, rebuilding the
"medieval" walls and adding gardens and wildfowl. The castle may not be authentic but the
gardens and the narrow streets of the Santa
Cruz district within the walls make a pleasant
stroll and the views are the finest in Lisbon.

Torre de Ulisses has a camera
obscura that projects views of Lisbon
onto the inside walls of the tower.

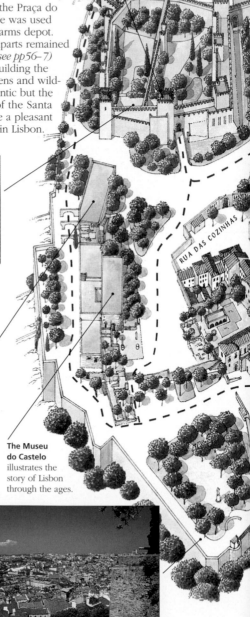

RUA DAS COZINHAS

★ Battlements
*Visitors can climb the towers and
walk along the reconstructed
ramparts of the castle walls.*

Casa do Leão Restaurant
*Part of the former royal residence
can be booked for evening meals
and parties (see p410).*

**The Museu
do Castelo**
illustrates the
story of Lisbon
through the ages.

★ Observation Terrace
*This large shaded square
affords spectacular views over
Lisbon and the Tagus. Local
men play backgammon and
cards under the trees.*

KEY

– – – Suggested route

◁ **Delightful hidden courtyard among the run-down houses in Santa Cruz, within the castle walls**

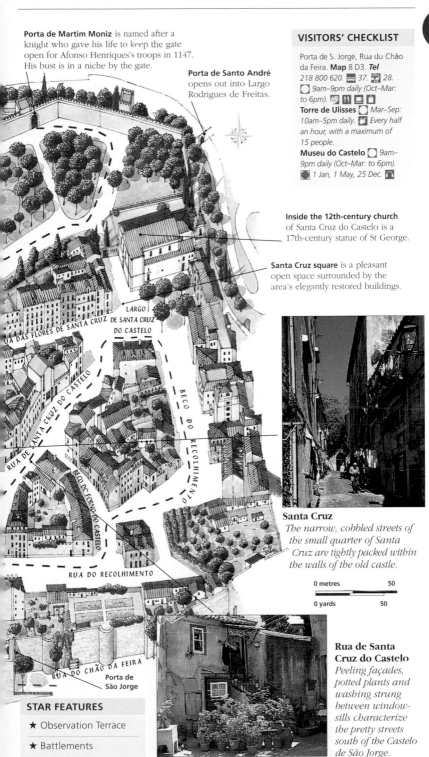

Porta de Martim Moniz is named after a knight who gave his life to keep the gate open for Afonso Henriques's troops in 1147. His bust is in a niche by the gate.

Porta de Santo André opens out into Largo Rodrigues de Freitas.

VISITORS' CHECKLIST

Porta de S. Jorge, Rua do Chão da Feira. **Map** 8 D3. *Tel* *218 800 620.* 37. 28. 9am–9pm daily (Oct–Mar: to 6pm). **Torre de Ulisses** Mar–Sep: 10am–5pm daily. Every half an hour, with a maximum of 15 people. **Museu do Castelo** 9am–9pm daily (Oct–Mar: to 6pm). 1 Jan, 1 May, 25 Dec.

Inside the 12th-century church of Santa Cruz do Castelo is a 17th-century statue of St George.

Santa Cruz square is a pleasant open space surrounded by the area's elegantly restored buildings.

LARGO DE SANTA CRUZ DO CASTELO

RUA DAS FLORES DE SANTA CRUZ

RUA DE SANTA CRUZ DO CASTELO

BECO DO RECOLHIMENTO

BECO DO FORNO DO CASTELO

RUA DO RECOLHIMENTO

RUA DO CHÃO DA FEIRA

Porta de São Jorge

Santa Cruz
The narrow, cobbled streets of the small quarter of Santa Cruz are tightly packed within the walls of the old castle.

| 0 metres | 50 |
| 0 yards | 50 |

Rua de Santa Cruz do Castelo
Peeling façades, potted plants and washing strung between window-sills characterize the pretty streets south of the Castelo de São Jorge.

STAR FEATURES

★ Observation Terrace

★ Battlements

For hotels and restaurants in this region see pp382–6 and pp408–12

BAIXA AND AVENIDA

Detail on statue of José I in Praça do Comércio

From the ruins of Lisbon, devastated by the earthquake of 1755 *(see pp62–3)*, the Marquês de Pombal created an entirely new centre. Using a grid layout of streets, he linked the stately, arcaded Praça do Comércio beside the Tagus with the busy central square of Rossio. The streets were flanked by uniform, Neo-Classical buildings and named according to the shopkeepers and craftsmen who traded there.

The Baixa (lower town) is still the commercial hub of the capital, housing banks, offices and shops. At its centre, Rossio is a popular meeting point with cafés, theatres and restaurants. The geometric layout of the area has been retained, but most of the buildings constructed since the mid-18th century have not adhered to Pombaline formality. The streets are crowded by day, particularly the lively Rua Augusta, but after dark the quarter is almost deserted.

SIGHTS AT A GLANCE

Museums and Galleries
Museu da Sociedade de Geografia **4**

Churches
Nossa Senhora da Conceição Velha **9**

Parks and Gardens
Jardim Botânico **1**

Lifts
Elevador de Santa Justa **7**

Historic Streets and Squares
Avenida da Liberdade **2**
Praça do Comércio **10**
Praça da Figueira **6**
Praça dos Restauradores **3**
Rossio **5**
Rua Augusta **8**

GETTING THERE

The area is extremely well served with buses from all directions, several Metro stations and Rossio mainline station (currently closed). Ferries from Cacilhas and Barreiro arrive at Terreiro do Paço.

KEY

- Street-by-Street: Baixa pp80–81
- **M** Metro station
- **R** Railway station
- Funicular
- Ferry boarding point
- **i** Tourist information

◁ **The triumphal arch in Praça do Comércio leading into Rua Augusta and the Baixa**

Street-by-Street: Restauradores

Tiled panel
on façade
of the
Tabacaria
Monaco

This is the busiest part of the city, especially
the central squares of Rossio and Praça
da Figueira. Totally rebuilt after the
earthquake of 1755 *(see pp62–3)*,
the area was one of Europe's first
examples of town planning.
Today, the large Neo-Classical
buildings on the wide streets
and squares house business
offices. The atmosphere
and surroundings are best
absorbed from one of the
busy pavement cafés. Rua
das Portas de Santo Antão,
a pedestrianized street
where restaurants
display tanks of live
lobsters, is more
relaxing for a stroll.

Palácio Foz, once a magnificent
18th-century palace built by the
Italian architect Francesco Fabri,
now houses a tourist office.

**The Elevador
da Glória** is a
bright yellow
funicular that
rattles up the hill
to the Bairro Alto as
far as the Miradouro
de São Pedro de
Alcântara *(see p92)*.

**Praça dos
Restauradores**
*This large tree-lined
square, named after
the men who fought
during the 1640 War of
Restoration, is a busy
through road with café
terraces on the pat-
terned pavements* ❸

Restauradores

KEY

– – – Suggested route

STAR SIGHT

★ Rossio

Rossio station,
designed by José
Luìs Monteiro, is
an eye-catching
late 19th-century
Neo-Manueline
building with two
Moorish-style
horseshoe arches.

For hotels and restaurants in this region see pp382–6 and pp408–12

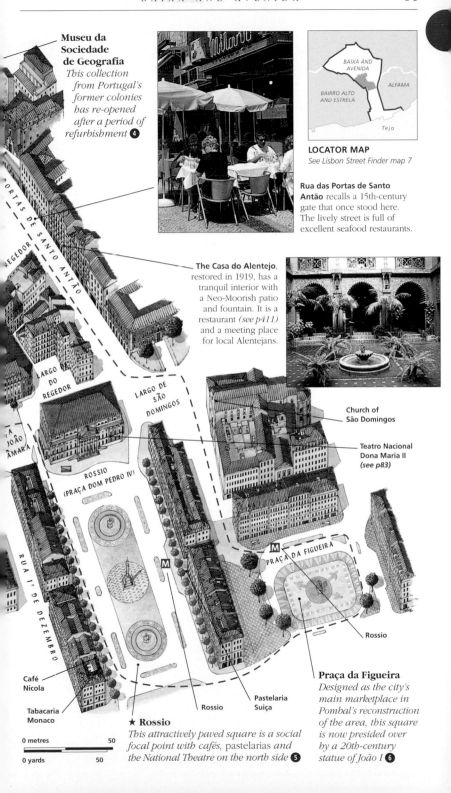

Museu da Sociedade de Geografia
This collection from Portugal's former colonies has re-opened after a period of refurbishment ❹

LOCATOR MAP
See Lisbon Street Finder map 7

Rua das Portas de Santo Antão recalls a 15th-century gate that once stood here. The lively street is full of excellent seafood restaurants.

The Casa do Alentejo, restored in 1919, has a tranquil interior with a Neo-Moorish patio and fountain. It is a restaurant *(see p411)* and a meeting place for local Alentejans.

Church of São Domingos

Teatro Nacional Dona Maria II *(see p83)*

LARGO DO REGEDOR

LARGO DE SÃO DOMINGOS

ROSSIO (PRAÇA DOM PEDRO IV)

RUA 1° DE DEZEMBRO

PRAÇA DA FIGUEIRA

Rossio

Café Nicola

Tabacaria Monaco

Rossio

Pastelaria Suiça

0 metres   50

0 yards   50

★ Rossio
This attractively paved square is a social focal point with cafés, pastelarias and the National Theatre on the north side ❺

Praça da Figueira
Designed as the city's main marketplace in Pombal's reconstruction of the area, this square is now presided over by a 20th-century statue of João I ❻

Bridge and pond shaded by trees in
the Jardim Botânico

Jardim Botânico ❶

Rua da Escola Politécnica 58. **Map**
4 F1. *Tel 213 921 892.* 🚌 *758.* Ⓜ
Rato. **Gardens** ◯ *Apr–Sep: 9am–*
8pm daily; Oct–Mar: 9am–6pm daily.
● *1 Jan, 25 Dec.* 🅿 🗟 *www.jb.ul.*
pt **Museu de História Natural** *Tel*
213 921 800. ◯ *10am–5pm Tue–Fri,*
11am–6pm Sat & Sun. ● *public hols.*
🗟 **Museu da Ciência** *Tel 213 921*
808. ◯ *10am–5pm Tue–Fri, 11am–*
6pm Sat & Sun. ● *public hols.* 🗟
www.museu-de-ciencia.ul.pt

The complex, owned by the
university of Lisbon, comprises
two museums and four hec-
tares (10 acres) of gardens.
The botanical gardens have
a distinct air of neglect. However, it is worth paying the
entrance fee to wander among
the exotic trees and dense
paths of the gardens as they
descend from the main entrance
towards Rua da Alegriato. A
magnificent avenue of lofty
palms connects the two levels.
The **Museu de História**
Natural (Natural History
Museum) opens only for temporary exhibitions and these
are well advertised throughout
the city. The **Museu da**
Ciência (Science Museum),
whose exhibits demonstrate
basic scientific principles, is
popular with school children.

Avenida da
Liberdade ❷

Map 7 A2. 🚌 *2, 9, 36 & many other*
routes. Ⓜ *Restauradores, Avenida.*

Following the earthquake
of 1755 *(see pp62–3)*, the
Marquês de Pombal created
the Passeio Público (public
promenade) in the area now
occupied by the lower part
of Avenida da Liberdade and
Praça dos Restauradores.

Despite its name,
enjoyment of the
park was restricted to
Lisbon's high society
and walls and gates
ensured the exclu-
sion of the lower
classes. In 1821,
when the Liberals
came to power, the
barriers were pulled
down and the
Avenida and square
became open to all.
The boulevard
you see today was
built in 1879–82
in the style of the
Champs-Elysées
in Paris. The wide
tree-lined avenue
became a focus for
pageants, festivities
and demonstrations.
A war memorial
stands as a tribute
to those who died
in World War I. The
avenue still retains
a certain elegance
with fountains and
café tables shaded by trees,
however, it no longer makes
for a peaceful stroll. The once
majestic thoroughfare, 90 m
(295 ft) wide and decorated
with abstract pavement patterns, is now divided by seven
lanes of traffic linking Praça
dos Restauradores and Praça
Marquês de Pombal to the
north. Some of the original
mansions have been preserved,
including the Neo-Classical
Tivoli cinema at No. 188, with
an original 1920s kiosk outside,
and Casa Lambertini with its
colourful mosaic decoration
at No. 166. However, many of
the Art Nouveau façades have
unfortunately given way to
newer ones occupied by
offices, hotels or shopping
complexes.

19th-century monument in honour of the
Restoration in Praça dos Restauradores

Praça dos
Restauradores ❸

Map 7 A2. 🚌 *2, 9, 36, 746 & many*
other routes. Ⓜ *Restauradores.*

The square, distinguished by
its soaring obelisk, erected
in 1886, commemorates the
country's liberation from the
Spanish yoke in 1640 *(see*
pp50–51). The bronze figures
on the pedestal depict Victory,
holding a palm and a crown,
and Freedom. The names and
dates inscribed on the obelisk
are those of the battles of the
War of Restoration.
On the west side, the
Palácio Foz houses a tourist
office and work premises.
It was built by Francesco
Savario Fabri in 1755–
77 for the Marquês
de Castelo-Melhor,
and was renamed
after the Marquês
de Foz, who
lived here in the 19th
century. The smart
Avenida Palace Hotel
on the southwest side of
the square, was designed
by José Lúis Monteiro
(1849–1942), who also
built Rossio railway
station *(see p82)*.

Detail from the memorial to the dead of
World War I in Avenida da Liberdade

Museu da Sociedade de Geografia ❹

Rua das Portas de Santo Antão 100. **Map** 7 A2. **Tel** 213 425 401. 🚌 2, 709, 711, 790. Ⓜ *Restauradores.* ⬜ *visits by appointment only.* ☑ *compulsory.* 📷 ♿

Located in the Geographical Society building, the museum houses an idiosyncratic ethnographical collection brought back from Portugal's former colonies. On display are circumcision masks from Guinea Bissau, musical instruments and snake spears. From Angola there are neckrests to sustain coiffures and the original *padrão* – the stone pillar erected by the Portuguese in 1482 to mark their sovereignty over the colony. Most of the exhibits are arranged along the splendid Sala Portugal.

Rossio ❺

Map 6 B3. 🚌 2, 36, 44, 745 & many other routes. Ⓜ *Rossio.*

Formally called Praça de Dom Pedro IV, this large square has been Lisbon's nerve centre for six centuries. During its history it has been the stage of bullfights, festival, military parades and gruesome *autos da fé (see p51)*. However, today there is little more than an occasional political rally, and the sober Pombaline buildings,

Teatro Nacional Dona Maria II in Rossio illuminated by night

disfigured on the upper level by the remains of neon signs, are occupied at street level by souvenir shops, jewellers and cafés. Centre stage is a statue of Dom Pedro IV, the first emperor of independent Brazil *(see p54)*. At the foot of the statue, the four female figures are allegories of Justice, Wisdom, Strength and Moderation.

In the mid-19 century the square was paved with wave-patterned mosaics which gave it the nickname of "Rolling Motion Square". The hand-cut grey and white stone cubes were the first such designs to decorate the city's pavements. Today, only a small central section of the design survives.

On the north side of Rossio is the Teatro Nacional Dona Maria II, named after Dom

Pedro's daughter. The Neo-Classical structure was built in the 1840s by the Italian architect Fortunato Lodi. The interior was destroyed by fire in 1964 and reconstructed in the 1970s. On top of the pediment is Gil Vicente (1465–1536), the founder of Portuguese theatre.

Café Nicola on the west side of the square was a favourite meeting place among writers, including the poet Manuel du Bocage (1765–1805), who was notorious for his satires. Café Suiça, on the opposite side, is popular with tourists for its sunlit terrace.

Praça da Figueira ❻

Map 6 B3. 🚌 60, 714, 759 & many other routes. 🚊 15. Ⓜ *Rossio.*

Before the 1755 earthquake *(see pp62–3)* the square next to Rossio was the site of the Hospital de Todos-os-Santos (All Saints). In Pombal's design for the Baixa, the square took on the role of the city's central marketplace. In 1885 a covered market was introduced, but this was pulled down in the 1950s. Today, the four-storey buildings are given over to hotels, shops and cafés and the square is no longer a marketplace. Perhaps its most eye-catching feature is the multitude of pigeons that perch on the pedestal supporting Leopoldo de Almeida's bronze equestrian statue of João I, erected in 1971.

Bronze statue of King João I in Praça da Figueira

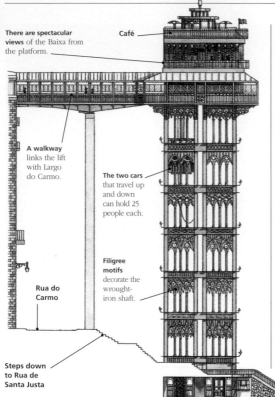

There are spectacular **views** of the Baixa from the platform.

Café

A walkway links the lift with Largo do Carmo.

The two cars that travel up and down can hold 25 people each.

Filigree motifs decorate the wrought-iron shaft.

Rua do Carmo

Steps down to Rua de Santa Justa

Elevador de Santa Justa **7**

Rua de Santa Justa & Largo do Carmo. **Map** 7 B3. **Tel** 213 613 000. ⬜ May–Sep: 7am–11pm daily; Oct–Apr: 7am–9pm daily. 🅿

Also known as the Elevador do Carmo, this Neo-Gothic lift was built at the turn of the 20th century by the French architect Raoul Mesnier du Ponsard, an apprentice of Alexandre Gustave Eiffel. Made of iron and embellished with filigree, it is one of the more eccentric features of the Baixa. Tickets can be purchased at the foot of the lift.

Passengers can travel up and down inside the tower in one of two smart wood-panelled cabins with brass fittings; they can also brave the walkway linking the lift to the Largo do Carmo in the Bairro Alto, 32 m (105 ft) above.

The very top of the tower, reached via a tight spiral stairway, is given over to café tables. This high vantage point commands splendid views of Rossio, the grid pattern of the Baixa, the castle on the opposite hill, the river and the nearby ruins of the Carmo church. The fire that gutted the Chiado district in 1988 (see p90) was extinguished very close to the lift.

Café on the top platform of the Elevador de Santa Justa

Rua Augusta **8**

Map 7 B4. Ⓜ Rossio. 🚌 2, 36, 40, 714 & many other routes.

A lively pedestrianized street decorated with mosaic pavements and lined with boutiques and open-air cafés, Rua Augusta is the main tourist thoroughfare and the smartest in the Baixa. Street performers provide entertain-ment, while vendors sell lottery tickets, street art, books and souvenirs. The triumphal Arco da Rua Augusta frames the equestrian statue of José I in Praça do Comércio. Designed by the architect Santos de Carvalho to commemorate the city's recovery from the earth-quake (see pp62–3), the arch was completed only in 1873.

The other main thorough-fares of the Baixa are Rua da Prata (silversmiths' street) and Rua do Ouro or Rua Aurea (goldsmiths' street). Cutting across these main streets full of shops and banks are smaller streets that give glimpses up to the Bairro Alto to the west and the Castelo de São Jorge (see pp76–7) to the east. Many of the streets retain shops that gave them their name: there are jewellers in Rua da Prata and Rua do Ouro, shoemakers in Rua dos Sapateiros and banks in Rua do Comércio.

The most incongruous sight in the heart of the Baixa is a small section of the Roman baths, located within the Banco Comercial Português in Rua dos Correeiros. The ruins and mosaics can be seen from the street window at the rear side of the bank; alternatively you can book ahead to visit the "museum" on 213 211 000.

Shoppers and strollers in the pedestrianized Rua Augusta

Nossa Senhora da Concceição Velha ❾

Rua da Alfândega. **Map** 7 C4.
Tel 218 870 202. 🚌 709, 746, 790.
🚊 15, 18. ⊘ 9am–5pm Mon–Fri,
10am–1pm Sat & Sun. 🚹 📷 ♿

The elaborate Manueline doorway of the church is the only feature that survived from the original 16th-century Nossa Senhora da Misericórdia, which stood here until the 1755 earthquake. The portal is decorated with a profusion of Manueline detail including angels, beasts, flowers, armillary spheres and the cross of the Order of Christ *(see pp22–3)*. In the tympanum, the Virgin Mary spreads her protective mantle over various contemporary figures. These include Pope Leo X, Manuel I *(see pp46–7)* and his sister, Queen Leonor, widow of João II. It was Leonor who founded the original Misericórdia (almshouse) on the site of a former synagogue.

Unfortunately, enjoyment of the portal is hampered by the stream of traffic hurtling along Rua da Alfândega and the cars that park right in front of the church. The gloomy interior has an unusual stucco ceiling; in the second chapel on the right is a statue of Our Lady of Restelo. This came from the Belém chapel where navigators prayed before embarking on their historic voyages east.

Detail from portal of Conceição Velha

library and 70,000 books, was destroyed in the earthquake of 1755. In the rebuilding of the city, the square became the *pièce de résistance* of Pombal's Baixa design. The new palace occupied spacious arcaded buildings that extended around three sides of the square. After the revolution of 1910 *(see pp54–5)* these were converted into government administrative offices and painted Republican pink. However, they have since been repainted royal yellow.

The south side, graced by two square towers, looks across the wide expanse of the Tagus. This has always been the finest gateway to Lisbon, where royalty and ambassadors would alight and take the marble steps up from the river. You can still experience the dramatic approach by taking a ferry across from Cacilhas on the southern bank. However, today the spectacle is spoilt by the busy Avenida Infante Dom Henrique, which runs along the waterfront. In the centre of Praça do Comércio is the equestrian statue of King José I erected in 1775 by Machado de Castro, the leading Portuguese sculptor of the 18th century. The bronze horse, depicted trampling on serpents, earned the square its third name of "Black Horse Square", used by English travellers and merchants. Over the years, however, the horse

Shaded arcades along the north side of Praça do Comércio

has acquired a green patina. The impressive triumphal arch on the north side of the square leads into Rua Augusta and is the gateway to the Baixa. Opened in January 2001, in the northwest of the square, the Lisboa Welcome Center has a tourist information service, gallery, restaurants and shops. In the opposite corner, stands Lisbon's oldest café, the Martinho da Arcada, formerly a haunt of the city's literati.

On 1 February 1908, King Carlos and his son, Luís Felipe, were assassinated as they were passing through the square *(see p55)*. In 1974 the square saw the first uprising of the Armed Forces Movement which overthrew the Caetano regime in a bloodless revolution *(see p57)*. For many years the area was used as a car park, but today is occasionally used for cultural events.

Praça do Comércio ❿

Map 7 C5. 🚌 2, 40, 709, 711, 714, 732, 746 & many other routes.
🚊 15, 18, 25.

More commonly known by the locals as *Terreiro do Paço* (Palace Square), this huge open space was the site of the royal palace for 400 years. Manuel I transferred the royal residence from Castelo de São Jorge to this more convenient location by the river in 1511. The first palace, along with its

The triumphal arch and statue of King José I in Praça do Comércio

BAIRRO ALTO AND ESTRELA

aid out in a grid pattern in
the late 16th century, the
hilltop Bairro Alto is one
of the most picturesque districts
of the city. First settled by rich
citizens who moved out of the
disreputable Alfama, by the
19th century it had become a
run-down area frequented by
prostitutes. Today, its small
workshops and family-run *tas-
cas* (cheap restaurants) exist
alongside a thriving nightlife.

**Tile panel in Largo
Rafael Bordalo
Pinheiro, Bairro Alto**

Very different in character to
the heart of the Bairro Alto is
the elegant commercial district known as the Chiado,
where affluent Lisboetas do
their shopping. To the northwest, the Estrela quarter is
centred on the huge domed
basilica and popular gardens.
The mid-18th century district
of Lapa, to the southwest, is
home to foreign embassies
and large, smart residences.

SIGHTS AT A GLANCE

Museums and Galleries
Museu do Chiado **5**
*Museu Nacional de Arte
Antiga pp94–7* **11**
Museu Nacional
da Marioneta **6**

Churches
Basílica da Estrela **13**
Igreja do Carmo **2**
São Roque **1**

**Historic Buildings
and Districts**
Chiado **3**
Palácio de São Bento **10**
Solar do Vinho
do Porto **7**
Teatro
Nacional
de São
Carlos **4**

Gardens and Belvederes
Jardim da Estrela **12**
Miradouro de São Pedro
de Alcântara **8**
Praça do Príncipe Real **9**

GETTING THERE
This area is reached via the
Elevador da Glória from Praça
dos Restauradores, the Elevador
de Santa Justa from the Baixa, or
by a steep, but pleasant walk.
There is also a metro station on
Largo do Chiado. Tram 28 passes
Bairro Alto on its way between
Graça and Estrela.

KEY

▨	Street-by-Street: Bairro Alto pp88–9
M	Metro station
▤	Railway station
▦	Funicular
⛴	Ferry boarding point
══	Railway line

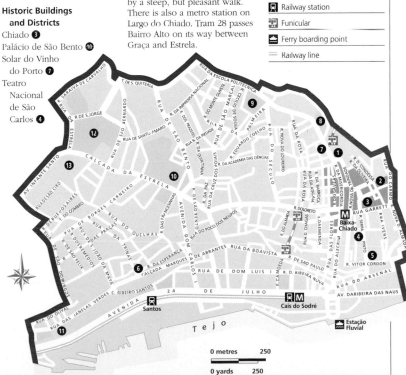

Street-by-Street: Bairro Alto and Chiado

Baroque cherub, Igreja do Carmo

The Bairro Alto (high quarter) is a fascinating area of cobbled streets, adjacent to the Carmo and Chiado areas. Since the 1980s, this has been Lisbon's best-known nightlife zone, with countless small bars and restaurants alongside the older *Casas de Fado*. Much restoration work has taken place around this area, and many modern buildings stand side by side with old, peeling houses and tiny grocery shops. In contrast, the Chiado is an area of elegant shops and old-style cafés that extends down from Praça Luís de Camões towards Rua do Carmo and the Baixa. Major renovation work has taken place since a fire in 1988 *(see p90)* destroyed many of the buildings.

Once a haunt of writers and intellectuals, Chiado is now an elegant shopping district. The 1920s Brasileira café, on Largo do Chiado, is adorned with gilded mirrors.

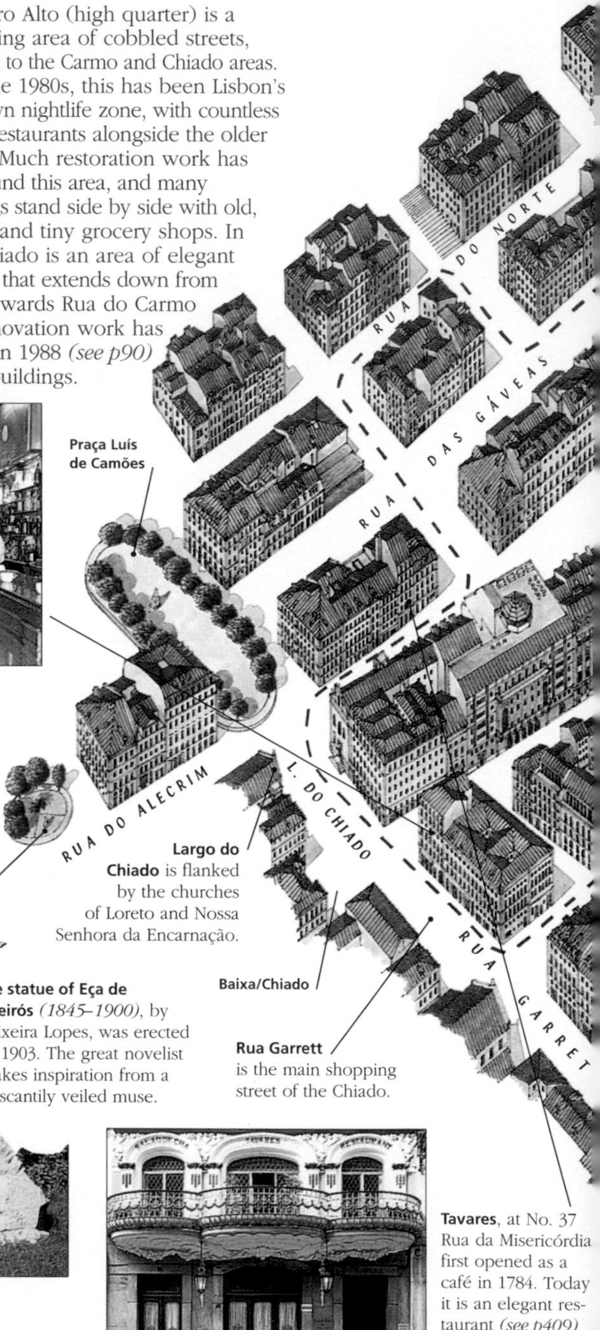

Praça Luís de Camões

Largo do Chiado is flanked by the churches of Loreto and Nossa Senhora da Encarnação.

The statue of Eça de Queirós *(1845–1900)*, by Teixeira Lopes, was erected in 1903. The great novelist takes inspiration from a scantily veiled muse.

Baixa/Chiado

Rua Garrett is the main shopping street of the Chiado.

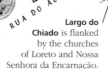

| 0 metres | 50 |
| 0 yards | 50 |

KEY

– – – Suggested route

Tavares, at No. 37 Rua da Misericórdia first opened as a café in 1784. Today it is an elegant restaurant *(see p409)* decorated at the turn of the century with mirrors and elaborate stucco designs.

The Museu de Arte Sacra has an interesting exhibition of religious artifacts and explains the history of the treasures in the church of São Roque next door.

Elevador da Glória

LOCATOR MAP
See Lisbon Street Finder map 7

Cervejaria Trindade is a popular beer hall and restaurant decorated with *azulejo* panels.

★ São Roque
Opulent mosaics and semiprecious stones adorn the Baroque Capela de São João inside the 16th-century church of São Roque ❶

Teatro da Trindade

The tile decoration on the façade of this house, erected in 1864 on Largo Rafael Bordalo Pinheiro, features allegorical figures of Science, Agriculture Industry and Commerce.

★ Igreja do Carmo
The graceful skeletal arches of this Carmelite church, once the largest in Lisbon, stand as a reminder of the earthquake of 1755. The chancel, and main body of the church house an archaeological museum ❷

The Elevador de Santa Justa has a walkway that links the Baixa with Largo do Carmo.

The shops in Rua do Carmo have been completely restored after the devastating fire in 1988 *(see p90)*.

STAR SIGHTS

★ São Roque

★ Igreja do Carmo

Ruins of the 14th-century Igreja do Carmo seen from the Baixa

São Roque **❶**

Largo Trindade Coelho. **Map** 7 A3.
Tel *213 235 380.* 🚌 *58 & Glória lift.*
⬛ *2–6pm Mon, 9am–6pm Tue–Sun
(to 9pm Thu).* ⬤ *public hols.* ✝
Museu de Arte Sacra Tel *213 235
444.* ⬛ *10am–6pm Tue, Wed & Fri–
Sun, 2–9pm Thu.* ⬤ *pub hols.* 📷

São Roque's plain façade
belies a remarkably rich
interior. The church
was founded at the
end of the 16th
century by the Jesuit
Order, then at the
peak of its power. In
1742 the Chapel of
St John the Baptist
(last on the left) was
commissioned by the
prodigal João V from
the Italian architects
Luigi Vanvitelli
and Nicola Salvi.   **Tile detail in the**
Constructed in Rome   **Chapel of St Roch**
and embellished with lapis
lazuli, agate, alabaster,
amethyst, precious marbles,
gold, silver and mosaics, the
chapel was given the Pope's
blessing in the church of
Sant'Antonio dei Portoghesi
in Rome, dismantled and sent
to Lisbon in three ships.

Among the many tiles in the
church, the oldest and most
interesting are those in the
third chapel on the right,
dating from the mid-16th
century and dedicated to São
Roque (St Roch), protector
against the plague. Other
features of the church are
the scenes of the Apocalypse
painted on the ceiling, and
the sacristy, with its coffered
ceiling and painted panels of
the life of St Francis Xavier,
the 16th-century missionary.

Treasures from the Chapel of
St John, including the silver
and lapis lazuli altar front,
are in the adjoining **Museu
de Arte Sacra**.

Igreja do Carmo **❷**

Largo do Carmo. **Map** 7 B3. **Tel** *213
460 473.* 🚋 *28 & Santa Justa lift.*
🚌 *758.* ⬛ *May–Sep: 10am–7pm
Mon–Sat; Oct–Apr: 10am–
6pm Mon–Sat.* ⬤ *public
holidays.* 📷

The Gothic ruins of
this Carmelite church,
built on a slope over-
looking the Baixa, are
evocative reminders
of the devastation left
by the earthquake of
1755. As the congre-
gation was attending
mass the shockwaves
caused the church to
collapse, depositing tons of
masonry on to the people
below. Founded in the late
14th century by Nuno Álvares
Pereira, the commander who
became a member of the
Carmelite Order, the church
was at one time the biggest
in the city of Lisbon.

Nowadays the main body
of the church and the chancel,
whose roof withstood the
violent shockwaves, house
an **archaeological museum**
with a small, heterogeneous
collection of sarcophagi,
statuary, ceramics and mosaics.

Among the more ancient
finds from Europe are a
remnant from a Visigothic
pillar and a Roman tomb
carved with reliefs depicting
the Muses. There are also
finds from Mexico and
South America, including
ancient mummies.

Outside the ruins, in the
Largo do Carmo, stands
the Chafariz do Carmo,
an 18th-century fountain
designed by Ângelo Belasco,
elaborately decorated with
four dolphins.

Chiado **❸**

Map 7 A4. 🚌 *100, 758.* 🚋 *28.*
Ⓜ *Baixa-Chiado.*

Hypotheses abound for the
origin of the word Chiado,
in use since 1567. One of the
most interesting recalls the
creak (*chiar*) of the wheels of
the carts as they negotiated the
area's steep slopes. A second
theory refers to the nickname
given to the 16th-century poet
António Ribeiro, "O Chiado".

THE CHIADO FIRE

On 25 August 1988 a disas-
trous fire began in a store in
Rua do Carmo, the street that
links the Baixa with the Bairro
Alto. Fire engines were unable
to enter this pedestrianized
street and the fire spread into
Rua Garrett. Along with shops
and offices, many important
18th-century buildings were
destroyed, the worst damage
being in Rua do Carmo. The
renovation project, which is
now complete, has preserved
many original façades, and
was headed by Portuguese
architect, Álvaro Siza Vieira.

Firemen attending the raging
fire in Rua do Carmo

Stalls and circle of the 18th-century Teatro Nacional de São Carlos

Various statues of literary figures can be found in this area, known for its intellectual associations. Fernando Pessoa, Portugal's most famous 20th-century poet, is seated at a table outside the Café Brasileira, once a favourite rendezvous of intellectuals.

The name Chiado is often used to mean just Rua Garrett, the main shopping street of the area, named after the author and poet João Almeida Garrett (1799–1854). This elegant street, which descends from Largo do Chiado towards the Baixa, is known for its clothes shops, cafés and bookshops. Devastated by fire in 1988, the former elegance of this quarter has now been restored.

On Largo do Chiado stand two Baroque churches: the Italian church, Igreja do Loreto, on the north side and opposite, Nossa Senhora da Encarnação, whose exterior walls are partly decorated with *azulejos*.

Teatro Nacional de São Carlos ❹

Rua Serpa Pinto 9. **Map** 7 A4.
Tel 213 253 000. 🚌 758, 790.
🚊 28. Ⓜ Baixa-Chiado. ☐ for performances. **www**.saocarlos.pt

Replacing a former opera house which was ruined by the earthquake of 1755, the Teatro de São Carlos was built in 1792–5 by José da Costa e Silva. Designed on the lines of La Scala in Milan and the San Carlo in Naples, the building has a beautifully proportioned façade and an enchanting Rococo interior. Views of the exterior, however, are spoiled by the car park that occupies the square in front. The opera season lasts from September to June, but concerts and ballets are also staged here at other times of the year.

Museu do Chiado ❺

Rua Serpa Pinto 4–6. **Map** 7
A5. **Tel** 213 432 148. 🚌 758,
790. 🚊 28. Ⓜ Baixa-Chiado.
☐ 10am–6pm Tue–Sun. ● 1 Jan,
Easter, 1 May, 25 Dec. 📷 **www**.
museudochiado-ipmuseus.pt

The National Museum of Contemporary Art, whose collection of 1850–1950 paintings could no longer be described as contemporary, changed its name in 1994 and moved to a stylishly restored warehouse. The paintings and sculpture are arranged over three floors in 12 rooms. Each room has a different theme illustrating the development

from Romanticism to Modernism. The majority are works by Portuguese, often showing the marked influence from other European countries. This is particularly noticeable in the 19th-century landscape painters who had contact with artists from the French Barbizon School. The few international works of art on display include a collection of drawings by Rodin (1840–1917) and some French sculpture from the late 19th century. There are also temporary exhibitions which are held for "very new artists, preferably inspired by the permanent collection".

Grotesque puppet in Museu da Marioneta

Museu da Marioneta ❻

Convento das Bernardas, Rua da Esperança 146. **Map** 4 D3. **Tel** 213 942 810. 🚌 49, 60, 713, 777 🚊 15. Ⓜ Cais do Sodré. ☐ 10am–noon & 2–5:30pm Tue–Sun. ● 1 Jan, 1 May, 25 Dec. 📷

This small puppet museum, housed in an elegantly refurbished convent building, includes characters dating from 17th- and 18th-century theatre and opera, among them devils, knights, jesters and satirical figures. Many of the puppets possess gruesome, contorted features that are unlikely to appeal to small children. The museum explains the history of the art form and runs videos of puppet shows. Call ahead to see if a live performance is being held on the small stage. There is also a space for children's entertainment and pedagogical activities.

Art Nouveau façade of the popular Café Brasileira in the Chiado

The wide selection of port at the Solar do Vinho do Porto

Solar do Vinho do Porto **7**

Rua de São Pedro de Alcântara 45.
Map 4 F2. **Tel** 213 475 707.
🚌 758. 🚋 28, Elevador da Glória
⭘ 11am–midnight Mon–Fri, 2pm–
midnight Sat. ⬤ public hols.

The Portuguese word *solar*
means mansion or manor
house and the Solar do Vinho
do Porto occupies the ground
floor of an 18th-century mansion. The building was once
owned by the German architect, Johann Friedrich Ludwig
(Ludovice), who built the
monastery at Mafra (*see p154*).
The port wine institute of
Oporto runs a pleasant if
dated bar here for the
promotion of port. Nearly 200
types of port are listed in the
lengthy drinks menu, with
every producer represented
and including some rarities.
Unfortunately, many of
the listed wines are often
unavailable. All but the
vintage ports are sold by the
glass, with prices ranging
from €1 for the simplest ruby
to €70 for a glass of 40-year-
old tawny.

Miradouro de São Pedro de Alcântara **8**

Rua de São Pedro de Alcântara.
Map 7 A2. 🚌 758. 🚋 28,
Elevador da Glória.

The Belvedere (*miradouro*)
commands a sweeping view
of eastern Lisbon, seen across
the Baixa. A tiled map placed
against the balustrade helps
you locate the landmarks in
the city below. The panorama
extends from the battlements
of the Castelo de São
Jorge (*see pp76–7*),
clearly seen surrounded
by trees on the hill to
the southeast, to the
18th-century church of
Penha da França in the
northwest. The large
monastery complex of
the Igreja da Graça (*see
p73*) is also visible on
the hill, and in the dis-
tance São Vicente de
Fora (*see p71*) is recognizable
by the symmetrical towers
that flank its white façade.

Benches and ample shade
from the trees make this
terrace a pleasant stop after
the steep walk up Calçada da
Glória from the Baixa. Alternatively, the yellow funicular,
Elevador da Glória, will drop
you off nearby.

The memorial in the garden,
erected in 1904, depicts
Eduardo Coelho (1835–89),
founder of the newspaper
Diário de Notícias, and below
him a ragged paper boy running with copies of the famous

daily. This area was once the
centre of the newspaper industry, however the modern
printing presses have now
moved to more spacious
premises west of the city.

The view is most attractive at
sunset and by night when the
castle is floodlit and the terrace
becomes a popular meeting
point for young Lisboetas.

Praça do Príncipe Real **9**

Map 4 F1. 🚌 758, 790.

Playing cards in Praça do Príncipe Real

Laid out in 1860 as a prime
residential quarter, the
square still retains an air of
affluence. Smartly painted mansions surround a particularly
pleasant park with an open-air
café, statuary and some splendid robinia, magnolia and
Judas trees. The branches of
a huge cedar tree have been
trained on a trellis, creating a
wide shady spot for the locals
who play cards beneath it. On
the large square, at No. 26, the
eye-catching pink and white
Neo-Moorish building with
domes and pinnacles is part
of Lisbon university.

View across the city to Castelo de São Jorge from Miradouro de São Pedro de Alcântara

Attractive wrought-iron music pavilion in Jardim da Estrela

Palácio de São Bento ⑩

Largo das Cortes. **Map** 4 E2. *Tel 213 919 000.* 🚌 49, 790. 🚋 28. ⬡ *by appt.* 🎟 *last Sat of month, 3–4pm, 213 919 446.* **www**.parlamento.pt

Also known as the Assembleia da República, this massive white Neo-Classical building is the seat of the Portuguese Parliament. It started life in the late 1500s as the Benedictine monastery of São Bento. After the dissolution of the religious orders in 1834, the building became the seat of Parliament, known as the Palácio das Cortes. The interior is suitably grandiose with marble pillars and Neo-Classical statues.

Museu Nacional de Arte Antiga ⑪

See pp94–7.

Jardim da Estrela ⑫

Praça da Estrela. **Map** 4 D2. 🚌 720, 738. 🚋 25, 28. ⬡ *7am–midnight daily.*

Laid out in the middle of the 19th century, opposite the Basílica da Estrela, the popular gardens are a focal part of the Estrela quarter. Local families congregate here at weekends to feed the ducks and carp in the lake, sit at the waterside café or wander among the flower beds, plants and trees. The formal gardens are planted with herbaceous borders and shrubs surrounding plane trees and elms. The central feature of the park is a green wrought-iron bandstand, decorated with elegant filigree, where musicians strike up in the summer months. This was built in 1884 and originally stood on the Passeio Público, before the creation of Avenida da Liberdade (*see p44*).

The English Cemetery to the north of the gardens is best known as the burial place of Henry Fielding (1707–54), the English novelist and playwright who died in Lisbon at the age of 47. The *Journal of a Voyage to Lisbon*, published posthumously in 1775, recounts his last voyage to Portugal made in a fruitless attempt to recover his failing health.

Basílica da Estrela ⑬

Praça da Estrela. **Map** 4 D2. *Tel 213 960 915.* 🚌 738. 🚋 25, 28. ⬡ *7:45am–8pm daily (large groups by appt only).* 🕇 📷

The tomb of the pious Maria I in the Basílica da Estrela

In the second half of the 18th century Maria I (*see p167*), daughter of José I, vowed she would build a church if she bore a son and heir to the throne. Her wish was granted and construction of the basilica began in 1779. Her son José, however, died of smallpox two years before the completion of the church in 1790. The huge domed basilica, set on a hill in the west of the city, is one of Lisbon's great landmarks. A simpler version of the basilica at Mafra (*see p154*), the church was built by architects from the Mafra School in late Baroque and Neo-Classical style. The façade is flanked by twin belltowers and decorated with an array of statues of saints and allegorical figures.

The spacious, somewhat awe-inspiring interior, where light streams down from the pierced dome, is clad in grey, pink and yellow marble. The elaborate Empire-style tomb of Queen Maria I, who died in Brazil, lies in the right transept. Locked in a room nearby is Machado de Castro's extraordinary Nativity scene, composed of over 500 cork and terracotta figures. (To see it, ask the sacristan.)

Neo-Classical façade and stairway of Palácio de São Bento

Museu Nacional de Arte Antiga ⓫

Portugal's national art collection is housed in a 17th-century palace that was built for the counts of Alvor. In 1770 it was acquired by the Marquês de Pombal and remained in the possession of his family for over a century. Inaugurated in 1884, the museum is known to locals as the Museu das Janelas Verdes, referring to the former green windows of the palace. In 1940 a modern annexe (including the main façade) was added. This was built on the site of the St Albert Carmelite monastery, which was partially demolished between 1910 and 1920. The only surviving feature was the chapel, now integrated into the museum.

15th-century wood carving of St George

★ **St Jerome**
This masterly portrayal of old age by Albrecht Dürer expresses one of the central dilemmas of Renaissance humanism: the ephemeral nature of man (1521).

St Augustine by Piero della Francesca

Stairs down to

GALLERY GUIDE

The ground floor contains 14th–19th-century European paintings, as well as some decorative arts and furniture. Oriental and African art, Chinese and Portuguese ceramics and silver, gold and jewellery are on display on the first floor. The top floor is dedicated to Portuguese art and sculpture.

St Leonard
This sculpture of the saint was made by Florentine sculptor Andrea della Robbia (1435–1525), the nephew of Luca della Robbia.

The Temptations of St Antony by Hieronymus Bosch

KEY TO FLOORPLAN

- ☐ European art
- ☐ Portuguese painting and sculpture
- ☐ Portuguese and Chinese ceramics
- ☐ Oriental and African art
- ☐ Silver, gold and jewellery
- ☐ Decorative arts
- ☐ Chapel of St Albert
- ☐ Textiles and furniture
- ☐ Non-exhibition space

STAR EXHIBITS

- ★ St Jerome by Dürer
- ★ Namban Screens
- ★ Adoration of St Vincent by Gonçalves

The Virgin and Child and Saints
Hans Holbein the Elder's balanced composition of a Sacra Conversazione *(1519) is set among majestic Renaissance architecture with saints in detailed contemporary costumes sewing or reading.*

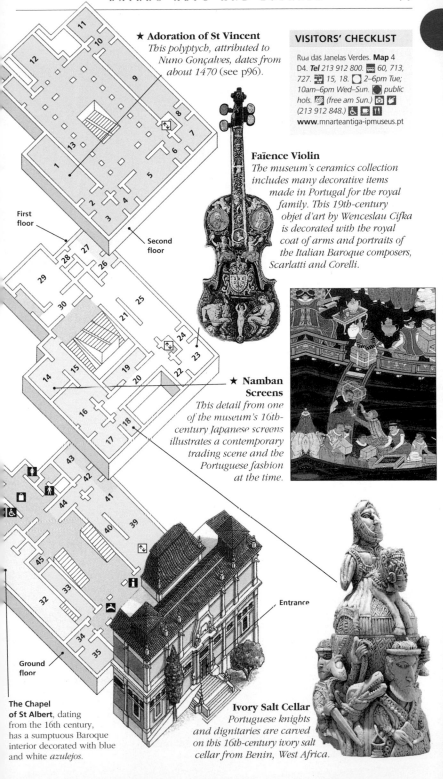

★ **Adoration of St Vincent**
*This polyptych, attributed to
Nuno Gonçalves, dates from
about 1470 (see p96).*

VISITORS' CHECKLIST

Rua das Janelas Verdes. **Map** 4
D4. *Tel* 213 912 800. 60, 713,
727. 15, 18. 2–6pm Tue;
10am–6pm Wed–Sun. public
hols. (free am Sun.)
(213 912 848.)
www.mnarteantiga-ipmuseus.pt

Faïence Violin
*The museum's ceramics collection
includes many decorative items
made in Portugal for the royal
family. This 19th-century
objet d'art by Wenceslau Cifka
is decorated with the royal
coat of arms and portraits of
the Italian Baroque composers,
Scarlatti and Corelli.*

First floor

Second floor

★ **Namban
Screens**
*This detail from one
of the museum's 16th-
century Japanese screens
illustrates a contemporary
trading scene and the
Portuguese fashion
at the time.*

Entrance

Ground floor

**The Chapel
of St Albert**, dating
from the 16th century,
has a sumptuous Baroque
interior decorated with blue
and white *azulejos*.

Ivory Salt Cellar
*Portuguese knights
and dignitaries are carved
on this 16th-century ivory salt
cellar from Benin, West Africa.*

Exploring the Collections of the Museu Nacional de Arte Antiga

The museum has the largest collection of paintings in Portugal and is particularly strong on early religious works by Portuguese artists. The majority of exhibits came from convents and monasteries following the suppression of religious orders in 1834. There are also extensive displays of sculpture, silverware, porcelain and applied arts giving an overview of Portuguese art from the Middle Ages to the 19th century, complemented by many fine European and Oriental pieces. The theme of the discoveries is ever-present, illustrating Portugal's links with Brazil, Africa, India, China and Japan.

ADORATION OF ST VINCENT

Cistercian monks from Alcobaça *(see pp180–81)* | Friar

Fisherman

EUROPEAN ART

Paintings by European artists, dating from the 14th to the 19th century, are arranged chronologically on the ground floor. Unlike the Portuguese art, most of these works were donated from private collections, contributing to the great diversity of works on display. The first rooms, dedicated to the 14th and 15th centuries, trace the transition from medieval Gothic taste to the aesthetic of the Renaissance.

The painters best represented in the European Art section are 16th-century German and Flemish artists. Notable works here include *St Jerome* by Albrecht Dürer (1471–1528), *Salomé* by Lucas Cranach the Elder (1472–1553), *Virgin and Child* by Hans Memling (c.1430–94) and *The Temptations of St Antony* by the great Flemish master of fantasy, Hieronymus

Bosch (1450–1516). Of the small number of Italian works here, the finest pieces are *St Augustine* by the Renaissance painter Piero della Francesca (c.1420–92) and a graceful early altar panel representing the Resurrection by Raphael (1483–1520).

PORTUGUESE PAINTING AND SCULPTURE

Many of the earliest works are by the Portuguese primitive painters, such as Josefa de Óbidos *(see p51)*, who were influenced by the realistic detail of Flemish artists. There had always been strong trading links between Portugal and Flanders, and in the 15th and 16th centuries several painters of Flemish origin, for example Frey Carlos of Évora, set up workshops in Portugal.

Also in this section is the São Vicente de Fora polyptych, the main painting of 15th-century Portuguese art and one that

has become a symbol of national pride in the Age of Discovery. Painted around 1470–80 and believed to be by Nuno Gonçalves, the altarpiece portrays the *Adoration of St Vincent*, patron saint of Portugal, surrounded by dignitaries, knights, monks, fishermen and beggars. The painting is an invaluable historical and social document.

Later works include a 16th-century portrait of the young Dom Sebastião *(see pp46–7)* by Cristóvão de Morais and paintings by Neo-Classical artist Domingos António de Sequeira.

The museum's sculpture collection has many Gothic polychrome stone and wood statues of Christ, the Virgin and saints. There are also statues from the 17th century and a nativity scene in the Chapel of St Albert painted by Barros Laborão between 1796 and 1807.

PORTUGUESE AND CHINESE CERAMICS

The extensive collection of ceramics enables visitors to trace the evolution of Chinese porcelain and Portuguese faïence and to see the influence of oriental designs on

Central panel of The *Temptations of St Antony* by Hieronymus Bosch

Nuno Gonçalves, self-portrait of the artist

Queen Eleonor of Aragon, the Queen mother

Henry the Navigator *(see p49)*

Archbishop of Lisbon, Jorge da Costa

Moorish knight

Jewish scholar

Beggar

Queen Isabel

Infante João (King João II)

King Afonso V

Infante Fernão, the king's brother

St Vincent

Knight

Duke of Bragança

Priest holding a fragment of St Vincent's skull

Portuguese pieces, and vice versa. From the 16th century Portuguese ceramics show a marked influence of Ming, and conversely the Chinese pieces bear Portuguese motifs such as coats of arms. By the mid-18th century individual potters had begun to develop an increasingly personalized, European style, with popular, rustic designs. The collection also includes ceramics from Italy, Spain and the Netherlands.

Chinese porcelain vase, 18th century

ORIENTAL AND AFRICAN ART

The collection of ivories and furniture, with their European motifs, further illustrates the reciprocal influences of Portugal and her colonies. The 16th-century predilection for the exotic gave rise to a huge demand for items such as carved ivory hunting horns from Africa. The fascinating 16th-century Japanese Namban screens show the Portuguese trading in Japan. *Namban-jin* (barbarians from the south) is the name the Japanese gave to the Portuguese.

SILVER, GOLD AND JEWELLERY

The collection of ecclesiastical treasures includes King Sancho I's gold cross (1214) and the Belém monstrance (1506) *(see p24)*. Also on display is the 16th-century Madre de Deus reliquary, which allegedly holds a thorn from the crown of Christ. Highlight of the foreign collection is a sumptuous set of rare 18th-century silver tableware. Commissioned by José I from the Paris workshop of François-Thomas Germain, the 1,200 pieces include intricately decorated tureens, sauce boats and salt cellars. The rich collection of jewels came from the convents, originally donated by members of the nobility and wealthy bourgeoisie on entering the religious orders.

APPLIED ARTS

Furniture, tapestries and textiles, liturgical vestments and bishops' mitres are among the wide range of objects on display. The furniture collection includes many Medieval and Renaissance pieces, as well as Baroque and Neo-classical items from the reigns of King João V, King José and Queen Maria I. Of the foreign furniture, French pieces from the 18th century are prominent.

The textiles include 17th-century bedspreads, tapestries, many of Flemish origin, such as the *Baptism of Christ* (16th century), embroidered rugs and Arraiolos carpets *(see p303)*.

Madre de Deus reliquary inlaid with precious stones (c.1510–25)

BELÉM

At the mouth of the River Tagus, where the caravels set sail on their voyages of discovery, Belém is inextricably linked with Portugal's Golden Age *(see pp46–9)*. When Manuel I came to power in 1495 he reaped the profits of those heady days of expansion, building grandiose monuments and churches that mirrored the spirit of the time. Two of the finest examples of the exuberant and exotic Manueline style of architecture *(see pp24–5)* are the Mosteiro dos Jerónimos and the Torre de Belém.

Generosity, statue at entrance to Palácio da Ajuda

Today Belém is a spacious, relatively green suburb with many museums, parks and gardens, as well as an attractive riverside setting with cafés and a promenade. On sunny days there is a distinct seaside feel to the embankment.

Before the Tagus receded, the monks in the monastery used to look out onto the river and watch the boats set forth. In contrast today several lanes of traffic along the busy Avenida da Índia cut central Belém off from the picturesque waterfront, and silver and yellow trains rattle regularly past.

SIGHTS AT A GLANCE

Museums and Galleries
Museu de Arte Popular ❿
Museu da Marinha ❼
Museu Nacional de Arqueologia ❺
Museu Nacional dos Coches ❷
Planetário Calouste Gulbenkian ❻

Parks and Gardens
Jardim Agrícola Tropical ❸
Jardim Botânico da Ajuda ⓮

Churches and Monasteries
Ermida de São Jerónimo ⓬
Igreja da Memória ⓭
Mosteiro dos Jerónimos pp106–7 ❹

Historic Buildings
Palácio de Belém ❶
Palácio Nacional da Ajuda ⓯
Torre de Belém p108 ⓫

Monuments
Monument to the Discoveries ❾

Cultural Centres
Centro Cultural de Belém ❽

KEY

	Street-by-Street: Belém pp100–101
	Railway station
	Ferry boarding point
	Railway line
	Tourist information

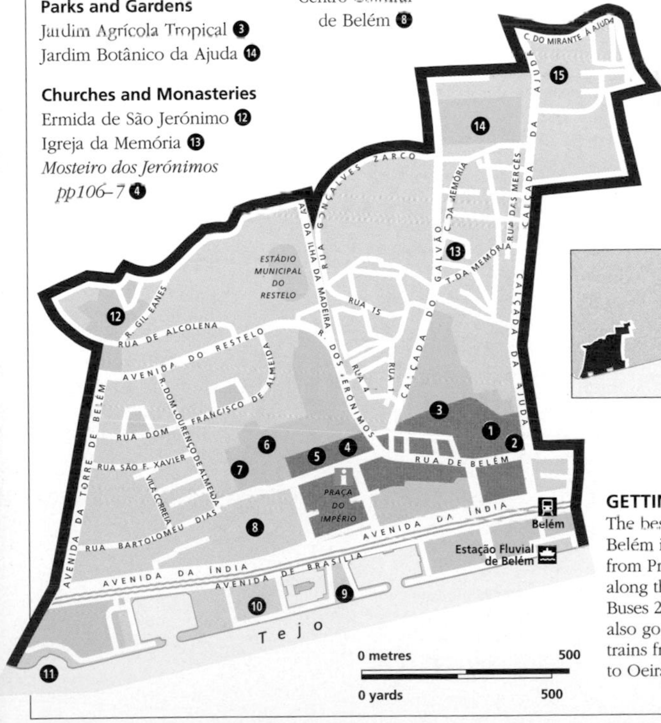

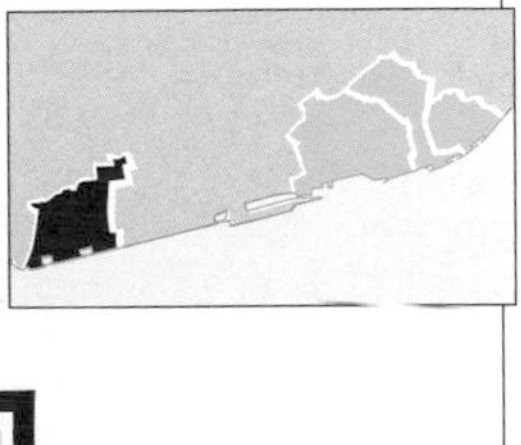

GETTING THERE
The best way to reach Belém is to take tram 15 from Praça do Comércio along the busy waterfront. Buses 28, 727, 729 and 751 also go to Belém. Slow trains from Cais do Sodré to Oeiras stop at Belém.

0 metres   500
0 yards   500

Tejo

◁ **Nave of Santa Maria de Belém, the church of the Jerónimos monastery**

Street-by-Street: Belém

Stone caravel, Jerónimos monastery

Portugal's former maritime glory, expressed in the imposing, exuberant buildings such as the Jerónimos monastery, is evident all around Belém. In Salazar's *(see p56)* attempted revival of Portugal's Golden Age, the area along the waterfront, which had silted up since the days of the caravels, was restructured to celebrate the former greatness of the nation. Praça do Império was laid out for the Exhibition of the Portuguese World in 1940 and Praça Afonso de Albuquerque was dedicated to Portugal's first viceroy of India. The royal Palácio de Belém, restored with gardens and a riding school by João V in the 18th century, briefly housed the royal family after the 1755 earthquake.

★ Mosteiro dos Jerónimos
Vaulted arcades and richly carved columns adorned with foliage, exotic animals and navigational instruments decorate the Manueline cloister of the Jerónimos monastery ④

LARGO

DOS

JERÓNIMOS

PRAÇA DO IMPÉRIO

Museu Nacional de Arqueologia
Archaeological finds ranging from an Iron Age gold bracelet to Moorish artefacts are among the interesting exhibits on display ⑤

Torre de Belém
(see p108)

STAR SIGHTS

★ Mosteiro dos Jerónimos

★ Museu Nacional dos Coches

Praça do Império, an impressive square that opens out in front of the monastery, is lit up on special occasions with a colourful light display in the central fountain.

KEY

– – – Suggested route

Rua Vieira Portuense runs along a small park.
Its colourful 16th- and 17th-century houses contrast with the typically imposing buildings in Belém.

Jardim Agrícola Tropical
Exotic plants and trees gathered from Portugal's former colonies fill these peaceful gardens that were once part of the Palácio de Belém ❸

LOCATOR MAP
See Lisbon Street Finder maps 1 & 2

Antiga Confeitaria de Belém, a 19th-century café, sells *pastéis de Belém*, rich custard in a flaky pastry cup.

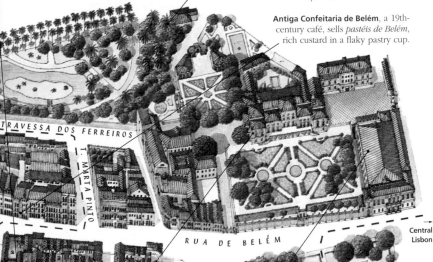

TRAVESSA DOS FERREIROS

T. MARTA PINTO

RUA DE BELÉM

→ Central Lisbon

RUA VIEIRA PORTUENSE

Palácio de Belém
Also known as the Palácio Cor de Rosa (pink palace) because of its faded pink façade, the former royal palace is the residence of the Portuguese president. It also houses the Museu da Presidencia ❶

0 metres   50
0 yards   50

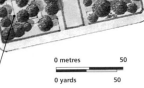

★ Museu Nacional dos Coches
This 18th-century coach used by the ambassador to Pope Clement XI is part of the collection in the old riding school of the Palácio de Belém ❷

Praça Afonso de Albuquerque is named after the first Portuguese viceroy of India. A Neo-Manueline column in the centre bears his statue, with scenes from his life carved on the base.

Palácio de Belém ❶

Praça Afonso de Albuquerque.
Map 1 C4. **Tel** *213 614 600.* 🚌 *28, 714, 727, 729, 751.* 🚊 *15.* 🚆
Belém. **Belém Palace** ⭕ *10am–5pm Sat.* 🎟 *compulsory (213 414 660).* 🎦 **Museu da Presidencia** ⭕ *10am–6pm Tue–Sun.* 🎦 📷
www.museu.presidencia.pt

Pink façade of the Palácio de Belém, home of the President of Portugal

Built by the Conde de Aveiras in 1559, this palace once had gardens bordering the river. In the 18th century it was bought by João V, who radically altered it, rendering the interior suitably lavish for his amorous liaisons.

When the 1755 earthquake *(see pp62–3)* struck, the king, José I, and his family were staying here. Fearing another earth tremor, they set up camp in tents in the palace grounds and the building was used as a hospital. Today the elegant palace is the residence of the President of Portugal. The Presidential Museum allows visitors to get acquainted with former presidents through their personal items and state gifts, as well as the official portrait gallery.

Museu Nacional dos Coches ❷

Praça Afonso de Albuquerque. **Map**
2 D4. **Tel** *213 610 850.* 🚌 *28, 714, 727, 729, 751.* 🚊 *15.* 🚆 *Belém.* ⭕
10am–6pm Tue–Sun. ⭕ *1 Jan, Easter, 1 May, 25 Dec.* 🎦 *(free 10am–2pm Sun).* 🎟 *available for groups.* 📷 ♿
www.museudoscoches-ipmuseus.pt

The museum's collection of coaches is arguably the finest in Europe. Occupying the east wing of the Palácio de Belém, this was formerly the riding school built by the Italian architect Giacomo Azzolini in 1726. Seated in the upper gallery, the royal family used to watch their beautiful Lusitanian horses *(see p298)* performing in the arena. In 1905 the riding school was turned into a museum by King Carlos's wife, Dona Amélia, whose pink riding cloak is on display.

Made in Portugal, Italy, France, Austria and Spain, the coaches span three centuries and range from the plain to the preposterous. The main gallery, in Louis XVI style with splendid painted ceiling, is the setting for two rows of coaches created for Portuguese royalty. The collection starts with the comparatively plain 17th-century red leather and wood coach of Philip II of Spain *(see pp50–51)*. The coaches become increasingly sumptuous, interiors lined with red velvet and gold, exteriors profusely carved and decorated with allegories and royal coats of arms. The rows end with three huge Baroque coaches made in Rome for the Portuguese ambassador to the Vatican, Dom Rodrigo Almeida e Menezes, the Marquês de Abrantes. The epitome of pomp and extravagance, these 5-tonne carriages are embellished with a plush interior and life-size gilded statues.

The neighbouring gallery has further examples of royal carriages, including two-wheeled cabriolets, landaus and pony-drawn chaises used by young members of the royal family. There is also a 19th-century Lisbon cab, painted black and green, the colours of

Rear view of a coach built in 1716 for the Marquês de Abrantes, the Portuguese ambassador to Pope Clement XI

taxis right up to the 1990s. The 18th-century Eyeglass Chaise, whose black leather hood is pierced by sinister eye-like windows, was made during the era of Pombal (*see pp52–3*) when lavish decoration was discouraged. The upper gallery has a collection of harnesses, court costumes and portraits of members of the royal family.

Jardim Agrícola Tropical ❸

Largo do Jerónimos. **Map** 1 C4. *Tel 213 609 665.* 🚌 *28, 49, 112, 727, 751.* 🚊 *15.* ⬚ *Apr–Sep: 9am–6pm Mon–Fri, 11am–7pm Sat & Sun; Oct–Mar: 9am–5pm Mon–Fri, 10am–5pm Sat & Sun.* ⬤ *public hols.* 📷 *Tue–Fri only.* **Palácio dos Condes da Calheta** ⬚ *as above.* ⬤ *12:30–2pm.*

Also known as the Jardim do Ultramar, this peaceful park with ponds, waterfowl and peacocks attracts surprisingly few visitors. Laid out at the start of the 20th century as the research centre of the Institute for Tropical Sciences, it is more of an arboretum than a flower garden. The emphasis is on rare and endangered tropical and subtropical trees and plants. Among the most striking are dragon trees, native to the Canary Islands and Madeira, monkey puzzle trees from South America and a handsome avenue of Washington palms. The oriental garden, with its streams, bridges and hibiscus, is heralded by a large Chinese-style gateway that represented Macau in the Exhibition of the Portuguese World in 1940 (*see p100*).

Visigothic gold buckle, Museu de Arqueologia

The research buildings are located in the **Palácio dos Condes da Calheta**, whose interior walls are covered with *azulejos* spanning three centuries. The palace is open to the public and houses temporary exhibitions.

Mosteiro dos Jerónimos ❹

See pp104–5.

Washington palms in the Jardim Agrícola Tropical

Museu Nacional de Arqueologia ❺

Praça do Império. **Map** 1 B4. *Tel 213 620 000.* 🚌 *28, 714, 727, 729, 751.* 🚊 *15.* 🚊 *Belém.* ⬚ *10am–6pm Tue–Sun.* ⬤ *1 Jan, Easter, 1 May, 25 Dec.* 📷 *(free 10am–2pm Sun).* 📷 ♿ www.mnarqueologia-ipmuseus.pt

The long west wing of the Mosteiro dos Jerónimos (*see pp104–5*), formerly the monks' dormitory, has been a museum since 1893. Reconstructed in the middle of the 19th century, the building is a poor imitation of the Manueline original. The museum houses Portugal's main archaeological research centre and the exhibits, from sites all over the country, include a gold Iron Age bracelet found in the Alentejo and Visigothic jewellery from Beja (*see p313*), Roman ornaments and early 8th-century Moorish artefacts. The main Egyptian and Greco-Roman section is strong on funerary art, featuring figurines, tombstones, masks, terracotta amulets and funeral cones inscribed with hieroglyphics alluding to the solar system. The dimly lit Room of Treasures has an exquisite collection of coins, necklaces, bracelets and other

jewellery dating from 1800–500 BC. This room has been refurbished to allow more of the magnificent jewellery, unseen by the public for decades, to be shown.

Planetário Calouste Gulbenkian ❻

Praça do Império. **Map** 1 B4. *Tel 213 620 002.* 🚌 *28, 49, 112, 727, 751.* 🚊 *15.* ⬚ *11am Wed, 4pm Thu, 3pm Sat & Sun.* 📷 📷 ♿ www.planetario.online.pt

Financed by the Gulbenkian foundation (*see p117*) and built in 1965, this modern building sits incongruously beside the Jerónimos monastery. Inside, the Planetarium reveals the mysteries of the cosmos. There are shows in Portuguese, English and French explaining the movement of the stars and our solar system, as well as presentations on more specialist themes, such as the constellations or the Star of Bethlehem (Belém).

The dome of the Planetário Calouste Gulbenkian

Mosteiro dos Jerónimos 4

Armillary sphere
in the cloister

A monument to the wealth of the Age of Discovery *(see pp48–9)*, the monastery is the culmination of Manueline architecture *(see pp20–21)*. commissioned by Manuel I in around 1501, after Vasco da Gama's return from his historic voyage, it was financed largely by "pepper money", a tax levied on spices precious stones and gold. Various masterbuilders worked on the building, the most notable of whom was Diogo Boitac, replaced by João de Castilho in 1517. The monastery was cared for by the Order of St Jerome (Hieronymites) until 1834, when all religious orders were disbanded.

Tomb of Vasco da Gama
The 19th-century tomb of the navigator (see p106) *is carved with ropes, spheres and other seafaring symbols.*

Refectory
The walls of the refectory are tiled with 18th-century azulejos. *The panel at the northern end depicts the Feeding of the Five Thousand.*

The fountain is in the shape of a lion, the heraldic animal of St Jerome.

The modern wing, built in 1850 in Neo-Manueline style, houses the Museu Nacional de Arqueologia *(see p103).*

The west portal was designed by the French sculptor Nicolau Chanterène.

Entrance to church and cloister

Gallery

View of the Monastery
This 17th-century scene by Felipe Lobo shows women at a fountain in front of the Mosteiro dos Jerónimos.

STAR FEATURES

★ South Portal

★ Cloister

★ **Cloister**
João de Castilho's pure Manueline creation was completed in 1544. Delicate tracery and richly carved images decorate the arches and balustrades.

VISITORS' CHECKLIST

Praça do Império. **Map** 1 R4
Tel 213 620 034. 🚌 727, 728, 729, 751. 🚊 15. 🚉 Belem. ⬜ May–Sep: 10am–6:30pm; Oct–Apr: 10am–5:30pm. ⬤ public hols. 🕆 🏛 (free am Sun). 📷

Nave
The spectacular vaulting in the church of Santa Maria is held aloft by slender octagonal pillars. These rise like palm trees to the roof creating a feeling of space and harmony.

The chapterhouse holds the tomb of Alexandre Herculano (1810–77), historian and first mayor of Belém.

The chancel was commissioned in 1572 by Dona Catarina, wife of João III.

The tombs of Manuel I, his wife Dona Maria, João III and Catarina are supported by elephants.

★ **South Portal**
The strict geometrical architecture of the portal is almost obscured by the exuberant decoration. João de Castilho unites religious themes, such as this image of St Jerome, with the secular, exalting the kings of Portugal.

Tomb of King Sebastião
The tomb of the "longed for" Dom Sebastião stands empty. The young king never returned from battle in 1578 (see p47).

Façade of the Museu de Marinha

Museu de Marinha ➐

Praça do Império. **Map** 1 B4.
Tel *213 620 019.* 🚌 *28, 727, 729,
751.* 🚊 *15.* 🚋 *Belém.* ⏱ *10am–
6pm Tue–Sun (Oct–Mar: to 5pm).*
⬤ *1 Jan, Easter, 1 May, 25 Dec.*
📷 *(free 10am–1pm Sun).* 📷 ♿
www.museu.marinha.pt

The Maritime Museum was
inaugurated in 1962 in the
west wing of the Jerónimos
monastery *(see pp104–5).* It
was here, in the chapel built by
Henry the Navigator *(see p49),*
that mariners took mass before
embarking on their voyages.
A hall about the Discoveries

illustrates the
progress in ship-
building from the
mid-15th century,
capitalizing on the
experience of long-
distance explorers.
Small replicas show
the transition from
the bark to the
lateen-rigged caravel,
through the faster
square-rigged caravel,
to the Portuguese
nau. Also here are
navigational instru-
ments, astrolabes and
replicas of 16th-cen-
tury maps showing
the world as it was
known then. The
stone pillars, carved
with the Cross of the
Knights of Christ,
are replicas of the
types of *padrão* set
up as monuments
to Portuguese
sovereignty on
the lands discovered.

A series of rooms displaying
models of modern Portuguese
ships leads on to the Royal
Quarters, where you can see
the exquisitely furnished
wood-panelled cabin of King
Carlos and Queen Amélia
from the royal yacht *Amélia,*
built in Scotland in 1900.

The modern, incongruous
pavilion opposite houses original royal barges, the most
extravagant of which is the
royal brig built in 1780 for
Maria I. The collection ends
with a display of seaplanes,
including the *Santa Clara*
which made the first crossing
of the South Atlantic in 1922.

Centro Cultural de Belém ➑

Praça do Império. **Map** 1 B5.
Tel *213 612 400.* 🚌 *28, 727, 729,
751.* 🚊 *15.* 🚋 *Belém.* **Berardo
Collection Museum** *Tel 213 612
878.* ⏱ *10am–7pm daily (last entry
at 6:30pm).* ♿ **www.**ccb.pt

Standing between the Tagus
and the Jerónimos monastery,
this stark, modern building was
erected as the headquarters of
the Portuguese presidency of
the European Community. In
1993 it opened as a cultural
centre offering performing
arts, music and photography.
The centre houses the **Berardo
Collection Museum**, which has
contemporary art by the likes
of Francis Bacon, Willem de
Kooning and Michel Basquiat.

Both the café and restaurant
spill out onto the ramparts of
the building, whose peaceful
gardens of olive trees and
geometric lawns look out
over the quay and river.

**The modern complex of the
Centro Cultural de Belém**

Monument to the Discoveries ➒

Padrão dos Descobrimentos,
Avenida de Brasília. **Map** 1 C5.
Tel *213 031 950.* 🚌 *28, 727.* 🚊 *15.*
🚋 *Belém.* ⏱ *10am–6pm Tue–Sun
(May–Sep: to 7pm).* ⬤ *1 Jan, 1 May,
25 Dec.* 📷 *for lift.* 📷 **www.**
padraodescobrimentos.egeac.pt

Standing prominently on the
Belém waterfront, this massive angular monument, the
Padrão dos Descobrimentos,
was built in 1960 to mark the
500th anniversary of the death
of Henry the Navigator *(see
p49).* The 52-m (170-ft) high
monument, commissioned by
the Salazar regime, commemorates the mariners, royal
patrons and all those who

VASCO DA GAMA (C.1460–1524)

In 1498 Vasco da Gama sailed
around the Cape of Good Hope
and opened the sea route to India
(see pp48–9). Although the Hindu
ruler of Calicut, who received him
wearing diamond and ruby rings,
was not impressed by his humble
offerings of cloth and wash basins,
da Gama returned to Portugal
with a cargo of spices. In 1502 he
sailed again to India, establishing
Portuguese trade routes in the
Indian Ocean. João III nominated
him Viceroy of India in 1524, but
he died of a fever soon after.

**16th-century painting of
Vasco da Gama in Goa**

The huge pavement compass in front of the Monument to the Discoveries

took part in the development of the Portuguese Age of Discovery. The monument is designed in the shape of a caravel, with Portugal's coat of arms on the sides and the sword of the Royal House of Avis rising above the entrance. Henry the Navigator stands at the prow with a caravel in hand. In two sloping lines either side of the monument are stone statues of Portuguese heroes linked with the Age of Discovery, such as Dom Manuel I holding an armillary sphere, the poet Camões with a copy of Os Lusíadas and the painter Nuno Gonçalves, as well as famous navigators, cartographers and kings.

On the monument's north side, the huge mariner's compass cut into the paving stone was a gift

from South Africa in 1960. The central map, dotted with mermaids and galleons, shows the routes of the discoverers in the 15th and 16th centuries. Inside the monument a lift whisks you up to the sixth floor where steps then lead to the top for a splendid panorama of Belém. The basement level is used for temporary exhibitions, but not necessarily related to the Discoveries.

The rather ostentatious Padrão is not to everyone's taste but the setting is undeniably splendid and the caravel design is imaginative. The monument looks particularly dramatic when viewed from the west in the light of the late afternoon sun.

Museu de Arte Popular ⑩

Avenida de Brasília. **Map** 1 B5.
Tel *213 011 282.* 🚌 *28, 727, 729.*
🚃*15.* 🚊 *Belém.* ⬤ *closed for refurbishment.* 📷

The drab building on the waterfront, between the Monument to the Discoveries and the Torre de Belém *(see p108)*, houses the museum of Portuguese folk art and traditional handicrafts, opened in 1948. While the rooms housing the permanent collections are closed for alterations indefinitely, a temporary exhibition space is open. The exhibits are arranged by province and include local pottery, costumes, agricultural tools, musical instruments, jewellery and brightly coloured saddles. The display gives a vivid indication of the diversity between the different regions. Each area has its speciality such as the colourful ox yokes and ceramic cocks from the Minho, basketware from Trás-os-Montes, cowbells and terracotta casseroles from the Alentejo and fishing equipment from the Algarve. If you are planning to travel around the country the museum offers an excellent preview to the traditional handicrafts of the provinces.

Traditional costume from Trás-os-Montes

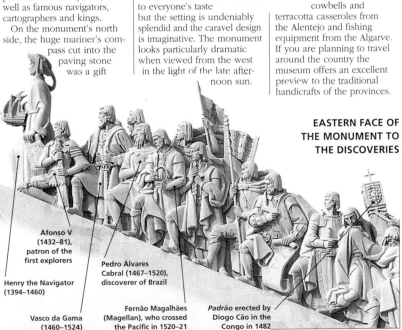

EASTERN FACE OF THE MONUMENT TO THE DISCOVERIES

Afonso V (1432–81), patron of the first explorers

Pedro Álvares Cabral (1467–1520), discoverer of Brazil

Henry the Navigator (1394–1460)

Vasco da Gama (1460–1524)

Fernão Magalhães (Magellan), who crossed the Pacific in 1520–21

Padrão erected by Diogo Cão in the Congo in 1482

Torre de Belém ⑪

Arms of Manuel I

Commissioned by Manuel I, the tower was built as a fortress in the middle of the Tagus in 1515–21. Starting point for the navigators who set out to discover the trade routes, this Manueline gem became a symbol of Portugal's great era of expansion. The real beauty of the tower lies in the decoration of the exterior. Adorned with rope carved in stone, it has openwork balconies, Moorish-style watchtowers and distinctive battlements in the shape of shields. The Gothic interior below the terrace, which served as a storeroom for arms and a prison, is very austere but the private quarters in the tower are worth visiting for the loggia and the panorama.

VISITORS' CHECKLIST

Avenida de Brasilia. **Map** 1 A5.
Tel 213 620 034. 🚌 729.
🚋 15. 🚆 Belém. ⏱ 10am–
6:30pm Tue–Sun (Oct–Apr:
to 5:30pm). ⬤ public hols.
📷 📷 ♿ ground floor only.

Renaissance Loggia
The elegant arcaded loggia, inspired by Italian architecture, gives a light touch to the defensive battlements of the tower.

Armillary spheres
and nautical rope are symbols of Portugal's seafaring prowess.

Royal coat of arms of Manuel I

Chapel

Battlements are decorated with the cross of the Order of Christ *(see pp24–5).*

Governor's room

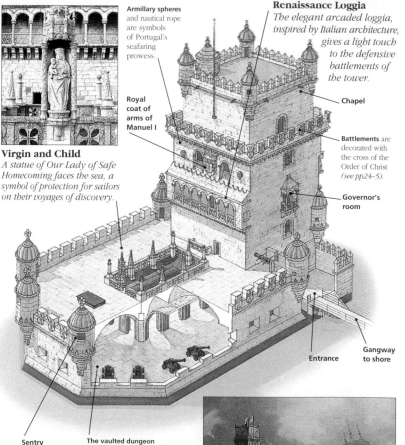

Virgin and Child
A statue of Our Lady of Safe Homecoming faces the sea, a symbol of protection for sailors on their voyages of discovery.

Entrance

Gangway to shore

Sentry posts

The vaulted dungeon was used as a prison until the 19th century.

The Torre de Belém in 1811
This painting of a British ship navigating the Tagus, by JT Serres, shows the tower much further from the shore than it is today. In the 19th century land on the north bank was reclaimed, making the river narrower.

The simple Manueline chapel, Ermida de São Jerónimo

Ermida de São Jerónimo ⑫

Rua Pero de Covilhã. **Map** 1 A3. **Tel** *213 018 648.* 🚌 *28, 49, 73, 714, 729, 751.* ⬜ *Mon–Sat (by appt).*

Also known as the Capela de São Jerónimo, this elegant little chapel was constructed in 1514 when Diogo Boitac was working on the Jerónimos monastery *(see pp104–5)*. Although a far simpler building, it is also Manueline in style and may have been built to a design by Boitac. The only decorative elements on the monolithic chapel are the four pinnacles, corner gargoyles and Manueline portal. Perched on a quiet hill above Belém, the chapel has fine views down to the River Tagus and a path from the terrace winds down the hill towards the Torre de Belém.

Igreja da Memória ⑬

Calçada do Galvão, Ajuda. **Map** 1 C3. **Tel** *213 635 295.* 🚌 *28, 714, 727, 732* 🚊 *18.* ⬜ *for mass 6pm Mon–Sat, 10am Sun.* ✝ &

Built in 1760, the church was founded by King José I in gratitude for his escape from an assassination plot on this site in 1758. The king was returning from a secret liaison with a lady of the noble Távora family when his carriage was attacked and a bullet hit him in the arm. Pombal *(see pp52–3)*, whose power had become absolute, used this as an excuse to get rid of his enemies in the Távora family,

accusing them of conspiracy. In 1759 they were savagely tortured and executed. Their deaths are commemorated by a pillar in Beco do Chão Salgado, off Rua de Belém.

The Neo-Classical domed church has a marble-clad interior and a small chapel containing the tomb of Pombal, who died a year after being banished from Lisbon.

Jardim Botânico da Ajuda ⑭

Calçada da Ajuda. **Map** 1 C2. **Tel** & **Fax** *213 622 503.* 🚌 *28, 73, 714, 727, 729, 732.* 🚊 *18.* ⬜ *Apr: 9am–7pm daily; May–Sep: 9am–8pm daily; Oct–Mar: 9am–6pm daily.* ⬤ *1 Jan, 25 Dec.* 🎫 & 🖼 *(fax your request).*

Laid out by Pombal *(see p19)* in 1768, these Italian-style gardens provide a pleasant respite from Belém's noisy suburbs. The entrance (wrought-iron gates in a pink wall) is easy to miss. The park has 5,000 plant species from Africa, Asia and America. Notable features are the 400-year-old dragon tree, native of Madeira, and the flamboyant 18th-century fountain decorated with serpents, winged fish, sea horses and mythical creatures. A majestic terrace looks out over the lower level of the gardens.

Palácio Nacional da Ajuda ⑮

Calçada da Ajuda. **Map** 2 D2. **Tel** *213 620 264.* 🚌 *60, 714, 732, 742.* 🚊 *18.* ⬜ *10am–5:30pm Thu–Tue (last entry 5pm).* ⬤ *public hols.* 🖼 *(free 10am–2pm Sun).* & 🖼

The royal palace, destroyed by fire in 1795, was replaced in the early 19th century by this Neo-Classical building. Left incomplete when the royal family was forced into exile in Brazil in 1807 *(see pp52–3)*, the palace only became a permanent residence of the royal family when Luís I became king in 1861 and married an Italian Princess, Maria Pia di Savoia. No expense was spared in furnishing the apartments, which are decorated with silk wallpaper, Sèvres porcelain and crystal chandeliers. A prime example of regal excess is the extraordinary Saxe Room, a wedding present to Maria Pia from the King of Saxony, in which every piece of furniture is decorated with Meissen porcelain. On the first floor the huge Banqueting Hall, with crystal chandeliers, silk-covered chairs and an allegory of the birth of João VI on the frescoed ceiling, is truly impressive. At the other end of the palace, Luís I's Neo-Gothic painting studio is a more intimate display of intricately carved furniture.

19th-century throne from the Palácio Nacional da Ajuda

Manicured formal gardens of the Jardim Botânico da Ajuda

FURTHER AFIELD

The majority of the outlying sights, which include some of Lisbon's finest museums, are easily accessible by bus or metro from the city centre. A ten-minute walk north from the gardens of the Parque Eduardo VII brings you to Portugal's great cultural complex, the Calouste Gulbenkian Foundation, set in a pleasant park. Few tourists go further north than the Gulbenkian, but the Museu da Cidade on Campo Grande is worth a detour for its fascinating overview of Lisbon's history.

Azulejo **panel from Palácio Fronteira**

The charming Palácio Fronteira, decorated with splendid tiles, is one of the many villas built for the aristocracy that now overlook the city suburbs. Those interested in tiles will also enjoy the Museu Nacional do Azulejo in the cloisters of the Madre de Deus convent.

Visitors with a spare half day can cross the Tagus to the Cristo Rei monument. Northeast of Lisbon is the vast oceanarium, Oceanário de Lisboa, in the Parque das Nações, which includes other family-oriented attractions, hotels and shops.

SIGHTS AT A GLANCE

Museums and Galleries
Centro de Arte Moderna ❼
Museu da Água ❾
Museu Calouste Gulbenkian pp114–17 ❻
Museu da Cidade ❸
Museu Nacional do Azulejo pp120–21 ❿

Modern Architecture
Centro Colombo ❸
Cristo Rei ❶
Parque das Nações ⓫
Ponte 25 de Abril ❷

Historic Architecture
Aqueduto das Águas Livres ⓯
Campo Pequeno ❽
Palácio Fronteira ⓰
Praça Marquês de Pombal ❹

Parks and Gardens
Parque Eduardo VII ❺
Parque do Monteiro-Mor ⓱

Zoos
Jardim Zoológico ⓮
Oceanário de Lisboa ⓬

KEY

▪ Main sightseeing areas
✈ Airport
⛴ Ferry boarding point
═ Motorway
═ Major road
═ Minor road

0 kilometres   4

0 miles   2

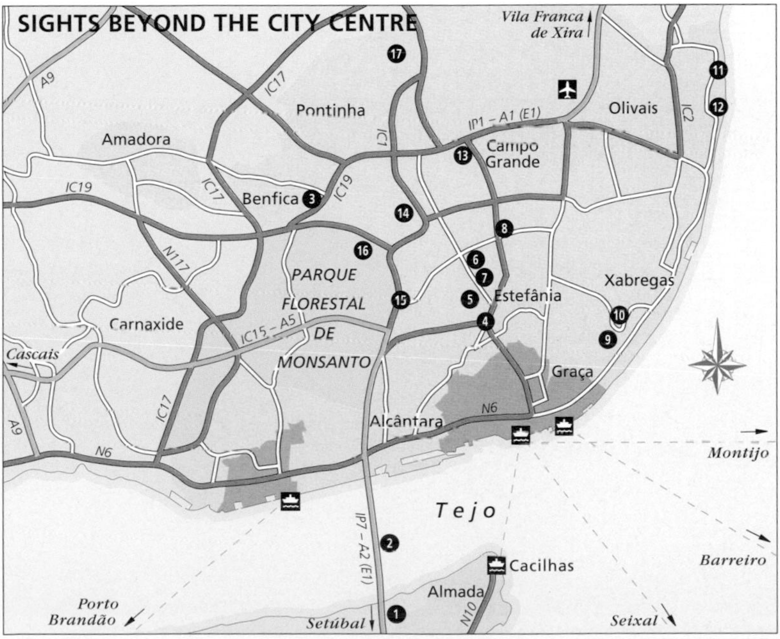

SIGHTS BEYOND THE CITY CENTRE

Vila Franca de Xira

⓱ A9 IC17 Pontinha Amadora ✈ IP1 – A1 (E1) Olivais ⓫ ⓬ IC2

IC19 IC17 Benfica ❸ IC19 ⓭ Campo Grande

N117 ⓮ ⓰ ❻ ❼ ❽ Xabregas

Carnaxide PARQUE FLORESTAL ⓯ ❺ Estefânia ❿ ❾

Cascais DE ❹ Graça

IC17 IC15 – A5 MONSANTO

N6 Alcântara N6 Montijo

N6 ❷ *Tejo* Cacilhas Barreiro

Porto Brandão Almada Seixal

Setúbal ❶

◁ **Nymph fountain among tropical vegetation inside the Estufa Fria, Parque Eduardo VII**

Cristo Rei ❶

Santuário Nacional do Cristo Rei,
Alto do Pragal, Almada. **Tel** 212 751
000. 🚢 Transtejo Cacilhas ferry from
Cais do Sodré to Cacilhas, then
🚌 101. **Lift** ◯ Jul–Sep: 9:30am–
6:30pm daily (to 7pm Sat & Sun);
Oct–Jun: 9:30am–6pm daily. 📷

Modelled on the more famous
Cristo Redentor in Rio de
Janeiro, this giant statue
stands with arms outstretched
on the south bank of the
Tagus. The 28 m (92 ft) tall
figure of Christ, mounted on
an 82 m (269 ft) pedestal, was
built by Francisco Franco in
1949–59 at the instigation of
Prime Minister Salazar.

You can see the monument
from various viewpoints in
the city, but it is fun to take a
ferry to the Outra Banda (the
other bank), then a bus or taxi
to the monument. A lift, plus
some steps, takes you to the
top of the pedestal, affording
fine views of the city.

**The towering monument of Cristo
Rei overlooking the Tagus**

Ponte 25 de Abril ❷

Map 3 A5. 🚌 52, 53.

Originally called the Ponte
Salazar after the dictator
who had it built in 1966,
Lisbon's suspension bridge
was renamed (like many other
monuments) to commemorate
the revolution of 25 April 1974
which restored democracy to
Portugal (see p57).

Inspired by San Francisco's
Golden Gate in the United
States, this steel construction
stretches for 2 km (half a mile).
The lower tier was modified

in 1999 to accommodate the
Fertagus, a much-needed
railway across the Tagus.

The bridge's notorious
traffic congestion has been
partly resolved by the
opening of the 11-km
(7-mile) Vasco da Gama
bridge. Spanning the river
from Montijo to Sacavém,
north of the Parque das
Nações, this bridge was
completed in 1998.

Centro Colombo ❸

Avenida Lusíada. **Tel** 217 113 636.
Ⓜ Colégio Militar. 🚌 3, 64, 729,
765, 799. ◯ 9am–midnight daily.
♿ www.colombo.pt

The huge Centro Colombo
in Benfica is the biggest
shopping centre in the
Iberian Peninsula, almost
matching the adjacent
Estádio da Luz football
stadium in size. With its 420
shops, 60 restaurants and 10
cinemas, this mall provides
the ultimate everything-
under-one-roof shopping
experience. The Funcenter
located on the second floor
is an indoor amusement
park catering for kids of all
ages with a roller coaster,
amusement arcade, carousels
and a 24-lane bowling alley.
Other amenities include a
well-equipped health club.

Ponte 25 de Abril linking central Lisbon with the Outra Banda, the south bank of the Tagus

Tropical plants in the Estufa Quente glasshouse, Parque Eduardo VII

Praça Marquês de Pombal ❹

Map 5 C5. Ⓜ *Marquês de Pombal.* 🚌 *12, 22, 36, 711, 720, 723, 727, 732, 738 & many other routes.*

At the top of the Avenida da Liberdade *(see p82)*, traffic thunders round the "Rotunda" (roundabout), as the praça is also known. At the centre is a 1934 monument to Pombal. The despotic statesman, who virtually ruled Portugal from 1750–77, stands on the top of the column, his hand on a lion (symbol of power) and his eyes directed down to the Baixa, whose creation he masterminded *(see pp62–3)*.

Detail representing agricultural toil on the base of the monument in Praça Marquês de Pombal

Allegorical images depicting Pombal's political, educational and agricultural reforms decorate the base of the monument. Standing figures represent Coimbra University, where he introduced a new Faculty of Science. Broken blocks of stone at the foot of the monument and tidal waves flooding the city are an allegory of the destruction caused by the 1755 earthquake.

An underpass, which is not always open, leads to the centre of the square where the sculptures on the pedestal and the inscriptions relating to Pombal's achievements can be seen. Nearby, the well-tended Parque Eduardo VII extends northwards behind the square. The paving stones around the Rotunda are decorated with a mosaic of Lisbon's coat of arms. Similar patterns decorate many of the city's streets and squares. A tunnel is being built under the roundabout to ease traffic. Until the work is completed, the area is likely to be heavily congested.

Parque Eduardo VII ❺

Praça Marquês de Pombal. **Map** 5 B4. *Tel 213 882 278.* Ⓜ *Marquês de Pombal.* 🚌 *12, 22, 36, 711.* **Estufa Fria** 🔴 *for renovation.* ♿

The largest park in central Lisbon was named in honour of King Edward VII of England who came to Lisbon in 1902 to reaffirm the Anglo-Portuguese alliance. The wide grassy slope that extends for 25 hectares (62 acres) was laid out as Parque de Liberdade, a continuation of Avenida da Liberdade *(see p82)* in the late 19th century. Neatly clipped box hedging, flanked by mosaic patterned walkways, stretches uphill from the Praça Marquês de Pombal to a belvedere at the top. Here, in the flower-filled landscaped garden dedicated to Amália Rodrigues *(see p65)*, you will find the *Fat Mama* sculpture by Botero. From here there are fine views of the city. On clear days it is possible to see as far as the Serra da Arrábida *(see p169)*.

Located at the northwest corner, the most inspiring feature of this rather monotonous park is the jungle-like **Estufa Fria**, or greenhouse, where exotic plants, streams and waterfalls provide an oasis from the city streets.

There are in fact two greenhouses: in the Estufa Fria (cold greenhouse), palms push through the slatted bamboo roof and paths wind through a forest of ferns, fuchsias, flowering shrubs and banana trees; the Estufa Quente, or hothouse, is a glassed-over garden with lush plants, water-lily ponds and cacti, as well as tropical birds in cages.

Near the estufas a pond with large carp and a play area in the shape of a galleon are popular with children. On the east side the **Pavilhão Carlos Lopes**, named after the 1984 Olympic marathon winner, is now a venue for concerts and conferences. The façade is decorated with a series of modern tiled scenes.

Museu Calouste Gulbenkian ❻

Thanks to a wealthy Armenian oil magnate, Calouste Gulbenkian *(see p117)*, with wide-ranging tastes and an eye for a masterpiece, the museum has one of the finest collections of art in Europe. Inaugurated in 1969, the purpose-built museum was created as part of the charitable institution bequeathed to Portugal by the multimillionaire. The design of the building, set in a spacious park allowing natural light to fill some of the rooms, was devised to create the best layout for the founder's varied collection.

Mustard Barrel
This 18th-century silver mustard barrel was made in France by Antoine Sébastien Durand.

Lalique Corsage Ornament
The sinuous curves of the gold and enamel snakes are typical of René Lalique's Art Nouveau jewellery.

★ Diana
This fine marble statue (1780) by the French sculptor Jean-Antoine Houdon, was once owned by Catherine the Great of Russia but was considered too obscene to exhibit. The graceful Diana, goddess of the hunt, stands with a bow and arrow in hand.

Entrance

Stairs to

★ St Catherine
This serene bust of St Catherine was painted by the Flemish artist Rogier Van der Weyden (1400–64). The thin strip of landscape on the left of the wooden panel brings light and depth to the still portrait.

STAR EXHIBITS

★ Portrait of an Old Man by Rembrandt

★ Diana by Houdon

★ St Catherine by Van der Weyden

★ Portrait of an Old Man
Rembrandt was a master of light and shade. In this expressive portrait, dated 1645, the fragile countenance of the old man is contrasted with the strong and dramatic lighting.

VISITORS' CHECKLIST

Avenida de Berna 45.
Map 5 B2. **Tel** *217 823 402.*
Ⓜ *Praça de Espanha or São Sebastião.* 🚌 *16, 56, 718, 726, 742.* ◻ *10am–6pm Tue–Sun.* ● *1 Jan, Easter, 1 May, 25 Dec.* 🎫 *(free Sun).*
♿ 🖥 🍴
www.museu.gulbenkian.pt

Renaissance art

Vase of a Hundred Birds
The enamel decoration that adorns this Chinese porcelain vase is known as Famille Verte. *This type of elaborate design is characteristic of the Ch'ing dynasty during the reign of the Emperor K'ang Hsi (1662–1722).*

GALLERY GUIDE
The galleries are laid out both chronologically and geographically, the first section (rooms 1–6) dedicated to Classical and Oriental art, the second section (rooms 7–17) housing the European collection of paintings, sculpture, furniture, silverware and jewellery.

Armenian art

Egyptian Bronze Cat
This bronze of a cat feeding her kittens dates from the Saite Period (8th century BC). Other stunning Egyptian pieces include a gilded mask of a mummy.

Persian faïence

Turkish Faïence Plate
The factories at Iznik in Turkey produced some of the most beautiful jugs, plates and vases of the Islamic world, including this 17th-century deep plate decorated with stylized animal forms.

KEY TO FLOORPLAN

☐	Egyptian, Classical and Mesopotamian art
☐	Oriental Islamic art
☐	Far Eastern art
☐	European art (14th–17th centuries)
☐	French 18th-century decorative arts
☐	European art (18th–19th centuries)
☐	Lalique collection
☐	Non-exhibition space

Exploring the Gulbenkian Collection

Housing Calouste Gulbenkian's unique collection of art, the museum ranks with the Museu de Arte Antiga *(see pp94–7)* as the finest in Lisbon. The exhibits, which span over 4,000 years from ancient Egyptian statuettes, through translucent Islamic glassware, to Art Nouveau brooches, are displayed in spacious and well-lit galleries, many overlooking the gardens or courtyards. The museum is quite small, however each individual work of art, from the magnificent pieces that make up the rich display of Oriental and Islamic art, to the selection of European paintings and furniture, is worthy of attention.

Late 16th-century Persian faïence tile from the School of Isfahan

EGYPTIAN, CLASSICAL AND MESOPOTAMIAN ART

Priceless treasures chart the evolution of Egyptian art from the Old Kingdom (c.2700 BC) to the Roman Period (lst century BC). The exhibits range from an alabaster bowl of the 3rd Dynasty to a surprisingly modern-looking blue terracotta torso of a statuette of *Venus Anadyomene* from the Roman period.

Outstanding pieces in the Classical art section are a magnificent red-figure Greek vase and 11 Roman medallions, found in Egypt. These are believed to have been struck to commemorate the Olympic games held in Macedonia in AD 242 in honour of Alexander the Great. In the Mesopotamian art section the large Assyrian

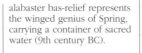
5th-century BC Greek vase

alabaster bas-relief represents the winged genius of Spring, carrying a container of sacred water (9th century BC).

ORIENTAL ISLAMIC ART

Being Armenian, Calouste Gulbenkian had a keen interest in art from the Near and Middle East. The Oriental Islamic gallery has a fine collection of Persian and Turkish carpets, textiles, costumes and ceramics. In the section overlooking the courtyard, the Syrian mosque lamps and bottles commissioned by princes and sultans, are beautifully decorated with coloured enamel on glass. The Armenian section has some exquisite illustrated manuscripts from the 16th to 18th centuries, produced by Armenian refugees in Istanbul, Persia and the Crimea.

FAR EASTERN ART

Calouste Gulbenkian acquired a large collection of Chinese porcelain between 1910 and 1930. One of the rarest pieces is the small blue-glazed bowl from the Yüan Dynasty (1279–1368), on the right as you go into the gallery. The majority of exhibits, however, are the later, more exuberantly decorated *famille verte* porcelain and the K'ang Hsi biscuitware of the 17th and 18th centuries. Further exhibits from the Far East are translucent Chinese jades and other semi-precious stones, Japanese prints, brocaded silk hangings and bound books, and lacquerwork.

EUROPEAN ART (14TH–17TH CENTURIES)

Illuminated manuscripts, rare printed books and medieval ivories introduce the section on Western art. The delicately sculpted 14th-century ivory diptychs and triptychs, made in France, show scenes from the lives of Christ and the Virgin.

The collection of early European paintings starts with panels of *St Joseph* and *St Catherine* by Rogier van der Weyden, leading painter of the mid-15th century in Flanders. Italian Renaissance painting is represented by Cima da Conegliano's *Sacra Conversazione* from the late 15th century and Domenico Ghirlandaio's *Portrait of a Young Woman* (1485).

The collection progresses to Flemish and Dutch works of the 17th century, including two works by Rembrandt: *Portrait of an Old Man* (1645),

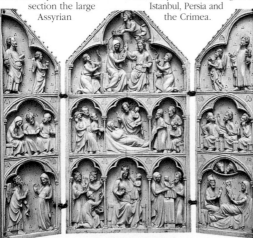
French ivory triptych of
Scenes from the Life of the Virgin **(14th century)**

a masterpiece of psychological penetration, and *Alexander the Great* (1660), said to have been modelled on Rembrandt's son, Titus, and previously thought to have portrayed the Greek goddess Pallas Athena. Rubens is represented by three paintings, the most remarkable of which is the *Portrait of Hélène Fourment* (1630), the artist's second wife.

The gallery beyond the Dutch and Flemish paintings has tapestries and textiles from Italy and Flanders, Italian ceramics, rare 15th-century medallions and sculpture.

FRENCH 18TH-CENTURY DECORATIVE ARTS

Some remarkably elaborate Louis XV and Louis XVI pieces, many commissioned by royalty, feature in the collection of French 18th-century furniture. The exhibits, many of them embellished with laquer panels, ebony and bronze, are grouped together according to historical style with Beauvais and "chinoiserie" Aubusson tapestries decorating the walls.

The French silverware from the same period, much of which once adorned the dining tables of Russian palaces, includes lavishly decorated soup tureens, salt-cellars and platters.

Louis XV chest of drawers inlaid with ebony and bronze

EUROPEAN ART (18TH–19TH CENTURIES)

The art of the 18th century is dominated by French painters, including Watteau (1684–1721), Fragonard (1732–1806) and Boucher (1703–70). The most celebrated piece of sculpture is a statue of *Diana* by Jean-Antoine Houdon. Commissioned in 1780 by the Duke of Saxe-Gotha for his

View of the Molo with the Ducal Palace (1790) by Francesco Guardi

gardens, it became one of the principal exhibits in the Hermitage in Russia during the 19th and early 20th centuries.

One whole room is devoted to views of Venice by the 18th-century Venetian painter Francesco Guardi, and a small collection of British art includes works by leading 18th-century portraitists, such as Gainsborough's *Portrait of Mrs Lowndes-Stone* (c.1775) and Romney's *Portrait of Mrs Constable* (1787). There are also two stormy seascapes by JMW Turner (1775–1851). French 19th-century landscape painting is well represented here, reflecting Gulbenkian's preference for naturalism, with works by the Barbizon school, the Realists and the Impressionists. The best-known paintings in the section, however, are probably Manet's *Boy with Cherries*, painted in about 1858 at the beginning of the artist's career, and *Boy Blowing Bubbles*, painted about 1867. Renoir's *Portrait of Madame Claude Monet* was painted in about 1872 when the artist was staying with Monet at his country home in Argenteuil, in the outskirts of Paris.

LALIQUE COLLECTION

The tour of the museum ends with an entire room filled with the flamboyant creations of French Art Nouveau jeweller, René Lalique (1860–1945). Gulbenkian was a close friend of Lalique's and he acquired many of the pieces of jewellery, glassware and ivory on display here directly from the artist. Inlaid with semi-precious stones and covered with gold leaf or enamel, the brooches, necklaces, vases and combs are decorated with the dragonfly, peacock or sensual female nude motifs characteristic of Art Nouveau.

CALOUSTE GULBENKIAN

Born in Scutari (Turkey) in 1869, Gulbenkian started his art collection at the age of 14 when he bought some ancient coins in a bazaar. In 1928 he was granted a 5 per cent stake in four major oil companies, including BP and Shell, in thanks for his part in the transfer of the assets of the Turkish Petroleum Company to those four companies. He thereby earned himself the nickname of "Mr Five Percent". With the wealth he accumulated, Gulbenkian was able to indulge his passion for fine works of art. During World War II, he went to live in neutral Portugal and, on his death in 1955, bequeathed his estate to the Portuguese in the form of a charitable trust. The Foundation supports many cultural activities and has its own orchestra, libraries, ballet company and concert halls.

A light-filled gallery at the Centro de Arte Moderna

Centro de Arte Moderna 🌑

Rua Dr Nicolau de Bettencourt.
Map 5 B3. *Tel* 217 823 000. Ⓜ *São Sebastião.* 🚌 *16, 56, 718, 726, 742, 746.* ◯ *10am–6pm Tue–Sun.* ● *1 Jan, Easter, 1 May, 25 Dec.* 🎟 *(free Sun).* **www**.gulbenkian.pt

The Modern Art Museum lies across the gardens from the Calouste Gulbenkian museum and is part of the same cultural foundation *(see p117)*.

The permanent collection features paintings and sculpture by Portuguese artists from the turn of the 20th century to the present day.

The most famous painting is the striking portrait of poet Fernando Pessoa in the Café Irmãos Unidos (1964) by José de Almada Negreiros (1893– 1970), a main exponent of Portuguese Modernism. Also of interest are paintings by Eduardo Viana (1881– 1967), Amadeo de Sousa Cardoso (1887–1910), as well as contemporary artists such as Paula Rego, Rui Sanches, Graça Morais and Teresa Magalhães.

The museum is light and spacious, with pleasant gardens and a busy cafeteria.

Campo Pequeno 🌑

Map 5 C1. Ⓜ *Campo Pequeno.* 🚌 *22, 745.* **Bullring** *Tel* 217 820 575. ◯ *Easter–Oct: for bullfights.* 🎟 ♿

This square is dominated by the red-brick Neo-Moorish bullring built in the late 19th century. A full renovation added a roof, a shopping and leisure centre and an underground car park. Much of the bullring's distinctive architecture, such as keyhole-shaped windows and double cupolas was retained.

Call the tourist office or the number listed above for information on this and other bullfight venues.

Renovated 19th-century steam pump in the Museu da Água

Museu da Água 🌑

Rua do Alviela 12. *Tel* 218 100 215. 🚌 *35, 107.* ◯ *10am–6pm Mon– Sat.* ● *public hols.* 🎟 📷

Dedicated to the history of Lisbon's water supply, this small but informative museum was imaginatively created around the city's first steam pumping station. It commemorates Manuel da Maia, the 18th-century engineer who masterminded the Águas Livres aqueduct *(see p122)*. The excellent layout of the museum earned it the Council of Europe Museum Prize in 1990.

Pride of place goes to four lovingly preserved steam engines, one of which still functions (by electricity) and can be switched on for visitors. The development of technology relating to the city's water supply is documented with photographs. Particularly interesting are the sections on the Águas Livres aqueduct and the Alfama's 17th-century Chafariz d'El Rei, one of Lisbon's first fountains. Locals used to queue at one of six founts, depending on their social status.

Neo-Moorish façade of the bullring in Campo Pequeno

Museu Nacional do Azulejo 🌑

See pp120–21.

The impressive Oriente Station, located next to Parque das Nações

Parque das Nações ⓫

Avenida Dom João II. *Tel 218 919 898.* Ⓜ *Oriente.* 🚌 *5, 21, 25, 28, 44, 750, 782.* 🚆 *Gare do Oriente.* ⬤ *daily.* ♿ 🍴 💻 **Pavilhão do Conhecimento – Ciencia Viva** *Tel 218 917 100.* ⬤ *10am–6pm Tue–Fri, 11am–7pm Sat & Sun.* ⬤ *1 Jan, 24, 25 & 31 Dec.* 💷 **Casino Lisboa** *Tel 218 929 000.* ⬤ *3pm–3am Sun–Thu, 4pm–4am Fri & Sat.* ⬤ *24 Dec.*

Originally the site of Expo '98, Parque das Nações has renewed the eastern waterfront, formerly an industrial wasteland, with its contemporary architecture and family-oriented attractions. The soaring geometry of the platform canopies over Santiago Calatrava's Oriente Station set the architectural tone for the development. The impressive **Portugal Pavillion**, designed by the Portuguese architect Álvaro Siza Vieira has an enormous reinforced-concrete roof suspended like a sailcloth above its forecourt.

The **Pavilhão do Conhecimento – Ciencia Viva** (Knowledge and Science Pavilion) is a modern museum of science and technology that houses several interactive exhibitions. Also in the park is the **Casino Lisboa**, located in the space formerly occupied by the Pavilion of the Future.

Views can be had from the cable car that lifts visitors from one end of the park to the other or the **Torre Vasco da Gama**, Lisbon's tallest building. The promenade along the river, which offers delightful views of the Tagus, is not to be missed.

The 10-mile (17-km) long Vasco da Gama bridge is the longest in Europe and was completed in 1998. Also in the area are the Sony Plaza and Pavilhão Atlantico, which host concerts and sporting events.

Oceanário de Lisboa ⓬

Esplanada D. Carlos 1, Parque das Nações. *Tel 218 917 002.* Ⓜ *Oriente.* 🚌 *5, 21, 28, 44, 750.* 🚆 *Gare do Oriente.* ⬤ *Apr–Oct: 10am–8pm daily; Nov–Mar: 10am–7pm daily.* 💷 ♿ www.oceanario.pt

Centrepiece of Expo '98 and now the main attraction at Parque das Nações, the somewhat aircraft carrier-like oceanarium was designed by American architect Peter Chermayeff, and is perched on the end of a pier, surrounded by water. It is the second-largest aquarium in the world, and holds an impressive array of species – birds and some mammals as well as fish and other underwater dwellers.

18th-century Indian toy, Museu da Cidade

Four separate sea- and landscapes represent the habitats of the Atlantic, Pacific, Indian and Antarctic oceans, with suitable fauna and flora. The main attraction for most visitors, though, is the vast central tank with a dazzling variety of fish, large and small, swimming round and round. Hammerhead sharks co-exist peaceably with bream, barracudas with rays.

Museu da Cidade ⓭

Campo Grande 245. *Tel 217 513 200.* Ⓜ *Campo Grande.* 🚌 *3, 36, 47, 701, 750.* ⬤ *10am–1pm, 2–6pm Tue–Sun.* ⬤ *public hols.* 💷 *(free Sun).* ♿

Palácio Pimenta was allegedly commissioned by João V (*see pp52–3*) for his mistress Madre Paula, a nun from the nearby convent at Odivelas. When the mansion was built, in the middle of the 18th century, it occupied a peaceful site outside the capital. Nowadays it has to contend with the teeming traffic of Campo Grande. The house itself, however, retains its period charm and the city museum is one of the most interesting in Lisbon.

The displays follow the development of the city, from prehistoric times, through the Romans, Visigoths and Moors, traced by means of tiles, drawings, paintings, models and historical documents.

Visits also take you through the former living quarters of the mansion, including the kitchen, decorated with blue and white tile panels of fish, flowers and hanging game.

Some of the most fascinating exhibits are those depicting the city before the earthquake of 1755, including a highly detailed model made in the 1950s and an impressive 17th-century oil painting by Dirk Stoop (1610–86) of *Terreiro do Paço* (Praça do Comércio, *see p85*). One room is devoted to the Águas Livres aqueduct (*see p122*) with detailed architectural plans for its construction as well as prints and watercolours of the completed aqueduct.

The earthquake theme is resumed with pictures of the city amid the devastation and various plans for its reconstruction. The museum brings you into the 20th century with a large colour poster celebrating the Revolution of 1910 and the proclamation of the new republic (*see pp54–5*).

Museu Nacional do Azulejo ⑩

Pelican on the Manueline portal

Dona Leonor, widow of King João II, founded the Convento da Madre de Deus in 1509. Originally built in Manueline style, the church was restored under João III using simple Renaissance designs. The striking Baroque decoration was added by João V. The convent cloisters provide a stunning setting for the National Tile Museum. Decorative panels, individual tiles and photographs trace the evolution of tile-making from its introduction by the Moors, through Spanish influence and the development of Portugal's own style *(see pp26–7)*, up to the present day.

Panorama of Lisbon
A striking 18th-century panel, along one wall of the cloister, depicts Lisbon before the 1755 earthquake (see pp62–3). This detail shows the royal palace on Terreiro do Paço.

Hunting Scene
Artisans rather than artists began to decorate tiles in the 17th century. This detail shows a naive representation of a hunt.

Level 2

Level 1

KEY TO FLOORPLAN

- ☐ Moorish tiles
- ☐ 16th-century tiles
- ☐ 17th-century tiles
- ☐ 18th-century tiles
- ☐ 19th-century tiles
- ☐ 20th-century tiles
- ☐ Temporary exhibition space
- ☐ Non-exhibition space

STAR FEATURES

- ★ Madre de Deus
- ★ Manueline Cloister
- ★ Nossa Senhora da Vida

★ Nossa Senhora da Vida
This detail showing St John is part of a fine 16th-century maiolica altarpiece. The central panel of the huge work depicts The Adoration of the Shepherds.

Tiles from the 17th century with oriental influences are displayed here.

Café Tiles
*The walls of the
restaurant are lined
with 19th-century tiles
showing hanging
game, including
wild boar and
pheasant.*

VISITORS' CHECKLIST

Rua da Madre de Deus 4.
Tel 218 100 340. 718, 742,
794. 2–6pm Tue, 10am–6pm
Wed–Sun (last adm: 30 mins
before closing). 1 Jan, Easter,
1 May, 25 Dec. (free 10am–
2pm Sun).

Level 3

Moorish Tiles
*Decorated with a
stylized animal
motif, this
15th-
century
tile is typical
of Moorish
azulejo patterns.*

Entrance

The Renaissance cloister
is the work of Diogo de
Torralva (1500–66).

★ Madre de Deus
*Completed in the mid-16th
century, it was not until two
centuries later, under João V,
that the church of Madre de
Deus acquired its ornate
decoration. The sumptuous
Rococo altarpiece was added
after the earthquake of 1755.*

GALLERY GUIDE

*The rooms around the central
cloister are arranged chronologically with the oldest tiles
on the ground floor. Access to
the Madre de Deus is via level
1 of the museum. The front
entrance of the church is used
only during religious services.*

**The carved
Manueline
portal** *(see p25)*
was recreated from
a 16th-century painting.

★ Manueline Cloister
*An important surviving feature of
the original convent is the graceful
Manueline cloister. Fine geometrical
patterned tiles were added to the
cloister walls in the 17th century.*

Jardim Zoológico ⓮

Estrada de Benfica 158–60. *Tel 217 232 900.* Ⓜ *Jardim Zoológico.* 🚌 *16, 54, 768 & other routes.* 🚆 *Sete-Rios.* ◯ *10am–6pm daily (Apr–Sep: to 8pm).* 🖼 ⧉ **www**.zoolisboa.pt

The gardens here are as much a feature as the actual zoo. Opened in 1905, the zoo has been revamped since, and most of its aviaries and cages provide more comfortable conditions for the specimens. The most bizarre feature is the dogs' cemetery, complete with tombstones and flowers. Other attractions include a cable car touring the park, a reptile house, dolphin shows and an amusement park. The area is divided into two zones, and the admission charge is based on how many you visit, or there is an all-inclusive ticket.

Aqueduto das Águas Livres ⓯

Best seen from Calçada da Quintinha. *Tel 218 100 215.* 🚌 *22, 49, 74, 720, 727, 738.* ◯ *Mar–Nov: 10am–6pm Mon–Sat.* ⬤ *public hols.*
Mãe d'Água das Amoreiras Praça das Amoreiras. *Tel 218 100 215.* ◯ *10am–6pm Mon–Sat.*

Considered the most beautiful sight in Lisbon at the turn of the century, the impressive structure of the Aqueduto das Águas Livres looms over the Alcântara valley to the northwest of the city. The construction of an aqueduct to bring fresh water to the city gave João V *(see pp52–3)* an

Dolphins performing in the aquarium of the Jardim Zoológico

ideal opportunity to indulge his passion for grandiose building schemes, as the only area of Lisbon with fresh drinking water was the Alfama. A tax on meat, wine, olive oil and other comestibles funded the project, and although not complete until the 19th century, it was already supplying the city with water by 1748. The main pipeline measures 19 km (12 miles), but the total length, including all the secondary channels, is 58 km (36 miles). The most visible part of this imposing structure are the 35 arches that cross the Alcântara valley, the tallest of which rise to a spectacular 65 m (213 ft) above the city.

The public walkway along the aqueduct, once a pleasant promenade, has been closed since 1853. This is partly due to Diogo Alves, a robber who threw his victims over the edge. Today, visitors may take

an informative guided tour over the Alcântara arches. There are also tours of the Mãe d'Água reservoir and trips to the Mãe d'Água springs, the source of the water supply. These tours can be irregular, so it is best to contact the Museu da Água *(see p118)* for details of the trip on offer.

At the end of the aqueduct, the **Mãe d'Água das Amoreiras** is a castle-like building which once served as a reservoir for the water. supplied from the aqueduct. The original design of 1745 was by the Hungarian architect, Carlos Mardel, who worked under Pombal *(see pp62–3)* in the rebuilding of the Baixa. Completed in 1834, it became a popular meeting place and acquired a reputation as the rendezvous for kings and their mistresses. Today the space is used for art exhibitions, fashion shows and other events.

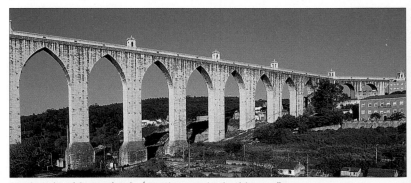

Imposing arches of the Aqueduto das Águas Livres spanning the Alcântara valley

For hotels and restaurants in this region see pp382–6 and pp408–12

Palácio Fronteira ⑯

Largo São Domingos de Benfica 1. **Tel** *217 782 023.* Ⓜ *Jardim Zoológico.* 🚌 *70.* 🚆 *Benfica.* 🕒 *Mon–Sat.* 📷 *compulsory. Jun–Sep: 10:30, 11 & 11:30am & noon; Oct–May: 11am & noon.* ● *public hols.* 📷

This delightful country manor house was built as a hunting pavilion for João de Mascarenhas, the first Marquês de Fronteira, in 1640. Although skyscrapers are visible in the distance, it still occupies a quiet spot, by the Parque Florestal de Monsanto. Both house and garden have *azulejo* decoration whose subjects include battle scenes and trumpet-blowing monkeys.

Although the palace is still occupied by the 12th Marquis, some of the living rooms and the library, as well as the formal gardens, are included in the tour. The Battles Room has lively tiled panels depicting scenes of the War of Restoration *(see pp50–51)*, with a detail showing João de Fronteira fighting a Spanish general. It was his loyalty to Pedro II during this war that earned him the title of Marquis. Interesting comparisons can be made between these naive 17th-century Portuguese tiles and the Delft ones from the same period in the dining room, depicting naturalistic scenes. The dining room is also decorated with frescoed panels and portraits of Portuguese nobility by artists such as Domingos António de Sequeira (1768–1837).

The late 16th-century chapel is the oldest part of the house. The façade is adorned with stones, shells, broken glass and bits of china. These fragments of crockery are believed to have been used at the feast inaugurating the palace and then smashed to ensure no one else could sup off the same set. Visits to the **garden** start at the chapel terrace, where tiled niches are decorated with figures personifying the arts and mythological creatures.

Bust of João I in gardens of Palácio Fronteira

Tiled terrace leading to the chapel of the Palácio Fronteira

In the formal Italian garden the immaculate box hedges are cut into shapes to represent the seasons of the year. To one end, tiled scenes of dashing knights on horseback, representing ancestors of the Fronteira family, are reflected in the waters of a large tank. On either side of the water, a grand staircase leads to a terrace above. Here, decorative niches contain the busts of Portuguese kings and colourful majolica reliefs adorn the arcades. More blue and white tiled scenes, realistic and allegorical, decorate the wall at the far end of the garden.

Entrance to the theatre museum in Parque do Monteiro-Mor

Parque do Monteiro-Mor ⑰

Largo Júlio Castilho. **Tel** *217 590 318.* 🚌 *3, 7, 36, 108, 701.* Ⓜ *Lumiar.* **Park** 🕒 *10am–6pm Tue–Sun.* ● *1 Jan, Easter, 1 May, 25 Dec.* **Museu Nacional do Traje Tel** *217 590 318.* 🕒 *10am–6pm Tue–Sun.* **Museu Nacional do Teatro Tel** *217 567 410.* 🕒 *2–6pm Tue, 10am–6pm Wed–Sun.* 📷 *combined ticket for park & museums; free 10am–2pm Sun.* 📷 📷

Monteiro-Mor Park was sold to the state in 1975 and the 18th-century palace buildings were converted into museums. The gardens are attractive and rather more romantic than the manicured box-hedge gardens so typical of Lisbon. Much of the land is wooded, though the area around the museums has gardens with flowering shrubs, duck ponds and tropical trees.

The rather old-fashioned **Museu Nacional do Traje** (costume museum) has a vast collection of textiles, accessories and costumes worn by musicians, politicians, poets, aristocrats and soldiers.

The **Museu Nacional do Teatro** has two buildings, one devoted to temporary exhibitions, the other containing a small permanent collection. Photographs, posters and cartoons feature famous 20th-century Portuguese actors and one section is devoted to Amália Rodrigues, the famous *fado* singer *(see pp64–5).*

SHOPPING IN LISBON

Lisbon offers excellent shopping opportunities for the visitor with its combination of elegant high street shops, large modern shopping centres and flea markets. The cobbled streets of the Baixa and the chic Chiado district are the city's traditional shopping areas and the wine merchants are the best in the country. The

Portuguese ceramic figure

more exclusive designer shops are found around the Avenida da Liberdade. The enormous indoor shopping centres are increasingly popular. The street and indoor markets offer more adventurous shopping if you are looking for something typically Portuguese, such as hand-woven tapestries, ceramics or clothes.

A delicatessen in the Bairro Alto

OPENING HOURS

Traditional shopping hours are Monday to Friday 9am to 1pm and 3pm to 7pm, and Saturday 9am to 1pm. However, in order to satisfy growing consumer demand, many shops, especially those in the Baixa, open during the lunch hour and on Saturday afternoons. Shopping centres are open daily from 10am to midnight.

HOW TO PAY

Most shops in Lisbon accept Visa but it is probably better to obtain a cash advance with a credit card from one of the many Multibanco teller machines (ATMs).

TAX FREE GOODS

Many shops are affiliated to the Tax Free for Tourists system and are identified by the logo of the same name. The shop assistant will issue a tax exemption form (*isenção na exportação*) which should be presented to customs on your departure from Portugal in order to obtain a rebate.

SHOPPING CENTRES

Shopping centres have had a dramatic impact on shopping in Lisbon. They combine vast supermarkets, restaurants, shops, cinemas and banks. Well-known centres include **Amoreiras**, **Vasco da Gama**, **Centro Colombo** and **El Corte Inglés**.

FOOD AND MARKETS

There are markets of every variety in Lisbon, from municipal markets selling fresh produce to the famous Feira da Ladra (*see p71*). Bargains can be found among the bric-a-brac, second-hand clothes and general arts and crafts. Coin collectors head for the Feira Numismática in Praça do Comércio (*see p85*). Other good spots are the **Feira de Antiguidades e Velharias** for antiques and **Feira dos Alfarrabistas** for old books.

Gourmets will find Lisbon's delicatessens (*charcutarias*) irresistible. They are lined with superb cheeses, tasty smoked meats and wild game, delicious sweets (*ovos* *moles*) and an assortment of dried and crystallized fruits.

Charcutaria Brasil, **Manuel Tavares**, which has a fine selection of port and madeira, and **Celeiro Dieta**, known for organic foods, are popular.

WINES AND SPIRITS

Portugal's large variety of wines and spirits is well represented in Lisbon's specialist shops.

Napoleão, the city's best-known wine merchants, has a number of outlets, with its oldest in the Baixa. For port specifically, visit Solar do Vinho do Porto (*see p92*) where it is possible to sample before deciding what to buy.

BOOKS AND MUSIC

The music scene in Portugal is a lively mix of traditions and the very latest. *Fado* music is hugely popular, while dance music has a dedicated following. **FNAC** is Lisbon's best music retailer. **Discoteca Amália** specialises in *fado*.

Bric-a-brac on display at the popular Feira de Ladra market

Brightly painted ceramic plates

shops in the Restauradores and Rossio areas of Lisbon and **Arte Rustica** in the Baixa. Portugal's ceramics are renowned for their quality and variety, and in Lisbon you can find eveything from delicate porcelain to rustic terracotta, and from tiles to tableware. Fine porcelain tableware from **Vista Alegre** makes for an excellent souvenir.

ANTIQUES

The majority of Lisbon's antique shops are located either on Rua Dom Pedro V or Rua São Bento. There are numerous religious artifacts to be found in the area and **Solar** specializes in antique tiles (*azulejos*). Beautiful prints sold at second-hand bookshops in the Bairro Alto are good value for money. **Livraria Olisipo** stocks books and also old prints of landscapes, fauna and maps. Look for shops that are members of APA (*Associação Portuguesa de Antiquário*), often indicated by a sign in the window.

Portugal also boasts a great literary tradition, with a range of authors including Luís de Camões, Fernando Pessoa, Eça de Queiróz and José Saramago. Translations of their works are found in most bookshops. **Livraria Portugal** and **Livraria Betrand** are among Lisbon's oldest bookshops.

CLOTHES

Most of the large chain stores have outlets in Lisbon, particularly in the shopping centres, The Spanish **Zara** chain sell affordable clothes for everyone. More exclusive shops, including designer outlets, can be found on and around Avenida de la Liberdade. **Ann Salazar** is one of an increasing number of known Portuguese designers.

REGIONAL CRAFTS

Portugal has a rich history of fine craftwork (*artesanato*), notably embroidery, fine lace, hand-knitted woollens and delicate gold and silver thread jewellery. Head for the gift

DIRECTORY

SHOPPING CENTRES

Amoreiras
Avenida Eng. Duarte Pacheco, Amoreiras.
Map 5 A5.
Tel 213 810 200.

Centro Colombo
Avenida Lusíada.
Tel 217 113 600.
www.colombo.pt

El Corte Inglés
Avenida António Augusto Aguiar 31. **Map** 5 B5.
Tel 213 711 700.
www.elcorteingles.pt

Vasco da Gama
Avenida Dom João II, Parque das Nações.
Tel 218 930 600.

FOOD & MARKETS

Celeiro Dieta
Avenida António Augusto de Aguiar 130, Saldanha.
Map 5 B3.
Tel 213 144 383.

Charcutaria Brasil
Rua Alexandre Herculano 90–92, Rato. **Map** 5 C5.
Tel 213 885 644.

Feira dos Alfarrabistas
Rua Anchieta, Chiado.
◻ *10am–6pm Sat.*

Feira de Antiguidades e Velharias
Estação Oriente.
◻ *10am–7pm 3rd Sun of month.*

Manuel Tavares
Rua da Betesga 1, Baixa.
Map 7 B3.
Tel 213 424 209.

WINES AND SPIRITS

Napoleão
Rua dos Fanqueiros 70, Baixa.
Map 7 C4.
Tel 218 872 042.

BOOKS AND MUSIC

Discoteca Amália
Rua do Ouro, 272.
Baixa. **Map** 7 B4.
Tel 213 420 939,

FNAC
Rua Nova do Almada 102, Chiado.
Map 7 B4
Tel 707 313 435.

Livraria Bertrand
Rua Garrett 73, Chiado.
Map 7 A4.
Tel 213 476 122.

Livraria Portugal
Rua do Carmo 70–74, Chiado.
Map 7 B4.
Tel 213 474 982.

CLOTHES

Ana Salazar
Rua do Carmo 85–87, Chiado.
Map 7 B3.
Tel 213 472 289.

Zara
Rua Garrett 1, Chiado.
Map 7 B4.
Tel 213 243 710.

REGIONAL CRAFTS

Arte Rústica
Rua do Ouro 246–8, Baixa. **Map** 7 B4.
Tel 213 421 127.

Vista Alegre
Largo do Chiado 20–21, Chiado. **Map** 7 A4.
Tel 213 461 401.

ANTIQUES

Livraria Olisipo
Largo Trindade Coelho 7–8, Bairro Alto. **Map** 7 A3.
Tel 213 462 771.

Solar
Rua Dom Pedro V 70, Bairro Alto. **Map** 4 F2.
Tel 213 465 522.

ENTERTAINMENT IN LISBON

For a smallish European capital, Lisbon has a good and varied cultural calendar. Musical events range from classical and opera performances to intimate *fado* evenings, and large rock concerts. Dance, both classical and modern, is well represented in Lisbon. The Gulbenkian Foundation, long the only major arts patron, has been joined by other private funds as well as state institutions.

Football is a consuming passion of the Portuguese, and Lisbon's Sporting and Benfica teams play regularly at home. Lisbon outparties many larger capitals, with a nightlife known for its liveliness.

BOOKING TICKETS

Tickets can be reserved by phoning the Agência de Bilhetes para Espectáculos Públicos (**ABEP**). Pay in cash when you collect them from the kiosk. Tickets are also sold at **FNAC**. Not all cinemas and theatres accept credit card bookings – check first.

ABEP kiosk selling tickets on Praça dos Restauradores

LISTINGS MAGAZINES

Previews of forthcoming cultural events plus listings and reviews of the city's latest bars and clubs appear each week in major newspapers. English-language publications on offer include the monthly *Follow Me Lisboa*, which can be obtained free from tourist offices. The monthly *Agenda Cultural* is in Portuguese.

CINEMA AND THEATRE

Movie-goers are very well served in Lisbon. Films are shown in their original language with Portuguese subtitles, and tickets are inexpensive. On Mondays most cinemas offer reductions. The city's older cinemas have now largely given way to modern multiplexes, usually located in shopping centres such as Amoreiras, Centro Colombo or El Corte Inglés. While these screen mainstream Hollywood fare, cinemas such as King Triplex show more European films. For classics and retrospectives, head to the **Cinemateca Portuguesa**; a programme is available at tourist offices. Theatre performances are most often in Portuguese, but large institutions such as the **Teatro Nacional Dona Maria II** and the **Teatro da Trindade** occasionally stage guest performances by visiting companies. Less formally, **Chapitô** sometimes has open-air shows.

CLASSICAL MUSIC, OPERA AND DANCE

Lisbon's top cultural centres are the modern **Centro Cultural de Belém** *(see p106)* and the **Fundação Calouste Gulbenkian** *(see pp114–17)*. They host national and international events such as ballet and concerts. Ballet is also the focus of the **Teatro Camões**. The **Teatro Nacional de São Carlos** is Portugal's national opera, with a varied season that mixes its own productions with guest performances. The **Coliseu dos Recreios** has no institution attached and so offers a variety of events.

Performance at the Chapitô, circus school, Alfama

WORLD MUSIC, JAZZ, POP AND ROCK

Lisbon's musical soul may be *fado (see pp64–5)*, but the city is no stranger to other forms of musical expression. African music, particularly that of former Portuguese colony Cape Verde, plays a big part in Lisbon's music scene. Venues such as **Bartô** and **Enclave** have frequent live performances.

The **Hot Clube** has been Lisbon's foremost jazz venue for as long as anyone can remember, and has the right intimate atmosphere.

The house orchestra playing at the Fundaeção Calouste Gulbenkian

Musician at Pé Sujo

Speakeasy is younger, slightly bigger, and varies live jazz with up-tempo blues, particularly at weekends.

Large rock and pop concerts are held at outdoor venues such as **Parque da Bela Vista** and football stadiums, or indoors at **Pavilhão Atlântico** or **Coliseu dos Recreios.**

NIGHTCLUBS

Bairro Alto remains a lively area for Lisbon nightlife, although its mostly small bars don't usually have dance floors or keep very late hours. There are a exceptions, including the doyen of Bairro Alto clubs, **Frágil.**

Among the larger and more mainstream dance venues are **Kremlin** and **Kapital**; the first a nearly historic house club, the second a very middle-of-the-road disco.

Farther westward by the Doca de Santo Amaro marina is the attractively housed **Buddha** restaurant, bar and nightclub. Inland, in the Alcântara area, are **W** and **Alcântara-Mar**, while eastwards along the river near Santa Apolónia station, is **Lux**, the cream of Lisbon's current club scene.

SPECTATOR SPORTS

Portugal hosted the 2004 European Football Championship, and Lisbon's two main teams, Sporting and Benfica, built new stadiums for the event, the **Estádio José Alvalade** and the **Estádio da Luz** respectively. Portuguese football cup finals, as well as other events such as the Estoril Open tennis tournament, are held at the **Estádio Nacional-Jamor**. The Pavilhão Atlântico is also used for indoor events such as tennis, volleyball and basket-ball. **The Autódromo do Estoril** is a motor-racing venue.

DIRECTORY

BOOKING TICKETS

ABEP
Praça dos Restauradores.
Map 7 A2.
Tel 213 425 360.

FNAC
Rua Nova do Almada 102.
Map 7 B4. **Tel** 707 313 435.

CINEMA AND THEATRE

Chapitô
Costa do Castelo 7.
Map 7 C3.
Tel 218 855 550.

Cinemateca Portuguesa
Rua Barata Salgueiro 39.
Map 5 C5.
Tel 213 596 262.

King Triplex
Avenida Frei Miguel
Contreiras 52a.
Map 6 E1.
Tel 218 480 808.

Teatro Nacional Dona Maria II
Praça Dom Pedro IV.
Map 7 B3.
Tel 213 250 800.

Teatro da Trindade
Largo da Trindade 9.
Map 7 A3.
Tel 213 423 200.

CLASSICAL MUSIC, OPERA AND DANCE

Centro Cultural de Belém
Praça do Império. **Map** 1 C5. **Tel** 213 612 400.

Coliseu dos Recreios
Rua das Portas de Santo Antão 92. **Map** 7 A2.
Tel 213 240 580.

Fundação Calouste Gulbenkian
Avenida de Berna 45. **Map** 5 B2. **Tel** 217 823 000.

Teatro Camões
Parque das Nações.
Tel 218 923 470.

Teatro Nacional de São Carlos
Rua Serpa Pinto 9. **Map** 7 A4. **Tel** 213 253 000.

WORLD MUSIC, JAZZ, POP AND ROCK

Bartô
Costa do Castelo 1. **Map** 7 C3. **Tel** 218 855 550.

Enclave
Rua do Sol ao Rato 71A.
Map 4 D1.
Tel 213 888 738.

Hot Clube
Praça da Alegria 38–9.
Map 4 F1.
Tel 213 467 369.

Parque da Bela Vista
off Avenida Gago Coutinho.

Pavilhão Atlântico
Parque das Nações.
Tel 218 918 409.

Speakeasy
Cais das Oficinas,
Armazém 115,
Rocha Conde d'Óbidos.
Map 4 D4.
Tel 213 909 166.

NIGHTCLUBS

Alcântara-Mar
Rua da Colina
Económica 11.
Tel 213 636 830.

Buddha
Gare Marítima de Alcântara.
Map 3 A5/B5.
Tel 213 950 555.

Frágil
Rua da Atalaia 128.
Map 4 F2.
Tel 213 469 578.

Kapital
Avenida 24 de Julho 68.
Map 4 E3.
Tel 213 957 101.

Kremlin
Escadinhas da Praia 5.
Map 4 D3.
Tel 213 957 101.

Lux
Avenida Infante
Dom Henrique.
Map 8 D5.
Tel 218 820 890.

W
Rua Maria Luísa
Holstein 13.
Map 3 A4.
Tel 213 636 830.

SPORTS

Autódromo Estoril
Tel 214 609 500.

Estádio José Alvalade
Rua Pr Fernando
da Fonseca 1600
Tel 217 516 000.

Estádio da Luz
Avenida Gen Norton
Matos 1500.
Tel 217 219 500.

Estádio Nacional-Jamor
Cruz Quebrada.
Tel 214 146 030.

LISBON STREET FINDER

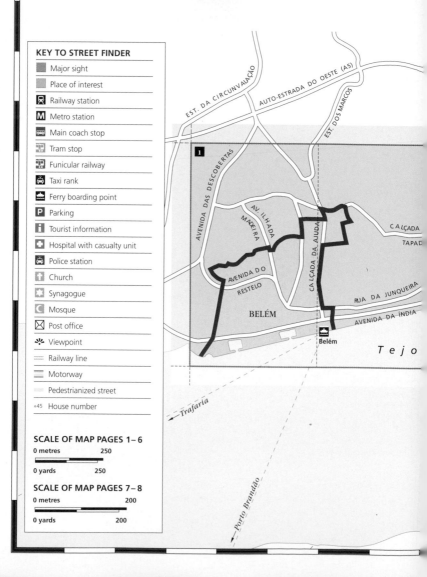

Map references given in this guide for sights and entertainment venues in Lisbon refer to the Street Finder maps on the following pages. Map references are also given for Lisbon's hotels (*see pp382–6*) and restaurants (*see pp408–12*). The first figure in the map reference indicates which Street Finder map to turn to, and the letter and number which follow refer to the grid reference on that map. The map below shows the area of Lisbon covered by the eight Street Finder maps. Symbols used for sights and useful information are displayed in the key below. An index of street names and all the places of interest marked on the maps can be found on the following pages.

KEY TO STREET FINDER

🟥	Major sight
🟦	Place of interest
🚆	Railway station
Ⓜ	Metro station
🚌	Main coach stop
🚋	Tram stop
🚋	Funicular railway
🚖	Taxi rank
⛴	Ferry boarding point
P	Parking
ℹ	Tourist information
✚	Hospital with casualty unit
🚓	Police station
✝	Church
✡	Synagogue
C	Mosque
⊠	Post office
☀	Viewpoint
=	Railway line
=	Motorway
	Pedestrianized street
«45	House number

SCALE OF MAP PAGES 1– 6

0 metres   250

0 yards   250

SCALE OF MAP PAGES 7– 8

0 metres   200

0 yards   200

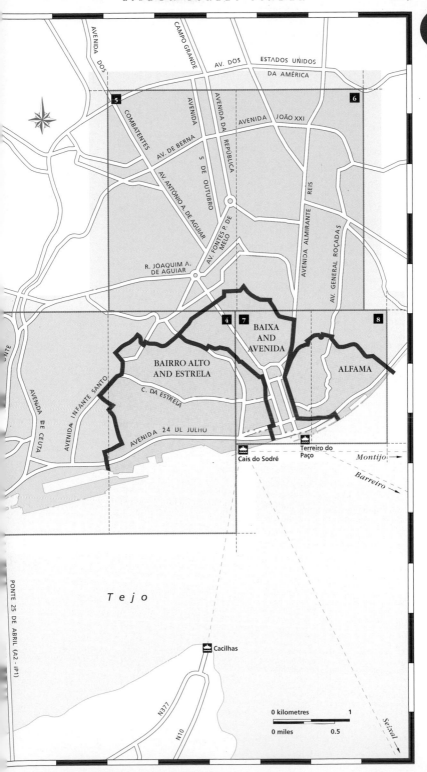

Street Finder Index

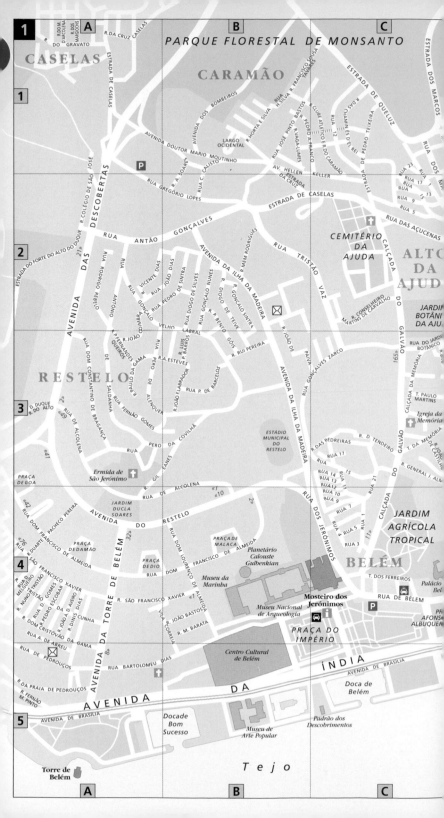

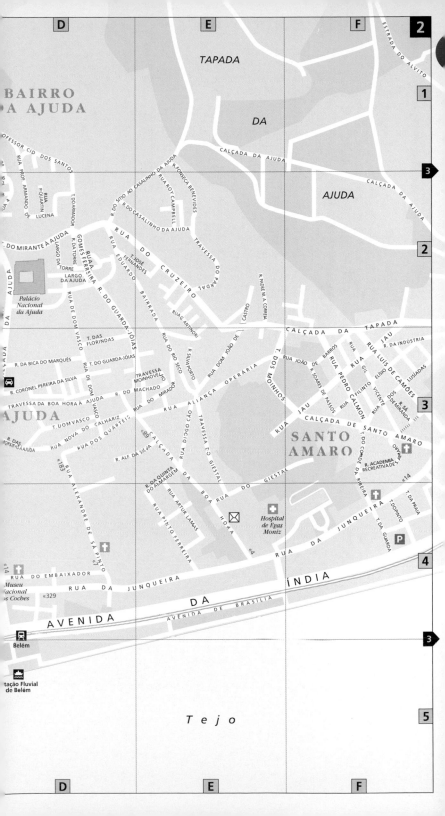

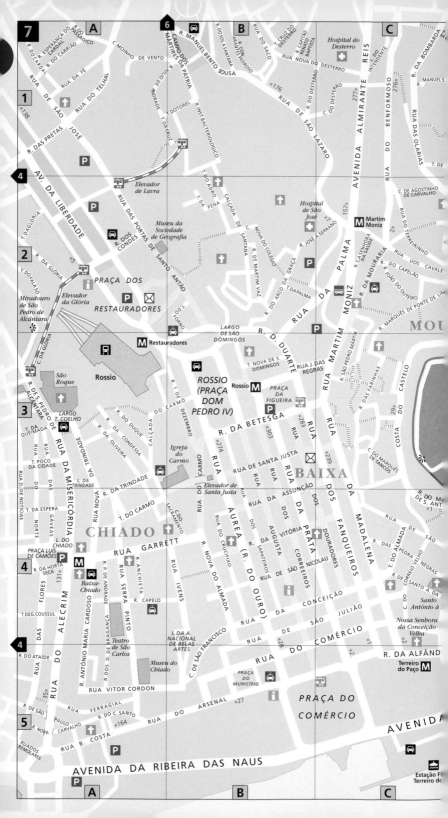

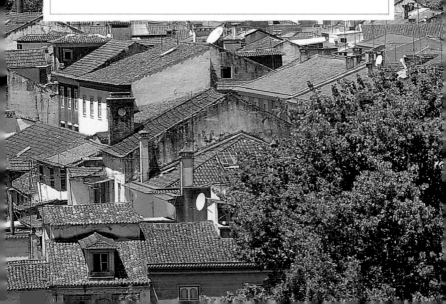

CENTRAL
PORTUGAL

Central Portugal at a Glance

Between Portugal's capital and its second city, Oporto, can be found some of the country's most impressive architecture and important historical sights. Near Lisbon are the fine palaces of Sintra and Queluz, and in Estremadura are several of Portugal's foremost religious sites. Estremadura and Beira Litoral mix empty beaches with quaint fishing villages and smart resorts, while the lush country stretching inland to the banks of the Tagus supports livestock and crops from grapes to fruit and rice. Further north, the Beiras are more varied, with the historic university town of Coimbra, the vine-clad valleys of the Dão wine region and the bleak highlands and fortress towns of Beira Alta and Beira Baixa. Dominating this remote region is the granite range of the Serra da Estrela.

Batalha *means "battle" and the monastery of Santa Maria da Vitória at Batalha was built to give thanks for victory over the Spanish at the Battle of Aljubarrota in 1385. Its delicate style makes it one of Portugal's finest Gothic buildings (see pp184–5).*

Alcobaça *is principally known for its abbey, founded in the 12th century by Portugal's first king, Afonso Henriques. The graceful, contemplative air of this great Cistercian house (see pp180–81) is exemplified by its huge vaulted dormitory.*

Sintra, *just west of Lisbon, is a cool wooded retreat from the heat of the capital. This is where the Portuguese monarchs chose to spend their summers. The Palácio Nacional is full of remarkable decorative effects, such as this painted "magpie" ceiling (see pp160–61).*

Estremadura

ESTREMADURA AND RIBATEJO
(See pp172–95)

LISBON
(See pp58–149)

THE LISBON COAST
(See pp150–71)

The Palácio de Queluz, *a masterpiece of Rococo architecture (see pp166–7), lies just outside Lisbon. The Lion Staircase leads up to the colonnaded pavilion named after its architect, Jean-Baptiste Robillion.*

0 kilometres

0 miles   50

◁ Tomar's Templar fortress of Convento de Cristo overlooking the town

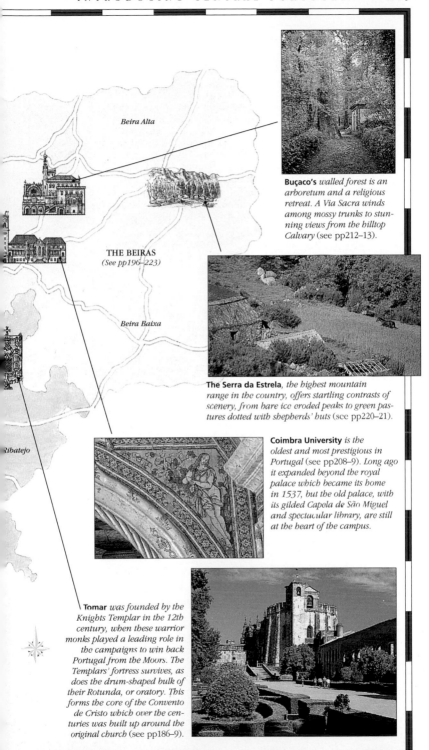

Beira Alta

Buçaco's *walled forest is an arboretum and a religious retreat. A Via Sacra winds among mossy trunks to stunning views from the hilltop Calvary (see pp212–13).*

THE BEIRAS
(See pp196–223)

Beira Baixa

The Serra da Estrela, *the highest mountain range in the country, offers startling contrasts of scenery, from bare ice eroded peaks to green pastures dotted with shepherds' huts (see pp220–21).*

Ribatejo

Coimbra University *is the oldest and most prestigious in Portugal (see pp208–9). Long ago it expanded beyond the royal palace which became its home in 1537, but the old palace, with its gilded Capela de São Miguel and spectacular library, are still at the heart of the campus.*

Tomar *was founded by the Knights Templar in the 12th century, when these warrior monks played a leading role in the campaigns to win back Portugal from the Moors. The Templars' fortress survives, as does the drum-shaped bulk of their Rotunda, or oratory. This forms the core of the Convento de Cristo which over the centuries was built up around the original church (see pp186–9).*

Horsemanship and Bullfighting

Classical dressage and bravura bullfighting in Portugal are linked to the Marquês de Marialva, the King's Master of the Horse from 1770 to 1799. He made famous the most advanced and difficult dressage techniques, including some in which the horse lifts itself off the ground like a ballet dancer. The Art of Marialva, as it is called, is of great use to horsemen in the bullring, and they will usually demonstrate some dressage movements for the entertainment of the crowd. The Ribatejo is the traditional centre of bullfighting, with events held from spring to autumn at annual fairs and towns such as Santarém, Vila Franca de Xira and Coruche. In Portugal, the bull is never killed in the arena.

Horseman at the national fair in Golegã

Advertising a summer bullfight in Santarém

Ribatejan herdsmen or campinos, *who round up the fighting bulls, here demonstrate their skills.*

Leading bullfighter João Moura salutes the crowd at a *tourada* with his tricorne hat.

The mane is plaited with ribbons for a beautifully groomed effect.

THE CAVALEIRO

The bullfighter or *cavaleiro* wears traditional 18th-century costume, including the satin coat of a grandee, and rides an elaborately adorned horse. He has to plant a number of darts *(farpas)* in the bull's shoulders, and his performance is judged on style and courage.

The costly saddle cloth is embroidered with João Moura's initials.

Tail tidying and decoration go back to the ornate French style of Louis XV.

Box stirrups are traditional, stylish and secure.

TRADITIONAL EQUESTRIAN SKILLS

Lisbon's Escola Portuguesa de Arte Equestre, and equestrian centres in the Ribatejo, today maintain the standards set by Marialva. The Lisbon school performs several times a year around the country. On Lusitanian horses of Alter Real stock *(see p298)*, riders in 18th-century costume give superb dressage displays. Their movements resemble these illustrations of 1790 from a book on equestrianism, dedicated to Dom João (later João VI), himself a keen horseman.

Plaque of Lezíria Grande Equestrian Centre (see p194)

The Marquês de Marialva trains his horse in the *croupade*, its hind legs tucked up beneath as it spring into the a

THE BULLFIGHT

The *corrida* or *tourada* combines drama and daring. First, a team of bullfighters on foot *(peões de brega)* distracts the bull with capes, preparing it for the *cavaleiro*. He is followed by eight volunteer *forcados*, who aim to overcome the bull with their bare hands in what is known as the *pega*. Finally the bull is herded from the ring among a group of farm oxen.

At this opening ceremony *in Montijo, the two* cavaleiros *line up with the* forcados *on either side.*

The *cavaleiro* lodges long darts in the bull's shoulders.

The bull charges, provoked by the *cavaleiro* and the prancing horse. The bull's horns are blunted and sheathed in leather.

Partnership between *man and horse is paramount. Most* cavaleiros *ride a Lusitanian, the world's oldest saddle horse and a classic warrior steed, famed for its courage, grace and strength. Its agility and speed are essential in the ring, and defenders of bullfighting believe the spectacle has helped preserve the breed.*

The horse's lower legs are strapped for support.

The leader of the *forcados* tackles the bull head on, throwing himself between its horns and gripping it around the neck.

The next in line assists the front man, while the others prepare to lend support.

The bullfight ends *with the* pega. *The leader of the* forcados *challenges the bull to charge, then launches himself over its head. The others try to hold him in place and use their combined weight to bring the bull to a standstill, with one of the men holding onto its tail. Eight times out of ten the* forcados *get tossed in all directions, then re-form to repeat the challenge. The crowd laughs, but applauds the men's skill and courage.*

Dom João himself demonstrates the *galope*, a difficult exercise with a change of direction at each step.

The Marquês de Marialva teaches his mount to turn in tight circles round a pole.

The horse leaps from a standstill, back legs outstretched, in the dramatic *capriole*.

The Flavours of Central Portugal

The geography of central Portugal ranges from a lagoon-dotted Atlantic coastline and a vast flood-plain to a hilly, then rocky, interior crowned by Portugal's highest mountains, The food here is equally varied, with roast suckling pig in the north, a rich choice of fish and seafood from the ports, unique cheeses and hearty stews from the mountains. One popular dish reflecting this diversity is *porco à alentejana*, a mixture of pork and clams. Cuisines old and new, exotic and familiar, rub along together in Lisbon, where cosmopolitanism has quietly thrived for half a millennium.

Sardines

Lisbon's famed lettuces take pride of place on a vegetable stall

LISBON

The capital is not just the place where all the flavours of Portugal come together, but also where the influences of Portugal's 16th-century overseas expansion get their strongest expression. This applies equally to older influences, long since assimilated into the local cuisine, and to newer phenomena, from Cape Verdean restaurants to sushi bars. One old favourite, barbecued chicken with chilli *(frango à piri-piri)*, originated in former colonies in Africa. The Lisbon speciality *peixinhos da horta*, runner beans coated in batter and deep fried, provide an interesting insight into influences going the other way. Japanese tempura is said to have developed from this Portuguese dish, introduced to Japan in the 16th century. The nickname *alfacinhas* for natives of Lisbon may have a connection with *alface* (lettuce) – city has long been famous for an especially delicious variety.

THE BAIRRADA AND SIERRA DA ESTRELA

The town of Mealhada, in the Bairrada region to the north, is known throughout Portugal for its *leitão*, spit-

Serra de Estrela   Quejo fresco   Alavão

Saloio   Palhais

Fine ewe's and goat's milk cheeses from central Portugal

REGIONAL DISHES AND SPECIALITIES

Chanfana is a speciality of Beira Litoral in which goat's meat is cooked slowly with wine and spices in an earthenware pot known as a *caçoilo*. *Cabrito à padeiro* is a similar dish using kid that, after a wine marinade, is roasted and continually basted with the marinade. Traditionally, this would be done in the local baker's large wood-fired oven, and the best restaurants to eat it in are the ones with such ovens. *Caldeirada de peixe* is cooked all over Portugal but does not get any better than in Nazaré or Peniche, preferably eaten outdoors within sight of the sea. *Feijoada* is one of Portugal's most versatile dishes, mixing beans with a wide range of ingredients, including cuttlefish and snails. The latter is a speciality of Tomar. *Favas à Portuguesa* is a Lisbon favourite.

Paprika

Feijoada *is a paprika-spiced stew of beans, vegetables and cured meat (usually pork), with many local variations.*

Meats, cheeses and sausages on sale at a market in Sintra

rolling hills of Estremadura give way, as you cross the Tejo eastwards, to the fertile Lezíria flood-plain of Ribatejo, land of bulls, horses and juicy melons. Vila Franca de Xira, back on the west bank of the river, is a good place to try the local bull meat. For the most part, the regional cuisine of Ribatejo is frugal and thrifty. A classic example is *magusto*, a thick purée of dry maize (corn) and white bread blended with water, olive oil, and boiled kale served with oven-baked *bacalhau* (salt cod).

roasted suckling pig. The local custom is to drink red sparkling wine, unique to this area, with the crisp-skinned but mild-tasting pig. Nearby Luso is the source of one of Portugal's finest mineral waters. The granite Serra da Estrela mountain range is home to Portugal's most famous cheese, the distinctive and buttery Serra. It is made from ewe's milk, and the rounds are wrapped in muslin to maintain their shape. Bay leaves are often used in Portuguese cooking, and the black-barked bay tree is common in these parts – though the scent in the air is not of bay but of eucalyptus. Bean stews are another common feature of the local cuisine, particularly *feijoada*, of which every town and village seems to have its own version.

ESTREMADURA AND RIBATEJO

Further south, in Estremadura, the fishing ports of Nazaré and Peniche boast a smaller catch than they once did, but the local sardines in particular are well worth sampling. The

Traditional Lisbon egg tarts, known as *Pasteis de Belem*

REGIONAL WINES

The Dão wine region now produces some of Portugal's finest red wines, often distinguishable from the wines of the Douro to the north by their greater elegance. The Bairrada region borders Dão but has only one authorized grape variety for making reds: Baga. There are some great examples of traditional style, with deep tannins and hints of pine and bonfire, but modernity features too, with fruitier, more approachable reds and fresh, light whites. Estremadura and Ribatejo once produced vast amounts of fairly unpalatable wine for mass consumption or distillation. Now they shine, with wines often made from foreign grape varieties. Of Lisbon's own appellations – Colares, Carcavelos and Bucelas – only the last remains commercially viable, making some of the country's most distinctive whites.

Caldeirada de peixe, *a fish stew, uses a selection of seafood along with potatoes, tomatoes and peppers.*

Favas à Portuguesa *combines broad (fava) beans with morcela (blood sausage) and chopped pork ribs.*

Arroz doce *is a delicious dessert of lemon-zest scented rice pudding topped with a decoration of cinnamon.*

THE LISBON COAST

Within an hour's drive northwest of Lisbon you can reach the rocky Atlantic coast, the wooded slopes of Sintra or countryside dotted with villas and royal palaces. South of Lisbon you can enjoy the sandy beaches and fishing towns along the coast or explore the lagoons of the Tagus and Sado river estuaries.

Traders and invaders, from the Phoenicians to the Spanish, have left their mark in this region, in particular the Moors whose forts and castles, rebuilt many times over the centuries, can be found all along this coast. After Lisbon became the capital in 1256, Portuguese kings and nobles built summer palaces and villas in the countryside west of the city, particularly on the cool, green heights of the Serra de Sintra.

Across the Tagus, the less fashionable southern shore (Outra Banda) could be reached only by ferry, until the suspension bridge was built in 1966. Now, the long sandy beaches of the Costa da Caparica, the coast around the fishing town of Sesimbra and even the remote Tróia peninsula have become popular resorts during the summer months. Fortunately, large stretches of coast and unspoilt countryside are being protected as conservation areas and nature reserves.

Despite the region's rapid urbanization, small fishing and farming communities still remain. Lively fish markets offer a huge variety of fresh fish and seafood; Palmela and the Sado region are noted for their wine; sheep still roam the unspoilt Serra da Arrábida, providing milk for Azeitão cheese; and rice is the main crop in the Sado estuary. Traditional industries also survive, such as salt panning near Alcochete and marble quarries at Pero Pinheiro.

Though the sea is cold and often rough, especially on west-facing coasts, the beaches are among the cleanest in Europe. As well as surfing, fishing and scuba diving, the region provides splendid golf courses, horse riding facilities and a motor-racing track. Arts and entertainment range from music and cinema festivals to bullfights and country fairs where regional crafts, such as hand-painted pottery, lace and baskets, are on display.

Tiled façades of houses in Alcochete, an attractive town on the Tagus estuary

◁ Brightly painted fishing boats moored in the harbour at Sesimbra

Exploring the Lisbon Coast

North of the Tagus, the beautiful hilltown of Sintra is dotted with historic palaces and surrounded by wooded hills, at times enveloped in an eerie sea mist. On the coast, cosmopolitan Cascais and the traditional fishing town of Ericeira are both excellent bases from which to explore the rocky coastline and surrounding country- side. South of the Tagus, the Serra da Arrábida and the rugged coast around Cabo Espichel can be visited from the small port of Sesimbra. Inland, the nature reserves of the Tagus and Sado estuaries offer a quiet retreat.

SIGHTS AT A GLANCE

Tours

0 kilometres   10

0 miles   5

Cabo da Roca on the western edge of Serra de Sintra

KEY

▬▬	Motorway
▬▬	Secondary road
▭▭▭	Minor road
▬▬	Scenic route
▬ ▪ ▬	Main railway
▬ ▪ ▬	Minor railway
▬▬	Regional border

For additional map symbols *see back flap*

Convento da Arrábida in the hills of the Serra da Arrábida

GETTING AROUND

Motorways give quick access from Lisbon to Sintra, Estoril, Palmela and Setúbal. Main roads are generally well signposted and surfaced, though traffic congestion can be a problem, particularly at weekends and holidays. Watch out for potholes on smaller roads. Fast, frequent trains run west from Lisbon's Cais do Sodré station to Estoril and Cascais, and from Roma Areeiro and Entrecampos stations to Queluz and Sintra. Trains south to Setúbal, Alcácer do Sal and beyond leave from Roma Areeiro, crossing the April 25 bridge. There are good bus services to all parts of the region, most of which leave from Sete Rios.

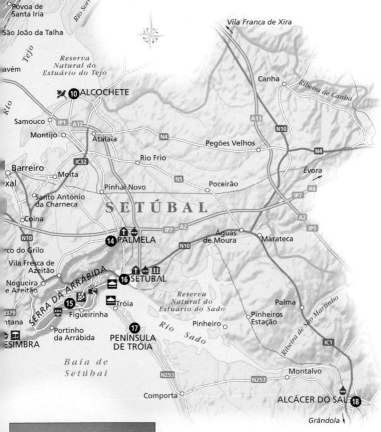

Fishing boats in the harbour at Sesimbra

The stunning library in the Palácio de Mafra, paved with chequered marble

Palácio de Mafra ❶

Road Map B5. Terreiro de Dom João V, Mafra. **Tel** 261 817 550. 🚌 Ericeira bus from Lisbon. Ⓜ Campo Grande, then 🚌 1 Mafrens. 🕙 10am–5pm Wed–Mon (last entry 4:30pm). ⬤ 1 Jan, Easter, 1 May, 25 Dec. ✝ 🎟 (free 10am–1pm Sun). 📷 compulsory.

The massive Baroque palace and monastery *(see also pp52–3)*, which dwarfs the small town of Mafra, was built during the reign of Portugal's most extravagant monarch, João V. It began with a vow by the young king to build a new monastery and basilica, supposedly in return for an heir (but more likely, to atone for his sexual excesses). Work began in 1717 on a modest project to house 13 Franciscan friars but, as wealth began to pour into the royal coffers from Brazil, the king and his Italian-trained architect, Johann Friedrich Ludwig

(1670–1752), made ever more extravagant plans. No expense was spared: 52,000 men were employed and the finished project housed not 13, but 330 friars, a royal palace and one of the finest libraries in Europe, decorated with precious marble, exotic wood and countless works of art. The magnificent basilica was consecrated on the king's 41st birthday, 22 October 1730, with festivities lasting for eight days.

The palace was only popular with those members of the royal family who enjoyed hunting deer and wild boar. Today, a wolf conservation project runs here. Most of the finest furniture and art works were taken to Brazil when the royal family escaped the French invasion in 1807.

The monastery was abandoned in 1834 following the dissolution of all religious orders, and the palace itself was abandoned in 1910, when the last Portuguese king, Manuel II, escaped from here to the Royal Yacht anchored off Ericeira.

Allow at least an hour for the tour, which starts in the rooms of the

The king's bedroom in the Royal Palace

monastery, through the pharmacy, with fine old medicine jars and some alarming medical instruments, to the hospital, where 16 patients could see and hear mass in the adjoining chapel without leaving their beds.

Upstairs, the sumptuous palace state rooms extend across the whole of the monumental west façade, with the King's apartments at one end and the Queen's apartments at the other. Halfway between the two, the long, imposing façade is relieved by the twin towers of the domed basilica. The interior of the church is decorated in contrasting colours of marble and furnished with six early 19th-century organs. Fine Baroque sculptures, executed by members of the Mafra School of Sculpture, adorn the atrium of the basilica. Begun by José I in 1754, many renowned Portuguese and foreign artists trained in the school under the directorship of the Italian sculptor Alessandro Giusti (1715–99). Further on, the Sala da Caça has a grotesque collection of hunting trophies and boars' heads. Mafra's greatest treasure, however, is its magnificent library, with a patterned marble floor, Rococo-style wooden bookcases, and a collection of over 40,000 books in gold embossed leather bindings, including a prized first edition of *Os Lusíadas* (1572) by the Portuguese poet Luís de Camões *(see p46)*.

Statue of St Bruno in the atrium of Mafra's basilica

Environs: Once a week, on Thursday mornings, the small country town of **Malveira**, 10 km (6 miles) east of Mafra, has the region's biggest market, selling clothes and household goods as well as food.

At the village of **Sobreiro**, 6 km (4 miles) west of Mafra, Zé Franco's model village is complete with houses, farms, a waterfall and working windmill, all in minute detail.

Tractor pulling a fishing boat out of the sea at Ericeira

Ericeira ❷

Road Map B5. 🏚 *7,500.* 🚌
ℹ️ *Rua Dr Eduardo Burnay 46*
(261 863 122). 🅐 *daily.*

Ericeira is an old fishing
village which keeps its
traditions despite an ever-
increasing influx of summer
visitors who enjoy the bracing
climate, clean, sandy beaches
and fresh seafood. In July and
August, when the population
leaps to 30,000, pavement
cafés, restaurants and bars
around the tree-lined Praça
da República are buzzing late
into the night. Red flags warn
when swimming is dangerous:
alternative attractions include
crazy golf in Santa Marta park
and an interesting museum of
local history, the **Museu da
Ericeira**, exhibiting models
of traditional regional boats
and fishing equipment.

The unspoilt old town, a
maze of whitewashed houses
and narrow, cobbled streets, is
perched high above the ocean.
From Largo das Ribas, at the
top of a 30-m (100-ft) stone-
faced cliff, there is a bird's-eye
view over the busy fishing
harbour below, where tractors
have replaced the oxen that
once hauled the boats out of
reach of the tide. On 16
August, the annual fishermen's
festival is celebrated with a
candlelit procession to the
harbour at the foot of the cliffs
for the blessing of the boats.

On 5 October 1910, Manuel
II, the last king of Portugal *(see
pp54–5),* sailed into exile from
Ericeira as the Republic was
declared in Lisbon; a tiled
panel in the fishermen's chapel
of Santo António above the

harbour records the event.
The banished king settled in
Twickenham, southwest Lon-
don, where he died in 1932.

🏛 Museu da Ericeira
Largo da Misericórdia. **Tel** *261 862
536.* ⬜ *call ahead for opening
times.* ⬤ *public hols.* 🈸

Colares ❸

Road Map B5. 🏚 *7,500.* 🚌
ℹ️ *Cabo da Roca (219 280 081).*

On the lower slopes of the
Serra de Sintra, this lovely
village faces the sea over a
green valley, the Várzea de
Colares. A leafy avenue winds
its way up to the village. Small
quantities of the famous
Colares wine are still made,
but current vintages lack the
character and ageing potential
of classic Colares and growers

face a financial struggle to
survive. Their hardy old vines
grow in sandy soil, with their
roots set deep below in clay;
these were the only vines in
Europe to survive the dis-
astrous phylloxera epidemic
brought from America in the
late 19th century with the first
viticultural exchanges. The
insect, which destroyed vineyards all over Europe by eating
the vines, could not penetrate
the dense sandy soil of the
Atlantic coast. Wine can be
sampled at the Adega Regional
de Colares on Alameda de
Coronel Linhares de Lima.

Environs: There are several
popular beach resorts west of
Colares. Just north of **Praia
das Maçãs** is the picturesque
village of **Azenhas do Mar**,
clinging to the cliffs; just to
the south is the larger resort
of **Praia Grande**. Both have
natural pools in the rocks,
which are filled by seawater
at high tide. The unspoilt
Praia da Adraga, 1 km (half
a mile) further south, has a
delightful beach café and
restaurant. In the evenings
and off-season, fishermen set
up their lines to catch bass,
bream and flat fish that swim
in on the high tide. A tram-
way that opened in 1910 links
the district of Estefânia, in
Sintra, to the Ribeira de Sintra
(Friday to Sunday). It then
continues on to Praia das
Maçãs (this part of the line is
currently under restoration).

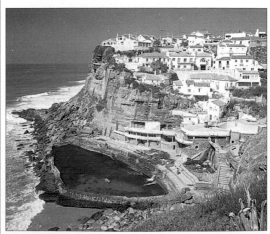

Natural rock pool at Azenhas do Mar, near Colares

Serra de Sintra Tour ❹

This round trip from Sintra follows a dramatic route over the top of the wooded Serra. The first part is a challenging drive with hazardous hairpin bends on steep, narrow roads that are at times poorly surfaced. It passes through dense forest and a surreal landscape of giant moss-covered boulders, with breathtaking views over the Atlantic coast, the Tagus estuary and beyond.

Tiled angels, Peninha chapel

After dropping down to the rugged, windswept coast, the route returns along small country roads passing through hill villages and large estates on the cool, green northern slopes of the Serra de Sintra.

Atlantic coastline seen from Peninha

Colares ⑥
The village of Colares rests on the lower slopes of the wooded Serra, surrounded by gardens and vineyards *(see p155)*.

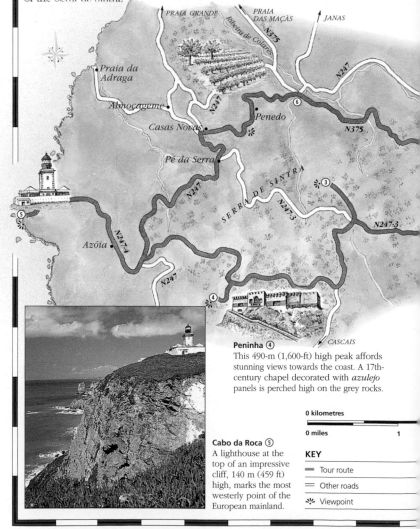

Peninha ④
This 490-m (1,600-ft) high peak affords stunning views towards the coast. A 17th-century chapel decorated with *azulejo* panels is perched high on the grey rocks.

Cabo da Roca ⑤
A lighthouse at the top of an impressive cliff, 140 m (459 ft) high, marks the most westerly point of the European mainland.

0 kilometres

0 miles   1

KEY

▬ Tour route

═ Other roads

❋ Viewpoint

Seteais ⑧
The elegant palace, now a luxury hotel and restaurant *(see p388 & p414)*, was built in the 18th century for the Dutch Consul, Daniel Gildemeester.

TIPS FOR DRIVERS

Length: 36 km (22 miles).
Stopping-off points:
At Cabo da Roca you will find a café, restaurant and souvenir shops; at Colares there are several delightful restaurants and bars. Due to fire risks, picnicking is no longer allowed in the Sintra woods and Parque da Pena.

Palace of Monserrate

Monserrate ⑨

Road map B5. Estrada de Monserrate. **Tel** 219 237 300. ▦ to Sintra then taxi. ◯ Apr–Sep: 9:30am–8pm daily; Oct–Mar: 10am–6pm daily. Last adm: 1 hr before closing time. ● 25 Dec. ▦ www.parquesdesintra.pt

Monserrate ⑦
The cool, overgrown forest park and elaborate 19th-century palace epitomize the romanticism of Sintra.

Sintra ①
From the centre of the old town the road winds steeply upwards past magnificent *quintas* (country estates) hidden among the trees.

ERICEIRA
MAFRA

N247

Palácio
da Pena

LISBOA

N249

CRUZ ALTA

ESTORIL
CASCAIS

Parque da Pena ②
This huge, exotic park can be explored on foot *(see p159)*. It is also possible to drive as far as Cruz Alta, the highest point of the Serra de Sintra.

Convento dos Capuchos ③
Two huge boulders guard the entrance to this remote Franciscan monastery, founded in 1560, where the monks lived in tiny rock-hewn cells lined with cork. There are stunning views of the coast from the hill above this austere, rocky hideaway.

The wild, romantic garden of this once magnificent estate is a jungle of exotic trees and flowering shrubs. Among the sub-tropical foliage and valley of tree ferns are a water-fall, a small lake and a chapel, built as a ruin, tangled in the roots of a giant *Ficus* tree. Its history dates back to the Moors, but it takes its name from a small 16th-century chapel dedicated to Our Lady of Montserrat in Catalonia, Spain. The gardens were landscaped in the late 18th century by a wealthy young Englishman, William Beckford. They were later immortalized by Lord Byron in *Childe Harold's Pilgrimage* (1812).

In 1856, the abandoned estate was bought by another Englishman, Sir Francis Cook, who built a fantastic Moorish-style palace (which now stands eerily empty) and trans-formed the gardens with a large sweeping lawn, camellias and sub-tropical trees from all over the world. These include the giant *Metrosideros* (Australian Christmas tree, covered in a blaze of red flowers in July), the native *Arbutus* (known as the strawberry tree because of its juicy red berries), from which the *medronheira* firewater drink is distilled, and cork oak, with small ferns growing on its bark.

The Friends of Monserrate is a group set up to help restore the sadly neglected house and gardens to their former glory.

Sintra ❻

Sintra's stunning setting on the north slopes of the granite Serra, among wooded ravines and fresh water springs, made it a favourite summer retreat for the kings of Portugal. The tall conical chimneys of the Palácio Nacional de Sintra *(see pp160–61)* and the fabulous Palácio da Pena *(see pp162–3)*, eerily impressive on its peak when the Serra is blanketed in mist, are unmistakable landmarks.

Today, the town (recognized as a UNESCO World Heritage site in 1995) draws thousands of visitors all through the year. Even so, there are many quiet walks in the wooded hills around the town, especially beautiful in the long, cool evenings of the summer months.

Fonte Mourisca on Volta do Duche

Exploring Sintra

Present-day Sintra is in three parts, Sintra Vila, Estefânia and São Pedro, joined by a confusing maze of winding roads scattered over the surrounding hills. In the pretty cobbled streets of the old town, Sintra Vila, which is centred on the **Palácio Nacional de Sintra**, are the museums and beautifully tiled **post office**. The curving **Volta do Duche** leads from the old town, past the lush **Parque da Liberdade**, north to the Estefânia district and the striking Neo-Gothic **Câmara Municipal** (Town Hall). To the south and east, the hilly village of São Pedro spreads over the slopes of the Serra. The fortnightly Sunday **market** here extends across the broad market square.

Exploring Sintra on foot involves a lot of walking and climbing up and down its steep hills. For a more leisurely tour, take one of the horse and carriage rides around the town. The **Miradouro da Vigia** in São Pedro offers impressive views, as does the cosy **Casa de Sapa** café, where you can sample *queijadas*, the local sweet speciality *(see p139)*.

The many fountains dotted around the town are used by locals for their fresh spring drinking water. Two of the most striking are the tiled **Fonte Mourisca** (Arab Fountain), named for its Neo-Moorish decoration, and **Fonte da Sabuga**, where the water spouts from a pair of breasts.

🏛 Museu do Brinquedo

Rua Visconde de Monserrate. *Tel* 219 242 171. ⭘ Tue–Sun. 🈲 ♿ **www.**museu-do-brinquedo.pt
This small museum has a fine collection of toys, ranging from model planes, cars and trains, including 1930s Hornby sets, to dolls and dolls' houses, tin toys and clockwork models of cars and soldiers. There is also a restoration workshop and a playroom with puppets and story tellers.

Toy Alfa Romeo, Museu do Brinquedo

🏛 Museu de Arte Moderna

Avenida Heliodoro Salgado. *Tel* 219 248 170. ⭘ 10am–6pm Tue–Sun. 🈲 (free 10am–2pm Sun). ♿ 🍴 ▢
Housed in a striking 1920s building, this museum showcases the Berardo Collection, an important compilation of modern European and US art. Now that the bulk of the collection has been moved to Lisbon's Centro Cultural de Belém *(see p106)*, the Sintra museum focuses largely on temporary exhibitions of modern and contemporary art.

▥ Quinta da Regaleira

Rua Barbosa du Bocage. *Tel* 219 106 650. ⭘ 10am–8pm daily (Jan & Dec: to 5:30pm; Feb & Mar: to 6:30pm; Oct & Nov: to 6pm). ⬤ 1 Jan, 24, 25 & 31 Dec. 📷 call to book. 🈲 🍴 ▢
Built in the 1890s, this palace and extensive gardens are a feast of historical and religious references, occult symbols and mystery. The obsession of the eccentric millionaire António Augusto Carvalho Monteiro, they are a must for anyone interested in esoterica.

Chimneys of the Palácio Nacional de Sintra above the old town

♣ Castelo dos Mouros

Estrada da Pena. *Tel* 219 107 970.
◻ daily. ● 1 Jan, 25 Dec.
Standing above the old town,
like a sentinel, the ramparts
of the 8th-century Moorish
castle, conquered by Afonso
Henriques in 1147, snake
over the top of the Serra. On
a fine day, there are breathtaking views from the castle
walls over the old town to
Palácio da Pena, on a neighbouring peak, and far along

the coast. Hidden inside the
walls are a ruined chapel and
an ancient Moorish cistern. For
walkers, a steep footpath
threads up through wooded
slopes from the 12th-century
church of **Santa Maria**. Follow
the signs to a dark green swing
gate where the footpath begins.
The monogram "DFII" carved
on the gateway is a reminder
that the castle walls were
restored by Fernando II *(see
p163)* in the 19th century.

Battlements of the Castelo dos Mouros perched on the slopes of the Serra

VISITORS' CHECKLIST

Road map B5. ⋔ 25,000. 🚌
🚌 Avda Dr Miguel Bombarda.
ℹ Praça da República 23 (219
236 922); train station (219 241
623). 🛒 2nd & 4th Sun of month.
🎭 Jun–Jul: Festival de Música.

♣ Parque da Pena

Estrada da Pena. *Tel* 219 237 300.
◻ daily. ● 1 Jan, 25 Dec. 🚹
www.parquesdesintra.pt
A huge park surrounds the
Palácio da Pena where footpaths wind among a lush
vegetation of exotic trees and
shrubs. Hidden among the
foliage are gazebos, follies
and fountains, and a Romantic
chalet built by Fernando II for
his mistress in 1869. Cruz Alta,
the highest point of the Serra
at 530 m (1,740 ft), commands
spectacular views. On a
nearby crag stands the statue
of Baron Von Eschwege, architect of the palace and park.

SINTRA TOWN CENTRE

Câmara Municipal ②
Casa de Sapa ③
Castelo dos Mouros ⑪
Fonte Mourisca ⑦
Fonte da Sabuga ⑨
Museu de Arte Moderna ①
Museu do Brinquedo ⑥
*Palácio Nacional de
Sintra pp160–61* ④
Parque da Pena ⑫
Post office ⑤
Quinta da Regaleira ⑧
Santa Maria ⑩

0 metres   250
0 yards   200

Key to Symbols see back flap

Palácio Nacional de Sintra

At the heart of the old town of Sintra (Sintra Vila), a pair of strange conical chimneys rises high above the Royal Palace. The main part of the palace, including the central block with its plain Gothic façade and the large kitchens beneath the chimneys, was built by João I in the late 14th century, on a site once occupied by the Moorish rulers. The Paço Real, as it is also known, became the favourite summer retreat for the court, and continued as a residence for Portuguese royalty until the 1880s. Additions to the building by the wealthy Manuel I, in the early 16th century, echo the Moorish style. Gradual rebuilding of the palace has resulted in a fascinating amalgamation of various different styles.

Swan panel, Sala dos Cisnes

★ **Sala das Pegas**
It is said that King João I had the ceiling panels painted as a rebuke to the court women for indulging in idle gossip like chattering magpies (pegas).

The Torre da Meca has dovecotes below the cornice decorated with armillary spheres and nautical rope.

The Sala das Galés (galleons) houses temporary exhibitions.

★ **Sala dos Brasões**
The domed ceiling of this majestic room is decorated with stags holding the coats of arms (brasões) of 72 noble Portuguese families. The lower walls are lined with 18th-century Delft-like tiled panels.

Jardim da Preta, a walled garden

Sala de Dom Sebastião, the audience chamber

TIMELINE

10th century Palace becomes residence of Moorish governor	**1281** King Dinis orders restoration of the Palácio de Oliva (as it was then known)	**1495–1521** Reign of Manuel I; major restoration and Manueline additions	**1683** Afonso VI dies after being imprisoned here for nine years by brother Pedro II	**1755** Parts of palace damaged in great earthquake *(see pp62–3)*

800	1000	1200	1400	1600	1800

1147 Christian reconquest; Afonso Henriques takes over palace

1385 João I orders complete rebuilding of central buildings and kitchens

1880s Maria Pia (grandmother of Manuel II) is last royal resident

8th century First palace established by Moors

Siren, Sala das Sereias (c.1660)

1910 Palace becomes a national monument

★ **Sala dos Cisnes**
The magnificent ceiling of the former banqueting hall, painted in the 15th century, is divided into octagonal panels decorated with swans (cisnes).

The Sala dos Árabes
is decorated with fine *azulejos*.

VISITORS' CHECKLIST

Largo Rainha Dona Amélia.
***Tel** 219 106 840.* 🕙 *9:30am–5:30pm Thu–Tue.* ⬤ *1 Jan, Easter, 1 May, 29 Jun, 25 Dec.* ✦ 💺 *(free 10am–2pm Sun).* **www**.imc-ip.pt

Sala das Sereias
Intricate Arabesque designs on 16th-century tiles frame this door in the Room of the Sirens.

The kitchens, beneath the huge conical chimneys, have spits and utensils once used for preparing royal banquets.

Entrance

 Sala dos Archeiros,
the entrance hall

Manuel I added the *ajimene* windows, a distinctive Moorish design with a slender column dividing two arches.

Chapel
Symmetrical Moorish patterns decorate the original 14th-century chestnut and oak ceiling and the mosaic floor of the private chapel.

STAR FEATURES

★ Sala dos Brasões

★ Sala dos Cisnes

★ Sala das Pegas

Sintra: Palácio da Pena

Triton Arch

On the highest peaks of the Serra de Sintra stands the spectacular palace of Pena, an eclectic medley of architectural styles built in the 19th century for the husband of the young Queen Maria II, Ferdinand Saxe-Coburg-Gotha. It stands over the ruins of a Hieronymite monastery founded here in the 16th century on the site of the chapel of Nossa Senhora da Pena. Ferdinand appointed a German architect, Baron Von Eschwege, to build his summer palace filled with oddities from all over the world and surrounded by a park. With the declaration of the Republic in 1910, the palace became a museum, preserved as it was when the royal family lived here. Allow at least an hour and a half to visit this enchanting place.

Entrance Arch
A studded archway with crenellated turrets greets the visitor at the entrance to the palace. The palace buildings are painted the original daffodil yellow and strawberry pink.

Manuel II's Bedroom
The oval-shaped room is decorated with green walls and stuccoed ceiling. A portrait of Manuel II, the last king of Portugal, hangs above the fireplace.

In the kitchen the copper pots and utensils still hang around the iron stove. The dinner service bears the coat of arms of Ferdinand II.

★ Ballroom
The spacious ballroom is sumptuously furnished with German stained-glass windows, precious Oriental porcelain and four lifesize turbaned torchbearers holding giant candelabra.

★ Arab Room
Marvellous trompe-l'oeil frescoes cover the walls and ceiling of the Arab Room, one of the loveliest in the palace. The Orient was a great inspiration to Romanticism.

VISITORS' CHECKLIST

Estrada da Pena, 5 km (3 mile) S of Sintra. *Tel 219 105 340.* 434 from Avenida Dr Miguel Bombarda, Sintra. Apr–Sep: 9:45am–7pm daily; Oct–Mar: 10am–6pm daily. 1 Jan, Easter, 1 May, 29 Jun, 25 Dec. **www**.parquesdesintra.pt

★ Chapel Altarpiece
The impressive 16th-century alabaster and marble retable was sculpted by Nicolau Chanterène. Each niche portrays a scene of the life of Christ, from the manger to the Ascension.

The Triton Arch is encrusted with Neo-Manueline decoration and is guarded by a fierce sea monster.

The cloister, decorated with colourful patterned tiles, is part of the original monastery buildings.

Entrance

STAR FEATURES

★ Arab Room

★ Ballroom

★ Chapel Altarpiece

FERDINAND: KING CONSORT

Ferdinand was known in Portugal as Dom Fernando II, the "artist" king. Like his cousin Prince Albert, who married the English Queen Victoria, he loved art, nature and the new inventions of the time. He was himself a watercolour painter. Ferdinand enthusiastically adopted his new country and devoted his life to patronizing the arts. In 1869, 16 years after the death of Maria II, Ferdinand married his mistress, the opera singer Countess Edla. His lifelong dream of building the extravagant palace at Pena was completed in 1885, the year he died.

Outdoor café in the popular holiday resort of Cascais

Cascais ❼

Road map B5. 🏘 *33,000.* 🚇 🚍
🛈 *Rua Visconde da Luz 14 (214 820 085).* 🔄 *1st & 3rd Sun of month.*

Having been a holiday resort for well over a century, Cascais possesses a certain illustriousness that younger resorts lack. Its history is most clearly visible in the villas along the coast, built as summer residences by wealthy *Lisboetas* during the late 19th century, after King Luís I had moved his summer activities to the 17th-century fortress here. The military importance of Cascais, now waned, is much older as it sits on the north bank of the mouth of the Tagus.

The sandy, sheltered bay around which the modern suburb has sprawled was a fishing harbour in prehistoric times. Fishing still goes on, and it was given a municipal boost with the decision to build a quay for the landing and initial auctioning of the fishermen's catch. But Cascais today is first of all a favoured suburb of Lisbon, a place of apartments with a sea view and pine-studded plots by golf courses. It may sometimes seem more defined by its ceaseless construction boom than by any historic or even touristic qualities, but the beautiful, windswept coastline beyond the town has been left relatively undeveloped.

The Museu do Conde de Castro Guimaraes is perhaps the best place to get a taste of Cascais as it was just over a century ago. A castle-like villa on a small creek by a headland, its grounds are today part of a park. The house and its contents were bequeathed to the municipality.

Across the road from the museum is the marina, one of the most emblematic developments in Cascais. With its small shopping centre, restaurants and cafés it is becoming a weekend magnet for today's car-borne Cascais residents and tourists.

🏛 **Museu do Conde de Castro Guimarães**
Avenida Rei Humberto de Itália.
Tel *214 815 308.* ⏰ *10am–5pm Tue–Sun (excl 1–2pm Sat & Sun).* 📷 ⬤ *public hols.*

Environs: At **Boca do Inferno** (Mouth of Hell) about 3 km (2 miles) west on the coast road, the sea rushes into clefts and caves in the rocks making a booming sound and sending up spectacular spray.

The magnificent sandy beach of **Guincho**, 10 km (6 miles) further west, has Atlantic breakers that make this a paradise for experienced windsurfers and surfers, though beware of the strong currents.

The **Ellipse Foundation Contemporary Art Collection** in Alcoitão has over 300 works by contemporary artists.

🏛 **Ellipse Foundation Contemporary Art Collection**
Rua das Fisgas, Pedra Furada, Alcoitão. **Tel** *214 691 806.*
⏰ *11am–6pm Fri–Sun.*

Spectacular view of the weatherbeaten coastline at Boca do Inferno, near Cascais

Estoril ❽

Road map B5. 🏘 *24,000.* 🚇
🚍 🛈 *Arcadas do Parque (214 672 280).*

Despite once being the haunt of exiled royalty and nobility fleeing European republicanism, the lovely resort town of Estoril does not rest on its historical laurels. Today, it is a tourist and business resort, and a place for comfortable retirement. As such, it relies equally on its historical reputation and on the natural attractiveness it has always possessed. There are also a number of good golf courses.

What separates Estoril from Cascais, besides a pleasant beach promenade of 3 km (2 miles) and a mansion-covered ridge known as Monte Estoril, is its sense of place. The heart of Estoril is immediately accessible from the train station. On one side of the tracks, the riviera-like

Sandy beach and promenade along the bay of Estoril

beach, on the other, a palm-lined park flanked by grand buildings, stretches up past fountains to what is said to be Europe's biggest casino. Dwarfing the casino is the Estoril Congress Centre, a vast multipurpose edifice that speaks confidently of Estoril's contemporary role.

Palácio de Queluz ❾

See pp166–7.

Alcochete ❿

Road map C5. 🏘 *9,000.* 🚆 🛈 *Largo da Misericórdia (212 348 655).*

This delightful old town overlooks the wide Tagus estuary from the southern shore. Salt has long been one of the main industries here, and saltpans can still be seen to the north and south of the town, while in the town centre a large statue of a muscular salt worker has the inscription: "Do Sal a Revolta e a Esperança" (From Salt to Rebellion and Hope). On the outskirts of town, is a statue of Manuel I *(see pp46–7)*, who was born here on 1 June 1469 and granted the town a Royal Charter in 1515.

Statue of a salt worker in Alcochete (1985)

Environs: The **Reserva Natural do Estuário do Tejo** covers a vast area of estuary water, salt marshes and small islands around Alcochete and is a very important breeding ground for water birds. Particularly interesting are the flocks of flamingos that gather here during the autumn and spring migration, en route from colonies such as the Camargue in France and Fuente de Piedra in Spain. Ask at the tourist office about boat trips to see the wildlife of the estuary, which includes wild bulls and horses.

🦌 **Reserva Natural do Estuário do Tejo**
Avenida dos Combatentes da Grande Guerra 1. **Tel** *212 348 021.*

Pilgrims' lodgings, Cabo Espichel

Costa da Caparica ⓫

Road map B5. 🏘 *12,000.* 🚆 *to Pragal, then 194 bus.* 🛈 *Avenida da República 18 (212 900 071).*

Long sandy beaches, backed by sand dunes, have made this a popular holiday resort for Lisboetas who come here to swim, sunbathe and enjoy the seafood restaurants and beach cafés. A railway, with open carriages, runs for 10 km (6 miles) along the coast during the summer months. The first beaches reached from the town are popular with families with children, while the furthest beaches suit those seeking quiet isolation. Further south, sheltered by pine forests, **Lagoa do Albufeira**, is a peaceful wind-surfing centre and camp site.

Cabo Espichel ⓬

Road map B5. 🚌 *from Sesimbra.*

Sheer cliffs drop straight into the sea at this windswept promontory where the land ends dramatically. The Romans named it Promontorium Barbaricum, alluding to its dangerous location, and a lighthouse warns sailors of the treacherous rocks below. Stunning views of the ocean and the coast can be enjoyed from this bleak outcrop of land but beware of the strong gusts of wind on the cliff edge.

In this desolate setting stands the impressive **Santuário de Nossa Senhora do Cabo**, a late 17th-century church with its back to the sea. On either side of the church a long line of pilgrims' lodgings facing inwards form an open courtyard. Baroque paintings, ex votos and a frescoed ceiling decorate the interior of the church. There are plans to fully restore the building and open it as a hotel. A domed chapel, tiled with blue and white *azulejo* panels, is located nearby.

The site became a popular place of pilgrimage in the 13th century when a local man had a vision of the Madonna rising from the sea on a mule. Legend has it that the tracks of the mule can be seen embedded in the rock. The large footprints, on Praia dos Lagosteiros below the church, are actually believed to be fossilized dinosaur tracks.

Spring flowers by the saltpans of the Tagus estuary near Alcochete

Palácio de Queluz ❾

In 1747, Pedro, younger son of João V, commissioned Mateus Vicente to transform his 17th-century hunting lodge into a Rococo summer palace. The central section, including a music room and chapel, was built, but after Pedro's marriage in 1760 to the future Maria I, the palace was again extended. The French architect, Jean-Baptiste Robillion, added the sumptuous Robillion Pavilion and gardens, cleared space for the Throne Room and redesigned the Music Room. During Maria's reign, the royal family kept a menagerie and went boating on the *azulejo*-lined canal.

A sphinx in the gardens

Corridor of the Sleeves
Painted azulejo panels (1784) representing the continents and the seasons, as well as hunting scenes, line the walls of the bright Corredor das Mangas (sleeves).

Neptune's Fountain

★ Sala dos Embaixadores
Built by Robillion, this stately room was used for diplomatic audiences as well as concerts. The trompe l'oeil ceiling shows the royal family attending a concert.

The Lion Staircase is an impressive and graceful link from the lower gardens to the palace.

STAR FEATURES

- ★ Throne Room
- ★ Sala dos Embaixadores
- ★ Palace Gardens

To canal

Shell Waterfall

The Robillion Pavilion displays the flamboyance of the French architect's Rococo style.

Don Quixote Chamber
The royal bedroom, where Pedro IV (see p54) was born and died, has a domed ceiling and magnificent floor decoration in exotic woods, giving the square room a circular appearance. Painted scenes by Manuel de Costa (1784) tell the story of Don Quixote.

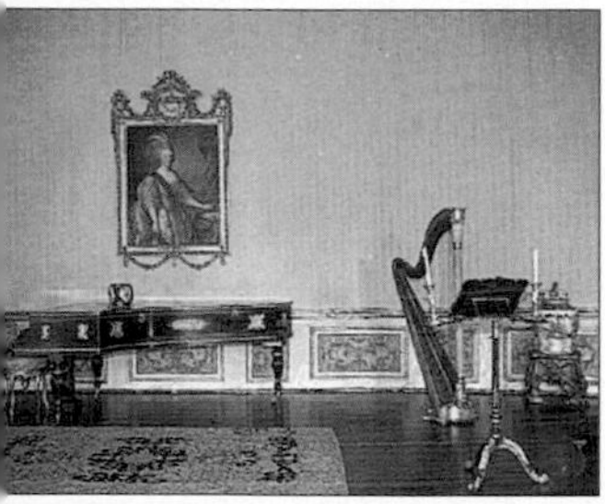

Music Room
Operas and concerts were performed here by Maria I's orchestra, "the best in Europe" according to English traveller, William Beckford. A portrait of the queen hangs above the grand piano.

VISITORS' CHECKLIST

Road Map B5. Largo do Palácio. ***Tel*** *214 343 860.* *Queluz-Belas or Queluz-Massama.* *from Lisbon (Colégio Militar).* *9am–5pm Wed–Mon.* *1 Jan, Easter, 1 May, 29 Jun, 25 Dec.* *(free 10am–2pm Sun).*

Chapel
Entrance
Malta Gardens

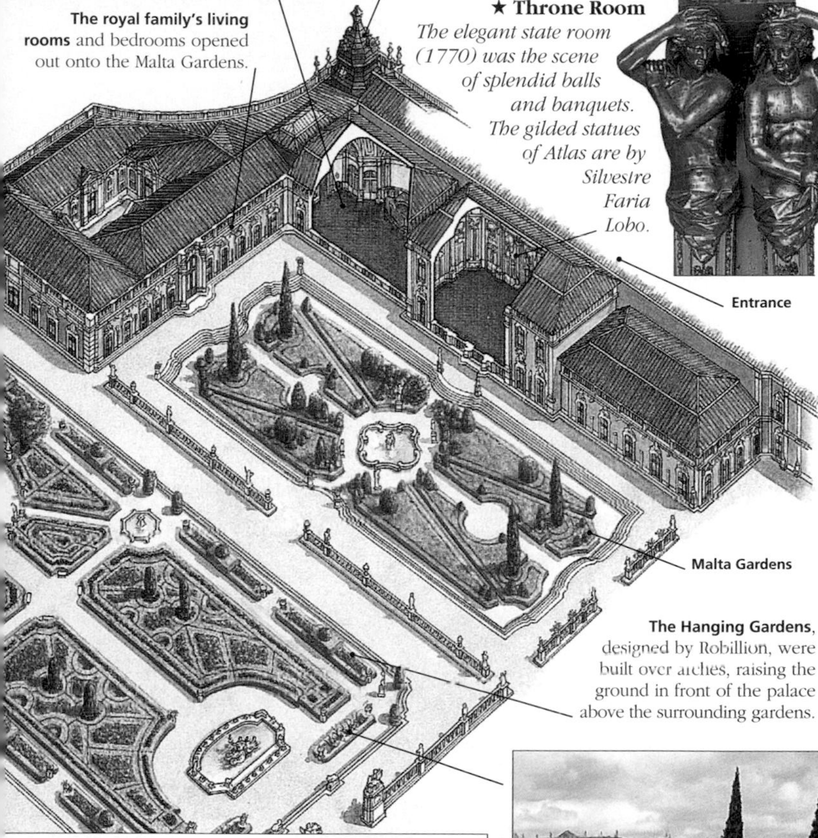

The royal family's living rooms and bedrooms opened out onto the Malta Gardens.

★ Throne Room
The elegant state room (1770) was the scene of splendid balls and banquets. The gilded statues of Atlas are by Silvestre Faria Lobo.

The Hanging Gardens, designed by Robillion, were built over arches, raising the ground in front of the palace above the surrounding gardens.

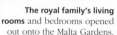

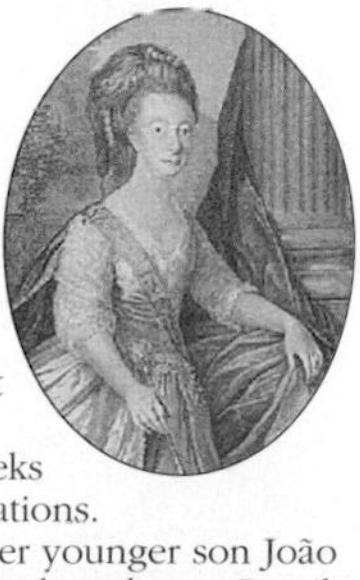

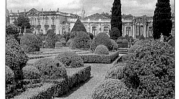

★ Palace Gardens
The formal gardens, adorned with statues, fountains and topiary, were often used for entertaining. Concerts performed in the Music Room would spill out into the Malta Gardens.

MARIA I (1734–1816)

Maria, the eldest daughter of José I, lived at the palace in Queluz after her marriage to her uncle, Pedro, in 1760. Serious and devout, she conscientiously filled her role as queen, but suffered increasingly from bouts of melancholia. When her son José died from smallpox in 1788, she went hopelessly mad. Visitors to Queluz were dismayed by her agonizing shrieks as she suffered visions and hallucinations. After the French invasion of 1807, her younger son João (declared regent in 1792) took his mad mother to Brazil.

Sesimbra ⑬

Road map C5. 🏘 *42,000.* 🚌
ℹ *Largo da Marinha 26–7 (212 280 027).* 🎡 *1st & 3rd Fri of month.*

A steep narrow road leads down to this busy fishing village in a sheltered south-facing bay. Protected from north winds by the slopes of the Serra da Arrábida, the town has become a popular holiday resort with Lisboetas. It was occupied by the Romans and later the Moors until King Sancho II *(see pp42–3)* conquered its heavily defended forts in 1236. The old town is a maze of steep narrow streets, with the **Santiago Fort** (now a customs post) in the centre overlooking the sea. From the terrace, which is open to the public during the day, there are views over the town, the Atlantic and the wide sandy beach that stretches out on either side. Sesimbra is fast developing as a resort, with holiday flats mushrooming on the surrounding hillsides and plentiful pavement cafés and bars that are always busy on sunny days, even in winter.

The fishing fleet of brightly painted boats is moored in the **Porto do Abrigo** to the west of the main town. The harbour is reached by taking Avenida dos Náufragos, a sweeping

Colourful fishing boats in the harbour at Sesimbra

promenade that follows the beach out of town. On the large trawlers *(traineiras)*, the catch is mainly sardines, sea bream, whiting and swordfish; on the smaller boats, octopus and squid. In the late afternoon, when the fishing boats return from a day at sea, a colourful, noisy fish auction takes place on the quayside. The day's catch can be tasted in the town's excellent fish restaurants along the shore.

High above the town is the **Moorish castle**, greatly restored in the 18th century when a church and small flower-filled cemetery were added inside the walls. There are wonderful views from the ramparts, especially at sunset.

Palmela ⑭

Road map C5. 🏘 *57,000.* 🚌 🚆
ℹ *Castelo de Palmela (212 332 122).* 🎡 *every other Tue.*

The formidable castle at Palmela stands over the small hilltown, high on a north-eastern spur of the wooded Serra da Arrábida. Its strategic position dominates the plain for miles around, especially when floodlit at night. Heavily defended by the Moors, it was eventually conquered in the 12th century and given by Sancho I to the Knights of the Order of Santiago *(see p43)*. In 1423, João I transformed the castle into a monastery for the Order, which has been restored and converted into a splendid *pousada (see p387)*, with a restaurant in the monks' refectory and a swimming pool for residents, hidden inside the castle walls.

From the castle terraces, and especially from the top of the 14th-century keep, there are fantastic views all around, over the Serra da Arrábida to the south and on a clear day across the Tagus to Lisbon. In the town square below, the church of **São Pedro** contains 18th-century tiles of scenes from the life of St Peter.

The annual wine festival, the Festa das Vindimas, is held on the first weekend of September in front of the 17th-century Paços do Concelho (town hall). Traditionally dressed villagers, press the wine barefoot and on the final day of celebrations there is a spectacular firework display from the castle walls.

The castle at Palmela with views over the wooded Serra da Arrábida

For hotels and restaurants in this region see 386–8 and pp412–15

Serra da Arrábida ⓯

Road map C5. 🚌 *Setúbal.*
🚹 *Parque Natural da Arrábida, Praça
da República, Setúbal (265 541 140).*

The Parque Natural da
Arrábida covers the small
range of limestone mountains
which stretches east-west along
the coast between Sesimbra
and Setúbal. It was established
to protect the wild, beautiful
landscape and rich variety of
birds and wildlife, including
eagles, wildcats and badgers.

The name Arrábida is from
Arabic meaning a place of
prayer, and the wooded hillsides are indeed a peaceful,
secluded retreat. The sheltered,
south-facing slopes are thickly
covered with aromatic and
evergreen shrubs and trees
such as pine and cypress, more
typical of the Mediterranean.
Vineyards also thrive on the
sheltered slopes and the town
of **Vila Nogueira de Azeitão** is
known for its wine, especially
the Moscatel de Setúbal.

The **Estrada de Escarpa**
(the N379-1) snakes across the
top of the ridge and affords
astounding views. A narrow
road winds down to **Portinho
da Arrábida**, a sheltered cove
with a beach of fine white sand
and crystal clear sea, popular
with underwater fishermen.
The sandy beaches of **Galapos**
and **Figueirinha** are a little
further east along the coast
road towards Setúbal. Just
east of Sesimbra, the Serra da
Arrábida drops to the sea in
the sheer 380-m (1,250-ft)
cliffs of Risco, the
highest in
mainland
Portugal.

Portinho da Arrábida on the dramatic coastline of the Serra da Arrábida

🏠 Convento da Arrábida

Serra da Arrábida. **Tel** *212 197 620.*
🕐 *by appt only at 3pm Wed–Sun.*
● *Aug.* 🌐
Half-hidden among the trees
of the Serra, this 16th-century
building was once a Franciscan
monastery. The five round
towers on the hillside were
probably used for meditation.
Today, the building houses
a cultural centre.

🏛 Museu Oceanográfico

Fortaleza de Santa Maria, Portinho
da Arrábida. **Tel** *212 189 791.*
○ *10am–4pm Tue–Fri, 3–6pm Sat
(except Aug).* ● *public hols.* 🌐
This small fort, just above
Portinho da Arrábida, was
built by Pedro, the Prince
Regent, in 1676 to protect
local communities from
attacks by Moorish pirates.
It now houses a Sea Museum
and Marine Biology Centre
where visitors can see
aquaria containing
many local sea creatures,
including sea urchins,
octopus and starfish.

🍷 José Maria de Fonseca

Rua José Augusto Coelho 11,
Vila Nogueira de Azeitão. **Tel** *212
198 940.* **Fax** *212 197 501.* ○
10am–1pm & 2:30–6:30pm daily.
● *1 Jan, 24 & 25 Dec.* 🌐 🍷 🏠
The Fonseca winery produces
quality table wines and is
famous for its fragrant dessert
wine, Moscatel de Setúbal
(see p29). Tours of the winery
explain the process of making
moscatel and a visit to a series
of old cellars containing huge
oak and chestnut vats. Tours
last about 45 minutes and
include a wine tasting.

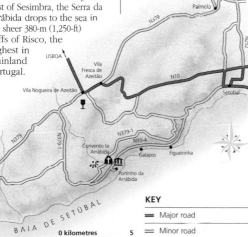

KEY

━━ Major road

═══ Minor road

═══ Other road

0 kilometres 5

0 miles 3

Manueline interior of Igreja de Jesus, Setúbal

Setúbal **⑯**

Road map C5. 🏠 *118,500.* 🚊 🚌
🚢 🚹 *Casa de Bahia, Avenida Luísa
Todi (265 534 222/402).*

Although this is an important
industrial town, and the
third largest port in Portugal
(after Lisbon and Oporto),
Setúbal can be used to
explore the area. To the south
of the central gardens and
fountains are the fishing harbour, marina and ferry port,
and a lively covered market.
North of the gardens is the
old town, with attractive
pedestrian streets and squares
full of shops and cafés. ·

The 16th-century **cathedral**,
dedicated to Santa Maria da
Graça, has glorious tiled panels
dating from the 18th century,
and gilded altar decoration.
Street names commemorate
two famous Setúbal residents:
Manuel Barbosa du Bocage
(1765–1805), whose satirical
poetry landed him in prison,
and Luísa Todi (1753–1833),
a celebrated opera singer.

In Roman times, fish-salting
was the most important industry here. Rectangular tanks,
carved from stone, can be
seen under the glass floor of
the Regional Tourist Office at
No. 10 Travessa Frei Gaspar.

🏠 Igreja de Jesus
Largo de Jesus. **Tel** *265 520 964.*
⏰ *9:30am–12:30pm & 2:30–5pm
Tue–Sun.* ♿ **Museum Tel** *265 537
890.* ⏰ *9am–12:30pm & 2–5:30pm
Tue–Sat.* ⏺ *public hols.*
To the north of the old town,
this striking Gothic church is
one of Setúbal's architectural

Fisherman's boat on the shallow mud flats of
the Reserva Natural do Estuário do Sado

treasures. Designed by the
architect Diogo Boitac in 1494,
the lofty interior is adorned
with twisted columns, carved
in three strands from pinkish
Arrábida limestone, and rope-
like stone ribs decorating the
roof, recognized as the earliest
examples of the distinctive
Manueline style *(see pp24–5)*.

On Rua do Balneário, in
the old monastic quarters, a
museum houses 14 remarkable paintings of the life of
Christ. The works are attributed to the followers of Jorge
Afonso (1520–30), influenced
by the Flemish school.

🏛 Museu de Arqueologia
e Etnografia
Avenida Luísa Todi 162. **Tel** *265 239
365.* ⏺ *9am–12:30pm & 2–5:30pm
Tue–Sat.* ⏺ *public hols.*
The archaeological museum
displays a wealth of finds from
digs around Setúbal, including
Bronze Age pots, Roman coins
and amphorae made to carry
wine and *garum*, a sauce
made from fish marinated
in salt and herbs. The
ethnography display shows
local arts, crafts and industries,
including the processing of salt
and cork over the centuries.

♦ Castelo de São Filipe
Estrada de São Filipe.
Tel *265 550 070.*
The star-shaped fort was built
in 1595 by Philip II of Spain
during the period of Spanish
rule *(see pp50–51)* to keep a
wary eye on pirates, English
invaders and the local population. A massive gateway
and stone tunnel lead to the
sheltered interior, which
houses a *pousada (see p388)*
and an exquisite small chapel,
tiled with scenes from the life
of São Filipe by Policarpo de
Oliveira Bernardes
(see p26). A broad
terrace offers mar-
vellous views over
the city and the
Sado estuary.

Environs: Setúbal is
an excellent starting
point for a tour by
car of the unspoilt
**Reserva Natural
do Estuário do
Sado**, a vast stretch
of mud flats, shallow

lagoons and salt marshes with patches of pine forest, which has been explored and inhabited since 3500 BC. Otters, water birds (including storks and herons), oysters and a great variety of fish are found in the reserve. The old tidal water mill at Mouriscas, 5 km (3 miles) to the east of Setúbal, uses the different levels of the tide to turn the grinding stones. Rice-growing and fishing are the main occupations today, and pine trees around the lagoon are tapped for resin.

✖ Reserva Natural do Estuário do Sado
ℹ *Praça da República, Setúbal (265 541 140).*

Península de Tróia ⑰

Road map C5. 🚌 ⛴ *Tróia.* **ℹ** *Tv Frei Gaspar 10, Setúbal (265 539 130).*

Thatched fisherman's cottage in the village of Carrasqueira

High-rise holiday apartments dominate the tip of the Tróia peninsula, easily accessible from Setúbal by ferry. The Atlantic coast, stretching south for 18 km (11 miles) of untouched sandy beach, lined with dunes and pine woods, is now the haunt of sun-seekers in the summer.

Near Tróia, in the sheltered lagoon, the Roman town of **Cetóbriga** was the site of a thriving fish-salting business; the stone tanks and ruined buildings are open to visit. To the south, smart holiday villas and golf clubs are springing up along the lagoon.

Further on, **Carrasqueira** is an old fishing community where you can still see traditional reed houses. The narrow fishing boats moored along the mud flats are

View over Alcácer do Sal and the River Sado from the castle

reached by walkways raised on stilts. From here to Alcácer do Sal, great stretches of pine forest line the road, and there are the first glimpses of the cork oak countryside typical of the Alentejo.

♠ Cetóbriga
N253-1. **Tel** *213 614 200.*
◯ *by appt only.*

Alcácer do Sal ⑱

Road map C5. 🏠 *13,700.* 🚌 🚌 **ℹ** *Largo Pedro Nunes (265 610 070).* 🞄 *1st Sat of month.*

Bypassed by the main road, the ancient town of Alcácer do Sal (*al-kasr* from the Arabic for castle, and *do sal* from its trade in salt) sits peacefully on the north bank of the River Sado. The imposing castle was a hillfort as early as the 6th century BC.

The Phoenicians established an inland trading port here, and the castle later became a stronghold for the Romans. Rebuilt by the Moors, it was finally conquered by Afonso II in 1217. The restored buildings have taken on a new life as a *pousada (see p386)*, with sweeping views over the rooftops and untidy storks' nests.

There are pleasant cafés along the riverside promenade and several historic churches. The small church of Espírito Santo now houses a **Museu Arqueológico** exhibiting local finds and the 18th-century **Santo António** holds a marble Chapel of the 11,000 Virgins. The bullring is a focus for summer events and hosts the agricultural fair in October.

🏛 Museu Arqueológico
Igreja do Espírito Santo, Praça Pedro Nunes. **Tel** *265 610 040.*
◯ *call ahead for opening times.*

BIRDS OF THE TAGUS AND SADO ESTUARIES

Many waterbirds, including black-winged stilts, avocets, Kentish plovers and pratincoles are found close to areas of open water and mud flats as well as the dried out lagoons of the Tagus and Sado estuaries. Reed-beds also provide shelter for nesting and support good numbers of little bitterns, purple herons and marsh harriers. From September to March, the area around the Tagus estuary is extremely important for wildfowl and wintering waders.

Black-winged stilt, a wader that feeds in the estuaries

ESTREMADURA AND RIBATEJO

etween the Tagus and the coast lies Estremadura, an area of rolling hills that tumble down to rugged cliffs and sandy beaches. In contrast, the Ribatejo is a vast alluvial plain stretching along the banks of the Tagus. Portugal's finest medieval monasteries bear witness to the illustrious, if turbulent past of these regions.

The name Estremadura comes from the Latin *Extrema Durii,* "beyond the Douro", once the border of the Christian kingdoms in the north. As Portugal expanded southwards in the 12th century, land taken from the Moors *(see pp42–3)* was given to the religious orders. The Cistercian abbey at Alcobaça celebrates Afonso Henriques's capture of the town of Santarém in 1147, and the Knights Templar began their citadel at Tomar *(see p187)* soon after.

Spanish claims to the Portuguese throne brought more fighting: Batalha's magnificent abbey was built near the site of João I's victory over the Castilians at Aljubarrota in 1385. More recently, in 1808–10, Napoleonic forces sacked many towns in the region, but were stopped by Wellington's formidable defences, the Lines of Torres Vedras.

Nowadays, Estremadura is an area of expanding commerce, where vineyards, wheatfields and market gardens flourish. In the Ribatejo (the name means "Banks of the Tagus") the river's vast flood plain provides fertile soil for agriculture and grazing land for Portugal's prized black fighting bulls and fine horses.

The area around Tomar and the river towns along the Tagus have thriving industries, while on the River Zêzere, the dam built at Castelo de Bode in the 1940s heralded a new era of hydro-electric power. The Atlantic coast is a popular holiday destination, especially the fishing village of Nazaré and the sandy beaches along the Pinhal de Leiria forest. Visitors also flock to Portugal's most important religious shrine at Fátima, scene of celebrated visions of the Virgin Mary in 1917.

Posters advertising the local bullfighting events in Coruche

◁ Austere Gothic columns in the nave of the Cistercian abbey church at Alcobaça

Exploring Estremadura and the Ribatejo

The impressive monuments in Estremadura recall the important role the region has played in Portugal's history. Tomar and Óbidos are convenient bases from which to visit the great abbeys at Batalha and Alcobaça or the modern shrine at Fátima. Leiria's charming old town is also a good place to stay and it is possible to make day trips from Lisbon. Those in search of more leisurely pursuits can enjoy boating on the Castelo de Bode lake or relaxing on the coast's stunning beaches. The fertile Leziria plain of the Ribatejo is an area famous for bull- and horse-breeding. Here visitors can enjoy bullfights at Santarém and lively local festivals.

SIGHTS AT A GLANCE

Abrantes ⑭
Alcobaça pp180–81 ⑤
Alenquer ㉒
Alpiarça ⑱
Barragem do
  Castelo de Bode ⑬
Batalha pp184–5 ⑧
Berlenga Islands ①
Caldas da Rainha ④
Castelo de Almourol ⑮
Coruche ⑳
Fátima ⑪
Golegã ⑰
Leiria ⑨
Nazaré ⑥
Óbidos ③
Peniche ②

Pombal ⑩
Porto de Mós ⑦
Santarém ⑲
Tomar pp186–9 ⑫
Torres Novas ⑯
Torres Vedras ㉓
Vila Franca de Xira ㉑

GETTING AROUND

Although trains connect many of the major towns in the region, stations are often located outside the town. There are local bus services and coach trips from Lisbon to such destinations as Alcobaça and Tomar. Driving is the most convenient option. The A1 (IP1) and A8 (IC1) allow easy north-south access. Avoid the N1 (IC2) as it is often congested. The A23 (IP6) runs eastwards from the A1 (IP1).

Colourful beach tents at São Martinho do Porto, near Nazaré

SEE ALSO

- *Where to Stay* pp388–90

- *Where to Eat* pp415–17

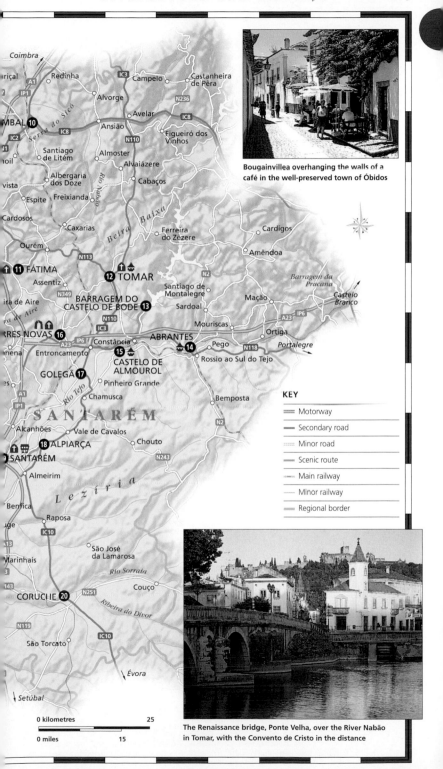

Coimbra
Redinha
Campelo
Castanheira
de Pêra
IC3
A1
IP1
Alvorge
N236
riçal
Avelar
MBAL **10**
Ansião
IC8
IC8
Figueiró dos
Vinhos
IC2
N110
Serra do Sicó
Almoster
Santiago
de Litém
Alvaiázere
noil
Albergaria
dos Doze
Cabaços
Rio Nabão
vista
Espite
Freixianda
Cardosos
Caxarias
Beira Baixa
Ferreira
do Zêzere
Cardigos
Ourém
Amêndoa
N113
11 FÁTIMA
12 TOMAR
Assentiz
N349
Santiago de
Montalegre
Barragem da
Pracana
ira de Aire
BARRAGEM DO
CASTELO DE BODE **13**
Sardoal
Mação
Castelo
Branco
ra de Aire
N110
A23 IP6
IC3
Mouriscas
RES NOVAS **16**
Constância
ABRANTES
Ortiga
IP6
A23
nena
Entroncamento
15
14
Pego
N118
Portalegre
CASTELO DE
ALMOUROL
Rossio ao Sul do Tejo
GOLEGÃ **17**
Pinheiro Grande
es
A1
Chamusca
Bemposta
IP1
Rio Tejo
SANTARÉM
Alcanhões
Vale de Cavalos
Chouto
N2
18 ALPIARÇA
SANTARÉM
N243
Almeirim
Leziria
Benfica
Raposa
uge
IC10
13
São José
da Lamarosa
Marinhais
Rio Sorraia
3
CORUCHE **20**
Couço
N251
N119
Ribeira do Divor
IC10
São Torcato
Évora
Setúbal

Bougainvillea overhanging the walls of a
café in the well-preserved town of Óbidos

KEY

▬▬	Motorway
▬▬	Secondary road
▭▭▭	Minor road
▬▬	Scenic route
▭▭▭	Main railway
―――	Minor railway
▬▬	Regional border

0 kilometres   25

0 miles   15

The Renaissance bridge, Ponte Velha, over the River Nabão
in Tomar, with the Convento de Cristo in the distance

Berlenga Islands ●

Road map B4. ⛴ *from Peniche.*
ℹ *Peniche.*

Monks, a lighthouse keeper, fishermen and biologists have inhabited this rocky archipelago that juts out from the Atlantic Ocean 12 km (7 miles) from the mainland. Berlenga Grande, the biggest island, can be reached by ferry in about an hour. This island is a nature reserve with nesting sites for seabirds including guillemots and herring gulls.

On the southeast side of the island is the 17th-century pentagonal **Forte de São João Baptista**. This stark, stone fort suffered repeated assaults from pirates and foreign armies over the years. Today it is a basic hostel. Small boats can be hired from the jetty to explore the reefs and marine grottoes around the island. **Furado Grande** is the most spectacular of these; a 70-m (230-ft) tunnel, opening into the Covo do Sonho (Dream Cove) framed by imposing red granite cliffs.

Stone fortress of São João Baptista on Berlenga Grande

Peniche ●

Road map B4. 🏘 *28,000.* 🚌
ℹ *Rua Alexandre Herculano (262 789 571).* 🛒 *Last Thu of the month (except Jul & Dec).*

Set on a peninsula, this small, pleasant town is partly enclosed by 16th-century walls. Totally dependent on its port, Peniche has good fish restaurants and deep-sea fishing facilities. At the water's edge on the

south side of town stands the 16th-century **Fortaleza**, used as a prison during the Salazar regime *(see pp56–7)*. The fortress was made famous by the escape in 1960 of the communist leader, Álvaro Cunhal. Inside, the **Museu de Peniche** caters to popular interest with a tour that includes a look into the prison cells. In Largo 5 de Outubro, the **Igreja da Misericórdia** has 17th-century painted ceiling panels depicting the *Life of Christ,* and patterned *azulejo* panels from the same period.

🏛 **Museu de Peniche**
Campo da República. **Tel** 262 780 116. 🕐 *Tue–Sun.* ⬤ *25 Dec.* 🎫

Environs: On the peninsula's western headland, 2 km (1 mile) from Peniche, **Cabo Carvoeiro** affords grand views of the ocean and the strange-shaped rocks along the eroded coastline. Here, the interior of the chapel of **Nossa Senhora dos Remédios** is faced with 18th-century tiles on the *Life of the Virgin* attributed to the workshop of António de Oliveira Bernardee *(see p26)*.

Along the coast, 2 km (1 mile) east of Peniche, **Baleal** is a small community with gorgeous beaches and an idyllic fishing cove across a causeway.

Óbidos ●

Road map B4. 🏘 *11,000.* 🚉 🚌
ℹ *Rua da Porta da Vila (Parque do Estacionamento Grande) (262 959 231).*

This enchanting hilltown with pretty whitewashed houses is enclosed within 14th-century walls. When King Dinis *(see pp44–5)* married Isabel of Aragon in 1282, Óbidos was among his wedding presents to her. At the time Óbidos was an important port, but by the 16th century the river had silted up and its strategic importance declined. It has since been restored and preserved.

Boats anchored in the old harbour at Peniche

The entrance into the town is through the southern gate, **Porta da Vila**, whose interior is embellished with 18th-century tiles. Rua Direita, the main shopping street, leads to Praça de Santa Maria. Here, a Manueline **pelourinho** (pillory) is decorated with a fishing net, the emblem of Dona Leonor, wife of João II. She chose this emblem in honour of the fishermen who tried in vain to save her son from drowning.

Opposite the pillory is the church of **Santa Maria**, with a simple Renaissance portal. The future Afonso V was married to his cousin Isabel here in 1441. He was ten years old, she eight. The interior of the church retains a simple clarity with a painted wooden ceiling and 17th-century tiles. In the chancel, a retable depicting the *Mystic Marriage of St Catherine* (1661) is by Josefa de Óbidos *(see p51)*. The artist lived most of her life in Óbidos and is buried in the church of **São Pedro** on Largo de São Pedro. Her work is also on display in the **Museu Municipal**.

Dominating the town is the **castle**, rebuilt by Afonso Henriques after he took the town from the Moors in 1148.

View of the castle over the whitewashed houses of Óbidos

Today it is a charming *pousada* *(see p390)*. The sentry path along the battlements affords fine views of the rooftops.

Southeast of town is the Baroque **Santuário do Senhor da Pedra**, begun in 1740 to a hexagonal plan. An early Christian stone crucifix on the altar remains a venerated item.

🏛 Museu Municipal
Praça de Sta Maria. *Tel* 262 955 500. ◯ daily. ● 1 Jan, 25 Dec.

Caldas da Rainha ❹

Road map B4. 🚶 22,000. 🚇 🚌
ℹ Rua Engº Duarte Pacheco (262 839 700). 🛒 Mon.

The "queen's hot springs", a sprawling spa town, owes its prosperity to three different fields: thermal cures, ceramics and fruit farming. The town is named after Dona Leonor, founder of the **Misericórdia** hospital on Largo Rainha Dona Leonor. The original hospital chapel later became the impressive Manueline **Igreja do Populo**, built by Diogo Boitac *(see pp104–5)*. Inside is the 15th-century chapel of São Sebastião, faced with 18th-century *azulejos*.

The shops in Rua da Liberdade sell local ceramics, including the local green majolica ware. Examples of the work of the caricaturist and potter Rafael Bordalo Pinheiro (1846–1905) can be seen in the **Museu de Cerâmica**, in the ceramics factory. The **Centro de Artes** on Rua Ilídio Amado showcases the work of four prominent Portuguese sculptors.

🏛 Museu de Cerâmica
Rua Dr Ilídio Amado. *Tel* 262 840 280. ◯ 10am–12:30pm & 2–5pm Tue–Sun. ● public hols. 🎫 (free 10am–12:30pm Sun).

Environs
Saltwater **Lagoa de Óbidos**, 15 km (9 miles) west, is a popular lagoon for sailing and fishing.

Pillory in front of the Igreja de Santa Maria in Óbidos

The fairytale town of Óbidos encircled by medieval crenellated walls ▷

Alcobaça ❺

Portugal's largest church, the Mosteiro de Santa Maria de Alcobaça, is renowned for its simple medieval architecture. Founded in 1153, this UNESCO World Heritage site is closely linked to the arrival of the Cistercian order in Portugal in 1138 as well as the birth of the nation. In March 1147, King Afonso Henriques *(see pp42–3)* conquered the Moorish stronghold of Santarém. To commemorate the victory, he fulfilled his vow to build a church for the Cistercians, a task completed in 1223. The monastery was further endowed by other monarchs, notably King Dinis who built the main cloister. Among those buried here are the tragic lovers King Pedro and his murdered mistress Inês.

Sacristy Doorway
Exotic foliage and elaborate pinnacles adorn the Manueline doorway, attributed to João de Castilho (see p104).

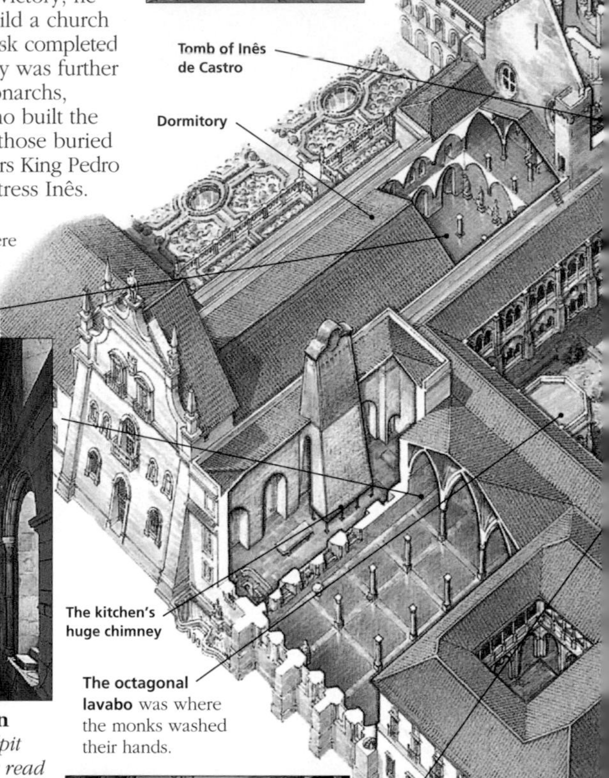

Tomb of Inês de Castro

Dormitory

The chapterhouse was where the monks met to elect the abbot and discuss issues regarding the monastery.

Refectory and Kitchen
Stairs lead up to the pulpit where one of the monks read from the Bible as the others ate in silence. In the vast kitchen next door, oxen could be roasted on the spit inside the chimney and a specially diverted stream provided a constant water supply.

The kitchen's huge chimney

The octagonal lavabo was where the monks washed their hands.

STAR FEATURES

★ Cloister of Dom Dinis

★ Tombs of Pedro I and Inês de Castro

★ **Cloister of Dom Dinis**
Also known as the Cloister of Silence, the exquisite cloister was ordered by King Dinis in 1308. The austere galleries and double arches are in keeping with the Cistercian regard for simplicity.

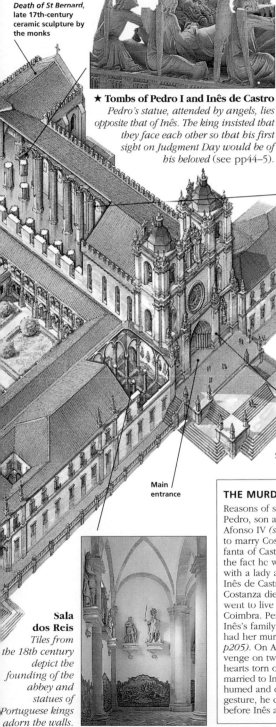

Death of St Bernard, late 17th-century ceramic sculpture by the monks

★ **Tombs of Pedro I and Inês de Castro**
Pedro's statue, attended by angels, lies opposite that of Inês. The king insisted that they face each other so that his first sight on Judgment Day would be of his beloved (see pp44–5).

Main entrance

Sala dos Reis
Tiles from the 18th century depict the founding of the abbey and statues of Portuguese kings adorn the walls.

Central Nave
The vaulted roof and soaring columns of the central nave create an impression of harmony and austere simplicity.

The façade is a richly decorated 18th-century addition. Marble statues of St Benedict and St Bernard flank the main doorway.

THE MURDER OF INÊS DE CASTRO

Reasons of state obliged Pedro, son and heir of Afonso IV *(see pp44–5)*, to marry Costanza, Infanta of Castile, despite the fact he was in love with a lady at court, Inês de Castro. When Costanza died, Pedro went to live with Inês in Coimbra. Persuaded that Inês's family was dangerous, Afonso IV had her murdered on 7 January 1355 *(see p205)*. On Afonso's death, Pedro took revenge on two of the killers by having their hearts torn out. Declaring that he had been married to Inês, Pedro had her corpse exhumed and crowned. In a final gruesome gesture, he compelled his court to kneel before Inês and kiss her decomposed hand.

The beach at Nazaré viewed from Sítio

Nazaré 6

Road map C4. 👥 *15,000.* 🚌
ℹ️ *Avenida da República 17 (262 561 194).* 🚍 *Fri.*

Beside a glorious beach in a sweeping bay backed by steep cliffs, this fishing village is a popular summer resort that has maintained some of its traditional character. Fishermen dressed in checked shirts and black stocking caps and fishwives wearing several layers of petticoats can still be seen mending nets and drying fish on wire racks on the beach. The bright boats with tall prows that once were hauled from the sea by oxen are still used, although now they have a proper anchorage south of the beach. According to legend the name Nazaré comes from

Baroque church of Nossa Senhora da Nazaré in Sítio

a statue of the Virgin Mary brought to the town by a monk from Nazareth in the 4th century.

High on the cliff above the town is **Sítio**, reached by a funicular that climbs 110 m (360 ft). At the cliff edge stands the tiny **Ermida da Memória**. According to legend, this is where the Virgin Mary saved Dom Fuas Roupinho, a local dignitary, and his horse from following a deer that leapt off the cliff in a sea mist in 1182. Across the square, the 17th-century church of **Nossa Senhora da Nazaré**, with two Baroque belfries and 18th-century tiles inside, contains an anonymous painting of the miraculous rescue. The church also contains the revered image of Our Lady of Nazaré. In September this statue is borne down to the sea in a traditional procession, a colourful reminder of the town's origins.

Environs: São Martinho do Porto, 13 km (8 miles) south of Nazaré, is a sandy beach on a curving, almost land-locked bay. The safe location makes it popular with families and children. The Visigothic church of **São Gião**, 5 km (3 miles) further south, has fine sculpting and well-proportioned arches.

Porto de Mós 7

Road map C4. 👥 *24,500.* 🚌
ℹ️ *Jardim Público (244 491 323).* 🚍 *Fri.*

Originally a Moorish fort, and rebuilt over the centuries by successive Christian kings, the rather fanciful **castle** perches on a hill above the small town of Porto de Mós. Its present appearance, with green cone-shaped turrets and an exquisite loggia, was the inspired work of King Afonso IV's master builders in 1420.

In the town below, the 13th-century church of **São João Baptista** retains its original

Romanesque portal. In the public gardens is the richly decorated Baroque church of **São Pedro**. Just off the Praça da República, the **Museu Municipal** displays a varied collection of local finds dating back to Roman remains and dinosaur bones. More modern exhibits include the local *mós* (millstones), as well as present-day ceramics and woven rugs.

🏛 **Museu Municipal**
Travessa de São Pedro. *Tel 244 499 615.* ⬤ *Tue–Sat.* ⬤ *public hols.*

Donkey in the Serra de Aire nature reserve, south of Porto de Mós

Environs: South of the town, the 38,900-ha (96,000-acre) **Parque Natural das Serras de Aire e Candeeiros** covers a limestone landscape of pastures, olive groves and stone walls and is a nesting place for the red-beaked chough.

The area is also dotted with vast and spectacular underground caverns with odd rock formations and festoons of stalactites and stalagmites. The **Grutas de Mira de Aire**, 17 km (10 miles) southeast of Porto de Mós, are the biggest, descending 110 m (360 ft) into tunnels and walkways around subterranean lakes. A tour through caverns with names such as the "Jewel Room", past bizarre rocks dubbed "Chinese Hat" or "Jellyfish", ends in a theatrical light and water show.

📷 **Grutas de Mira de Aire**
Av. Dr Luciano Justo Ramos. *Tel 244 440 322.* ⬤ *daily.* 📷

Batalha 8

See pp184–5.

Leiria ❾

Road map C4. 👥 123,000. 🚗 🚆
ℹ️ *Jardim Luís de Camões (244 848 770).* 🏪 *every second Tue & Sat.*
www.rt-leiriafatima.pt

Episcopal city since 1545, Leiria is set in attractive countryside on the banks of the River Lis. Originally the Roman town of Collipo, it was recaptured from the Moors by Afonso Henriques *(see pp42–3)* in the 12th century. In 1254 Afonso III held a *cortes* here, the first parliament attended by common laymen.

The resplendent hilltop **castle** houses a library and meeting rooms. Along with Pombal, Ourém and Tomar, the Leiria castle was part of the defence system of central Portugal. In the early 1300s, King Dinis turned it into a royal residence for himself and his queen, Isabel of Aragon. Within the castle battlements is the Gothic church of **Nossa Senhora da Pena**, today little more than a roofless shell of dark granite walls. The view from the castle loggia overlooks the wide expanse of pine forest, the Pinhal de Leiria, and the rooftops of the town below.

The old town below the castle is full of charm, with tiny dwellings over archways, graceful arcades and the small 12th-century church of **São Pedro** on Largo de São Pedro.

The Romanesque portal is all that remains of the original church. The muted 16th-century **Sé** above Praça Rodrigues Lobo has an elegant vaulted nave and an altarpiece in the chancel painted in 1605 by Simão Rodrigues. From Avenida Marquês de Pombal, climbing the hill opposite the castle, an 18th-century stairway takes you up to the elaborate 16th-century **Santuário de Nossa Senhora da Encarnação**. The small Baroque interior is tightly packed with colourful geometric *azulejo* panels and 17th-century paintings of the *Life of the Virgin*.

♜ Castle
Largo de São Pedro. **Tel** 244 813 982.
🕐 *Tue–Sun.* 🔴 *1 Jan, 25 Dec.* 🏷️

Environs: West of Leiria is the long coastal pine forest, the **Pinhal de Leiria**, planted by King Dinis to supply wood for ship building. The Estádio Dr Magalhães Pessoa, built for the Euro 2004 championship, stands in the middle of this pine forest, which extends northwards to the beach of Pedrogão. **São Pedro de Muel**, 22 km (13 miles) to the west of Leiria, is a small resort on a marvellous beach.

Exposed and rugged coastline west of Leiria

Pombal ❿

Road map C4. 👥 58,000. 🚗 🚆
ℹ️ *Viaduto Guilherme Santos (236 213 230).* 🏪 *Mon & Thu.*

Closely associated with the Marquês de Pombal *(see pp52–3)* who retired here in disgrace in 1777, this small town of whitewashed houses is overlooked by the stately and well-preserved **castle**, founded in 1161 by the Knights Templar *(see p187)*.

In the Praça Marquês de Pombal the old prison and the *celeiro* (granary) are adorned with the Pombal family crest. The **Museu Marquês de Pombal** features a collection of documents and artworks focusing on the Marquis.

🏛️ Museu Marquês de Pombal
Praça Marquês de Pombal. **Tel** 236 210 564. 🕐 *daily (weekends by appt only).* 🔴 *public hols.* 🏷️

Arcaded loggia and castle towers guarding the town of Leiria

Batalha 🔞

João I's coat of arms on portal

The Dominican abbey of Santa Maria da Vitória at Batalha, a UNESCO World Heritage site, is a masterpiece of Portuguese Gothic architecture famous for its Manueline elements. The pale limestone monastery celebrates João I's 1385 victory over Castile at Aljubarrota. Today, two unknown soldiers from World War I lie in the chapterhouse. The abbey was begun in 1388 under master builder Afonso Domingues, succeeded in 1402 by David Huguet. Over the next two centuries successive kings left their mark on the monastery: João's son, King Duarte, ordered a royal pantheon behind the apse, and Manueline additions include the Unfinished Chapels and much of the decoration of the abbey buildings.

Chapterhouse
Guards keep watch by the Tomb of the Unknown Soldiers beneath David Huguet's striking star-vaulted ceiling.

★ Royal Cloister
Gothic arches by Afonso Domingues and David Huguet around the cloister are embellished by Manueline tracery (see pp24–5) to achieve a harmony of form and decoration.

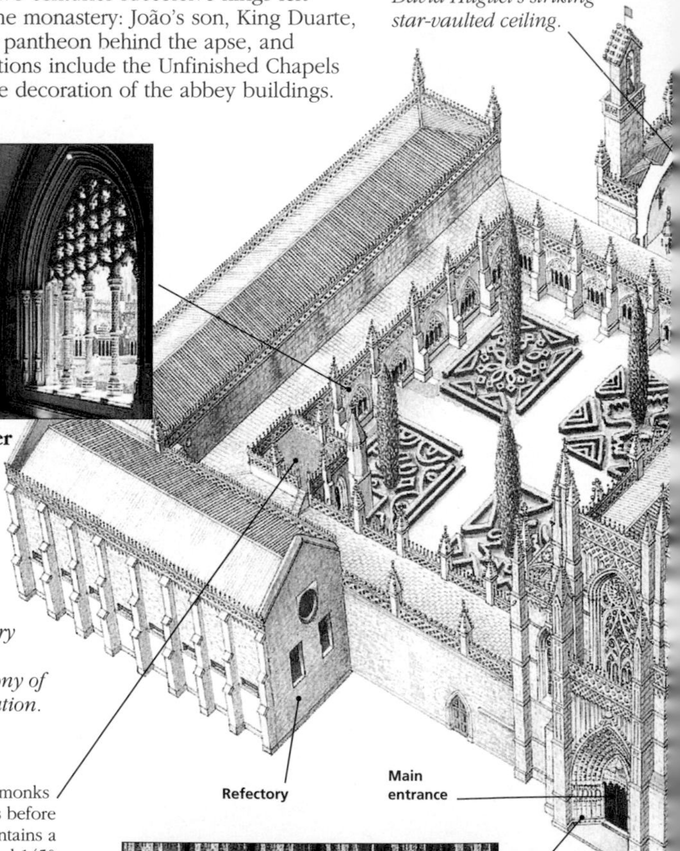

The lavabo, where monks washed their hands before and after meals, contains a fountain built around 1450.

Refectory

Main entrance

Portal
The portal was decorated by Huguet with religious motifs and statues of the apostles in intricate late Gothic style.

STAR FEATURES

- ★ Founder's Chapel
- ★ Royal Cloister
- ★ Unfinished Chapels

★ **Unfinished Chapels**

Begun under King Duarte, the octagonal mausoleum was abandoned by Manuel I in favour of the Jerónimos monastery in Belém (see pp104–5).

VISITORS' CHECKLIST

Road map C4. Mosteiro de Santa Maria da Vitória, Batalha. **Tel** *244 765 497.* 🚌 *from Lisbon, Leiria, Porto de Mós & Fátima.* ⬤ *9am–6pm (Oct–Mar: to 5pm) daily.* ⬤ *1 Jan, Easter, 1 May, 25 Dec.* ⬤ *(free 9am–2pm Sun).* 📷

The stained-glass window behind the choir dates from 1514.

Manueline Portal

Most of the decoration of the Unfinished Chapels dates from the reign of Manuel I. This delicate portal was carved in 1509 by Mateus Fernandes.

Lofty nave by Afonso Domingues

The chapel is topped by an octagonal lantern.

★ **Founder's Chapel**

The tomb of João I and his English wife Philippa of Lancaster, lying hand in hand, was begun in 1426 by Huguet. Their son, Henry the Navigator, is also buried here.

João I's motto, *Por bem* (for good), is inscribed on his tomb.

THE BATTLE OF ALJUBARROTA

In 1383 Portugal's direct male line of descent ended with the death of Fernando I *(see pp44–5)*. Dom João, the illegitimate son of Fernando's father, was proclaimed king, but his claim was opposed by Juan of Castile. On 14 August 1385 João I's greatly outnumbered forces, commanded by Nuno Álvares Pereira, faced the Castilians on a small plateau near Aljubarrota, 15 km (9 miles) south of Batalha. João's spectacular victory ensured 200 years of independence from Spain. The monastery now stands as a symbol of Portuguese sovereignty and the power of the house of Avis.

Commander Nuno Álvares Pereira

Curved limestone gallery around the vast esplanade in front of the basilica at Fátima

Fátima ⓫

Road map C4. 🏛 9,000. 🚌
🛈 Avenida Dom José Alves Correia da Silva (249 531 139). 🚏 Sat.
www.santuario-fatima.pt/portal

The sanctuary of Fátima is a devotional shrine on a prodigious scale, a pilgrim destination on a par with Lourdes in France. The Neo-Baroque limestone **basilica**, flanked by statues of saints, has a 65-m (213-ft) tower and an esplanade twice the size of St Peter's Square in Rome.

On 12 and 13 of May and October vast crowds of pilgrims arrive to commemorate appearances of the Virgin to three shepherd children (the three *pastorinhos*). On 13 May 1917, 10-year-old Lucia Santos and her young cousins, Jacinta Marta and Francisco, saw a shining figure in a holm oak tree. She ordered them to return to the tree on the same day for six months and by 13 October 70,000 pilgrims were with the children by the tree.

Only Lucia heard the "Secret of Fátima", spoken on her last appearance. The first part of the secret was a vision of hell; the second was of a war worse than World War I. The third part, a vision of papal assassination, was finally revealed by Pope John Paul II on the occasion of the Millennium. The Pope beatified Jacinta and Francisco in 2000. Their tombs are inside the basilica. Lucia, who became a nun, died in 2005. The stained-glass windows show scenes of the sightings. In the esplanade, the **Capela das Aparições** marks the site of the apparition. Inside, the crown of the Virgin holds the bullet used in the 1981 assassination attempt on Pope John Paul II. East of the sanctuary, the childrens' homes have been preserved in the **Casa dos Pastorinhos**. Waxworks and a multimedia show complete the experience.

For most people, however, the most impressive sight is the intense emotion and faith of the penitents who approach the shrine on their knees. Wax limbs are burned as offerings for miracles performed by the Virgin and thousands of candles light the esplanade in the night-time masses.

🏛 **Casa dos Pastorinhos**
Rua dos Pastorinhos de Aljustrel.
Tel 249 532 828. 🔲 daily. 🚻

Environs: The medieval town of **Ourém**, 10 km (6 miles) northeast of Fátima, is a walled citadel, dominated by the 15th-century castle of Ourém built by Afonso, grandson of Nuno Álvares Pereira *(see p185)*. His magnificent tomb is in the 15th-century Igreja Matriz. The town's name is said to derive from Oureana, a Moorish girl who, before she fell in love with a Christian knight and converted, was called Fátima.

Ruined secret passage connecting the towers of the castle in Ourém

Tomar ⓬

Road map C4. 🏛 43,000. 🚉 🚌
🛈 Avenida Dr Cândido Madureira (249 322 427). 🚏 Fri.

Founded in 1157 by Gualdim Pais, the first grand master of the Order of the Templars in Portugal, the town is dominated by the 12th-century castle containing the Convento de Cristo *(see pp188–9)*. The heart of this charming town is a neat grid of narrow streets. The lively shopping street, Rua Serpa Pinto, leads to the Gothic church of **São João Baptista** on Praça da República, the town's main square. The late 15th-century church has an elegant Manueline portal and is capped by an octagonal spire. Inside, there is a carved stone pulpit and 16th-century paintings including a *Last Supper* by Gregório Lopes (1490–1550). A particularly gory beheading of John the Baptist is also attributed to Lopes.

The area outside the church is the focus of the spectacular Festa dos Tabuleiros, a festival with pagan origins held

Church and clocktower of São João Baptista in Tomar's main square

in July, every two or three years, in which girls in white carry towering platters of bread and flowers on their heads. The festival has similar roots to the Festa do Espírito Santo (see p368), popular in the Azores.

Nearby, in Rua Dr Joaquim Jacinto, stands one of the oldest **synagogues** in Portugal, built in 1430–60 with four tall columns and a vaulted ceiling. The building was last used as a place of worship in 1497 after which Manuel I (see pp46–7) banished all Jews who refused to convert to Christianity. It has since been a prison, a hay loft and a warehouse. Today, it holds a small Jewish museum, the **Museu Luso-Hebraico de Abraham Zacuto**, named after a renowned 15th-century astronomer and mathematician.

Further south stands the 17th-century church of São Francisco. Its former cloisters now house the **Museu dos Fósforos**, a match museum proudly boasting the largest collection in Europe – over 43,000 matchboxes from 104 countries of the world.

On the east side of the River Nabão, just off Rua Aquiles da Mota Lima, is the 13th-century church of **Santa Maria do Olival**, with a distinctive three-storey belltower.

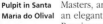

Restored various times over the centuries, the church preserves its Gothic façade and rose window. Inside are the graves of Gualdim Pais (died 1195) and other Templar Masters, and an elegant Renaissance

Pulpit in Santa Maria do Olival

pulpit. The church once had significance far beyond Tomar as the mother church for mariners in the Age of Discovery.

Heading north, Rua Santa Iria takes you to the **Capela de Santa Iria**, beside the 15th-century bridge, **Ponte Velha**. This Renaissance chapel is said to have been built where the saint was martyred in the 7th century (see p193). A powerful stone retable depicting Christ on the Cross (1536) stands

Tomar's main shopping street, Rua Serpa Pinto, overlooked by the castle

above the altar in the Capela dos Vales. On an island in the river the shaded **Parque do Mouchão** is a pleasant walk; an allegedly Roman water wheel turns with the passing water. Continuing northwards, past the octagonal 16th-century **Ermida de São Gregório** with its wild Manueline doorway, a huge flight of steps leads to a 17th-century chapel, **Nossa Senhora da Piedade**.

On the slopes of the hill leading up to the Convento do Cristo is the Renaissance basilica, **Nossa Senhora da Conceição**, built between 1530 and 1550. Its exterior simplicity contrasts with the elegantly proportioned and delicately carved Corinthian columns of the interior. The architect is believed to be Francisco de Holanda (1517–84), who worked for King João III.

🏛 **Museu Hebraico (Synagogue)**
📍 Rua Joaquim Jacinto. **Tel** 249 322 427. ☐ daily. ● public hols.

🏛 **Museu dos Fósforos**
Av. General Bernardo Faria. **Tel** 249 329 814. ☐ daily. ● pub hols. ♿

THE ORDER OF CHRIST

During the 12th and 13th centuries, the crusading Order of the Knights Templar helped the Portuguese in their battle against the Moorish "infidels". In return they were rewarded with extensive lands and political power. Castles, churches and towns sprang up under their protective mantle. In 1314, Pope Clement V was forced to suppress this rich and powerful Order, but in Portugal King Dinis turned it into the Order of Christ, which inherited the property and privileges of the Templars. Ideals of Christian expansion were revived in the 15th century when their Grand Master, Prince Henry the Navigator, invested the order's revenue in exploration. The emblem of the order, the squared cross, adorned the sails of the caravels that crossed the uncharted waters (see pp46–7).

Cross of the Order of Christ

Tomar: Convento de Cristo

Founded in 1160 by the Grand Master of the Templars, the Convent of Christ still retains some reminders of these monk-knights and the inheritors of their mantle, the Order of Christ (see p187). Under Henry the Navigator, the Governor of the Order from 1418, cloisters were built between the Charola and the Templars' fortress, but it was the reign of João III (1521–57) that saw the

St Jerome, south portal

greatest changes. Architects such as João de Castilho and Diogo de Arruda, engaged to express the Order's power and royal patronage in stone, built the church and cloisters with dazzling Manueline flourishes, which reached a crescendo with the window in the west front of the church.

★ **Manueline Window**
Marine motifs entwine round this elaborate window. The carving at base is thought to be either the architect (see p24) or the Old Man of the Sea.

Cloister of the Crows, flanked by an aqueduct

★ **Great Cloister**
Begun in the 1550s, probably by Diogo de Torralva, this cloister reflects João III's passion for Italian art. Concealed spiral stairways in the corners lead to the Terrace of Wax.

The **"Bread" Cloister** was where loaves were handed out to the poor who came to beg at the monastery.

The **Terrace of Wax**, where honeycombs were left to dry

THE CHAROLA

The nucleus of the monastery is the 12th-century Charola, the Templars' oratory. Like many of their temples, its layout is based on the Rotunda of Jerusalem's Holy Sepulchre, with a central octagon of altars. In 1356, Tomar became the headquarters of the Order of Christ in Portugal, and the Charola's decoration reflects the Order's wealth. The paintings and frescoes (mostly 16th-century biblical scenes) and the gilded statuary below the Byzantine cupola have undergone much careful restoration.

The gilded octagon

When the Manueline church was built, an archway was created in the side of the Charola to link the two, making the Charola the church's main chapel.

STAR FEATURES

★ Charola

★ Manueline Window

★ Great Cloister

Manueline Church
Diogo de Arruda's church, begun in the early 16th century, is on two levels: this is the upper choir. The ornate ribbed vaulting incorporates the insignia and initials of Manuel I.

★ **Charola**
The original Templar church, sometimes called the Rotunda, was built in the shape of a 16-sided drum.

Internal octagon of the Charola

Cemetery Cloister
Monks' tombstones pave the perimeter of this early 15th-century cloister, the first to be built here. In one corner stands a well.

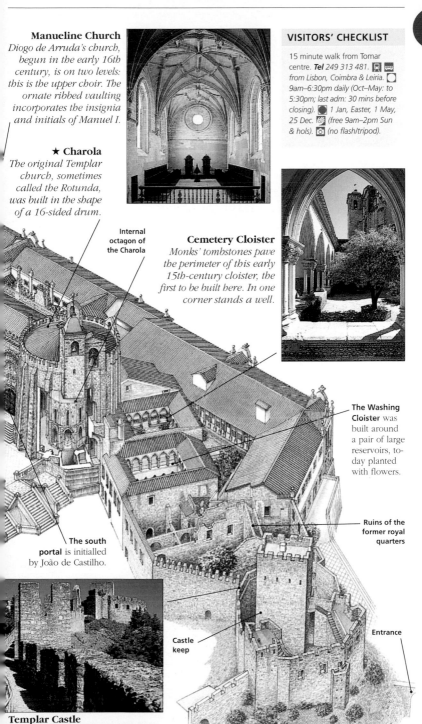

The Washing Cloister was built around a pair of large reservoirs, to-day planted with flowers.

Ruins of the former royal quarters

The south portal is initialled by João de Castilho.

Entrance

Castle keep

Templar Castle
In 1160 the Templars' Grand Master built this castle on land given to the Order for services in battle.

The defensive walls of the early 13th-century fortress at Abrantes

Barragem do Castelo de Bode **⑬**

Road map C4. 🚌 to dam. 🚌 from Castanheira. ⬜ by appt (249 380 200). ℹ️ Tomar (249 322 427).

Perhaps there once was a "Castle of the Billygoat", but today the name refers to a large dam *(barragem)* that blocks the flow of the River Zêzere 10 km (6 miles) up-stream from its confluence with the Tagus. Construction of the dam began in 1946 to serve the first of Portugal's hydroelectric power stations. Above it, a long, sprawling lake nestles between hills covered in pine and eucalyptus forests in which lie small, isolated villages. The valley is a secluded area popular for boating, fishing and water sports and it is possible to hire equipment from centres along the lake shore. Canoes, windsurf boards and water skis can be found at

the Centro Naútico do Zêzere, in Castanheira on the western side of the lake, and yachting facilities are usually available from the lakeside hotels such as the peaceful Estalagem Lago Azul *(see p388)*. A cruise can also be taken from the hotel, stopping at the sandy beaches and the small islands.

Abrantes **⑭**

Road map C4. 🏔️ 41,500. 🚉 🚌 ℹ️ Esplanada 1º de Maio (241 362 555). 🛒 Mon.

Grandly situated above the Tagus, the town was once of strategic importance. It had a vital role in the Reconquest *(see pp42–3)*, and during the Peninsular War *(see p54)* both the French General Junot and the Duke of Wellington made it a base. The ruined **fortress** that overlooks the town and the surrounding flatlands is a reminder of its status.

The 15th-century church of Santa Maria do Castelo, within the castle walls, is now the small **Museu Dom Lopo de Almeida**. Besides local archaeological finds, it houses the tombs of the Almeida family, counts of Abrantes. On Rua da República, the **Misericórdia** church, constructed in 1584, has six magnificent religious panels attributed to Gregório Lopes (1490–1550).

🏛️ **Museu Dom Lopo de Almeida**
Rua Capitão Correia de Lacerda. *Tel 241 371 724.* ⬜ Tue–Sun.

Whitewashed houses in Constância above the banks of the Tagus

Environs: The 16th-century church of São Tiago e São Mateus, in the unspoiled town of **Sardoal**, 8 km (5 miles) north of Abrantes, holds a compelling thorn-crowned Christ by the 16th-century painter, the Master of Sardoal. An 18th-century tile panel on the façade of the Capela do Espírito Santo, in Praça da República, honours Gil Vicente, the 16th-century playwright born here.

The pretty whitewashed town of **Constância**, 12 km (7 miles) west of Sardoal, nurtures the memory of the poet Luís Vaz de Camões. Sent away from court for misbehaving with a court lady, he lived here briefly after 1546. The **Casa Memória de Camões**, the poet's home on the river bank, can be visited.

🏚️ **Casa Memória de Camões**
Rua do Tejo. *Tel 249 739 066.* ⬜ call for opening times.

LUÍS VAZ DE CAMÕES (1524–80)

The author of Portugal's celebrated epic poem, *Os Lusíadas*, had a passionate nature and was often in trouble. Banished from court, he enlisted in 1547 and set sail for North Africa, where he lost an eye. Imprisoned after another brawl, he agreed to serve his country in India, but his was the only ship from the fleet to survive the stormy seas. This experience gave his subsequent poem its vibrant power. A unique record of the Discoveries, this Classical-style epic charts the voyage of Vasco da Gama to India and recounts events and legends from Portuguese history. There was to be no success for Camões, however, and he passed bleak years in India yearning for **Statue of Camões on the** Lisbon. His poem was published in **river bank at Constância** 1572 but he died almost unnoticed.

Castelo de Almourol

Road map C4. 🚌 *to Barquinha then taxi then ferry.* ⬜ *daily during daylight hours.* ℹ️ *Largo 1 Dezembro, Barquinha (249 720 358).*

Dramatically set on a tiny island in the Tagus, this enchanting castle was built over a Roman fortress in 1171 by Gualdim Pais *(see p187)*. Legends of this magical place abound. A 16th-century verse romance called *Palmeirim de Inglaterra* weaves a tale of giants and knights and the fight of the crusader Palmeirim for the lovely Polinarda. Some say the castle is haunted by the ghost of a princess sighing for the love of her Moorish slave.

Over the centuries, the castle, surrounded by ramparts and nine towers, has never been taken by invading forces.

The evocative ruins of the island fortress of Almourol

Torres Novas ⑯

Road map C4. 🏛 *16,000.* 🚌 ℹ️ *Largo dos Combatentes 4–5 (249 813 019).* 🛒 *Tue.*

Animated streets and many fine churches cluster beneath the castle walls of this handsome town. The ruins of the 12th-century **fortress**, scene of bitter fighting between Moors and Christians during the Reconquest, now enclose a garden. Just below the castle is the 16th-century **Misericórdia** church with a Renaissance portal and an interior lined with colourful "carpet" *azulejos* from 1674. The **Igreja de Santiago**, on Largo do Paço, was probably built in 1203, although tiles and a gilded retable with a wood carving of the young Jesus assisting Joseph in his carpentry are 17th-century additions.

In the centre of town is the **Museu Municipal de Carlos Reis**, named after the painter Carlos Reis (1863–1940) who was born here. The museum contains paintings by 19th- and early 20th-century artists, a 15th-century Gothic figure of Nossa Senhora do Ó, as well as coins and bronze and ceramic artefacts from the Roman ruins at Vila Cardílio.

🏛 **Museu Municipal de Carlos Reis**
Rua do Salvador. **Tel** 249 812 535. ⬜ *Tue–Sun.* ⬛ *public holidays.*

Environs: Roman ruins dating from the 4th century AD at **Vila Cardílio**, 3 km (2 miles) southwest of Torres Novas, retain some superb mosaics and baths. On the northeast outskirts of town the **Grutas das Lapas**, large Neolithic caves, can be seen carved out of the rock. The small wetland **Reserva Natural do Paúl de Boquilobo**, 8 km (5 miles) south, between the Tagus and Almondo rivers, was declared a nature reserve in 1981. The willow trees and aquatic plants along the river shelter wildfowl in winter, and nesting egrets and herons in spring.

🏛 **Vila Cardílio**
Estrada Municipal de St António da Caveira. **Tel** 249 813 019. ⬜ *daily.* ♿

🏛 **Grutas das Lapas**
Largo das Catacumbas. **Tel** 249 813 060. ⬜ *daily (ask for key at No.16).*

Remains of the hypocaust, the Roman underfloor heating system, at Vila Cardílio outside Torres Novas

Portal of the Igreja Matriz in Golegã

Golegã ⑰

Road map C4. 🏠 *9,000.* 🚌
ℹ *Rua de D. Afonso Henriques,
Largo da Imaculada Conceição
(249 977 361).* 🛒 *Wed.*

Usually a quiet town, Golegã
is overrun during the first
two weeks of November by
thousands of horse enthusiasts
who throng to the annual Feira
Nacional do Cavalo. This horse
fair, which attracts Portugal's
finest horses, breeders and
equestrians, coincides with
the tasting of the year's new
wine on St Martin's day (11
November). The atmosphere is
enlivened by the consumption
of the young wine known as
agua-pé (literally, foot water).

In the centre of town, the
16th-century **Igreja Matriz**,
attributed to Diogo Boitac *(see
pp104–5)*, has an exquisite
Manueline portal and a calm
interior. The small **Museu de
Fotografia Carlos Relvas**
is housed in the elegant Art
Nouveau house and studio of
the photographer (1838–94).
A vivid modern art collection
can be seen in the **Museu de
Pintura e Escultura Martins
Correia** in the old post office.

🏛 **Museu de Fotografia
Carlos Relvas**
Largo Dom Manuel I. **Tel** 249 979
000. 🕐 *10am–12:30pm & 2–6pm
Tue–Sun.* ⬤ *public hols.* 📷

🏛 **Museu de Pintura e
Escultura Martins Correia**
Rua D João IV. **Tel** *as above.* 🕐 *as
above.* ⬤ *as above.* ♿ *limited.* 📷

Alpiarça ⑱

Road map C4. 🏠 *8,000.* 🚌
ℹ *Praça José Rodrigues Faustino
Pinho (243 556 000).* 🛒 *Wed.*

Set in the vast, fertile plain
known as the Lezìria, which
stretches east of the Tagus and
is famous for horse breeding,
Alpiarça is a small, neat town.
The fine twin-towered parish
church, on Rua José Relvas, is
dedicated to **Santo Eustáquio**,
patron saint of the town. Built
in the late 19th century, it
houses paintings from the 17th
century, including a charming *Divine Shepherdess* in
the sacristy in which the
young Jesus is shown
conversing with a sheep.
The stone cross in the
courtyard is dated 1515.

On the southern outskirts
of town is the striking **Casa
Museu dos Patudos** sur-
rounded by vineyards. This
was the residence of the
wealthy and cultivated José
Relvas (1858–1929), an art
collector and diplomat as well
as a politician and – briefly –
premier of the Republic. The
exterior of this eye-catching
country house, built for him
by Raúl Lino in 1905–9, has
simple whitewashed walls
and a green and white striped
spire. The colonnaded loggia,
reached via an outside staircase, is lined with *azulejo*
panels. The museum contains
Relvas's personal collection of
fine and decorative art. Renaissance paintings include
Virgin with Child and St John
by the school of Leonardo da

Vinci and *Christ in the Tomb*
by the German school. There
are also paintings by Delacroix
and Zurbarán as well as many
works by 19th-century Portuguese artists, including 30 by
Relvas's friend, José Malhôa
(see p55). Relvas also collected
exquisite porcelain, bronzes,
furniture and Oriental rugs, as
well as early Portuguese
Arraiolos carpets, including a
particularly fine one in silk.

🏛 **Casa Museu dos Patudos**
2 km (1 mile) S, N.118. **Tel** 243 558
321. 🕐 *Tue–Sun.* ⬤ *public hols.* 📷

**Elegant façade of the country manor,
Quinta da Alorna, outside Almeirim**

Environs: Almeirim, 7 km
(4 miles) to the south, was a
favourite abode of the House
of Avis *(see pp46–7)*. Today
little of its royal past remains
and most visitors come here
to sample the famous *sopa
de pedra* (stone soup).

Many large estates and fine
stables extend across the vast
flat plains of this fertile horse
and cattle breeding area. The
Quinta da Alorna, a handsome 19th-century manor
house within walled gardens
and well known for its wines,
lies just outside Almeirim.

Tiled loggia of the Casa Museu dos Patudos, Alpiarça

The Tagus seen from the Jardim das Portas do Sol in Santarém

Santarém ⑲

Road map C4. 🏛 *30,000.* 🚉 🚌
🛈 *Rua Capelo Ivens 63 (243 304
437).* 🏪 *2nd & 4th Sun of month.*

The lively district capital of
the Ribatejo, overlooking
the Tagus, has an illustrious
past. To Julius Caesar it was an
important bureaucratic centre,
Praesidium Julium. To the
Moors it was the stronghold
of Xantarim – from Santa Iria,
the 7th-century martyred nun
from Tomar *(see pp186–7)*
whose body was thrown into
the River Nabão and allegedly
reappeared here on the Tagus
shore. To the Portuguese kings,
who ousted the Moors in 1147,
Santarém was a pleasing abode
and the site of many gatherings
of the *cortes* (parliaments).

At the centre of the old town,
in Praça Sá da Bandeira, is the
vast **Igreja do Seminário**, a
multi-windowed Baroque
edifice built by João IV for the
Jesuits in 1640 on the site of a
royal palace. The huge interior
has a painted wooden ceiling
and marble and gilt ornamentation. From here, Rua Serpa
Pinto runs southeast past a
cluster of older buildings. The
lofty **Igreja de Marvila**, built
in the 12th century and later
altered, has a Manueline portal
and is lined with dazzling
early 17th-century diamond-
patterned *azulejo* panels. The
medieval, although much restored 22-m (72-ft) high **Torre
das Cabaças**, was once a
clock tower and now houses
a small museum of time,
**Núcleo Museológico do
Tempo**. Opposite the tower,
the **Museu Arqueológico**
was formerly the Romanesque

church of São João de Alporão.
Unfortunately, the museum
has been closed because of
unstable foundations, and has
no reopening date as yet.

Rua Serpa Pinto leads into
Rua 5 de Outubro and up to
the **Jardim das Portas do
Sol**, built on the site of a
Moorish castle. The gardens
are enclosed by the city's
medieval walls, and a
terrace affords a panorama
of the river and its vast
meadowlands. Returning
into town, on Largo Pedro
Álvares Cabral, the 14th-
century **Igreja da Graça**
has a spectacular rose
window carved from

a single stone. The church
contains the tombstone of
Pedro Álvares Cabral, who
discovered Brazil *(see p48)*.
Further south, the 14th-
century **Igreja do Santíssimo
Milagre**, on Rua Braamcamp
Freire, has a Renaissance
interior and 16th-century
azulejos. A small crystal flask
in the sacristy is said to
contain the blood of Christ.
The belief stems from a 13th-
century legend in which a
holy wafer intended to help
persuade a husband to stop
beating his wife was miraculously transformed into blood.

Santarém is an important
bullfighting centre with a
modern bullring at the southwest corner of town. During
the first ten days of June, the
town hosts the Ribatejo Fair,
Portugal's largest agricultural
fair, in which there are bullfights and contests between the
colourfully dressed herdsmen,
campinos. In the autumn
(Oct/Nov) Portugal's
biggest gastronomy
festival is held here,
with lots of informal
eating at stands
representing the
country's regions
and types of food.

Tomb of Duarte de Meneses in the Museu Arqueológico, Santarém

Fields and vineyards in the low-lying Lezíria extending beyond Coruche

Coruche ❷⓪

Road map C5. 🚶 3,500. 🚌 🚆
🏢 Rua Júlio Maria de Sousa (243
610 820). 🛒 last Sat of month.

Coruche is an attractive little
town in the heart of the
bullfighting country with a
riverside location overlooking
the Lezíria, the wide open
plain that stretches east of the
Tagus. The town, inhabited
since Palaeolithic times, was
razed to the ground in 1180 by
the Moors as reprisal against
the reconquering Christians.

In the central pedestrian
street, Rua de Santarém, the
O Coruja café is lined with
vivid modern *azulejo* panels
showing bulls in the Lezíria,
the town's bullring and scenes
of local life. A short walk up
the street stands the tiny
church of **São Pedro**. Its interior is completely covered with
17th-century blue and yellow
carpet tiles. An *azulejo* panel
on the altar front shows St
Peter surrounded by birds
and animals. Above the town

Chancel in the church of São Pedro
covered in *azulejos*, Coruche

stands the simple 12th-century
blue and white church of
Nossa Senhora do Castelo.
From here there are excellent
views over the fertile agricultural land and cork oaks of the
Sorraia valley and the Lezíria.

Bull-running *(largada)* in Vila Franca de Xira

Vila Franca de Xira ❷①

Road map C5. 🚶 130,600. 🚌 🚆
🏢 Praça Afonso de Albuquerque 12
(263 285 605). 🛒 Tue & Fri.

Sitting beside the Tagus,
surrounded by the riverside
industries that dominate this
area, the town has a reputation
larger than its modest appearance suggests. Traditionally
the area has been the centre
for bull and horse rearing communities. Twice a year crowds
flock here to participate in the
bull-running through the
streets and watch the *tourada*
and traditional horsemanship.
The animated and gaudy Festa
do Colete Encarnado (named
after the red waistcoat worn
by *campinos*, the Ribatejo

herdsmen) takes place over
several days in early July. The
festival is a lively occasion with
folk dancing, boat races on the
Tagus and sardines grilled in
the street. A similar festival,
the Feira de Outubro, takes
place in October.
The brightly col-
oured traditional
costumes of the
campinos and other
exhibits related to
bullfighting in Por-
tugal are on display
in the small **Museu
Etnográfico**.
The town centre
retains an exuber-
antly tiled covered
market dating from
the 1920s. Further
east, on Largo da Misericórdia,
striking 18th-century *azulejos*
adorn the chancel of the
Misericórdia church. South
of town, the **Ponte Marechal
Carmona**, built in 1951, is the
only bridge across the River
Tagus between Santarém to the
north and Lisbon to the south.

🏛 **Museu Etnográfico**
Praça de Touros. *Tel* 263 273 057.
⬜ Tue–Sun. ⬤ public hols.

Environs
At the **Centro Equestre da
Lezíria Grande** in Povos, 3 km
(2 miles) south, you can watch
stylish dressage displays on
Lusitanian horses *(see p298)*.

⬤ **Centro Equestre da
Lezíria Grande**
N.1. *Tel* 263 285 160. ⬜ Tue–Sun.
⬤ 1 Jan, Easter, Aug, 25 Dec.

Alenquer ❷

Road map C5. 👥 *42,000.* 🚉
ℹ *Parque Vaz Monteiro (263 733 663).* 🗓 *2nd Mon of month.*

Vila Alta, the old part of town, climbs steeply up the slopes of the hillside, high above the newer town by the river. In the central Praça Luìs de Camões, the 15th-century church of **São Pedro** contains the tomb of the humanist chronicler and native son, Damião de Góis (1501–74). Pêro de Alenquer, a navigator for the explorers Bartolomeu Dias in 1488 and Vasco da Gama in 1497 *(see pp48–9)*, was also born here. Uphill, near the ruins of a 13th-century castle, the monastery church of **São Francisco** retains a Manueline cloister and a 13th-century portal. Founded in 1222, this was Portugal's first Franciscan monastery.

Environs

At **Meca**, 5 km (3 miles) northwest, is the huge pilgrimage church of Santa Quitéria, where a blessing of animals takes place each May.

Defensive walls and the castle overlooking Torres Vedras

Torres Vedras ❷

Road map B5. 👥 *74,800.* 🚉 🚌
ℹ *Rua 9 de Abril (261 314 094).* 🗓 *3rd Mon of month.*

The town is closely linked with the Lines of Torres Vedras, fortified defenses built by the Duke of Wellington to repel Napoleon's troops during the Peninsular War *(see p54)*. North of the town, near the restored fort of **São Vicente**, traces of trenches and bastions are still visible, but along most of the lines the forts and earthworks have gone, buried by time and rapid change.

Above the town, the restored walls of the 13th-century **castle** embrace a shady garden and the church of Santa Maria do Castelo. Down in the town, on Praça 25 de Abril, a memorial to those who died in the Peninsular War stands in front of the 16th-century Convento da Graça. Today the monastery houses the well-lit **Museu Municipal**. A room devoted to the Peninsular War displays a model of the lines; other interesting exhibits include a 15th-century Flemish School *Retábulo da Vida da Virgem*. Open for mass at weekends, the monastery church, **Igreja da Graça**, has a 17th-century gilded altarpiece. In a niche in the chancel is the tomb of São Gonçalo de Lagos *(see p322)*.

Beyond the pedestrian Rua 9 de Abril, the Manueline church of **São Pedro** greets the visitor with an exotic winged dragon on the portal. The interior has a painted wooden ceiling, and colourful 18th-century *azulejo* panels depicting scenes of daily life adorn the walls. Behind the church, on Rua Cândido dos Reis, is a 16th-century water fountain, the **Chafariz dos Canos**.

THE LINES OF TORRES VEDRAS

In October 1809, to save Lisbon from Napoleonic invasion, Arthur Wellesley (later the Duke of Wellington) ordered an arc of defensive lines *(Linhas de Torres)* to be built. When complete, over 600 guns and 152 redoubts (masonry forts) lay along two lines stretching from the sea to the River Tagus. One was 46 km (29 miles) long, from the Sizandra river mouth, west of Torres Vedras, to Alhandra, south of Vila Franca de Xira. The second line, running behind the first as far as the sea, was 39 km (24 miles) long. A short third line covered the possibility of retreat and embarkation. Construction of the lines took place in extraordinary secrecy: rivers had to be dammed, earthworks raised, hills shifted and homes and farms demolished, but within a year the chain of hilltop fortresses was complete. On 14 October 1810, General Masséna, at the head of 65,000 French troops, saw with astonishment the vastly altered and fortified landscape and realized it was impregnable. In November, the invaders fell back to Santarém *(see p193)* and in 1811, suffering hunger and defeat, withdrew beyond the Spanish border.

Flintlock pistol from Peninsular War

Portrait of the Duke of Wellington, 1814

🏛 **Museu Municipal**
Praça 25 de Abril. **Tel** 261 310 484.
⭘ *Tue–Sun.* ⬤ *public hols.* 📷

THE BEIRAS

*S*tretching from the Spanish frontier to the sea, the Beiras are a
bulwark between the cool green north and the parched south.
This diverse region encompasses the heights of the Serra da Estrela
and the salt marshes of the Ria de Aveiro, and its towns vary from lively
Figueira da Foz to the stately old university town of Coimbra.

The three provinces of the Beiras (also called Centro) may not be a hub of tourism, but their past commercial and defensive significance has left its mark. In Beira Litoral, the prows of Aveiro's seaweed boats are a legacy of trade with the Phoenicians. All over Beira Baixa, from Castelo Branco to little granite villages, are relics of foreign occupations, and Viseu, Beira Alta's capital, grew up at a crossroads of Roman trading routes.

The Romans were never as firmly entrenched here as further south, but the ruins of Conímbriga speak eloquently of the elegant city that once stood here, and which gave its name to Coimbra, the principal city of Beira Litoral. Afonso Henriques, as king of the new nation of Portugal *(see p42)*, moved his court to Coimbra, the young country's capital for over a century.

The upheavals of the nation's founding and a hard-won independence have left a rich heritage of castles and fortified towns. Conscious of Spain's proximity and claim on their land, successive Portuguese kings constructed a great defensive chain of forts along the vulnerable eastern border. The seemingly impregnable walls of Almeida still stand as a reminder of the region's unsettled history. These border fortresses continued to prove vital in the fight for independence from Spain in the 17th century, and again against Napoleon's forces *(see p54)*. Even Buçaco, revered for the peace and sanctity of its forest, is known also as the site of Wellington's successful stand against Masséna.

Despite the unforgiving terrain and 20th-century depopulation, the Beiras are the source of some gastronomic treats: Portugal's favourite cheese is made in the Serra da Estrela, and the lush Bairrada district around Mealhada is renowned for its *leitão*, sucking pig. The region's red wines are among Portugal's best known: elegant Bairradas and powerful Dãos *(see pp28–9)*.

Distinctive candy-striped beach houses in Costa Nova, between the Ria de Aveiro and the sea

◁ A stone *pelourinho* (pillory) in a quiet corner of Castelo Mendo, one of the border towns in Beira Alta

Exploring the Beiras

The Beiras, encompassing some of Portugal's finest scenery, comprise three regions. Along the Beira Litoral are the sleepy backwaters of the Ria de Aveiro and, in contrast, the busy seaside resort of Figueira da Foz. The stately old university city of Coimbra repays exploration, and is a convenient base for visiting the historic forest of Buçaco and several of Portugal's spas.

Inland lies Viseu, the charming capital of Beira Alta, on the route to the medieval strongholds of Guarda, Trancoso and the border castles. The country's highest mountains, the Serra da Estrela, separate the Beira Alta from the little-visited Beira Baixa, where Monsanto, voted "most Portuguese village", and the handsome little city of Castelo Branco are contrasting attractions.

Coimbra's Museu Nacional Machado de Castro, with a fine sculpture collection

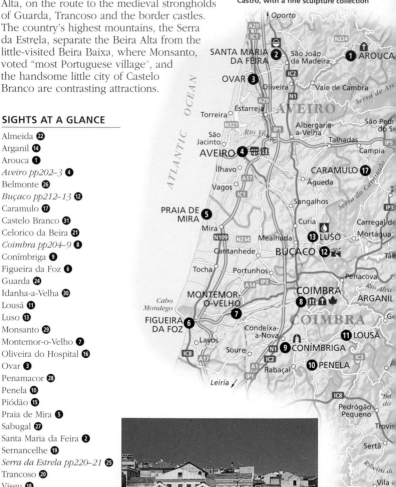

0 kilometres 25

0 miles 15

Summer at the seaside in popular Figueira da Foz

Dão vineyards between Viseu and Mangualde

GETTING AROUND

A rail network links the principal cities to smaller towns, but stations are often outside the town. Buses run from Coimbra to outlying areas, and local buses link villages and towns throughout the region. The most convenient way to explore the Beiras, however, is by car. The Oporto-Lisbon A1 (E2) motorway passes close to Coimbra and Aveiro, while the A25 motorway links Aveiro and the eastern uplands. Long inclines and bad bends make the A25 Portugal's worst road for accidents. All but the major routes are relatively traffic-free and a pleasure to drive, but unpaved surfaces can still be expected.

Steep terraces in the Serra de Açor, around Piódão

KEY

⚍	Motorway
━	Major road
⚌	Minor road
⚊	Scenic route
⌁	Main railway
─	Minor railway
▬	National border
▬	Regional border
△	Summit

SEE ALSO

- **Where to Stay** pp390–93
- **Where to Eat** pp417–19

Arouca ❶

Road map C2. 🏠 24,000. 🚌
🛈 Rua Alfredo Vaz Pinto (256 943 575). 🔁 5 & 20 of month.

This small town in a green valley owes its principal attraction, the great **Convento de Arouca**, to its saintly royal benefactor, Mafalda. Princess Mafalda was born in 1195, the daughter of Sancho I. She was betrothed to the teenage Prince Enrique of Castile, but when he died in an accident, Mafalda took the veil in Arouca. Under her, the convent became Cistercian and Mafalda's wealth and dedication made the house highly influential. She died in 1256, and her incorrupt corpse was discovered in 1616, leading to her beatification in 1793.

For over a thousand years the convent has stood beside Arouca's church on the cobbled main square. In the early 18th century the church underwent costly redecoration: 104 carved choir stalls are surmounted by paintings in sumptuous gilded panels, and the organ and chancel retable are also heavily gilded. Honoured with its own altar is a recumbent effigy of Santa Mafalda in a silver and ebony casket; her mummified remains lie below the casket.

Guided tours take visitors round the convent's museum, in which are displayed some exquisite silver monstrances, furniture and religious works of art, including two paintings

by 18th-century artist André Gonçalves, showing Mafalda saving the monastery from fire. The Neo-Classical double cloister, begun in 1781, the large refectory and kitchen and a chapterhouse covered with cheerful Coimbra tiles of rural scenes can also be visited.

🔒 Convento de Arouca
Largo de Santa Mafalda. **Tel** 256 943 321. 🕐 Tue–Sun. 🔴 Wed am, Jan, 2 May, 25 Dec. 🎟 📷

Silver and ebony casket in the convent church at Arouca, containing the effigy of Santa Mafalda

Santa Maria da Feira ❷

Road map C2. 🏠 140,500. 🚉 🚌
🛈 Praça da República (256 370 802). 🔁 20 of month.

Prosperous from cork and its thriving markets, Santa Maria derives its name from long tradition – a document from 1117 refers to "Terra de Santa Maria, a place people call Feira", after the fairs held here. A large market each month in the broad Rossio upholds the town's reputation.

A double stairway leads from the Rossio to the **Igreja dos Lóios**, with blue 17th-century tiles decorating the façades of its two symmetrical belltowers. On the opposite side of the Rossio, winding streets of solid merchants' houses from the 18th and 19th centuries lead to a decorative stairway with an ornamental fountain. This rises up to the 18th-century **Misericórdia** church.

Crowning a wooded hill on the southern edge of the town is the fairytale **castle**. Although much is a 20th-century recon-struction, it follows the 15th-century design of a local, Fernão Pereira, and his son. They added crenellations and towers to an 11th-century fort which in turn had been built over a temple to a local god. The title of Conde da Feira was bes-towed on Pereira, and the castle remained in his family until 1700. There is not much inside the castle now, but it retains its romantic air.

⛰ Castle
Largo do Castelo. **Tel** 256 372 248. 🕐 Tue–Sun. 🎟

Ovar ❸

Road map C2. 🏠 56,300. 🚉 🚌
🛈 Rua Elias Garcia (256 572 215). 🔁 Tue, Thu & Sat (general), 3rd Sun of month (antiques).

Varinas, the hardworking Portuguese fishwives, take their name from Var, or O Var, this small town which earned its living from the sea and the Ria de Aveiro that spreads out to the south (see p203). Indus-try has arrived in the shape of foundries and steel mills, but oxen still plod along the roads.

Gleaming tiles cover many of the small houses, as well as the twin-towered 17th-century **Igreja Matriz** in Avenida do Bom Reitor. In the town centre the Calvary chapel of the 18th-century **Capela dos Passos** is adorned with woodcarvings carrying a shell motif.

Ovar's Carnaval parade is one of the most colourful in Portugal, and its sponge cake,

The pinnacled and crenellated castle crowning Santa Maria da Feira

House façades in Ovar with their traditional eye-catching blue tiles

pão-de-ló, is highly esteemed. Tableaux in the **Museu de Ovar** recreate the lifestyle of a bygone era, alongside displays of regional costume and dolls. There are also mementoes of Júlio Dinis, a popular Portuguese novelist who lived in Ovar in the 19th century.

🏛 Museu de Ovar
Rua Heliodoro Salgado 11.
Tel 256 572 822. ⬜ Mon–Fri & Sat am. ⬤ public hols. 🖼

Aveiro ❹

See pp202–3.

Praia de Mira ❺

Road map C3. 🏚 5,000. 🚌
🛈 Av. da Barrinha (231 472 566).
🎪 11, 23 & 30 of month.

Fishing boat on the beach at Praia de Mira

Tourism is only now making an impact on this stretch of coast backed by a wooded reserve, the Mata Nacional das Dunas de Mira, with the dunes and Atlantic on one side and the peaceful lagoon of Barrinha de Mira on the other, is a pretty fishing village developing as a resort. High-prowed fishing boats are still drawn up the spectacular beach by oxen, but leisure craft now cruise the shore and the

inland waterways, and the fishermen's striped *palheiros (see p22)*, popular as seaside cottages, are fast vanishing amid shops, bars and cafés.

Figueira da Foz ❻

Road map C3. 🏚 63,000. 🚉
🚌 🛈 Avenida 25 de Abril (233 422 610). 🎪 daily.

Lively and cosmopolitan, this popular resort has a busy marina, a casino and a wide, curving beach with breakers that attract intrepid surfers.

General jollity is the keynote, but the **Museu Municipal Dr Santos Rocha** has a notable archaeological collection, and an eclectic display extending to Arraiolos carpets *(see p303)*, religious art, Indo-Portuguese furniture, a musical archive, fans and photographs.

The amazing interior of the **Casa do Paço** is lined with 8,000 Delft tiles taken from a shipwreck in the late 1600s. The 16th-century fortress of **Santa Catarina** stands where the Mondego meets the sea. The Duke of Wellington briefly made this little fort his base when he landed to retake Portugal from Napoleon in 1808 *(see p54)*.

🏛 Museu Municipal Dr Santos Rocha
Rua Calouste Gulbenkian.
Tel 233 402 840. ⬜ 9:30am–5:15pm Tue–Fri, 2–6:45pm Sat.
⬤ 1 Jan, Easter, 1 May, 25 Dec.
🏛 Casa do Paço
Largo Professor Vitor Guerra. **Tel** 233 401 320. ⬜ 9:30am–12:30pm & 2–6pm Mon–Fri. ⬤ public hols.

Montemor-o-Velho ❼

Road map C3. 🏚 2,600. 🚌
🛈 Castelo de Montemor-o-Velho (239 680 380). 🚢 every other Wed.

This attractive and historic hillside town rises out of fields of rice and maize beside the River Mondego. Its **castle**, which served as a primary defence of the city of Coimbra *(see pp204–9)* is mostly 14th century, but it had previously been a Moorish stronghold, and the keep has fragments of Roman stonework. The church of **Santa Maria de Alcaçova** within its walls was founded in 1090. Restored in the 15th century, its naves and arches reflect the Manueline style.

Montemor was the birthplace of Fernão Mendes Pinto (1510–83), famous for the colourful accounts of his travels in the east. Another explorer, Diogo de Azambuja (died 1518), is buried here. Columbus is said to have sailed with Azambuja, who intrepidly navigated along the West African coast. His tomb, by the Manueline master Diogo Pires, is in the **Convento de Nossa Senhora dos Anjos** in the square of the same name (ask at the tourist office for key). Its 17th-century façade hides an earlier, more lavish interior, with Manueline and Renaissance influences.

♣ Castle
Rua do Castelo. ⬜ daily.

Enjoying café life in the spring sunshine of Figueira da Foz

Aveiro ❹

This little city, once a great sea port, has a long history – Aveiro's salt pans were featured in the will of Countess Mumadona in AD 959. By the 16th century it was a considerable town, rich from salt and the *bacalhoeiros* fishing for cod off Newfoundland. When storms silted up the harbour in 1575 this wealth vanished rapidly, and the town languished beside an unhealthy lagoon, the *ria*. Only in the 19th century did Aveiro regain some of its prosperity; it is now ringed with industry and is home to an important university. The *ria* and canals give Aveiro its individual character.

Wooden barrel of *ovos moles*

Old Quarter

Tucked in between the Canal das Pirâmides and the Canal de São Roque are the neat, whitewashed houses of Aveiro's fishermen. In the early morning the focus of activity is the **Mercado do Peixe**, where the fish from the night's catch is auctioned.

Bridge across the Canal de São Roque

Skirting the Canal Central, along Rua João de Mendonça, are Art Nouveau mansions and some of the many *pastelarias* selling Aveiro's speciality: *ovos moles*. Literally "soft eggs", these are a rich confection of sweetened egg yolk in candied casings shaped like fish or barrels. As so often in Portugal, the original recipe is credited to nuns. *Ovos moles* are sold by weight or in little barrels.

Across the Canal Central

South of the Canal Central and the bustling Praça Humberto Delgado are the principal historic buildings of Aveiro. The **Misericórdia** church in the Praça da República dates from the 16th century, its façade of *azulejos* framing a splendid Mannerist portal. In the same square stands the stately 18th-century **Paços do Concelho**, or town hall, with its distinctive Tuscan-style pilasters.

Nearby, opposite the museum, is Aveiro's modest 15th-century cathedral of **São Domingos**. The figures of the Three Graces over the door on the Baroque façade were added in 1719.

A short walk south lies the **Igreja das Carmelitas**, its nave and chancel decorated with paintings of the life of the Carmelite reformer, St Teresa.

🏛 Museu de Aveiro

Ave Santa Joana Princesa. **Tel** *234 423 297.* ⬜ *10am–noon & 2–5:30pm Tue–Sun.* ⬛ *1 Jan, 25 Dec.* 🎦

The former Mosteiro de Jesus is full of mementoes of Santa Joana, who died here in 1490. The daughter of Afonso V, Joana retreated to the convent in 1472 and spent the rest of her life here. She was beatified in 1693 and her ornamental Baroque marble tomb, completed 20 years later, is in the lower choir. Simpler in style are the 18th-century paintings in the chapel, showing scenes of her life. This was once the needlework room where Santa Joana died. Among Portuguese primitive paintings is a superb 15th-century full-face portrait of the princess in court dress.

Also part of the museum are the superb gilded chancel (1725–9), 15th-century cloisters and refectory faced in Coimbra tiles. Between the refectory and chapterhouse lies the Gothic tomb of an armoured knight, Dom João de Albuquerque.

Colourful seaweed-collecting *moliceiros* moored along the Canal Central

Raking the salt as it dries in the pans fringing the Ria de Aveiro

Environs: Lying about 8 km (5 miles) south of Aveiro, at Ílhavo, is the modern block of the **Museu Marítimo e**

Regional de Ílhavo, where the region's long seafaring history is told through displays of fishing craft and equipment, with maritime memorabilia from shells to model boats.

About 4 km (2 miles) further south a small sign points to the **Museu Histórico da Vista Alegre**. A name renowned in the world of porcelain (*see p24*), the Vista Alegre factory was established in 1824 and samples of its fine porcelain can be bought from the factory shop. The museum traces the history of the factory, and has displays of porcelain (together with some crystal glass) from the 1850s to the present day.

RIA DE AVEIRO

Old maritime charts show no lagoon here, but in 1575 a terrible storm raised a sand bar that blocked the harbour. Denied access to the sea, Aveiro declined, its population cut down by the fever bred in the stagnant waters. It was not until 1808 that the *barra nova* was created, linking Aveiro once more to the sea.

The lagoon which remains covers some 65 sq km (25 sq miles), and is nearly 50 km (30 miles) long, from Furadouro south past Aveiro's salt pans and the *Reserva Natural das Dunas de São Jacinto* (nature reserve of São Jacinto) to Costa Nova. The reserve includes beaches, dunes and woods as well as the lagoon, and is home to a large and varied bird population, including pintails and goshawks. Of the boats seen here the most elegant is the *moliceiro*. Despite the bright, often humorous, decoration on its high, curving prow, this is a working boat, harvesting *moliço* (seaweed) for fertilizer. Chemical fertilizers have drastically cut demand for *moliço*, but a few of the stately craft survive; the Festa da Ria is a chance to see them in full sail.

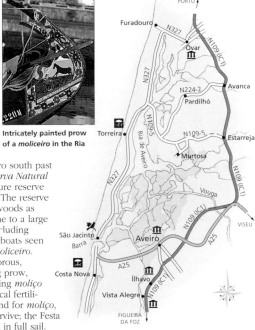

Intricately painted prow of a *moliceiro* in the Ria

KEY

▬	Motorway
▬	Major road
▬	Minor road
▬	Other road
▢	Salt marsh

0 kilometres 10

0 miles 5

The seaward waterfront at the fishing village of Torreira

Coimbra ⑧

The birthplace of six kings and the seat of Portugal's oldest university, Coimbra arouses an affection in the Portuguese shared by no other city. To the Romans the town founded on Alcaçova hill was Aeminium, but as its importance grew it took on the mantle and name of nearby Conìmbriga *(see p210)*. Coimbra was wrested from the Moors in AD 878, only to come under their control again a century later, until finally freed by Ferdinand the Great of Castile in 1064. When Afonso Henriques, the first king of Portugal, decided to move his capital south from Guimarães in 1139 *(see pp42–3)*, his choice was Coimbra, an honour it retained until 1256. For the Portuguese, Coimbra carries the roots of nationhood and, for visitors, a wealth of fascinating historic associations.

Student in May celebrations

Orientation

In the historic heart of the city, high above the Mondego, lie the cathedrals, university and a fine museum, but a first impression of Coimbra is likely to be of commerce, not culture. Shops, traffic and the railway rule the riverside and around the Praça do Comércio. The Largo da Portagem is a useful starting point, and river trips depart from nearby, alongside the Parque Dr Manuel Braga.

Tomb of Portugal's first king, Afonso Henriques, in Santa Cruz

The Lower Town

From Largo da Portagem, Rua Ferreira Borges leads past shops, lively bars, restaurants and *pastelarias* to the Praça do Comércio. In one corner of this bustling square stands the church of **São Tiago**. Its plain façade is a restoration of the 12th-century original, but inside is an exuberant Rococo altarpiece in gilded wood.

Running north of the Praça do Comércio, Rua Visconde da Luz leads to the Praça 8 de Maio and the historic church of **Santa Cruz** *(see p207)*. Portugal's first two kings are buried here, and monks from the adjacent monastery of Santa Cruz tutored the first students at Coimbra university.

Beyond Praça 8 de Maio is Rua da Sofia, the "street of wisdom", named after the theological colleges that once stood here. The convent churches to which they were attached remain: the **Igreja do Carmo** (1597), with a 16th-century retable, and the **Igreja da Graça**, founded by João III in 1543. The nearby Pátio da Inquisição is a reminder that Coimbra, like Lisbon and Évora, was a seat in the 16th century of the fiercely intolerant Inquisition *(see p51)*.

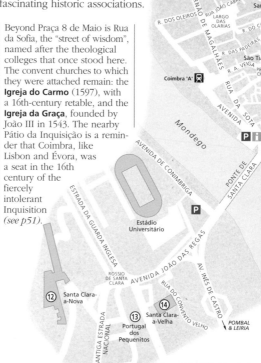

Café tables in the Praça do Comércio, overlooked by São Tiago

Pátio das Escolas, at the heart of Portugal's oldest university

Key to Symbols see back flap

0 metres 200
0 yards 200

COIMBRA CITY CENTRE

Arco de Almedina ⑥
Igreja do Carmo ②
Igreja da Graça ①
Jardim Botânico ⑪
Museu Nacional Machado
  de Castro ⑧
Portugal dos Pequenitos ⑬
Santa Clara-a-Nova ⑫
Santa Clara-a-Velha ⑭
Santa Cruz ③
São Tiago ④
Sé Nova ⑨
Sé Velha ⑦
Torre de Anto ⑤
University ⑩

VISITORS' CHECKLIST

Road map C3. 👥 *143,800.* 🚉
Coimbra A, Avda Emídio Navarro;
Coimbra B, N of city, on N11. 🚌
Avda Fernão de Magalhães. 🛈
Edifício da Biblioteca Geral, Univer-
sidade de Coimbra (239 859 884);
Largo da Portajem (239 488 120).
🎫 *Mon–Sat.* 🎭 *May: Queima*
das Fitas; Nov: Festa das Latas.

16th-century sculptor Jean de
Rouen. The tower now houses
an arts and crafts gallery.

Among the houses lining the
maze of steep alleys that wind
up to the top of the hill are a
number of *repúblicas*, student
lodgings since medieval times.

Coimbra's two cathedrals, **Sé
Velha** and **Sé Nova** *(see p206)*,
lie in the shadow of the hilltop
university *(see pp208–9)*. Beyond is the upper town's main
square, Praça da República.

Across the Mondego

It is worth crossing the river
just to admire the view of old
Coimbra. The two convents
of **Santa Clara** *(see p207)* on
the southern bank have close
ties with Santa Isabel, and
with Inês de Castro, Pedro I's
luckless lover, who was
stabbed to death here in 1355
(see p181). A romantic legend
tells how a spring, the **Fonte
dos Amores**, rose on the spot.
This can be seen in the
garden of the 18th-century
Quinta das Lágrimas, now a
hotel *(see p399)*, just south
of Santa Clara-a-Velha.

The Upper Town

The altered and restored 12th-
century **Arco de Almedina**,
off the Rua Ferreira Borges,
is the gateway to the old city (in
Arabic *medina* means town).
Steps lead up past the **Torre
de Anto**, whose Renaissance
windows and medallions
are from the workshop of the

The Arco de Almedina arching
over the steps to the upper town

Exploring Coimbra

That the citizens of Coimbra fondly call their river, the Mondego, "O Rio dos Poetas" gives a clue to the affection they have for their vibrant and beautiful city. From the university *(see pp208–9)* at the top of Alcáçova hill, down the narrow streets and stairways to the lower town, the city is crammed with historic buildings and treasures (and, all too often, slow-moving traffic). Most sights are within walking distance of each other, and despite its steep hill, Coimbra is a city best appreciated on foot. Across the Mondego there are further historic sights and an unusual theme park for children.

Elaborate façade of the Sé Nova

The Sé Velha's gilded altarpiece

🏛 Sé Velha

Largo da Sé Velha. *Tel 239 825 273.* ◯ 9:30am–7pm daily (to 5pm in winter). ⬤ 1 Jan, Easter, 1 May, 25 Dec. 🖼 to cloister.

The fortress-style Old Cathedral is widely regarded as the finest Romanesque building in Portugal, a celebration in stone of the triumph over the Moors in 1064. The nation's first king, Afonso Henriques, made the city of Coimbra his capital and his son, Sancho I, was crowned here in 1185, soon after the cathedral was completed.

Inside, square piers lead the eye up the nave to the flamboyant retable over the altar. The work of Flemish woodcarvers in about 1502, this depicts the birth of Christ, the Assumption and many saints. A 16th-century altarpiece in the south transept is also highly decorated, as is the Manueline font, thought to be by Diogo Pires the Younger. In contrast is the quiet restraint of the cloister, built in 1218 but restored in the 18th century.

The tomb of the city's first Christian governor, Sisinando (a Moslem convert who died in 1091), lies in the chapterhouse, and in the north aisle is the tomb of the Byzantine Dona Vetaça (died 1246), tutor to the wife of King Dinis, the saintly Queen Isabel *(see p45).*

🏛 Sé Nova

Largo da Feira. *Tel 239 823 138.* ◯ 9am–noon, 2–7pm Tue–Sat. ⬤ public hols. ✚ 6pm Sat, 11am Sun.

New is a relative term, as this church, a short walk from the university, was founded by the Jesuits in 1598. (Their adjacent Colégio das Onze Mil Virgens is today part of the sciences faculty.) The Jesuit Order was banned by the Marquês de Pombal in 1759 *(see p52)* but their church became the episcopal seat in 1772. Jesuit saints still look out from the façade.

The interior, more spacious than the Sé Velha, is barrel-vaulted, with a dome over the crossing. To the left of the entrance is a Manueline-style octagonal font brought, like the choir stalls, from the Sé Velha. The paintings above the stalls are copies of Italian masters. The altarpiece in the 17th-century chancel, featuring more Jesuit saints, is flanked by a pair of 18th-century organs.

Coimbra seen from the Mondego, with the university's landmark belltower crowning Alcáçova hill

For hotels and restaurants in this region see pp390–93 and pp417–19

🏛 Museu Nacional Machado de Castro

Largo Dr José Rodrigues. *Tel 239 823 727.* ⬜ *10am–6pm Tue–Sun.* ⬤ *1 Jan, Easter, 25 Dec.* 🖼

The elegant 16th-century loggias and courtyards of the former bishops' palace are the setting for the display of some of Portugal's finest sculpture – Joaquim Machado de Castro (1731–1822) was himself a master sculptor. Among the medieval pieces is an endearing knight holding a mace. Also in the collection, along with furnishings and vestments, are paintings from the 12th to 20th centuries, including an early 16th-century work, *The Assumption of Mary Magdalen*, by the Master of Sardoal.

An intriguing feature is the Criptoportico de Aeminium, a maze of underground passages holding a collection of Roman sculpture and stelae and Visigothic artifacts.

Claustro do Silêncio (Cloister of Silence) in the monastery of Santa Cruz

⛪ Santa Cruz

Praça 8 de Maio. *Tel 239 822 941.* ⬜ *9am–noon & 2–5:45pm Mon–Sat, 4–6pm Sun.* 🖼 *to cloister.*

Founded by the canons of St Augustine in 1131, the church and monastery of Santa Cruz are rich in examples of the city's early 16th-century school of sculpture. Carvings by Nicolau Chanterène and Jean de Rouen adorn the church's Portal da Majestade, designed by Diogo de Castilho in 1523. The chapterhouse by Diogo Boitac is Manueline in style, as are the Claustro do Silêncio and the choir stalls, carved in 1518 with a frieze about exploration. Portugal's first two kings, Afonso Henriques and Sancho I, were reinterred here in 1520. Their elaborate tombs are thought to be by Chanterène, also buried here.

🌿 Jardim Botânico

Calçada Martim de Freitas. *Tel 239 855 233.* ⬜ *daily.*

These, Portugal's largest botanical gardens, were created in 1772 when the Marquês de Pombal introduced the study of natural history at the University of Coimbra.

The entrance, near the 16th-century aqueduct of São Sebastião, leads into 20 ha (50 acres) devoted to a remarkable collection of some 1,200 plants, including many rare and exotic species. The gardens are used for research, but are laid out as pleasure gardens, with greenhouses and a wild area overlooking the Mondego.

Open-air study in the Jardim Botânico

⛪ Santa Clara-a-Velha

Santa Clara. *Tel 239 801 160.* ⬜ *10am–7pm Tue–Sun (to 5pm in winter).* ⬤ *1 Jan, 1 May, 25 Dec.*

Santa Isabel, the widow of King Dinis, had the convent of Santa Clara rebuilt for her retreat. She died in 1336 in Estremoz *(see p302)* but was buried here, in the convent church. Inês de Castro was also laid to rest here 20 years later, but was re-entombed at Alcobaça *(see pp180–81)*.

Almost from the day it was built, Santa Clara suffered from flooding, but was finally abandoned in 1677. In 1696 Santa Isabel's remains were moved to the Convent of Santa Clara-a-Nova. The original Gothic church, in silted ruins since the late 1600s, is at last being restored.

⛪ Santa Clara-a-Nova

Alto de Santa Clara. *Tel 239 441 674.* ⬜ *8:30am–6pm daily (Apr–Sep: to 7pm).* 🖼 *to cloister.*

The vast "new" convent of the Poor Clares was built between 1649 and 1677 to house the nuns from Santa Clara-a-Velha on drier land uphill. The building was designed by a mathematics professor, João Turriano, and although intended as a convent, now serves in part as a barracks for the army. In the richly Baroque church, pride of place is given to the silver tomb of Santa Isabel, installed in 1696 and paid for by the people of Coimbra. The saint's original tomb, a single stone, lies in the lower choir and polychrome wooden panels in the aisles tell the story of her life. The convent's large cloister, built by the Hungarian Carlos Mardel, was contributed in 1733 by João V, a generous benefactor who was well-known for his charity to nuns.

🏰 Portugal dos Pequenitos

Santa Clara. *Tel 239 801 170.* ⬜ *daily. Feb & mid-Oct–Dec: 10am–5pm; Mar–May: 10am–7pm; Jun–mid-Sep: 9am–8pm; mid-Sep–mid-Oct: 9am–7pm.* ⬤ *Jan, 25 Dec.* 🖼 ♿ **www**.portaldospequenitos.pt

At this world in miniature, children and adults alike can explore scaled-down versions of Portugal's finest national buildings, whole villages of typical regional architecture, and pagodas and temples representing the far-flung reaches of the former Portuguese empire.

Child-sized model of an Algarve manor house in Portugal dos Pequenitos

Coimbra University

An Atlas on the Via Latina

In response to an ecclesiastical petition, in 1290 King Dinis founded a university in Lisbon, one of the world's oldest and most illustrious. In 1537 it was transferred to Coimbra and located in what used to be King Afonso's palace. Study was mostly of theology, medicine and law until the reforms by the Marquês de Pombal in the 1770s broadened the curriculum. Several 19th-century literary figures, including Eça de Queirós *(see p55)*, were alumni of Coimbra. Many buildings were replaced after the 1940s, but the halls around the Pátio das Escolas echo with 700 years of learning.

Museu de Arte Sacra
As well as works of art on religious themes, this museum has vestments, chalices and books of early sacred music. It is currently closed.

★ Capela de São Miguel
Although begun in 1517 the chapel's interior is mostly 17th and 18th century. The azulejos, ornate ceiling, even the fine Mannerist altar, are eclipsed by the dazzling organ, angels trumpeting its Baroque glory.

The portal of Capela de São Miguel is Manueline in style, the work of Marcos Pires before his death in 1521.

Portrait of João V (c.1730)

STAR FEATURES

★ Biblioteca Joanina

★ Capela de São Miguel

★ Biblioteca Joanina
Named after its benefactor, João V (whose coat of arms is over the door), the library was built in the early 18th century. Its rooms, rich in gilt and exotic wood, are lined with 300,000 books.

The belltower, symbol of the university, can be seen from all over the city. The best-known of its three bells, called *a cabra*, the goat, has summoned generations of students to lectures since the tower was completed in 1733.

VISITORS' CHECKLIST

Universidade de Coimbra, Paço das Escolas. *Tel 239 859 800.*
103 from train station.
9am–7pm daily. 1 Jan, 25 Dec. www.uc.pt

Sala Grande dos Actos

Also known as the Sala dos Capelos, this is where major events such as investitures are celebrated. Dons' benches line the walls below portraits of Portuguese monarchs.

The Via Latina is a colonnaded walkway added to the original palace in the 18th century. The Portuguese coat of arms above the double staircase is crowned by a statue of Wisdom, while below, figures of Justice and Fortitude flank José I, in whose reign (1750–77) the Marquês de Pombal modernized the university.

To ticket office

Sala do Exame Privado

José Ferreira Araújo's exuberant ceiling, painted in 1701, arcs above a frieze of portraits of past rectors in the private examination hall.

STUDENT TRADITIONS

When the university was first founded, the only subjects studied were canon and civil law, medicine and letters – grammar and philosophy. To indicate which faculty they belonged to, students began to pin coloured ribbons to their gowns: red for law, yellow for medicine, dark blue for letters. Much has changed in 700 years, but students are still initiated in rites whose origins are long forgotten, and in May, as the academic year ends, there is a ceremonial burning of ribbons, the Queima das Fitas.

Burning faculty ribbons in best scholastic tradition

Porta Férrea

Built in 1634, this heavy iron gate to the university pátio is flanked by figures representing the original faculties.

Conímbriga 9

Road map C3. 2 km (1 mile) S of
Condeixa-a-Nova. ▦ *from Coimbra.*
Site ◻ *10am–8pm daily (Oct–May:
to 6pm).* ● *25 Dec.* **Museum Tel**
239 941 177. ◻ *10am–8pm Tue–
Sun (Oct–May: to 6pm).* ● *public
hols.* ▨ ♿ *museum only.*

This, the largest and most
extensively excavated
Roman site in Portugal *(see
pp40–41)*, was on the Roman
road between Lisbon (Olisipo)
and Braga (Bracara Augusta).
There is evidence of Roman
habitation as early as the 2nd
century BC, but even before
then there was
a Celtic settle-
ment here.
Under the
Roman
emperor
Augustus, from
about 25 BC,
Conímbriga
became a sub-
stantial town:
baths, a forum

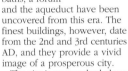

**Detail of a bedroom floor in a
house near the entrance**

and the aqueduct have been
uncovered from this era. The
finest buildings, however, date
from the 2nd and 3rd centuries
AD, and they provide a vivid
image of a prosperous city.

The site is approached along
a section of Roman road that
led into the city from the east.
Just to the left cluster the out-
lines of shops, baths and two
once-luxurious houses, both
with exquisite mosaic floors.

At Conímbriga is one of the
largest houses discovered in
the western Roman empire.
This opulent villa, known as

the Casa de Cantaber, is built
around ornamental pools in
superb colonnaded gardens,
with its own bath complex and
a sophisticated heating system.
Some of the fine mosaics in
the museum probably came
from this huge residence.

The Casa das Fontes, dating
from the early 2nd century, is
under a protective cover but
walkways provide good views.
Its mosaics and fountains, rare
survivals, which give the house
its name, form a strong image
of the Roman taste for good
living. The city's pools, and
the baths and steam rooms of
Trajan's *thermae*, were fed by
a spring 3.5 km
(2 miles) away via
a mostly subter-
ranean aqueduct.

Official exca-
vation was begun
here in 1912, but
a considerable
part of the 13-ha
(32-acre) site has
yet to be explor-
ed, including an
amphitheatre north of the city.
In the 3rd or early 4th century,
buildings were plundered for
stone as defensive walls were
hastily raised against Barbarian
hordes. In a successful assault
in AD 468, the Suevi burned
the city and murdered the inhabitants. Excavated skeletons
may date from this episode.

An informative museum
explains the history and layout
of the site, and has exhibits
of Roman busts, mosaics and
coins alongside more ancient
Celtic artefacts. There is also
a restaurant and picnic site.

**View of the church of São Miguel
within the castle walls at Penela**

Penela 10

Road map C3. ▓ *6,500.* ▦
🛈 *Praça do Município (239 560
120).* ▣ *Thu.*

Penela's thickest **castle** was
built in 1087 by Sisinando,
governor of Coimbra, as part
of the line of defences of the
Mondego valley. Its squat
towers provide wonderful
views over the village and, to
the east, of the wooded Serra
da Lousã. The church within
the castle walls, **São Miguel**,
dates back to the 16th century.
Below, in Penela itself, **Santa
Eufémia**, dated 1551 above
its decorative doorway, has a
Roman capital used as a font.

Environs: Among walnut and
olive groves 5 km (3 miles) to
the west, is the tiny village of
Rabaçal, whose tasty cheese,
made with a mixture of sheep's
and goat's milk, is a regional
speciality. Some village
women still mature the
cheese rounds in darkened
rooms in their homes.

Lousã 11

Road map C3. ▓ *16,700.* 🚉 ▦
🛈 *Rua João Luso (239 990 040).*
▣ *Tue & Sat.*

The paper factory at Lousã,
on the forested banks of
the River Arouce, was opened
in 1716 and is still working.
Skilled papermakers imported
from Italy and Germany by the
Marquês de Pombal *(see p52)*
brought prosperity, still evident
in the handsome 18th-century

The central garden of the Casa das Fontes in Conímbriga

The castle at Arouce, near Lousã, oddly defenceless in its deep valley

houses. Most elegant of these is the **Palácio dos Salazares**, a private home in Rua Viscondessa do Espinhal. Also notable is the **Misericórdia**, with a 1568 Renaissance portal, in Rua do Comércio.

Environs: Deep in a valley, 3 km (2 miles) south of Lousã, is the **Castelo de Arouce**. Legend says it was built in the 11th century by a King Arunce who took refuge in the valley when fleeing from raiders. Permission to visit the castle is available from the town hall. Near the castle are the three shrines of the **Santuário de Nossa Senhora da Piedade**.

A viewpoint on the tortuous road south towards Castanheira de Pêra gives a splendid view across the valley. A turning east leads up to **Alto do Trevim** which, at 1,204 m (3,950 ft), is the highest point in the Serra de Lousã.

Buçaco ⑫

See pp212–13.

Luso ⑬

Road map C3. 👥 3,000. 🚌
🅸 Rua Emídio Navarro (231 939 133). 📅 Mon–Sat.

In the 11th century Luso was just a village linked to a monastery at Vacariça, but it developed into a lively spa town in the 18th century as

its hot-water springs became a focus for tourism. The thermal waters, which originate from a spring below the **Capela de São João**, are said to be of therapeutic value in the treatment of a wide range of conditions, from bad circulation and muscle tone to renal problems and rheumatism.

There are a number of grand, if somewhat faded, hotels here, and an elegant Art Nouveau lobby adorns the former casino, but the main reason for visiting the resort is to enjoy its spa facilities. An additional attraction of Luso is the proximity of the treasured national forest of Buçaco, which is a powerful presence above the town.

Environs: Between Luso and Curia, **Mealhada** is an attractive small town in the heart of a region famous for *leitão*, sucking pig. This enormously popular dish is prominently advertised at numerous hotly competing restaurants in the area.

Arganil ⑭

Road map D3. 👥 13,300. 🚌
🅸 Avenida das Forças Armadas (235 200 137). 📅 Thu.

Tradition says that this was a Roman city called Argos. In the 12th century, Dona Teresa, the mother of Afonso Henriques *(see pp42–3)*, gave the town to the bishopric of Coimbra, whose incumbent also acquired the title of Conde de Arganil. Most of the town's architecture is unremarkable, but the church of **São Gens**, the Igreja Matriz in Rua de Visconde de Frias, dates back perhaps to the 14th century.

Environs: One of the most curious local sights is kept in the sanctuary of Mont'Alto, 3 km (2 miles) above the town. Here, the **Capela do Senhor da Ladeira** harbours the Menino Jesus, a Christ Child figure in a bicorne hat (part of a full wardrobe). He comes out for *festas* but the chapel key is otherwise available from the last house on the right.

Menino Jesus in Mont'Alto sanctuary, Arganil

Taking the spa waters at the Fonte de São João, Luso

THERMAL SPAS

In response to the Portuguese enthusiasm for thermal waters and health-orientated holidays, spa resorts have developed across the northern half of the country, with several of them in the Beiras, near Luso. All offer extensive sports facilities and a calm ambience as well as treatments for all the body's major systems. Most spas close for the winter, but Curia, 16 km (10 miles) northwest of Luso, is open all year for relaxation and treatments. Luso itself produces the country's best-known bottled mineral water.

Buçaco ⑫

Viewpoint of Cruz Alta

Part ancient woodland, part arboretum, the National Forest of Buçaco is a magic place. As early as the 6th century it was a monastic retreat, and in 1628 the Carmelites built a house here, walling in the forest to keep the world at bay (women had already been banned by the pope in 1622). In their secluded forest the monks established contemplative walks, chapels – and trees. The trees, added to by Portuguese explorers, gained papal protection in 1632, and the 105 ha (260 acres) contain some 700 native and exotic species, including the venerable "Buçaco cedar". The peace of the forest was disturbed in 1810 as British and Portuguese troops fought the French on Buçaco ridge. In 1834 the monastery closed, but the forest endures, with its shady walks, hermits' grottoes and the astonishing Palace Hotel Bussaco at its centre.

★ **Fonte Fria**
This impressive cascade, fed by t greatest of the forest's six sprin tumbles down to a magnolia-fringed pool.

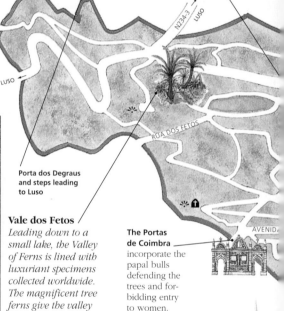

Porta dos Degraus and steps leading to Luso

Vale dos Fetos
Leading down to a small lake, the Valley of Ferns is lined with luxuriant specimens collected worldwide. The magnificent tree ferns give the valley a tropical air.

The Portas de Coimbra incorporate the papal bulls defending the trees and forbidding entry to women.

PALACE HOTEL BUSSACO

King Carlos, who commissioned this extravaganza in 1888, never lived to see his creation. His son, Manuel II, visited only briefly before his exile in 1910 *(see p55)* – he is said to have brought the French actress, Gaby Deslys, here for a romantic interlude. Its rebirth as a luxury hotel, serving its own renowned wines, was the inspiration of the royal chef and it became a fashionable rendezvous for socialites; in World War II it was also rumoured to be frequented by spies. It is now one of the great hotels of Portugal *(see p391)*.

Gaby Deslys, with whom Manuel II reputedly had a brief romance

KEY

▬	Wall
•••	Route of Via Sacra
P	Parking
⬛	Chapel
❋	Viewpoint

STAR SIGHTS

★ Palace Hotel Bussaco

★ Fonte Fria

Monastery

Only the cloisters, chapel and a few monks' cells of the Carmelite monastery remain. A plaque records that Wellington slept in one of the cork-lined cells.

Porta da Rainha was made for Catherine of Bragança, but when her visit in 1693 was cancelled the gateway was sealed up for 11 years.

Tasmanian eucalyptus (1876)

Museu Militar, devoted to the Peninsular War

N234

RUA DA RAINHA

★ Palace Hotel Bussaco

Completed in 1907, the Neo-Manueline folly of a hunting lodge built by Luigi Manini includes murals and tiles by prominent artists. Azulejos in the hall feature scenes of the Battle of Buçaco.

The Monument to the Battle of Buçaco marks Wellington's victory on the ridge of Buçaco on 27 September 1810. As the nearby Museu Militar explains, this decisive battle halted the French march on Coimbra.

Cruz Alta, the forest's highest point, has glorious views as far as the sea.

Porta da Cruz Alta

The Buçaco cedar, now 26 m (85 ft) high, is believed to have been planted in 1644.

Via Sacra

Chapels containing life-size figures mark the Stations of the Cross along this winding pathway. They were installed by the Bishop of Coimbra in 1693.

0 metres	250
0 yards	250

The village of Piódão, blending with the granite of the surrounding Serra de Açor

Piódão ⑮

Road map D3. 🚌 60 🚌 to Coja
20 km (12 miles) away. 🛈 Largo
Cónego Manuel Fernando Nogueira
(235 732 787).

The Serra de Açor (hills of the goshawk) is a place of bleak beauty, where solitary villages cling to precipitous terraces. Piódão is the most striking of these dark schist and slate hamlets. Seemingly remote, Piódão was, until the late 19th century, on the main commercial route from Coimbra to Covilhã, but with newer roads the village was forgotten. With help from EU funds, it is coming back to life: shops are opening, houses are being repainted with traditional blue trim, and in the main square the bright white **Igreja Matriz** stands out against the surrounding dark stone. Happily, Piódão retains its old-world charm.

Oliveira do Hospital ⑯

Road map D3. 🚌 22,000. 🚌
🛈 Casa da Cultura, Rua do Colégio
(238 609 269). 🗓 2nd Mon & last
Sun of month.

These lands once belonged to the Knights Hospitallers, a gift in 1120 from the mother of Afonso Henriques. The 13th-century **Igreja Matriz** in Largo Ribeira do Amaral, houses a magnificent reminder of the era of these warrior monks. One of the founders of the

town, Domingues Joanes, lies in a large tomb surmounted by a charming equestrian statue.

Today, this lively industrial town is perfectly situated for exploring the valleys of the Mondego and the Alva.

Environs: At Lourosa, 12 km (7 miles) to the southwest, the 10th-century church of **São Pedro** reflects the changing fate of Portugal over the centuries. A cemetery excavated beneath the church dates from the Roman era; the porch is Visigothic, while inside are ten impressive Roman arches and an *ajimene* (Moorish window).

Caramulo ⑰

Road map C3. 🚌 2,000. 🚌
🛈 Avenida Dr Jerónimo de Lacerda
750 (232 861 437).

In a grassy rolling serra west of Viseu, this small town was once, with its clear mountain air, a centre for sanatoria.

Interior of São Pedro at Lourosa, near Oliveira do Hospital

It is better known today for two very disparate museums in a single institutional block.

In the **Museu do Caramulo**, the exhibits range from 16th-century Flemish tapestries, sculpture, porcelain, silver and ivory to Egyptian bronzes from 1580 to 900 BC. The paintings are as varied: from Portuguese primitives to the 20th century. Chagall and Dalí are represented, as is the Portuguese Maria Helena Vieira da Silva (1908–92). One of Picasso's haunting still lifes was donated by the artist in 1947.

The collection in the **Museu do Automóvel** is just as eclectic: a working 1899 Peugeot, Bugattis and Rolls-Royces, and a bullet-proof 1938 Mercedes-Benz ordered for Salazar when he was prime minister *(see pp56–7)* but never used.

> 🏛 **Museu do Caramulo**
> **(Fundação Abel de Lacerda)**
> **and Museu do Automóvel**
> Caramulo. **Tel** 232 861 270.
> ◯ 10am–1pm & 2–6pm daily
> (Oct–Mar: to 5pm). ● Easter Sun,
> Easter Mon, 24 Dec, 25 Dec am. 🈚

Environs: From the museum the road winds southwest up to two viewpoints and picnic spots in the Serra do Caramulo. About 4 km (2 miles) from Caramulo are the wild-flower pastures of **Cabeça da Neve**, at 970 m (3,200 ft). A little further on, signposted to the West, is the boulder-strewn upland of **Caramulinho**, rising to 1,074 m (3,524 ft). The views from here are magnificent.

Viseu ⑱

Road map D3. 🏘 *19,500.* 🚌
🛈 *Avenida de Gulbenkian (232 420 950).* 🛒 *Tue.*

An enthralling old town is at the heart of this lively regional capital. Viseu has been a major northern crossroads since the time of the Romans and is the centre of the Dão wine-growing region *(see p29).*

On a visit to Viseu it is hard to miss that this was the home town of one of Portugal's great 16th-century artists. The name of Grão Vasco graces a hotel, a museum, even a wine label.

On the western side of the old town is the striking 15th-century **Porta do Soar de Cima**, a remnant of the original walls. In the Rossio, the main square, the **Igreja dos Terceiros de São Francisco** (1773) has an Italianate façade and gilded interior. The 1887 town hall on the west side has a grand stairway and *azulejos* featuring the history of Viseu and its personalities. Just north is Rua Augusto Hilário, named after the originator of Coimbra-style *fado (see pp64–5)* who was born here.

The two-towered 17th-century façade of Viseu's cathedral

🛉 Sé

Largo da Sé. **Tel** *232 436 065.*
🕐 *8am–noon & 2–7pm daily.*
Viseu's cathedral still retains a few Romanesque features, but it has been altered over the centuries in a variety of styles which work together surprisingly well. The façade is a 17th-century replacement of a Manueline frontage that fell down in 1635. Inside, the vaulted roof is supported by 16th-century knotted ribs on 13th-century columns. In the

The graceful Rococo façade of the church of the Misericórdia, Viseu

north chapel are fine *azulejos* from the 18th century, while those in the two-storey cloister date from a century earlier. The sacristy has a lavishly painted ceiling and early "carpet" tiles *(see p26).* In the chancel, choir stalls in Brazilian jacaranda contrast with a startling modern altar, an inverted pyramid in polished granite and steel.

The Sé's treasury, housed in the chapterhouse, includes a 12th-century Gospel and a 13th-century Limoges coffer.

Facing the cathedral is the **Misericórdia** church, with its 18th-century Rococo façade. It houses a temporary exhibition from the Museu de Grão Vasco.

🏛 Museu de Grão Vasco

Largo da Sé. **Tel** *232-42 20 49.*
🕐 *10am–5:30pm Tue–Sun (from 2pm Tue).* ● *public hols.*
🎟 *(free 10am–2pm Sun).*
In the 16th-century former bishops' palace abutting the cathedral is the Museu de Grão Vasco, Viseu's "great Vasco". The paintings of Vasco Fernandes (c.1475–1540) and his fellow artists of the Viseu School are highly esteemed for their naturalism, background landscapes, drapery and attention to detail. Their treatment of light betrays the marked influence of Flemish painters.

On the top floor of the three-storey museum are the masterpieces that once adorned the cathedral's chancel altarpiece, including Grão Vasco's monumental *St Peter* and, from a series of 14 panels on the life of Christ, *The Adoration of the Magi.* Painted around 1503–5, it is memorable for the inclusion of a Brazilian Indian among those paying homage to the newborn Christ *(see p48).* Some of the other panels are thought to be by fellow artists in the Viseu School.

Among other masterpieces here are works by Grão Vasco's great rival, Gaspar Vaz, including a *Last Supper.* On the lower floors are works by Portuguese artists from the 19th and 20th centuries, including Columbano Bordalo Pinheiro.

St Peter (1503–5) by Vasco Fernandes in the Museu de Grão Vasco, Viseu

Sernancelhe ⓙ

Road map D2. 🏠 *6,200.* 🚌
ℹ️ *Avenida das Tílias (254 598 300).*
🗓️ *every other Thu.*

Small whitewashed houses
cluster around the granite
heart of this modest Beira
town which was established
on the banks of the Távora in
the 10th century. In the central
Praça da República stands the
Romanesque **Igreja Matriz**.
The granite statues in its façade
niches, survivors from the
12th century, flank a notable
arched portal embellished by
a semicircle of carved angels.
The pillory that stands across
the square is dated 1554.

The grandest house here is
the Baroque **Solar dos
Carvalhos** behind
the church. Long
and low, with
carved granite
portals against
whitewashed
walls, it is where
the local noble
family lived in
the 18th century.
It is still a private house.

Only a few stubs of castle
wall remain on the rocky outcrop overlooking the square,
but a small battlemented house
has been built into them.

Environs: In the Serra da Lapa,
which rises to the south of
Sernancelhe, stands a popular
shrine known as the
**Santuário da Nossa
Senhora da Lapa**. The
story tells of a dumb
shepherd girl, Joana,
who found a statue of
the Virgin Mary on a
great boulder and took
it home. Irritated, her
mother threw it on the
fire, at which moment
the child miraculously
spoke: "Don't burn it,"
cried Joana. "It is the
Senhora da Lapa."

A chapel was built
to enshrine the boulder,
and the image, now
with a slightly scorched
face, looks down from
an ornamental recess.
The space below her
niche is packed with
images and offerings
left by pilgrims.

The main gateway into the old walled town of Trancoso

*Carved arch over the portal of
the Igreja Matriz, Sernancelhe*

The castle at **Penedono** is captivating. Perched on rocks in
the middle of this small town
17 km (11 miles) northeast of
Sernancelhe, it has survived
since at least the 10th century.
The castle is mentioned
in the medieval tale of
a knight known as
O Magriço, who
went to England
with 11 other
knights to joust
in honour of 12
English ladies.
There is little to
see inside the
castle – if closed, the key is in
the store beside the *pelourinho*
(pillory), but there are splendid
views from the walls.

🏰 Santuário da Nossa Senhora da Lapa
Quintela da Lapa, 11 km (7 miles)
SW of Sernancelhe.
Tel 232 688 993. 🕐 *daily.*

The castle of Penedono, near Sernancelhe,
with its imposing medieval battlements

Trancoso ⓚ

Road map D2. 🏠 *6,000.* 🚌
ℹ️ *Avenida Heróis de São Marcos
(271 811 147).* 🗓️ *Fri.*

When King Dinis married
Isabel here in 1283 *(see
pp44–5),* he gave her Trancoso
as a wedding gift. He was also
responsible for the impressive
walls that still encircle the town
and, in 1304, established here
the first unrestricted fair in Portugal. Left in peace after 1385,
the town became a lively commercial centre. Trancoso once
had a large Jewish population,
and in the old Judiaria, houses
survive with one broad and
one narrow door, separating
domestic life from commerce.

From the southern gate, Rua
da Corredoura leads to **São
Pedro**, restored after 1720. A
tombstone in the church commemorates Gonçalo Anes,
a local shoemaker who, in the
1580s, wrote the celebrated
Trovas under the name of
Bandarra. These prophesied
the return of the young King
Sebastião *(see p105).*

Environs: Tumbledown ruins
above a humble village are all
that remain of the medieval
citadel of **Marialva**, 14 km
(9 miles) to the northeast of
Trancoso. Granite walls, fragments of stone carvings and
a striking 15th-century pillory
emanate an aura of lost grandeur. Probably founded by
Ferdinand of León and Castile
early in the 11th century and
fortified by Sancho I, it is not
known why Marialva fell into
ruin. No battle destroyed it
and it seems merely to have
been abandoned as townsfolk
moved to more fruitful lands.

SERRA CHEESE

Serra, made from the milk of ewes grazing in the Serra da Estrela *(see pp220–21)*, is Portugal's finest cheese. It is made in the winter – its success was once governed by the temperature of the women's hands as they worked in their cool granite kitchens – and traditionally the milk is coagulated with *flor do cardo*, thistle. Now the small factories producing the cheese, in rounds of 1.5–2 kg (about 3–5 lb), are certified to ensure quality and authenticity (fakes are not uncommon). At room temperature Serra becomes runny. The cheese is scooped out with a spoon through a hole cut into the top.

A shepherd with his flock on the slopes of the Serra da Estrela

Celorico da Beira ㉑

Road map D3. 🏘 *8,800*. 🚊 🚌 🛈 *Estrada Nacional 16 (271 742 109)*. 🗓 *Tue, Dec–May: alternate Fri.*

In the lee of the Serra da Estrela, the pastures around Celorico da Beira have long been a source of the region's famous Serra cheese. From December to May the cheese market is held in the Praça Municipal and every February there is a cheese fair. Around Rua Fernão Pacheco, running

from the main road up to the castle, is the old centre of Celorico, a cluster of granite houses with Manueline windows and Gothic doors. Of the 10th-century **castle**, battered by a long succession of frontier disputes with Spain, only a tower and the outer walls remain. Its stark silhouette is less dramatic at close quarters. The **Igreja Matriz**, restored in the 18th century, has a painted coffered ceiling. During the Peninsular War, the church served briefly as a makeshift hospital for the English forces.

Almeida ㉒

Road map E2. 🏘 *1,500*. 🚌 🛈 *Portas de São Francisco (271 574 204)*. 🗓 *8th day & last Sat of month.*

Formidable defences in the form of a 12-pointed star guard this small, delightfully preserved border town.

Almeida was recognized by Spain as Portuguese territory under the Alcañices Treaty on 12 September 1297, but this did not stop further incursions. The present Vauban-style stronghold *(see p299)* was designed in 1641 by Antoine Deville after Spain's Philip IV, in post-Restoration rage, destroyed the earlier defences protecting the town and its medieval castle.

From 1742 to 1743 Almeida was in Spanish hands again, and then during the Peninsular War was held in turn by the French under Masséna and the British under the Duke of Wellington. In 1810, a French shell lit a powder trail that destroyed the castle.

To breach the town's fortifications today, it is necessary to cross a bridge and pass through a tunnel. The underground **casamatas**, soldiers' barracks, can be visited and an armoury in the main gateway, the Portas de São Francisco, holds further mementoes of Almeida's military past. In the town itself are a 17th-century parish church and a **Misericórdia** church of a similar age, attached to one of Portugal's oldest almshouses. A walk around the grassy walls gives rewarding views of the town.

's complex fortifications, still discernible despite the incursion of grass and wild flowers

Border Castles Tour ㉓

Defending Portugal's frontiers was a vital priority of the nation's early kings. The greatest period of castle-building was in the reign of King Dinis (1279–1325). All along the shakily held border, Spanish incursions were frequent and loyalties divided. Castles were constantly being assaulted, besieged and rebuilt, and the 20 that survived are a lasting reminder of this long period of dispute. Much of the terrain, especially in the Serra da Marofa, is bleak and rocky, but near Pinhel and beyond Castelo Mendo the scenic valley of the River Côa provides a dramatic backdrop.

Castelo Rodrigo ②
This tiny fortified village still has its encircling walls built by King Dinis in 1296. But the fine palace of its lord, the Spanish sympathizer Cristóvão de Moura, was burnt down at the Restoration in 1640 *(see pp50–51).*

Figueira de Castelo Rodrigo ③
From the 18th century, Castelo Rodrigo was largely abandoned in favour of less isolated Figueira, now a flourishing little town known for its almond blossom. Just to the south, topped by a huge stone Christ the King, is the highest point of the Serra da Marofa, 977 m (3,205 ft).

Almeida ①
The town's star-shaped defences are a finely preserved example of the complex but effective style of fortifications developed by the French engineer, Vauban, in the 17th century *(see p299).*

VILA NOVA DE FOZ CÔA

SERRA DA MAROFA

Vale Verde

Aldeia Nova

Ribeira de Tourões

IP5

SALAMANCA

Vilar Formoso   Fuentes de Oñoro

GUARDA   N16

SABUGAL

Pinhel ④
Part of the region's defences since Roman times, Pinhel formed the fulcrum for a network of fortresses, and in the early 14th century King Dinis built it up into an impressive citadel. Much of this ring of walls survives, as do two towers.

TIPS FOR DRIVERS

Length: 115 km (72 miles).
Stopping-off points: Most villages have cafés, and Pinhel and Almeida have restaurants.
Road conditions: The tour uses well-surfaced roads; short cuts are deceptive and not recommended. (See also pp460–61.)

KEY

■ Tour route
= Other roads
-.- International boundary
☀ Viewpoint

0 kilometres   10

0 miles   5

Castelo Mendo ⑤
Beyond the main gate, guarded by two stone boars, little survives of the castle here, but the distant views make its role as a frontier fort easy to appreciate.

The soaring triple-aisled interior of Guarda's Gothic cathedral

🏛 **Museu de Guarda**
R. Alves Roçadas 30. **Tel** 271 213 460.
⭘ Tue–Sun. ⬤ public hols. 📷

Serra da Estrela 🛇

See pp218–19.

Belmonte 🛇

Road map D3. 🛈 3,500. 🚉 🚌
🛈 Castelo de Belmonte (275 911
488). 🛄 1st & 3rd Mon of month.

Belmonte was for generations
the fiefdom of the heroic
Cabral family. Pedro Álvares
Cabral, the first navigator to
land in Brazil, had forebears
who fought at Ceuta (see p48)
and Aljubarrota (see p185).
Fernão, an earlier ancestor,
was famed for his feats of
strength. The family crest,
incorporating a goat (cabra),
can be seen in the castle and
adjacent chapel.

The **castle**, begun
in 1266, retains
its keep and, a
later addition, an
ornate Manueline
window. The little
church of **São
Tiago** nearby
has preserved its
Romanesque sim-
plicity: the frescoes
above the altar

Cabral family crest in
the chapel, Belmonte

and, in a tiny side chapel, a
serene granite pietà date from
the 13th century. Beside the
church is the 15th-century
Capela dos Cabrais which
holds the Cabral family tombs.

The modern **Igreja da
Sagrada Família** (1940) is
the repository for a treasured
statue of Nossa Senhora da
Esperança said to have
accompanied Cabral on his
voyage to Brazil. A museum
charting the development of
the Jewish community in the
region is due to open soon.

Environs: Just northeast of
Belmonte is a Roman tower,
Centum Cellas, also called
Torre de Colmeal. The role
of this square, three-storeyed
structure is uncertain and
archaeologists' theories have
suggested a range of functions
from hostel or military base
to mansion and temple.

Guarda 🛇

Road map D3. 🛈 26,000. 🚉 🚌
🛈 Praça Luis de Camões (271 205
530). 🛄 1st & last Wed of month.

Spread over a bleak hill on
the northeast flank of the
Serra da Estrela, Guarda is Portugal's highest city, at 1,056 m
(3,465 ft). Founded in 1197 by
Sancho I, the city's original
role as frontier guard explains
its name and its rather forbidding countenance. Some of its
arcaded streets and squares
are lively and interesting, but
the great fortress-like **Sé**, with
its flying buttresses, pinnacles
and gargoyles, could never be
described as lovely. Master
architects who worked on the
cathedral, begun in 1390 and
completed in 1540, included
Diogo Boitac (from 1504 to
1517) and the builders of
Batalha (see pp184–5). The
interior, by contrast, is light
and graceful. The 100 carved
figures high on the altarpiece
in the chancel were worked
by Jean de Rouen in 1552.

On display in the nearby
Museu de Guarda are two
floors of paintings, artefacts,
archaeological discoveries and
a section on the city's own
poet, Augusto Gil (1873–1929).

From the cathedral square,
a do Comércio leads down
he 17th-century **Miseri-
ia** church. Inside the orna-
l portal are Baroque
nd pulpits. Just north
athedral, in the historic
tre, is the 18th-century

church of **São Vicente**, which
has 16 elaborate azulejo panels
depicting the life of Christ.

Guarda used to support a
thriving Jewish community and
in Rua Dom Sancho I is a key
shop that may once
have served as a
synagogue. History
records that João I,
on a visit to Guarda,
was smitten by Inês
Fernandes, the beau-
tiful daughter of a
Jewish shoemaker.
From their liaison
a son, Afonso, was
born. In 1442 the
title of first Duke of
Bragança was bestowed on
Afonso, and 200 years later his
descendant would take the
throne as João IV, first of the
Bragança monarchs (see p301).

Centum Cellas, a curious Roman
landmark near Belmonte

Serra da Estrela ㉕

Haymaking near the town of Linhares

These "star mountains" are the highest range on mainland Portugal, with much of the Serra over 1,500 m (5,000 ft). The highest point rises to 1,993 m (6,539 ft) but is topped by a small stone tower – the Torre – to "stretch" it to 2,000 m. The exposed granite of the upper slopes is good for little but grazing sheep, and stone shepherds' huts form part of the landscape, their thatched roofs renewed each year after the harsh winter. Sheep have shaped the fortunes of the area, providing wool for a textile industry and supplying milk for Portugal's best-known cheese. A designated nature reserve, the Serra's long-distance paths and stunning flora attract walkers and nature enthusiasts, while a winter snowfall brings skiers to the slopes around Torre.

Cabeça do Velho
The granite of the mountain tops has been eroded into many weird shapes, such as this "old man's head" near Sabugueiro. It is matched by an "old woman's head" south of Seia.

Valezim
In Valezim are several old water mills of a type not often found in Portugal. Two of them are still used to grind grain.

Seia is one of the main entry points to the Parque Natural da Serra da Estrela.

(Map) Gouve · Viseu · Alva · Seia · Cabeça do Velho · Sabugueiro · Valezim · Curral Martir · N33.9 · Rodeio Grande · Zê · N231 · Coimbra · Muro · Vide · Penha dos Abutres · Ribeira de Alvoco · Torre · Pe da S · N230 · N231 · Unhais da Serra · Alto da Pedrice · N230 · N230

Serra Cheese Shop
The best Serra cheese, prized for its rich flavour (see p217), is still made by hand. Farmers sell their produce at cheese fairs and at stalls or small shops such as this one near the summit of Torre.

Penhas de Saúd
once a health s
is now pop
with sk

Torre
*Despite the unpre
bility of snow, th
below Torre are
skiing, tobogg
just fun in the*

STAR SIGHTS

★ Zêzere Valley

★ Linhares

★ **Linhares**
Guarded by the towers of its medieval castle, Linhares is like a living museum. The forum, from which medieval justice was dispensed, survives, as do many fine houses from its 15th-century heyday.

KEY

═══ Major road

═══ Minor road

ℹ️ Tourist information

🔆 Viewpoint

Celorico
da Beira

Celorico
da Beira

Prados

Linhares

Cabeça Alta ▲

Folgosinho

Videmonte

Guarda

Galhardos ▲

Mondego

Guarda

Manteigas,
at the heart of the Serra, is a textile centre. Just to the west there is a *pousada (see p392).*

Manteigas

N232

N18-1

Zêzere

Valhelhas

Belmonte

Poço
do Inferno
🔆

0 kilometres   5

0 miles   2

★ **Zêzere Valley**
The Zêzere eventually joins the Tagus, but here, near its source, the young river flows through a classic glacier-cut valley. The golden broom growing here is used to thatch mountain huts.

Covilhã, the largest town in the area, is known for its fine textiles woven from locally produced wool. The textile museum here deserves a visit.

Poço do Inferno
This cascade in a gorge of the River Leandros is a spectacular sight, especially when it freezes in winter.

SHEEPDOG OF THE SERRA

Intelligent, loyal and brave, the Serra da Estrela sheepdog embodies all the qualities required in this wild region. Its heavy coat, as shaggy as its charges, helps it survive the bitter high altitude winters and in the past its strength was called upon to defend the flock from wolves. Pedigree Serra da Estrela dogs (reputedly with some wolf's blood introduced in their breeding) are raised at kennels near Gouveia and west of Manteigas.

Sabugal ㉗

Road map E3. 🏠 3,000. 🚌
ℹ️ Câmara Municipal, Praça da
República (800 262 788).
🗓 1st Thu & 3rd Tue of month.

In 1296, when this small town
beside the River Côa was
confirmed as Portuguese in the
Treaty of Alcañices, the **castle**
was refortified by the ever-
industrious King Dinis *(see
p44)*. Its imposing towered
walls and unusual five-sided
keep survive from this era,
although the castle suffered
in peacetime from villagers
raiding it for building stone.

Peopled since prehistoric
times, Sabugal still has part of
its medieval walls, reinforced
in the 17th century and now
ringed by newer houses. In
the Praça da República stands
a granite **clocktower**, reconstructed in the 17th century.

The castle at Sabugal, with its distinctive five-sided keep

Environs: Wrapped in its ring
of walls, **Sortelha**, 20 km (12
miles) west, is enchanting. It
sits on a granite outcrop and
the views from the high keep
of its gem of a 13th-century
castle are stunning. In front of
the arched castle entrance is a
16th-century pillory with an
armillary sphere on top. In the
tiny citadel are a school and
stony lanes of granite houses,
some discreetly converted into
restaurants *(see p419)*.

The local fondness for bullfights *(see pp146–7)* is reflected
in names of nearby villages

such as **Vila do Touro**. In a
local variation, the *capeia*, bulls
were taunted into charging into
a huge fork of branches.

Penamacor ㉘

Road map D3. 🏠 6,200. 🚉 🚌
ℹ️ Rua S. Pedro (277 394 058).
🗓 1st & 3rd Wed of month.

Fought over by successive
waves of Romans, Visigoths
and Moors, this frontier town
was fortified in the 12th century by Gualdim Pais, Master
of the Knights Templar *(see
pp186–7)*. Today the weather-
beaten castle walls rise above
a quiet town at the heart of
hardy, sparsely inhabited country where the main attraction
is the hunting of small game.

From the main square, the
road up to the old town passes
beside the former town hall,

built over a medieval archway.
Beyond lie the restored **castle
keep** and the 16th-century
Igreja da Misericórdia, with
an elegant Manueline portal
capped by armillary spheres,
the emblem of Manuel I.

Environs: Penamacor is the
headquarters of the **Reserva
Natural da Serra da Malcata**.
These 20 sq km (8 sq miles)
of forested wilderness shelter
wolves, otters and, most im-
portantly, are one of the last
refuges of the Iberian lynx.
Visitors should first call at the
information centre for advice.

🦌 **Reserva Natural
da Serra da Malcata**
🚌 to Penamacor or Sabugal. ℹ️ Rua
Ribeiro Sanches 60, Penamacor (277
394 467). 📷 by appt.

Monsanto ㉙

Road map E3. 🏠 1,500. 🚌
ℹ️ Rua Marquês de Graciosa
(277 314 642). 🗓 3rd Sat.

An odd fame hit Monsanto
in 1938 when it was voted
"most Portuguese village in
Portugal". The village is at one
with the granite hillside on
which it perches: its lanes
blend into the grey rock, the
houses squeezed between
massive boulders. Tiny gardens
sprout from the granite and
dogs drink from granite bowls.

The ruined **castle** began as
a *castro*, a Lusitanian fortified
settlement, and suffered a long
history of sieges and battles
for its commanding position.
It was finally destroyed by a
19th-century gunpowder

Monsanto's houses, dwarfed by immense granite boulders

explosion. Cars cannot venture beyond the village centre, but the view alone is worth the walk up to the ruined walls.

A story is told of how a long siege by the Moors drove the hungry villagers to a desperate ploy. They threw their last calf, full of their last grain, over the walls, a show of profligacy that convinced the Moors to give up. Each May there is a mock re-enactment of this victory amid much music and singing.

Idanha-a-Velha ⑳

Road map D3. 🏠 90. 🚌 🅸 *Rua da Sé (277 914 280).*

This modest hamlet among the olive groves encapsulates the history of Portugal. Discreet signposts and explanations in Portuguese, French and English guide visitors round the landmarks of this fascinating living museum.

Idanha-a-Velha was, it is said, the birthplace of the Visigothic King Wamba, and had its own bishop until 1199. The present appearance of the **cathedral** comes from early 16th-century restoration, but in the echoing interior are stacked inscribed and sculpted Roman stones.

In the middle of the village stand several historic monuments: a 17th-century pillory and the Renaissance **Igreja Matriz**, while near an early 20th-century olive press is a ruined **Torre dos Templários**, a relic of the Templars. This order of religious knights held sway in Idanha until the 14th century *(see pp186–7).*

Statue-lined Stairway of the Apostles in the unusual Jardim Episcopal, Castelo Branco

Castelo Branco ㉑

Road map D4. 🏠 32,500. 🚆 🚌 🅸 *Alameda da Liberdade (272 330 339).* 🛒 *Mon.*

This handsome, busy old city, overlooked by the vestiges of a Templar castle, is the most important in the Beira Baixa.

Much the greatest attraction is the extraordinary **Jardim Episcopal** beside the former bishops' palace. Created by Bishop João de Mendonça in the 18th century, the garden's layout is conventionally formal; its individuality lies in its dense population of statues. Baroque in style and often bizarre in character, stone saints and apostles line the box-edged paths, lions peer at their reflections in pools and monarchs stand guard along the balustrades – the hated kings of the 60-year Spanish rule *(see p50)* conspicuously half-size.

The 17th-century Paço Episcopal itself now houses the **Museu Francisco Tavares Proença Júnior**. Its wide-ranging collection includes archaeological finds, displays of 16th-century tapestries and Portuguese primitive art. Castelo Branco is also well known for its fine silk-embroidered bedspreads, called *colchas,* and examples of these are also exhibited in the museum.

In the mainly 18th-century Convento da Graça opposite there is a small **Museu de Arte Sacra** with a varied collection of religious art, including an ivory Christ. Beside the road back to the town centre stands a 15th-century cross known as the **Cruzeiro de São João**.

🌸 **Jardim Episcopal**
Rua Bartolomeu da Costa. ◯ *daily.* 🅰

🏛 **Museu Francisco Tavares Proença Júnior**
Largo Doutor José Lopes Dias, **Tel** 272 344 277. ◯ *10am–12:30pm & 2–5:30pm Tue–Sun.* ● *public hols.*

🏛 **Museu de Arte Sacra**
Rua Bartolomeu da Costa. **Tel** 272 348 420, ext. 237. ◯ *9am–noon & 2–5:30pm Mon–Fri.* ● *public hols.* ♿

The historic little village of Idanha-a-Velha, among its olive groves beside the River Ponsul

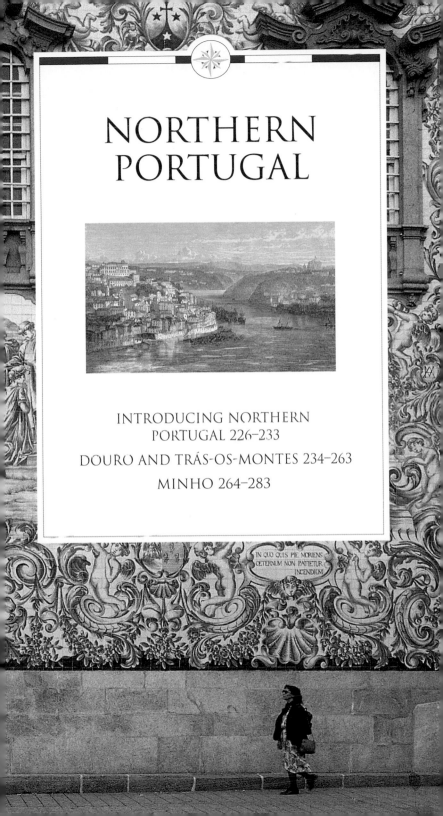

NORTHERN PORTUGAL

IN QUO QUIS PIE MORIENS
CETERNUM NON PATIETUR
INCENDIUM

Northern Portugal at a Glance

Portugal north of the River Douro is rural and unspoilt, yet offers splendid opportunities for cultural sightseeing, walking and water sports. Beyond the cultivated valley of the Douro and the fertile Minho rises the remote and romantically named Trás-os-Montes ("Behind the Mountains"), with its tracts of wilderness and tiny medieval townships. It could be said the nation was conceived between the Minho and the Douro, and historic cities such as Oporto, Bragança and Braga give fascinating insights into the country's past.

In the Parque Nacional da Peneda-Gerês *scenery ranges from dramatic forested valleys to flowery meadows. Local farmers store their grain in curious stone espigueiros (see pp272–3).*

Viana do Castelo, *at the mouth of the River Lima, is elegant and relaxed (see pp276–7). The stately buildings in the Praça da República, including the arcaded* Paços do Concelho *(the old town hall), reflect the town's wealthy past.*

MINHO
(See pp264–83)

Bom Jesus do Monte, *near Braga, attracts worshippers, penitents and tourists, who all come to climb 116 m (380 ft) up the Baroque staircase (see pp280–81). This is the Staircase of the Five Senses, with fountains depicting each of the senses.*

Douro Litoral

Oporto, *set on Penaventosa Hill above the River Douro, is Portugal's second city (see pp236–47). Alongside a wealth of historic sights and sophisticated shopping, it offers the charm of its steep medieval alleys tumbling down to the lively riverside quays, and a chance to taste port at its point of origin.*

◁ **Azulejos** on the Igreja do Carmo in Oporto, depicting the founding of the Carmelite Order

The Casa de Mateus, *familiar to many from the Mateus Rosé wine label, lies in the hills above the valley of the Douro. This Baroque solar, or manor house, is set in beautifully manicured formal gardens, its distinctive pinnacles rising above the orchards and vineyards that surround it (see pp256–7).*

Bragança, *capital of Trás-os-Montes, gave its name to Portugal's last and longest-ruling royal dynasty. The keep and walls of this remote citadel, founded in the 12th century, look out over the valley of the River Fervença (see pp260–61).*

Trás-os-Montes

DOURO AND TRÁS-OS-MONTES
(See pp234–63)

Alto Douro

0 kilometres 25

0 miles 10

Port Country, *as the scenic valley of the Upper Douro is commonly called, is the nursery of Portugal's port industry. A tour of a quinta, or wine estate, with its steeply terraced riverside vineyards, is highly recommended (see pp254–5).*

The Festivals of the North

Portuguese cities, towns and villages all have their own particular saints' days. These are primarily religious occasions, particularly in the Minho and across the devout north, but are also a chance to put aside the cares of life for a day or two. It is a popular maxim that a holy day is best celebrated by eating, drinking, dancing and merrymaking, as well as worshipping and giving thanks. The most solemn and spectacular celebrations of Holy Week, Semana Santa, can also be seen in the north, especially in Braga *(see pp278–9)*, Portugal's ecclesiastical capital.

Dressing up for Holy Week

Street procession during the Festa das Cruzes in Barcelos

A solemn moment as Easter candles are lit in Braga

EASTER

Holy Week, culminating in Easter Sunday, is the major religious festival of the year. In Braga, processions snake round the city walls to the great cathedral, and every village has its own ceremonies.

The start of Holy Week is heralded by Palm Sunday, when branch-waving faithful line the streets to commemorate the entry of Christ into Jerusalem. Good Friday evening is palpably solemn, as innumerable processions follow the 14 Stations of the Cross, many believers doing public penance as they recall Christ's suffering. In some villages an effigy of the lifeless and bleeding Christ is carried through the streets.

On Easter Sunday, after an uplifting mass proclaiming the risen Christ, every parish priest processes around his village with a crucifix on a tall staff for parishioners to kiss the feet of Jesus. While the priest takes a customary glass of wine, his entourage ecstatically let off rockets. Families then traditionally lunch on roast kid *(cabrito)*.

After Easter, in early May, the passion of Christ is recalled in Barcelos *(see p275)*. Crosses are erected the length of a petal-strewn route for the **Festa das Cruzes**.

SÃO JOÃO

Oporto's celebration of São João *(23–24 Jun)* is one of Portugal's most exuberant festival. It coincides with the summer solstice, and to celebrate, people eat, drink and dance all night, playfully hitting each other over the head with giant garlic-leeks (or sometimes, even more strangely, with squeaky plastic hammers). Bonfires are lit and a spectacular display of fireworks explodes over the Douro.

Wielding a São João hammer

COSTUME IN THE MINHO

Gold necklets

Embroidered apron pockets

Festivals are important vehicles for keeping alive tradition, particularly regional costume. These days, rock music and designer clothes are as much part of young people's life in Minho villages as elsewhere in western Europe, but traditional dress is worn with pride on days of celebration. The Minho's costume is the most colourful in Portugal, with exquisitely embroidered scarves and aprons in colours denoting village loyalties. Messages of love and friendship are stitched on to pockets, and bodices are half-lost under tiers of gold filigree.

A tradition that has become a part of São João over the last few decades is the annual regatta of the *barcos rabelos*, the boats in which port used to be shipped down the Douro *(see p254)*.

ROMARIAS

Any kind of celebration or party can be described as a *festa*, but one billed as a *romaria* implies a religious dimension. Most *festas* in the north are *romarias*; they begin with a special mass, then saints' statues are brought from the church to be paraded through the streets on litters. Blessings are dispensed in all directions – fire engines and ambulances frequently also getting the treatment – followed by a spraying with some Raposeira sparkling wine. Many *romarias* take place in the summer, and in August few days go by without a celebration. **Assumption Day** *(15 Aug)*

Nossa Senhora da Agonia, Viana do Castelo

is fêted all over Portugal with dancing and music. *Gigantones*, grotesque giants of pre-Christian origin, join street processions and fireworks light the sky. A few days later, around 20 August, one of the year's most spectacular *romarias* takes place in Viana do Castelo *(see pp272–3)*. The festivities celebrating **Nossa Senhora da Agonia** include a bullfight and an afternoon devoted to a kaleidoscopic display of regional costume,

which may include more than a thousand participants. As a finale, fireworks are let off from the bridge over the River Lima to cascade down into the water as a fiery waterfall.

On the coast just to the west of Braga, villagers in São Bartolomeu do Mar mark the end of their *romaria (22–24 Aug)* by dipping their children in the sea, as a mock sacrifice to the waves.

STICK DANCING

Stick dancers, or *pauliteiros*, can still be seen at village festival in Trás-os-Montes. The dances are of ancient origin, probably associated with fertility rites, and the sticks may once have been swords. The most famous troupe comes from the village of Duas Igrejas, near Miranda do Douro *(see p262)*.

Dancers performing at a *festa*

Outlandish costumes and masks donned for the Dia dos Rapazes

CHRISTMAS AND WINTER

On Christmas Eve, families gather to enjoy enormous quantities of *bacalhau* (salt cod) and mulled port, and to exchange presents, before attending midnight mass.

Between Christmas and Epiphany, Trás-os-Montes village boys dress in crazy, fringed suits to take part in the rite-of-passage **Dia dos Rapazes**.

The Christmas season ends on **Dia de Reis** *(6 Jan)*, when the *bolo rei*, or "king cake", rich with crystallized fruit "jewels", is eaten *(see p33)*.

...ical giants leading an Assumption Day parade in Peso da Régua

The Story of Port

The "discovery" of port dates from the 17th century when British merchants added brandy to the wine of the northern Douro region to prevent it souring in transit. They found that the stronger and sweeter the wine, the better flavour it acquired. Methods of maturing and blending continue to be refined by the main port producers. Croft was one of the first big shippers, followed by other English and Scottish firms. Despite the consolidation of the global drinks industry, much of the port trade is still in British hands, and some firms are still family-run.

Barco rabelo ferrying port down the Douro river

THE PORT REGION

Port comes only from a demarcated region of the upper Douro valley, stretching 100 km (62 miles) to the Spanish border. Régua and Pinhão are the main centres of production, but most top-quality vineyards lie on estates or *quintas* in the harsh eastern terrain.

STYLES OF PORT

There are essentially two categories of port: red and wood-aged. The former are deeper in colour and will develop after bottling; the latter, which include tawney ports, are ready to drink when they are bottled. White port is in a category of its own.

Vintage, *the star of any shipper's range, is made from wines of a single year, from the best vineyards. It is blended and bottled after two years in wood, and may then mature for a very long time in the bottle.*

Vintage

Late Bottled Vintage (LBV) *is wine of a single ye bottled between f and six years aft the harvest. Filter LBV does not requ decanting but may have less flavo than unfiltered, "traditional" LBV*

LBV

Aged tawny *port is blended from top-quality wines that have been aged in wood for a long time. The age on the label is not precise, but the older it is, the paler, more delicate, less fruity and more expensive the port is likely to be.*

Aged Tawny

Tawny *port without ind ation of age may not hat been in woo for long enough to develop the co plex flavours of aged tawny; its st is light and its price fairly low. It m be a blend of red and white ports*

Tawny

Ruby port *is deep red and should be full of lively fruit flavour. It has been aged for two or three years, sometimes in wood, sometimes not. It is less complex than either LBV or Vintage, but costs considerably less.*

Ruby

White port *is made from white grapes and may sweet or not so sweet. It is main drunk chilled as an aperitif. Some types of white p have a slightly lower alcohol cont than the normal 20% for port.*

White

lecting grapes in tall wicker baskets for transport to the wineries

OW PORT IS MADE

e climax of the Douro farmers' year comes in late Septem-
r when bands of pickers congregate to harvest the grapes.

More than 40 varieties are used for
making port, but there are five
recommended top varieties.

ading the grapes *in stone
ks or* lagares *to extract the
e is a feature of very tradi-
al quintas. Some shippers
eve it adds a special quality.*

Fermentation *in cement or
steel tanks is a more common
method. Carbon dioxide builds
up within the tank, forcing the
fermenting must (juice from
the grapes) up a tube into an
open trough at the top. The gas
is released and the must sprays
back over the pips and skins, in
a process similar to treading.*

In the fortification *process,
the semi-fermented must is run
into a second vat where brandy
– actually grape spirit – is
added. This arrests the fermentation, leaving the wine sweet
from natural grape sugar.*

usands of bottles *of
ham's vintage port from
7 await full maturation in
cellars of the Vila Nova de
a lodge.*

Quality tawny port *is
matured in oak casks in the
port lodges. Once bottled, it is
ready for drinking and does
not require decanting.*

VINTAGE PORT

In the interests of
maintaining the
highest standards of
quality – and of not
saturating the market
– port producers do not
"declare" a vintage every year.
Each year, the wine from the
best vineyards is closely moni-
tored for 18 months, other
producers are consulted about
their quality, and then a decision is taken. If a vintage is
not declared, the wine may
remain in wood to be blended
as tawny or LBV in future, or
it may be bottled as a "single
quinta" port – a kind of
second-label vintage. On
average, producers declare
a vintage three times in a
decade, though not always
in the same years.

A good vintage needs time in
bottle to reveal itself. Fifteen
years is seen as a minimum,
although many impatient
drinkers do not actually wait
that long; there is even a fashion for drinking young vintage
port. The nature of vintage
port's aging process results
in a continuously evolving
list of great vintages. Most
experts agree, however, that
no vintage has yet equalled
that produced in 1963.

Pre-war vintages
1927, 1931, 1935.
All great and now very rare.

Post-war vintages
1945, 1947, 1948, 1955:
For the very rich and
extremely lucky.
1963 Perhaps the greatest
post-war vintage.
1994 A fine vintage,
particularly
from producers
Dow, Taylor
and Quinta
do Noval.
1997 Another fine
vintage.
2000 A very pro-
mising year.
2003 A superb
vintage with
attractive ripe
fruit flavours.

Taylor's 1994 vintage

The Flavours of Northern Portugal

There is a smoky flavour to the rustic food of the north. This seems to come not only from the area's wealth of cured, often smoked, pork products (frequently used to add spice to other dishes), but from the woodsmoke-scented air of the quiet valleys of the interior, too. The cuisine consists of rich stews and thick soups, beans, chestnuts and cabbage, and crusty maize bread. The prized pig does service in everything from the pale, lightly cured hams of Amarante to clove- and cumin-spiced *morcela* (blood sausage). Local beef is renowned, and *cabrito* (kid) is a favourite in roasts and stews.

Maize bread (cornbread)

Sheets of salt cod drying in the sun and coastal breezes

MINHO

Northernmost Portugal is a landscape of dense greenery, punctuated with granite and traversed by rivers. Trout, eel and lamprey all still feature prominently on local menus, even if the trout nowadays is mostly farmed and the lamprey often imported. The Minho region is also home to *caldo verde*, the best-known of Portugal's soups. It is made with *couve galega*, the tall-growing, open-leafed kale typical of the Minho. The Portuguese love affair with *bacalhau*, dried salted cod, is as ardent here as it is anywhere in the country, despite the availability of fresh fish throughout the region. Try it *com broa* – baked with a crust of the rich maize bread *(broa de milbao)*, another speciality of the north.

DOURO AND TRÁS-OS-MONTES

These are meatier regions, famed for their *embutidos* or *enchidos* (cured pork products). Vila Real is a centre for the production of spiced, salted, sometimes marinated and smoked meats and sausages, but each area makes its own, often on a small scale. *Presunto* (cured ham) from Chaves, traditionally covered

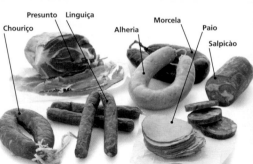

Presunto   Linguiça

Chouriço   Alheria   Morcela   Paio

Salpicào

Some of the cured and smoked pork produce of Northern Portugal

REGIONAL DISHES AND SPECIALITIES

Portuguese cabbage

Caldo verde is by far the best-known dish from the north, and its simple composition and strong flavours, though sometimes diluted by too much potato, are representative of the northern style of cooking. Combinations of fish and meat, in particular cured pork, are another feature, as in *lampreia à moda do Minho* (lamprey cooked in white wine with *chouriço*), *trutas com presunto* (trout with cured ham) and *bacalhau à Transmontana* (salt cod with pork belly). *Cozido* is a pan-Portuguese dish whose origins are thought to be in the north or across the border in Spain. It is a stew of beef, vegetables and sausages, including *morcela*. Traditionally, the meat and vegetables are served separately, with rice and beans respectively, and the stock is served on the side.

Caldo Verde *is a hearty soup of cale or cabbage with spicy* chouriço *sausage. The colour is as vibrant as the flavour.*

Weekly regional market at Barcelos in the Minho

in paprika powder after salting and drying, has a long-standing reputation as among the country's best. Serra do Barroso, the mountainous area bordering the Minho, gives its name to the Barrosã breed of cow, made tasty by grazing the high pastures of this wet area.

EXTREME CLIMATES

The rows of vines that line the slopes of the upper Douro valley, neatly tracing its contours, give this once remote region a tamed appearance that belies its extremes of climate. Cold winters, slow warming in spring, and blistering-hot summers bring out the best in the thick-skinned grape varieties that go into making port. On the valley's northern side are the olive groves and orchards of

the Terra Quente, the "hot lands" of the lower Trás-os-Montes region. Interestingly, the olive oils from here are prized for their mildness of flavour. Farther north, beyond Bragança, lie the drier and colder high plains of the Terra Fria, where some

The shop window of a Porto *pastelaria* (pastry shop)

inhabitants still spend the winter indoors, warmed by their animals and living off their stocks of chestnuts, cabbages and cured meats.

PORTO

Modern cooking is largely confined to Porto, where some of the country's most innovative chefs work, but the city also retains culinary traditions such as cooking tripe, which has earned its citizens the nickname *tripeiros* – tripe-eaters. It is also famed for its egg-based pastries.

REGIONAL WINES

Vinho verde, the familiar light white and slightly fizzy wine from the Minho, has made something of a comeback after a period of neglect by producers as well as consumers. Its appeal lies in its acidity (the "crispness" and "freshness" of wine writing), its carbon dioxide sparkle and its relatively low alcohol content – around 10 per cent. There is also a fuller-bodied, more complex style, made from the Alvarinho grape in and around the town of Monção. The red version of *vinho verde* is rarely found outside the region. Port wine (*see pp230–31*) is the other highlight among northern Portuguese drinks, but modern wines from the Douro also merit serious attention. They match the regional cuisine admirably, and their distinctive character includes rare wine flavours such as violets and heather.

Trutas con presunto *wraps fat river trout in lean cured ham before they are fried in bacon fat until golden.*

Cozido à Portuguesa *is a winter stew of beef, sausage and root vegetables, suited to the cold northern plains.*

Toucinho do céu *translates as "heavenly bacon" but is actually a rich and mouth-watering almond cake.*

DOURO AND TRÁS-OS-MONTES

O*n its way to the Atlantic, the Douro or "Golden River" weaves its scenic path through deep-cleft gorges, terraced with thousands of vineyards, to the historic city of Oporto, home of port. To the northeast, the high plateaus and mountain ranges of Trás-os-Montes, "Behind the Mountains", form Portugal's wildest region.*

As early as the 9th century BC, Phoenician merchants arrived in the Douro estuary to trade. The Romans later developed the settlements of Portus and Cale on either side of the river, and the names subsequently united, as Portucale, to denote the region between the Minho and Douro rivers. This was the nucleus of the kingdom of Portugal *(see pp42–3)*. The estuary and coastal strip, or Douro Litoral, is now a mix of fishing ports, beach resorts and industrial zones, while Portus, at the river's mouth, became Oporto, the regional capital and Portugal's second city.

Rich from centuries of trade, cosmopolitan Oporto is at once modern and steeped in the past, its waterfront and higgledy-piggledy streets a delight to explore. From its hillside, Oporto looks across the Douro to the lodges which nurture the precious wine to which the city gave its name: port.

The upper reaches of the river are devoted to the cultivation of grapes for port, the landscape shaped by endless vineyards and wine estates *(quintas)*.

In contrast with the thriving Douro valley, Trás-os-Montes is remote and untamed, a refuge in the past of religious and political exiles. The hard life and lack of opportunity to better it have depopulated the land; those who remain till the fields and herd their flocks in the unforgiving climate, according to the rhythm of the seasons.

The rural north clings closely to tradition and local *festas* are some of the country's most colourful *(see pp228–9)*. Outside influences are beginning to make an impact on Trás-os-Montes, but for the visitor it remains a land of quiet stone villages amid fields of rye and moorland, where the wild Parque Natural de Montesinho stretches from Bragança to the Spanish border.

Terraced vineyards covering the hillsides between Pinhão and Alijó, in the valley of the Upper Douro

◁ Oporto's Barredo district, where houses are squeezed into the steep maze of ancient alleys

Exploring the Douro and Trás-os-Montes

Oporto itself is so full of interest that many visitors venture no further. But to follow the Douro upstream is to discover a world of neat terraced vineyards and prosperous *quintas* all dedicated to producing wine and port. Oporto apart, either Peso da Régua or the pilgrimage town of Lamego would make a convenient base from which to explore the area.

Trás-os-Montes is Portugal's poorest and least-known region. Its isolated capital, Bragança, is full of historic associations, and lies on the edge of the wild terrain of the Montesinho reserve. Between here and Chaves is spectacular country seldom visited by tourists.

Rocky outcrops of the Parque Natural do Alvão

SIGHTS AT A GLANCE

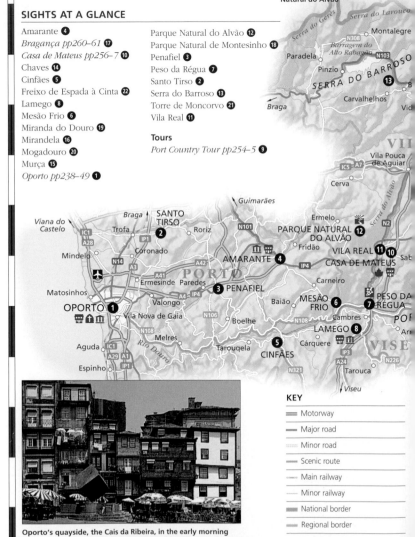

Oporto's quayside, the Cais da Ribeira, in the early morning

KEY

▬▬	Motorway
▬▬	Major road
▭▭	Minor road
▬▬	Scenic route
▬▬	Main railway
▬▬	Minor railway
▬▬	National border
▬▬	Regional border

Port country near Pinhão, where vineyards clothe the banks of the Douro

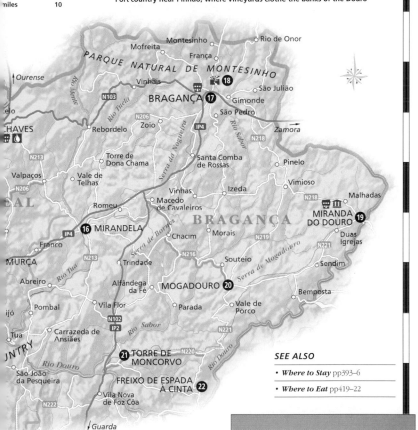

kilometres 25

miles 10

PARQUE NATURAL DE MONTESINHO

Ourense

Montesinho
Mofreita
França
Rio de Onor
Vinhais
São Julião
BRAGANÇA **17**
18
Gimonde
São Pedro

CHAVES

N103

N206
Rebordelo
Zoio
IP4
Rio Sabor
Zamora
N218

N213

Torre de
Dona Chama
Santa Comba
de Rossas
Pinelo

Valpaços
Vale de
Telhas
Vinhas
Izeda
Vimioso

N206

Romeu
Macedo
de Cavaleiros
BRAGANÇA
N218
Malhadas

MIRANDA
DO DOURO **19**

IP4 **16** MIRANDELA
Morais
Duas
Igrejas

Franco
Chacim
N219
N221

MURÇA
N213
Trindade
Souteio
Sendim

Abreiro
Alfândega
da Fé
MOGADOURO **20**
Bemposta

ijó
Pombal
Vila Flor
Parada
Vale de
Porco

Tua
Carrazeda de
Ansiães
N102
IP2
Rio Sabor
N221

UNTRY
Rio Douro
21 TORRE DE
N220
MONCORVO

São João
da Pesqueira
FREIXO DE ESPADA
À CINTA **22**

N222
Vila Nova
de Foz Côa

Guarda

SEE ALSO

- **Where to Stay** pp393–6
- **Where to Eat** pp419–22

GETTING AROUND

With the frenetic tempo of traffic in Oporto, it is best to negotiate the inner city by bus, taxi or on foot. Boat trips from Oporto are a good way to see the varied Douro landscape at a relaxed pace. Trains link Oporto to the major towns of the north and also run along the Douro valley. Services are less frequent beyond Peso da Régua, but a trip alongside the Douro is highly recommended. In Trás-os-Montes, public transport is minimal and driving is the most convenient way to explore this remote region, especially now the IP4 (E82) links Vila Real and Bragança. However, the state of repair of many minor roads leaves a lot to be desired.

The Sabor near Bragança, on the southern edge of the Parque Natural de Montesinho

Oporto ❶

Ever since the Romans built a fort here, where their trading route crossed the Douro, Oporto has prospered from commerce. Quick to expel the Moors in the 11th century and to profit from provisioning crusaders en route to the Holy Land, Oporto took advantage of the wealth generated by Portugal's maritime discoveries in the 15th and 16th centuries. Later, the wine trade with Britain compensated for the loss of the lucrative spice trade. Still a thriving industrial centre and Portugal's second-largest city, Oporto, known locally as Porto, blends industry with charm. In 2001 the city, the historic centre of which is a UNESCO World Heritage site, was the European Capital of Culture.

Lion and eagle statue, Rotunda da Boavista

The cathedral (Sé) and statue of Vimara Peres *(see p42)*

The Cathedral District

Oporto's cathedral *(see p242)* crowns the city's upper level and in the surrounding streets are a variety of monuments to the city's past, including the

Washing hanging out to dry in a typical street in the Ribeira district

Renaissance church of Santa Clara *(see p241)* and the turn-of-the-century railway station of São Bento *(see p241)*, alongside bustling street markets.

Beneath the towering cathedral lies the crowded Barredo, a quarter seemingly unchanged since medieval days, where balconied houses cling to each other and to the vertiginous hillside, forming a maze of ancient alleys; some are no more than outside staircases.

Ribeira

This riverside quarter is a warren of narrow, twisting streets and shadowy arcades. Behind brightly tiled or pastel-painted façades, many in faded glory, a working population earns its living, hangs out the washing, chats and mixes in lively street scenes. Restoration of this atmospheric district is attracting a growing number of restaurants and nightclubs.

Cordoaria

The Cordoaria gardens lie in the lee of the hilltop landmark of the Torre dos Clérigos *(see p243)*. Nearby streets are full of interesting shops.

A shop specializing in *Bacalhau* (dried salted cod)

Looking north up the Avenida dos Aliados to the Câmara Municipal

VISITORS' CHECKLIST

Map C2. 🏛 245,000. ✈
*Francisco Sá Carneiro, Pedras
Rubras 20 km (12 miles) N (229
432 400).* 🚉 *National & Inter-
national: Campanhã; Regional: São
Bento (808 208 208).* 🚌 *Praceta
Régulo Megoanha; Rua Alexandre
Herculano; Rua da Restauraçao;
Praça da Galiza; Campo 24 de
Agosto; Praça General H. Delgado.*
🛈 *Rua Clube dos Fenianos 25
(223 393 472); Rua Infante Dom
Henrique 63 (222 060 412).*
🎭 *2nd half of Jun: Festas da
Cidade.* www.portoturismo.pt

concentration of the city's
banks and offices, and
thriving outdoor cafés.
To the east, the Baixa
or "lower level" district
attracts shoppers, especially
to the fashionable jewellery
and leather shops in
and around the
pedestrianized
Rua de

Boavista

Avenida da Boavista is lined
with hotels, homes and shops.
In the centre of the Rotunda da
Boavista, as Praça de Mouzinho
de Albuquerque is known
locally, a statue of a lion (the
Luso-British forces) crushing
an eagle (the French) marks
the victory in the Peninsular
War. South of here is some of
the best shopping in the city.

OPORTO CITY CENTRE

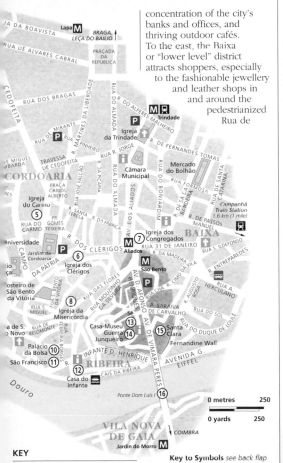

KEY

■ Cathedral District pp240–1

Key to Symbols *see back flap*

Central and Baixa

The civic centre of Oporto
ranges along the Avenida dos
Aliados, leading up to the
modern Câmara Municipal, or
town hall. Along this broad
double avenue is a high

Santa Catarina and the parallel
Rua Sá da Bandeira. Between
them lies the two-tier covered
Bolhão market. Exuberant and
noisy, it provides an entertaining view of Oporto daily life.
Everything can be bought here,
from fresh fruit and vegetables
to household goods and pets.

**Fresh fruit and vegetables in the
colourful Bolhão market**

Street-by-Street: Oporto's Cathedral District

Archaeological excavations show that
Penaventosa Hill, now the site of
Oporto's cathedral, or Sé, was inhabited
as early as 3,000 years ago. In its elevated
position, the cathedral is a useful landmark
and its terrace provides an excellent orientation point. The broad Avenida de Vímara
Peres, named after the military hero who
expelled the Moors from the city in AD 868,
sweeps south past the huddle of steep alleys
and stairways of the Barredo. The view
to the north is towards the extraordinarily
embellished São Bento station and the busy
commercial heart of the city.

Rua das Flores
*Behind the traditional shop-
fronts in the Street of Flowers
are many of the city's best
jewellers and goldsmiths.*

A semi-covered market
near the Sé offer fresh
fish, fruit and vegetables
alongside household
goods, bric-a-brac
and souvenirs.

Terreiro da Sé
*This broad open terrace offers a
wonderful panorama of the city.
In one corner stands a Manueline
pillory, complete with hooks.*

RUA ESCURA

CALÇADA DE VANDOMA

TERREIRO
DA SÉ

RUA DE DOM HUGO

★ Sé
*Although imposing and perhaps a little
forbidding, Oporto's cathedral contains
many small-scale treasures. This 17th-
century gilded painting of the Last Supper
is in the Capela de São Vicente (see p242).*

**Former
bishops'
palace**

**The Casa-Museu Guerra
Junqueiro** is a charming museum
in a house that once belonged to
the 19th-century poet *(see p242).*

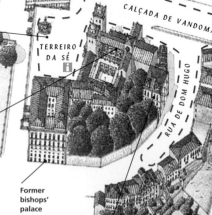

**Ponte de
Dom Luís I**

Praça da Liberdade

Praça de Almeida Garrett
Traffic hurries by oblivious to the architectural diversity of this busy square in the centre of Oporto.

PRAÇA DE ALMEIDA GARRETT

RUA DO LOUREIRO

A DOM AFONSO HENRIQUES

RUA CHÃ

RUA SARAIVA DE CARVALHO

★ São Bento Station
Oporto's central railway station, on the site of an earlier monastery, was completed in 1916. Inside is a feast of azulejos by Jorge Colaço (see p27), depicting early modes of transport, rural festivities and historic scenes.

The Fernandine Wall, named after Fernando I, was built in the 14th century; only fragments here and along the Cais da Ribeira *(see p238)* remain.

Santa Clara
The Mannerist church of Santa Clara presents a strong contrast between its simple external façade and the opulent gilded woodwork of its interior.

0 metres 50
0 yards 50

KEY

– – – Suggested route

STAR SIGHTS

★ Sé

★ São Bento Station

Exploring Oporto

Throughout Oporto there is evidence of the wealth that flowed into the city from the 15th century onwards. Trade in the commodities from Portugal's newly claimed lands *(see pp48–9)* brought Brazilian gold and exotic woods to embellish Oporto's churches, and prosperous merchants spent prodigiously on paintings and *azulejos*. Recently the city authorities restored footpaths, cobbled streets and stone steps to create five historical walks between the Jardim do Palácio de Cristal and the river.

The magnificently gilded Arabian Room in Oporto's Palácio da Bolsa

🔒 Sé

Terreiro da Sé. *Tel 222 059 028.*
⭕ *9am–12:30pm & 2:30–6pm daily (Apr–Oct: to 7pm).* ✝ *9am, 11am.*
Cloisters ⭕ *9am–12:30pm & 2:30–5pm daily (only pm Sun); Apr–Oct: 9am–12:15pm & 2:30–6pm daily (only pm Sun).* 📷

Built as a fortress church in the 12th and 13th centuries, the cathedral has been modified several times. The beautiful rose window in the west front is from the 13th century. The small chapel to the left of the chancel has a dazzling silver retable, saved from invading French troops in 1809 by a hastily raised plaster wall. The south transept gives access to the 14th-century cloisters and the Capela de São Vicente. An 18th-century staircase leads to the upper levels, where *azulejo* panels depict the life of the Virgin and Ovid's *Metamorphoses*.

Portuguese water jug, Museu Guerra Junqueiro

The Gothic cloisters on the south side of the Sé

🏛 Casa-Museu Guerra Junqueiro

Rua de Dom Hugo 32. *Tel 222 003 689.* ⭕ *10am–12:30pm & 2–5:30pm Tue–Sun.* ⚫ *public hols.* 📷

The former home of the poet and fiery Republican activist Guerra Junqueiro (1850–1923) is an 18th-century Baroque gem. The poet's private collection ranges from rare ceramics and Portuguese furniture to Flemish tapestries and a remarkable set of English alabaster sculptures. In the Dom João V Room there is a colourful parade of Chinese dogs.

🏺 Casa do Infante

Rua da Alfândega 10. *Tel 222 060 400.* ⭕ *10am–noon & 2–5pm Tue–Sun.* ⚫ *public hols.* 🎫 *compulsory; book ahead.* ♿

Legend has it that Prince Henry the Navigator was born in this house on Oporto's riverfront. Today the building houses Oporto's city archives, which include historical documents, among them Prince Henry's christening certificate, photographs and archaeological finds.

🏺 Palácio da Bolsa

Rua Ferreira Borges. *Tel 223 399 000.* ⭕ *Apr–Oct: 9am–7pm daily; Nov–Mar: 9am–1pm & 2–6pm daily.* ⚫ *1 Jan, 25 Dec.* 📷 🎫 *compulsory*

Where the monastery of São Francisco once stood, the city's merchants built the stock exchange, or Bolsa, in 1842. The Tribunal do Comércio, where

Oporto's mercantile law was upheld, is full of historic interest, and has a small adjoining picture gallery. The glittering highlight is the Arabian Room. This galleried salon, its convoluted blue and gold arabesques inspired by Granada's Alhambra, makes a setting fit for Scheherazade.

🏛 Museu dos Transportes e Comunicações

Rua Nova da Alfândega, Edifico da Alfândega. *Tel 223 403 000.* ⭕ *10am–6pm Tue–Fri, 3–7pm Sat & Sun.* ⚫ *public hols.* 📷 ♿ www.amtc.pt

Housed in a vast Neo-Classical building on the riverfront, this museum includes a permanent exhibition on the automobile and interactive exhibitions on media, science, new technologies and art. The building also houses a restaurant, various spaces for cultural events and the customs service.

🔒 Igreja da Misericórdia

Rua das Flores 15. *Tel 222 074 710.* ⚫ *for restoration.* 📷

This religious hospice, alongside its imposing church, was founded in the 1500s. Its most precious possession is the *Fons Vitae* (Fountain of Life), donated by Manuel I in about 1520. It shows the king and his family kneeling before the crucified Christ. The artist's identity remains unproven, but both Van der Weyden and Holbein have been suggested.

SÃO FRANCISCO'S TREE OF JESSE

Illustrating biblical episodes, either in stained-glass windows or as elaborate carvings, was a common form of "Bible teaching" before literacy became widespread. A popular subject was Christ's genealogy, showing his descent from the kings of Judah and Israel. This was commonly rendered as an actual tree, tracing the family line back through Joseph to the father of King David, Jesse of Bethlehem.

São Francisco's Tree, in gilded and painted wood, was carved between 1718 and 1721 by Filipe da Silva and António Gomes. Its sinuous branches and trunk, sprouting from a reclining Jesse, support a dozen expressive figures, culminating in Christ flanked by His mother, Mary, and St Joseph.

Virgin Mary

Jesus Christ

Joseph

Solomon, who succeeded his father, David, was famed for his wisdom and for the building of the Temple in Jerusalem.

Jesse is shown with the roots of the Tree springing from his loins. His youngest son was David, the slayer of Goliath, who became king of Israel and Judah.

King David, identified by his harp

🏛 São Francisco

Rua do Infante D Henrique. *Tel 222 062 100.* 🕐 9am–7pm daily (Jul–Sep: to 8pm; Nov–Feb: to 5:30pm). 🚫 25 Dec. 📷 🎫 Catacombs incl.

This Gothic church was begun in the 1300s, but it is the 18th-century Baroque interior that amazes visitors. Over 200 kg (450 lb) of gold encrusts the high altar, columns and pillars, wrought into cherubs and garlands, culminating with the Tree of Jesse on the north wall. A tour includes the catacombs and treasures from the church's monastery, destroyed in 1832.

🏛 Igreja dos Congregados

Rua da Sá da Bandeira 11. *Tel 222 002 948.* 🕐 7am–7pm Mon–Sat, 7am–1pm & 6–8pm Sun. 🚫 public hols.

The modern tiles on the façade of this 17th-century church are by Jorge Colaço (*see p27*). They depict scenes from the life of St Antony, and provide a dignified presence amid the traffic that clogs this part of the city.

🏛 Igreja dos Clérigos

Rua São Filipe de Nery. *Tel 222 001 729.* 🕐 daily. 🕐 at lunchtime. **Tower** 🕐 daily. 📷

This unmistakable hilltop landmark was built in the 18th century by Niccolò Nasoni.

The soaring Torre dos Clérigos with which the architect complemented his design is, at 75 m (246 ft), still one of the tallest buildings in Portugal. The dizzying 240-step climb is worth it for the superb views of the river, the coastline and the Douro valley.

Torre dos Clérigos, Oporto's landmark and panoramic viewpoint

São Francisco's extravagant interior

Detail of the *azulejo* panel on the side wall of the Igreja do Carmo

🔒 Igreja do Carmo

Praça Carlos Alberto 32. *Tel 222
078 400.* ◯ *8am–noon & 2–5pm
Mon–Fri, 8am–noon Sat, 8am–1pm
Sun.* 👤

This typical example of Portuguese Baroque architecture
was built by José Figueiredo
Seixas between 1750 and 1768.
The immense *azulejo* panel
covering one outside wall, designed by Silvestro Silvestri,
depicts the legendary founding of the Carmelite order.

The older Igreja das Carmelitas
next door was completed
in 1628 in a combination of
Classical and Baroque styles.
It is now part of a barracks.

🏛 Museu Soares dos Reis

Rua Dom Manuel II. *Tel 223 393 770.*
◯ *10am–6pm Tue–Sun (from 2pm
Tue).* ⬤ *public hols.* 📷
The elegant Carrancas Palace,
built in the 18th century, has
been a Jewish textile workshop, a royal abode and a

military headquarters. In 1809
Oporto was in French hands,
and Marshal Soult and his
troops were quartered here.
They were ousted in a surprise
attack by Arthur Wellesley,
later Duke of Wellington, who
then calmly installed himself
at the marshal's dinner table.

Today, the palace provides
an appropriate setting for an
outstanding museum, named
after António Soares dos Reis,
the country's leading 19th-
century sculptor. Pride of place
goes to the display of Portuguese art. This includes
paintings by the 16th-
century master, Frey
Carlos, and the
Impressionist,
Henrique Pousão.
Also hung here
are landscapes of
Oporto by the
French artist, Jean
Pillement (1728–
1808). The star
sculpture exhibit,
O Desterrado (The
Exile), is Soares
dos Reis's own
marvel of pensive
tension in marble,
completed in
1874. Further
sections display

*O Desterrado ▶
Soares dos Re...*

A River View of Oporto

Flowing over 927 km (576 miles) from
its source in Spain to the Atlantic, the
Douro has been linked with the fortunes
of Oporto since time immemorial. There
is an unsubstantiated story that Henry the
Navigator, patron of Portuguese explorers,
(see p49), was born in the waterfront
Casa do Infante. The days are long since
gone when ships laden with port or goods
from overseas would moor here, but the
river continues to be a focal point of the
city. A river cruise is a chance to appreciate Oporto from a different viewpoint.

Most river-boat operators are based in
the shadow of the swooping curve of the
splendid two-tier Ponte de Dom Luís I,
built in 1886 by an assistant of Gustave
Eiffel, to link the city to Vila Nova de
Gaia on the southern bank. The city
recently inaugurated a largely above
ground metro system, which uses the
upper level of the Dom Luís I bridge.
Just upriver, the new Infante Dom
Henrique bridge is for cars.

Vila Nova de Gaia
is home of the port
lodges *(see p249).*

**Ponte da
Arrábida**

**Quayside
of the Cais
da Estiva**

Portuguese pottery, Limoges enamels, porcelain and decorative art. Historical exhibits in the museum include an appealing 15th-century silver bust of São Pantaleão, patron saint of Oporto, and a sword which was once owned by the first king of Portugal.

🔒 Igreja de São Martinho de Cedofeita

Largo do Priorado. **Tel** *222 005 620.* ☐ *phone to check.* ♿

Constructed in Romanesque style in the 12th century, this plain little church is thought to be the oldest in the city. It is said to have been built on the site where Theodomir, the King of the Suevi (a Germanic tribe who occupied the area), was converted to Christianity in the 6th century by Saint Martin.

🏛 Museu Romântico

Rua de Entre-Quintas 220. **Tel** *226 057 033.* ☐ *10am–12:30pm & 2– 5:30pm Tue–Sun.* ● *public hols.* 📷
Solar do Vinho do Porto Tel *226 094 749.* ☐ *4pm–midnight Mon– Sat.* ● *public hols.*

The Quinta da Macieirinha was briefly the residence of the abdicated King Carlo Alberto of Sardinia (1798–1849), who lived here for the final two

Temporary exhibits in the billiards room of the Museu Romântico

months of his life. In 1972 the upper floor of the mansion was converted into a museum. The well-proportioned rooms looking out over the river display French, German and Portuguese furniture, as well as rugs, ceramics and miscellaneous exhibits. Among the oil paintings and watercolours on show here are portraits of Baron Forrester *(see p254)* and Almeida Garrett, the great Portuguese Romantic poet, playwright and author.

On the ground floor of the Quinta, the Port Wine Institute operates the Solar do Vinho do Porto. In this bar it

is possible to choose from a tasting list of over 150 varieties of port, then relax in the secluded garden and enjoy the view across the Douro.

🍃 Jardim do Palácio de Cristal

Rua Dom Manuel II. ☐ *8am–9pm daily (Oct–Mar: to 7pm).*
Inspired by the Crystal Palace of London's Great Exhibition in 1851, Oporto's own crystal palace was begun in 1861. The steel and glass structure of the original was replaced in the 1950s by the Pavilhão Rosa Mota, an ungainly shape dubbed "the half-orange". Concerts are occasionally held here and the leisure gardens are enlivened by a fair at *festa* time.

Cyclists in the Jardim do Palácio de Cristal

Cais da Ribeira is one of the quays at which river boats moor.

Former bishops' palace

Torre dos Clérigos *(see p243)*

Sé *(see p242)*

Ponte de Dom Luis I

Oporto: Further Afield

A way from the city centre, Oporto has many additional places of interest. Crossing the Ponte de Dom Luís I brings you to Vila Nova de Gaia, the home of port, and the Mosteiro da Serra do Pilar, with one of the finest views of the old city. In the northern and western suburbs are several fascinating attractions, from the great church of the Hospitallers at Leça do Bailio, north of Oporto, to the latest developments in Portuguese art exhibited in the beautifully modern setting of the Museu Serralves.

Along the coast, beyond the river-mouth castle at Foz do Douro, lies Matosinhos which, despite its industrial port, is renowned for its seafood.

The beaches, such as Espinho, are the main draw along the coast south of Oporto.

A tram, once such a feature of Oporto, in the Museu do Carro Eléctrico

🔒 Mosteiro da Serra do Pilar
Serra do Pilar. **Tel** 223 795 385.
◯ Jun–Sep (cloisters by appt only).
From the terrace of this circular 16th-century church, the future Duke of Wellington planned his surprise attack on the French in 1809. The view takes in the port lodges below, the sweep of the River Douro and the old city on the far side.

⛁ Museu do Carro Eléctrico
Alameda Basilio Teles 51. **Tel** 226 158 185. ◯ Tue–Sun (only pm Sat & Sun). 🖼
Among the trams on show here is No. 22, introduced in 1895 as the first electric tram on the Iberian Peninsula. A ride on No. 18, Oporto's last tram, takes a scenic route along the river to Rua Infante Dom Henrique and back.

⛁ Casa da Música
Avenida da Boavista. **Tel** 220 120 220. 📷 11am & 3:30pm Mon–Fri (Eng/Port); 10:30am & 4pm Sat & Sun (Eng/Port); also 3pm (Port). **www**.casadamusica.com
The Casa da Musíca is a venue for all types of music, from classical to fado, from electronica to jazz. It also promotes research into the origins of Portuguese music.

⛁ Fundação de Serralves Museu de Arte Contemporânea
Rua Dom João de Castro 210. **Tel** 226 156 500 or 808 200 543 (toll free). ◯ 10am–7pm Tue–Sun (Apr–Sep: to 8pm). ● 1 Jan, 25 Dec. 🖼 ♿ **www**.serralves.pt
Portugal's main institution for contemporary art is responsible for both the Art Deco Casa de Serralves and the Museu de Arte Contemporânea. Housed in a long, white building, the museum has a permanent collection including works by Christian Boltanski, Bruce Nauman and Julião Sarmento.

⛁ Casa-Museu Fernando de Castro
Rua Costa Cabral 716. ◯ by appt (223 393 770). **Tel** 225 094 625. 🖼
The former residence of poet, businessman and collector Fernando de Castro (1888–1950) houses his collection, which ranges from religious sculpture to works of modern art. Among the highlights are a painting of the infant Jesus attributed to Josefa de Óbidos (see p51) and figurines from the 19th and 20th centuries by Teixeira Lopes, father and son.

Environs: Forts around the river mouth, such as **Castelo da Foz** at Foz do Douro and **Castelo do Queijo** just to the north, are reminders that for centuries the coast and ships were under constant threat from the Spanish and pirates.

The church of **Bom Jesus**, near Matosinhos, was reconstructed by Niccolò Nasoni in the 18th century. Each June, pilgrims come here to honour a wooden statue of Christ allegedly carved by the disciple Nicodemus.

The 14th-century fortified **Igreja do Mosteiro** at Leça do Bailio, 8 km (5 miles) north of Oporto, was Portugal's first headquarters of the Order of Hospitallers. The church has elegant Gothic arches and a splendid rose window.

The Art Deco Casa de Serralves

◁ **Barcos rabelos** moored beside the quary at Vila Nova de Gaia

Vila Nova de Gaia

Afonso III, in dispute with the Bishop of Oporto over shipping tolls, established a rival port at Vila Nova de Gaia. In 1253, they reluctantly agreed to share the levies. Today the heart of Vila Nova de Gaia is devoted mostly to the maturation and shipping of port *(see pp254–5)*. Although the

Taylor's port regulation that port could be made only in Vila Nova de Gaia was relaxed in 1987, this is still very much the centre of production. Every alley is lined with the lodges or *armazéns* (there are no cellars here) in which port is blended and aged.

Guided tours *are a chance to see how port is made (see pp230–31) and often end with a tasting to demonstrate the different styles.*

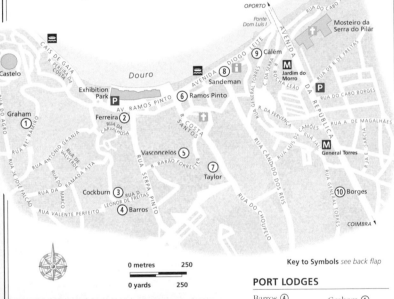

Key to Symbols *see back flap*

PORT LODGES

Barros ④
Borges ⑩
Cálem ⑨
Cockburn ③
Ferreira ②

Graham ①
Ramos Pinto ⑥
Sandeman ⑧
Taylor ⑦
Vasconcelos ⑤

VISITING THE LODGES

Joining a tour: Lodges listed here are among those offering tours. Booking is not usually necessary, but contact a lodge beforehand to confirm times; the tourist office at Avenida Diogo Leite 242 (223 773 080) can supply addresses and telephone numbers.
Opening times: Variable. Usually Mon–Fri; some also at weekends. Most close on public holidays.

The port lodges *dominate Vila Nova de Gaia. Over 50 port companies are based in these narrow streets, ageing and blending most of the world's supply of port beneath a sea of red roofs emblazoned with world-famous names.*

The former monastery of São Bento at Santo Tirso, now a college

Santo Tirso ❷

Road map C2. 🏠 *13,900.* 🚊 🚌
ℹ️ *Praça 25 de Abril (252 830 411).*
🗓️ *Mon.*

Santo Tirso, a major textile centre, lies beside the River Ave. The town's most notable building is the former monastery of **São Bento**. Founded by the Benedictines in the 8th century, the monastery was later rebuilt, then modified in the 17th century. The pairs of columns in the 14th-century Gothic cloister are graced with richly carved capitals.

The monastery, now an agricultural college, also houses the **Museu Abade Pedrosa**, featuring local archaeological finds, including stone axes, bronze armlets and ceramics.

🏛️ Museu Abade Pedrosa
Rua Unisco Godiniz 100. *Tel 252 830 400.* ⭕ *Tue–Sun.* ⬤ *public hols.*

The sanctuary of Nossa Senhora da Piedade in Penafiel

Environs: At Roriz, 13 km (8 miles) east of Santo Tirso, the Romanesque church of **São Pedro** perches above the Vizela valley. A date of 1228 is carved in the porch, although there are claims that a church may have stood here as early as the 8th century. Above the portal is a fine rose window. Set apart from the church are an attractive belltower and the ruins of the monastic cloister.

Sanfins de Ferreira, 5 km (3 miles) further east, is the hilltop site of a *citânia*, an Iron Age citadel, probably inhabited from around the 6th century BC. Traces remain of a triple ring of defensive walls around about 100 huts, and there is also a small museum on the site. The guard next door will let you in on public holidays.

🏛️ Sanfins de Ferreira
Sanfins, signposted off N209.
Tel 255 862 029. ⭕ *Tue–Sun.*

Penafiel ❸

Road map C2. 🏠 *8,000.* 🚌
ℹ️ *Rua do Passo (255 712 561).*
🗓️ *10 & 20 of month.*

The granite town of Penafiel stands on a hilltop above the River Sousa. Apart from an elegant Renaissance-style **Igreja Matriz**, there is also a sanctuary, **Nossa Senhora da Piedade**, built in 1908 in a curious medley of Neo-Gothic and Byzantine styles. Penafiel is chiefly known, however, as the regional centre for *vinho verde* production.

Environs: One of the region's foremost estates producing *vinho verde* is **Quinta da Aveleda**, just north of Penafiel.

Boelhe, around 17 km (11 miles) south of Penafiel, merits a detour for the 12th-century church of São Gens. Only 10 m (33 ft) high, and a mere 7 m (23 ft) in width and length, it is claimed to be the smallest Romanesque church in the country. Its simple design enhances the aesthetic appeal.

In the 13th-century church of São Salvador at **Paço de Sousa**, 8 km (5 miles) southwest of Penafiel, is the tomb of Egas Moniz. A figure of legendary loyalty, he was counsellor to Afonso Henriques (1139–85), the first king of Portugal.

🍷 Quinta da Aveleda
Signposted from N115. *Tel 255 718 200.* ⭕ *Mon–Fri.* ⬤ *public hols.* 🎦 ♿ 📷 *compulsory.*

The tiny church of São Gens at Boelhe, south of Penafiel

Amarante ❹

Road map D2. 🏠 *70,000.* 🚊 🚌
ℹ️ *Alameda Teixeira de Pascoães (255 420 246).* 🗓️ *Wed & Sat.*

The pretty, riverside town of Amarante is one of the gems of northern Portugal. Rows of 17th-century mansions with brightly painted wooden balconies line Amarante's narrow streets, and restaurants seat diners on terraces overhanging the river. The origins of the town are uncertain but the first settlement here was probably around 360 BC. Much of the town was burnt down in 1809, after a two-week siege by the French forces under Marshal Soult.

A recurring name in Amarante is that of São Gonçalo, a very popular saint born at the end of the 12th century. There are many stories of the dancing and festivities he organized to keep ladies from temptation by finding them husbands, and he has become associated with matchmaking and fertility. On the first weekend in June, the Festa de São Gonçalo begins with prayers for a marriage partner, followed by dancing, music and the giving of phallic-shaped São Gonçalo cakes.

When the old Roman bridge across the Tâmega collapsed during floods in the 13th century, it was São Gonçalo who was credited with replacing it. The present Ponte de São Gonçalo crosses to the 16th-century **Igreja de São Gonçalo**, where his memory lives on. In the chapel to the left of the chancel, the image on his tomb has been eroded through the embraces of thousands of devotees in search of his intercession.

The **Museu Amadeo de Sousa-Cardoso** is housed in the old monastery cloister next to the church. One of the exhibits describes a fertility cult that predates even São Gonçalo. The *diabo* and *diaba* are a pair of bawdy devils carved in black wood, and are 19th-century replacements for a more ancient duo destroyed in

The Ponte de São Gonçalo across the Tâmega at Amarante

the Peninsular War. They gradually became the focus of a type of local fertility rite, and were threatened with burning by an outraged bishop of Braga; the *diabo* was "castrated" instead.

The museum's other prized possession is the collection of Cubist works by the artist after whom the museum is named. Amadeo de Sousa-Cardoso (1887–1918), one of Portugal's leading 20th-century artists, was a native of Amarante.

⌂ Igreja de São Gonçalo
Praça da República.
Tel 255 422 050. ☐ daily.

🏛 Museu Amadeo de Sousa-Cardoso
Alameda Teixeira de Pascoães.
Tel 255 420 272. ☐ Tue–Sun.
⬤ public hols. 🔷

Cinfães ❺

Road map D2. 🏠 4,000. 🚌
ℹ Rua Dr Flávio Resende 43 (255 560 571). ⬤ 10 & 26 of month.

Cinfães lies just above the Douro, tucked below the foothills of the Serra de Montemuro whose peaks rise over 1,000 m (3,300 ft). The town is a gateway to Lamego and the Upper Douro to the east *(see pp254–5)* and is surrounded by verdant scenery. Cinfães itself is an agricultural centre and local handicrafts include weaving, lacework, basketry, and the production of miniature *rabelos*, the boats that used to ship port down the river to Oporto *(see p252)*.

Environs: Around 16 km (10 miles) west of the town, at Tarouquela, is the 12th-century church of **Santa Maria Maior**. Romanesque columns flank the portal, while later additions include the 14th-century Gothic mausoleum beside the chancel.

In the village of **Cárquere**, between Cinfães and Lamego, stands another church dedicated to the Virgin Mary. Legend tells how the sickly young Afonso Henriques, future king of Portugal, was healed at Cárquere by his devoted aide, Egas Moniz. In about 1110, guided by a dream, Moniz unearthed a buried statue of the Virgin and built a church for her. Miraculously, his young charge was cured overnight. The present church dates from the 14th or 15th century, but the finest of its treasures is a minute ivory carving of the Virgin, of unknown date.

The 12th-century church of Nossa Senhora de Cárquere, near Cinfães

Painted ceiling panels in São Nicolau, Mesão Frio's Igreja Matriz

Mesão Frio ⑥

Road map D2. 4,900. ⓘ Avenida Conselheiro José Maria Alpoim (933 911 043). Fri.

This scenic gateway to the port wine-growing region enjoys a fine setting above the River Douro. Around it, the majestic tiers of the Serra do Marão rise to form a natural climatic shield for the vineyards to the east. Mesão Frio itself is known for its wickerwork and a culinary speciality, *falachas* or chestnut cakes.

The Igreja Matriz of **São Nicolau** was rebuilt in 1877, but has fortunately retained its magnificent late 16th-century ceiling panels, each one featuring an individual portrait of a saint. The tourist office and town hall are housed in the 18th-century **cloisters** of a former Franciscan monastery.

On the western edge of the town, the lavish Baroque **Casa da Rede** can be seen from the roadside, but not visited.

Peso da Régua ⑦

Road map D2. 21,000. ⓘ Rua da Ferreirinha (254 312 846). Wed & Sat.

Developed from the villages of Peso and Régua in the 18th century, Peso da Régua is the major hub for rail and road connections in the region.

In 1756, Régua, as the town is invariably called, was chosen by the Marquês de Pombal as the centre of the demarcated region for port production. From here, *rabelos*, the traditional wooden sailing ships, transported the barrels of port through hazardous gorges to Vila Nova de Gaia (*see p249*). They continued to ply the river even after the advent of the Douro railway in the 1880s. Régua suffered frequently in the past from severe floods, and these are still a threat, although they have lessened since dams were built across the Douro in the 1970s and 1980s.

Visitors to Régua usually pause only briefly on their way to explore the "port country" (*see pp254–5*), but it is worth seeking out the **Casa do Douro**, the administrative headquarters of the Port Wine Institute. Its modern stained-glass windows, created by Lino António, vividly depict the history and production of port. Also of interest is the **Museu do Douro**, which portrays the region's rich heritage through paintings, writings and other forms of local culture.

 Casa do Douro
Rua dos Camilos. **Tel** 254 320 811. ◯ by appt. ⬤ public hols.

Museu do Douro
Rua Marquês de Pombal. **Tel** 254 310 190. ◯ by appt. ⬤ public hols.

Environs: In the surrounding countryside are some beautiful *quintas*, country estates where port is produced. The **Quinta da Pacheca** is at Cambres, 4 km (2 miles) to the south-west. Dating from the 18th century, this well-known winery produces reds and whites, in addition to port. Visitors can tour the cellars.

Quinta da Pacheca
Apt 3, 5051 Régua. **Tel** 254 313 228.

Stained-glass window of the Casa do Douro, Peso da Régua, showing loaded *rabelos*

Lamego ⑧

Road map D2. 11,000. ⓘ Avenida Visconde Guedes Teixeira (254 612 005). Thu.

An attractive town within the demarcated port area, Lamego also produces wines, including Raposeira, Portugal's premier sparkling wine. This fertile region is also known for its fruit and choice hams.

In its more illustrious past, Lamego claims to have been host in 1143 to the first *cortes*, or national assembly, to recognize Afonso Henriques as first king of Portugal. The town's later economic decline was halted in the 16th century, when it turned to wine and textile production, and handsome Baroque mansions from this prosperous period are still a feature of the town. Today, the main focus of Lamego is as a pilgrimage town.

Vineyards on the slopes of the Serra do Marão around Mesão Frio

For hotels and restaurants in this region see pp393–6 and pp419–22

The grand staircase leading up to Nossa Senhora dos Remédios, Lamego

🏛 Nossa Senhora dos Remédios

Monte de Santo Estêvão. ☐ *daily.*
A small hilltop chapel, originally dedicated in 1391 to St Stephen, became the focus of pilgrims devoted to the Virgin, and in 1761 Nossa Senhora dos Remédios was built on the spectacular site. The church is reached via an awe-inspiring double stairway, similar to Braga's even larger Bom Jesus *(see pp280–81).* Its 686 steps and nine terraces, embellished with *azulejos* and urns, rise to the Pátio dos Reis, a circle of noble granite figures beneath the twin-towered church. The church itself is of marginal interest, but there is a well-earned view across the town to the Douro and its tributaries.

In early September pilgrims arrive in their thousands for Lamego's Romaria de Nossa Senhora dos Remédios *(see p32),* many of them climbing the steps on their knees.

🏛 Sé

Largo da Sé. **Tel** *254 612 766.*
☐ *daily.*
Lamego's Gothic cathedral, founded in 1129, retains its original square tower, while the rest of the architecture reflects modifications between the 16th and 18th centuries, including a Renaissance cloister with a dozen arches.

🏛 Museu de Lamego

Largo de Camões. **Tel** *254 600 238.*
☐ *Tue–Sun.* ☐ *public hols.* 🈺
One of the country's best local museums is housed in the former bishops' palace. Pride of place goes to the strikingly original *Criação dos Animais*

(Creation of the Animals), part of a series of masterly altar panels attributed to the great 16th-century Portuguese artist, Grão Vasco *(see p215).* Finely worked 16th-century Flemish tapestries include a vividly detailed life of Oedipus.

Environs: At the foot of the valley 4 km (2 miles) east, the **Capela de São Pedro de Balsemão** is said to be the oldest church in Portugal. Although much modified, the 7th-century sanctuary, of Visigothic origins, remains. Here, in an ornate tomb, lies Afonso Pires, a 14th-century bishop of Oporto. A statue of Nossa Senhora do Ó, the pregnant Virgin, is from the 15th century.

The 12th-century monastery of **São João de Tarouca,** the first Cistercian house in Portugal, lies 16 km (10 miles) south of Lamego. The interior of the church has many fine 18th-century *azulejo* panels, notably those in the chancel depicting the founding of the monastery, and in the sacristy, where none of the 4,709 tiles has the same design. The church also contains a remarkable *St Peter* by Grão Vasco. The Count of Barcelos, bastard son of King Dinis, is buried here, his tomb adorned with vigorous scenes of a boar hunt.

Just to the northeast, **Ucanha** is famed for its fortified tollgate and bridge, imposing survivals from the 12th century.

🏛 São João de Tarouca

Signposted from N226. **Tel** *254 678 766.* ☐ *Tue–Sun.* ♿

The monastery church of São João de Tarouca in its peaceful setting

Port Country Tour ❾

The barrels of port maturing in the port lodges of Vila Nova de Gaia *(see p249)* begin their life here, on the wine estates *(quintas)* of the Upper Douro *(see pp230–31)*. Centuries of toil on the poor schist have created thousands of terraces along the steep river banks, many no wider than a person's outstretched arms. Many vineyards have had their terraces widened to allow tractor access, but some of the oldest ones are protected as part of the cultural heritage. Many *quintas*, including those shown on the map, welcome visitors. Early autumn is the most rewarding time to tour; workers sing as they pick, and celebrate a good *vindima* or harvest.

Bottles of Graham's port

The village and vineyards of Vale de Mendiz just before sunset

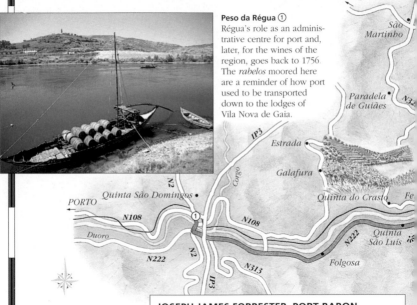

Peso da Régua ①
Régua's role as an administrative centre for port and, later, for the wines of the region, goes back to 1756. The *rabelos* moored here are a reminder of how port used to be transported down to the lodges of Vila Nova de Gaia.

VILA REAL
São Martinho
Paradela de Guiães
Estrada
Galafura
Quinta São Domingos
PORTO
Quinta do Crasto
Fe
Quinta São Luís
Folgosa
Duoro
N108
N108
N2
N222
N313
IP3
Corgo

0 kilometres   5
0 miles   3

KEY
▬ Tour route
= Other roads
— Railway
⚜ Viewpoint

JOSEPH JAMES FORRESTER, PORT BARON
In 1831, Joseph Forrester arrived from Britain to join his uncle's wine company in Oporto, and enthusiastically set about reforming the port trade. In his 1844 treatise, *A Word or Two on Port*, he waged war on shippers who adulterated the wine. He also studied the vine blight, *Oidium tuckeri*, drew up remarkably detailed maps of the Douro valley and found time to become a talented watercolourist. His contribution was such that in 1855 Pedro V bestowed on him the title of Barão. In 1862, Forrester's boat capsized at Cachão de Valeira. Dragged down by his moneybelt, he drowned, but the ladies in his company survived, buoyed up by their crinolines.

Pinhão ②

Many of the most famous names in port production have *quintas* close to this small town. Its railway station is decorated with 24 dazzling *azulejo* panels depicting local scenes and folk culture.

TIPS FOR DRIVERS

Tour length: *125 km (78 miles). Beyond Pinhão, steep, narrow roads can make the going slow.* **Stopping-off points:** *The drive beside the Douro has several fine viewpoints. Alijó, Régua and Sabrosa make good overnight stops (see pp393–5) and many quintas offer tours and port-tasting (see also pp460–61).*

Sabrosa ③

The village of Sabrosa, set among vineyards above the River Pinhão, has a wealth of 15th-century houses. It was in one of these that the explorer Magellan *(see p48)* was born in about 1480.

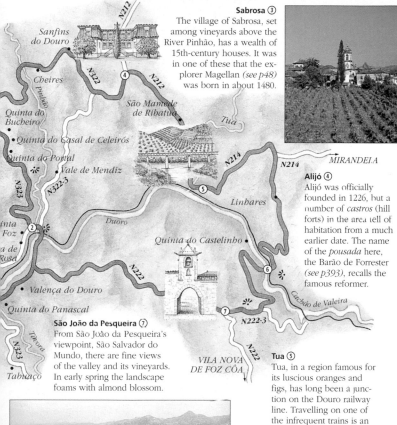

Sanfins do Douro

Cheires

Quinta do Bucheiro

Quinta do Casal de Celeirós

Quinta do Portal

Vale de Mendiz

São Mamede de Ribatua

Tua

MIRANDELA

N214

Linbares

Duoro

Quinta Foz

a de Rosa

Quinta do Castelinho

Valença do Douro

Quinta do Panascal

Cachão de Valeira

Alijó ④

Alijó was officially founded in 1226, but a number of *castros* (hill forts) in the area tell of habitation from a much earlier date. The name of the *pousada* here, the Barão de Forrester *(see p393)*, recalls the famous reformer.

São João da Pesqueira ⑦

From São João da Pesqueira's viewpoint, São Salvador do Mundo, there are fine views of the valley and its vineyards. In early spring the landscape foams with almond blossom.

Tabuaço

VILA NOVA DE FOZ CÔA

Tua ⑤

Tua, in a region famous for its luscious oranges and figs, has long been a junction on the Douro railway line. Travelling on one of the infrequent trains is an enjoyable way of seeing the valley's terraced vineyards.

Barragem de Valeira ⑥

Until the end of the 18th century the Douro was unnavigable beyond Cachão de Valeira. Even when engineers had bypassed the worst of the rapids, this stretch of water remained treacherous – it was here that Baron Forrester met his death – until the water was tamed by the Valeira dam in 1976.

Casa de Mateus ⑩

The splendid manor house, or *solar*, depicted on the labels of Mateus Rosé *(see p28)* epitomizes the flamboyance of Baroque architecture in Portugal. It was built in the early 18th century, probably by Niccolò Nasoni, for António José Botelho Mourão, whose descendants still live here. The house, which was declared a national monument in 1911, is also a breeding ground for creativity, offering 11 six-month residencies to budding artists.

English 17th-century cupboard in the Tea Salon

The wood-panelled library, repository of many valuable works

The Manor House

Inside and out, the Casa de Mateus was conceived to present carefully created vistas and series of mirror images. A formal pool added in the 1930s continues this spirit of harmonious repetition, reflecting the main façade and its two wings.

Tours start in the first-floor entrance salon, a well-proportioned room graced by a pair of sedan chairs and with a magnificent wooden ceiling featuring family coats of arms. Doorcases and ceilings throughout the house are of richly carved chestnut. The Tea Salon has a 17th-century William and Mary cupboard and

Coat of arms on the entrance hall ceiling

matching longcase clock from England, while the Salon of the Four Seasons gets its name from the large 18th-century paintings on its walls. Many of the paintings in the house were contributed by the 4th Morgado's uncle, an archdeacon in Rome who was also responsible for the original gardens. The library, remodelled in the mid-20th century, contains volumes dating back to the 16th century, but the rarest book is in the small museum: an 1817 copy of *Os Lusíadas* *(see p190)*, with engravings by leading artists. It is one of a

limited edition produced by the colourful diplomat grandson of the 3rd Morgado (his tomb is in the family chapel beside the house). Also on display in the museum is family correspondence with famous figures of the era, including Frederick the Great and Wellington.

The Gardens

Beneath the entrance staircase a dark passageway leads between the stables to an inner courtyard and out to the formal gardens on the far side of the house. Little remains of the original gardens planted by the horticultural archdeacon, and the present gardens were laid out in the 1930s and 1940s. The style, however, is of an earlier, romantic era and the complex parterres and formal beds edged with tightly clipped dwarf box hedges form a living tapestry which

The principal façade of the Casa de Mateus, its pinnacled symmetry reflected in a rectangular pool

For hotels and restaurants in this region see pp393–6 and pp419–22

**Immaculate box-edged flower beds
in the Casa de Mateus gardens**

reflects perfectly the ornate
symmetry of the house. In
winter the grand old camellias,
relics from the 19th century,
are a highlight of the gardens,
but for most visitors the lasting
memory is of the vast cedar
tunnel, greatest among the
many pieces of topiary here.

Beyond the formal gardens
lie the well-ordered orchards
and fields of the estate.

THE CEDAR TUNNEL

This celebrated feature in
the Casa de Mateus garden
was formed from cedars
planted in 1941. It is 35 m
(115 ft) long and 7.5 m
(25 ft) high, the tight-knit
greenery providing an aromatic walk in summer. To
keep it in shape, gardeners
have to scale specially
fashioned outsize ladders.

Vila Real ⓫

Road map D2. ☗ 20,000. ☐ ☐
☐ Avenida Carvalho Araújo 94 (259
322 819). ☐ Tue & Fri.

Perched over a gorge cut by
the confluence of the Cabril
and Corgo rivers, Vila Real is
a busy commercial centre. As
the communications hub of
the Upper Douro, it makes a
convenient starting point from
which to explore the valley of
the Douro to the south and the
Parque Natural do Alvão to the
northwest. Vila Real also has
a motor-racing circuit, which
hosts major events each year
during June and July.

Midway along the broad
main street, Avenida Carvalho
Araújo, is the 15th-century
Sé. This fine Gothic cathedral
was originally the church of
a Dominican friary. The other
monastic buildings burnt down
in suspicious circumstances in
the mid-19th century.

At the southern end of the
avenue, a plaque on the wall at
No. 19 marks the birthplace of
Diogo Cão, the explorer who
discovered the mouth of the
Congo in 1482 *(see pp48–9)*.

The **Igreja dos Clérigos**, in
nearby Rua dos Combatentes
da Grande Guerra, is also
known as Capela Nova. It
presents a pleasing Baroque
façade attributed to Niccolò
Nasoni and an interior of fine
blue and white *azulejos*.

Environs: The small village of
Bisalhães, 6 km (4 miles) to
the west, is famed for its
boldly designed black pottery
(see p25). Examples can be

seen displayed for sale at the
annual Festa de São Pedro,
celebrated in Vila Real each
year on 28–9 June. Also seen
at this time is the fine linen
from nearby Agarez.

Parque Natural do Alvão ⓬

Road map D1. ☐ to Ermelo via
Campeã. ☐ Lago dos Freitas, Parque
Natural do Alvão (259 302 830).

The scenic Parque Natural do Alvão

Within the 72 sq km (28 sq
miles) of the nature re-
serve between the Corgo and
Tâmega rivers, the scenery
ranges from verdant, cultivated
lowlands to bleak heights that
reach 1,339 m (4,393 ft) at
Alto das Caravelas. Despite
hunters and habitat encroach-
ment, hawks, dippers and
otters can still be spotted. Between the picturesque hamlets
of **Ermelo** and **Lamas de Olo**,
where maize is still kept in
espigueiros (see p273), the Olo
drops in a spectacular cascade,
the **Fisgas de Ermelo**. From
Alto do Velão, just southwest
of the park, are splendid views
west over the Tâmega valley.

Vila Real seen across the deep gorge of the Corgo and Cabril rivers

A farmer and his grazing ox near Carvalhelhos, Serra do Barroso

Serra do Barroso ⑬

Road map D1. 🚌 *to Montalegre or Boticas.* 🛈 *Praça do Município, Montalegre (276 511 010).* **www**.rt-atb.pt

Just southeast of the Parque Nacional da Peneda-Gerês *(see pp272–3)* is the wild and remote Serra do Barroso. The landscape of heathery hillsides is split by the immense Barragem do Alto Rabagão, the largest of many reservoirs in the area created by the damming of rivers for hydroelectric power. Water is a mainstay of the local economy: a high rainfall enables farmers to eke out an existence on the poor soil, and the artificial lakes attract fishing and watersports enthusiasts. The source of one of the country's most popular bottled mineral waters is at **Carvalhelhos**.

The village of **Boticas** nearby produces a beverage with a more original claim to fame. In 1809, the locals buried their wine rather than have it fall into the hands of the invading French. When the enemy departed, the wine was retrieved and found to have improved. The bottles were colloquially termed *mortos* ("dead"), hence the name of the wine – *vinho dos mortos*. The practice continues and bottles are usually buried for up to two years.

The area's principal town is **Montalegre**, on a plateau to the north. Its most notable feature is the imposing keep, 27 m (88 ft) high, of the ruined 14th-century castle.

Oxen are bred in the Serra, and inter-village *chegas dos bois* (ox fights) are a popular pastime. The contest is usually decided within half an hour, when the weaker ox takes to its heels.

Chaves ⑭

Road map D1. 🏰 *18,000.* 🚌 🛈 *Terreiro da Cavalaria (276 340 661).* 🗓 *Wed.* **www**.rt-atb.pt

Beside the upper reaches of the Tâmega stands historic Chaves, attractively sited in the middle of a fertile plain.

Thermal springs and nearby gold deposits encouraged the Romans to establish Aquae Flaviae here in AD 78. Its strategic position led to successive invasion and occupation by the Suevi, Visigoths and Moors, before the Portuguese gained final possession in 1160. The name Chaves ("keys") is often associated with the keys of the north awarded to Nuno Álvares Pereira, hero of Aljubarrota *(see p185)*. A likelier but more pedestrian explanation is that Chaves is simply a corruption of the Latin "Flaviae".

Today Chaves is renowned for its spa and historic centre, and for its smoked hams. A curiosity of the north, the distinctive black pottery *(see p25)*, is made in nearby Nantes.

The old town focuses on the Praça de Camões. The 14th-century **keep** overlooking this pleasant medieval square is all that remains of the castle given to Nuno Álvares Pereira by João I. On the south side of the square stands the **Igreja Matriz** with its fine Romanesque portal. The Baroque

Tiled and gilded Misericórdia church at Chaves

Misericórdia church opposite has an exquisite interior lined with 18th-century *azulejos*. Attributed to Policarpo de Oliveira Bernardes *(see p26)*, the huge panels depict scenes from the New Testament.

The 14th-century keep of Chaves castle, set in formal gardens

🏛 Museu Militar and Museu da Região Flaviense
Praça de Camões. *Tel 276 340 500.* ◯ *daily.* ⬤ *public hols.* 🎟 *joint ticket.*

Within the castle keep is a small military museum, where suits of armour, uniforms and associated regalia are on display. Also exhibited are military memorabilia from the city's defence against the attack by Royalists from Spain in 1912. In the flower-filled garden surrounding the keep are a few archaeological finds from Chaves's long history, but most are to be found in the Museu da Região Flaviense behind the keep. Here, in the Paço dos Duques de Bragança, are displayed a variety of local archaeological discoveries. Items of interest include souvenirs of the Roman occupation, such as milestones and coins, alongside an oxcart and a straw mantle of the type worn by shepherds for protection in the rain or the hot sun.

🏛 Ponte Romana

The 16-arch Roman bridge across the Tâmega was completed around AD 100, at the time of the Emperor Trajan. Its construction brought added importance to Chaves as a staging post on the route between Braga and Astorga (in northwestern Spain). On the bridge are Roman milestones which record that funds to build it were raised locally.

🏛 Thermal springs

Largo Tito Flávio Vespasiano.
Tel 276 332 445. ☐ daily. 🚻
A few minutes on foot from the city centre is one of the hottest springs in Europe. Water here bubbles up at a temperature of 73°C (163°F) and the spa's facilities attract both holiday-makers and patients seeking treatment *(see p211)*. Chaves water is recommended for the treatment of ailments as diverse as rheumatism, kidney dysfunction and hypertension.

The huge cleft Pedra Bolideira near Chaves

Environs: Close to the village of Soutelo, 4 km (2 miles) northwest of Chaves (the route is signposted), is the strange **Outeiro Machado Boulder.** It measures 50 m (165 ft) in length and is covered with mysterious hieroglyphs and symbols of unknown meaning. These may be Celtic in origin.

Another gigantic boulder, the **Pedra Bolideira**, lies near Bolideira, 16 km (10 miles) east of Chaves. Split in two, the massive larger section balances lightly, needing only a gentle push to rock it to and fro.

The spa town of **Vidago**, 17 km (11 miles) southwest of Chaves, is well known for its therapeutic water. The Vidago Palace Hotel *(see p396),* once the haunt of royalty, has been renovated but retains the regal charm of its park, lakes and pump room.

Murça's Misericórdia chapel, with its vine-embellished pillars

Murça ⓱

Road map D2. 🏘 7,000. 🚌
🛈 Alameda do Paço (259 510 120).
📅 13 & 28 of month.

The market town of Murça is famed for its honey, goat's cheese and sausage. Its major attraction, and the focal point of the garden in the main square, is its **porca**, an Iron Age granite pig with a substantial girth of 2.8 m (9 ft) *(see p40)*. The role of *berroes*, as beasts such as these are called, is enigmatic, but they may have been linked to fertility cults. Smaller versions survive in Bragança, Chaves and elsewhere. In more recent times the Murça *porca* has been pressed into service at elections, when the winning political parties would paint her in their colours.

The **Misericórdia** chapel on the main street is notable for its early Baroque façade, attractively ornamented with designs of vines and grapes.

Mirandela ⓰

Road map D1. 🏘 11,000. 🚉 🚌
🛈 Rua D Afonso III (278 203 143).
📅 Thu.

Mirandela, at the end of the Tua narrow-gauge railway line, has pretty gardens running down to the River Tua and an elegant Roman bridge with 20 asymmetrical arches. Built for the deployment of troops and to aid the transport of ore from local mines, it was rebuilt in the 16th century and is now for pedestrians only.

Displayed in the **Museu Municipal Armindo Teixeira Lopes** are sculpture, prints and paintings, including views of Lisbon and Mirandela by the local 20th-century artist after whom the museum is named.

The 17th-century **town hall** once belonged to the Távoras, but the family was accused of attempted regicide in 1759 and all trace of them was erased.

🏛 Museu Municipal Armindo Teixeira Lopes
Rua Coronel Sarmento Pimentel.
Tel 278 201 590. ☐ Mon–Fri;
Sat pm. ● public hols.

Environs: In a pretty valley 15 km (9 miles) northeast of Mirandela lies **Romeu.** Its **Museu das Curiosidades,** as the name implies, is a hotch-potch of exhibits from the turn of the century onwards. The collection of the local Menéres family, it includes Model-T Fords, musical boxes and early photographic equipment. Next door is the famed Maria Rita restaurant *(see p422).*

🏛 Museu das Curiosidades
Jerusalém do Romeu. **Tel** 278 939 134. ☐ Tue–Sun. ● pub hols. 🎫

The River Tua at Mirandela, with its Roman bridge and waterside parks

Bragança: the Citadel ⑰

This strategic hilltop was the site of
a succession of forts before Fernão
Mendes, brother-in-law to King Afonso
Henriques, built a walled citadel here in
1130. Like several predecessors, it was
named Brigantia. Within the walls still
stand Sancho I's castle, built in 1187, with
its watchtowers and dungeons, and the
pentagonal 12th-century Domus Municipalis beside the church of Santa Maria.

The town gave its name to Portugal's
final royal dynasty, descended from an
illegitimate son of João I who was created
first Duke of Bragança in 1442 *(see p301).*

Bragança's walled citadel
on its isolated hilltop

Porta da Traiçã

The Museu Militar in the robust Gothic
keep includes memorabilia from the
Africa campaigns (1895) of a local
regiment. The keep is 33 m
(108 ft) high.

The medieval pillory
has the appearance of
skewering a hapless
porca, an ancient
stone pig *(see
p40),* to the
pedestal.

★ **Castle**
*The castle's Torre da
Princesa, scene of many
tragic tales, was refuge
to Dona Sancha, un-
happy wife of Fernão
Mendes, and prison to
other mistreated wives.*

Porta
da Vila

RUA DOM FERNÃO O BRAVO

To town

Porta
de Santo
António

Santa Maria
*The church's elaborately
carved portal dates from
its 18th-century restoration.*

★ **Domus Municipalis**
*This, the only surviving
example of Romanesque
civic architecture in
Portugal, served as a
hall where the* homens
boms *("good men")
settled disputes. Below
was the town's cistern.*

STAR SIGHTS

★ Castle

★ Domus Municipalis

KEY

– – – Suggested route

0 metres   50

0 yards   50

Porta do Sol

Museu Abade de Baçal gardens, where archaeological finds are displayed

Houses within the Citadel
*Bragança had outgrown the
citadel by the 15th century,
but streets of small houses
still cluster within the walls.*

Beyond the Citadel

By the 15th century, Bragança
had expanded west along the
banks of the River Fervença.
The Jewish quarter in Rua dos
Fornos survives from this era,
when Jews from North Africa
and Spain settled here and
founded the silk industry.

Despite its royal links, the
town never overcame its isolation, the Bragança monarchs
preferring Vila Viçosa *(see
pp300–301)*. Only now are
the investments of returning
emigrants and the completion
of the Oporto-Spain motorway reviving trade. A cathedral "for the millennium" was
inaugurated in 1996, another
indicator of the city's rebirth.
Near the modest old cathedral in the town centre is a
lively covered market where
delicacies such as smoked
hams and *alheiras* (chicken
sausages) are sold.

🏛 Museu Abade de Baçal

Rua Abílio Beça 27. *Tel 273 331
595.* ◯ *Tue–Sun.* ⬤ *public hols.*
📷 *(free 10am–2pm Sun).*

The Abbot of Baçal (1865–
1947) was a prodigious scholar
whose definitive researches
into the region's history and
customs, including its Jewish
connections, were published
in 11 volumes. Bragança's
museum is named after him.
Highlights among the paintings are *The Martyrdom of St
Ignatius*, an unsigned triptych
of the 16th century, and watercolours by Aurélia de Sousa
(1865–1922), including *A
Sombra* (In the Shade). In
another section are colourful
pauliteiros costumes *(see p229)*
and instruments of torture.

In the garden are a variety
of archaeological discoveries
including *porcas* and tablets
with Luso-Roman inscriptions.

🔰 São Bento

Rua de São Francisco. *Tel 273 325
876.* ◯ *by appt.* ♿
Founded in 1590 by Bishop
António Pinheiro, São Bento
has two startlingly contrasting
ceilings: a splendid canopy of
Moorish-influenced geometric
carving in the chancel, and a
richly coloured 18th-century
trompe l'oeil over the nave.

🔰 São Vicente

Largo do Principal. ◯ *variable hours.*
The secret wedding between
Inês de Castro and Dom Pedro
is reputed to have taken place
here in 1354 *(see p181)*. The
original 13th-century church
was reconstructed in the 17th
century with the addition of a
great deal of sumptuous gilt-
work. The *azulejo* panel to the
right of the main door depicts
General Sepúlveda exhorting
the citizens of Bragança to
free themselves from French
occupation in 1809.

Street in the old Jewish quarter,
sloping steeply down to the river

The sparsely inhabited landscape of the Parque Natural de Montesinho

Parque Natural de Montesinho ⓲

Road map E1. 🚌 to Rio de Onor & Vinhais. ℹ️ Bairro Salvador Nunes Teixeira 5, Bragança (273 300 400).

One of the wildest areas in Europe, the reserve covers 70,000 ha (175,000 acres) between Bragança and the border with Spain. The region, understandably, is known as Terra Fria (Cold Land). Bleak mountains rise to 1,481 m (4,859 ft) above heather and broom, descending to oak forests and valleys of alder and willow.

Spectacular views of the park can be enjoyed from **Vinhais**, on its southern fringe, and the wilderness attracts walkers and riders – mountain bikes and horses can be hired locally.

The population clusters in farming communities on the lowlands, leaving much of the Serra an undisturbed habitat for rare species such as wolves and golden eagles, as well as boars, otters and falcons.

Little changed from medieval times, villages such as **França** and **Montesinho** are typical

in their stone houses, wooden balconies and cobbled streets. Ancient practices such as herbal cures and reverence for the supernatural linger, and ties are communal rather than national: in **Rio de Onor** Spanish and Portuguese have been welded into a unique dialect, Rionorês.

Farm parlour, Museu da Terra de Miranda

Miranda do Douro ⓳

Road map E1. 🏠 3,000. 🚌 ℹ️ Largo do Menino Jesus da Cartolinha (273 431 132). 🗓️ 1st of month.

This medieval outpost stands on top of the Douro gorge, which here forms an abrupt border with Spain. Its key

position and the establishment of a bishopric here in 1545 paved the way for the town's development into the cultural and religious centre of Trás-os-Montes. But in 1762, during the Seven Years' War against France and Spain, the powder store exploded, claiming 400 lives and destroying the castle (only the keep remains). This mishap, compounded by the transfer of the bishopric to Bragança, led the town into a deep economic decline, only halted by trade links with the coast and Spain.

The lovely twin-towered **Sé** was founded in the 16th century. The graceful wood-carvings of the chancel retable depict, among other themes, the Apostles and the Virgin attended by angels. But the cathedral's most original feature is a wooden figure of the Boy Jesus in the south transept. The Menino Jesus da Cartolinha represents a boy who, legend tells, appeared during a Spanish siege in 1711 to rally the demoralized Portuguese to miraculous victory. Devotees dressed the statue in 17th-century costume and later gave him a top hat (cartolinha).

The excellent **Museu da Terra de Miranda** houses an eclectic display of archaeological finds, folk costume, a reconstruction of a Mirandês farmhouse parlour and curious rural devices such as an inflated pig's-bladder cosh.

🏛️ **Museu da Terra de Miranda**
Largo Dom João III. **Tel** 273 431 164. 🕐 Tue pm & Wed–Sun. 🟢 public hols. 🎫 (free 10am–2pm Sun).

Environs: Just southwest of Miranda, the village of **Duas Igrejas** is famed for its stick dancers, or pauliteiros, who perform at local festivals and overseas (see p229). The tradition is in decline, but for the Festa de Santa Bárbara, on the third Sunday in August, the dancers don their distinctive black and white costumes and are accompanied in their energetic display by drums and gaita de foles (bagpipes).

A distinctive pombal or dovecote still found around Montesinho

THE DOVECOTES OF MONTESINHO

Doves supply not only food, but also droppings, which are highly prized as fertilizer. In this part of Trás-os-Montes the traditional horseshoe-shaped dovecote or pombal is still a familiar sight, although many are now disused. The birds nest in rough cells inside the whitewashed schist walls and enter and leave through gaps in the tile or slate roof. They are fed via a small raised door at the front of the pombal.

The church and town of Mogadouro, viewed from beside the ruins of its 13th-century castle

Mogadouro ⑳

Road map E2. 🏛 *3,000.* 🚌
🛈 *Largo Trindade Coelho (279 340 100).* 🔔 *2 & 16 of month.*

Apart from the hilltop tower, little remains of the great castle founded here by King Dinis and presented to the Templars in 1297. From the top there are fine views over the drowsy little market town known for its handicrafts, particularly leather goods.

Mogadouro's 16th-century **Igreja Matriz** features a 17th-century tower, while lavishly gilded retables from the 18th century decorate the altars.

Torre de Moncorvo ㉑

Road map E2. 🏛 *3,000.* 🚌
🛈 *Travessa Dr Campos Monteiro 21 (279 252 289).* 🔔 *8 & 23 of month.*

Famed for the white mantle of almond blossom that fleetingly covers the valleys in early spring (egg-shaped *amêndoas cobertas*, sugared almonds, are an Easter treat), Moncorvo also offers an atmospheric stroll through its maze of medieval streets. Its name is variously attributed to a local nobleman, Mendo Curvo, or perhaps to his raven *(corvo)*.

The ponderous 16th-century **Igreja Matriz**, the largest in Trás-os-Montes, boasts a 17th-century altarpiece depicting scenes from the life of Christ.

Environs: The fate of the Côa valley, south of Moncorvo, was finally decided in 1996 when plans for a dam were dropped to preserve the world's largest collection of open-air Stone Age rock art. Discovered in 1933 and estimated to be 20,000 years old, it features bulls, horses, fish and a naked man, the Homem de Pisco. Vila Nova de Foz Côa, Castelo Melhor and Muxagata offer several guided tours a day into the Parque Arqueológico do Vale do Côa, and visits must be booked in advance.

🏛 Parque Arqueológico do Vale do Côa
Avenida Gago Coutinho 19a, Vila Nova de Foz Côa. **Tel** *2/9 768 260.* 🔲 *Tue–Sun.* ⬤ *public hols.* 📷 ♿

Rich interior of the Igreja Matriz at Freixo

Freixo de Espada à Cinta ㉒

Road map E2. 🏛 *5,000.* 🚌
🛈 *Avenida do Emigrante (279 653 480).* 🔔 *5 of month.*

Several stories try to explain the curious name of this remote border town. "Ash tree of the girt sword" may derive from the arms of a Spanish nobleman, or a Visigoth called Espadacinta, or from a tale that, when founding the town in the 14th century, King Dinis strapped his sword to an ash.

Dominating the skyline is the heptagonal **Torre do Galo**, a relic from the 14th-century defences. Views from the top are splendid, especially in spring when the almond blossom attracts a great many tourists. The cultivation of silkworms shows a revival of the 18th-century industry.

The intricate 16th-century portal of the **Igreja Matriz** leads into a splendid small-scale version of Belém's Mosteiro dos Jerónimos *(see pp104–5).* Panels of the altarpiece, attributed to Grão Vasco *(see p215),* include a fine *Annunciation*.

⛪ Torre do Galo
Praça Jorge Álvares. 🔲 *daily.* ⬤ *public hols.*

MINHO

Known as the birthplace of the nation, the Minho has two of Portugal's most historic cities: its first capital, Guimarães, and Braga, the country's main religious centre. Life in the province is still firmly rooted in tradition. Agriculture thrives thanks to abundant rainfall that makes this the greenest area in Portugal.

The province of Minho occupies land between the River Douro in the south and the River Minho in the north. Fortified hilltop stone forts *(castros)* remain as evidence of the Neolithic history of the region. When Celtic peoples migrated into the area in the first millennium BC, these sites developed into *citânias* (settlements) such as Briteiros.

During the 2nd century BC, advancing Roman legions conquered the land, introduced vine-growing techniques and constructed a network of roads. Roman milestones are still visible in Peneda-Gerês National Park. When Christianity became the official religion of the Roman empire in the 4th century AD, Braga became an important religious centre, a position it holds to this day. The Suevi swept aside the Romans in the 5th century, followed by the Visigoths, who were ousted in turn by the Moorish invasion of 711. The Minho was won back from the Moors in the 9th century. The region rose to prominence in the 12th century under Afonso Henriques *(see pp42–3)*, who proclaimed himself the first king of Portugal and chose Guimarães as his capital.

The Minho's fertile farms and estates have been handed down within families for centuries, each heir traditionally receiving a share of the land. This custom results in plots of land too small to support their owners, many of whom emigrate in search of work. The economy of the Minho, under pressure from high local unemployment, concentrates on medium-scale industry around Braga and Guimarães. Agriculture in the valleys includes production of the area's distinctive *vinhos verdes* or "green wines". Despite the growth of tourism, the Minho has maintained its strong folk traditions. Carnivals and street markets pervade everyday life and ox-drawn carts are still in use.

Cows being herded across a bridge near the Brejoeira Palace, south of Monção

The sanctuary of Nossa Senhora da Peneda, in the Parque Nacional da Peneda-Gerês

Exploring the Minho

In the south of the Minho lie Braga and Guimarães, the two major cities of the region, both rich in historic sights. From Braga, the Baroque splendour of Bom Jesus or the ruins of Citânia de Briteiros, the country's largest Iron Age site, are within easy reach. Between Braga and the coast lies Barcelos, the ceramics centre of the region, famed for its weekly market. Travelling north, the pretty town of Viana do Castelo is a useful base from which to explore the coast. Turning inland again, the picturesque market town of Ponte de Lima, beside the River Lima, is one of many places in the Minho that provide accommodation in traditional manor houses. In the north of the Minho, the River Minho forms the border with Spain. Along the river, fortified towns offer magnificent views into Spain. To the northeast, walkers and wildlife enthusiasts should not miss the dramatic mountain ranges of the Parque Nacional da Peneda-Gerês.

Foal grazing in the Parque Nacional da Peneda-Gerês

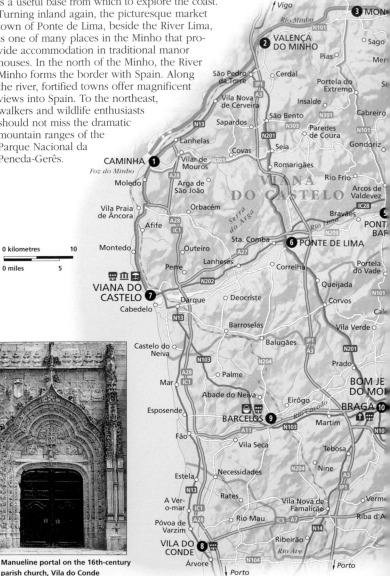

0 kilometres   10

0 miles   5

Manueline portal on the 16th-century parish church, Vila do Conde

SIGHTS AT A GLANCE

Vinho verde **vineyards near Monção**

GETTING AROUND

The road system is efficient, with motorways joining Oporto with Braga, Guimarães, Valença on the Spanish border and Viana do Castelo along the coast. Elsewhere in the region, potholes are a common hazard, and motorists need to allow time for the scenic routes winding through the mountains in the east. Train routes link Oporto to Barcelos and Viana do Castelo, en route to the border with Spain; separate lines run to Guimarães and Braga from Oporto. A bus network provides frequent service to the main towns, but it is reduced for more isolated destinations, especially those in the east.

SEE ALSO

- **Where to Stay** pp396–8
- **Where to Eat** pp422–4

Map labels

Ourense
São Gregório
gaço
N202
so
balhão
Lamas de Mouro
Castro Laboreiro
Rio Trancoso
Senhora da Peneda
Serra da Peneda
PARQUE
NACIONAL
ezio
oajo
N203
re
bos-os-Rios
Lindoso
Portela do Homem
Tourém
Pitões
DA PENEDA-GERÊS
Serra do Gerês
Outeiro
Paradela
ampo do Gerês
Caldas do Gerês
erras do Bouro
Vilar da Veiga
Cabril
Salamonde
N103
Caniçada
Chaves
s Cerdeirinhas
N304
Vieira do Minho
RAGA
Póvoa de Lanhoso
Rossas
Serra do Barroso
Eiró
N205
Arosa
TÂNIA DE RITEIROS
Freitas
CABECEIRAS DE BASTO **14**
N206
das
São Torcato
Moreira de Rei
Baúlhe
Vila Pouca de Aguiar
2 GUIMARÃES
Fafe
IC5 A7
NZ10
N206
Penha
Mondim de Basto
aldas de zeia
N101
Celorico de Basto
Felgueiras
Vila Real
Amarante

KEY

▬▬	Motorway
▬▬	Major road
═══	Minor road
▬▬	Scenic route
▬▬▬	Main railway
▬▬▬	Minor railway
▬▬	National border
▬▬	Regional border

Popular cafés in Praça do Conselheiro Silva Torres, Caminha's attractive main square

Caminha ❶

Road map C1. ⚞ 2,000. 🚉 🚍 🚌
ℹ️ *Rua Ricardo Joaquim de Sousa (258 921 952).* 🛒 *Wed.*

This ancient fortress town perches beside the Minho with fine views across the river to Spain. Occupied in Celtic and Roman times for its strategic position, Caminha developed into a major port until the diversion of its trade to Viana do Castelo in the 16th century. Today it is a small port, with a daily ferry connection to A Guarda in Spain.

On the main square is the 15th-century **Torre do Relógio** clock tower, once a gateway in the medieval defensive walls, and the 17th-century **Paços do Concelho** with its attractive loggia supported by pillars. Cross to the other side of the square, past the Renaissance fountain, to admire the seven Manueline windows on the upper storey of the **Solar dos Pitas** mansion (15th century).

The Rua Ricardo Joaquim de Sousa leads to the Gothic **Igreja Matriz**. Begun in the late 15th century, it has a superb inlaid ceiling of panels carved in Mudéjar (Moorish) style. Renaissance carvings above the side doors depict the Apostles, the Virgin, and several figures in daring poses, including one man with his posterior bared towards Spain.

Environs: Foz do Minho, the mouth of the Minho, lies 5 km (3 miles) southwest of town. From here local fishermen will take groups (by prior arrangement) to the ruined island fortress of **Forte da Ínsua.**

The small walled town of **Vila Nova de Cerveira**, 12 km (7 miles) northeast of Caminha on the road to Valença, has a 16th-century castle, refurbished as the luxurious Pousada Dom Dinis *(see p398).* The tranquil atmosphere is ideal for a stroll in narrow streets lined with 17th- and 18th-century mansions, or along the river-front, where a car ferry runs to the Spanish town of Goián.

Valença do Minho ❷

Road map C1. ⚞ 3,000. 🚍 🚌
ℹ️ *Paiol do Campo de Marte (251 823 329).* 🛒 *Wed.*

Set in a commanding position on a hilltop overlooking the River Minho, Valença is an attractive border town with an old quarter set in the narrow confines of two double-walled forts, shaped like crowns and linked by a causeway. During the reign of Sancho I (1185–1211), the town was named *Contrasta*, due to its position facing the Spanish town of Tui.

The **forts** date from the 17th and 18th centuries and were designed according to the principles of the French archi-tect, Vauban. There are fine

views from the ramparts across the river into Galicia. Although the town was briefly captured by Napoleonic troops in 1807, its formidable bastions resisted subsequent shelling and attacks from across the river in 1809.

Lining the cobbled alleys of the old quarter are shops full of linen, wickerwork, pottery and handicrafts to tempt the thousands of Spanish visitors who stroll across the bridge to shop. South of the ramparts is the newer part of town.

In Praça de São Teotónio, **Casa do Eirado** (1448) boasts a crenellated roof and late Gothic window, adorned with the builder's signature. The 18th-century **Casa do Poço** presents symmetrical windows and wrought-iron balconies.

A quiet sunlit corner in the old quarter of Valença do Minho

Environs: The **Convento de Ganfei**, 5 km (3 miles) east of Valença on the N101, was re-constructed in the 11th century by a Norman priest. It retains pleasing Romanesque features, including ornamental animal and plant motifs and vestiges of medieval frescoes. To visit the chapel, ask for the key at the house opposite.

Part of the walls and ramparts surrounding Valença do Minho

Monção ❸

Road map C1. 🏛 25,000. 🚌
ℹ *Casa do Corro 1950 (251 652
757).* 🛒 *Thu.*

A remote and charming town,
Monção once formed part
of the string of fortified border
posts standing sentinel on the
River Minho. Both the town's
main squares are lined with old
houses, and decorated with
chestnut trees, flowerbeds and
mosaic paths.

The 13th-century **Igreja
Matriz** in Rua João de Pinho
boasts an outstanding Romanesque doorway of sculpted
acanthus flowers. Inside, to
the right of the transept is the
cenotaph of the valiant Deu-
la-Deu Martins, the town's
heroine, erected in 1679 by
a descendant. A leafy avenue
east of the town leads to the
hot mineral springs used for
the treatment of rheumatism.

A colourful element in the
June Corpus Christi festival
is the Festa da Coca, when
St George engages the dragon
(coca) in comic ritual combat
before giving the final blow.

Environs: The countryside
around Monçao produces excellent *vinho verde (see p29)*;
one of the best-known estates
is the privately owned Neo-
Classical Palácio de Brejoeira,
5 km (3 miles) south of town.

About 5 km (3 miles) southeast of Monção, the monastery
of **São João de Longos Vales**
was built in Romanesque style

Bridge across the Lima at Ponte da Barca, with the town behind

in the 12th century. The exterior capitals and interior apse
have fantastical sculpted figures, including serpents and
monkeys. Visits are arranged
by the tourist office in Monção.

The town of **Melgaço**, 24 km
(15 miles) east of Monção provides a useful gateway to the
Peneda-Gerês National Park.

Parque Nacional da Peneda-Gerês ❹

See pp272–3.

Ponte da Barca ❺

Road map C1. 🏛 2,000. 🚌
ℹ *R.D. Manuel I (258 452 899).*
🛒 *every other Wed.*

The town of Ponte da Barca
derives its name from the
graceful 15th-century bridge
that replaced the boat once
used to ferry pilgrims across
the River Lima *(ponte* means

bridge, and *barca* means boat).
A stroll through the tranquil
town centre leads past the pillory (crowned with sphere and
pyramid), the graceful arcades
and noble mansions from the
16th and 17th centuries. The
Jardim dos Poetas (Poets'
Garden) and riverside parks
are ideal for picnics, and the
huge open-air market along
the river is well worth a visit.

Carved relief on the tympanum of
the small parish church at Bravães

Environs: Some of Portugal's
finest Romanesque carvings
are on the 13th-century church
at **Bravães**, 4 km (2 miles)
west of Ponte da Barca. Sculpted monkeys, oxen, and birds
of prey decorate the columns
of its main portal; the tympanum shows Christ in majesty
flanked by two angels.

The town of **Arcos de
Valdevez**, 5 km (3 miles) north
of Ponte da Barca, nestles by
the banks of the River Vez and
lies within convenient reach of
Peneda-Gerês National Park.
The impressive church of
Nossa Senhora da Lapa was
built in 1767 by André Soares.
This Baroque showpiece has
an oval exterior, yet transforms
the interior into an octagon.

Hiking enthusiasts should
ask the tourist office for directions to follow the circuit of
elevated viewpoints and local
villages from the hamlet of
São Miguel, 11 km (7 miles)
east of Ponte da Barca.

DEU-LA-DEU MARTINS

In 1368, when a Spanish army had besieged Monção to the
verge of starvation, Deu-la-Deu Martins used the last of
the town's flour to bake rolls that she flung over the walls
to the Spaniards, with taunts that there were plenty more

The heroic Deu-la-Deu Martins
on Monção's coat of arms

to throw at them. Thinking
their time was being wasted in
a futile siege, the troops soon
withdrew. In gratitude for
saving the town, Deu la Deu
(the name means "God gave
her") is remembered on the
town's coat of arms, where
she is shown with a loaf of
bread in each hand. *Pãezinhos*
(bread rolls) *de Deu-la-Deu*
used to be baked to honour
her memory, but the tradition
is no longer followed.

Vinho verde **vineyards near Monção** ▷

Parque Nacional da Peneda-Gerês ❹

Broom in Peneda Mountains

Peneda-Gerês National Park, one of Portugal's greatest natural attractions, stretches from the Gerês Mountains in the south to the Peneda range and the Spanish border in the north. Established in 1971, it extends over about 700 sq km (270 sq miles) of wild, dramatic scenery, with windswept peaks and wooded valleys of oak, pine and yew. It also hosts rare wolves and golden eagles among its rich variety of fauna. In the park's villages, everyday life remains firmly rooted in tradition.

Lamas de Mouro, at the northern entrance to the park, serves as an information centre and offers accommodation.

Castro Laboreiro is best known for the breed of sheepdog to which it gives its name. The ruins of a medieval castle can be seen in the village.

★ **Nossa Senhora da Peneda**
Surrounded by massive rocks, this elaborate sanctuary is a replica of Bom Jesus (see pp280–81). The site is visited in early September by pilgrims from all over the region.

Castelo Lindoso, in the frontier village of Lindoso, is a fine 13th-century castle that has been renovated to house an art gallery.

Soajo
The traditional village of Soajo, surrounded by terraced hillsides, is known for its collection of espigueiros. *The village's local festival takes place in the middle of August.*

Nossa Senhora da Peneda

Melgaço

Arcos de Valdevez

Mezio

N202

Soajo

N304-1

Entre Ambos-os-Rios

Albufeira de Vilarinho das Furnas

Campo do Gerês

Braga

0 kilometres 5
0 miles 2

Vilarinho das Furnas
Beautifully set in a rocky landscape, the Vilarinho das Furnas reservoir was formed by the damming of the River Homem. The reservoir is good for swimming as well as hikes along its shores.

Caldas do Gerês, known since Roman times for its spa, now serves as an information centre and base for excursions from the centre of the park.

Pitões das Júnias Monastery

Dating to 1147, the picturesque ruins of this monastery lie approximately 3 km (2 miles) south of the road leading into Pitões das Júnias village.

VISITORS' CHECKLIST

Road map C1. 🚌 *from Braga to Caldas do Gerês; from Arcos de Valdevez to Soajo & Lindoso; from Melgaço to Castro Laboreiro & Lamas de Mouro.* 🛈 *Caldas do Gerês: on main road (253 390 110); Lamas do Mouro: next to camp site; Arcos de Valdevez: Rua Padre Manuel Himalaia (258 515 338). Information on camp sites, hiking & pony trekking is available at these offices and at Montalegre (see p258).* **Castelo Lindoso** ⬭ *daily.* ⬤ *public hols.* 🎫

Inverneiras in Seara

Migration during the summer from these solidly built winter houses to brandas, stone shelters high in the mountains, is still practised in some villages.

★ Roman Road

Sections of the old Roman road that ran from Braga to Astorga in Spain, can still be seen at points along the Homem river valley.

STAR SIGHTS

★ Nossa Senhora da Peneda

★ Roman Road

ESPIGUEIROS

The tomb-like architecture of *espigueiros* (granaries) appears in several areas of the park, especially in the villages of Lindoso and Soajo. Constructed either of wood or granite, they are raised on columns and slatted for ventilation. The design keeps grain and maize at the right humidity as well as off the ground, out of reach of hens and rodents. Topped with an ornamental cross or pyramid, the design of *espigueiros* has scarcely changed since the 18th and 19th centuries.

Granite *espigueiro*, Lindoso

KEY

═══ Road

--- Long-distance footpath

-·-·- National boundary

🛈 Tourist information

☼ Viewpoint

Ponte de Lima ⑥

Road map C1. 🏘 *3,200.* 🚌
ℹ️ *Paço do Márquês de Ponte de Lima
(258 942 335).* 🅿️ *every other Mon.*

This attractive riverside
town takes its name from
the ancient bridge over the
River Lima. During the Middle
Ages, the town played a
pivotal role in the defence of
the Minho against the Moors.

The Roman **bridge** has only
five of its original stone arches;
the rest were rebuilt or restored
in the 14th and 15th centuries.
The 15th-century church of
Santo António houses the
Museu dos Terceiros, a
museum of sacred art. The
Museu Rural has antique farming equipment, an authentic
regional kitchen and gardens.

Ponte de Lima's remaining
medieval fortifications
include the 15th-century
**Palácio dos Marqueses
de Ponte de Lima**.

The town's market,
a tradition dating back
to 1125, takes place
on the river's wide
and sandy left bank.
In mid-September
crowds gather in the
town to celebrate the
Feiras Novas (new
fairs), a combined
religious festival and
folkloric market.

**Stone carving of
a musician, Museu
dos Terceiros**

🏛 **Museu Rural**
Largo da Arnado. **Tel** *258 900 414.*
⏲️ *2–6pm Tue–Sun.* ⚫ *public hols.*

Viana do Castelo ⑦

See pp276–7.

Former dormitory of the Mosteiro de Santa Clara, Vila do Conde

Vila do Conde ⑧

Road map C2. 🏘 *21,000.* 🚉 🚌
ℹ️ *Rua 25 de Abril 103 (252 248
473/474/475).* 🅿️ *Fri.*

The small town of Vila do
Conde enjoyed its boom
years as a shipbuilding
centre in the Age of
Discovery *(see pp46–
7)*; today it is a quiet
fishing port. By the
river, in the historic
centre, the main attrac-
tion is the **Mosteiro de
Santa Clara**, founded in
1318. The principal
dormitory building,
dating from the 18th
century, was used
for some time as a
correctional institu-
tion for teenagers. The Gothic
church contains the tombs of
the nunnery's founders, Dom
Afonso Sanches (son of King
Dinis) and his wife Dona
Teresa Martins. The entire
building is now closed for
redevelopment and will re-

open as a *pousada*. By the
Mosteiro de Santa Clara are
parts of the imposing 5-km
(3-mile) **aqueduct**, built in
1705–14, with 999 arches.

At the heart of the historic
centre is Praça Vasco da
Gama, with an unusual
pillory in the shape of an
arm with thrusting sword –
a vivid warning to potential
wrongdoers. Bordering the
square by the pillory is the
16th-century **Igreja Matriz**,
notable for its wonderfully
ornate Manueline portico,
attributed to João de Castilho.

The town is a centre for lace-
making (bone lace or *rendas
de bilros*). Visitors can buy
samples and see the skills
at the **Escola de Rendas** (lace-
making school). The same
building also houses the Museu
de Rendas (lace museum).

🏛 **Escola de Rendas**
Rua de São Bento 70. **Tel** *252 248
470.* ⏲️ *Mon–Fri.* ⚫ *public hols.*

Environs: The town of **Póvoa
de Varzim**, 3 km (2 miles)
north of Vila do Conde, is
a resort with sandy beaches,
amusements and nightlife.

In the village of Rates, 10
km (6 miles) northeast, the
13th-century church of **São
Pedro de Rates** boasts a portal
surmounted by gracefully
sculpted statues of saints, and
a rose window. Its nearby
counterpart at Rio Mau, the
church of **São Cristóvão de
Rio Mau**, was finished in
1151. Above the door is a
bishop (possibly St Augustine)
flanked by helpers.

Ponte de Lima's Roman bridge, leading to the church of Santo António

THE LEGEND OF THE BARCELOS COCK

A Galician pilgrim, as he was leaving Barcelos en route to Santiago de Compostela, was accused of stealing silver from a landowner, and sentenced to death by hanging. As a final plea to save himself, the prisoner requested a meeting with the judge, who was about to tuck into a meal of roast cockerel. The Galician vowed that as proof of his innocence the cockerel would stand up on the plate and crow.

The judge pushed aside his meal and ignored the plea. But as the prisoner was hanged, the cockerel stood up and crowed. The judge, realizing his mistake, hurried to the gallows and found that the Galician had miraculously survived thanks to a loose knot. According to legend, the Galician returned years later to carve the Cruzeiro do Senhor do Galo, now housed in the Museu Arqueológico in Barcelos.

Traditional Barcelos cock

Azulejos of St Benedict's miracle of the sickle, Nossa Senhora do Terço

Barcelos ❾

Road map C1. 🏛 *10,000.* 🚉 🚌 🛈 *Largo Dr José Novais 8 (253 811 882).* 🛒 *Thu.*

A pleasant riverside town, Barcelos is famed as the country's leading ceramics and crafts market and the source of the legendary cock that has become Portugal's national symbol. From its origins as a settlement in Roman times, the town of Barcelos developed into a flourishing agricultural centre and achieved political importance during the 15th century as the seat of the First Duke of Bragança. The town's star attraction is the Feira de Barcelos, a huge weekly market held on Campo da República. Anything from clothes to livestock can be bought here. Pottery enthusiasts can browse amongst bright designs including pagan figurines and the famous clay cockerels.

North of the square stands **Nossa Senhora do Terço**, the 18th-century church of a former Benedictine nunnery. In contrast to its plain exterior, the interior is beautifully decorated with panels of *azulejos* illustrating St Benedict's life.

In the southwest corner of the square, a graceful cupola crowns the **Igreja do Senhor da Cruz**, built around 1705 on the site where two centuries earlier João Pires, a cobbler, had a miraculous vision of a cross etched into the ground. The Festa das Cruzes (festival of crosses), the town's most spectacular event, is held at the beginning of May to celebrate the vision. During the celebrations thousands of flowers are laid on the streets to welcome a procession to the church, and events include magnificent displays of local folk costumes, dancing and fireworks.

The other historic attractions in the town are clustered together in a tranquil setting beside the 15th-century granite bridge that crosses over the River Cávado. The privately owned **Solar dos Pinheiros** is an attractive mansion on Rua Duques de Bragança, built in 1448. The sculpted figure plucking his beard on the south tower is known as Barbadão, the "bearded one". So incensed was this Jew when his daughter bore a child to a gentile (King João I) that he vowed never to shave again, hence his nickname.

A rich Gothic pillory stands in front of the ruined Counts' Palace or Paço dos Condes, destroyed by the earthquake of 1755. The ruins provide an open-air setting for the **Museu Arqueológico**, which displays stone crosses, sculpted blazons, sarcophagi, and its famous exhibit, the Cruzeiro do Senhor do Galo, a cross paying tribute to the Barcelos cock legend. Next to the palace, the **Igreja Matriz** is Romanesque with Gothic influences, and dates from the 13th century. There are 18th-century *azulejos* inside as well as an impressive rose window. The nearby **Museu de Olaria** illustrates the history of ceramics in the region.

🏛 **Museu Arqueológico**
Paços dos Condes. *Tel 253 824 741*
🔲 *Tue–Sun.* ⬤ *public hols.*

🏛 **Museu de Olaria**
Rua Cónego J Gaiolas.
Tel 253 824 741. 🔲 *Tue–Sun.*
⬤ *public hols.* 📷 ♿

16th-century pillory on terrace overlooking the River Cávado at Barcelos

Street-by-Street: Viana do Castelo ➐

Viana do Castelo lies in a beautiful setting on the Lima estuary. This 13th-century town gained prominence as a fishing centre in the 1400s; later it provided ships and seafarers for the great maritime discoveries of the 16th century *(see pp48–9)*. From here João Velho set off to explore the Congo, and João Álvares Fagundes charted the rich fishing grounds of Newfoundland. Wealth derived from trade with Europe and Brazil funded the town's many opulent mansions built in Manueline, Renaissance and Baroque styles. Today the main interest lies in the winding streets and intimate squares of the city centre, easily explored on foot.

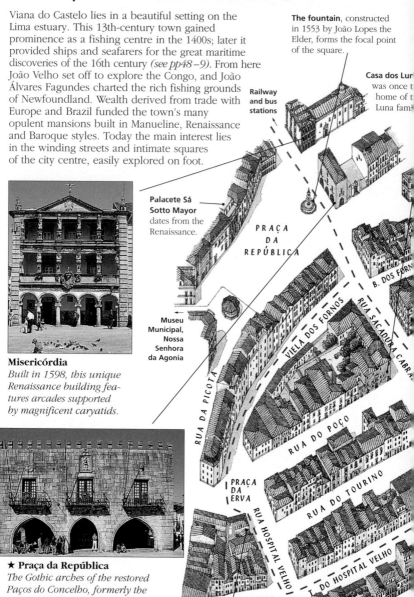

The fountain, constructed in 1553 by João Lopes the Elder, forms the focal point of the square.

Casa dos Lun was once t home of t Luna fam

Railway and bus stations

Palacete Sá Sotto Mayor dates from the Renaissance.

PRAÇA DA REPÚBLICA

B. DOS FORN

VIELA DOS FORNOS

RUA SACADURA CABRA

Museu Municipal, Nossa Senhora da Agonia

RUA DA PICOTA

RUA DO POÇO

RUA DO TOURINO

PRAÇA DA ERVA

RUA HOSPITAL VELHO

DO HOSPITAL VELHO

VIELA DA PARENTA

Misericórdia
Built in 1598, this unique Renaissance building features arcades supported by magnificent caryatids.

★ Praça da República
The Gothic arches of the restored Paços do Concelho, formerly the town hall, dominate the head of Viana's main square. Manueline motifs include the arms of João III.

STAR SIGHTS

★ Igreja Matriz

★ Praça da República

The Hospital Velho was originally a pilgrims' hospice. It now houses the Alto Minho tourist office.

0 metres   50
0 yards   50

KEY

– – – Suggested route

Casa da Praça, a magnificent Baroque mansion

Casa de João Velho
is a 15th-century
house, said to
have belonged
to the town's
most famous
navigator.

GAGO COUTINHO

T. DOS CLÉRIGOS

V. DO SEQUEIRO

★ **Igreja Matriz**
*The arch surrounding the
west door of Viana's 15th-
century, fortress-like parish
church is adorned with
Gothic reliefs of the apostles.*

The fountain in Praça da República, the centre of daily life in Viana

Exploring Viana do Castelo

Both a busy fishing port and
holiday resort, Viana is overlooked by the peak of Monte
de Santa Luzia. The town is
the capital of Minho folk culture, playing host to lively
festivals and supporting a
thriving handicrafts industry.

🏛 Museu Municipal

Largo de São Domingos. **Tel** *258
820 377.* ⬜ *Tue–Sun.* ⬛ *public
hols.* 📷 ♿ *new wing only.*
Viana's Museu Municipal
is housed in the 18th-
century Palacete dos
Barbosas Maciéis
and has an excellent
collection of rare
ceramics, furniture,
archaeological
finds and paintings.
In one of the upstairs
rooms, the walls are
tiled with animated
allegorical depictions
of the continents,
while the chapel is
lined with tiles signed
by the 18th-century
artist Policarpo de
Oliveira Bernardes,
(see p26). Among
the exhibits are a
17th-century Indo-
Portuguese cabinet
magnificently deco-
rated with inlaid ivory, and
pieces of Oporto faïence from
the Massarelos district, embellished with fine brushwork.

**Early 19th-
century ceramic,
Museu Municipal**

🛐 Nossa Senhora da Agonia

Campo de Nossa Senhora da Agonia.
Tel *258 824 067.* ⬜ *daily.* ♿
Northwest of the centre, the
mid-18th century Romanesque
chapel of Nossa Senhora da
Agonia houses a statue of Our

Lady of Sorrows *(agonia).* The
chapel, with façade and altar
designed by André Soares,
draws enormous crowds for
the *romaria* of Nossa Senhora
da Agonia, a three-day festival
held each year in the month
of August *(see p229).* The
statue is carried in procession
through the town amid much
feasting and celebration.

Environs: In order to enjoy
exceptional views, take the
zig-zag road to **Monte
de Santa Luzia**, 5 km
(3 miles) north of the
town centre. (A funicular
runs on winter weekends
from the station.) The
basilica, completed in
1926 and modelled on
the Sacré Coeur in Paris,
is a pilgrimage site with
little aesthetic appeal.
The steep climb, how-
ever, is well rewarded
by the superb views from
the top of the dome.
Behind the church you
can wander along
woodland paths or visit
the Pousada de Santa
Luzia *(see p398).* From
the *pousada* it is a short
walk to the top of the
hill, where there are
traces of a Celtiberian
settlement *(citânia).*
The excellent beach of
Praia do Cabedelo lies to
the south of the town. The
beach is accessible by road
via the bridge or by a five-
minute ferry crossing from
the riverside dock on Avenida
dos Combatentes da Grande
Guerra. To the north lies **Vila
Praia de Âncora**, another
popular beach resort.

Braga

Churches, grand 18th-century houses and pretty gardens provide the focus for the charm and interest of Braga's centre, once past the urban development on the city outskirts.

Known in Roman times as Bracara Augusta, Braga has a long history as a religious and commercial centre. In the 12th century, it became the seat of Portugal's archbishops, and the country's religious capital. The city lost some influence in the 19th century, but today continues as the ecclesiastical capital of Portugal and main city of the Minho.

Symbol of the city, Our Lady of the Milk

Not surprisingly, Braga hosts some of Portugal's most colourful religious festivals. Semana Santa (Holy Week) is celebrated with dramatic, solemn processions, while the lively festival of São João in June sees dancing, fairs and fireworks.

The west façade of the Sé, with its 15th-century galilee, or porch

Exploring Braga

The compact historic centre borders **Praça da República**, the central square. Within the square stands the 14th-century **Torre de Menagem**, all that remains of the city's original fortifications. A short walk leads to Rua do Souto, a narrow pedestrian street lined with elegant shops and cafés, including the **Café Brasileira**, furnished in 19th-century salon style. Towards the end of the road stands the impressive **Sé**, the cathedral of Braga. Other churches worth a visit include the small, 16th-century **Capela dos Coimbras**, and the 17th-century Baroque **Santa Cruz**. Many of the finest mansions in Braga also date from the Baroque period, such as the **Palácio do Raio** and the **Câmara Municipal** (the town hall). Both buildings are attributed to the 18th-century architect André Soares da Silva.

The blue-tiled façade of the Palácio do Raio, also known as the Casa do Mexicano

🏛 Sé

R. Dom Paio Mendes. ☐ *daily.*
Museu de Arte Sacra Tel *253 263 317.* ☐ *Tue–Sun.* 📷
Braga's cathedral was begun in the 11th century, when Henry of Burgundy decided to build on the site of an older church, destroyed in the 6th century. Since then the building has seen many changes, including the addition of a graceful galilee (porch) in the late 15th century. Outstanding features

include the chapel to the right, just inside the west door, housing the ornate 15th-century tomb of the first-born son of João I *(see pp46–7)*, Dom Afonso, who died as a child. Also of interest are the upper choir, with its carved wooden stalls, and the ornate, gilded, Baroque organ cases.

The cathedral also houses the Treasury or **Museu de Arte Sacra**, which contains a rich collection of ecclesiastical treasures as well as, statues, carvings and *azulejo* tiles.

Several chapels can be seen in the courtyard and cloister. The Capela dos Reis houses the tombs of the founders, Henry of Burgundy and his wife Dona Teresa, as well as the preserved body of the 14th-century archbishop Dom Lourenço Vicente.

From Rua de São João you can admire a statue of Nossa Senhora do Leite (Our Lady of the Milk), symbol of the city of Braga, sheltered under an ornate Gothic canopy.

🏛 Antigo Paço Episcopal

Praça Municipal. **Tel** *253 601 135.*
Library ☐ *Mon–Fri.*
Near the Sé is the former archbishops' palace. The façades date from the 14th, 17th and 18th centuries, but a major fire destroyed the interior in the 18th century. The palace is now used as a

The Jardim de Santa Bárbara by the walls of the Antigo Paço Episcopal

library and archives. Beside it are the immaculate gardens of the Jardim de Santa Bárbara.

⚜ Palácio dos Biscainhos
Rua dos Biscainhos. **Tel** *253 204 650.*
◯ *Tue–Sun.* 🈯

To the west of the city centre is the Palácio dos Biscainhos. Built in the 16th century and modified over the centuries, this imposing aristocratic mansion houses the city's Museu Etnográfico e Artístico (Ethnography and Arts Museum) with displays of foreign and Portuguese furniture. An unusual detail is the ribbed, paved ground floor, designed to allow

carriages inside the building to deposit guests and drive on to the stables beyond.

Environs: The attractively simple chapel of **São Frutuoso de Montélios**, 3.5 km (2 miles) northwest of Braga, is one of the few remaining examples of pre-Romanesque architecture to be found in Portugal. Built around the 7th century, it was destroyed by the Moors and rebuilt in the 11th century. West of Braga, 4 km (2.5 miles) from the centre and on the road to Barcelos, is the former Benedictine **Mosteiro de Tibães**. Dating back to the 11th century, this magnificent

Interior of the old coach stable at the Palácio dos Biscainhos

architectural complex with its gardens and cloisters, was rebuilt in the 19th century and is being refurbished to house a historical centre.

At Falperra, 6 km (4 miles) southeast of Braga, stands the church of **Santa Maria Madalena**. Designed by André Soares da Silva in 1750, it is known for its ornate exterior, perhaps the country's finest expression of the Rococo.

The sanctuary at **Sameiro**, 6.4 km (4 miles) from Braga, is second only to Fatima (*see p186*) in the Marian geography of Portugal. It was built in 1863 to honour the dogma of the Immaculate Conception.

✿ São Frutuoso de Montélios
Av. São Frutuoso. **Tel** *(Tourist office) 253 282 707.* ◯ *Tue–Sun.*

🏛 Mosteiro de Tibães
Lugar de Tibães. **Tel** *253 622 670.* ◯ *Tue–Sun.* 🈯 *to museum.* ♿

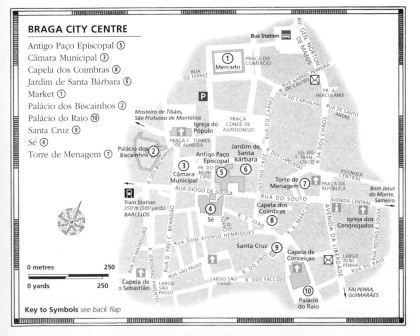

BRAGA CITY CENTRE

Antigo Paço Episcopal ⑤
Câmara Municipal ③
Capela dos Coimbras ⑧
Jardim de Santa Bárbara ⑥
Market ①
Palácio dos Biscainhos ②
Palácio do Raio ⑩
Santa Cruz ⑨
Sé ④
Torre de Menagem ⑦

0 metres	250
0 yards	250

Key to Symbols *see back flap*

Bom Jesus do Monte ⑪

Fountain on Staircase of the Three Virtues

On a forested slope east of Braga stands Portugal's most spectacular religious sanctuary. In 1722 the Archbishop of Braga devised the giant Baroque Escadaria (stairway) of Bom Jesus as the approach to a small existing shrine. The stairway and the church of Bom Jesus were completed by Carlos Amarante in 1811. The lower section features a steep Sacred Way with chapels showing the 14 Stations of the Cross, the scenes leading up to Christ's crucifixion. The Escadório dos Cinco Sentidos, in the middle section, depicts the five senses with ingenious wall-fountains and statues of biblical, mythological and symbolic figures. This is followed by the similarly allegorical Staircase of the Three Virtues.

At the summit, an esplanade provides superb views and access to the church. Close by are several hotels, a café and a boating lake hidden among the trees. Both a pilgrimage site and tourist attraction, the sanctuary attracts large festive crowds at weekends.

★ **Escadaria**
The staircase is built of granite accentuated by whitewashed walls. The steps represent an upward spiritual journey.

Chapel of the Crucifixion

Chapel of Jesus before Pilate

Chapel of the Road to Calvary

Chapel of the Flagellation

Entrance Portico
At the foot of the giant stairway stands a portico bearing the coat of arms of Dom Rodrigo de Moura Teles, the archbishop who commissioned the work.

★ **Funicular Railway**
The funicular (elevador) dates back to 1882. Hydraulically operated, it makes the ascent to the terrace beside the church in three minutes.

Chapel of Christ's Agony in the Garden

Chapel of the Kiss of Judas

Chapel of the Last Supper

Chapel of Darkness

For hotels and restaurants in this region see pp396–8 and pp422–4

The Hotel do Elevador *(see p396)* stands near the top of the funicular.

Hotel do Parque

Pelican fountain

VISITORS' CHECKLIST

Road map C1. 5 km (3 miles) E of Braga. **Tel** *253 676 636.* 🚌
🚠 *funicular to the top.* ⭕ *daily.*
📷 🚻 🍴 ⛪ *daily.*

The church of Bom Jesus was built on the site of a 15th-century sanctuary. In front of it stand eight statues of people who condemned Christ, including Herod and Pilate.

Chapel of the Descent from the Cross
Each chapel has a tableau of life-size terracotta figures in a scene from Christ's last journey.

On the Staircase of the Five Senses are five fountains, each representing a bodily sense: sight, hearing, smell, taste and touch.

Statues, symbols and inscriptions elaborate on the theme of the senses.

Staircase of the Three Virtues
The final stretch of staircase represents the gaining of Faith, Hope and Charity, symbolized by fountains and various allegorical figures.

Chapel of Simon the Cyrenian

Chapel of the Crown of Thorns

0 metres	25
0 yards	25

Fountain of the Five Wounds of Christ
The fountains positioned at various points on the long ascent symbolize the water of life and purification of the body and spirit. In the fountain at the foot of the Staircase of the Five Senses, water spills from the five bezants on the Portuguese coat of arms, a symbolic reference to Christ's wounds.

STAR FEATURES

★ Escadaria

★ Funicular Railway

Guimarães ⓬

A UNESCO World Heritage site, the town of Guimarães is celebrated as the birthplace of the nation. When Afonso Henriques proclaimed himself king of Portugal in 1139 *(see pp42–3)*, he chose Guimarães as his capital, and the distinctive outline of its proud castle appears on the Portuguese coat of arms. In the well-preserved city centre, the narrow streets of the medieval quarter are ideal for exploration on foot. The cobbled Rua de Santa Maria, lined with old town houses embellished with ornate statuary, leads up from the main square, the Largo da Oliveira, past the Paço dos Duques to the castle. To feel the hustle and bustle of the Middle Ages, visit the town in the first week of August for the Festas Gualterianas, a festival of medieval art and costume.

Baroque candle-holder, Paço dos Duques

♤ Castelo de Guimarães

Rua Conde Dom Henrique. *Tel 253 412 273.* ◻ *Tue–Sun.* ● *public hols.* 🖾

The castle's huge square keep, encircled by eight crenellated towers, dominates the skyline. First built to deter attacks by Moors and Normans in the 10th century, it was extended by Henry of Burgundy two centuries later and, according to tradition, was the birthplace of Portugal's first king, Afonso Henriques. The font where he was reputedly baptized is kept in the tiny Romanesque chapel of **São Miguel,** situated at the western end of the castle.

♛ Paço dos Duques

Rua Conde Dom Henrique. *Tel 253 412 273.* ◻ *Tue–Sun.* ● *1 Jan, Easter, 1 May, 25 Dec.* 🖾

Constructed in the 15th century by Dom Afonso (first Duke of Bragança), the Burgundian

style of the Paço dos Duques reflects Dom Afonso's taste acquired on his travels through Europe. The palace fell into disuse when the Bragança family moved to Vila Viçosa *(see pp300–301)*. In 1933, under Salazar's dictatorship *(see pp56–7)*, it was renovated as an official presidential residence.

On view in a small museum inside the palace, are lavish displays of Persian rugs, Flemish tapestries and paintings, such as the impressive *O Coreiro Pascal* (Paschal Lamb) by Josefa de Óbidos *(see p51)*. Paying unusual homage to the nation's maritime exploits, the chestnut ceiling in the banqueting hall imitates the upturned hull of a Portuguese caravel.

🏛 Museu de Alberto Sampaio

Rua Alfredo Guimarães. *Tel 253 423 910.* ◻ *Tue–Sun.* ● *1 Jan, Easter, 1 May, 25 Dec.* 🖾

This museum, housed in the beautiful Romanesque cloister and adjoining rooms of Nossa Senhora da Oliveira, displays some outstanding religious art, *azulejos* and ceramics, all from local churches.

The star exhibits, donated to the church by João I, are his tunic worn at the battle of Aljubarrota in 1385 *(see p185)*, and a 14th-century silver altarpiece, comprising a triptych of the Visitation, Annunciation and Nativity, reportedly taken from the defeated Spanish king. The Santa Clara room contains gilt carving, the work of local craftsmen, taken from the former convent of Santa Clara, now the town hall.

Largo da Oliveira, centre of old Guimarães

⚑ Nossa Senhora da Oliveira

Largo da Oliveira. *Tel 253 416 144.* ◻ *daily.*

This former monastery lies on the square's east side. Founded by Afonso Henriques, the church was restored by João I in gratitude to Our Lady of the Olive Tree for his victory at Aljubarrota *(see p185)*. The Manueline tower is from 1515.

In front of it is the Padrão do Salado, a 14th-century Gothic shrine housing a cross. It commemorates the legend of how the church and square acquired their name. An olive tree was transplanted here to supply the altar lamp with oil, but it withered. In 1342, the merchant Pedro Esteves placed the cross on it, whereupon the tree flourished. The tree that stands in the square today dates only from 1985.

The massive battlements surrounding the keep of Castelo de São Miguel

🏛 **Museu Martins Sarmento**

Rua Paio Galvão. **Tel** *253 414 011.*
⭕ *Tue–Sun.* ⚫ *public hols.* 🎫
Named after the archaeologist
who excavated major Iron
Age sites in the north, notably
Citânia de Briteiros, the museum is housed in the Gothic
cloister of the 14th-century
convent of São Domingos. Specializing in finds from these
sites, some dating to the Stone
Age, the museum contains
a wealth of archaeological,
ethnological and numismatic
exhibits. These include a rare
pair of Lusitanian granite
warriors, a bronze votive oxcart, and the Pedras Formosas,
two stone slabs inscribed with
human figures. The most striking exhibit is the Colossus of
Pedralva, a stone figure that
stands 3 m (10 ft) tall.

🏛 **São Francisco**

Largo de São Francisco. **Tel** *253 439
850.* ⭕ *Tue–Sun.* ⚫ *public hols.*
Built in 1400 in Gothic style,
the elegant church of São Francisco was reconstructed in the
18th century. The interior of
the church boasts a chancel
covered in magnificent 18th-
century *azulejos* with scenes
from the life of St Antony.

Environs: The former monastery of **Santa Marinha da
Costa** is one of Portugal's top
pousadas (see p379). It stands
5 km (3 miles) southeast of
Guimarães, and was founded
in 1154. The gardens and
chapel are open to the public.

Renaissance stone fountain at Santa
Marinha da Costa monastery

Reconstructed huts at the Iron Age site of Citânia de Briteiros

Citânia de Briteiros 🔟

Road map C1. 15 km (9 miles) N of
Guimarães, off N101. **Tel** *253 415
969.* 🚌 *from Guimarães & Braga.*
⭕ *Apr–Sep: 9am–6pm daily;
Oct–Mar: 9am–5pm daily.* 🎫

This Iron Age settlement
is one of Portugal's most
impressive archaeolo-
gical sites. Excavated by
Martins Sarmento (1833–
99), who devoted his life
to the study of Iron Age
sites, are the foundations
of 150 stone dwellings,
a number of which have
since been reconstructed.
   From about the 4th
century BC to the
4th century AD, the
site was inhabited by
Celtiberians, but was
most probably under
Roman rule from c.20
BC. A network of
paths leads visitors
past paved streets,
subterranean cisterns,
sewers and water supply ducts.
The Museu Martins Sarmento
in Guimarães displays various
excavated artifacts.

Cabeceiras de Basto 🔟

Road map D1. 🏠 *17,000.* 🚌
ℹ️ *Praça da República (253 669
100).* 🛒 *Mon.*
The Terras de Basto, once
a region of refuge from
Moorish invasion, lie east of
Guimarães among mountains

The *basto* statue
of Cabeceiras
de Basto

and forests. Statues known as
bastos, believed to represent
Celtic warriors, are found in
various parts of the Terras de
Basto where they served as
territorial markers. In the main
town, Cabeceiras de Basto,
the prime attraction is the
Baroque **Mosteiro de
Refojos**, with its splendid
dome 33 m (108 ft) high,
surrounded by statues of
the Apostles, and sur-
mounted by a statue of
the archangel Michael.
The town also owns the
best of the *basto* statues,
albeit with a French
head; it was changed by
troops as a joke during
the Napoleonic Wars.

Environs: The fine
hiking country of
the Terras de Basto,
carpeted with flowers
in spring, has other
villages worth visiting. **Mondim de Basto**,
overlooking the River
Tâmega some 25 km
(15 miles) south of
Cabeceiras, is a convenient
base for climbing **Monte
Farinha** which, at 966 m
(3,169 ft) is the highest peak
in the region. Then climb the
steps to the top of the church
of Nossa Senhora da Graça on
the summit, for splendid views.
   Over the Tâmega, the village
of **Celorico de Basto** has a
small castle and several manor
houses in the surrounding area.
Most are private but some,
such as the **Casa do Campo**
(see p396), are part of the
Turismo de Habitação scheme
(see p378) and take in guests.

SOUTHERN PORTUGAL

Southern Portugal at a Glance

South of the Tagus the vast wheatfields and rolling plains of the Alentejo stretch almost uninterrupted to the horizon. There is a rich legacy of early civilization here, dating back to prehistory, but visitors to Elvas, Beja or even the World Heritage city of Évora will usually be untroubled by mass tourism – until reaching the southern coast. Many visitors know nothing of Portugal except the tourist playground of the Algarve, yet it is least typical of the country. The sandy beaches are a year-round attraction but the historic town centres such as Faro, and the quieter hinterland, are well worth exploring.

Évora, *the Alentejo's historic university city, has monuments dating back to the Roman era. Gleaming white arcades and balconies of finely wrought ironwork are reminders that for over 450 years, until 1165, Évora was inhabited by the Moors (see pp304–7).*

Beja *flourished under the Moors and its museum is housed in a former convent resplendent with Hispano-Arab tiles, such as these in the chapter-house (see p313).*

Baixo Alentejo

Lagos, *principal town of the western Algarve, is flanked by inviting cove beaches, such as Praia de Dona Ana, which make it easy to understand why sunseekers flock here (see pp322–3).*

ALGARVE
(See pp316–33)

| 0 kilometres | 25 |
| 0 miles | 10 |

◁ Sandy beach and calm waters at the popular resort of Albufeira

Marvão, *within a stone's throw of the Spanish border, sits like a miniature fortress high in the Serra de São Mamede. The granite walls which protect the tiny town merge imperceptibly with the rock and have kept Marvão safe through centuries of dispute (see p296).*

Alto Alentejo

Elvas *has some of the best-preserved fortifications in Europe (see p299). At the centre of the walled old town lies the Praça da República, where Elvas's former cathedral looks out over the square's striking geometric mosaics.*

ALENTEJO
(See pp292–315)

Vila Viçosa *was chosen in the 15th century as the seat of the dukes of Bragança. Here they built their Paço Ducal (see pp300–301), in front of which stands a bronze equestrian statue of the 8th Duke, who became King João IV in 1640.*

Faro, *the gateway to the Algarve thanks to its international airport, is nevertheless bypassed by many visitors. Much was destroyed by the 1755 earthquake, but the town still has a pleasant historic centre beside the harbour. In spring the streets and squares are scented with the sweetness of orange blossom (see pp328–9).*

The Beaches of the Algarve

Facing North Africa to the south, and exposed to the force of the Atlantic in the west, the Algarve has a varied coastline. The Barlavento (windward side) includes the west coast and the south coast almost as far as Faro. Beaches around the promontory of Sagres are backed by cliffs and on the west coast many beaches are deserted. The sea here is colder and rougher than on the south coast, with dangerous currents. Between Sagres and Lagos is the start of a series of beautiful sandy coves, punctuated with grottoes, overlooked by tightly packed holiday resorts. East of Faro, the *Sotavento* (leeward side) has long, sandy beaches washed by warmer calmer water.

Sunbathing on the beach

Arrifana ①

The gracefully curving beach of Arrifana is one of the most stunning on the west coast. Sheltered below high cliffs, the approach by road offers dramatic views *(see p320)*.

Castelejo ②

This long, deserted beach of soft sand can only be reached via a dirt road by bicycle, car or jeep. Its remote location, how-ever, ensures peace and quiet *(see p321)*.

Beliche ③

Despite being at the "world's end", Beliche is sheltered by Cabo de São Vicente. The sandy beach is backed by fascinating caves and rock formations *(see p322)*.

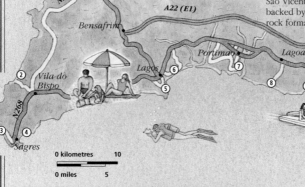

Alfezur · N268 · N120 · A22 (E1) · Bensafrim · Portimão · Lagoa · Armação de Pêra · Vila do Bispo · Lagos · Albufeira · N268 · Sagres · ICI · A2 (E1)

0 kilometres 10
0 miles 5

KEY

▬	Motorway
▬	Major road
	Minor road

For key to symbols see back flap

Martinhal ④

Martinhal is a wide, sheltered expanse of sand east of Sagres. The area is popular for water sports of all kinds, and the beach boasts an aquatic school with parasailing, water-skiing and windsurfing *(see p322)*.

Dona Ana ⑤

A tiny cove on the way to Ponta da Piedade, Dona Ana is one of the prettiest beaches in the Algarve, although crowded during the summer. A boat trip to see nearby caves and grottoes is highly recommended *(see p323)*.

Meia Praia ⑥

A vast expanse of sand stretching for 4 km (2 miles), the sheltered Meia Praia is the longest beach in the Algarve. Easily reached by road, there is also a boat trip from Lagos during the summer months *(see p323)*.

Praia da Rocha ⑦

Framed by ochre cliffs and lapped by calm water, this spacious beach is justifiably famous – and crowded in high season. Water sports can be practised here in a gentler sea than the extreme southwest and visitors are well catered for *(see p324)*.

Ilha de Tavira ⑪

In summer, boats go from Quatro Águas to the sandy Ilha de Tavira. The beach facing the coast has calm water, whereas the beaches on the ocean side, that run the length of the island, offer good swimming and windsurfing *(see p332)*.

Carvoeiro ⑧

Carvoeiro is a fishing village with a diminutive cove. The whole area is great for cove beaches, and a boat trip or a walk along the cliff will take you to spectacular sandy beaches with excellent swimming and snorkelling.

A22 (E1)

A22 (E1)
25
amoura
N2
arteira
N2

N125

N125 *Olhão*

Faro

Tavira ⑪

Castro Marim

⑫

Monte Gordo ⑫

The warm water and balmy climate, combined with vast stretches of clean sand backed by pine woods, make Monte Gordo a very popular resort.

Senhora da Rocha ⑨

Senhora da Rocha, named after a small chapel on its eastern promontory, is actually three small, sheltered beaches. Typical of this part of the coast, these half-moons of sand tucked below eroded yellow cliffs are reached via steep steps.

São Rafael ⑩

The small, popular beach of São Rafael offers soft sand and shallow water, with spectacular caves and eroded rock formations to explore. For those without a car, it is a steep walk down from the bus stop on the main road *(see p 325)*.

The Flavours of Southern Portugal

Alentejan cuisine is one of the country's most loved. The landscape is a powerful source of culinary inspiration, with its abundant wheat fields, its silvery olive groves and its wide oaks that provide acorns for pigs giving an intense flavour to local pork meat. The Portuguese trinity of olive oil, garlic and coriander is at its holiest here, and some of the country's tastiest fish and seafood is caught off the region's rocky western coast. The Algarve boasts a wide variety of fish, a wealth of fruit and vegetables, a unique pan, the *cataplana,* and the culinary cosmopolitanism that comes with tourism.

Fresh figs

Algarve chef cooking with a *cataplana* **pan**

THE ALENTEJO

For a region whose history and identity is bound up with a poor and landless peasantry, the Alentejo has a surprisingly rich culinary heritage. Dishes are varied and use basic ingredients imaginatively, leaving little to waste. One example is Alentejan bread, that famously keeps for a long time. Even when at last it begins to go stale it still has uses. Slices are placed in a broth of hot water, olive oil, garlic and coriander, mashed and topped with a poached egg to make *açorda*.

The ewe's milk cheeses of Serpa, Évora and Nisa are eaten when they are freshly made, soft and even runny, or after prolonged maturing, which hardens them and sharpens their flavour. Shepherds also herd Ibérico pigs, or *porcos pretos* as they are often called. These are fattened up by foraging for acorns, which gives the meat and fat a delicious intensity of flavour to make most other pork seem insipid in comparison.

Olives are a staple of the Alentejo, and the area around Moura is famous for its olive oil. Small, hot chillies known as *piri-piri* make their way into many local dishes and

Oysters Clams Crab Dourada (bream) Giant prawns Mussels Squid Red mullet

Harvest of fish and seafood from the southern Portuguese coastline

REGIONAL DISHES AND SPECIALITIES

Olives

It might seem strange that one of the great dishes of the Alentejo is a fish soup, but *sopa de cação* masterfully transforms the humble dogfish into a velvety soup with a sweet-and-sour streak. *Ensopado* is a quintessentially Alentejan type of dish, a sort of soupy stew, often served with a slice of bread at the bottom of the bowl. The lamb version, *ensopado de borrego*, is the most popular. *Porco preto* is prepared in any number of ways, from the classic *pézinhos de coentrada* (pig's trotters with coriander), to *lombo de porco em presunto* – tenderloin wrapped in cured ham. The Algarvian *cataplana* pan is often used to cook a rich fish and seafood stew, *cataplana de peixe e mariscos*. Figs feature in many of the region's desserts, including the fudge-like *morgado de figo*.

Lombo de porco em presunto *is often served with baby turnips. The ham keeps the tenderloin moist.*

Fresh char-grilled sardines and giant prawns

pickles, while large, sweet red peppers are char-roasted and peeled to add to salads, or mashed into a paste with salt to be preserved as *massa de pimentão*.

The coast yields delicacies such as *sargo* (white bream) and *perceves*, the odd-looking goose barnacle, which is pried off steep cliffsides at low tide. Deep-fried dried eel is popular, and tastes similar to pork crackling.

THE ALGARVE

Portugal's tourist hub is often condescendingly regarded as a culinary cliché of grilled sardines, vinegary salads, grilled chicken and chips, but that misses a few crucial points. In the *cataplana*, a wok-shaped copper pan with a hinged, domed lid, the region has its own cooking utensil and technique as well as a link to its Arabic past. Though many restaurants use it like any other pan, the *cataplana* is above all a steaming device, particularly suited to the coast's many delicious edible shells, such as *ameijoas* and *conquilhas*

Oranges ripening in a citrus grove in the Algarve

(types of cockle) and *ostras* (oysters). Tuna is rarer now than it was, but the range at any fish market remains vast.

Inland from its popular beaches, the region is a fertile garden for almost every kind of vegetable – peppers and beefsteak tomatoes are particularly good – and a large variety of fruits including citrus, figs and melons. The *serras*, mostly low mountain ranges forming a natural border with the Alentejo, provide traditional cheeses, herbs, honey and sweets.

REGIONAL WINES

The Alentejo is Portugal's favourite wine region, and accounts for about one-third of the country's vineyards. Parts of it date back to Roman times. It produces wines with styles ranging from traditional, farmyard-scented light reds to deep, berry-flavoured and oaked ones, often made from grapes that are new to the region, including Syrah and the Douro variety Touriga Nacional. The leap in quality that the Alentejo has performed over the last couple of decades is perhaps most noticeable in the whites, which are strikingly fresh and fruity for a region of extreme heat. The Algarve has begun a process of renewal and modernization as well, with a few individual producers leading the way, and some co-operatives are now making very palatable reds. Wines tend to be soft and aromatic with a high alcohol content.

Ensopado de Borrego *uses cheap cuts of lamb marinated with cumin and cloves and simmered until very tender.*

Cataplana *is named for the pan. Shellfish, squid, prawns and fish are steamed with white wine, garlic and herbs.*

Morgado de Figo *is a rich, sticky cake of dried figs, almonds, sugar, chocolate, cinnamon and aniseed.*

ALENTEJO

The sun-baked Alentejo occupies nearly one-third of Portugal, stretching all the way from the Tagus south to the Algarve. Its vast rolling plains, golden with wheat or silver with olive trees, its whitewashed villages, megaliths and castles, and above all the space and tranquillity, are the Alentejo's great attractions for visitors.

Stone circles, dolmens and other relics of Stone Age life pepper the Alentejan plain, particularly around Évora, a historical gem of a city at the region's geographical centre.

Évora, like Beja, Vidigueira and other towns, was founded by the Romans, who valued this land beyond the Tagus – *além Tejo* – for its wheatfields. Introducing irrigation systems to overcome the soil's aridity, they established enormous farms to grow grain for the empire. Worked by peasant farmers, these huge estates, or *latifúndios*, still exist, some of them now being run as co-operatives.

Grain apart, the vast plains yield cork from the bark of cork oaks and olives – Elvas is prized for these as well as its candied greengages. Vineyards around Reguengos and Vidigueira have long produced powerful wines, and the Alentejo has a number of demarcated wine regions *(see pp28–9)*. Since 1986, Portugal's membership of the European Union has increased the rate of investment and modernization, although the region is still sparsely populated, supporting only ten per cent of the population. Land tenure has always been a concern here, and communism has a strong appeal – the Alentejans were solid supporters of the 1974 revolution *(see p57)*.

Many towns and villages, especially in the south, carry echoes of the long Moorish occupation in the cube-like white houses, while to the north and east the plains give way to a rocky terrain of fortified villages and scrubland grazed by flocks of sheep.

Portuguese from other regions mock the amiable *alentejanos* for their slow ways, but they are widely admired for their singing and their handicrafts.

An Alentejan house in Odemira, with the traditional blue trim typical of the region

◁ Cork oaks and olive trees breaking up the wheatfields of the Alentejo plains

Exploring the Alentejo

The ancient city of Évora, with its exceptional historic centre and location in the heart of the Alentejo, is an obvious starting point for exploring this varied and beautiful region.

To the northeast lie the white towns of Estremoz and Vila Viçosa, where local marble has been used in the construction of some fabulous façades, and Alter do Chão, home of Portugal's royal horse, the Alter Real. Nearer the formerly-disputed Spanish frontier, towns and villages still shelter within massive fortifications, while travelling south the legacy of the Moors becomes ever more apparent; Beja and Mértola, especially, are full of Moorish history.

On the west coast there are some lovely beaches, with many stretches still relatively untouched by tourism.

The cromlech of Almendres, one of many prehistoric sites around Évora

SIGHTS AT A GLANCE

0 kilometres   25

0 miles   10

The fertile farmland and orchards of the northern Alentejo, seen from Estremoz

Montalvão

Nisa

CASTELO
DE VIDE **4**

2 MARVÃO

Alpalhão

1

Cáceres

N245

Flor da Rosa

Fortios

3

44

Ponte de Sor

CRATO **5**

PORTALEGRE

Vila Formosa

6 ALTER
DO CHÃO

Urra

N246

PORTALEGRE

Arronches

N371

Vaiamonte

Monforte

Avis

Fronteira

IP2

Santa Eulália

7 CAMPO
MAIOR

Sousel

Veiros

Vila
Fernando

Badajoz

Casa Branca

N245

8 ELVAS

Pavia
Ribeira de Tera

N4

12 ESTREMOZ

A6 IP7

Vimieiro

N373

ÉVORAMONTE **13**

Serra de Ossa

9 VILA VIÇOSA

Pardais

Rio Guadiana

14 ARRAIOLOS

10 ALANDROAL

São Miguel
de Machede

N254

11 REDONDO

São Matias

ÉVORA

Terena

17 ÉVORA **16**

N255

ALITHS
ÚR

Montoito

São
Manços

18 MONSARAZ

Reguengos
de Monsaraz

Mourão

ANA DO
ENTEJO

N256

IP2

Oriola

Portel

Amieira Barragem
d'Alqueva

Granja

N358

Alvito

Póvoa

Amareleja

DIGUEIRA **20**

Alqueva

N384

Cuba

N258

MOURA **21**

N258

Barrancos

Pedrógão

Sáfara

Beringel

Serra da Adiça

Baleizão

N255

Pias

Sobral da Adiça

23 BEJA

nta
tória

Trindade

22 SERPA

IP8

Vila Nova
de São Bento

pa
Ribeira de Terges

Santa Iria

BEJA

Rio Chança

tradas

N122

N265

N123

MÉRTOLA **28**

Mina de
São Domingos

N267

Espírito
Santo

odôvar

Faro

GETTING AROUND
Exploration by road is a more
feasible option than by rail, although trains run between the
major towns of Évora, Beja
and some of the smaller
centres. The bus network links
most towns and villages, but
time and patience are needed
to cope with the logistics. For
motorists, the A6 (E90) provides fast access from Lisbon
right through the Alentejo to
the Spanish border, while the
IP2 (E802) bisects the region
from north to south. Links on
to minor roads are generally
well marked and roads are
mainly in good condition.

Serpa's Nossa Senhora de Guadalupe,
startlingly white in the hot sun

SEE ALSO

• *Where to Stay* pp398–400

• *Where to Eat* pp424–6

KEY

▬▬	Motorway
▬▬	Major road
▬▬	Minor road
▬▬	Scenic route
▬▬	Major railway
▬▬	Minor railway
▬▬	National border
▬▬	Regional border

A sea of wheat surrounding a farmhouse near Moura

Serra de São Mamede ❶

Road map D4. 🚌 to Portalegre.
ℹ️ Portalegre.

The diverse geology and capricious climate of this remote range, caught between the Atlantic and the Mediterranean, encourage a fascinating range of flora and fauna. In 1989, 320 sq km (120 sq miles) of the Serra were designated a *parque natural*, and griffon vultures and Bonelli's eagles soar overhead. Red deer, wild boar and the cat-like genet live among the sweet chestnut trees and holm oaks, and streams attract otters and amphibians, such as the Iberian midwife toad. The reserve is also home to one of the largest colonies of bats in Europe.

The Serra's apparent emptiness is deceptive: megaliths suggest that it was settled in prehistoric times, and in the south of the reserve, rock paintings survive in the Serra de Cavaleiros and Serra de Louções. Below Marvão is the Roman town of Amaia (São Salvador de Aramenha), and the Roman network of roads still winds among the trim white villages, offering grand views at every curve.

From Portalegre, the road climbs for 15 km (9 miles) to the Pico de São Mamede at 1,025 m (3,363 ft). A minor road leads south to Alegrete, a fortified village crowned by its ruined 14th-century castle.

Sheep in the summer pastures of the Serra de São Mamede

Marvão ❷

Road map D4. 🏠 185. 🚊 🚌
ℹ️ Largo de Santa Maria (245 909 131). 🗓️ Thu.

This serene medieval hamlet is dramatically set at 862 m (2,828 ft) on a spectacular escarpment facing Spain. Its 13th-century walls and 17th-century buttresses blend seamlessly into the granite of the mountains, making it an impregnable stronghold. The Romans, who called the outcrop Herminius Minor, were followed by the Moors – the name may have come from Marvan, a Moorish leader – whom the Christians evicted with difficulty only in 1166.

The walls completely enclose the little collection of whitewashed houses, a *pousada* (*see p399*) and the 15th-century **Igreja Matriz**. Rua do Espírito

Santo leads past the former governor's house (now a bank) with its 17th-century iron balcony, and a Baroque fountain, up towards the **castle**.

Built by King Dinis in about 1299, the castle dominates the village. Its walls enclose two cisterns, a museum displaying historic weapons and a keep. The castle offers spectacular views south and west towards the Serra de São Mamede and east to the Spanish frontier.

The **Museu Municipal**, in the former church of Santa Maria, retains the main altar, and has an interesting exhibition of traditional remedies and local archaeological finds dating from Palaeolithic to Roman times.

🏛️ **Museu Municipal**
Largo de Santa Maria. **Tel** 245 909 132. ◯ Tue–Sun. ● 25 Dec. 🎦

Portalegre ❸

Road map D4. 🏠 12,000. 🚊 🚌
ℹ️ Rua Guilherme Gomes Fernandes 22 (245 307 445). 🗓️ Wed & Sat (food); 2nd Wed of month (clothes).
www.rtsm.pt

Strategically positioned on a low plateau of the Serra de São Mamede, Portalegre is of Roman origin. At the end of the 13th century, King Dinis (*see pp44–5*) built a **castle** on the city's highest point. The castle keep houses the city museum (Rua Luís Barahona; open Tue–Sun).

Textile, tapestry and silk industries brought prosperity

Looking out over the plain from the heights of Marvão's castle

in the 16th and 17th centuries, reflected in the Renaissance and Baroque mansions found along Rua 19 de Junho, the main street of the old town. Near the new town's central square, the Rossio, a former Jesuit monastery is now the only tapestry factory still in use. Cork production is also an important industry here.

Uphill lies the cathedral, or **Sé**. Built in 1556, it acquired its Baroque façade and twin pinnacles in the 18th century. The late Renaissance interior has a sacristy lined with striking *azulejo* panels. These blue and white tile pictures, dating from the first years of the 17th century, depict scenes from the life of the Virgin Mary and the flight of the Holy Family into Egypt.

In an adjacent 18th-century mansion is the small **Museu Municipal**, where the eclectic collection on display ranges from religious art to Portuguese ceramics.

The home of José Régio (1901–69), the eminent Portuguese poet and dramatist, is near the Praça da República. Now the **Museu José Régio**, it contains some fascinating folk art objects in a variety of media as well as his collection of crucifixes and a recreated Alentejan kitchen.

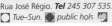

Folk crucifix, Museu José Régio, Portalegre

🏛 Museu Municipal
Rua José Maria da Rosa. **Tel** 245 307 535. ● for restoration. 🖼

🏛 Museu José Régio
Rua José Régio. **Tel** 245 307 535. ☐ Tue–Sun. ● public hols 🖼

Castelo de Vide ❹

Road map D4. 🏠 3,000. 🚍 🚆
🛈 Praça Dom Pedro V (245 901 361). 🛍 Fri (clothes).

Sprawled on a green slope of the Serra de São Mamede, this pretty spa town enjoyed by the Romans has worn well. It is fringed by modern development but the lower town, around Praça Dom Pedro V, retains its Baroque church of **Santa Maria**, the 18th-century town hall and pillory, and handsome mansions from the same era. In the Largo Frederico Laranjo is one of several sources of the town's curative waters: the **Fonte da Vila**, a carved stone fountain with a pillared canopy. Just above is the maze-like **Judiaria**, where small white houses sprout vivid pots of geraniums. Its cobbled alleys conceal a 13th-century **synagogue** and are lined with fine Gothic doorways. The town's oldest chapel, the 13th-century **Salvador do Mundo** on the Estrada de Circunvalação, has a much admired *Flight into Egypt* by an unknown 18th-century artist.

In the upper town, the tiny **Nossa Senhora da Alegria** offers a feast of 17th-century polychrome floral tiles. It stands within the walls of the **castle** that gave the town its name. This was rebuilt in 1310 by King Dinis, who negotiated here to marry Isabel of Aragon. Much of the castle was lost in an explosion in 1705.

Red-tiled roofs of Castelo de Vide

Crato ❺

Road map D4. 🏠 2,000. 🚍 🚆 🛈
Mosteiro de Santa Maria de Flor da Rosa, next to the pousada (245 997 341). 🛍 3rd Thu of month.

Modest houses under outsize chimneys give no hint of Crato's past eminence. Part of a gift from Sancho II to the powerful crusading Order of Hospitallers, Crato was the Order's headquarters by 1350. Its prestige was such that Manuel I and João III were both married here, and João III's nephew was Grand Prior.

In 1662, invading Spanish forces sacked and burned the town, which never recovered. The Hospitallers' **castle** remains in ruins, and in Praça do Município the 15th-century **Varanda do Grão-Prior** marks the entrance to what was the Grand Prior's residence.

Rua de Santa Maria leads, via an avenue of orange trees, to the **Igreja Matriz**, much altered since its 13th-century origins. In the chancel, 18th-century *azulejos* depict fishing, hunting and travelling scenes.

Environs: Just north of Crato are the imposing monastery and church of **Flor da Rosa**. Built in 1356 by the Grand Prior of Crato, father of Nuno Álvares Pereira (*see p185*), the monastery was restored and in 1995 opened as a *pousada* (*see p398*). A tapestry in the dining room shows the monastery surrounded by pine forests, as it was until the 20th century.

The crenellated monastery, now a *pousada*, of Flor da Rosa, near Crato

Alter do Chão 6

Road map D4. ☗ 3,900. ⊟
ℹ Palácio do Álamo (245 610 004).
🗓 1st Thu of month.

The Romans founded Elteri (or Eltori) in 204 BC, but razed it under the Emperor Hadrian after the inhabitants were accused of disloyalty. The town was re-established in the 13th century.

Dominating the town centre is the five-towered **castle** (closed for restoration). It has a Gothic portal built in 1359 by Pedro I. The flower-filled market square, the Largo Doze Melhores de Alter, lies at its feet.

Several streets northwest of the castle are graced by fine Baroque town houses, many trimmed with Alentejan style yellow paintwork. The 18th-century **Palácio do Álamo** (open daily) houses an art gallery and library.

☗ Castle
Largo Barreto Caldeira.
◻ Tue–Sun.

Environs: Alter is best known for the **Coudelaria de Alter**, founded in 1748 to breed the Alter Real. The stud extends to 300 ha (740 acres) around attractive stables painted in the royal livery of white and ochre.

Spanning the Seda 12 km (7 miles) west along the N369 is the robust six-arched **Ponte de Vila Formosa**. This bridge carried the Roman road from Lisbon to Mérida in Spain.

⋃ Coudelaria de Alter
3 km (2 miles) NW of town.
Tel 245 610 060. ◻ Tue–Sun.
◉ public hols. 🎟 ♿

Campo Maior's macabre but compelling Capela dos Ossos

Campo Maior 7

Road map E5. ☗ 8,500. ⊟
ℹ Largo da Barata (268 689 413).
🗓 2nd Sat of month.

According to legend, this town got its name when three families settled in *campo maior*, the "bigger field". King Dinis fortified the town in 1310 and the monumental Porta da Vila was added in 1646.

Disaster struck in 1732 when a gunpowder magazine, ignited by lightning, destroyed the citadel and killed 1,500 people. It seems likely that after a decent period, the victims provided the material for the morbid **Capela dos Ossos**, entirely faced in human bones. Dated 1766, it bears an inscription on mortality spelt out in collar bones.

Each September the streets are dressed with paper flowers for the joyful Festa das Flores.

⛪ Capela dos Ossos
Largo Dr. Regala 6. **Tel** 268 686 168.
◻ daily (if closed, ask priest to open).

Elvas 8

Road map D5. ☗ 20,000. 🚉 ⊟
ℹ Praça da República (268 622 236).
🗓 2nd & 4th Mon of the month.

Only 12 km (7 miles) from the Spanish border, Elvas feels like a frontier town. The sprawl of modern Elvas caters for busy cross-border traffic, but the old town's fortifications are among the best preserved in Europe. Within the walls a few architectural features and many of the street names are reminders that for 500 years the town was in Moorish hands.

Elvas was liberated from the Moors in 1230, but for another 600 years its fate was to swing between periodic attacks from Spain and the witnessing of numerous peace treaties.

Despite its dramatic history, Elvas is nowadays associated in Portuguese minds with Elvas plums.

Summer roses brightening an Elvas street

ALTER REAL: HORSE OF KINGS

Most Lusitano horses – Portugal's national breed – are grey, but those called Alter Real ("real" means royal) are purebred bay or brown. King José (1750–77), who yearned for a quality Portuguese horse, imported a stock of Andalusian mares, from which the gracious, nimble Alter Real was bred. The equestrian statue in Lisbon's Praça do Comércio *(see p85)* is of José astride his beloved Alter, Gentil. The stud prospered until the Napoleonic Wars (1807–15), when horse stealing and erratic breeding sent the Alter into decline. By 1930, the royal horse was practically extinct, but years of dedication have ultimately revived this classic breed.

THE FORTIFICATIONS OF ELVAS

A walk around the top of the battlements gives a fine view of the old town and a vantage point from which to appreciate the ingenious design of the fortifications. Using the principles of the French military architect, the Marquis de Vauban, a series of pentagonal bastions and free-standing angled ravelins form a multi-faceted star, protecting the walls from every angle. What survives dates mostly from the 17th century, when the defences held off Spanish troops in the War of Independence (see pp50–51). Elvas also served as Wellington's base to besiege Badajoz across the Guadiana.

Two surviving satellite forts indicate the strategic importance of Elvas: just to the southeast lies **Forte de Santa Luzia** (1641–87), and 2 km (1 mile) to the north is the 18th-century **Forte de Graça**, which is still a military post.

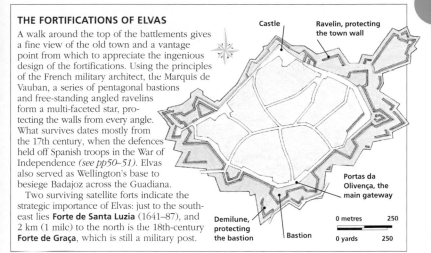

Castle

Ravelin, protecting the town wall

Portas da Olivença, the main gateway

Demilune, protecting the bastion

Bastion

0 metres 250
0 yards 250

♣ Castle
Parada do Castelo. ◐ Mon–Fri.
Romano-Moorish in origin, the castle was rebuilt for Sancho II in 1226. It underwent further remodelling over the years, mainly by King Dinis and then, in the late 15th century, under João II, whose arms, which incorporate a pelican, can be seen above the entrance. Until the late 1500s the castle was used as the residence of the mayors of Elvas.

⌂ Nossa Senhora da Assunção
Praça da República. **Tel** 268 625 997.
◐ Tue pm–Sun. ♿ (via side door).
Until 1882, this was the cathedral of Elvas. Built in the early 16th century, its architect was Francisco de Arruda, who also designed the town's impressive aqueduct. His Manueline south portal survives, but much of the church has been modified. The azulejos in the nave date from the early 17th century.

⌂ Museu Arqueológico and Biblioteca
Largo do Colégio. **Tel** 268 622 404.
◑ for renovation. 🖼
This archaeological museum is set to move to a new site in Rua do Açolges (no date as yet). The cool rooms in the present building display a collection that ranges from Roman water pots to prehistoric artifacts. The associated library contains more than 50,000 books, including a number of rare early works.

⌂ Museu de Arte Contemporânea de Elvas
Rua da Cadeia. **Tel** 268 637 150.
◐ Tue pm–Sun.
The only national museum that displays exclusively contemporary Portuguese art occupies a former hospital. The collection includes works by artists such as Adriana Molder and André Gomes.

⌂ Nossa Senhora dos Aflitos
Largo do Pelourinho. ◐ Tue–Sun.
The plain exterior belies the wealth within the walls of this little 16th-century church. Its appeal is in the fine marble columns and spectacular azulejos added in the 17th century. These line the walls and reach up into the cupola.

Just behind the church is the archway of the Arab Porta da Alcáçova, a vestige of Elvas's

Largo do Dr Santa Clara, with its pillory

Moorish fortifications. In the adjacent Largo do Dr Santa Clara is a pillory, carved in Manueline style (see pp24–5) and still armed with its hooks.

The arches of the great aqueduct

⌂ Aqueduto da Amoreira
Until the 16th century the only source of drinking water in Elvas was the Alcalá well in the west of the town. When this began to fail, alarmed citizens conceived the notion of an aqueduct to bring water from the spring at Amoreira, some 8 km (5 miles) away. Work, begun in 1498, was not finished until 1622. The great round buttresses and arches of architect Francisco de Arruda march across the valley and still deliver water to the fountain in the Largo da Misericórdia. The aqueduct has a total of 843 arches in up to five tiers and in places towers to over 30 m (100 ft).

Vila Viçosa: Paço Ducal

The Dukes of Bragança owned vast estates, but the lavish palace at Vila Viçosa, begun by Dom Jaime in 1501, became their favoured residence.

When the 8th Duke became king in 1640, many of the furnishings accompanied him to Lisbon, but the long suite of first-floor rooms is still splendid, from the Sala da Cabra-Cega, where royal parties played blind man's buff, to the heroic Sala de Hércules. More intimate are the rooms of King Carlos and his wife, which are much as he left them the day before his assassination in 1908.

Chapel
Despite later additions the chapel has retained its coffered ceiling and other features from the early 16th century. It was here, on 3 December 1640, that the 8th Duke learnt that he was to become king.

Dining room

First floor

The vast kitchen, which once regularly fed several hundred people, gleams with over 600 copper pots and pans, some large enough to bathe in.

★ Sala dos Duques
Lining the ceiling of the Room of the Dukes are portraits of all the dukes of Bragança by the Italian Domenico Dupra (1689–1770), commissioned by João V. On the walls are Brussels tapestries of scenes from the life of Achilles.

Sala da Cabra-Cega

The armouries, in a series of vaulted rooms, display swords, crossbows, halberds and suits of armour.

Ground floor

The library is contained in several rooms and includes precious early works collected by King Manuel II in exile *(see p57)*

Formal Gardens
The Jardim da Duquesa and the Jardim do Bosque are partly enclosed by palace walls, but can be seen from the dining-room windows. Their geometric formality reflects the palace's architectural style.

Entrance

STAR FEATURE

★ Sala dos Duques

VISITORS' CHECKLIST

Terreiro do Paço. *Tel 268 980 659.*
2:30–5:30pm Tue; 10am–1pm,
2:30–5:30pm Wed–Fri; 9:30am–
1pm, 2:30–6pm Sat & Sun (Oct–
Mar: 2–5pm Tue; 10am–1pm, 2–
5pm Wed; 9:30am–1pm, 2–5pm
Thu–Sun). 1 Jan, Easter, 25
Dec, 1 May. compulsory.

KEY TO FLOORPLAN

☐ Royal rooms

☐ Library

☐ Chapel

☐ Armouries

☐ Kitchen

☐ Treasury

☐ Public areas

PALACE GUIDE

*Guided tours, which last
about an hour, take in the
royal rooms ranged along the
first floor and ground-floor
areas such as the kitchen and
the treasury. Entry to the coach
museum, on the north side of
the palace, and armoury is
by separate tickets. From
time to time areas may
be closed for restora-
tion and rooms
can be shut off
without notice.*

Vila Viçosa 9

Road map D5. 8,700.
Praça da República (268 881
101). Wed.

After the expulsion of the
Moors in 1226, this hill-
side town was named Val
Viçosa – "fertile valley". In the
15th century it became the
country seat of the dukes of
Bragança, and when the 8th
Duke became King João IV,
Vila Viçosa was expanded to
meet the needs of nobles
and visiting ministers. Substantial houses, built from the
local white marble, in streets
lined with orange trees, reflect
its prosperous royal past.

The town is full of reminders
of the Braganças. Dominating
the west side of the Terreiro do
Paço is the long façade of the
Paço Ducal, which stretches
for 110 m (360 ft). Visitors to
the palace emerge through the
Porta do Nó, a marble and
schist gateway formed into the
knot symbol of the Braganças.

In the centre of the square a
statue of João IV on horseback
looks across to the **Igreja dos
Agostinhos** (not open to the
public). Founded in 1267 but
rebuilt in the 17th century, the
church was intended as the last
resting place of the dukes, but
despite their affection for Vila
Viçosa, most Bragança monarchs are buried in Lisbon, at
São Vicente de Fora (see p70).

**View from the castle at Vila Viçosa,
looking towards the Paço Ducal**

In the Renaissance **Convento
das Chagas**, on the south side
of the square, are the tombs of
the Bragança wives. Founded
by the 4th Duke's second wife
in 1530, the convent is being
converted to a *pousada*.

Alongside the Paço Ducal, an
18-km (11-mile) wall rings the
tapada real, or royal chase.
Uphill from the Terreiro do
Paço is the **castle**, where an
exhibition explains the history
of the hunt. The castle, built by
King Dinis, was the Braganças'
residence from 1461 until the
Paço Ducal became habitable.

In the nearby 14th-century
church of **Nossa Senhora da
Conceição** stands a Gothic
image of the Virgin, said to be
from England. During the 1646
cortes João IV crowned her as
patron saint of Portugal, after
which no Portuguese monarch
ever wore a crown.

🏰 **Castle**
Avenida Duques de Bragança.
Tel 268 980 128. same as Paço
Ducal. public hols.

THE ROYAL HOUSE OF BRAGANÇA

**Catherine, born at
Vila Viçosa in 1638**

Afonso, illegitimate son of João I, was
created Duke of Bragança in 1442,
first of an influential but bloodstained
dynasty. Fernando, the 3rd Duke, was
executed in 1483 by his cousin, João
II, who feared his power. Jaime, the
unstable 4th Duke, locked up his wife
in Bragança castle (see p260), then
killed her at Vila Viçosa. It was Dom
Jaime who initiated the building of
the palace at Vila Viçosa, an ambitious
work embellished by later dukes to
reflect their aspirations and affluence.
The 8th Duke only reluctantly relinquished a life of music
and hunting here to take up the throne (see p50).

The Braganças ruled Portugal for 270 years, accumulating
wealth and forging alliances (João IV's daughter, Catherine,
married Charles II of England), but inbreeding enfeebled the
bloodline (see p167). The last monarch, Manuel II, fled to
exile in 1910, two years after his father and brother were shot
by Republicans. The present duke farms quietly near Viseu.

**The Porta do Nó, its carved knots
the symbol of the Braganças**

Alandroal, surrounded by groves of cork oaks

Alandroal ⑩

Road map D5. 🏚 *2,500.* 🚌 🚹
*Praça da República (268 440
045).* 🕑 *Wed.*

The low-lying little town of
Alandroal, wrapped tidily
around its **castle** ruins, was
built by the Knights of Avis,
who settled here from 1220.
Little remains inside, but a surviving inscription shows it was
completed in 1298. The **Igreja
Matriz** within its walls dates
from the 16th century.

The **Misericórdia** church near
the castle walls contains beautiful *azulejos* reputed to be the
work of Policarpo de Oliveira
Bernardes (1695–1778).

Environs: Terena, 10 km (6
miles) south of Alandroal, is
well known for its pottery.
The 14th-century sanctuary of
Nossa Senhora de Boa Nova
has frescoes covering its walls
and ceiling; dating from 1706,
these depict saints and Portuguese kings. For access ask at
the house opposite the church.

MARBLE: ALENTEJO'S WHITE GOLD

Portugal is the world's second largest exporter of marble,
and even Italy, the biggest producer, buys Portugal's quality
stone. Around 90 per cent – over 500,000 tonnes a year – is
quarried around Estremoz. The marble from Estremoz and
nearby Borba is white or pink, while the quarries at Viana do

Quarrymen near Estremoz, working on
elephantine blocks of prized marble

Alentejo yield green
stone. Marble has
been used for con-
struction since Roman
times and in towns
such as Évora *(see
pp304–7)* and Vila
Viçosa *(see pp300–
301)*, palaces and
humble doorsteps
alike gleam with the
stone often referred
to as "white gold".

Redondo ⑪

Road map D5. 🏚 *4,000* 🚌 🚹
Praça da República (266 909 100).
🕑 *1st Sun of month (antiques);
2nd Thu of month (general).*

The centre of one of the
Alentejo's wine regions *(see
p29)*, medieval Redondo is
also renowned for its pottery.
Roman-style water jugs,
casseroles and bowls painted
with humorous folk-art motifs
(see p25) are sold from the
tiny white houses leading up
to the ruins of the **castle**
founded by King Dinis.

Environs: The **Convento de
São Paulo** in the Serra de
Ossa, 10 km (6 miles) north,
was built in 1376; Catherine
of Bragança stayed here on her
return home in 1692 after the
death of her husband, King
Charles II of England. It is now
a luxury hotel *(see p399)*, but
retains its wonderful 16th- to
18th-century *azulejos*.

Estremoz ⑫

Road map D5. 🏚 *9,000.* 🚌
🚹 *Rossio Marquês de Pombal
(268 333 541).* 🕑 *Sat.*

A key stronghold in the War
of Restoration *(see p50)*
and then in the War of the Two
Brothers *(see p54)*, Estremoz
looks out from its hilltop over
groves of gnarled olive trees.

The medieval upper town,
set within stout ramparts, is
dominated by a 13th-century
marble keep, rising to 27 m
(89 ft). This is the **Torre das
Três Coroas**, the Tower of
the Three Crowns, recalling the
kings (Sancho II, Afonso III
and Dinis) in whose reigns
it was built. The adjoining
castle and palace complex,
built for Dona Isabel, is now
a *pousada (see p399)*. The
saintly Isabel *(see p45)*, wife of
King Dinis, died here in 1336
and the **Capela da Rainha
Santa** dedicated to her is lined
with *azulejos* recording her life.

Today the bustling weekly
market in the Rossio, the main
square in the lower town, is a
reflection of local farming life.
Across the square are the remains of King Dinis's once-fine

palace and the town's **Museu Municipal**, with a display of archaeological finds, restored living rooms and a parade of *bonecos*, the charming pottery figurines for which Estremoz is famous *(see p25)*.

🏛 **Museu Municipal**
Largo Dom Dinis. *Tel 268 333 608.*
⭕ Tue–Sun. ⬤ public hols. ⬤

⛪ **Capela da Rainha Santa**
Largo Dom Dinis. (Access via adjacent Design Gallery.) ⭕ Ask at the Igreja de Santa Maria, on Largo Dom Dinis.

Évoramonte 𝟙𝟛

Road map D5. 🏘 *1,000.* 🚌
ℹ Rua Santa Maria (268 959 227).

Stone "rope" embellishing the castle walls at Évoramonte

Above the doorway of No. 41, along Évoramonte's single street, is a historic plaque. It records that here, on 26 May 1834, Dom Miguel ceded the throne, ending the conflict with his older brother *(see p54)*.

Évoramonte's eye-catching **castle**, its walls bound by bold stone "ropes", largely replaced an earlier castle that fell in an earthquake in 1531. The 16th-century walls, however, have been controversially "restored" with concrete. An exhibition explains the castle's history.

⛫ **Castle**
⭕ Tue pm–Sun. ⬤ last weekend of month. ⬤

Arraiolos 𝟙𝟜

Road map D5. 🏘 *3,500.* 🚌
ℹ Praça Lima e Brito (266 490 254).
📅 1st Sat of month.

The foundation of Arraiolos is attributed either to Celts or perhaps to local tribes in about 300 BC. Its 14th-century **castle** seems overwhelmed by the town walls and looming 16th-century **Igreja do Salvador**. Typically, houses in Arraiolos are low and white, and are painted with a blue trim to ward off the devil.

The principal sight in Arraiolos, however, is of women stitching at their bright wool rugs in the shadowy rooms behind the main street. Carpets have been woven in Arraiolos since the 13th century and decorate countless manor houses and palaces throughout Portugal. The craft may have begun with the Moors, but floral designs of the 18th century are thought to be the finest. At the many carpet shops here it is also possible to see a range of contemporary designs with their bright colours and less elaborate patterns.

Environs: At **Pavia**, 18 km (11 miles) to the north, is the startling sight of a tiny chapel built into a dolmen. It is signposted as Anta de São Dinis; if closed, ask at the café nearby.

Montemor-o-Novo 𝟙𝟝

Road map C5. 🏘 *9,000.* 🚌
ℹ Largo Calouste Gulbenkian (266 898 103). 📅 2nd Sat of month.

Montemor was fortified by the Romans and then by the Moors – the Arab warrior Al-Mansur is remembered in the name of the nearby River

The view down the nave of the Igreja Matriz in Montemor-o-Novo

Almançor. The town, regained from the Moors in the reign of Sancho I, was awarded its first charter in 1203. The **castle**, rebuilt in the late 13th century, is now a ruin crowning the hill.

Montemor's 17th-century **Igreja Matriz** stands in Largo São João de Deus, named after the saint who was born nearby in 1495. The Order of Brothers Hospitallers that St John of God founded evolved from his care for the sick, especially foundlings and prisoners.

A former convent in the upper town is now the **Museu de Arqueologia** and **Museu Regional**. The former has local archaeological finds and antique farming tools, the latter has a series of themed rooms on pottery and sacred art.

🏛 **Museu de Arqueologia**
Convento de São Domingos, Largo Professor Dr Banha de Andrade. *Tel* 266 890 235. ⭕ Tue–Sun. ⬤ ⬤

Arraiolos, crowned by its castle and the Igreja do Salvador

Street-by-Street: Évora ⑯

Rising out of the Alentejan plain is the enchanting walled city of Évora. The town rose to prominence under the Romans and flourished throughout the Middle Ages as a centre of learning and the arts. It was a popular residence of Portuguese kings, but fell out of favour after Spain's annexation of Portugal in 1580. Its influence waned further when the Jesuit university closed in the 18th century. Students once again throng Évora's streets, joined by visitors who come to discover its many historical sites and enjoy the atmosphere of the old town. The city's historic legacy was officially recognized in 1986, when UNESCO declared Évora a World Heritage Site.

★ Roman Temp
Popularly believe to have been ded cated to the godd Diana, this templ was erected in th 2nd or 3rd centu AD. It was used a armoury, theatre and slaughterhou before being rescued in 1870.

Rua 5 de Outubro
The shops along this street sell curios and handicrafts, from painted chairs to carved cork.

RUA DO SALVADOR

RUA DE DONA ISABEL

RUA DAS CASAS PINT ADAS

PRAÇA DO SERTÓRIO

RUA DE VASCO DA GAM

RUA JOÃO DE DEUS

RUA NOVA

RUA 5 DE OUTU

```
0 metres        50
0 yards         50
```

KEY

– – – Suggested route

PRAÇA DO GIRALDO

Tourist information

RUA DA REPÚBLICA

Praça do Giraldo
The fountain in Évora's main square was erected in 1571. Its marble predecessor received the first water delivered by the town's aqueduct (see p307).

STAR SIGHTS

★ Sé

★ Roman Temple

★ Museu de Évora

To railway and bus stations

For hotels and restaurants in this region see pp398–400 and pp424–6

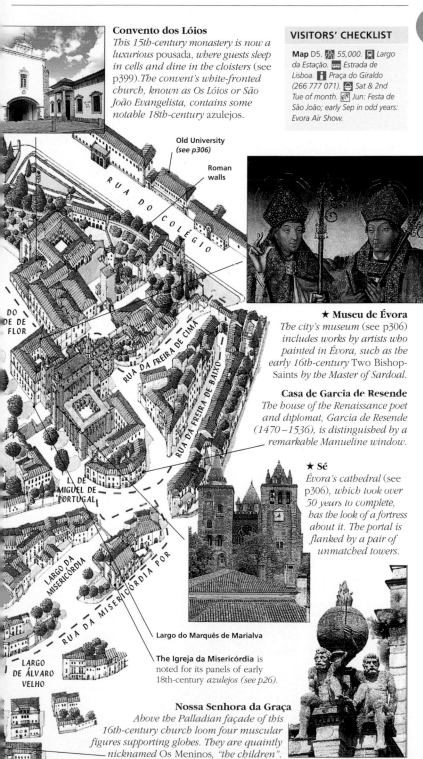

Convento dos Lóios

This 15th-century monastery is now a luxurious pousada, where guests sleep in cells and dine in the cloisters (see p399). The convent's white-fronted church, known as Os Lóios or São João Evangelista, contains some notable 18th-century azulejos.

Old University
(see p306)

Roman walls

RUA DO COLÉGIO

DO
DE DE
FLOR

RUA DA FREIRA DE CIMA

RUA DA FREIRA DE BAIXO

L. DE
MIGUEL DE
PORTUGAL

LARGO DA
MISERICÓRDIA

RUA DA MISERICÓRDIA POR

RUA DA MISERICÓRDIA

LARGO
DE ÁLVARO
VELHO

VISITORS' CHECKLIST

Map D5. 55,000. Largo da Estação. Estrada de Lisboa. Praça do Giraldo (266 777 071). Sat & 2nd Tue of month. Jun: Festa de São João; early Sep in odd years: Évora Air Show.

★ Museu de Évora

The city's museum (see p306) includes works by artists who painted in Évora, such as the early 16th-century Two Bishop-Saints by the Master of Sardoal.

Casa de Garcia de Resende

The house of the Renaissance poet and diplomat, Garcia de Resende (1470–1536), is distinguished by a remarkable Manueline window.

★ Sé

Évora's cathedral (see p306), which took over 50 years to complete, has the look of a fortress about it. The portal is flanked by a pair of unmatched towers.

Largo do Marquês de Marialva

The Igreja da Misericórdia is noted for its panels of early 18th-century azulejos (see p26).

Nossa Senhora da Graça

Above the Palladian façade of this 16th-century church loom four muscular figures supporting globes. They are quaintly nicknamed Os Meninos, "the children".

Exploring Évora

Squeezed within Roman, medieval and 17th-century walls, Évora's web of streets is an architectural and cultural cornucopia. From the forbidding cathedral, a stroll down past the craft shops of Rua 5 de Outubro leads to Praça do Giraldo, the city's lively main square, whose arcades are a reminder of Moorish influence. Évora's religious dedication is reflected in the number and variety of its churches – over 20 churches and monasteries, including a grisly chapel of bones. On a happier note, Évora's restaurants are excellent and the pleasure of wandering the historic streets is enhanced by evocative names such as Alley of the Unshaven Man and Street of the Countess's Tailor.

Azulejos at the Old University, depicting Aristotle teaching Alexander

🛐 Sé

Largo do Marquês de Marialva.
Tel 266 759 330. ⬭ daily (museum Tue–Sun). 🈸 to cloister & museum.
Begun in 1186 and consecrated in 1204, the granite cathedral of Santa Maria was completed by 1250. Romanesque melds with Gothic in this castle-like cathedral whose towers, one turreted, one topped by a blue cone, give the façade an odd asymmetry. Flanking the portal between them are superb 14th-century sculpted Apostles. The 18th-century high altar and marble chancel are by JF Ludwig, the architect of the monastery at Mafra *(see pp52–3)*. A Renaissance portal in the north transept is by Nicolau Chanterène. In the cloisters, which date from about 1325, statues of the Evangelists stand watch at each corner.

A glittering treasury houses sacred art. The most intriguing exhibit here is a 13th-century ivory Virgin whose body opens out to become a triptych of tiny carved scenes: her life in nine episodes.

🏛 Museu de Évora

Largo do Conde de Vila Flor (currently in Igreja do Convento de Santa Clara). **Tel** 266 708 095. ⬭ Tue pm–Sun. 🔘 some public hols. 🈸
This 16th-century palace, once the residence of governors and bishops, is now the regional museum. Évora's history is all here, from Roman columns to modern sculpture in local marble. A beautiful Moorish window came from the old town hall, and a stone frieze probably from the Roman temple. Notable upstairs are *The Life of the Virgin*, a 16th-century

Carved figures of the Apostles decorating the Gothic entrance to the Sé

Flemish polyptych in 13 panels and works by the Portuguese painter known as the Master of Sardoal, especially his *Two Bishop-Saints* and a *Nativity*.

🏫 University

Largo dos Colegiais 2. **Tel** 266 740 875. ⬭ Mon–Sat. 🔘 public hols. 🈸
With the establishment of the Jesuits' Colégio do Espírito Santo, Évora, already noted for its architecture and sacred art, became a seat of learning. The school, which was inaugurated in 1559 by Cardinal Henrique, brother of João III, flourished for 200 years, but was closed in 1759 when the reforming Marquês de Pombal banished the Jesuits *(see p53)*.

Today part of the University of Évora, the school still has a graceful cloister and notable *azulejos* – in the classrooms they depict suitably studious themes such as Plato lecturing to disciples (1744–9). The 18th-century Baroque chapel, now the Sala dos Actos, is used for graduation ceremonies.

🏫 Praça do Giraldo

Évora's bustling main square is bounded along its eastern side by a series of graceful Moorish arcades. The name Giraldo, some say, stems from Geraldo Sem-Pavor (the Fearless), an outlaw who in 1165 ousted the Moors for King Afonso Henriques.

The square has witnessed some bloody acts: João II watched the beheading of his brother-in-law, the Duke of Bragança, here in 1483, and it was the site in 1573 of an Inquisitional burning. Today, it is a favourite meeting-place, especially on market days.

🛐 São Francisco

Praça 1° de Maio. **Tel** 266 704 521. ⬭ daily. 🈸 to Capela dos Ossos.
The principal fascination of this 15th-century church is its Capela dos Ossos. This gruesome chapel of bones was created in the 17th century from the remains of 5,000 monks. Two leathery corpses, one of a child, dangle from a chain, and a mordant reminder at the entrance reads: *Nós ossos que aqui estamos, pelos vossos esperamos* (We bones that are here await yours).

Largo da Porta de Moura, with its striking Renaissance fountain

🏛 Largo da Porta de Moura
The western entrance to this
square is guarded by the vestiges of a Moorish gateway.
Both the domed Casa Soure
and the double arches of the
belvedere on Casa Cordovil at
the opposite end, show the
Arab influence on architecture
in Évora. The central fountain,
looking like some futuristic
orb, surprisingly dates back to
1556. Just south of the square,
the portal of the Convento do
Carmo features the knot symbol, denoting it once belonged
to the Braganças (see p301).

🌿 Jardim Público
◻ daily. ♿
On the southern edge of the
old town, Évora's public gardens are set out on the site of
the grandiose Palácio de Dom
Manuel, built for Afonso V
(1438–81) and embellished by
successive kings. It was the
venue for grand banquets and
ceremonies but fell into dis-
repair and finally disappeared
in 1895. All that remains is the
graceful Galeria das Damas, a
20th-century reconstruction of
a walkway and pavilion built
for Manuel I (1495–1521).

⛰ Walls
The fortifications that have
protected Évora down the
centuries form two incomplete
concentric circles. The inner
ring, of which only fragments
are discernible, is Roman, from
perhaps as early as the 1st
century AD, with Moorish and
medieval additions – the two
stubby towers that give the
Largo da Porta de Moura its
name mark an Arab gate.
  In the 14th century, new
walls were built to encompass
the growing town. Completed
under Fernando I, these had 40
towers and ten gates, including
the Porta de Alconchel, which
still faces the Lisbon road.
  When João IV was defiantly
declared king in 1640 (see
p50), major fortifications were
erected on this outer ring in
anticipation of Spanish attack,
and it is these 17th-century
walls which are most evident
today. The fear of attack was
not unfounded, and the walls
withstood much battering from
the besieging Spanish in 1663.

Surviving arches of Évora's 16th-
century aqueduct

🏛 Aqueduto da Água de Prata
Évora's aqueduct, evocatively
called "of the silver water", was
built between 1531 and 1537
by the town's own eminent
architect, Francisco de Arruda.
The construction was regarded
with wonder, and is even described in Os Lusíadas, the epic
by Luís de Camões (see p190).
It originally carried water as far
as the Praça do Giraldo. Like
the walls, it was damaged in
the 17th century during the
Restoration War with Spain, but
a surviving stretch, some 9 km
(5 miles) long, can still be seen
approaching from the northwest: there is a good view of
it from Rua Cândido dos Reis.

THE ROMANS IN THE ALENTEJO
Once the Romans gained dominance over Lusitania (see
pp40–41), they turned the Alentejo into a vast wheatfield:
their very name for the principal town – Ebora Cerealis
(Évora) – reflects the importance of the region's grain supply.
Latifúndios, large farms instigated by the Romans, survive
to this day, as do Roman open-cast copper and iron mines.
Local marble was used in the construction of the finest villas,
and Roman remains are to be found scattered throughout
the region, particularly in Évora and Beja (see p313) and
in more isolated sites such as São Cucufate, near Vidigueira
(see p312) and Miróbriga, near Santiago do Cacém (see p314).

Roman bridge over the Odivelas, near Vidigueira

Megaliths Tour ⑰

Archaeologists date the *pedras talhas,* hewn stones, near
Évora to between 4000 and 2000 BC. Their symbolism
remains mysterious. Dolmens are thought to be where Neolithic communities buried their dead, together with their
possessions – more than 130 have been found in the region.
Tall phallic menhirs jutting from olive groves immediately
suggest fertility rites, while cromlechs, carved stones standing
in regulated groups, probably had religious significance.
This tour includes examples of each; more can be found
further east, near Monsaraz, and the museum in Montemor-
o-Novo *(see p303)* has finds related to the area.

**Menhir of
Almendres** ②
Standing 2.5 m (8 ft)
tall, this solitary stone
is located away from
the cromlech, in an
olive grove behind a
row of tall Cooperativa
Agrícola storage bins.

**Cromlech of
Almendres** ③
This oval, made up of
95 ellipitical stones, is
believed to have been
a temple dedicated to
a solar cult. The route
to the cromlech is sign-
posted from the N114.

Grutas do Escoural ⑥
Discovered in 1963, these
caves contain paintings
about 15–20,000
years old.

Évora ①
In the undulating farmland
around the historic city of
Évora *(see pp304–7)* at
least 150 megalith sites
have been found.

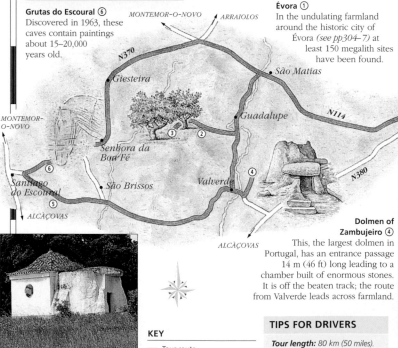

**Dolmen of
Zambujeiro** ④
This, the largest dolmen in
Portugal, has an entrance passage
14 m (46 ft) long leading to a
chamber built of enormous stones.
It is off the beaten track; the route
from Valverde leads across farmland.

**Dolmen-chapel
of São Brissos** ⑤
Beyond the hamlet of Brissos,
this tiny chapel has been
created from an *anta* or
dolmen. Another is to be
found at Pavia *(see p303).*

KEY

━━ Tour route

══ Other roads

0 kilometres 5

0 miles 3

TIPS FOR DRIVERS

Tour length: 80 km (50 miles).
Access to sites: The only guarded
site is Escoural. The caves are
closed at lunchtime, on Mondays
and at some other times. Access
roads to the sites are often no
more than tracks, and signposting
can be erratic. (See pp460–61.)

Riding through the narrow streets of Monsaraz on the day of a bullfight

Monsaraz ⑱

Road map D5. 👥 150. 🚌
🛈 Largo Dom Nuno Álvares Pereira 5 (266 557 136).

The tiny medieval walled town of Monsaraz perches above the River Guadiana on the frontier with Spain. Now a pretty backwater, it has known more turbulent times. Regained from the Moors in 1167 by the intrepid adventurer Geraldo Sem-Pavor (the Fearless), the town was handed over to the militant Knights Templar. Its frontier position continued to expose it to Spanish attack, but in 1381 assault came from an unexpected quarter. Troops of the Earl of Cambridge, Portugal's ally, were enraged by lack of pay and the annulment of the earl's betrothal to Fernando I's daughter, and unleashed their wrath on Monsaraz.

Principal access to the town is through the massive Porta da Vila. Rua Direita, the main street, leads up to the **castle**. Built by Afonso III and Dinis in the 13th century as part of the border defences, it was reinforced in the 17th century. The keep commands glorious views in all directions and at its foot is the garrison court-yard which today serves on occasion as a bullring.

The 16th-century **Igreja Matriz** in Rua Direita is worth visiting for its tall gilded altars and painted pillars. The 17th- and 18th-century houses along here display coats of arms. In

the Gothic Paços da Audiência, now the **Museu de Arte Sacra**, is a collection of vestments, religious books and sculpture. Its earlier role as a law court is reflected in an unusual secular fresco: *O Bom e o Mau Juiz* (The Good and Bad Judge).

🏛 Museu de Arte Sacra
Largo Dom Nuno Álvares Pereira.
Tel 266 550 120. ◯ Tue–Sun. 🎫

Environs: Surrounded by vineyards, **Reguengos de Monsaraz**, 16 km (10 miles) west, lies at the heart of one of the region's demarcated wine areas *(see p29)*. Its 19th-century church, Santo António, was built in flamboyant Neo-Gothic style by the architect of Lisbon's bullring *(see p118)*.

A number of striking megaliths are found near Monsaraz. The spectacular **Menhir of Outeiro**, 5.6 m (18 ft) tall, and the strangely inscribed **Menhir of Belhôa** are signposted in Telheiro, just north of Monsaraz. About 4 km (2 miles) south is the **Cromlech of Xerez**, a menhir in a square of lesser stones. The tiny houses of **Mourão**, some 8 km (5 miles) further on, have huge chimneys. The town's 14th-century castle looks out over the River Guadiana and vast new Alqueva Dam.

Viana do Alentejo ⑲

Road map D6. 👥 3,500. 🚌
🛈 Praça da República (266 930 012). 🛒 2nd & last Thu of month.

The natural springs of Viana do Alentejo have offered an abundant water source in the Alentejo's dry heartland since Roman times. Its **castle,** begun in 1313, was built to the design of King Dinis, the height of the outer wall exactly calculated to protect soldiers from attacking lancers. The unusual cylindrical towers show a Moorish influence and much of the later remodelling dates from João II, who held a *cortes* here in 1481–2.

Mirroring the castle walls are the crenellations and pinnacles of the adjacent 16th-century **Igreja Matriz**. The highly carved Manueline entrance to this splendid fortified church leads into a majestic triple-naved interior.

Ten minutes' walk east of the town stands the vast pilgrimage church of **Nossa Senhora de Aires**, rebuilt in the 1700s. Inside, the chancel's golden canopy contrasts with pilgrims' humble ex votos.

Environs: The Moorish-style castle at **Alvito**, 10 km (6 miles) south of Viana, was built in 1482 for the newly ennobled Barão de Alvito; it now operates as a *pousada (see p398)*.

The low roofs and distinctive pepperpot chimneys of Mourão, near Monsaraz

A bullfight in the shadow of the 13th-century keep of Monsaraz castle ▷

The vineyards around Vidigueira caught in the evening light

Vidigueira ⑳

Road map D6. 🏠 2,800. 🚌
🛈 Piscinas Municipais (284 437 410). 🎪 2nd Sat of month.

Fine wines from Vidigueira make it a leading centre of wine production in the Alentejo. Less well known is the fact that the explorer Vasco da Gama was Conde de Vidigueira. His remains, now in the Mosteiro dos Jerónimos *(see pp104–5)*, lay from 1539 to 1898 in the Convento do Carmo, now private property. A mediocre statue of the town's most famous son stands in the flowery square named after him. The main features of this unpretentious little town are a **Misericórdia** church dated 1620, and a clocktower from Vasco da Gama's time.

Environs: One of Portugal's most notable Roman sites, **São Cucufate**, named after a later monastery, lies 4 km (2 miles) west. The vaulting belonged to a 4th-century villa, but excavations have revealed the baths of a 2nd-century house, whose wine presses, reservoir and temple indicate a sumptuous Roman residence.

Moura ㉑

Road map D6. 🏠 7,000. 🚌
🛈 Pátio dos Rolins (285 251 375). 🎪 1st Sat of month.

Legend mingles with history in this quiet town among oak and olive trees. Salúquia, daughter of a Moorish governor is said to have thrown herself from the castle tower on learning that her lover had been killed. From this tragedy the town acquired its name – Moura, the Moorish girl. The town's old Moorish quarter is an area of narrow streets and low, whitewashed houses.

Even after the Reconquest in the 12th century, Moura's frontier position left it open to attack. A siege in 1657, during the War of Restoration *(see pp50–51)*, levelled much of it. The 13th-century **castle** survived, only to be blown up by the Spanish in 1707 – just a skeletal keep and wall remain.

Nossa Senhora do Carmo, near the castle, was founded in 1251, the first Carmelite convent in the country. Its two-storey cloister shows Gothic and Renaissance influence and the chancel ceiling frescoes are early 18th century.

View over Moura's quaint Moorish quarter

Serpa ㉒

Road map D6. 🏠 6,000. 🚌
🛈 Largo Dom Jorge de Melo 2–3 (284 544 727). 🎪 last Tue of month.

Serpa's stout walls are topped by an arched aqueduct. Beside the monumental **Porta de Beja** is a *nora*, or Arab water wheel. Won from the Moors in 1232, Serpa successfully resisted foreign control until a brief Spanish occupation in 1707.

Today, Serpa is a quiet agricultural town known for ewe's-milk cheese. Pleasing squares and streets of whitewashed houses are overlooked by a Moorish **castle**, rebuilt in the late 13th century. The **Watch Museum**, in the Convento do Mosteirinho, boasts some 1,800 timepieces, all of them mechanical and some dating from the 17th century.

🏛 **Watch Museum**
Convento do Mosteirinho. *Tel 284 543 194.* ◯ *Tue–Sun.*

Serpa's great Porta de Beja

Environs: Serpa is just 35 km (22 miles) from the Spanish border. The Moors, and later Spain, fought for control of the region, which was finally ceded to Portugal in 1295. Continued disputes have left the legacy of a chain of watch-towers and a peppering of fortresses across these hills. One of the most remote, the deserted fort at **Noudar**, was built in 1346, but even in this isolated corner, evidence of pre-Roman habitation has been uncovered.

On the border at **Barrancos**, an incomprehensible mix of Spanish and Portuguese is spoken. A speciality here is *pata negra* (black trotter), a ham from the local black pigs.

LOVE LETTERS OF A HEARTSICK NUN

Mariana's window

Lettres Portugaises, published in French in 1669, are celebrated for their lyric beauty. They are the poignant letters of a nun whose French lover deserted her: she was Mariana Alcoforado, born in Beja in 1640; he was the Comte de Saint-Léger, later Marquis de Chamilly, fighting in the Restoration wars with Spain. The true authorship of the five letters may be in doubt, but the story of the lovelorn nun endures – Matisse even painted her imaginary portrait. Sentimental visitors to the convent of Nossa Senhora da Conceição (now the Museu Regional) in Beja still sigh over "Mariana's window".

Beja

Road map D6. 🏛 *35,000.* 🚉
🚌 ❗ *Rua Capitão João Francisco de Sousa 25 (284 311 913).* 🛒 *Sat.*

Capital of the Baixo (lower) Alentejo, Beja is a city of historic and social importance. It is also a major centre for the production of wheat, olives and cork, which are grown on the Bejan plains and provide the city's lifeblood.

The town became a regional capital under Julius Caesar, who called it Pax Julia after the peace made here with the Lusitani *(see p40).* The Praça da República marks the site of the Roman forum. The Moors arrived in AD 711, giving the town its present name and a lively, poetic culture until they were forced out in 1162.

Beja has been the scene of struggles against oppressive regimes. In 1808, occupying French troops massacred the inhabitants and, in 1962, during the Salazar regime *(see pp56–7),* General Delgado led an unsuccessful uprising here.

Beja's old town, an area of narrow, often cobbled, streets, stretches from the castle keep southeast to the 13th-century convent of São Francisco, now a superb *pousada (see p398).*

🏛 Museu Regional Rainha Dona Leonor

Largo da Conceição. **Tel** 284 323 351. ☐ *Tue–Sun.* ⬤ *public hols.* 🎫
In the heart of the old town, the former Convento de Nossa Senhora da Conceição houses the regional museum. A little marble ossuary near the entrance contains the bones of the convent's first abbess. Exhibits are mostly paintings and coats of arms, but the building itself is a remarkable blend of architectural styles, with a Gothic church portal, Manueline windows and a dazzling Baroque chapel. Its *azulejos* are especially beautiful, the most notable being the Hispanic-Arab tiles in the chapterhouse and the early 16th-century examples in the cloister. Upstairs is a section on local archaeology and the romantic "Mariana's window".

♣ Torre de Menagem

Largo do Lidador. **Tel** 284 311 800. ☐ *Tue–Sun.* ⬤ *public hols.* 🎫
The unmistakable landmark of the castle keep marks the northwest limit of the old quarter. This work of King Dinis in the late 13th century towers 36 m (118 ft) high. The 183-step climb up through its three storeys provides a rewarding panorama from the top.

Beja's landmark castle keep

🏛 Museu Visigótico

Largo de Santo Amaro. **Tel** 284 321 465. ☐ *Tue–Sun.* ⬤ *public hols.* 🎫 *joint ticket with Museu Regional.*
Just beyond the castle keep stands Beja's oldest church, Santo Amaro, its columns surviving from its Visigothic origins. Appropriately, the church now serves as an exhibition area for the Museu Regional's collection of relics from this early but important period of Portugal's history.

Environs: The remains of the luxurious **Roman villa** at Pisões, 10 km (6 miles) south-west of Beja, date from the 1st century AD. Excavation is far from complete, but extensive floor mosaics and fragments of decorated walls, baths, a bathing pool and hypocaust have been uncovered.

🏛 Roman villa

Herdade de Almocreva, Estrada de Aljustrel (follow signs). ☐ *Tue–Sun.*

Chapterhouse of the former convent, now Beja's Museu Regional

Igreja Matriz, Santiago do Cacém

Santiago do Cacém ㉔

Road map C6. ⛰ 7,000.
🚌 ❗ Largo do Mercado (269
826 696). ⛵ 2nd Mon of month.

Santiago do Cacém's Moorish castle was rebuilt in 1157 by the Templars (see pp186–7). Its walls, which enclose the cemetery of the adjacent 13th-century **Igreja Matriz**, afford panoramic views of the Serra de Grândola to the northeast. The attractive main square is enhanced by the elegant 18th-century mansions built by rich landowners who came here to escape the heat of the plains.

The **Museu Municipal** still retains some cells from its days as a Salazarist prison (see p56). Exhibits here include Roman finds from nearby Miróbriga.

🏛 Museu Municipal
Largo do Município. **Tel** 269 827 375.
☐ Tue–Fri, Sat (pm only).
🌑 public hols.

Environs: On a hill just to the east of Santiago do Cacém lies the site of the Roman city of **Miróbriga**. Excavations, still in progress, have uncovered a forum, two temples, thermal baths and a circus which had seating for 25,000 spectators.

⌂ Miróbriga
Signposted off N121. **Tel** 269 818 460.
☐ Tue–Sun. 🌑 public hols. 🎟

Sines ㉕

Road map C6. ⛰ 26,000. ⛴ 🚌
❗ Largo Poeta Bocage (269 634
472). ⛵ 1st Thu of month.

The birthplace of Vasco da Gama (see p106) is now a major industrial port and tanker terminal ringed with refinery pipelines. Once past this heavy industrial zone, visitors reach the old town with its popular sandy beach, but it is not always possible to escape the haze of pollution.

A prominent landmark above the beach is the modest medieval **castle**, restored in the 16th century by King Manuel. It was here that Vasco da Gama, son of the _alcaide-mor_, or mayor, is reputed to have been born in 1469. A multimedia museum dedicated to the great navigator, the **Casa Vasco da Gama**, is housed in the castle keep. A modern statue of Vasco da Gama stands looking out over the bay.

🏛 Casa Vasco da Gama
Castle of Sines. **Tel** 269 632 237.
☐ Tue–Sun.

Environs: North and south of Sines are attractive beaches. About 10 km (6 miles) south, **Porto Covo** is a picturesque village with an old fort above a cove beach. A little further to the south and a short boat ride offshore is the low hump of **Ilha do Pessegueiro**, Peach Tree Island. Treeless and windswept, with the ruins of a fort, the little island is rather less romantic than it sounds.

More appealing are two sea-blue lagoons, **Lagoa de Santo André** and **Lagoa de Melides**, set in a long stretch of sandy coast about 20 km (12 miles) north of Sines. The lagoons attract a commune of campers, but vast open spaces remain for seekers of privacy.

Whitewashed houses with the traditional blue trim at Porto Covo, south of Sines

Vila Nova de Milfontes ㉖

Road map C6. ⛰ 11,000. 🚌 ❗ Rua
António Mantas (283 996 599). ⛵
2nd & 4th Sat of month in Brunheiras.

One of the loveliest places on Portugal's west coast is where the River Mira meets the sea. The popular resort of Vila Nova de Milfontes, on the sleepy estuary, is low-key and unassuming, but offers many places to stay. Its small castle overlooking the bay once defended the coast from pirates, and is now a hotel. In contrast to the quiet river are the pretty beaches with their crashing waves, a major summer attraction, especially with surfers.

Environs: To the south about 10 km (6 miles) is the unspoilt beach of **Almograve**, backed by impressive cliffs.

The calm, sunny face of the sandy coast near Vila Nova de Milfontes

Zambujeira do Mar

Road map C7. 🏘 *1,000*. 🚌
ℹ️ *Rua Miramar (283 961 144)*.

A narrow strip of sheltered land divides the plains of the Alentejo from the bracing Atlantic. Here lies the solitary village of Zambujeira do Mar, the whiteness of its gorgeous beach enhanced by the dark backdrop of high basalt cliffs. Traditionally, families come here for Sunday beach outings, joined nowadays by campers and more adventurous tourists.

Mértola ⓴

Road map D6. 🏘 *1,200*. 🚌
ℹ️ *Rua da Igreja 1 (286 610 109)*.
📅 *1st Thu of month*.

Pretty, whitewashed Mértola is of great historical interest. The whole of this small town is a *vila museu*, a museum site, with discoveries from different eras exhibited in *núcleos*, or areas where a concentration of treasures from that period can be found. The tourist office has details of each *núcleo*.

Mértola's origins date back to the Phoenicians, who created a thriving inland port here on the Guadiana, later enjoyed by the Romans and the Moors. Roman artefacts can be seen

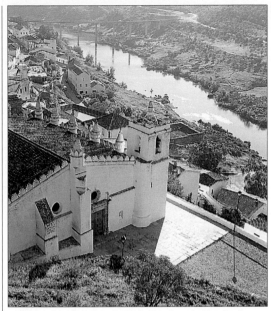
Mértola's unusual Moorish-style church, high above the River Guadiana

at the **Núcleo Romano**, based at an excavation beneath the municipal council buildings.

The post-Roman period in Mértola is on display in the **Núcleo Visigótico** and in an early Christian **basilica** whose ruins adjoin the Roman road to Beja *(see p313)*. The influence bequeathed by several centuries of Moorish domination is seen in Mértola's **Núcleo Islâmico** which houses one of the country's best collections of Portuguese Islamic art, and includes ceramics, coins and jewellery. The **Igreja Matriz** below the Moorish walls was formerly a mosque, unique in Portugal for being so little altered. Among surviving Arab features are the five-nave layout, four horseshoe arches and a *mihrab* or prayer niche.

Overlooking the town is the crumbling hilltop **castle**, with its keep of 1292, offering lovely views of the river valley.

Environs: The copper mines at **Minas de São Domingos**, 16 km (10 miles) to the east, were the main employer in the area from 1858 to 1965, when the vein was exhausted. An English company ran the mine under the harshest conditions, with miners' families living in one windowless room. The village's population has now fallen from 6,000 to 800, and the ghost-town atmosphere is relieved only by a reservoir and surrounding lush greenery.

Around Mértola, 600 sq km (230 sq miles) of the wild Guadiana valley is a **Parque Natural** that is home to the black stork, azure-winged magpie and raptors such as the red kite.

THE VERSATILITY OF CORK

Groves of evergreen cork oak *(Quercus suber)* provide the Alentejo with welcome shade and a thriving industry. It was Dom Pérignon, the wine-making monk, who in the 17th century revived the use of cork as a tasteless, odourless seal for wine. Portugal, the world's largest cork producer, has almost 7,000 sq km (2,700 sq miles) under cultivation and turns out some 30 million corks a day. In rural areas, this versatile bark is fashioned into waterproof, heatproof food containers and these decorated boxes are a traditional craft of the Alentejo.

Harvesting cork is a skilled task. Mature trees, stripped in summer every ten years or so, reveal a raw red undercoat until their new bark grows.

The glowing red of a stripped tree in an Alentejan cork grove

ALGARVE

Enclosed by ranges of hills to the north, the Algarve has a climate, culture and scenery very different from the rest of Portugal. Its stunning coastline and year-round mild weather, maintained by warm sea and air currents from nearby North Africa, make it one of the most popular holiday destinations in southern Europe.

The Algarve's fertile soil and strategic headlands and rivers have attracted visitors since the time of the Phoenicians. Five centuries of Arab rule, from AD 711, left a legacy that is still visible in the region's architecture, lattice chimneys, *azulejos*, orange groves and almond trees. Place names beginning with Al are also of Moorish origin; Al-Gharb ("the West") denoted the western edge of the Islamic empire.

When the Algarve was reclaimed by the Christians in 1249, the Portuguese rulers designated themselves kings "of Portugal and of the Algarves", emphasizing the region's separateness from the rest of the country. It was the Algarve, however, that shot Portugal to prominence in the 15th century, when Henry the Navigator *(see p49)* is said to have set up a school of navigation at Sagres, and launched the age of exploration from these southern shores.

The earthquake of 1755 *(see pp62–3)* had its epicentre just south of Lagos, then the region's capital. Virtually all the towns and villages were destroyed or badly damaged, which explains why very few buildings in the region predate this period.

Since the 1960s, when Faro airport was opened, international tourism has replaced agriculture and fishing as the region's main industry. A few stretches of the southwestern seashore are now cluttered with high-rise complexes catering for the yearly influx of tourists. However, the whole western seaboard exposed to the Atlantic and the lagoons east of Faro have been less affected by development. Trips inland, to the pretty whitewashed village of Alte or the border town of Alcoutim in the east, provide a welcome reminder that, in places, the Algarve's rural way of life continues virtually uninterrupted.

Colourful ceramic plates for sale outside a local craft shop in Alte

◁ Strolling along the sandy Praia da Rocha near Portimão

Exploring the Algarve

The Algarve is a delight to visit all year round. In summer, the coast between Faro and Lagos attracts thousands of visitors; but even near popular resorts such as Albufeira and Portimão it is possible to escape the crowds. Though often bypassed, Faro itself is well worth a visit. Picturesque Tavira is an ideal centre for the lagoons of the eastern Algarve, while from Lagos you can reach the beaches on the rugged southwest coast. Inland, the hillside villages are peaceful, with lush vegetation, both wild and cultivated. The wooded Serra de Monchique is an area of outstanding beauty offering lovely walks.

Wooded slopes around the vast lake created by the Bravura dam, north of Lagos

Praia de Odeceixe
↑ Odemira
Odeceixe
N120
Ribeira de Seixe
Carriagem
Rogil
Foz do Farelo
São Marcos da Serra
Baião Velho
Bej
Praia de Monte Clérigo
ALJEZUR ❶
Marmelete
❷ ❸ MONCHIQUE
IC1
Praia de Arrifana
SERRA DE MONCHIQUE
N267
Casais
Caldas de Monchique
Ribeira de Odelouca
Barragem do Funcho
Ribeira d
Alfambras
São Bartolomeu de Messines
N268 N120
Barragem da Bravura
N266
Barragem do Arade
N124
Porte de Messin
Bordeira
Vidigal
Porto de Lagos
Carrapateira
Serra do Espinhaço de Cão
Bensafrim
A22 IC4
❿ SILVES
Tune
Pedralva
Odiáxere
PORTIMÃO
Lagoa
Algoz
Praia de Castelejo
N268
Budens
N125
❼ LAGOS
❽ ALVOR ❾
Ferragudo
Alcantarilha
N125
Ferrei
VILA DO BISPO ❹
Figueira
Luz
Burgau
Praia da Rocha
Carvoeiro
Senhora da Rocha
ALBUFEIRA
❺ CABO DE SÃO VICENTE
❻ SAGRES

KEY

═══ Motorway

─── Major road

‧‧‧ Minor road

─── Scenic route

---- Minor railway

▬▬ National border

▬▬ Regional border

Brightly painted fishing boats in the harbour at Sagres

For additional map symbols see back flap

of the delightful sandy coves near Albufeira

SIGHTS AT A GLANCE

GETTING AROUND

The A22 (E1) runs from
Albufeira to Spain and has
relieved the N125, which can
become congested in summer.
Roads branch off to beaches,
coastal towns and inland villages.

A frequent but slow rail service
connects the main towns, but
stations are sometimes far from
the centre. Reliable buses link
coastal resorts and inland towns,
though progress can be slow.

0 kilometres   10

0 miles   5

SEE ALSO

Whitewashed house and lattice-
work chimney in Cacela Velha

Commanding view of the countryside from Aljezur's Moorish castle

Aljezur ●

Road map 7C. 🏛 *7,000.* 🚌
🛈 *Largo do Mercado (282 998 229).*
🏪 *3rd Mon of month.*

The small village of Aljezur
is overlooked by a 10th-
century **Moorish castle**,
reached via the old quarter.
Although in ruins, a cistern
and towers remain, and there
are splendid views towards
the Serra de Monchique.

Aljezur's **Igreja Matriz**, much
rebuilt after the earthquake of
1755 *(see pp62–3)*, has a fine
Neo-Classical altarpiece. Dating
from about 1809, it was probably executed in the workshop
of José da Costa of Faro.

Environs: From Aljezur, the
wild and deserted beaches of
the Algarve's west coast are
easily explored, although a car

The mountains of the Serra de Monchique
rising above meadows of wild flowers

is essential. Open to the strong
currents of the Atlantic, **Praia
de Arrifana** 10 km (6 miles)
southwest, and **Praia de
Monte Clérigo**, 8 km (5 miles)
northwest, are sandy, sweeping
beaches backed by cliffs. On
the Alentejo border, **Praia de
Odeceixe** is a sheltered cove
that is popular with surfers.

Serra de Monchique ●

Road map 7C. 🚌 *Monchique.*
🛈 *Monchique (282 911 189).*

Providing shelter from the
north, this volcanic mountain range helps to ensure the
mild southern climate of the
Algarve. The highest point is
Fóia at 902 m (2,959 ft). This,
however, is less pleasantly
wooded than **Picota**, which, at
773 m (2,536 ft), is the
second highest peak.
An impressive 4-km
(2-mile) walk to this
peak from Monchique
passes among chestnut
trees and fields of wild
flowers. A spectacular
panorama sweeps
down to the Ponta
de Sagres *(see p322)*
and there are stunning
views of the rest of the
range. Whether you
explore the Serra on
foot or by car, there
is a wonderful variety
of vegetation to enjoy
with rhododendron,
mimosa, chestnut, pine,
cork oak and patches
of terraced fertile land
in the valleys. The

increased planting of fast-
growing eucalyptus trees
has given cause for concern.
This highly flammable species
is one of the reasons for the
serious fires that break out
all too often in the Serra.

The 68-km (42-mile) run
along the N267 from Nave, just
below Monchique, to Aljezur
in the west, leads through a
beautiful part of the Serra.
The landscape is a mixture
of woods and moorland, kept
fertile by an abundant water
supply. Cork oak grows here,
home to the nuthatch and
lesser-spotted woodpecker.

Monchique ●

Road map 7C. 🏛 *7,000.* 🚌
🛈 *Largo de São Sebastião (282 911
189).* 🏪 *2nd Fri of month.*

Manueline portal of the Igreja
Matriz in Monchique

The small market town of
Monchique is primarily
famous for its altitude, 458 m
(1,500 ft), and consequently
spectacular views. It is also
known for its wooden handicrafts, particularly the folding
chairs which are believed to
date back to Roman times.

The 16th-century **Igreja
Matriz**, on the cobbled Rua da
Igreja behind the main square,
has an impressive Manueline
doorway whose knotted
columns end in unusual pinnacles. Above the town is the
ruined monastery of **Nossa
Senhora do Desterro**. This
Franciscan house, founded in
1632 by Dom Pero da Silva, is
now only a shell but it is worth
visiting for the stunning views
across to the peak of Picota.

Environs: A delightful, tiny spa, 6 km (4 miles) south, **Caldas de Monchique** is set in the foothills of the Serra in peaceful wooded surroundings.

The hot, curative waters have attracted the ailing since Roman times, and even though João II died soon after taking them in 1495, their reputation has remained undiminished. In the summer, people come to be treated for skin, digestive and rheumatic complaints. As well as the wholesome spring water, the bars here offer the local firewater, *medronheira*.

The shady main square has a large, attractive handicraft centre and there are some pretty walks in the woods.

Promontory of Cabo de São Vicente jutting into the Atlantic Ocean

Vila do Bispo ❹

Road map 7C. 👥 7,000. 🚌
🛈 *Rua Comandante Matoso, Sagres (282 624 873).* 🔄 *1st Thu of month.*

The grand name of "The Bishop's Town" today refers to a peaceful village, rather remote in feel, which makes the crowds of central Algarve seem very far away. It acquired its name in the 17th century when it was donated to the see of Faro. The town's parish church, **Nossa Senhora da Conceição**, has a delightful interior decorated with 18th-century *azulejos* from the floor up to the wooden, painted ceiling, and a Baroque altarpiece dating from 1715.

Environs: The beaches in the area are remote and unspoiled. **Praia do Castelejo**, 5 km (3 miles) to the west, is accessible by a dirt road that

Baroque altarpiece inside Nossa Senhora da Conceição, Vila do Bispo

winds up from the village over moorland. The beach, set at the foot of steep cliffs, is large, sandy and surf-fringed. The intrepid can turn off this track for the 6 km (4 miles) journey to **Torre de Aspa**, an obelisk at 156 m (512 ft) marking the spot for spectacular views over the ocean. The road is quite rough, so it is advisable to walk the last 2 km (1 mile).

Cabo de São Vicente ❺

Road map 7C. 🚌 *to Sagres then taxi.* 🛈 *Sagres (282 624 873).*

In the Middle Ages, this windblown cape at the extreme southwest of Europe was believed to be the end of the world. The Romans called it the *Promontorium Sacrum* (Sacred Promontory), and today, with its 60-m (200-ft) cliffs fronting the Atlantic, it still presents a most awe-inspiring aspect. The ocean waves have created long, sandy beaches and carved deep caves into the cliffs.

Since the 15th century, Cabo de São Vicente has been an important reference point for shipping, and its present lighthouse has a 95-km (60-mile) range, said to be the most powerful in Europe. For even longer it has had religious associations, and its name arises from the legend that the body of St Vincent was washed ashore here in the 4th century. Prince Henry the Navigator *(see p49)* was also reputed to have lived here, but, if so, all traces of his Vila do Infante have disappeared. A number

of important naval battles have taken place off the Cape, including the defeat of a Spanish fleet in 1797 by the British admirals Jervis and Nelson.

Since 1988 the coast from Sines in the north to Burgau in the east has been made a nature reserve, providing important nesting grounds for Bonelli's eagle, kestrel, white stork, heron and numerous other bird species. There is also a colony of sea otters.

Clump of scented thyme near Cabo de São Vicente

FLOWERS OF THE WESTERN ALGARVE

The remote headlands of Cabo de São Vicente and Sagres are renowned in botanical circles for their flowers, which put on a strikingly colourful and aromatic display from February to May. The climate, underlying rock and comparative isolation of these headlands have given an intriguing, stunted appearance to the local vegetation. There is a great array of different species, including cistuses, squills, an endemic sea pink, junipers, lavenders, narcissi, milk-vetches and many other magnificent plants.

The enormous Rosa dos Ventos wind compass on Ponta de Sagres

Sagres ⑥

Road map 7C. 🏃 3,500. 🚌
🛈 Rua Comandante Matoso (282
624 873). 🚙 1st Fri of month.

The small town of Sagres
has little to offer except a
picturesque harbour. Essentially
it is a good base from which
to explore the superb beaches
(see p288) and isolated peninsula west of the town. Henry
the Navigator (see p49) built
a fortress on this windswept
promontory and, according to
tradition, a school of navigation
and a shipyard. From here he
realized his dream "to see what
lay beyond the Canaries and
Cape Bojador… and attempt
the discovery of things hidden
from men". From 1419–60, he
poured his energy and the revenues of the Order of Christ
(see p185), of which he was
master, into building caravels
and sending his fear-stricken
sailors into unknown waters.
 In 1434 Gil Eanes of Lagos
was the first sailor to round
the dreaded Cape Bojador, in
the region of Western Sahara.
With this feat, the west coast
of Africa was opened up for
exploration (see pp48–9) and
Portugal poised for expansion.
 Little remains of Prince
Henry's original fortress: the
walls that can be seen today
are part of a 17th-century fort.
Still visible is the giant pebble
wind compass, the **Rosa dos
Ventos**, 43 m (141 ft) in dia-
meter, said to have been used
by Henry. The simple chapel
of **Nossa Senhora da Graça**
was also built by him. The
whole site, looking across to
Cabo de São Vicente and out
towards the open Atlantic, is
exhilarating and atmospheric.

Environs: The town is also
within easy reach of many
superb beaches. Some,
such as **Telheiro**, 9 km
(5 miles) west of Sagres,
and **Ponta Ruiva** 2 km
(1 mile) further up the
west coast, are only
accessible by car.
Nearer to Sagres,
Beliche is surprisingly
sheltered, **Tonel**, on the
tip of the promontory,
has wonderful surf and
Martinhal, 1 km (half
a mile) east, has a watersports school offering
water-skiing, surfing
and wind surfing.

Lagos ⑦

Road map 7C. 🏃 16,000. 🚊 🚌
🛈 Sítio de São João (282 763 031).
🚙 1st Sat of month.

Set on one of the largest bays
in the Algarve, Lagos is an
attractive, bustling town. In
the 8th century it was conquered by the Arabs, who left

Moorish archway leading onto
Avenida dos Descobrimentos, Lagos

behind fortifications that were
extended in the 16th century.
A well-preserved section and
archway can be seen near Rua
do Castelo dos Governadores,
where there is a monument to
the navigator Gil Eanes.
 The discoveries of the 15th
century (see pp48–9), pioneered by Henry the Navigator,
whose statue gazes scowlingly
out to sea, turned Lagos into
an important naval centre. At
the same time a most deplor-
able period of history began,
with the first slaves brought
back from the Sahara in 1441
by Henry's explorer Nuno
Tristão. The site of the first
slave market in Europe
is marked by a plaque
under the arcades on Rua
da Senhora da Graça.
 The city was the
capital of the Algarve
from 1576–1756. Ex-
tensive damage was
caused by the earth-
quake of 1755 (see
pp62–3), so that today
the centre consists
primarily of pretty
18th- and 19th-century
buildings. The citizens
of Lagos continue to
make their living from
fishing, which helps the town
to retain a character independent of the tourist trade.
 The smart marina on the
east side of town provides
the first safe anchorage on
the south coast for boats
coming in from the Atlantic.

São Gonçalo in
Santa Maria, Lagos

♣ Forte Ponta da Bandeira
Avenida dos Descobrimentos.
Tel 282 761 410. ◯ Tue–Sun.
🔵 public hols. 🎟
On the seafront stands the
17th-century fortress which
defended the entrance to the
harbour. Its imposing ramparts
afford far-reaching views over
the town and the bay.

🔒 Santa Maria
Praça Infante Dom Henrique.
Tel 282 762 723. ◯ daily. 🔵 🎟
The parish church of Lagos
originated in the 16th century,
and still retains a Renaissance
doorway. Of local interest is a
statue of São Gonçalo of Lagos,
a fisherman's son born in 1360
who became an Augustinian
monk, preacher and compos-
er of religious music.

🔒 Santo António

Rua General Alberto Silveira. *Tel 282 762 301.* ◯ *Tue–Sun.* ● *public hols.*

This 18th-century church is an Algarvian jewel. The lower section of the walls is covered in blue and white *azulejos*, the rest in carved, gilded and painted woodwork, an inspirational and riotous example of Baroque carving. Cherubs, beasts, flowers and scenes of hunting and fishing, surround eight panel paintings of miracles performed by St Antony.

A statue of the saint stands above the altar, surrounded by gilded pillars and arches adorned with angels and vines. St Antony was patron and honorary colonel-in-chief of the local regiment and, according to tradition, this statue accompanied it on various campaigns during the Peninsular War (1807–11) *(see p54).*

Near the altar is the grave of Hugh Beatty, an Irish colonel who commanded the Lagos regiment during the 17th-century wars with Spain. He died here in 1709 and his motto "Non vi sed arte" (Not with force but with skill) adorns the tomb.

🏛 Museu Municipal Dr José Formosinho

Rua General Alberto Silveira. *Tel 282 762 301.* ◯ *Tue–Sun.* ● *public hols.* 📷

This eclectic ethnographic museum displays local handicrafts and artifacts, traditional costumes and – most oddly – pickled creatures, including animal freaks such as an eight-legged goat kid. The custodian provides an informal guided tour.

Ochre sandstone rocks on the sheltered beach of Praia de Dona Ana, Lagos

Environs: The promontory, called the **Ponta da Piedade**, sheltering the bay of Lagos to the south has a series of wonderful rock formations, caves and calm, transparent waters. Accessible by road and sea, and most spectacular at sunset, this area is not to be missed. The prettiest beach is **Praia de Dona Ana**, 25 minutes' walk from the centre of town, but **Praia do Camilo**, further round to the tip of the promontory, may be less crowded. The long **Meia Praia** stretches for 4 km (2 miles) east of Lagos; a regular bus service leaves from the centre of town.

A 10-km (6-mile) drive due north of Lagos leads to the huge **Barragem de Bravura** reservoir. It is peaceful and especially picturesque seen from a viewpoint high up.

Alvor ❽

Road map 7C. 🏘 *5,000.* 🚌 🚆 ℹ️ *Rua Dr Afonso Costa 51 (282 457 540).*

This pretty fishing town of white houses is popular with holiday-makers, but in low season retains its charm. It was a Roman port, and later the Moorish town of Al-Bur. By the 16th century it was again a prosperous town, but it suffered much damage in the earthquake of 1755. The town was rebuilt with stone from the Moorish castle, so little of that fortress remains.

At the top of the town the 16th-century church, **Divino Salvador**, has a Manueline portal, carved with foliage, lions and dragons. The outermost arch is an octopus tentacle.

Church of Divino Salvador overlooking the whitewashed houses and the harbour at Alvor

Nossa Senhora da Conceição, Portimão

Portimão **9**

Road map 7C. 🐎 *40,000.* 🚉 🚌
ℹ️ *Avenida Zeca Afonso (289 470
732).* 🦐 *1st Mon of month.*

One of the largest towns in
the Algarve, Portimão is
not renowned for its beauty
but has plenty of character and
a long history as a port. The
Romans settled here, attracted
by the natural harbour on the
wide estuary of the Rio Arade.

Portimão's sprawling
outskirts are graced with a
marina and shopping centre.
Its 18th-century town centre
has excellent shopping as
well as a large, bustling market.

The centre lies around the
pedestrianized **Rua Vasco da
Gama**, with numerous shops
specializing in leather goods.
Along Rua Diogo Tomé, the
church of **Nossa Senhora da
Conceição** occupies a low
hill. Rebuilt after the earthquake of 1755 *(see pp62–3)*,
its 14th-century origins are still
visible in the portico with its
carved capitals. Inside, there

are 17th- and 18th-
century *azulejo* panels.
In Largo 1° de Dezem-
bro there are benches
adorned with brightly
coloured 19th-century
tiles. The waterfront is
always lively and res-
taurants serve fresh
sardines and sea bass.

Environs: Just 3 km
(2 miles) south lies
Portimão's touristic
neighbour, **Praia da
Rocha**, a series of
sandy coves amongst protruding red and ochre rocks. At its
east end is the **Fortaleza de
Santa Catarina**, a castle built
in the 16th century to protect
Portimão and Silves. From here
there is a superb view of the
lovely, sweeping beach backed
by 70-m (230-ft) cliffs, and
overlooked by a swathe of
high-rise hotels. These are
multiplying, and visitors will
find themselves fighting for
space in high season.

Silves **10**

Road map 7C. 🐎 *10,000.* 🚉 🚌
ℹ️ *Parque das Merendas (282 442
255).* 🦐 *3rd Mon of month.*

Silves's commanding position
made it the ideal fortified
settlement. The Romans built
a castle here, but it was under
the Arabs that the city flourished, becoming the Moorish
capital, Xelb. In the mid-12th
century the Arab geographer
Idrisi praised its beauty and
its "delicious, magnificent" figs.

Silves was renowned as a
centre of culture in Moorish
Al-Gharb until the Knights of
Santiago *(see pp42–3)* took
the city in 1242.

Today, the red walls of the
castle stand out against the
skyline. Next to the castle, the
Fábrica do Inglés houses a
cork museum. the **Museu da
Cortiça**, which tells the story
of cork production in Portugal.

🏛 **Museu da Cortiça**
Rua Gregório Mascarenhas.
Tel *282 440 480.* ⏰ *Mon–Fri.* ♿

Quiet cobbled street in Silves

♟ **Castle**
Castelo de Silves. **Tel** *282 445 624.*
⏰ *daily.* ♿ 🦽 *(garden only).*
The red sandstone castle
dates back mainly to Moorish
times, though it has done
duty as a Christian fortress
and a jail. It was the site of
the Palace of the Verandahs,
abode of Al-Mu'tamid from
1053 when he was ruler of
Seville and Wali of Al-Gharb.

There are superb views of
the town and countryside from
the massive, polygonal ramparts. Inside, there are gardens
and the impressive vaulted
Moorish **Cisterna da Moura
Encantada** (Cistern of the
Enchanted Moorish Girl).

The castle and town of Silves rising above a fertile valley of orange groves

⛪ Sé

Largo da Sé. ◯ *daily.* ● *public hols.*
Built on the site of a mosque,
the cathedral dates from the
13th century, but has been
much altered over the years.
In the chancel, light falls from
lovely double windows with
stained-glass borders, on a jas-
per statue of Nossa Senhora
da Conceição, believed to date
from the 14th century.

Opposite the Sé, the 16th-
century **Misericórdia** church
has a Manueline side door and
a Renaissance altarpiece.

🏛 Museu Arqueológico

Rua das Portas de Loulé 14. *Tel 282
444 832.* ◯ *Mon–Sat.* 🈺
Situated down the hill from
the cathedral, the Municipal
Museum was opened in 1990.
Its exhibits include Stone and
Iron Age tools, sculpted Roman
capitals, surgical instruments
from the 5th–7th centuries, a
13th-century anchor and items
of 18th-century ceramics. The
museum is built around its
star exhibit, a large Arab
well-cistern of about the
12th century that was
uncovered here in
1980. The staircase
built into the structure
descends 15 m (49 ft) to
the bottom of the well.

Environs: One kilometre
(half a mile) east of Silves
is the **Cruz de Portugal**,
an ornate 16th-century
granite cross. This may have
been given to the city by
Manuel I, when João II's
body was transferred
from Silves Cathedral to
Batalha *(see pp184–5).*
The faces are intricately carved
with the Crucifixion and the
Descent from the Cross.

*Silves's Cruz
de Portugal*

Albufeira ⓫

Road map 7C. 🏘 *31,000.* 🚌 🚏
🛈 *Rua 5 de Outubro (289 585 279).*
🗓 *1st & 3rd Tue of month.*

It is hardly surprising that
this charming fishing town
of whitewashed houses, overlooking a sheltered beach, has
become the tourist capital of
the Algarve. The Romans liked
it too, and built a castle here.
For the Arabs it was Al-Buhar

Colourful fishing boats on the beach at Albufeira

(The Castle on the Sea), and
under them it prospered from
trade with North Africa. The
Knights of Santiago *(see p43)*
took it in the 13th century,
but the consequent loss of
trade almost ruined it. In
1833 it was set on fire by
supporters of Dom
Miguel during the
War of the Two
Brothers *(see p54).*
Much of the town centre
is pedestrianized, including the oldest part around
Rua da Igreja Velha where
some of the buildings still
have original Moorish
arches. The church of **São
Sebastião**, on Praça Miguel
Bombarda, has a Manueline
doorway. Rua 5 de Outubro
leads through a tunnel
to the beach, east of
which is the **Praia dos
Barcos** where the fishermen
ply their trade. From **Praia de
São Rafael**, 2 km (1 mile) west
of Albufeira, to **Praia da Oura**
due east, the area is punctuated by small sandy coves set
between eroded ochre rocks.

Alte ⓬

Road map 7C. 🏘 *500.* 🚌 🚏
🛈 *Estrada da Ponte 17 (289 478
666).* 🗓 *3rd Thu of month.*

Perched on a hill, Alte is one
of the prettiest villages of
the Algarve. The approach
from the east along the N124

is the most picturesque, with
sweeping views of rolling hills.
The focus of this steep, white
village is the 16th-century
Nossa Senhora da Assunção,
which has a Manueline doorway and baptismal fonts, and
a fine gilded altarpiece celebrating the Assumption. The
chapel of São Sebastião has
beautiful, rare 16th-century
Sevillian *azulejos*.

About ten minutes' walk
from the church, and clearly
marked, is the River Alte, over-
hung with trees, and a water
source known as the **Fonte
Grande**. This leafy setting is
ideal for picnicking. On the
steep slopes, about 700 m (half
a mile) from the village is a
mill (converted into a restaurant) and a 5-m (16-ft) high
waterfall, **Queda do Vigário**.

One of many filigree chimneys
that adorn the rooftops of Alte

Vilamoura ⓫

Road map C7. 👥 *9,000.* 🚌
ℹ️ *Praça do Mar, Quarteira
(289 389 209).*

The coast between Faro and Lagos has effectively become a strip of villa complexes and high-rise hotels. Vilamoura is a prime example of this kind of development and is set to become Europe's largest leisure complex. Its 1,600 ha (4,000 acres) encompass four golf courses, tennis courts, a riding school, fishing and shooting facilities, and indoor and outdoor sports complexes. There is even a small landing strip. Its hotels and apartment blocks are still on the rise, and the already well-established complex is still under construction.

The focal point is the large **marina**, which bristles with powerboats and is fronted by restaurants, cafés and shops. It makes a diverting excursion, attracting many Portuguese visitors, including Lisbon's jet set. Due east is the crowded **Praia da Marina**. You can also visit the nearby Roman ruins of **Cerro da Vila**, which date from the 1st century AD and include a bath complex and a house with mosaics depicting fish.

⋂ Cerro da Vila
Avenida Cerro da Vila. **Tel** *289 312 153 (museum).* ◻ *daily.* 📷

Luxury yachts and powerboats moored at the smart marina at Vilamoura

18th-century tile panels and gilded altar in São Lourenço, Almancil

Almancil ⓬

Road map D7. 👥 *2,000.* 🚌 🚌 ℹ️
Rua de Vale (289 392 659). 🔼 *1st & 4th Sun of month, antiques 2nd Sun.*

Outside the undistinguished town of Almancil lies one of the Algarve's gems, the 18th-century **Igreja Matriz de São Lourenço**. Its interior is an outstanding masterpiece of decoration in *azulejo* panels. The church was commissioned by local inhabitants in gratitude to St Laurence, who answered their prayers for water.

The copious blue and white tiles were probably designed by master craftsmen in Lisbon and shipped down. They cover the cupola, the walls of the chancel, nave, and nave vault, to stunning effect. The wall panels depict episodes from the life of St Laurence; on one side of the altar the saint is shown healing two blind men, and on the other, giving money to the poor. The nave arches show the saint conversing with Pope Sixtus II; arguing for his Christian belief with the Roman Emperor Valerian; and refusing to give up his faith. The story culminates in his martyrdom. In the last panel on the right, in which the saint is placed on a gridiron to be burned, an angel comforts him. The nave vault depicts the *Coronation of St Laurence*,

and the cupola has decorative, *trompe-l'oeil* effects of exceptional quality. The last tiles were put in place in 1730.

The altarpiece, dated around 1735, was the work of Manuel Martins and was gilded by leading local painters. Astonishingly, the 1755 earthquake *(see pp62–3)* only dislodged five tiles from the vault.

Today, Almancil houses a large community of British expats, and is noted for its property agents and holiday and construction-related shops and services. The town is also within striking distance of some of the best restaurants in the Algarve *(see p426).*

Loulé ⓭

Road map D7. 👥 *20,000.* 🚌 🚌
ℹ️ *Avenida 25 de Abril (289 463 900).* 🔼 *Sat.*

Loulé is an attractive market town and thriving craft centre. Its Moorish origins are still visible in the belltower of the church of São Clemente. The **castle**, on the north side of town, is also Moorish in origin, rebuilt in the 13th century. Remnants of the walls behind the castle afford an overview of the town and the many pretty filigree chimneys, typical of the Algarve.

The heart of the town lies immediately south of Praça da República and encompasses the busy, pink-domed market. On Saturdays the area is particularly lively when gypsies run a simultaneous outdoor

For hotels and restaurants in this region see pp400–403 and pp426–9

market. From Rua 9 de Abril to the Igreja Matriz you can watch handicraft workers carving wood, weaving hats, making lace, decorating horse tackle and painting pottery and tiles.

The 13th-century **São Clemente**, on Largo da Silva, was badly damaged in three earthquakes, the last in 1969, but its triple nave, defined by Gothic arches, has been conserved. There are two beautiful side chapels dating from the early 16th century. The Capela de Nossa Senhora da Consolação is decorated from floor to vault with superb blue and white *azulejo* panels, while the Capela de São Brás, has a Manueline arch and a blue and gold Baroque altarpiece.

Other churches of note are the **Igreja da Misericórdia**, on Avenida Marçal Pacheco, which has a Manueline doorway, and the chapel of **Nossa Senhora da Conceição**, close to Praça da República. Here, the Baroque altarpiece (1745) by Miguel Nobre of Faro is complemented by scenes in blue and white *azulejos*.

Environs: The 16th-century, hilltop chapel of **Nossa Senhora da Piedade**, adorned with *azulejo* panels, lies 2 km (1 mile) west of Loulé. Behind it stands a modern white church of the same name built to replace the old chapel but which never became a popular place of worship. The spot also affords spectacular views.

Colourful tiled fountain on the terrace of the Patamar da Casa do Presépio, Estoi

Estoi ⑯

Road map D7. 🏛 *4,300.* 🚌
ℹ️ *Faro (289 803 604).*
📅 *2nd Sun of month.*

The quiet village of Estoi has two notable sights, separated by a short distance and about 1,800 years. Just off the main square is the **Palácio de Estoi**, an unashamedly pretty Rococo pastiche. The palace was the brainchild of a local nobleman, who died soon after work was begun in the mid-1840s. Another wealthy local later acquired the place, and completed it in 1909. For the vast amount of money and energy he expended on his new home, he was made Viscount of

Estoi. The work was supervised by the architect Domingos da Silva Meira, whose interest in sculpture is evident everywhere. The palace underwent restoration of its interior, a feast of pastel and stucco, and is now a *pousada.*

🌸 **Palace gardens**
Rua do Jardim. **Tel** *289 990 150.* ⭕ *daily.* ♿
Dotted with orange trees and palms, the gardens continue the joyful Rococo spirit of the palace. The lower terrace features a blue and white tiled pavilion, the Casa da Cascata, inside which is a copy of Canova's *Three Graces.* The main walled terrace above, the Patamar da Casa do Presépio, has a large pavilion with stained-glass windows, fountains adorned with nymphs and tiled niches.

Detail of fish mosaic in the baths of the Roman ruins at Milreu

🏛 **Milreu**
N2-6. ⭕ *Tue–Sun.* ⚫ *public hols.*
A ten-minute walk downhill from the other end of the main square leads to Estoi's second sight: the Roman complex of Milreu, which dates from the 1st or 2nd century AD. The buildings probably began as a large farmhouse that was converted in the 3rd century into a luxurious villa, built around a central courtyard.

Ebullient fish mosaics still adorn the baths, alongside the living quarters, but most portable archaeological finds are now housed in Faro's Museu Municipal *(see p329).* The importance of the villa, which may have belonged to a wealthy patrician, is indicated by the remains of a temple overlooking the site. This was converted into a Christian basilica in the 5th century.

Pink Rococo façade of the Palácio de Estoi

Faro 🟡

Capital of the Algarve since 1756, Faro has been reborn several times over the centuries – following invasion, fire and earthquake. A prehistoric fishing village, it became an important port and administrative centre under the Romans, who named it Ossonoba. Captured from the Moors in 1249 by Afonso III, Faro prospered until 1596, when it was sacked and burned by the Earl of Essex, favourite of Elizabeth I of England. A new city rose from the ashes, only to be badly damaged in the earthquake of 1755 *(see pp62–3)*. Although vestiges of the ancient city walls are still standing, the finest buildings date mainly from the late 18th and 19th centuries.

Azulejo crucifix in exterior chapel of Nossa Senhora do Pé da Cruz

Statue of Dom Francisco Gomes do Avelar in Largo da Sé

Exploring the Old City

The centre of Faro is attractive and easily explored on foot. It fans out from the small harbour to encompass the compact Old City to the southeast. Partly encircled by ancient walls, this is reached via the **Arco da Vila**. The arch was built on the site of a medieval castle gate in the 19th century for the bishop, Dom Francisco Gomes do Avelar, who had taken it upon himself to re-design the city in decline. The portico is originally Moorish, and a statue of St Thomas Aquinas, patron saint of Faro, surveys the scene. At the heart of the Old City, the Largo da Sé is a peaceful square, lined with orange trees and flanked by the elegant 18th-century seminary and **Paço Episcopal** (bishops' palace), still in use and closed to the public. Just outside the walls, through another archway of Moorish origin, the Arco do Repouso, is the 18th-century church of **São Francisco**, impressively decorated with tiled scenes of the life of St Francis. Further north is the 17th-century **Nossa Senhora do Pé da Cruz** with fanciful oil panels of stories from Genesis, such as the creation of the sun and stars. At the rear is an interesting exterior chapel or *humilhadero*.

🔒 Sé

Largo da Sé. ⬜ *Mon–Sat.* ◗ *Sat pm, public hols.*

The first Christian church here, built on the site of a mosque, was all but destroyed in the attack by the English in 1596. The base of the belltower, its medieval doorway and two chapels survived, and long-term reconstruction resulted in a mixture of Renaissance and Baroque styles.

By the 1640s a grander building had emerged which included a chancel decorated with *azulejos* and the Capela

Orange trees in front of the 18th-century bishops' palace along the Largo da Sé

For hotels and restaurants in this region see pp400–403 and pp426–9

de Nossa Senhora dos Prazeres, decorated with ornate gilded woodcarving. One of the cathedral's most dashing and eccentric features is the large 18th-century organ decorated with Chinese motifs. Its range includes an echoing horn and a nightingale's song, and it has often been used by leading European organists.

🏛 Museu Arquológico

Largo Dom Afonso III. **Tel** 289 897 400. ◯ Tue–Sun. ⬤ public hols. 🈚
Since 1973 the Municipal Museum has been housed in the former convent of Nossa Senhora da Assunção, founded for the Poor Clares by Dona Leonor, sister of Manuel I. Her emblem, a fishing net, adorns the portico.

A variety of local archaeological finds are displayed in the museum, partly in the lovely two-storey Renaissance cloister built by Afonso Pires in 1540. The collection contains Roman,

17th-century chancel of Faro's Sé

medieval and Manueline stone carvings and statuary. However, the most attractive exhibit is a huge, Roman floor mosaic featuring a magnificently executed head of the god Neptune (3rd century AD), found near the railway station.

🏛 Museu Marítimo

Rua da Comunidade Lusiada. **Tel** 289 894 990. ◯ Mon–Fri. ⬤ public hols. 🈚
The Museu Marítimo is housed in part of the harbour master's building on the waterfront. Its small and curious collection of maritime exhibits centres on models of boats from the Age of Discovery (see pp46–9) onwards, including the squarerigged *nau*, prototype of the galleon. One example is Vasco da Gama's *São Gabriel*, the flagship on his voyage to India in 1498. There are also displays of traditional fishing methods from the Algarve.

FARO CITY CENTRE

Arco da Vila ⑤
Igreja do Carmo ①
Museu Etnográfico ⑩
Museu Marítimo ④
Museu Municipal ⑧
Paço Episcopal ⑥
Palácio Bivarin ③
São Francisco ⑨
São Pedro ②
Sé ⑦

0 metres   250

0 yards   250

Key to Symbols see back flap

Exploring Faro

The lively centre of Faro along Rua de Santo António is a stylish, pedestrianized area full of shops, bars and restaurants. Between here and the Largo do Carmo are some fine 18th-century buildings, such as the **Palácio Bivarin**. The early morning market on Largo de Sá Carneiro, to the north, offers fresh produce, clothing and local crafts. From here, a brisk walk uphill to the **Ermida de Santo António do Alto** brings a panorama of Faro with the sea and saltpans to the south.

🏛 Museu Etnográfico
Praça da Liberdade 2. **Tel** 289 878 238. ⬭ Mon–Fri. ⬤ public hols. 🖼 📷

The Ethnographic Museum takes a nostalgic look at the Algarve's traditional way of life showing ceramics, looms and decorative horse tackle. Old photographs document peasant farming techniques, with their heavy reliance on manpower, donkeys and oxen. The most charming exhibit is the cart used by the last waterseller in Olhão, in operation until 1974.

Imposing twin-towered façade of the Baroque Igreja do Carmo

⛪ Igreja do Carmo
Largo do Carmo. **Tel** 289 824 490. ⬭ Mon–Sat. 🖼 to Capela dos Ossos.

The impressive façade of this church was begun in 1713. Inside, the decoration is Baroque run wild, with every scroll and barley-sugar twist covered in precious Brazilian gold leaf.

In sombre contrast, the Capela dos Ossos (Chapel of Bones), built in 1816, has walls lined with skulls and large bones taken from the friars' cemetery. It is a stark reminder of the transience of human life.

Sumptuous Baroque decoration of the main altarpiece in São Pedro

⛪ São Pedro
Largo de São Pedro. **Tel** 289 805 473. ⬭ daily.

The parish church of Faro is dedicated to St Peter, patron saint of fishermen. Though restored with Italianate columns after the earthquake of 1755, much original Baroque decoration has survived, including the main altarpiece (1689).

Highlights include the chapel of the Santíssimo Sacramento, with a dazzling altarpiece (c.1745) featuring a bas-relief of the Last Supper, and a sculpture of St Anne teaching the young Virgin Mary to read. The altar of the Capela das Almas is surrounded by stunning *azulejos* (c.1730) showing the Virgin and other saints pulling souls out of purgatory.

⛪ Cemitério dos Judeus
Estrada da Penha. **Tel** 289 829 525 or 925 071 509. ⬭ Mon–Fri. ⬤ public hols. ♿

At the far northeast corner of town is the Jewish cemetery, created for the Jewish community brought here in the 1700s by the Marquês de Pombal (*see pp52–3*) to revitalize the economy. The cemetery is laid out in the traditional Sephardic way, with children nearest the entrance, women in the centre and men at the back. It served from 1838 until 1932, during which time 60 local families prospered, then moved away. Today there is no Jewish community in Faro.

Olhão ⑱

Road map D7. 🚶 15,000. 🚃 🚌 ℹ Largo Sebastião Martins Mestre 6A (289 713 936). ⬤ daily (fish); Sat (general).

Olhão has been involved in fishing since the Middle Ages, and today is one of the largest fishing ports and tuna and sardine canning centres in the Algarve. In 1808 the village was elevated to the status of town, after 17 of its fishermen crossed the Atlantic Ocean without charts, expressly to bring the exiled King João VI, in Rio de Janeiro, the news that Napoleon's troops had been forced out of the country.

Olhão's square, whitewashed houses with their flat roof terraces and box-like chimneys are reminiscent of Moorish architecture. The best view is from the top of the belltower of the parish church, **Nossa Senhora do Rosário**, on Praça da Restauração, built between 1681 and 1698 with donations from the local fishermen. The custodian lets visitors through the locked door leading from the nave. In 1758 the parish priest remarked on the fishermen's great devotion to "Our Lady of the Rosary in their grief and danger at sea, especially in summertime when North African pirates often sail off this coast." At the rear of the church is the external chapel of **Nossa Senhora dos Aflitos**, where women pray for their men's safety in stormy weather. The narrow, pedestrianized streets of the old town wind down from here to the waterfront, the

Whitewashed chapel of Nossa Senhora dos Aflitos behind the parish church in Olhão

The wide lagoon of the Parque Natural da Ria Formosa

scene of one of the region's most lively and picturesque markets. The noisy covered fish market sells the morning's catch, while on Saturdays outside stalls line the quay, with local farmers selling other produce such as fruit, nuts, honey and live chickens.

Shop selling local basketware in Olhão

Environs: At the eastern end of the quay, beyond the market, boats take you out to the islands of **Armona** (15 min), **Culatra** (30 min) and **Farol** (45 min). These flat, narrow bars of sand provide shelter to the town, and excellent sandy beaches for visitors, particularly on the ocean side. The islands are part of the Parque Natural da Ria Formosa.

Parque Natural da Ria Formosa ⑲

Road map D7. 🛈 *Centro de Educação Ambiental de Marim (289 704 134/135).* 🚌 *East of Olhão on N125.* ⛴ *from Faro, Olhão & Tavira.*

Stretching from Praia de Faro to Cacela Velha *(see p333)*, this nature reserve follows 60 km (37 miles) of coastline. It was created in 1987 to protect the valuable ecosystem of this area, which was under serious threat from uncontrolled

building, sand extraction and pollution, all by-products of the massive rise in tourism. The lagoon area of marshes, saltpans, islets and channels is sheltered from the open sea by a chain of barrier islands – actually sand dunes. Inlets between the islands allow the tide to ebb and flow into the lagoon.

The lagoon waters are rich in shellfish, such as oysters, cockles and clams: bred here, they make up 80 per cent of the nation's mollusc exports. The fish life and warm climate attract many wildfowl and waders; snakes, toads and chameleons also live here. Apart from fish and shellfish farming and salt panning, all other human activities which might encroach on the park's ecosystem are strictly controlled or forbidden.

Centro de Educação Ambiental de Marim, about 3 km (2 miles) east of Olhão, is an environmental education centre. Its 60 ha (148 acres) of dune and pinewoods are home to various sights, including a restored farmhouse, a tidal mill, a centre for injured birds, as well as exhibitions and aquariums. The web-footed Portuguese water dog, once much used by fishermen, has been bred back from near-extinction here. At the eastern end of the park are Roman tanks where fish was salted before being exported to the empire.

Cattle egrets *feed among cattle and are often seen perched on their backs pecking off insects and flies.*

The purple gallinule *is a dark-coloured relative of the moorhen. It can run fairly fast on its extremely long legs but is a poor flier.*

The red-crested pochard *is a brightly coloured duck originally from central Europe.*

🗡 Centro de Educação
Quelfes. **Tel** *289 704 134/135.*
◯ *Mon–Fri.* ● *1 Jan, 25 Dec.*

Houses with four-sided roofs, along the river Gilão in Tavira

Tavira ⑳

Road map D7. 🕍 *10,000.* 🚉 🚌
ℹ️ *Rua da Galeria 9 (281 322 511).*
🗓️ *3rd Sat of month.*

The pretty town of Tavira, full
of historic churches and fine
mansions with filigree balconies, lies along both sides
of the Gilão river, linked by a
bridge of Roman origin. This
was part of the coastal Roman
road between Castro Marim
and Faro *(see pp328–31)*.

Tavira's early ascendancy
began with the Moors, who
saw it as one of their most
important settlements in the
Algarve, along with Silves and
Faro. It was conquered in 1242
by Dom Paio Peres Correia,
who was outraged at the murder of seven of his knights by
the Moors during a truce.

Tavira flourished until the
16th century, after which a
slow decline set in, aggravated
by a severe plague (1645–6)
and the silting up of the

Beach on Ilha de Tavira, an island
off the Algarve's eastern coast

harbour. The town now
accommodates tourists, without compromising either its
looks or atmosphere.

The best view of the town is
from the walls of the **Moorish
castle** in the old Arab quarter
on top of the hill. From here
the distinctive four-sided roofs
of the houses that line Rua da
Liberdade are clearly visible.
These pyramid-like roofs
possibly evolved to allow the
sudden torrential rain of the
Algarve to run off easily. From
the castle walls, the nearby
clock tower of the church of
Santa Maria do Castelo also
acts as a landmark. The church
itself occupies the site of what
was once the biggest mosque
in the Algarve. Its façade retains a Gothic doorway and
windows, and its interior,
restored in the 19th century,
houses the tombs of Dom Paio
Peres Correia and his seven
knights. Santa Maria do Castelo
and **Igreja da Misericórdia**
are the only two of Tavira's
21 churches to be open outside service hours. Below the
castle, is the 1569 convent of
Nossa Senhora da Graça.

Renaissance architecture
was pioneered in the town by
André Pilarte, and can be seen
on the way up to the castle,
in the Igreja da Misericórdia
(1541–51), with its lovely doorway topped by saints Peter
and Paul, and in the nearby
Palácio da Galeria (open for
temporary exhibitions). Rua da
Liberdade and Rua José Pires
Padinha have a sprinkling of
16th-century houses. The river
embankments are graced by
a few 18th-century mansions.

Environs: The sandy, offshore
Ilha de Tavira, provides excellent swimming. A popular
resort in summer, it is reached
by ferry from Quatro Águas.

Blue and white houses, Cacela Velha

Cacela Velha ㉑

Road map D7. 🕍 *50.* ℹ️ *Junta de
Freguesia de Vila Nova de Cacela
(281 951 228).*

This hamlet perches on a
cliff overlooking the sea,
reached via a landscape of
fields and olive trees. It has
remained untouched by mass
tourism, and retains a peaceful
atmosphere. Charming blue
and white fishermen's houses
cluster around the remains of
afort and a whitewashed
18th-century church.

The beach is sheltered by a
long spit of sand, and fishing
boats are dotted about. The
Phoenicians and Moors used
this protected site until it was
taken over by the Knights of
Santiago in 1240 *(see p43)*.

Vila Real de Santo António ㉒

Road map D7. 🏠 *10,000.*
🚉 🚌 🚶 *Avenida Marginal, Monte Gordo (281 544 495).*

Built to a plan by the Marquês de Pombal in 1774, Vila Real de Santo António is a little like a miniature version of Lisbon's Baixa *(pp78–81),* rebuilt after the 1755 earthquake also under the auspices of Pombal. The symmetrical grid of fairly wide streets, the equal-sized blocks with similar façades, the well-ordered naming system for the streets, all speak of Pombal's practical and political ideals.

Today, the town is one of the most important fishing ports on the Algarve coast, as well as a border town with its markets geared towards visiting Spaniards. Its centre now seems too grand for its size, all of which makes it an interesting place to drop in on.

Vila Real's Igreja Matriz, famous for its stained glass windows

Castro Marim ㉓

Road map D7. 🏠 *4,000.* 🚌 🚶 *Rua José Alves Moreira 2–4 (281 531 232).*

Castro Marim has attracted "visitors" since ancient times. The Phoenicians, Greeks and Romans all made use of its commanding location above the River Guadiana. It was the gateway to the Moorish Al-Gharb and for centuries it was a sanctuary for fugitives from the Inquisition *(see p51).* The **castle** above the town is of Moorish origin, the outlying walls a 13th-century addition.

Moorish castle and the abandoned Misericórdia church, Castro Marim

Environs: The town was also a centre for salt production and the surrounding *salinas* are now home to the wildlife reserve, **Reserva Natural do Sapal**, established in 1975. Extending for 2,090 ha (5,160 acres) south and east of town, this is an area of saltpans and marshes with a large variety of bird species including flamingos, avocets, and black-winged stilts, symbol of the reserve. Group tours may be booked on 281 510 680.

Alcoutim ㉔

Road map D7. 🏠 *400.* 🚌
🚶 *Rua 1° de Maio (281 546 179).*

The tiny, gem-like, unspoilt village of Alcoutim lies 15 km (9 miles) from the border with the Alentejo, and on the natural border with Spain, the River Guadiana. The drive there along the N122-2, a rough, winding road which sometimes runs alongside the Guadiana, provides stunning views of the countryside and across the river to Spain.

The size of Alcoutim belies its history. As a strategic location and river port, it was seized on by the Phoenicians, Greeks, Romans and, of course, the Moors who stayed until the reconquest in 1240. Here, in 1371, on flower-decked boats midway between Alcoutim and its Spanish counterpart, Sanlúcar de Guadiana, King Fernando I of Portugal signed the peace of Alcoutim with Enrique II of Castile. By the late 17th century, when its political importance had waned, the town had acquired a new reputation – for smuggling tobacco and snuff from Spain.

The walls of the 14th-century **castle** give an excellent view over the small village and its idyllic setting. Near the main square, by the river, is the refreshingly simple 16th-century church of **San Salvador**.

Environs: Visitors can take a scenic trip 15 km (9 miles) downriver to **Foz de Odeleite** by fishing boat from the jetty. The boat passes orchards and orange groves and, at Álamo, there is a Roman dam.

View from Alcoutim across the Guadiana to Sanlúcar in Spain

PORTUGAL'S ISLANDS

Portugal's Islands at a Glance

Once remote outposts of a maritime empire, today Madeira and the Azores are easily accessible by air from mainland Portugal. The fertile islands of Madeira and Porto Santo, 600 km (375 miles) off the African coast, are popular holiday destinations, with subtropical flora and high mountains. The Azorean archipelago lies further west, close to the Mid-Atlantic Ridge. The climate here is more temperate and the active volcanoes have created a fascinating scenery of moon-like landscapes and collapsed craters.

THE AZORES

MADEIRA

Terceira *is a relatively flat island famous for its bull-running festivals, the "tourada à corda". On the southern coast, the twin-towered church of São Mateus, built at the turn of the century, overlooks the harbour of São Mateus.*

Corvo

Flores

THE AZORES
(See pp360–73)

Graciosa

São Jor

Faial

Pico

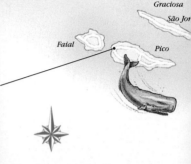

Pico *is the summit of a steep volcano protruding from the sea. On the lower slopes of the mountain that fall towards the sea, the fields are crisscrossed with a patchwork of drystone walls made from black volcanic basalt.*

◁ Fertile pastures sloping down to volcanic cones and the sea on the Azorean island of Faial

MADEIRA
(See pp342–59)

Funchal *is the capital of Madeira, famous for its flowers. Exotic blooms are sold along the main street, Avenida Arriaga, which is lined with tall jacaranda trees.*

Porto Santo

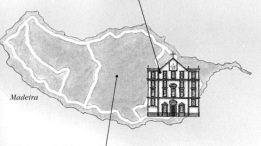

Madeira

Ilhas Desertas

0 kilometres		20
0 miles		10

Pico Ruivo, *at 1,961 m (6,105 ft), is the highest point on the island of Madeira. The slopes below are dotted with small farms.*

Terceira

0 kilometres		50
0 miles		25

São Miguel

São Miguel *is popular for its therapeutic spa treatments in hot pools of mineral water. At Caldeira das Furnas, in the east of the island, steaming mud springs bubbles from the ground.*

Santa Maria

The Landscape and Flowers of Madeira

Madeira has a mild, moist climate which promotes a rich cover of vegetation. At first glance, the flowers and foliage appear to harmonize with the environment. The well-travelled botanist, however, will soon become aware of the strange assortment of flowers from around the world. For example, over the past few centuries, many flowers from South Africa's Cape region and exotic blooms from South America have been introduced, which now thrive alongside indigenous plants.

Pride of Madeira

MADEIRA'S GARDENS

The sub-tropical climate and mix of indigenous and imported pla combine to produce gardens th are the envy of horticulturalists all over th world. Gardens such the Botanical Gardens Funchal *(see p346)* a awash with colour year. Here are some of th most striking plants that c be found in Madeira's garde

Magnolia in bloom

AROUND THE COAST

In many coastal areas the cliffs are spectacular, such as this stretch at Ponta de São Lourenço *(see p352)*. A rich and varied flora, both native and introduced, can be found along Madeira's coast despite the dry and stony habitat.

Hottentot fig *is a coastal, ground-cover plant originating from South Africa.*

Lampranthus spectabilis *is a South African plant which flowers on the coast between May and July.*

Canary Island date palms *are a familiar sight, especially along the sunny south coast.*

AGRICULTURAL AND WAYSIDE GROU

An irrigation system using man-made chann called *levadas*, such as this one near Curral Freiras *(see p356)*, allows the islanders to culti many otherwise unpromising areas. The mar of agricultural land are often rich with flowe

Mimosa trees *grow especially well in wood parts of Madeira, whe they bloom in winter.*

Parrot's Beak *is a large, striking flower that appears in March and April.*

Hibiscus syriacus, *from the Far East, flowers between June and October.*

Lady's slipper orchids come in a variety of colours and are great favourites among Madeira's more serious gardeners.

Cymbidium orchids from Southeast Asia thrive when they are grown in sheltered sites and in partial shade.

Coral trees originate from southern Brazil, and on Madeira flower between January and March.

Camellia thrives in partial shade and grows to the size of a small tree.

Protea cynaroides comes from South Africa where it is known as the Cape artichoke or king protea.

HIGH GROUND

The views from the summit of Pico Ruivo, the island's highest point *(see p356)*, are spectacular. In upland areas, the vegetation harbours a higher proportion of native species than in the lowlands.

TERRACED PLANTATIONS

Plantations, such as this one growing bananas near Calheta *(see p358)*, are made by digging terraces into the hillside. A wide range of crops are grown, for home consumption and export.

Isoplexis sceptrum, known as the yellow foxglove, is a flowering shrub native to Madeira.

Sweet chestnuts grow well in Madeira and produce an abundant autumn harvest.

Broom flowers are colourful and popular with pollinating insects.

Pawpaws produce fruit all year round. The plant originates from South America.

Prickly juniper is a hardy, spiny evergreen shrub covered in tough red berries.

Sword aloe has spiky leaves which provide a good physical barrier around plantations.

The Azores: Volcanic Islands Rising from the Ocean Bed

Situated on either side of the Mid-Atlantic Ridge, the Azores are a result of 20 million years of volcanic activity. As the plates of the earth's crust pull apart, volcanic eruptions form a giant ridge of mountains beneath the Atlantic. In places, the ridge is buckled and cut by perpendicular fractures, known as transform faults. Molten rock (magma) has been forced through these faults to form the Azores. These islands, among the youngest on earth, emerged above the waves less than five million years ago. Their striking landscape tells of their volcanic past and is still shaped by volcanic activity today.

The Mid-Atlantic Ridge *is a line of submarine volcanoes that runs the whole length of the Atlantic Ocean.*

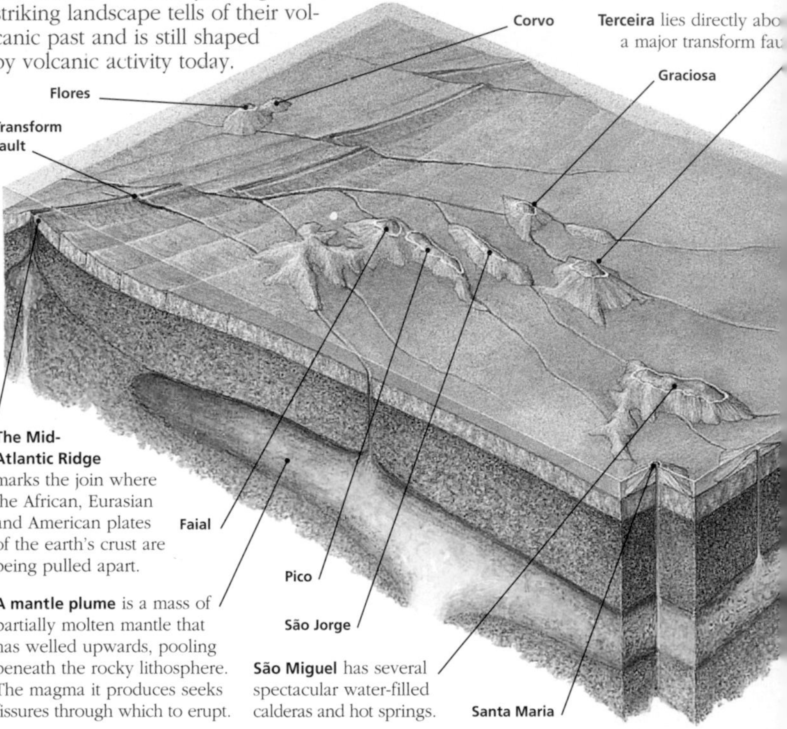

Corvo

Terceira lies directly abo a major transform fau

Graciosa

Flores

Transform fault

The Mid-Atlantic Ridge marks the join where the African, Eurasian and American plates of the earth's crust are being pulled apart.

Faial

Pico

São Jorge

A mantle plume is a mass of partially molten mantle that has welled upwards, pooling beneath the rocky lithosphere. The magma it produces seeks fissures through which to erupt.

São Miguel has several spectacular water-filled calderas and hot springs.

Santa Maria

VOLCANIC RESOURCES OF THE AZORES

The dramatic formation of the Azores has left the islands with abundant natural resources. Hot springs, strong building materials and, eventually, fertile soil, are all the result of the ongoing volcanic activity. A wet, temperate climate gradually breaks down the volcanic rocks into fertile soils. Older soils support luxuriant vegetation and are excellent for arable farming, but younger soils, like those found on Pico, support little agriculture yet.

These stone cottages *on Pico, like many on the islands, make use of the plentiful basalt rock as a durable building material.*

Furnas, on São Miguel, *is an area of sulphur and hot mud springs used for bathi and for medicinal purposes*

sing high above the clouds, *the still-active ▪lcanic peak of Pico Alto dominates the island of ▪co, which is itself the top of a giant underwater ▪lcano. At 2,350 m (7,700 ft) above sea level, Pico ▪to is the highest peak in the whole of Portugal.*

HE GEOLOGY OF THE AZORES

▪e Azores lie along transform fault lines, cracks ▪ the earth's crust which cross the Mid-Atlantic ▪dge. These faults are weak points through ▪hich magma can rise. Successive volcanic erup-▪ions have formed hundreds of undersea
mountains on either side of the ridge. The highest peaks of these mountains are the nine islands of the Azores. Their emergence above the sea has been aided by the swelling of the mantle plume beneath the ocean crust, which lifts the sea floor closer to the surface of the sea.

Thin ocean crust

Atlantic Ocean

The upper mantle is a layer of dense rock. With the crust above, it forms the lithosphere, a series of semi-rigid moving plates.

The lower mantle, or asthenosphere, is a deep layer of partially molten rock that surrounds the earth's core.

▪salt lava blocks *used for vines and dry-stone walls provide ▪elter for vines and protect against soil erosion on ▪co. Volcanic soil here is of relatively recent for-▪ation and suitable for few crops except grapes.*

THE FORMATION OF A CALDERA

A caldera is a large crater that forms during or after a volcanic eruption, when the roof of the magma chamber collapses under the weight of the volcano's cone. Water collecting in the natural bowl of a caldera can form a crater lake.

Caldeira das Sete Cidades on the island of São Miguel

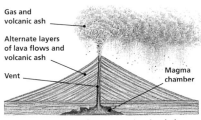

Gas and volcanic ash

Alternate layers of lava flows and volcanic ash

Vent

Magma chamber

In an active volcano, the magma chamber below the cone is full of molten rock. As pressure forces this magma up through the volcano's vent, it is expelled to the surface as a volcanic eruption.

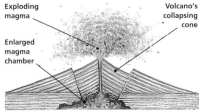

Exploding magma

Volcano's collapsing cone

Enlarged magma chamber

As magma is expelled, the level in the magma chamber drops. This may cause the volcano's cone to collapse under its own weight, leaving behind the characteristic bowl-shaped crater, or caldera.

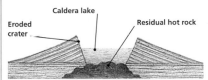

Caldera lake

Eroded crater

Residual hot rock

After the volcano has died down and is eroded, the caldera can fill with water and form a lake. Residual hot rock near the magma chamber may continue to heat the surrounding ground water.

MADEIRA

adeira is a green, subtropical paradise of volcanic origin, its soils formed from lava and ash, completely different in character from the Portuguese mainland. Blessed with an equable daytime temperature that varies only by a few degrees either side of 20°C (68° F), the island has an all-year-round appeal.

Madeira is a mere dot in the Atlantic Ocean, 608 km (378 miles) from Morocco, and nearly 1,000 km (621 miles) from Lisbon. Despite this, Madeira and Porto Santo appear on a Genoese map of 1351, so there is no doubt that sailors had long known about the islands. They remained unclaimed, however, until 1418 when João Gonçalves Zarco was blown out into the Atlantic by violent storms while exploring the coast of Africa. Zarco counted his blessings at having found safe harbour in Porto Santo, set up the Portuguese flag and returned to Lisbon. A year later he returned on a voyage of discovery sponsored by Henry the Navigator *(see p49)*. Early in 1420, after a winter on Porto Santo, he set sail for the mist-shrouded land on the horizon. He found a beautiful, thickly wooded island *(madeira* means wood), with abundant fresh water.

The bird-of-paradise flower *(Strelitzia reginae)*

Within seven years the island had attracted a pioneer colony and the early settlers exploited the fertile soil and warm climate to grow sugar cane. The islanders grew rich on this "white gold", and slaves were brought in to work the land and create the terraced fields and irrigation channels *(levadas)* that still cling to the steep hillsides. Today, despite the gradients, Madeirans make use of every spare patch of land, growing bananas, flowers and grapes (although tourism is the main industry).

In the late 19th century, Madeira became a popular winter holiday spot for northern Europeans. The start of commercial flights in 1964 introduced the rest of the world to its charms. Today Madeira appeals to keen walkers, plant lovers and sun seekers, although it lacks the sandy beaches of its sister island, Porto Santo.

Triangular-shaped houses, typical of the town of Santana on the north coast of Madeira

◁ Footpath winding through the spectacular mountain scenery of Pico do Arieiro

Exploring Madeira

Funchal is the island's capital and the only town of any size. This is where most of the museums and historic buildings are to be found, as well as the best hotels, restaurants and shops. Most of Madeira's agricultural crops are grown along the sunny, prosperous south coast. The cooler, wetter north side has fewer settlements and more cattle. Many parts of the mountainous and volcanic interior remain wild, and some are accessible only on foot. Pico Ruivo, the highest peak on the island, is a favourite destination for walkers.

Terraces near Boa Ventura, on the road from Santana to São Vicente

Ponta do Tristão

15 PORTO MONIZ

Santa
Lamaceiros
Achadas da Cruz
Ribeira da Janela

R101

ATLANTIC OCEAN

Seixal
Ponta Delgada

Ribeira da Vaca

R110

R101
Boaventu

Ponta do Pargo
Senhora do Amparo

14 SÃO VICENTE

R101

Cabeço da Roseira

Remal 1320m

Ginjas
Lameiros

R104

Achada da Madeira

Fajã da Ovelha

R210

Pico Ruivo do Paúl 1640m

Ponta do Pesqueiro

Raposeira

13 RABAÇAL WALKS

PAUL DA SERRA

Bica da Cana 1620m

Boca da Encumeada 1007m

Casa 1725

Paúl do Mar

Prazeres

R211

12

R110

Fajã Car

Jardim do Mar

R222

Lombo dos Reis

Chã da Quebrada

Pico Grande 1657m

Serra de Água

CALHETA 16

R101

R209

Lombo das Tercas

Lombo do Mouro

CURRA DAS FREIRA

Arco da Calheta

R104

Jard da S

0 kilometres   5

0 miles   3

Madalena do Mar

R222

Candelária

Lugar da Serra

Ponta do Sol
Tabúa
São João

RIBEIRA BRAVA 17

R101

Campanário

Quinta Grande

CÂMARA DE LOBOS

Early morning view across the rooftops of Funchal, with the mountainous interior beyond

GETTING AROUND

Madeira's international airport, Santa Catarina, is at Santa Cruz, 18 km (11 miles) northeast of Funchal. Buses operate to all corners of the island from Funchal but are not geared to tourists. Taxis can be used, but for flexibility car hire is best. From north to south the island is 22 km (14 miles) wide and from east to west just 57 km (35 miles) long. Even so, travelling times are magnified by the mountainous terrain. To reach the nearby island of Porto Santo, you can either fly from Santa Cruz or take the ferry from Funchal to Porto de Abrigo (near Vila Baleira). *(See also pp460–61.)*

PORTO SANTO 19

Ilhéu da Fonte da Areia
Camacha
Serra de Dentro
Ponta do Varadouro
Farrobo
Serra de Fora
Ponta dos Ferreiros
Campo de Cima
Tanque
Ponta da Galé
Ilhéu de Ferro
Vila Baleira
Ilhéu de Cima
Zimbralinho
Ponta
Cabeço da Ponta
Ponta da Calheta
ATLANTIC OCEAN
Ilhéu de Baixo ou da Cal

THE AZORES

MADEIRA

The wild cliffs of Ponta de São Lourenço, near Caniçal

Ponta de São Jorge
São Jorge
Ponta de Santana
Ribeira Funda
Achada da Cruz
7 SANTANA
Ilha
R101
Achada Marques
Faial
Queimadas
anário
R116
R103
Achada do Teixeira
ICO RUIVO
Cruzinhas
Porto da Cruz
Referta
Maiata
Ponta do Espigão Amarelo
Pico das Torres 1851m
Pico da Coroa 738m
Ponta de São Lourenço
Balcões 860m
Portela
CANIÇAL 6
CO DO RIEIRO
9
8 RIBEIRO FRIO
Maroços
R109
Prainha
R202
Ribeira de Machico
R108
Ribeira Seca
os
Passo de Poiso 1400m
Santo António da Serra
R202
m
R102
5 MACHICO
Pico Alto 1129m
João Ferino
Água de Pena
Choupana
R203
Águas Mansas
Terça
R103
3 MONTE
Santa Cruz
tio
São João de Latrão
4 CAMACHA
R101
Gaula
R102
nio
2 QUINTA DO PALHEIRO FERREIRO
R101
São Gonçalo
Caniço
ho
1 FUNCHAL
Garajau
Caniço de Baixo
Ponta da Oliveira

KEY

═══	Motorway
══	Motorway under construction
───	Major road
⋯⋯	Minor road
───	Scenic route
-- --	Path
△	Summit

SIGHTS AT A GLANCE

Calheta 16
Camacha 4
Câmara de Lobos 18
Caniçal 6
Curral das Freiras 11
Funchal pp346–9 1
Machico 5
Monte 3
Paúl da Serra 12
Pico do Arieiro 9
Pico Ruivo 10
Porto Moniz 15
Porto Santo 19
Quinta do Palheiro Ferreiro 2
Ribeira Brava 17
Ribeiro Frio 8
Santana 7
São Vicente 14

Walks and Tours

Rabaçal Walks 13

SEE ALSO

• *Where to Stay* pp403–4
• *Where to Eat* pp429–30

Street-by-Street: Funchal ●

Tiling on Palácio do Governo Regional, Avenida M. Arriaga

The deep natural harbour of Madeira's capital, Funchal, attracted early settlers in the 15th century. The historic core of the capital still overlooks the harbour and boasts fine government buildings and stately 18th-century houses with shady courtyards, iron balconies and carved black basalt doorways. Visitors have justly called Funchal a "little Lisbon" because of the town's steep cobbled streets and overall air of grandeur.

The Igreja do Colégio
(Collegiate Church) was foun[ded] by the Jesuits in 1574. The pl[ain] exterior contrasts with the ric[hly] decorated high altar, framed [by] carved, gilded wood (1641–6[...])

Rua da Carreira and Rua do Surdo
have preserved many of their original elegant balconied houses.

São Pedro church

The Museu Municipal houses an aquarium and is a favourite with children.

RUA DAS PRETAS

RUA DO SURDO

RUA DA CARREIRA

RUA S. FRANCISCO

The Old Blandy Wine Lodge *(see p349)*

The monument to João Gonçalves Zarco, the man who claimed Madeira for Portugal, was created by the sculptor Francisco Franco in 1927.

Toyota Showroom
The building's exterior is decorated with 20th-century tiles depicting various Madeiran scenes including the famous Monte toboggan (see p350).

AVENIDA M. ARRIAGA

AVEN[...]

RUA DAS FONTES

0 metres	50
0 yards	50

The Palácio de São Lourenço is a 16th-century fortress housing Madeira's military headquarters.

Yacht Marina
Lined with seafood restaurants, the yacht marina on Avenida do Mar is ideal for an evening stroll. The sea wall around the marina offers good views.

Avenida do Mar

STAR SIGHTS

★ Sé

★ Praça do Município

Câmara Municipal
Funchal's city hall is an imposing 18th-century mansion with a fountain in its courtyard depicting Leda and the Swan. *Inside, a small museum traces the history of Funchal in photographs.*

The Museu de Arte Sacra includes Flemish paintings, embroidered vestments and statues among the displays of religious art *(see p348).*

SÃO TAVIRA

RUA DO ALJUBE

RUA DA ALFÂNDEGA

Bus station

Palácio do Governo Regional

The Alfândega Velha (Old Customs House) was built in 1477 and is now home to the island's regional parliament.

KEY

– – – Suggested route

VISITORS' CHECKLIST

120,000. ✈ Santa Catarina 18 km (11 miles) NE. ⛴ 🚌 Avenida do Mar. 🛈 Avenida Arriaga 16 (291 211 902). 🚌 Mon–Sat. 🎉 Apr/May: Flower Festival; mid-Sep: Wine Festival; 31 Dec: Fireworks. **Museu Municipal** Rua da Mouraria 31. **Tel** 291 229 761. ◯ Tue–Sun (only pm Sat & Sun). ⬤ public hols. 📷

★ Praça do Município
Contrasting black and white stones pave the attractive municipal square. On the northeast side of the square is the Câmara Municipal.

Rua do Aljube
Alongside the Sé, flower sellers in traditional costumes offer a colourful array of exotic flowers.

★ Sé
São Tiago (St James) is one of many gilded figures that adorn the wonderfully carved wooden choir stalls in Funchal's 15th-century cathedral (see p348).

Exploring Funchal

Funchal extends in a crescent along the coastline of Funchal Bay, with the Zona Velha or Old Quarter, a warren of former fishermen's houses, at the eastern end and the Hotel or Tourist Zone, dominated by hotels and restaurants, at the western end and beyond. Between is the heart of Funchal, with its attractive historic centre around the gracious Avenida Arriaga. It has a lively marina and working port, where a small fishing fleet is overshadowed by cruise liners. Funchal also has two scenic cable cars. A few blocks inland, the city fans out in a dense web of red-tiled roofs and subtropical greenery.

Carved Manueline-style lions in the garden at Quinta das Cruzes

🏛 Sé

Largo da Sé. *Tel 291 228 155.*
◻ *daily.*

The cathedral is one of the few buildings in Madeira to have survived virtually untouched since the early days of the island's colonization. In the 1490s, King Manuel I *(see pp46–9)* sent the architect Pêro Anes from the mainland to work on the design of the colony's cathedral. The Sé was finally completed in 1514.

The highlights are the ceiling and the choir stalls, though neither is easy to see in the dark interior. The ceiling of inlaid wood is best seen from the south transept, where enough light filters in to illuminate the intricate patterning. The choir stalls depict saints, prophets and apostles in 16th-century costume. Aspects of Madeiran life feature in the decorative details of the armrests and seats: one cherub carries a bunch of bananas, another a goatskin full of wine.

Clock tower of Funchal's Sé

🏛 Museu de Arte Sacra

Rua do Bispo 21. *Tel 291 228 900.*
◻ *10:30am–12:30pm & 2:30–6pm Tue–Sat, 10am–1pm Sun.*
● *public hols.* 🎫

Madeiran merchants, who grew rich on the profitable sugar trade, sought to secure their salvation by commissioning paintings, statues, embroidered vestments and illuminated hymn books for their local churches. Hundreds of examples now fill this museum which is housed in the former bishops' palace, a building dating from 1600. There are some masterpieces in the collection, including the late-Gothic processional cross donated by King Manuel I, and religious paintings by major Flemish artists of the 15th and 16th centuries. Some works include portraits of the dignitaries who commissioned them. *Saints Philip and James* is a 16th-century painting showing Simão Gonçalves de Câmara, Zarco's *(see p343)* grandson.

🏛 Quinta das Cruzes

Calçada do Pico 1. *Tel 291 740 670.*
◻ *Tue–Sun.* ● *public hols.* 🎫

It is said that Zarco, the man who claimed Madeira for Portugal *(see p341)*, built his house where the Quinta das Cruzes now stands. The elegant 19th-century mansion is now the Museum of Decorative Arts, furnished as a wealthy merchant's house with Indian silk wall hangings, Regency sideboards and oriental carpets. In the basement is furniture made from mahogany packing cases used in the 17th century for shipping sugar, and turned into chests and cupboards when the sugar trade died.

The garden is dotted with ancient tombstones and architectural fragments. These include two window frames from 1507 carved with rope motifs, acrobatic figures and man-eating lions in a Madeiran version of the Manueline style of architecture *(see pp20–21)*.

🏛 Convento de Santa Clara

Calçada de Santa Clara. *Tel 291 742 602.* ◻ *Mon–Sat (ring doorbell).*

Opposite Quinta das Cruzes is the Convento de Santa Clara, founded in 1496 by João Gonçalves de Câmara, one of Zarco's grandsons. Zarco himself is buried under the high altar, and Martim Mendes Vasconcelos, his son-in-law, has a tomb at the rear of the church. Precious 17th-century *azulejo* tiles cover the walls.

🌿 Jardim Botânico

Quinta do Bom Sucesso, Caminho do Meio. *Tel 291 211 200.* ◻ *daily.*
● *25 Dec.* 🎫

The Botanical Gardens display plants from all over the world. Desert cacti, rainforest orchids and South African proteas grow here as well as Madeiran dragon trees. There are contrasting sections: formal areas of bedding plants, quiet carp ponds and wild wooded parts.

The intricately patterned formal gardens of the Jardim Botânico

For hotels and restaurants in this region see pp403–4 and pp429–30

▼ The Old Blandy Wine Lodge

Avenida Arriaga 28. *Tel 291 740 110.*
◯ *9:30am–6:30pm Mon–Fri, Sat am.*
● *public hols.* 🎫 ✓ *compulsory.*
In the cobbled courtyards of
the St Francis wine lodge, visitors are greeted by the scents
of ancient wood and Madeira.
Some of the buildings in this
maze of coopers' yards, wine
vaults and sampling rooms go
back to the 17th century when
the site was part of Funchal's
Franciscan friary. It is possible
to sample wines made on the
premises more than 150 years
ago as well as more recent
(and cheaper) vintages. Included in the guided tour is a visit
to the warming rooms where
Madeira is "cooked" by hot
water pipes *(see p351).*

**Tasting Madeira wine at The Old
Blandy Wine Lodge**

🏛 Mercado dos Lavradores

Largo dos Lavradores. *Tel 291 214
080.* ◯ *Mon–Sat.* ● *public hols.*
The Mercado dos Lavradores is
where flower growers, basket
weavers, farmers and fishermen from all over Madeira
bring their products to market.
The covered market
building, situated on
three floors around an
open courtyard, is full
of the colour and bustle
of island life. Stall-
holders offer slices of
mango or custard fruit
to prove that theirs are
the sweetest and best.
In the basement, marble
tables are draped with
great slabs of tuna and
black-skinned scabbard
fish with huge eyes
and razor-sharp teeth.
   On Fridays the mar-
ket spills out into the
back streets of the Zona
Velha (Old Town), the
former fishermen's
quarter and now an
area of small shops

and lively cafés. The simple,
single-storey dwellings at the
pedestrianized eastern end of
Rua Dom Carlos I are said to
date from the 15th century. The
little Corpo Santo chapel was
built by 16th-century fishermen in honour of their patron,
St Peter, and is said to be the
oldest such building in Funchal.

⚓ Fortaleza de São Tiago

Rua do Portão de São Tiago.
Tel 291 213 340. **Museum**
◯ *10am–12:30pm & 2–5:30pm
Mon–Sat.* ● *public hols.* 🎫
Along the seafront is the
Fortaleza de São Tiago, built
in 1614, with additions dating
from 1767. The fortress, with
its maze of passages and
staircases, commands views
over Funchal and houses a
Museum of Contemporary
Art and a restaurant.

House and gardens of the Quinta do Palheiro Ferreiro

Quinta do Palheiro Ferreiro ②

Sítio do Balançal, São Gonçalo.
Tel 291 790 350. 🚌 ◯ *9am–
4:30pm Mon–Fri.* ● *1 Jan, Easter,
1 May, 25 Dec.* 🎫

The Quinta do Palheiro
Ferreiro is Madeira's finest
garden and a place of pilgrimage for flower-lovers. A French
landscape architect laid out the
gardens in the 18th century for
the wealthy Count of Carvalhal,
who built the elegant mansion
(not open to visitors) overlooking the garden and the Baroque
chapel in the garden itself.
   The estate was acquired in
1885 by the long-established
Anglo-Madeiran Blandy family,
hence its English name: Blandy's Gardens. New species
were introduced from
South Africa, China and
Australia, resulting in a
garden that combines
the clipped formality of
late 18th-century layout
with the profusion of
English-style herba-
ceous borders, plus
the combination of
tropical and temperate
climate varieties.
   Quite apart from its
horticultural interest,
the garden is a peaceful
wildlife haven, full of
beauty and contrast as
you pass from the for-
mality of the Ladies'
Garden to the tropical
wilderness of the ravine
ominously signposted
"Inferno" (Hell).

**Fishmonger chopping tuna into huge steaks in the
basement of Funchal's Mercado dos Lavradores**

The contrasting façade of Nossa Senhora do
Monte, created by basalt against whitewash

Monte ❸

🏚 10,000. 🚋 ℹ️ *Caminho de Ferro
182, Junta da Freguesia (291 782 555).*

Monte has been a favourite
destination for visitors to
Madeira since the late 19th
century, when a rack and pin-
ion railway was built to haul
cruise liner passengers up the
hillside from Funchal. Coming
down they would take the famous **Monte toboggan** ride.

An alternative way to get
to the Monte is by the cable
car that runs from Jardim do
Almirante Reis, below the old
town, up to the Caminho das

Babosas, by the Monte
Palace Gardens. The
ascent takes 15
minutes, and the
car operates between
10am and 6pm daily.
The railway closed in
1939, but the station
and a viaduct survive,
now forming part of
the luxuriant **Jardim
do Monte** public gar-
dens. It is a short stroll
through the gardens to
the church of **Nossa
Senhora do Monte**,
whose twin-towered
façade looks down on
the island's capital.
The present church
was built in 1818 on
the site of a chapel
built in 1470 by Adam
Gonçalves Ferreira.

The Virgin of Monte
is Madeira's patron
saint and this church is the
focal point of the pilgrimage
that takes place annually on
15 August (the Feast of the
Assumption) when penitents
climb the church's 74 steps
on their knees. The object of
their worship is a tiny statue
of the Virgin on the high altar.

Left of the nave is a chapel
housing a mortuary chest, containing the remains of the last
Hapsburg Emperor, Karl I, who
was deposed in 1918. Exiled
in Madeira he died of pneu-
monia in 1922, aged only 35.

Toboggan drivers in straw
hats wait for passengers every
day on the corner of Caminho

do Monte, and they run (for a
fee) to Livramento and on to
Funchal. From the church
steps, past the drivers' corner, a
left turn signposted "Old Monte
Gardens" leads to the **Monte
Palace Tropical Gardens**. These
superb gardens, laid out in
1894, will delight children
with their maze of pathways
and bridges, follies, fountains,
cascades and black swans.
The gardens extend for 7 ha
(17 acres) down a lush valley
with areas devoted to Madeiran
flora, South African proteas,
plants from Japan and China,
azaleas, camellias and orchids.

🌿 **Monte Palace
Tropical Gardens**
***Tel** 291 782 339.* ◯ *daily.* 🖼️

One of the skilled wicker workers
of Camacha constructing a table

Camacha ❹

🏚 9,000. 🚋 ℹ️ *Junta da Freguesia,
Complexo de Habitação dos Casais
de Além 2 (291 922 466).*

Most of the wicker products
sold in Funchal are made in
and around Camacha, and
the sole attraction in this
otherwise sleepy village is a
large shop packed with everything wicker, from picture
frames, bedsteads and cradles
to peacock-backed armchairs.
It is often possible to see
weavers at work, bending
the pliant stripped willow
round a frame to produce
a linen basket or plant-pot
container. A Noah's Ark
full of paired animals is
displayed on the middle floor,
along with a full-sailed galleon, as an advertisement of
the local wicker weavers' skills.

THE MONTE TOBOGGAN

Sliding in a wicker basket mounted on wooden runners, it
is possible to cover the 2-km (1-mile) descent from Monte to
Livramento in 10 minutes. The trip
is made by thousands every year,
fascinated by the experience
of travelling at speed down a
public highway on a wooden
sled. Ernest Hemingway once
described it as "exhilarating".
A cushioned seat softens the
ride and passengers are in the
safe hands of the toboggan
drivers, who push and steer
from the rear, using their
rubber-soled boots as
brakes. Madeiran tobog-
ganing was invented as
a form of passenger
transport around 1850.

The famous Monte Toboggan ride

Madeira Wine

Wicker-covered Madeira bottle

In the 16th century, ships stopping at Funchal would take on barrels of local wine. This unfortified Madeira often spoiled during the voyage, so shippers started adding spirit to make it better. The wine now seemed to improve after a long, hot voyage, and quality Madeira began to be sent on round trips as an alternative to maturing it in Funchal's lodges. This expensive method was replaced with the *estufa* system, still very much in use today. Large volumes of wine are heated to between 30 and 50°C for a period of three months to a year. The effect is to hurry up the ageing process: the best wines are "cooked" more gently and slowly. The finest Madeirans are heated by the sun, maturing slowly in the attics of the wine lodges.

Most Madeira is made from the Tinta Negra Mole grape, often blended with one of the four noble varieties listed below.

Making barrels for Madeira, Funchal

THE FOUR TYPES OF MADEIRA

Sercial *is made from white grapes grown at heights up to 1,000 m (3,280 ft). Good-quality Sercial is aged for at least ten years, giving it its amber colour. A dry wine – it is mostly drunk as an aperitif or with soup, and is best served chilled.*

Verdelho *grapes are grown in cool vineyards at lower heights than the Sercial. This medium- dry tawny wine is also drunk as an aperitif. Sweeter than Sercial, Verdelho goes well with a slice of Madeira cake (invented by the English for just this purpose).*

The barrels *in the Adegas de São Francisco (see p347), where Madeira is warmed, need frequent repair as do the wooden floors that bear their huge weight.*

These casks of Verdelho *are being aged after the addition of brandy to the wine. Vintage wine must spend at least 20 years in the cask and two in the bottle.*

Bual *(or Boal) grapes are grown in lower, warmer conditions. Dark, rich and nutty, it is a medium-sweet wine that can be served as an alternative to port. It goes very well with cheeses and dessert, and is best drunk at room temperature.*

Malmsey, *the most celebrated Madeira, is made from Malvasia grapes grown in sunny vineyards backed by cliffs, where the heat absorbed by the rock by day warms the grapes by night. The result is a rich dark wine drunk as an after-dinner digestive.*

Vintage Madeira *from every decade as far back as the mid-19th century is still available for sale. The oldest surviving bottle of Madeira dates from 1772.*

Machico ❺

🏛 22,000. 🚌 ℹ️ Forte de Nossa Senhora do Amparo, Rua Dr José António de Almada (291 962 289).

Legend has it that Machico was named after Robert Machim, a merchant from Bristol, who eloped with the aristocratic Anne of Hertford and set sail for Portugal. Caught in a storm and shipwrecked on Madeira, the two lovers died from exposure and were buried. The rest of the crew repaired the boat and sailed to Lisbon, where their story inspired Prince Henry the Navigator (see p49) to send João Gonçalves Zarco (see p343) in search of this mysterious wooded island.

Machico has been Madeira's second most important town since the first settlements, when the island was divided into two captaincies: Zarco ruled the west from Funchal whilst his fellow navigator, Tristão Vaz Teixeira, ruled the east from Machico. However, Funchal's superior location and harbour soon ensured that it

developed as the capital of Madeira while Machico became a sleepy agricultural town.

The **Igreja Matriz** on Largo do Município, Machico's main square, dates from the 15th century. Above the high altar is a statue of the Virgin Mary, donated by Manuel I (see pp46–9), as were the three marble pillars used in the construction of the Gothic south portal. Inside, there is a fine example of Manueline-style stone masonry in the Capela de São João Baptista, whose arch shows Teixeira's coat of arms, with a phoenix rising from the flames.

Across the River Machico, on Largo dos Milagres, is the **Capela dos Milagres** (Chapel of the Miracles). The present structure dates from 1815, but it stands on the site of Madeira's first church, where Robert Machim and Anne of Hertford are supposedly buried. The earlier church of 1420 was destroyed in a flood in 1803, but the 15th-century crucifix was found floating out at sea. Machico celebrates the return of its cross with a procession every year on 8 October.

Main altar in the Capela dos Milagres, Machico

View from Ponta de São Lourenço promontory, east of Caniçal

Caniçal ❻

🏛 5,000. 🚌 ℹ️ (as for Machico) (291 962 289).

Caniçal was once the centre of Madeira's whaling industry: the whaling scenes for John Huston's film version of Moby Dick (1956) were shot here. Whaling ceased in June 1981, and since then the waters around Madeira have been declared a marine mammal sanctuary – killing whales, dolphins and seals is forbidden. Fishermen who once hunted whales now help marine biologists at the Society for the Protection of Sea Mammals understand whale migrations.

The old whaling company's office is now the **Museu da Baleia** (Whaling Museum). It shows a 45-minute video on whale hunting with commentaries by retired fishermen.

Caniçal is still a busy fishing port, and the stony beach is used by tuna fishermen to repair their colourful boats.

🏛 **Museu da Baleia**
Largo Manuel Alves. **Tel** 291 961 859. ⬤ for restoration. 🎥 ♿

Environs: The easternmost tip of Madeira, the **Ponta de São Lourenço**, is characterized by dramatic wave-battered cliffs plunging 180 m (590 ft) to the Atlantic. Walkers are attracted by footpaths which meander from one clifftop to another, with wild flowers growing in sheltered hollows. The treeless landscape contrasts totally with the island's wooded interior.

On the road from Caniçal to Ponta de São Lourenço, look out for the signpost to the bay of **Prainha**, Madeira's only naturally sandy beach.

Fishing boats hauled up on the beach at Caniçal

Santana ⓞ

🏚 10,500. 🚌 ℹ️ *Sitio do Serrado (291 572 992).*

Santana (named after St Anne, mother of the Virgin) has more than 100 thatched triangular houses, several of which, restored and brightly painted, can be visited by the public. The hillsides above the broad valley in which Santana sits are also dotted with triangular thatched byres, where cows are tethered to stop them from wandering along narrow terrace paths and harming themselves or crops.

The valley is intensively farmed both for fruit and vegetables, and osiers, the willow branches that are the raw material for the wicker workers of Camacha *(see p350).*

Ribeiro Frio ⓞ

🏚 45. 🚌 *from Funchal.*

Bridge across a *levada* on the walk from Ribeiro Frio to Balcões

Ribeiro Frio is a pretty spot consisting of a couple of restaurants, shops and a trout farm, fed by the "cold stream" after which the place is named.

Surrounding the trout farm is an attractive garden full of native trees and shrubs. This is the starting point for two of the island's best *levada* walks *(see p357).* The 12-km (7-mile) path signposted to **Portela** (on the right heading downhill past the restaurants) passes through dramatic mountain scenery but is best left to experienced walkers because of the long tunnels and steep drops in places. Far easier is

Sunrise over the mountains, seen from Pico do Arieiro

the 20-minute walk on the left (going downhill) signposted to **Balcões** (Balconies). This viewpoint gives panoramic views across the valley of the River Ametade to Penha de Águia (Eagle Rock), the sheer-sided hill that projects from Madeira's northern coast.

Pico do Arieiro ⓞ

🚌 *to Camacha, then taxi.*

From Funchal it is about a 30-minute drive up the Pico do Arieiro, Madeira's third highest mountain at 1,810 m (5,938 ft). The route leads through steep hillsides cloaked in fragrant eucalyptus and bay laurel. At around 900 m (2,950 ft), you will often meet the cloudline and pass for a few minutes through swirling mists and possibly rain, before emerging into a sunlit landscape of volcanic rocks. At the top, the spectacular view is of clouds in the valleys and dramatic mountain ridges with knife-edge peaks. Just visible on a clear day is Pico Ruivo *(see p356),* connected to Pico do Arieiro by a 10-km (6-mile) path. On especially clear days you may be able to see the neighbouring island of Porto Santo, some 48 km (30 miles) north of Madeira.

THE TRIANGULAR HOUSES OF SANTANA

Simply constructed from two A-shaped timber frames, with a wood-panelled interior and thatched roof, these triangular houses are unique to Madeira. They are first mentioned in the 16th century, but most of the surviving examples are no more than 100 years old. Today their doors and windows are often painted a cheerful red, yellow or blue. In the warm year-round climate of Madeira, cooking and eating take place out of doors, and the toilets are placed well away from the house. To the inhabitants, therefore, the triangular houses serve principally as shelter from the rain and for sleeping in. The interior is deceptively spacious, with a living area downstairs and sleeping space up in the loft.

Panoramic view of the mountains from the Pico Ruivo summit

Pico Ruivo ⑩

🚌 *to Santana or Faial, then taxi to Achada do Teixeira, then walk.*

Madeira's highest mountain at 1,861 m (6,105 ft), Pico Ruivo is only accessible on foot. The easiest way to scale its heights is via a well signposted footpath which begins at the village of Achada do Teixeira and leads visitors on a 45-minute walk to the top.

Alternatively, follow the walk from the top of Pico do Arieiro *(see p353)* along one of the island's most spectacular footpaths. Awe-inspiring mountain scenery and glorious views can be enjoyed all along the 10-km (6-mile) walk. This takes two to three hours and is really only suitable for experienced, well-equipped walkers. Vertigo sufferers should not attempt the path, as it involves negotiating narrow ridges with sheer drops on either side.

Curral das Freiras ⑪

🏘 3,000. 🚌 ℹ *Câmara de Lobos (291 943 470).*

Curral das Freiras means "Nuns' Refuge" and the name refers to the nuns of the Santa Clara convent who fled to this idyllic spot when pirates attacked Funchal in 1566. The nuns have left now, but the village remains. Visitors first glimpse Curral das Freiras from a viewpoint known as the **Eira do Serrado**, perched some 800 m (2,625 ft) above the scattered village.

The valley is surrounded on all sides by jagged mountain peaks. Until 1959 the only access to the village was by a steep zig-zagging path, but road tunnels now make the journey much easier and allow local people to transport their produce to the capital. Television arrived in 1986.

The sweet chestnuts that grow in profusion around the village are turned into sweet chestnut bread, best eaten still warm from the oven, and *licor de castanha*, a chestnut-flavoured liqueur. Both can be sampled in local bars.

Paúl da Serra ⑫

🚌 *to Canhas, then taxi.*

Sheep grazing on the wide plateau of Paúl da Serra, east of Rabaçal

The Paúl da Serra (literally "high moorland") is a large, boggy plateau, 17 km (11 miles) in length and 6 km (4 miles) in width. The plain contrasts dramatically with the jagged mountains that characterize the rest of Madeira.

Electricity for the north of the island is generated here by wind turbines. Only gorse and grass grow on the thin soil, and the sponge-like volcanic substrata act as a natural reservoir for rainfall. Water filters through the rock to emerge as springs which then feed the island's *levada* system.

THE LEVADAS OF MADEIRA

Madeira possesses a unique irrigation system that enables the plentiful rainfall of the north of the island to be distributed to the drier, sunny south. Rainfall is stored in reservoirs and lakes, or channelled from natural springs, and fed into the network of *levadas* that ring the island. These narrow channels carry water long distances to banana groves, vineyards and market gardens. Altogether there are 1,500 km (932 miles) of canals, some dating back to the 1500s. Maintenance paths run alongside the *levadas*, providing a network of footpaths reaching into remote parts of the island inaccessible by road.

Levada do Risco, one of many walking routes across Madeira

◁ Terraced hillsides around the village of Curral das Freiras

Rabaçal Walks ⑬

Reached down a single-track road near the Paúl
da Serra plateau, Rabaçal is the starting point
for two, equally magical, *levada* walks. One is a
simple 30-minute, there-and-back stroll to the Risco
waterfall, while the other is a more demanding
two- to three-hour walk to the
beauty spot known as Vinte
e Cinco Fontes (25 Springs).

TIPS FOR WALKERS

Length: These two walks can
be combined to create a circular
route of 8 km (5 miles), taking
around three and a half hours.
Note: The levadas can be slippery
and sometimes very narrow. In
places the path is only 30 cm (1 ft)
wide, but the channel runs at
waist height and you can hold on.

Levada da Rocha Vermelha ⑥
Wild, mountainous terrain forms
the backdrop to the steep path
down to the lower *levada*.

25 Fontes ⑤
A 30-minute walk brings
you to a mossy, fern-hung
area with a main cascade
and many smaller ones.

Ribeira da Janela ④
Cross the bridge and
then tackle the steep
uphill climb on
the left.

Levada da Rocha Vermelha

Levada Nova do Rabaçal

Levada Nova do Rabaçal

Levada das 25 Fontes

Ribeira da Janela

Levada do Risco

Levada das 25 Fontes

Levada do Risco

PAÚL DA
SERRA

Rabaçal ①
The starting point of the walk
has a car park and government
rest house with picnic tables
and views down the secluded
valley. Follow the signposted
path down to the right to
meet the Levada do Risco.

Risco Waterfall ③
At this magnificent spot,
a torrent of water cascades
from the rocky heights down
into the green depths of the
Risco valley far below.

KEY

- -	Walk route
=	Road
=	River
=	Levada
P	Parking

Levada do Risco ②
The course of the *levada*,
which leads to the waterfall,
is shaded by tree heathers
draped with hair-like lichens.

0 metres   250

0 yards   250

Simple stone font in the attractively tiled baptistry of the Igreja Matriz in São Vicente

São Vicente ⑭

🏠 *8,000.* 🚌 🛈 *Câmara Municipal, Vila de São Vicente (291 840 020).*

The agricultural town of São Vicente has grown prosperous over the years by tempting travellers to break their journeys here as they explore Madeira's northern coast.

To see how the village looked before development began, visit the **Igreja Matriz** (originally built in the 17th century), and look at the painting on the ceiling of St Vincent blessing the town. St Vincent appears again over the elaborately carved and gilded main altar, this time blessing a ship.

Around the church, cobbled traffic-free streets are lined with boutiques, bars and shops selling sweet cakes, including the popular Madeiran speciality *bolo de mel,* the so-called "honey cake" (actually made with molasses and fruit).

São Vicente marks the starting point of the coastal road northwest to Porto Moniz, one of the island's most exhilarating drives. The road, little more than a ledge cut into the sheer cliffs, sometimes passes through tunnels, sometimes through waterfalls. The 19-km (12-mile) road took 16 years to build without the aid of machinery.

The only village along this lonely road is **Seixal.** Despite the Atlantic storms that can batter the island's northern coast, Seixal occupies a remarkably sheltered spot where vineyards cling to the hillside terraces, producing excellent wine.

Porto Moniz ⑮

🏠 *4,000.* 🚌 🛈 *Rua dos Emigrantes, Vila do Porto Moniz (291 852 555).*

Although it is only 75 km (47 miles) from Funchal, visitors arriving in Porto Moniz feel a great sense of achievement after the long journey to this remote coastal village, on the northwest tip of Madeira.

Porto Moniz is surrounded by a patchwork pattern of tiny fields. The fields are protected by fences made from tree heather and dried bracken, a necessary precaution against the heavy, salt-laden air that blows in off the Atlantic.

Apart from its picturesque charm, the main attraction at Porto Moniz is the series of natural rock pools joined by concrete paths on the foreshore, where you can paddle or immerse yourself in sun-warmed water while being showered by spray as waves break against the nearby rocks.

Calheta ⑯

🏠 *3,500.* 🚌 🛈 *Câmara Municipal, Vila da Calheta (291 820 200).*

Bananas, a prolific crop in Calheta

Calheta stands among flourishing vineyards and banana plantations. It is also at the centre of what little sugarcane production survives on Madeira, and the sweet smell of cane syrup being extracted and turned into rum hangs around the village from the **factory** (visitors are welcome; the best time is March to April).

The **Igreja Matriz** looks unpromisingly modern, but it dates from 1430 and contains a large ebony and silver tabernacle donated by Manuel I *(see pp46–7).* There is also a fine wooden ceiling.

🏭 **Factory**
Vila da Calheta. **Tel** *291 822 264.* ⭕ *daily.*

Environs: About 2 km (1 mile) east of Calheta, at **Loreto,** the 15th-century chapel has a Manueline south portal and geometrically patterned ceiling. Outside Estreito da Calheta, 3 km (2 miles) northwest of Calheta, is **Lombo dos Reis.** Here the Capela dos Reis Magos (Chapel of the Three Kings) has a lively 16th-century Flemish altar carving of the *Adoration of the Magi.*

The warm, natural rock pools at Porto Moniz

Part of Porto Santo's splendid sandy beach

Ribeira Brava ⑰

🏃 13,500. 🚌 ℹ️ Forte de São Bento (291 951 675). 🛥️ daily.

Ribeira Brava is a small, attractive resort town, situated on the sunny south coast of Madeira. It has a pebble beach and a fishing harbour, which is reached through a tunnel to the east of the main town.

Overlooking the principal square, **São Bento** remains one of the most unspoiled churches on Madeira. Despite restoration and reconstruction, several of its 16th-century features are still intact. These include a stone-carved font and ornate pulpit decorated with wild beasts such as wolves, the Flemish painting of the *Nativity* in the side chapel, and the wooden statue of the Virgin over the main altar. The church's clock tower has a beautifully tiled roof.

São Bento's clock tower, Ribeira Brava

This is one of Madeira's main centres for catching scabbard fish *(peixe espada)*, which feature on every local menu. Long lines are baited with octopus to catch these fish that dwell at depths of between 800 m (2,600 ft) and 1,600 m (5,250 ft). The fishermen live in dwellings along the harbour front, and their tiny **chapel** dates from the 15th century, but was rebuilt in 1723. The chapel is dedicated to St Nicholas, the patron saint of seafarers, and is decorated with scenes from the saint's life, as well as vivid portrayals of drownings and shipwrecks.

Environs: The second highest sea cliff in Europe is **Cabo Girão**, located 10 km (6 miles) west of Câmara de Lobos. It peaks at a dramatic 580 m (1,900 ft) above sea level.

Câmara de Lobos ⑱

🏃 15,000. 🚌 ℹ️ Rua Padre Eduardo Clemente Nunes Pereira (291 943 470). 🛥️ Mon–Sat.

Visitors to this pretty fishing village are not allowed to forget that it was several times painted by Winston Churchill, who often visited Madeira in the 1950s. Bars and restaurants are named in his honour and a plaque marks the spot on the main road, east of the harbour, where the great statesman set up his easels. The town has not changed greatly since then.

Porto Santo ⑲

🏃 5,000. ✈️ ⛴️ ℹ️ Avenida Dr Manuel Gregório Pestana Júnior (291 985 189).

Porto Santo, the island that lies 37 km (23 miles) northeast of Madeira, is smaller, flatter and drier than its sister island. It also possesses something that Madeira lacks: a 9-km (6-mile) beach of golden sand, running the entire length of the island's south coast. There is a daily ferry service between Funchal and Porto Santo, which takes 2 hours and 30 minutes. There are also daily flights, shortening the trip to 15 minutes.

Porto Santo is a popular holiday destination for Madeirans, mainland Portuguese and growing numbers of foreign tourists. There are five big, but mostly discreet hotels, and several holiday resorts with villas and apartments. Snorkelling is good here and bicycles can be hired.

The one historic site of note on the island is the **Casa de Colombo** (house of Christopher Columbus), located behind Nossa Senhora da Piedade in Vila Baleira. The restored house is built from rough stone, and contains exhibits that tell Columbus's story, including maps, paintings and engravings.

🏛️ **Casa de Colombo**
Travessa da Sacristia 2, Vila Baleira. **Tel** 291 983 405. ☐ Tue–Sat & Sun am.

CHRISTOPHER COLUMBUS ON PORTO SANTO

Historical records vouch for the fact that Christopher Columbus came to Madeira in 1478, probably as an agent for sugar merchants in his native Italian town of Genoa. He went to Porto Santo to meet Bartolomeu Perestrelo, also from Genoa and the island's governor. There he met Filipa Moniz, Perestrelo's daughter. The two were married in 1479, but Filipa died soon after while giving birth to their son. Nothing else is known about Columbus's visit to the island, though this has not prevented local people from identifying his house.

Christopher
Ridolfo Ghirlan

THE AZORES

*F*ar out in the Atlantic, 1,300 km (800 miles) west of Portugal's mainland, the nine islands of the Azores are known for their spectacular volcanic scenery, abundant flora and peaceful way of life. Once wild and remote, they are now a popular destination for travellers who enjoy walking, sailing and getting away from it all.

Santa Maria was the first island discovered by the Portuguese in 1427. The archipelago was named after the buzzards the early explorers saw flying overhead and mistook for goshawks (*açores*). The islands were settled during the 15th and 16th centuries by colonists from Portugal and Flanders who introduced cattle, maize and vines.

Império chapel on Pico

The Azores have profited from their far-flung position in the Atlantic. Between 1580 and 1640, when Portugal came under Spanish rule (*see pp50–51*), the ports of Angra do Heroísmo on Terceira and Ponta Delgada on São Miguel prospered from the trade with the New World. In the 19th century the islands were a regular port of call for American whaling ships. During the 20th century they have benefited from their use as stations for transatlantic cable companies, meteorological observatories and military air bases.

Today the majority of islanders are involved in either dairy farming or fishing, and close links are maintained with both mainland Portugal and the sizeable communities of emigrant Azoreans in the United States and Canada. Many emigrants return to their native island for the traditional annual festivals, such as the *festas* of the Holy Spirit, celebrated in the colourful *impérios*. With few beaches, a capricious, often wet climate and no large-scale resorts, the Azores have escaped mass tourism. Most travellers come here to explore the green mountains embroidered with blue hydrangeas and relax in quiet ports adorned with cobbled streets and elegant Baroque churches. Once a brave new world of pioneer communities, the Azores are now an autonomous region of Portugal and an exotic corner of the European Union, where life remains refreshingly civil and unhurried.

Small fishing boats on the quayside at Lajes on the southern coast of Pico

◁ Terceira's walled pastures sloping down to the sea with the two small Ilhéus das Cabras in the distance

Exploring the Azores

The islands of the Azores are spread 650 km (400 miles) apart and fall into three distinct groups. In the east lie Santa Maria and São Miguel, the largest island and home to the regional capital, Ponta Delgada. The main towns in the central group of five islands are Horta on Faial, a popular stopover port for boats crossing the Atlantic, and Angra do Heroísmo on Terceira, a charming, historic town. From here visitors can travel to the other islands of São Jorge, Graciosa and Pico, the last dominated by a towering volcanic peak 2,351 m (7,700 ft) high. Further west lie the remote, weather-beaten islands of Flores and Corvo.

Transatlantic sailing boat moored in Faial's fine marina at Horta

9 CORVO
Vila do Corvo

Ponta Delgada
Fajã Grande
Santa Cruz das Flores
Fajãzinha
8 FLORES
Lajes

Santa Cruz da Graciosa
Praia
GRACIOSA 4
Luz

SIGHTS AT A GLANCE

FAIAL 7 Cedros
Capelo
Cabeço Gordo 1045m
Horta

Pico da Velha 495m
Velas R1-2
Manadas
Calheta
5 SÃO JORGE
R2-2
Santo Antão

Madalena
São Roque do Pico
Candelaria
Pico Alto 2350m
São Mateus R1-2 R2-2
Piedade
PICO 6 Lajes do Pico

0 kilometres 25
0 miles 10

Distances between islands are not shown to scale

Walking among Pico's black volcanic lava rock

KEY

— Major road
⋯ Minor road
— Scenic route
△ Summit

SEE ALSO

• *Where to Stay* pp404–5
• *Where to Eat* pp430–31

GETTING AROUND

São Miguel, Faial and Terceira have international airports and the local airline, SATA, flies between all the islands. A year-round ferry service runs between Faial, Pico and São Jorge; in the summer, it also connects with Terceira (www.transmacor. pt). Atlanticoline connects all the islands, including a special service between Corvo and Flores. All ferry services are subject to the weather. Bus services on the islands are designed for the locals and therefore not always practical for tourists. Car hire is more convenient and available on all islands except Corvo. *(See also p463.)*

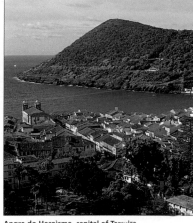

Angra do Heroísmo, capital of Terceira

Biscoitos

de Santa Bárbara
1022m

Santa Bárbara

R3-1   R1-1   Praia da Vitória

São Mateus   Angra do Heroísmo

3

TERCEIRA

Sete Cidades   R1-1   Ribeira Grande   Porto Formoso   R1-1   Nordeste

Capelas

Candelaria   Furnas

Ponta Delgada   Lagoa   R1-1   Vila Franca do Campo   Povoação

1

SÃO MIGUEL

Ponta Delgada's elegant waterfront, São Miguel

SANTA MARIA **2**

Anjos   Santa Bárbara

Vila do Porto

São Miguel ●

With its historic maritime capital, rich green fields
and dramatic volcanic scenery, this *ilha verde* (green
island) provides a rewarding introduction to the Azores.
The largest and most populated of the archipelago's nine
islands, São Miguel is 65 km (40 miles) long and was
originally two separate islands. The capital, Ponta
Delgada, is a good base from which to make day tours
of the rugged coast or visit the volcanic crater lakes and
steaming thermal springs in the interior of the island.

The 18th-century city gates leading onto Ponta Delgada's central square

Ponta Delgada

Lined with many impressive
churches, convents and trim
white houses, the cobbled
streets of the Azorean capital
recall the wealthy days when
the port was a crucial staging
post between Europe and the
New World *(see pp48–9)*. Its
hub is the arcaded Praça de
Gonçalo Velho Cabral, named
after the first governor of the
island in 1444, which looks
out onto the seafront. It is
dominated by three imposing
arches, dating from 1783, that
once marked the entrance to
the city. To the north, in Largo
da Matriz, stands the parish
church of **São Sebastião**.
Founded in 1533 it has a graceful Manueline portal intricately
carved in limestone. The sacristy is decorated with *azulejo*
panels and beautiful 17th-
century furniture made of
jacaranda wood from Brazil.

A short walk west lies the
Praça 5 de Outubro, a shaded,
tree-lined square overlooked
by the **Forte de São Brás**.
This Renaissance fortress, built
on a spur overlooking the sea,
was greatly restored in the 19th
century. Also on the square,
the immense **Convento da
Esperança** becomes the focus

of intense festivities when the
city celebrates the festival of
Santo Cristo dos Milagres on
the fifth Sunday after Easter. A
statue of Christ, wearing a red
robe decorated with sumptuous
diamond and gold ornaments,
leads the procession through
the streets. The statue can be
seen in the lower church along
with other religious treasures,
including reliquaries and
jewels. Colourful tiles, dating
from the 18th century, by
António de Oliveira Bernardes
(see p26) decorate the choir.

The **Museu Carlos Machado**,
in the former monastery of
Santo André, spotlights the
local fishing and farming
industries. Of particular
interest are the paintings by
Domingos Rebelo (1891–1975)
showing scenes of Azorean
life. The natural history wing
is packed with an encyclo-
pedic array of stuffed animals,
varnished fish, skeletons and
a large relief model of the
island. The museum's Núcleo
de Arte Sacra houses sacred
art treasures.

🏛 **Museu Carlos Machado**
Rua João Moreira. *Tel 296 28 38 14.*
⬤ *for refurbishment.* **Núcleo de
Arte Sacra** ◯ *Tue–Sun.* 📷

West of the Island

The northwest of São Miguel
is punctured by a giant volcanic crater, **Caldeira das Sete
Cidades**, with a 12-km (7-mile)
circumference. In places its
sheer walls drop like green
curtains for 300 m (1,000 ft).
When not obscured by cloud,
the crater is best seen from the
viewpoint of **Vista do Rei**
from where a walk leads west
around its rim. The crater floor
contains the small village of
Sete Cidades and six dark
green lakes. The crater is
believed to have been formed
in the 1440s when an eruption
destroyed the volcanic peak
that had formed the western
part of the island. In contrast
to the lush vegetation that
covers the crater now, the first
settlers described the area as
a burnt-out shell.

The main town on the north
coast, **Ribeira Grande** has a
small **Casa da Cultura** (cultural centre) housed in the
restored 17th-century Solar de
São Vicente. *Azulejos* from the
16th to 20th century are on display and in other rooms the
crafts and rural lifestyle of the
islanders are recorded, including a period barber's shop
rescued from Ponta Delgada.

🏛 **Casa da Cultura**
Rua São Vicente Ferreira 10, Ribeira
Grande. *Tel 296 470 768.* ◯ *8:30am–
5:30pm Mon–Fri.* ⬤ *public hols.*

KEY

═══ Main road

══ Other road

Turquoise waters of the crater lake, Lagoa do Fogo

East of the Island

The **Lagoa do Fogo**, "Lake of Fire", was formed in the island's central mountains by a volcanic eruption in 1563. On sunny days its remote sandy beach is a tranquil picnic spot.

Further east, the spa resort of **Furnas** is the perfect place to admire the geothermal activity taking place beneath the surface of the Azores *(see pp340–41)*. Scattered around the town are the **Caldeiras das Furnas** where visitors will see the hot bubbling springs that provide the therapeutic mud and mineral water used for the spa's treatments. In the 18th century, Thomas Hickling, a prosperous merchant from Boston, laid out gardens in Furnas which have now grown into the glorious **Parque Terra Nostra**. Covering 12 ha (30 acres), the gardens have a rich collection of mature trees and plants, including hibiscus and hydrangeas, as well as a bizarre swimming pool with warm, mustard-coloured water.

The volcanic ground on the northern shores of the **Lagoa das Furnas**, 4 km (2 miles) south, is so hot the islanders come here to cook *cozido*.

The rich meat and vegetable stew is cooked underground for up to six hours.

The far east of São Miguel is a beautiful area of deep valleys. Two immaculately kept viewpoints, **Miradouro do Sossego** and **Miradouro da Madrugada**, have fine gardens – the latter is a popular spot for watching the sunrise.

🏛 **Caldeiras das Furnas**
Off R1-1. 🛈 Rua Dr Frederico Moniz Pereira 15. **Tel** 296 58 45 25.

Pristine gardens and picnic area of the Miradouro da Madrugada

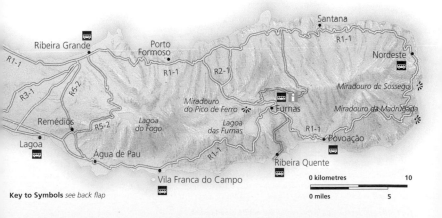

Ribeira Grande
Porto Formoso
Santana
R1-1
Nordeste
R1-1
R1-1   R2-1
Miradouro do Sossego
R3-1
R5-2
Miradouro do Pico de Ferro
Furnas
Miradouro da Madrugada
Remédios   R5-2   Lagoa do Fogo   Lagoa das Furnas
R1-1
Lagoa
Povoação
Água de Pau   R1-1
Ribeira Quente
Vila Franca do Campo

| 0 kilometres | | 10 |
| 0 miles | | 5 |

Key to Symbols *see back flap*

The wide bay of São Lourenço on Santa Maria

Santa Maria ❷

🏛 6,000. ✈ 3 km (2 miles) NW of Vila do Porto. 🚢 Vila do Porto. 🚌 Rua Dr Luís Bettencourt, Vila do Porto. 🚹 Aeroporto de Santa Maria, Vila do Porto (296 886 355). 📅 Festas do Espírito Santo (see p368); 15 Aug: Nossa Senhora da Assunção (Vila do Porto). **www**.visitazores.org

Lying 55 km (34 miles) south of São Miguel, Santa Maria was the first island in the archipelago to be discovered by the Portuguese around 1427. Though only 18 km (11 miles) long, it has great scenic variety and boasts sandy beaches, tranquil countryside and the warmest climate in the Azores.

Nossa Senhora da Purificação studded with black basalt in Santo Espírito, Santa Maria

The island's capital, **Vila do Porto**, is on the south coast and consists of a long main street that runs down to a small harbour. The west of the island is a dry, flat plateau with a vast airstrip built in World War II. To the north lies the fishing town of **Anjos**, where a statue commemorates a visit made by Christopher Columbus in 1493 on his return from discovering the New World. Next to it, the small,whitewashed chapel of **Mãe de Deus** is the oldest in the Azores.

The highest point of Santa Maria is the central **Pico Alto**, 590 m (1,935 ft) above sea level, which on a clear day offers fine views over the green and hilly east side of the island. Towards the east coast, the village of **Santo Espírito** is worth visiting for the white Baroque façade of its church of Nossa Senhora da Purificação adorned with black lava decoration, while the vine-covered half-crater of **Baía de São Lourenço**, north of here, is a delightful summer beach resort.

Terceira ❸

🏛 60,000. ✈ 3 km (2 miles) NW of Praia da Vitória. 🚢 Angra Alvaro Martins Homem. 🚌 Avenida 1° de Maio, Angra do Heroísmo. 🚹 Rua Direita 70–74, Angra do Heroísmo (295 213 393, 295 216 109) Praia da Vitoria Aerogare Civil das Lajes (295 513 140). 📅 Festas do Espírito Santo (see p368); late Jun: Festas de São João. **www**.visitazores.org

Terceira, meaning "third" in Portuguese, is so named because it was the third island to be discovered, in 1427. It is the most developed of the five central islands – a result in part of the large American-run airbase that has been operating at Lajes since World War II. Terceira is famous for its unusual form of bull-running, the *tourada à corda* (bullfight with a rope), in which a bull is taunted while tied to a rope held tight by teams of men. It is also renowned for the brightly painted chapels devoted to the cult of the Holy Spirit *(see p368)*. Terceira's interior is mainly green pastureland, while the coast has barren areas of black lava.

Taunting a bull with umbrellas during a *tourada à corda*, Terceira

Angra do Heroísmo
This attractive and historic town was declared a UNESCO World Heritage site in 1983, in recognition of the strategic role the port has played in the Atlantic. For over three centuries the town was a stopover point on the routes between Europe, America and Africa. It was here in 1499 that Vasco da Gama *(see p106)* buried his brother Paulo after their pioneering journey to India, and in the early 17th century its harbour glittered with Spanish fleets returning laden with treasure

The 16th-century Sé (cathedral) at the centre of Terceira's capital, Angra do Heroísmo

from the Americas. Maria II gave the town its name for the bravery *(heroísmo)* it demonstrated during the struggles for Liberalism in the early 19th century *(see pp54–5)*. Despite the severe damage caused by an earthquake in 1980, the city's wealthy past is reflected in the pretty streets lined with monumental churches and balconied houses.

The most spectacular view of the harbour is from **Monte Brasil**, a volcanic crater on the western side of the bay. Beside this popular picnic spot stands the fort, **Castelo de São João Baptista**, built during Spain's annexation of Portugal *(see pp50–51)* as a treasure store, and still in military use. A second rewarding viewpoint is from the **Alto da Memória** at the south end of Rua São João de Deus, from where the twin towers of the 16th-century **Sé** (restored after a fire in 1983) are easily seen. A path leads down into the **Jardim Municipal**, the city's restful public gardens. These once formed part of the 15th-century Convento de São Francisco which now houses the **Museu de Angra do Heroísmo**. The museum's exhibits reflect the history of the Azores and the city and include armour, maps, paintings and sculptures.

Wooden John the Baptist, Museu de Angra

🏛 Museu de Angra do Heroísmo
Ladeira de São Francisco. *Tel 295 213 147.* 9:30am–5pm Tue–Fri, 2–5pm Sat & Sun. pub hols.

Around the Island
Terceira is a large, oval-shaped island with a gentle green interior of forested hills and farmland. Its centre bears witness to its volcanic origins: the **Caldeira de Guilherme Moniz** is an eroded crater 3 km (2 miles) wide, the largest in the Azores. Nearby, the **Algar do Carvão** is a dramatic volcanic blast-hole, thick with dripping moss where visitors can tour an enormous subterranean cave. West of here, the **Furnas do Enxofre** are hot steaming geysers where the heavy sulphur vapours crystallize into brightly coloured formations.

Two viewpoints overlooking the island can be reached by car: in the west, a road bordered with blue hydrangeas winds up through the **Serra de Santa Bárbara** to a vast lonely crater at 1,022 m (3,353 ft), while the eastern **Serra do Cume**, at 545 m (1,788 ft), overlooks the airport and **Praia da Vitória**. This port has a large bay with a sandy beach. Its name pays tribute to a famous victory in 1581 when the Spanish attempted to seize the island at Baía da Salga, 10 km (6 miles) south, and were thwarted by the release of a herd of cattle onto the shore.

On the north coast, **Biscoitos** (which means biscuits) takes its name from the rubble of biscuit-like lava spread along the shore. Exhilarating swimming pools, popular in the summer, have been created amongst the rocks. The area is also known for its wine, and the land is covered in a chessboard of stone-walled pens *(curraletas)* built to shelter vines. The friendly **Museu do Vinho** explains the simple production methods used to produce the rich *verdelho* wine that was once exported to the Russian court, and provides an opportunity to taste and purchase today's vintages.

Algar do Carvão
Off R5-2. *Tel 295 212 992.* 21 Mar–1 Nov: daily; hours vary.

🏛 Museu do Vinho
Canada do Caldeiro, Biscoitos. *Tel 295 908 404.* Mon–Sat.

Patchwork of stone-walled fields in the northeast of Terceira, near Praia da Vitória

The Holy Spirit Festivals

Festivals are a vibrant feature of life in the Azores and have helped foster the deep sense of community that is a hallmark of the islands' culture. Emigrants and relatives from North America and mainland Portugal often return to their native island to celebrate the most popular *festas*.

The islands' most traditional festivals are associated with the Holy Spirit *(Festas do Espírito Santo)*. Brought to the Azores by the first Portuguese settlers, who called upon the Holy Spirit to

A girl wearing the emperor's crown

protect them against natural disasters, the rituals have remained almost unchanged. An "emperor", usually a child, is crowned in the parish church. With a sceptre and silver plate as insignia of the Holy Spirit, the "emperor" presides over the festivities that take place each Sunday for seven weeks after Easter. The seventh Sunday, Whit Sunday, the day of Pentecost when Christ's disciples were filled with the Holy Spirit, is the occasion of a great feast in the village.

The distribution of bread *for the Festival of the Holy Spirit originates in the donation of food to the poor introduced by saintly Queen Isabel (see p45). On the last day of celebrations, the seventh Sunday after Easter, a Holy Spirit soup is made from beef and vegetables and is handed out along with bread to everyone outside the local* império.

THE IMPÉRIOS OF THE HOLY SPIRIT

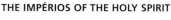

Império with Gothic windows in Praia da Vitória, Terceira (1861)

Flamboyantly decorated *império* in São Sebastião, Terceira (1918)

Simple *império* in Terra Chã, Terceira (1954)

The focus of the ceremonies is a small chapel or *império* (empire) which is used for the distribution of the Holy Spirit soup on the seventh Sunday. Here, the emperor's crown, sceptre and plate are displayed on the altar on the last day of the festivities. On Terceira, where the cult of the Holy Spirit is particularly strong, many of the 68 *impérios* are painted in bright colours every spring. Up to 500 islanders gather for a village feast accompanied by dancing, brass bands and lavish floral displays. In many places a *tourada à corda* will be held, where a bull, tied to the end of a long rope, is let loose in the street.

An emperor's crown on ceremonial display in an *império* on São Miguel

For hotels and restaurants in this region see pp404–5 and pp430–31

Traditional ox-drawn cart on the island of Graciosa

Graciosa ❹

🏠 *4,500.* ✈ *2 km (1 mile) W of Santa Cruz da Graciosa.* ⛴ *Praia de São Mateus.* 🛈 *Rua Castilho 7, Santa Cruz (295 712 509).* 🎭 *Festas do Espírito Santo; Aug: Santo Cristo.* **www**.visitazores.org

The "gracious" island is one of the most peaceful in the Azores. Only 12 km (7 miles) long, most of its low-lying land is given over to farms and vineyards where ox-drawn carts and ploughs are still in use. The capital, **Santa Cruz da Graciosa**, on the northern coast, has a simple quayside backed by rows of stark, two-storey, whitewashed houses with wrought-iron balconies and oval windows. A small **Museu da Graciosa** recalls life on this sleepy island with a homely miscellany of toys, sea chests, kitchenware, wine presses, furniture and mementoes sent back by emigrants to North America. A building next door houses a whaling boat *(see pp370–71)*.

The picturesque Monte da Ajuda that rises behind the town is capped by a 16th-century fortified chapel, **Nossa Senhora da Ajuda**, decorated with 18th-century tiles. Nearby, a small *vigia* (whalers' lookout) faces the sea.

In the southeast lies the island's principal sight, **Furna do Enxofre**, where visitors can descend flights of steps into the bowels of a volcanic crater. At the bottom is a huge cave with a deep, sulphurous lake and peep-holes where bubbling brews of evil grey liquid can be spied beneath the rocks. The best time to visit is late morning when the sun shines through the small cave mouth and lights the interior.

Above the cave, at **Furna Maria Encantada**, a natural tunnel through the rock leads to the edge of the crater. From here there are stunning views over the island. Treatments using the island's geothermal waters are available at the coastal resort of **Carapacho**, at the foot of the volcano.

🏛 **Museu da Graciosa**
Rua das Flores 2, Santa Cruz. *Tel 295 712 429.* ⏱ *9:30am–12:30pm, 2–5:30pm Tue–Fri.* ⬛ *pub hols.* 🎫

🌋 **Furna do Enxofre**
2 km (1 mile) E of Luz, follow signs to Caldeira. ⏱ *Mon–Sat.* 🎫

The rich Baroque interior of Santa Bárbara in Manadas, São Jorge

São Jorge ❺

🏠 *11,000.* ✈ *7 km (4 miles) E of Velas.* ⛴ *Velas & Calheta.* 🛈 *Rua Conselheiro Dr José Pereira 1, Velas (295 412 440).* 🎭 *23 Apr: Festa de São Jorge; Festas do Espírito Santo; Jul: Semana Cultural de Velas (Velas).* **www**.visitazores.org

São Jorge is a mountainous island that stretches for 56 km (35 miles) but is only 8 km (5 miles) wide. On its north coast, sheer cliffs drop 480 m (1,575 ft) to the sea. Over the centuries these cliffs have collapsed in places, creating tongues of land known as *fajãs*. It was on these coastal promontories that the island's Flemish colonists first settled in the mid-15th century.

Today many islanders on São Jorge are engaged in the production of a cured cheese, *Queijo de São Jorge*. The pace of life is leisurely, and most visitors come to enjoy the walking along the paths that climb between the *fajãs*. The most popular route is in the northeast of the island from Serra do Topo 10 km (6 miles) down to Fajã dos Cubres.

Most of the settlements lie along the gentler south coast, including the capital, **Velas**, and **Calheta**, where the **Museu Francisco de Lacerda** displays objects of local history such as the ornate breads baked for the Holy Spirit festival, a honey press, agricultural utensils and religious sculptures. West of Calheta, in the pretty village of **Manadas**, the 18th-century church of **Santa Bárbara** has an atmospheric carved and painted interior. In **Urzelina**, 2 km (1 mile) further west, the tower of a church buried by lava in 1808 protrudes defiantly from the ground. In the west of the island there is a pleasant forested picnic area at **Sete Fontes**, and on a clear day the nearby summit of **Pico da Velha** offers superb views of the central Azorean islands.

🏛 **Museu Francisco de Lacerda**
Rua José Azevedo da Cunha, Calheta. *Tel 295 416 323.* ⏱ *Mon–Fri.* ⬛ *public hols.*

Dramatic cliffs along the north coast of São Jorge

Pico ❻

🏘 15,500. ✈ 8 km (5 miles) E of Madalena. ⛴ Madalena. 🚌 Avenida Machado Serpa, Madalena. ℹ Gare Maritima, Madalena (292 623 524). 🎎 Festas do Espírito Santo (see p368); 22 Jul: Santa Maria Madalena. www.visitazores.org

The full majesty of Pico, the highest mountain in Portugal, becomes apparent when it is seen from the neighbouring central islands. Only then

Rustic house and well on Pico made from black lava rocks

does one realize how gracefully this volcanic peak soars out of the Atlantic, shooting up 2,350 m (7,700 ft) to form the summit of the greatest mountain range in the world, the Mid-Atlantic Ridge (see pp340–41).

The island's capital, **Madalena**, is a relaxed port that lies opposite Faial's capital, Horta. A regular ferry service crosses the 8 km (5 miles) between the two islands, making a day trip feasible. The entrance to the harbour is guarded by two rocks, Em Pé (standing) and Deitado (lying down) where colonies of birds have made their home.

Many people come to Pico to climb its eponymous peak. It is a strenuous climb, best done alongside a guide, and advance permission is needed. At 1,200 m (3,950 ft), the Casa

The summit of Pico's volcano

da Montanha offers refuge and support to hikers and climbers. For further details, contact the tourist office.

The other main draw to Pico in summer is whale watching. From **Lajes do Pico** groups are taken out in small boats for three-hour trips organized by the **Espaço Talassa**. They are guided by radio messages

In Pursuit of the Whale

Every summer the waters around the Azores are visited by a great variety of whales and dolphins. Until 1984 whaling was a traditional part of Azorean life – in the 18th century American whaling vessels frequently called here to pick up crew for their expeditions, and from the 1870s the Azoreans took up large-scale hunting in their own waters. Flags were waved from clifftop *vigias* (lookouts) giving coded directions so that other villagers would not get to the prize first.

Since whaling was banned in the 1980s, the Azoreans have applied their knowledge gained from hunting to whale watching and conservation.

Scrimshaws *are carvings made on the teeth and bones of whales and often depict whaling scenes. This fine example from the Museu do Scrimshau on Faial (see p372) shows the long, narrow boats called canoas that could hold up to 7 men.*

Whale watching *today takes place in small boats that allow fast and safe access to the whales. As well as trips out to sea, the whales can be observed from the vigias. These land-based towers afford spectacular views of the whales in their natural habitat. Expeditions run from Pico and Faial (see p372).*

from men who scan the sea for a fluke (tail) from the former *vigias* (lookouts). The history of Azorean whaling is recalled at the **Museu dos Baleeiros**, also in Lajes, where boats, tackle and whalebone artifacts are displayed. The whales were processed at a vast factory (closed down in 1984) on the north side of the island, at São Roque do Pico. The factory has been preserved as a piece of industrial heritage and now houses the **Museu da Indústria Baleeira**.

A coastal road encircles Pico, offering a slow drive that reveals the charm of this island. Minor eruptions have covered parts of its landscape with black mole-hills of lava that the islanders christened *mistérios* (mysteries). The black lava has been used to build houses and grids of stone walls that enclose fields or shelter vines. In some places, notably around **Cachorro** on the north coast,

the eroded lava has formed curious arches in the sea.

The island vineyards are a UNESCO World Heritage site. Pico's famous *Verdelho* wine is similar to the one made in Madeira *(see p351)* and was once exported to mainland Europe. There has been a revival of viticulture on the island, and the production of new reds and whites – such as the much acclaimed *Terras da Lava* – allows visitors a refined alternative to the

ubiquitous *vinho de cheiro* (wine of smell) traditionally drunk by the Azoreans.

Espaço Talassa
Rua do Saco, Lajes. *Tel* 292 672 010.
Boat trips: Apr–Oct.

Museu dos Baleeiros
Rua dos Baleeiros, Lajes. *Tel* 292 679 340. 9am–12:30pm & 2–5:30pm Tue–Sun (pm only Sat & Sun).

Museu da Indústria Baleeira
São Roque do Pico. *Tel* 292 642 096. daily (am only Sat, Sun & hols).

West coast of Pico with Faial in the distance

MARINE LIFE IN THE AZORES

Some 20 species of cetaceans can be found in the waters of the Azores. These warm-blooded animals follow the warm currents of the Gulf Stream to feed in the region's abundant, unpolluted waters. Schools of playful and gregarious dolphins are often seen scything through the waves at incredible speeds, but the most impressive sights are sperm whales. These large, sociable animals dive to great depths for giant squid and live in family groups called pods. Like all whales and dolphins they must come to the surface to breathe and this is when whale-watching expeditions make their sightings.

Atlantic spotted dolphins, fast and graceful swimmers

Sperm whales *are huge, tear-shaped creatures, the largest of the toothed whales. They can be seen breaching (diving out of the water), spy hopping (raising their head to have a look around) and socializing by rubbing bodies.*

Pilot whales *belong to the dolphin family and are recognizable from their strong blow of up to 1 m (3 ft).*

Risso's dolphins *have a squat head and light grey colouring. Older ones are often crisscrossed with white scars.*

Bottlenose dolphins *are the best known. These playful animals love to ride the waves at the bow of a moving vessel.*

Loggerhead *turtles, born on Florida's beaches, are frequent visitors to the warm Azorean waters.*

Transatlantic yachts moored in the marina at Horta, Faial, with the pointed summit of Pico in the distance

Faial ❼

🏚 15,000. ✈ 10 km (6 miles) SW of Horta. 🚢 Horta. 🚌 Rua Vasco da Gama, Horta. 🛈 Rua Vasco da Gama, Horta (292 292 237). 🎎 Festas do Espírito Santo (see p368); 1st–2nd Sun in Aug: Semana do Mar (Horta). www.visitazores.org

Faial was settled by Flemish farmers in the 15th century and prospered with the development of Horta harbour as a stopover for ships and – more recently – flying boats crossing the Atlantic. Today it is a fertile island with an international atmosphere and a mild climate, famous as a yachting destination and for the endless rows of colourful hydrangeas that bloom in June and July.

Horta

Stretching around a wide bay, Faial's capital has been a convenient anchorage for caravels, clippers and sea planes over the centuries. Captain Cook commented on Horta's fine houses and gardens when he called here in 1775. Today, visiting crews crossing between the Caribbean and Mediterranean paint a calling card on the quayside and celebrate their safe passage in **Peter's Café Sport**, which also organizes whale- and dolphin-watching excursions (see pp370–71) in the waters around the island.

In the upstairs rooms of the café, an engrossing **Museu do Scrimshaw** exhibits engraved whales' bones and teeth dating back to 1884 (see p370). In the **Museu da Horta** displays of antique furniture, portraits, nautical memorabilia and nostalgic photographs of the island's port are upstaged by miniature sculptures of liners and scenes of daily life, painstakingly carved

Ship's calling card on the quayside in Horta, Faial

from the white pith of fig trees. These virtuoso examples of a traditional island craft are by the Faial-born Euclides Silveira da Rosa (1910–79).

➤ **Peter's Café Sport**
Rua T Valadim 9.
www.whalewatchingazores.com

🏛 **Museu do Scrimshaw**
Peter's Café Sport, Rua T Valadim 9.
Tel 292 292 327. ◯ Mon–Sat. 📷

🏛 **Museu da Horta**
Largo Duque D'Ávila e Bolama.
Tel 292 392 784. ◯ Tue–Fri, Sat & Sun pm. ● public hols. 📷

Barren ash-covered volcanic landscape at Capelinhos, the westernmost point of Faial

Around the Island
Two viewpoints overlook Horta – to its south rises the volcanic peak of **Monte da Guia**, while the northern **Mira-douro da Espalamaca** is guarded by a huge statue of Nossa Senhora da Conceição. If the cloud cover permits, it is well worth driving 15 km (9 miles) to see Faial's central **Caldeira do Cabeço Gordo** – a vast green crater 2 km (1 mile) wide and 400 m (1,300 ft) deep. The path winding around its rim takes about two hours to walk and has magnificent views.

Faial's other spectacular natural sight is the **Vulcão dos Capelinhos** in the far west of the island. A volcano erupted here in 1957–8, smothering a lighthouse which can now be seen buried in ash. Around it lies a scorched and barren landscape that has, not surprisingly, been used as the location for a German post-nuclear holocaust film. The story of the eruption is told in the nearby **Centro de Interpretação do Vulcão dos Capelinhos**, where photographs and maps trace the area's geological activity. Also shown are the lava formations created in the eruption.

🏛 **Centro de Interpretação do Vulcão dos Capelinhos**
Farol dos Capelinhos. **Tel** 292 200 470. ◯ 10am–7pm Tue–Fri, 11am–6pm Sat, Sun & hols. 📷

Flores 8

4,000. *1km (Half a mile) N of Santa Cruz* *Lajes.* *Centro de Saúde, Santa Cruz.* *Rua Dr Armas da Silveira 1, Santa Cruz (292 592 369).* *Festas do Espírito Santo (see p368); 24–26 Jun: Festas de São João. (hols: am).* **www**.visitazores.org

Often cut off by stormy weather, the island of "Flowers" is a romantic outpost that was not permanently settled until the 16th century. A notorious hideout for pirates waiting to raid the treasure-laden Spanish galleons on their return to Europe, Flores was the scene of an epic battle in 1591 between the ship of the English commander Sir Richard Grenville and a fleet of Spanish ships. The battle was immortalized in a poem by Alfred Tennyson, *The Revenge* (the name of Grenville's ship).

This westernmost island of the Azores is 17 km (10 miles) long and extremely mountainous. Its name derives from the abundance of flowers growing in its ravines, and the prospect of wilderness draws adventurous walkers here during the summer. The capital, **Santa Cruz**, is enlivened by the enthusiastically run **Museu das Flores**, housed in the former Franciscan convent. Its displays include shipwreck finds, Azorean pottery, furniture and agricultural tools, as well as fishing rods and a guitar made from whalebone. The convent church of **São Boaventura**, erected in 1641, has a beautiful carved cedarwood chancel.

Hydrangeas growing in the mountains of Flores

The southern half of the island is the most scenic. The deep, verdant valleys are punctuated with dramatic peaks and volcanic crater lakes and caves. Yams and sweet potatoes grow in the fertile soil. The tranquil **Lagoa Funda** (Deep Lake), 25 km (15 miles) southwest of Santa Cruz, is a large crater lake at the base of a mountain. Visible from the main road just west of the lake, are the strange vertical rock formations of the **Rocha dos Bordões** formed by solidified basalt.

The winding road continues northwards over the mountains and, as the road descends towards the west coast, there are stunning views of the green valley and village of **Fajãzinha**. The resort of **Fajã Grande**, ringed by cliffs, is a popular base for walkers and impressive waterfalls plunge into the sea from the high cliffs. A short walk north from the town is the **Cascata da Ribeira Grande**, a towering jet of water that divides into smaller waterfalls before collecting in a still pool.

Museu das Flores
Largo da Misericórdia, Santa Cruz. **Tel** 292 592 159. 9am–noon & 2–5pm Mon–Fri. public hols.

Corvo 9

450. *Vila do Corvo.* *Rua da Matriz, Vila do Corvo.* *Câmara Municipal, Rua J da Bola, Vila do Corvo (292 590 200).* *Festas do Espírito Santo (see p368).* **www**.visitazores.org

Corvo lies 24 km (15 miles) northeast of Flores. The smallest island in the Azores, it has just one settlement, **Vila do Corvo**, and is blissfully undeveloped, with only one hotel and two restaurants. The entire island is the blown top of a marine volcano. A green crater, the **Lagoa do Caldeirão**, squats at its northern end. Its rim can be reached by road, after which there is a steep descent down to the crater floor 300 m (984 ft) below. In its centre, the crater is dotted with serene lakes and islands; a patchwork of stone-walled fields covers part of the slopes.

The island of Corvo seen from the rocky shore of Flores

TRAVELLERS' NEEDS

WHERE TO STAY

Portugal offers a wide range of accommodation, from luxury hotels and restored palaces to family-run hostels and self-catering apartments. The majority of the country's hotels are in Lisbon, Oporto and on the Algarve and Estoril coasts. Elsewhere, outside of the main towns, hotels are relatively scarce. This shortage is made up for by a number of schemes offering accommodation in traditional or historic buildings often set in lovely countryside. These all require advance booking, as rooms are in short supply.

Porter at Lisbon's Olissippo Lapa Palace *(see p384)*

Self-catering options include purpose-built apartments in cities and resorts, and converted country villas and farmhouses, all offering flexibility and good value. It is worth remembering that all rooms are cheaper outside high season. Accommodation in Lisbon divides between top-flight hotels and basic lodging with little choice in between. The hotels listed on pages 382–405 have been selected from every price category and represent the best value in each area.

TYPES OF HOTEL

Lodgings in Portugal come at all levels of comfort and cost. There are two main types, as classified by the Portuguese tourist authority: hotels and *pensões*. Hotels are distinguished mainly by the fact that they take up an entire building and are often purpose-built. *Pensões* are always housed in shared premises, typically occupying several floors of a residential building. *Apart-hotels* are essentially hotels with self-catering apartments, offering most or all of the services that normal hotels do.

All hotels and *pensões* are meant to provide meals. If they only offer breakfast their name must have *residencial* added to it. It is always best to check, however, as the official regime is often merely

official. There are also plenty of lodgings that operate without classification. *Estalagens (estalagem* in the singular), are usually located outside of city centres and must have a garden. *Albergarias* are the top category of *pensão,* which means that their facilities are on the same level as 4- or 5-star hotels (see page 377 for information on gradings).

Bedroom at the York House Hotel in Lisbon, a converted 16th-century convent *(see p384)*

POUSADAS

Pousadas are a special type of lodgings. They come in four categories: historic, historic design, charm and nature. Historic *pousadas* are housed in converted castles, convents or palaces and offer excellent

service and luxury accommodation, as well as memorable historical and architectural surroundings. The other types of *pousada* are country inns offering a high level of comfort, often located in scenic, sometimes remote, areas. With the exception of two mountain inns on Madeira that use *"pousada"* in their names, all *pousadas* are state-owned, and are run as a chain by the **Pestana** company.

HOTEL CHAINS

International luxury groups such as Le Meridien and Orient-Express are represented in the Algarve and Madeira, as well as in Oporto and the Lisbon area. Smaller luxury groups include **Tivoli Hotels** – with three hotels in Lisbon, two in Sintra, five in the Algarve and one each in Madeira and Coimbra – and the **Pestana Group**, with ten hotels in Madeira, nine in the Algarve,

Hotel Tivoli Carvoeiro in the resort of Carvoeiro, the Algarve *(see p401)*

◁ **Breakfasting beneath the wisteria at the Pousada de Palmela** *(see p387)*

and one each in Cascais, Lisbon, Oporto and Sintra.

Lower down the scale, **Choice Hotels Portugal** operates a number of hotels in its **Comfort Inn** and **Quality Inn** categories in the Lisbon area and the north of the country, while **Best Western** has nine hotels countrywide. **IBIS** hotels are also well represented with hotels that are frequently located outside cities and towns, but offer very good value for money.

GRADINGS

The Portuguese tourist authority rates hotels with one to five stars (five being the top rating) and *pensões* in four categories (*albergaria* is the top rating, followed by 1st to 3rd category). *Apart-hotels* are rated with two to five stars. These ratings are based on a fixed set of criteria which covers most aspects of comfort. They do not, however, take into account more subjective factors such as view, atmosphere or the staff's service-mindedness.

It is important to remember that hotels and *pensões* are rated separately from top to bottom. In other words, a one or two-star hotel will always have a lower level of comfort – and lower prices – than an *albergaria* or even a 1st-category *pensão*. All rated establishments are meant to have a sign by the entrance showing their rating, but as the system has been changed recently, these are not always up to date.

PRICES

In Portugal, establishments are free to decide their own prices, but all tariffs must be clearly displayed at reception and in the rooms. The cost of the room usually includes all taxes and a continental

View from the Tivoli Palácio de Seteais, Sintra, a luxury hotel *(see p388)*

breakfast. Other meals are charged as extras. It is sometimes possible to bargain for a better rate, especially outside the high season. As a rule, the cost of a single room is around 60 to 75 per cent of the cost of a double room.

Tourist areas, such as the Algarve and Estoril coasts, and Madeira and the Azores, can be expensive. But prices drop substantially outside the peak months of the summer. In Lisbon and Oporto however, many business-oriented hotels charge the same rates throughout the year.

Pousadas have three rates: low season (Nov–Mar except New Year, Carnival and Easter), high season (Apr–Oct) and August. In Madeira, Christmas and New Year are seen as high season.

BOOKINGS

You will need to book in advance for all tourist areas in the high season. Much of the accommodation in the Algarve and around the Estoril coast is mass booked by tour operators. For Madeira, Lisbon and Oporto, book ahead regardless of the season. Most receptionists speak English so it should not be a problem to book by phone. Deposits are not usually required, but a written confirmation by email or fax, including a credit card number, may be requested.

Pousadas can be booked through Pestana or at the *pousadas* website, which also has plenty of information. The Portuguese tourist authority, **Turismo de Portugal**, publishes two official guides which are revised regularly: *Alojamento Turístico* (Tourist Accommodation) and *Turismo no Espaço Rural* (Tourism in the Country). These list all of the establishments rated by the authority, but only the latter contains any descriptions of individual settings, services or surroundings.

Reid's Palace in Funchal, Madeira *(see p404)*

Casa do Campo, a manor house in Celorico de Basto *(see p396)*

RURAL ACCOMMODATION

The choice of accommodation in Portugal is vastly enhanced by the possibility for visitors to stay in private manors, country houses or on farms, usually, but not always, situated in the countryside and usually, but not always, with the owners in residence.

This *Turismo no Espaço Rural* (Tourism in the Country) falls into four main categories: *Turismo de Habitação* (TH), which are manors or palatial houses of recognised historical and/or architectural value, including interiors and furnishings; *Turismo Rural* (TR), country houses typical of their region and located in or near a village; *Agroturismo* (AG), houses that form part of a working farm; and *Casas de Campo* (CC), country houses that offer lodging in which the owners may be in residence.

Most of the grandest *Turismos de Habitação* are to be found in the Minho region in the north. However, there are now four owner's associations in Portugal who offer information and a booking facility.

The annual publication *Turismo no Espaço Rural* lists all the houses. Bookings can be made through agents or directly through the owners.

RESORT ACCOMMODATION

Portugal's resort accommodation is mainly situated along the Algarve and Estoril coasts. The most convenient way to book accommodation is to make prior arrangements through a travel agent or tour operator. Hotel prices can drop considerably outside high season, and it is often possible to get a very good deal at less popular times of the year, when there are also fewer crowds to contend with.

The tourist village or *Aldeamento Turístico* is a unique feature of resort areas such as the Algarve. These self-contained complexes offer well-furnished and fitted private apartments and usually provide a range of sports facilities, beaches, pools, restaurants, bars and sometimes a supermarket.

These complexes are graded from three to five stars.

Apartamentos Turísticos (Tourist Apartments) do not have the hotel-style facilities of the tourist villages but are ideal for those who require flexibility and independence. They are generally purpose-built modern buildings in resort areas that offer self-catering accommodation. These Tourist Apartments also carry quality gradings of between two and five stars.

The luxurious Tivoli Marina Marinotel at the resort of Vilamoura in the Algarve *(see p403)*

BUDGET ACCOMMODATION

Youth hostels in Portugal *(Pousadas de Juventude)* are mainly dotted along the coast, and include three each in the Azores and Madeira. There are 54 in total, and they are open all through the year, but advance booking is advisable in the summer. They require a valid IYHF card, which can be obtained from any Youth Hostel Association. Facilities vary greatly, and may include the use of a kitchen, bar and swimming pool. Some also offer facilities for disabled travellers. Information is available from **Movijovem**, the head office of the Portuguese Youth Hostel Association.

Almost as cheap as youth hostels, and offering greater privacy, are rooms *(quartos)* in private houses. This type of accommodation is often rented out in resorts, and lists of *quartos* are available from the local tourist office.

Elegant dining room in a rural hotel setting

CAMPING AND CARAVANNING

There are over 100 official campsites in Portugal in total. Most are along the coast, usually in attractive locations. The largest is at Albufeira in the Algarve, but most are small and quiet. There is a national chain of campsites run by the company **Orbitur**.

Generally you pay a rate for the tent and per person, and an extra charge for showers and parking. The Portuguese Tourist Office will provide lists of campsites and information. You will need an international camping carnet, available from motoring organizations or the **Camping and Caravanning Club** in Great Britain. This provides third party insurance cover and entitles holders to some out-of-season discounts.

Setting up camp outside official camping sites in

São Miguel campsite, near Odemira in the Alentejo region

the countryside is severely restricted in order to curb the danger of forest fires.

CHILDREN

Children are as welcome as adult visitors to Portugal and families are well catered for. Some hotels give children under eight years old a 50 per cent discount on the price of accommodation and meals.

DISABLED TRAVELLERS

Hotels with facilities for the disabled are listed by the Portuguese National Tourist Office, who also produce a leaflet with useful information. Some campsites and youth hostels provide special facilities and these are listed by relevant organizations, and in a guide published by the **Secretariado Nacional de Reabilitação**.

DIRECTORY

HOTEL CHAINS

Best Western
Tel *0845 776 7676 (UK)*.
Tel *800 839 361 (Portugal)*.
www.bestwestern.pt

Choice Hotels
Tel *800 277 277*.
www.choicehotels
europe.com/portugal

IBIS
112–114 Bath Road,
Hayes, Middlesex UB3 5AL.
Tel *0208 283 45 50*.
www.ibishotel.com

Pestana Group
Rua Jau 54, 1300-314
Lisbon. Tel *213 615 600*.
www.pestana.com

Pestana-Pousadas de Portugal
Tel *218 442 001*.
Fax *218 442 085*.
www.pousadas.pt

Tivoli Hotels
Avenida da Liberdade 185,
1269-050 Lisbon.
Tel *213 198 900*.
Fax *213 198 950*.
www.tivolihotels.com

NATIONAL TOURIST AGENCIES

Direcção Regional de Turismo dos Açores
Rua Ernesto Rebelo 14,
9900-112 Horta, Faial.
Tel *292 200 500*.
Fax *292 293 664*.
www.visitazores.org

Direcção Regional de Turismo da Madeira
Avenida Arriaga 18,
9004-519 Funchal.
Tel *291 211 900*.
www.madeiratourism.org

Turismo de Portugal
Rua Ivone Silva 6,
1050-126 Lisbon.
Tel *211 140 200*.
Fax *217 937 537*.
www.turismode
portugal.pt

RURAL ACCOMMODATION

ANTER
Associação Nacional de
Turismo no Espaço Rural,
Travessa do Meguê 4, 1º,
7000-631 Évora.
Tel & Fax *266 744 555*.

PRIVETUR
Rua da Capela,
3850-365 Alquerubim.
Tel *234 108 543*.
Fax *234 938 703*.

TURIHAB
Praça de República,
4990-062 Ponte
de Lima.
Tel *258 931 750 or
258 742 827*.
www.turihab.pt

YOUTH HOSTELS

Movijovem
Rua Lúcio de Azevedo 27,
1600-146 Lisbon.
Tel *217 232 100*.
Fax *217 232 101*.
www.movijovem.pt

CAMPING AND CARAVANNING

UK: Camping and Caravanning Club
Greenfields House,
Westwood Way,
Coventry CV4 8JH.
Tel *0845 130 7631*.
www.campingand
caravanningclub.co.uk

Portugal: Camping and Caravanning Albufeira
Estrada de Ferreiras,
8200-555 Albufeira,
Algarve.
Tel *289 587 629*.
Fax *289 587 633*.

Lisboa Camping
Estrada da Circuvalação,
1400-061 Lisbon.
Tel *217 628 200*.
Fax *217 628 299*. www.
lisboacamping.com

Orbitur Intercâmbio de Turismo
Avenida da Boavista
1681-3º, Salas 5 a 8,
4100-132 Oporto.
Tel *226 061 360*.
Fax *226 063 590*.

DISABLED TRAVELLERS

Secretariado Nacional de Reabilitação
Avenida Conde de
Valbom 63, 1069 Lisbon.
Tel *217 959 545*.
Fax *217 929 596*.

The Pousadas of Portugal

Pousada symbol

The concept of the *pousada* dates from the 1940s, when the Portuguese government decided to establish a national network of state-run country inns, offering "hospitality in keeping with the style and tradition of the region". *Pousadas* are often set in remote, scenic locations, and most have fewer than 30 rooms, so visitors can expect friendly, personalized service and a high degree of comfort. This map does not show all of Portugal's *pousadas*, just the 39 that are particularly recommended.

Pousada de Murtosa/ Torreira-Ria *near the port of Aveiro has 20 bedrooms, most with balconies overlooking the lagoon of Ria de Aveiro (see p391).*

Pousada Conde de Ourém, *located within the medieval walled town of Ourám, offers breathtaking views of the Seica River valley. This pousada is the ideal base from which to explore this interesting area of Portugal, including the Shrine of Fatima and the Convento do Cristo at Tomar (see p390).*

Pousada do Castelo, *in the walled town of Óbidos, is situated in a beautifully restored palace inside the 15th-century castle keep. The* pousada *combines a medieval atmosphere with all modern comforts and a highly recommended restaurant (see p389).*

Pousada de Palmela *boasts an elegant interior, commanding hilltop views over the town of Palmela and the Atlantic Ocean, and an illustrious history. It is a thoughtful conversion of a monastery which was the headquarters of the Portuguese Knights of Santiago in the 13th century (see p387).*

Pousada do Infante *occupies a spectacular clifftop position in the most southwesterly town of Europe, Sagres. The terrace restaurant of this purpose-built* pousada *has magnificent views over the Atlantic Ocean (see p402).*

Pousada de Santa Marinha da Costa, *housed in a medieval monastery near the city of Guimarães, is one of Portugal's most impressive and historic pousadas (see p397).*

0 kilometres 50

0 miles 25

Pousada do Barão de Forrester, *named after JJ Forrester, an influential figure in 19th-century port production (see p254), enjoys a peaceful setting among vineyards in the small Douro town of Alijó (see p393).*

HO
erês
aniçada
ares

Bragança P

DOURO AND
TRÀS-OS-MONTES

P

o

Almeida P

P Viseu

ateigas P

P
Belmonte

THE BEIRAS

Pousada da Rainha Santa Isabel *dominates the town of Estremoz and the surrounding countryside. In the 13th century, the site of the pousada was home to King Dinis and his wife Queen Isabel (see p399).*

Marvão P

P

P Sousel

P
P Elvas
Vila Viçosa
P

ão

P Alvito

P

Pousada dos Lóios *in Évora has been converted from a 15th-century monastery. Adjacent to the remains of a Roman temple of Diana, it features an elegant dining room set in the original monastic cloisters and a Neo-Classical façade that dates from the mid-18th century (see p399).*

NTEJO

São Brás
e Alportel
P

P Tavira
P Estoi

Pousada de São Francisco *is located in the heart of the old Roman town of Beja at the centre of the sun-baked plains of the southern Alentejo. The building incorporates parts of a former Franciscan convent, dating back to the 13th century. It was opened as a pousada in 1994 (see p398).*

Choosing a Hotel

The hotels in this guide have been selected across a wide price range for their good value, facilities and location. Hotels are listed by region, beginning with Lisbon, and alphabetically within each price category. Map references refer to the Lisbon Street Finder on pages 134-141.

PRICE CATEGORIES
For a standard double room per night, including breakfast.

€ Under €60
€€ €60–€90
€€€ €90–€140
€€€€ €140–€200
€€€€€ Over €200

LISBON

ALCANTÂRA Pestana Palace Hotel
⬚ 🅷 ♒ 🍴 🗐 🅿 ♿   €€€€€
Rua Jau 54, 1300-314 **Tel** *213 615 600* **Fax** *213 615 601* **Rooms** *190*   **Map** *2 F3*

This magnificent hotel is partly housed in the 19th-century Palácio Valle-Flor and features luxuriously appointed rooms and suites. Most are located in a modern accommodation wing where there is also a conference centre, health club and indoor swimming pool. A Chinese pavilion in the landscaped gardens overlooks a pool. **www.pestana.com**

AVENIDA Alegria
🗐   €
Praça da Alegria 12, 1250-004 **Tel** *213 220 670* **Fax** *213 478 070* **Rooms** *35*   **Map** *4 F1*

A homely feel pervades this basic, good-value pensão that offers clean and tidy rooms, some with their own balcony. The smart façade, which dates from 1865, overlooks a palm-laden garden and borders the red-light district, although the police station is next door and the vicinity is fairly quiet. **www.alegrianet.com**

AVENIDA VIP Inn Veneza
⬚ 🗐 🅿   €€€
Avenida da Liberdade 189, 1250-141 **Tel** *213 522 618* **Fax** *213 526 678* **Rooms** *37*   **Map** *5 C5*

This charming and elegantly designed property is distinguished by an ornate staircase lined with colourful murals, by Pedro Luiz-Gomes. The hotel was built in 1886 and the interior retains a wonderful 19th-century atmosphere. The rooms are spacious and well appointed and there's a wonderfully intimate bar. **www.viphotels.com**

AVENIDA NH Liberdade
⬚ 🅷 ♒ 🛠 🗐 🅿 ♿   €€€€
Avenida da Liberdade 180B, 1250-146 **Tel** *213 514 060* **Fax** *213 143 674* **Rooms** *83*   **Map** *4 F1*

Decorated in the sober, modern style that is the trademark of the Spanish NH chain, this sophisticated hotel has a rooftop pool with superb views of the city. Rooms on the higher floors also have good views over the Avenida da Liberdade. Comforts include a good range of pillows. Breakfast is included. **www.nh-hotels.pt**

AVENIDA Tivoli Jardim
⬚ 🅷 ♒ 🍴 🗐 🅿   €€€€
Rua J. César Machado, 1250-135 **Tel** *213 591 000* **Fax** *213 591 245* **Rooms** *119*   **Map** *4 F1*

Popular with business executives, this is the baby sister of the nearby Tivoli Lisboa. The hotel is named after the tropical gardens at the rear of the building where guests can relax and take a dip in the pool. Alternatively, you can take advantage of big sister's neighbouring sports facilities. **www.tivolihotels.com**

AVENIDA Britânia
⬚ 🗐 🅿   €€€€€
Rua Rodrigues Sampaio 17, 1150-278 **Tel** *213 155 016* **Fax** *213 155 021* **Rooms** *33*   **Map** *5 C5*

This small boutique property is unique as the only surviving Art Deco hotel in Lisbon. The building was designed by the architect Cassiano Branco in 1944 and has been lovingly restored. Period detail has been faithfully maintained, with some modern whimsical touches. The polished marble lobby is beautiful. **www.heritage.pt**

AVENIDA Lisboa Plaza
⬚ 🅷 🗐 🅿   €€€€€
Travessa do Salitre 7, 1269-066 **Tel** *213 218 218* **Fax** *213 471 630* **Rooms** *112*   **Map** *4 F1*

Built in 1953, and situated off Praça da Alegria and Av. da Liberdade, this boutique hotel possesses an air of informal good taste and understated charm. The decor is by the Portuguese interior designer Graça Viterbo, and her characteristic colour-coordinated fabrics and furnishings are carried through the entire property. **www.heritage.pt**

AVENIDA Sofitel Lisboa
⬚ 🅷 🗐 🅿 ♿   €€€€€
Avenida da Liberdade 127, 1269-038 **Tel** *213 228 300* **Fax** *213 228 310* **Rooms** *171*   **Map** *4 F1*

Comfort and modernity are the bywords here. The bedrooms feature opulent mattresses and soft, downy quilts that guarantee a good night's sleep. Slick, contemporary design, a first-class restaurant and a top floor terrace with a terrific downtown view are all qualities that make this deluxe hotel a city centre favourite. **www.sofitel-lisboa.com**

AVENIDA Tivoli Lisboa
⬚ 🅷 ♒ 🍴 🗐 🅿 ♿   €€€€€
Avenida da Liberdade 185, 1269-050 **Tel** *213 198 900* **Fax** *213 198 950* **Rooms** *329*   **Map** *4 F1*

One of Lisbon's most emblematic hotels, the Tivoli holds court over Avenida da Liberdade and is renowned for its high levels of service and personal attention. The 329 rooms are fully insulated and sound proofed, and the rooftop Terrace Grill is a gourmet hotspot. The property regularly hosts VIP conferences. **www.tivolihotels.com**

Key to Symbols *see back cover flap*

BAIRRO ALTO Pensão Londres

€€

Rua Dom Pedro V 53, 1250-092 **Tel** *213 462 203* **Fax** *213 465 682* **Rooms** *40* **Map** *4 F2*

Housed in a lofty, angular building, the rooms here are sparsely decorated but are clean, tidy and all have satellite TV. Those on the 4th floor command glorious panoramic views of the city. The owners can provide laundry service and helpful advice on where to go and what to see. **www.pensaolondres.com.pt**

BAIXA Beira Minho

€

Praça da Figueira 6, 1100-240 **Tel** *213 461 846* **Fax** *218 867 811* **Rooms** *19* **Map** *7 B3*

Probably the most colourful entrance you would be ever likely to make, the corridor leading to this comfortable and centrally located pensão arrows straight through a flower shop, and the bouquet is wonderful. Facilities here have improved, with the ensuite rooms equipped with TV and direct dial telephone. There's even an elevator.

BAIXA Duas Nações

€

Rua da Vitória 41, 1100-618 **Tel** *213 460 710* **Fax** *213 470 206* **Rooms** *54* **Map** *7 B4*

The Two Nations is a rather grand building straddling the corner of Rua Augusta and Rua da Vitória, both pedestrianized, and the property is fashioned as a traditional Lisbon boarding house. The rooms are well appointed and have private bathroom facilities. Those overlooking Rua Augusta can be noisy at times. **www.duasnacoes.com**

BAIXA Norte

€

Rua dos Douradores 161, 1100-205 **Tel** *218 878 941* **Fax** *218 868 462* **Rooms** *34* **Map** *7 B3*

Wedged in between a row of shops on a semi-pedestrianized street near Praça de Figueira, this centrally positioned functional Pensão offers spotless rooms with private bathroom facilities and TV but no breakfast. Guests will have no problem finding a café or restaurant however, as the area is full of them.

BAIXA Portugal

€€

Rua João das Regras 4, 1100-294 **Tel** *218 877 581* **Fax** *218 867 343* **Rooms** *59* **Map** *7 C3*

The rather drab façade of this hotel situated off Praça Martim Moniz belies a fairly stylish old-fashioned décor. The large ensuite rooms are light and airy and carpeted throughout. An attractive, well-stocked bar provides a handy meeting point and the hotel is within easy reach of Rossio metro station. **www.hotelportugal.com**

BAIXA Evidência Tejo Creative Hotel

€€€

Rua dos Condes de Monsanto 2, 1100-159 **Tel** *218 866 182* **Fax** *218 865 163* **Rooms** *58* **Map** *7 B3*

This modern, stylish hotel is situated in the heart of the downtown Baixa district, close to the metro station and surrounded by several good-value restaurants. The rooms are bright and comfortable, and there is even a Moorish well in the lobby. Breakfast is included. **www.evidenciatejo.com**

BAIXA Internacional Design Hotel

€€€

Rua da Betesga 3, 1100 090 **Tel** *213 240 990* **Fax** *213 240 999* **Rooms** *54* **Map** *7 B3*

Thanks to a multidisciplinary team of architects, decorators, designers and artists, the four floors of this hotel each convey a special theme: minimalism; Zen philosophy; pop culture; and Afro-style. This radical concept is based on a holistic perspective and the hotel only uses organic products. **www.internacionaldesignhotel.com**

BAIXA Mundial

€€€€

Praça Martim Moniz 2, 1100-341 **Tel** *218 842 000* **Fax** *218 842 110* **Rooms** *350* **Map** *7 B3*

This typical 4-star property has comfortable rooms, modern facilities and the added bonus of a private car park. The hotel looms large over Praça Martim Moniz but extends far enough back to take in some fine cityscapes. The best views though are from the top floor restaurant, particularly at night. **www.hotel-mundial.pt**

CASTELO Ninho das Águias

€

Costa do Castelo 74, 1100-179 **Tel** *218 854 070* **Rooms** *16* **Map** *7 C3*

Easily identified by its rooftop turret, the unusual Eagle's Nest *pensão* perches under the castle walls. A huge stuffed eagle greets visitors at reception. The bright and sometimes breezy rooms are very popular so it's wise to book ahead. The terraced flower garden offers peace and solitude. No breakfast.

CASTELO Solar do Castelo

€€€€€

Rua das Cozinhas 2, 1100-181 **Tel** *218 806 050* **Fax** *218 870 907* **Rooms** *14* **Map** *7 C3*

Hidden within the walls of the castle is this sparkling gem of a hotel, incorporated into the architecture of a renovated 18th-century mansion, itself constructed on the site of the former Alcáçova Palace. Some rooms face a central courtyard and guests can enjoy a complimentary decanter of port upon arrival. **www.heritage.pt**

CHIADO Hotel do Chiado

€€€€€

Rua Nova do Almada 114, 1200-290 **Tel** *213 256 100* **Fax** *213 256 161* **Rooms** *40* **Map** *B4*

Japanese silk-screen prints adorn the lobby of this prestigious boutique hotel in Lisbon's most fashionable district. It was designed by Portuguese architect Álvaro Siza Vieira who has cleverly blended Oriental and colonial Portuguese influences with a modern and stylish functionality. Some rooms offer outstanding views. **www.regency-hotels-resorts.com**

GRAÇA Senhora do Monte

€€€

Calçada do Monte 39, 1170-250 **Tel** *218 866 002* **Fax** *218 877 783* **Rooms** *28* **Map** *7 D1*

This unique little hilltop *albergaria* is somewhat off the beaten track, but rewards those who make the effort with some memorable views. The interior features tufted sofas and oversize tables and lamps and all guest rooms have a veranda. Little touches like the brass shower fixtures make all the difference. **www.maisturismo.pt/sramonte**

LAPA York House

▥ 🍽   €€€€

Rua das Janelas Verdes 32, 1200-691 **Tel** *213 962 435* **Fax** *213 972 793* **Rooms** *32*   **Map** *4 D3*

Behind the rose-pink walls of this enchanting pensão are luxurious rooms with wooden or terracotta floors, and elegant antique furniture. The accommodation is housed in the 17th-century Covento dos Marianos and is set around a charming, plant-filled patio. Peaceful, serene and wholly inviting. **www.yorkhouselisboa.com**

LAPA As Janelas Verdes

▤ 🅿   €€€€€

Rua das Janelas Verdes 47, 1200-690 **Tel** *213 968 143* **Fax** *213 968 144* **Rooms** *29*   **Map** *4 D3*

This romantic and luxurious *pensão* is housed in an 18th-century mansion, once owned by the Portuguese novelist Eça de Queirós *(see p55)*. It has Neo-Classical decor and a peaceful, charming patio. The property has its own library and is a short walk from the Museu Nacional de Arte Antiga. **www.heritage.pt**

LAPA Olissippo Lapa Palace

🖥 🍽 ≅ 🎦 ▤ 🅿 ♿   €€€€€

Rua do Pau da Bandeira 4, 1249-021 **Tel** *213 949 494* **Fax** *213 950 665* **Rooms** *109*   **Map** *3 C3*

The Grand Dame of Lisbon hotels, this gracious, historical property dates from 1870. The palace was once the home of the Count of Valanças and each room in the Palace Wing is uniquely decorated in its own Portuguese style – from 18th-century Neo-Classical to Art Deco. Leisure options include a spa. **www.lapapalace.com**

MARQUÊS DE POMBAL Castilho

🖥 ▤   €

Rua Castilho 57, 1250-068 **Tel** *213 860 822* **Fax** *213 862 910* **Rooms** *24*   **Map** *4 F1*

A stone's throw from the Marquês de Pombal metro station, this is an ideal option for those seeking a city-centre location at an out-of-town price. The *pensão* is on the fourth floor of a building and the comfortable rooms, some with three or four beds, are well equipped. **pensaocastilho@hotmail.com**

MARQUÊS DE POMBAL Jorge V

🖥 ▤ 🅿 ♿   €€€

Rua Mouzinho da Silveira 3, 1250-165 **Tel** *213 562 525* **Fax** *213 150 319* **Rooms** *49*   **Map** *5 C5*

Considering the central location, this pleasant, comfortable hotel offers good value for money. Roughly half the rooms have balconies, so request one when checking in. There are also six suites. The downstairs bar is a good place to mingle with fellow guests, and there are Internet facilities in the lobby. **www.hoteljorgev.com**

MARQUÊS DE POMBAL VIP Executive Diplomático

🖥 🏃 ▤ 🅿   €€€

Rua Castilho 74, 1250-071 **Tel** *213 839 020* **Fax** *213 862 155* **Rooms** *90*   **Map** *5 B5*

Furnished throughout in a classical style, this hotel is a popular choice for business conferences, but the leisure traveller will be equally at home in the modern surroundings. Families are also welcome and there is a babysitting service available on request. The rooms and suites offer complimentary tea, coffee and chocolate. **www.viphotels.com**

MARQUÊS DE POMBAL Nacional

🖥 ▤ 🅿 ♿   €€€

Rua Castilho 34, 1250-070 **Tel** *213 554 433* **Fax** *213 561 122* **Rooms** *61*   **Map** *5 B5*

This interesting glass-fronted hotel has comfortable rooms, including two suites and one for guests with disabilities, and all the services you'd expect from a 3-star property, including a private car parking facility. Its location near Praça Marquês de Pombal makes it a handy base from which to explore the city. **www.hotel-nacional.com**

MARQUÊS DE POMBAL Ritz Four Seasons

🖥 🍽 ≅ 🎦 ▤ 🅿 ♿   €€€€€

Rua Rodrigo da Fonseca 88, 1099-039 **Tel** *213 811 400* **Fax** *213 831 783* **Rooms** *282*   **Map** *5 B5*

Hospitality at the legendary Ritz combines luxury and elegance in a grand style. The hotel is a prominent landmark and a stunning locale from which to experience the city. A major draw is the spa. Designed in marble and rich oak, the facility offers a wealth of treatments and therapies. **www.fourseasons.com**

MARQUÊS DE POMBAL Tiara Park Atlantic Lisboa

🖥 🍽 ≅ 🎦 ▤ 🅿 ♿   €€€€€

Rua Castilho 149, 1099-034 **Tel** *213 818 700* **Fax** *213 890 500* **Rooms** *331*   **Map** *5 B4*

The generous rooms and superb suites here are of contemporary design, with signature Philip Stark bathrooms. Guests can enjoy full privileges at the nearby Club VII private health club and indulge in some fine dining at the Restaurante L'Appart. Cocktails and lighter meals are available at the sophisticated Ganesh Bar. **www.tiara-hotels.com**

PARQUE DAS NAÇÕES Tivoli Oriente

🖥 🍽 ≅ 🎦 ▤ 🅿 ♿   €€€

Avenida Dom João II, 1990-083 **Tel** *218 915 100* **Fax** *218 915 345* **Rooms** *279*   **Map**

Parque das Nações, on the riverfront east of the city centre, boasts major attractions like the Oceanarium and the Pavilhão Atlântico concert hall, all within easy reach of this handsome property. The impressive Vasco da Gama shopping mall is opposite, and there's a delicious choice of nearby bars and restaurants. **www.tivolihotels.com**

RATO Amazónia Lisboa

🖥 🍽 ≅ ▤ 🅿 ♿   €€€

Travessa Fábrica dos Pentes 12-20, 1250-106 **Tel** *213 877 006* **Fax** *213 879 090* **Rooms** *192*   **Map** *5 B5*

Conveniently close to the city centre but with an informal side-street ambiance, this mid-range hotel has an attractive interior decorated with ethnic artwork and sculpture. The guest rooms are comfortable, and the grounds incorporate a modest swimming pool that closes during the winter months. **www.amazoniahoteis.com**

RATO Altis

🖥 🍽 ≅ 🎦 ▤ 🅿 ♿   €€€€€

Rua Castilho 11, 1269-072 **Tel** *213 106 000* **Fax** *213 106 262* **Rooms** *303*   **Map** *4 F1*

This huge hotel has every expected facility, including a well-equipped health club that offers massage and physiotherapy among its many treatments, and an indoor swimming pool. Other leisure options include a rooftop grill and the Herald Bar where guests can unwind over a drink while listening to live piano music. **www.altishotels.com**

Key to Price Guide *see p382* **Key to Symbols** *see back cover flap*

RESTAURADORES Florescente 🗐 🅿 €

Rua das Portas de Santo Antão 99, 1150-226 **Tel** *213 425 062* **Fax** *213 427 733* **Rooms** *68* **Map** *7 A2*

For a modest pensão, the rooms here put a 3-star hotel to shame. They are spotless and well appointed and all have ensuite bathrooms. Florescente stands on a pedestrianized street and is near the Coliseu dos Recreios concert venue so the *pensão's* exclusive car parking option is a real plus. **www.residencialflorescente.com**

RESTAURADORES Nova Goa 🗐 €

Rua do Arco do Marquês do Alegrete 13, 1100-034 **Tel** *218 881 137* **Fax** *218 867 811* **Rooms** *42* **Map** *7 C3*

Just around the corner from Praça da Figueira, and almost opposite the Hotel Portugal, this pensão is like many in the vicinity: clean, comfortable and fairly basic. The rooms do, however, have ensuite bathrooms and cable TV. Some knowledge of Portuguese will help foreign guests as little English is spoken. **www.pensaonovagoa.com**

RESTAURADORES Restauradores 🗐🔲🗐 €

Praça dos Restauradores 13, 1250-187 **Tel** *213 475 660* **Rooms** *30* **Map** *7 A2*

If the elevator is out of order it will be a bit of a hike to the fourth floor where this small pensão is situated. The ensuite rooms are surprisingly well furnished, with those at the front of the building commanding a giddy view of the busy street below. No breakfast.

RESTAURADORES Roma 🗐 €

Travessa da Glória 22a, 1250-118 **Tel** *213 460 557* **Fax** *213 460 557* **Rooms** *24* **Map** *7 A2*

A first-class pensão that differs from many others in that some of the rooms are in fact small apartments, complete with kitchenette with microwave. A 24-hour reception means guests can arrive any time of day or night, and there is a secure luggage room. Restaurants and bars are close at hand. **www.residenciaroma.com**

RESTAURADORES Turim Suisso Atlântico 🔲🗐🅿 €

Rua da Glória 3, 1250-114 **Tel** *213 461 713* **Fax** *213 469 013* **Rooms** *84* **Map** *7 A2*

In a small side street by the Elevador da Glória, this slightly outdated hotel has large old-fashioned rooms and public areas with stone arches and wooden beams. It's great advantage is the location, a quick step away from bustling Praça dos Restauradores. Note that room 117 does not have a window. **turimsuissoatlantico@turimhoteis.com**

RESTAURADORES Executive Suites Eden 🔲🎔🗐🔥 €€€€

Praça dos Restauradores 24, 1250-187 **Tel** *213 216 600* **Fax** *213 216 666* **Rooms** *134* **Map** *7 A2*

This building used to be a theatre-cinema and part of the interior is decorated with old movie posters. The refurbishment project won its architects a 'Best Tourism Project in Portugal' award for the 75 studios and 59 apartments they incorporated into the original structure. All have private bathroom and kitchen. **www.viphotels.com**

RESTAURADORES Avenida Palace 🔲🗐🔲 €€€€€

Rua 1 de Dezembro 123, 1200-359 **Tel** *213 218 100* **Fax** *213 422 884* **Rooms** *82* **Map** *7 B3*

Built in 1892, this sumptuous building with its Neo-Classical façade is the oldest hotel in Lisbon. The stunning interior retains many charming period details and evokes images of Paris during the Belle Epoch. The rooms are decorated in a classical style. Japan's wartime monarch Emperor Hirohito was a guest here. **www.hotel-avenida-palace.pt**

ROSSIO Metrópole 🔲🗐 €€€€

Praça Dom Pedro IV 30, 1100-200 **Tel** *213 219 030* **Fax** *213 469 166* **Rooms** *36* **Map** *7 B3*

Inaugurated in 1917, this hotel was a favourite haunt of spies and double agents during World War II. The individually styled and elegant rooms are partly furnished with original pieces from the 1920s, and the whole building exudes a distinctly retro atmosphere. The balcony views across Rossio are picture postcard. **www.almeidahotels.com**

SALDANHA Horizonte 🗐 €

Av António Augusto de Aguiar 42, 1050-017 **Tel** *213 539 526* **Fax** *213 538 474* **Rooms** *53* **Map** *5 B4*

This large pensão offers good value for money for this area, situated as it is near Parque Eduardo VII. Accommodation is roomy and amenities include satellite TV and safe. There's also a daily laundry service. The pensão faces the Parque metro station and rooms at the front can be noisy. **www.hotelhorizonte.com**

SALDANHA Marisela €

Rua Filipe Folque 19, 1050-111 **Tel** *213 533 205* **Fax** *213 160 423* **Rooms** *19* **Map** *5 C3*

The drapes and curtains may not be to everyone's taste, but this good-value pensão has one unique attribute: a waterbed! For those who'd rather not experience that sinking feeling, there are plenty of conventional doubles and singles to choose from, and all rooms are ensuite with cable TV. No breakfast. **www.residencialmarisela.pt**

SALDANHA Olissippo Marquês de Sá 🔲🔢🗐🅿🔥 €€€

Avenida Miguel Bombarda 130, 1050-167 **Tel** *217 911 014* **Fax** *217 936 983* **Rooms** *164* **Map** *6 B2*

An adequate and inexpensive 3-star property, the hotel's modern, symmetrical edifice stands proud over the older townhouses that characterize this area of Lisbon. The interior design is conventional, save for some fetching abstract carpet designs. The hotel is a short walk from the Museu Calouste Gulbenkian *(see pp76-9)*. **www.olissippohotels.com**

SALDANHA Real Parque 🔲🔢🧍🗐🅿🔥 €€€

Avenida Luis Bívar 67, 1069-146 **Tel** *213 199 000* **Fax** *213 570 750* **Rooms** *153* **Map** *5 C3*

Smart and impressive, this hotel loves children and can even supply kid's toys and furniture, and a special minors' menu. The adults meanwhile can make use of a health and fitness centre, decorated with lovely turquoise and aquamarine mosaic tiles. There are seven rooms for guests with disabilities. **www.hoteisreal.com**

SALDANHA Sheraton Lisboa Hotel & Spa

€€€€

Rua Latino Coelho 1, 1069-025 **Tel** *213 120 000* **Fax** *213 575 073* **Rooms** *369*   **Map** *5 C3*

Housed in central Lisbon's tallest building, the Sheraton hotel has a redesigned lobby, a mouth-watering choice of gourmet and bistro restaurants and several stylish bars. The chic guest rooms and suites are complemented in mood and design by a state-of-the-art spa, boasting ten specialist treatment rooms. **www.sheraton.com/lisboa**

THE LISBON COAST

ALCÁCER DO SAL Pousada Dom Afonso II

€€€€€

Castelo de Alcácer do Sal, 7580-123 **Tel** *265 613 070* **Fax** *265 613 074* **Rooms** *35*   **Road map** *C5*

This historic *pousada* occupies a converted castle on a strategic hilltop whose foundations overlay vestiges of Roman, Moorish, Phoenician and even Neolithic remains. Chunky, whitewashed walls embrace tidy rooms with floor-to-ceiling shuttered windows that open to sweeping views of the town and the River Sado. **www.pousadas.pt**

ALCOCHETE Quinta da Praia das Fontes

€€

Largo do Marquês de Soydos, 2890-032 **Tel & Fax** *212 340 191* **Rooms** *9*   **Road map** *C5*

A charming 16th-century former manor house of the Marquês de Soydos, located in its own grounds in the centre of this picturesque riverside town. The building was later enriched with magnificent 17th- and 18th-century *azulejo* tiles. The interior includes a wonderful country style kitchen, where breakfast is taken. **www.quintapraiafontes.com.pt**

CARCAVELOS Praia Mar

€€€

Rua do Gurué 16, 2775-581 **Tel** *214 585 100* **Fax** *214 573 130* **Rooms** *154*

You can almost keep one foot in the swimming pool while dipping the other in the sea, such is the proximity to the beach of this wonderful hotel. The ultra-modern rooms and suites are as stylish as their flat screen TVs, with ocean views or garden vistas fitted as standard. **www.almeidahotels.com**

CASCAIS Solar Dom Carlos

€€

Rua Latino Coelho 104, 2750-408 **Tel** *214 828 115* **Fax** *214 865 155* **Rooms** *12*   **Road map** *B5*

This wonderful building is a former Royal Cottage and was once the summer residence of King Carlos I. As befitting a monarch, some of the bedrooms are very grand. So, too, is the breakfast room, which is decorated with wall-to-ceiling frescos. The rear gardens contain an historic chapel. **www.solardomcarlos.com**

CASCAIS Casa da Pérgola

€€€

Avenida Valbom 13, 2750-508 **Tel** *214 840 040* **Fax** *214 834 791* **Rooms** *10*   **Road map** *B5*

A beautiful 19th-century Mediterranean-style mansion replete with white marble floors and staircase, stucco ceiling and ornate furniture. The façade is adorned with decorative handpainted tiles, and the property stands in its own landscaped gardens. Owned by the same family for over a century. Closed Dec-Feb. **www.pergolahouse.com**

CASCAIS Cidadela

€€€

Avenida 25 de Abril, 2754-517 **Tel** *214 827 600* **Fax** *214 867 226* **Rooms** *115*   **Road map** *B5*

An easy walk from the town centre, most of the rooms and suites at this typical holiday hotel offer spectacular views over the bay. T1 and T3 apartments are also available, complete with kitchenette. The swimming pool is surrounded by pretty gardens where themed barbeques take place during the evening. **www.hotelcidadela.com**

CASCAIS Albatroz

€€€€€

Rua Frederico Arouca 100, 2750-353 **Tel** *214 847 380* **Fax** *214 844 827* **Rooms** *59*   **Road map** *B5*

Built in the 19th century as a retreat for the Portuguese royal family, the Albatroz sits perched on the rocks directly overlooking the ocean. Notable for its traditional style of luxury and exceptional design, the service is first class and discreet. The hotel has its own outdoor salt-water swimming pool. **www.albatrozhotels.com**

CASCAIS Cascais Miragem

€€€€€

Avenida Marginal 8554, 2754-536 **Tel** *210 060 600* **Fax** *210 060 601* **Rooms** *192*   **Road map** *B5*

Opulent and stylish, this luxury hotel overlooking Cascais bay has three restaurants, one of which serves gourmet cuisine, and an impressive swimming pool that features the revolutionary infinity Edge system, which gives bathers the sensation of actually swimming in the ocean. Children are especially welcome. **www.cascaismirage.com**

CASCAIS Farol Design Hotel

€€€€€

Avenida Rei Humberto II de Itália 7, 2750-461 **Tel** *214 823 490* **Fax** *214 841 447* **Rooms** *33*   **Road map** *B5*

A 19th-century oceanfront mansion given an eye-catching 21st-century makeover. The hotel's close association with the fashion industry has led to the innovative "dress a room" concept, with rooms designed by 10 different Portuguese and international designers. The result is a chic, stylish and inventive property singular in its appeal. **www.farol.com.pt**

COSTA DA CAPARICA Praia do Sol

€

Rua dos Pescadores 12, 2825-386 **Tel** *212 900 012* **Fax** *212 902 541* **Rooms** *54*   **Road map** *B5*

A small hotel, Praia do Sol offers comfortable rooms specially designed for leisure stays. The interior design, all puffy leather armchairs and tiled flooring, is not the most stylish but the hotel is located in a popular resort town near one of the largest beaches in Portugal. **hotelpraiadosol@netcabo.pt**

Key to Price Guide *see p382* **Key to Symbols** *see back cover flap*

COSTA DA CAPARICA Hotel Costa da Caparica
€€€€

Avenida General Humberto Delgado 47, 2829-506 **Tel** *212 918 900* **Fax** *212 910 687* **Rooms** *353* **Road map** *B5*

This attractive hotel, with an unusual semi-circular entrance, has a spa that offers guests hot-stone massage, among other treatments and therapies. Many of the rooms, some non-smoking and seven of which are adapted for the disabled, overlook the beach. A piano bar and à la carte restaurant entertain and sustain. **www.hotelcostacaparica.pt**

ERICEIRA Vilazul
€€

Calçada da Baleia 10, 2655-238 **Tel** *261 860 000* **Fax** *261 862 927* **Rooms** *21* **Road map** *B5*

Only 500 m (550 yds) from the sea, this bright and airy hotel is family-owned and the staff friendly and helpful. Though basic, the rooms are spotless and some have great panoramic views of the beach. The hotel has its own restaurant. Book ahead if planning a stay during summer. **www.hotelvilazul.com**

ESTORIL Hotel Alvorada
€€€

Rua de Lisboa 3, 2765-240 **Tel** *214 649 860* **Fax** *214 687 250* **Rooms** *51* **Road map** *B5*

The bright, flashing neon from the casino opposite is reflected in the lobby windows of this conveniently located property. The Estoril Congress Centre is situated on the other side of the square and accommodation at the hotel is at a premium during seminars and conferences, so check ahead for availability. **www.hotelalvorada.com**

ESTORIL Hotel Inglaterra
€€€€

Rua do Porto 1, 2765-271 **Tel** *214 684 461* **Fax** *214 682 108* **Rooms** *55* **Road map** *B5*

This impressive and charismatic hotel started life in the early 20th century as a palace mansion and is endowed with some fine examples of period furniture. Carefully modernized over the years, the hotel features an excellent gymnasium and massage facility, and an outdoor swimming pool. There's even a playground. **www.hotelinglaterra.com.pt**

ESTORIL Palácio
€€€€

Rua da Particular, 2769-504 **Tel** *214 648 000* **Fax** *214 648 159* **Rooms** *161* **Road map** *B5*

Its impressive façade, classically styled interiors and gourmet restaurant makes Estoril's landmark hotel a favourite with visiting heads of state, film stars and royalty. Most of the elegantly appointed rooms and suites benefit from garden and sea views and guests have access to an 18-hole golf course and tennis courts. **www.palacioestorilhotel.com**

GUINCHO Fortaleza do Guincho
€€€€€

Estrada do Guincho, 2750-642 **Tel** *214 870 491* **Fax** *214 870 431* **Rooms** *27* **Road map** *B5*

The most westerly hotel on the European mainland, this magical property is perched on a windy bluff near Cabo da Rocha and overlooks the ocean. Renovated from the shell of an old fortress, the arched ceilings and medieval decor enrich an already atmospheric interior. The restaurant is Michelin-starred. Reservations essential. **www.guinchotel.pt**

GUINCHO Senhora da Guia
€€€€

Estrada do Guincho, 2750-642 **Tel** *214 869 239* **Fax** *214 869 227* **Rooms** *41* **Road map** *B5*

This fashionable *estalagem* is set in its own beautiful and carefully maintained grounds alongside the Quinta da Marinha golf course. Guests passionate about the sport can buy a Golf Passport that allows play on five different courses. A luxury health club provides an alternative leisure pursuit. Most rooms have sea views. **www.senhoradaguia.com**

MAFRA Castelão
€€

Avenida 25 de Abril, 2640-456 **Tel** *261 816 050* **Fax** *261 816 059* **Rooms** *30* **Road map** *B5*

Convenient as a base when visiting the town's fabulous Baroque palace and monastery – one of Portugal's great historical treasures – this hotel is well regarded and has tidy and attractive rooms with all modern conveniences, including mini bar, direct dial telephone and satellite TV. The restaurant serves typical Portuguese fare. **www.hotelcastelao.com**

PALMELA Pousada do Castelo de Palmela
€€€€€

Castelo de Palmela, 2950-317 **Tel** *212 351 226* **Fax** *212 330 440* **Rooms** *28* **Road map** *C5*

The fortified walls of this 12th-century castle enclose a tranquil *pousada* of stunning beauty and great historical interest. Housed in a former convent, the *pousada's* graceful, whitewashed rooms are large and comfortable, with incredible views. The 15th-century Igreja de Santiago, lined with 17th-century *azulejo* tiles, stands next door. **www.pousadas.pt**

QUELUZ Pousada Dona Maria
€€€€

Largo do Palácio Nacional, 2745-191 **Tel** *214 356 158* **Fax** *214 356 189* **Rooms** *26* **Road map** *B5*

This impressive *pousada* is located in a building traditionally referred to as the Clock Tower, which was once used by staff serving the Royal Court at the nearby 18th-century Palácio de Queluz. Careful renovation has preserved the character of the annexe while making sure guests are afforded every modern amenity. **www.pousadas.pt**

SESIMBRA Hotel do Mar
€€€

Rua General Humberto Delgado 10, 2970-628 **Tel** *212 288 300* **Fax** *212 233 888* **Rooms** *168* **Road map** *C5*

It's easy to lose your way in this sprawling complex. The hotel is built on different levels on the cliffside and is linked by a catacomb of corridors and several elevators. Rooms are clean and simply furnished, though if you stay in the presidential suite you get your own private pool. **www.hoteldomar.pt**

SETÚBAL IBIS Setúbal
€

Rua do Alto da Guerra, 2914-518 **Tel** *265 700 900* **Fax** *265 700 909* **Rooms** *102* **Road map** *C5*

Featuring the usual combination of IBIS comforts and economy, this hotel is an ideal base from which to explore the Arrábida Natural Park and the Sado Estuary Nature Reserve. The friendly staff can also arrange dolphin-watching excursions. Guests have the use of a swimming pool and a free car park. **www.ibishotel.com**

SETÚBAL Pousada de São Filipe   🔢📱📶 €€€€€

Castelo de São Filipe, 2900-300 **Tel** *265 550 070* **Fax** *265 539 240* **Rooms** *16*   **Road map** *C5*

This historic *pousada* is integrated within the Castelo de São Filipe, built on the orders of Philip of Spain *(see p50)* in 1590. Guests can tread the ramparts and admire fine views over the estuary and the Tróia peninsula. Five of the rooms are located in the castle's former cells. **www.pousadas.pt**

SINTRA Residencial Sintra   📶👤📱 €€

Travessa dos Avelares 12, 2710-506 **Tel** *219 230 738* **Fax** *219 230 738* **Rooms** *15*   **Road map** *B5*

This rambling, family-run *pensão* is blessed with a serene location just east of town centre, in the verdant São Pedro residential area. Spruce, comfortable rooms gaze over lush grounds, an amazingly narrow swimming pool and a splendid view of Sintra's Moorish castle. Private car parking available. **www.residencialsintra.blogspot.com**

SINTRA Tivoli Sintra   📺🔢📱📶♿ €€

Praça da República, 2710-616 **Tel** *219 237 200* **Fax** *219 237 245* **Rooms** *77*   **Road map** *B5*

Tucked away in a corner of the main square, this modern hotel is an unbeatable location for exploring Sintra's wealth of historical palaces and monuments, as well as the town itself – all classified as a UNESCO World Heritage Site. Rooms and suites offer magnificent views of the surrounding hills. **www.tivolihotels.com**

SINTRA Lawrence's   🔢📶📱♿ €€€€€

Rua Consigliéri Pedroso 38-40, 2710-550 **Tel** *219 105 500* **Fax** *219 105 505* **Rooms** *16*   **Road map** *B5*

Dating from 1764, Lawrence's is believed to be the oldest hotel on the Iberian Peninsula. Guest rooms are not numbered but instead are named after personalities from the world of art, theatre and literature including Lord Byron, who is said to have stayed here in 1809 while writing *Childe Harold*. **www.lawrenceshotel.com**

SINTRA Penha Longa   📺🔢📶📺📱♿ €€€€€

Estrada da Lagoa Azul-Linhó, 2714-511 **Tel** *219 249 011* **Fax** *219 249 007* **Rooms** *194*   **Road map** *B5*

A luxury hotel and golf resort, Penha Longa is famed for its outstanding blend of culture and leisure. Rooms and suites are fabulously appointed, with many facing the Atlantic golf course designed by Robert Trent Jones Jr. The Midori restaurant serves Japanese gourmet cuisine, and Six Senses operates the lavish spa. **www.penhalonga.com**

SINTRA Tivoli Palácio de Seteais   🔢📶📱 €€€€€

Avenida Barbosa do Bocage 10, 2710-517 **Tel** *219 233 200* **Fax** *219 234 277* **Rooms** *30*   **Road map** *B5*

One of the most cherished and romantic hotels in the country, this splendid property is a magnificent example of 18th-century architecture, with rooms that dazzle in the classical style of the era. Rare period furniture graces the public areas and guests are free to wander the beautifully landscaped topiary gardens. **www.tivolihotels.com**

ESTREMADURA AND RIBATEJO

ABRANTES Best Western Hotel de Turismo   📺🔢📶📱 €€

Largo de Santo António, 2200-349 **Tel** *241 361 261* **Fax** *241 365 218* **Rooms** *40*   **Road map** *C4*

This hotel, decorated in bright, classic colours, is found in a very pleasant location on a hill overlooking the Tagus river valley. Set in its own attractive gardens, the relaxing atmosphere is further enhanced by a good restaurant and a friendly bar, with an open fireplace and a summer veranda. **www.hotelabrantes.pt**

ABRANTES Herdade de Cadouços   🔢📶👤📶📱♿ €€

Água Travessa, Bemposta, 2205-163 **Tel** *241 760 000* **Fax** *241 760 019* **Rooms** *24*   **Road map** *C4*

Set in the Abrantes countryside, this enchanting estate offers a true taste of country living, amid lakes, forests and vineyards. The rooms and suites are furnished in typically Ribatejan style and afford splendid views. On-site amenities include a tennis court, outdoor pool and fitness circuit. Other activities are available nearby. **www.herdadedecadoucos.com**

BALEAL Casa das Marés II   📄📶📱 €€

Praia de Baleal, Peniche, 2520-009 **Tel** *262 769 255* **Fax** *262 769 255* **Rooms** *12*   **Road map** *B4*

The family-run "House of Tides" is unmistakeable in appearance. The whitewashed property with dark green window shutters is set on a promontory with dramatic sea views. The front ground-floor bedrooms have their own private patios that look over the beach. Breakfast is served on the terrace above the cove. **www.casadasmares2.com**

BARRAGEM DO CASTELO DE BODE Estalagem Lago Azul   🔢📶👤📶📱 €€€

Castanheira, Ferreira do Zêzere, 2240-132 **Tel** *249 361 445* **Fax** *249 361 664* **Rooms** *20*   **Road map** *C4*

The rooms of this *estalagem* are tidy and functional and some have their own balconies that peer over an enormous lake formed by the dam of Castelo de Bode. The lakeside setting is spectacular and affords opportunities for sailing and boating. There are tennis courts within the hotel grounds. **lagoazul@hoteldostemplarios.pt**

BATALHA Estalagem do Mestre Afonso Domingues   🔢📶📱 €€€

Largo do Mestre A. Domingues 6, 2440-102 **Tel** *244 765 260* **Fax** *244 765 247* **Rooms** *22*   **Road map** *C4*

Modern in design but discreet in appearance, this *estalagem* stands next to the town's impressive abbey, declared a UNESCO World Heritage Site. The inn owes its name to the Portuguese architect who became renowned as the original designer of the 14th-century monument. The hotel's tidy rooms are traditionally furnished. **www.mestreafonso.com**

CALDAS DA RAINHA Caldas Internacional €€

Rua Dr Figueirôa Rego 45, 2500-186 **Tel** *262 830 500* **Fax** *262 844 482* **Rooms** *83* **Road map** *B4*

Patterned floor tiles in the reception area welcome the visitor to this efficient and modern hotel. Popular with business travellers, Caldas offers rooms for seminars, conferences and meetings. Recreational facilities include a swimming pool, jacuzzi, gym and sauna. The region is rich in vibrant scenery. **www.caldasinternacionalhotel.com**

CONSTÂNCIA Quinta de Santa Bárbara €€

Constância, 2250-092 **Tel** *249 739 214* **Fax** *249 739 373* **Rooms** *8* **Road map** *C4*

A fine 18th-century manor house with Gothic stone-vaulted refectory, the Quinta de Santa Bárbara has been converted into a distinguished inn, with cosy, rustic rooms. The furnishings are original and there is a real sense of history. Cooked breakfast is served in the principal salon, noted for its highly decorative ceiling. **www.quinta-santabarbara.com**

FÁTIMA Verbo Divino €

Praça João Paulo VI, 2495-908 **Tel** *249 533 043* **Fax** *249 532 263* **Rooms** *208* **Road map** *C4*

Built to guarantee a revenue for the Divine Word Missionaries, this is a large, simply decorated hotel for pilgrims to Fátima. The hotel has its own chapel available to guests for private worship. Verbo Divino is very busy during the pilgrimages in May and October, so booking ahead is advisable. **hotel.verbo.divino@verbodivino.pt**

FÁTIMA Dom Gonçalo Hotel & Spa €€

Rua Jacinto Marto 100, 2495-450 **Tel** *249 539 330* **Fax** *249 539 335* **Rooms** *71* **Road map** *C4*

A delightful *estalagem* set in peaceful, well-manicured gardens and verdant woods, yet still close to the sanctuary of Fátima. Dom Gonçalo is always full on the dates surrounding the twice-yearly pilgrimages, in May and October, so advance reservation is essential if you plan to visit during this period. **www.hoteldg.com**

GOLEGÃ Casa da Azinhaga €€

Rua da Misericórdia 26, 2150-021 **Tel** *249 957 146* **Fax** *249 957 182* **Rooms** *7* **Road map** *C4*

This classic 18th-century manor house belongs to the Marquês do Rio Maior and is set deep in the countryside 7 km (4 miles) south of Golegã, known for its annual horse fair. Remodelled in the 20th century, it retains its traditional rural character and offers comfortable rooms in a pleasant ambience. **casadaazinhaga@clix.pt**

LEIRIA Leiriense €

Rua Afonso Alburquerque 8, 2400-080 **Tel** *244 823 054* **Fax** *244 823 073* **Rooms** *24* **Road map** *C4*

This clean, welcoming and quite charming *residencial* is housed in a typical late 19th-century townhouse found tucked away in the narrow side streets of the old area of Leiria. The ensuite rooms are small and lightly furnished but are equipped with TV. Those facing the front have their own balconies.

LEIRIA Eurosol Residence €€

Rua Comissão da Iniciativa 13, 2410-098 **Tel** *244 860 460* **Fax** *244 860 469* **Rooms** *58* **Road map** *C4*

Conveniently located in the centre of town, the Eurosol Residence offers clean, modern and tastefully decorated studios and apartments, each with kitchenette, cable TV and many other mod cons. The outdoor pool is a rare treat for a downtown hotel in this part of Portugal, and there is also a health club with gym and sauna. **www.eurosol.pt**

NAZARÉ Albergaria Mar Bravo €€€

Praça Sousa Oliveira 71, 2450-159 **Tel** *262 569 160* **Fax** *262 569 169* **Rooms** *16* **Road map** *C4*

Situated on a tidy square off Nazaré's esplanade just 10 m (6 ft) from the beach, this popular *albergaria* has been welcoming guests for over 50 years. The tidy and well-appointed rooms all have balconies with panoramic views over the picturesque town and the sea. Book one on the top floor. **www.marbravo.com**

ÓBIDOS Rainha Santa Isabel €€

Rua Direita 61, 2510-010 **Tel** *262 959 323* **Fax** *262 959 115* **Rooms** *20* **Road map** *B4*

Overlooking a cobblestoned, pedestrianized street and enclosed within the ancient castle walls of this pretty town, this handsome *albergaria* has attractive wood-panelled rooms with lovely *azulejo* tiles. The cosy, lived-in feel is accentuated by armchairs, generously lined with padded leather, and an old stone fireplace in the sitting room. **www.arsio.com**

ÓBIDOS Estalagem do Convento €€€

Rua D João de Ornelas, 2510-074 **Tel** *262 959 214* **Fax** *262 959 159* **Rooms** *30* **Road map** *B4*

Housed in a former 19th-century convent, the rooms of this tastefully converted and wonderfully atmospheric *estalagem*, known locally as the Cloisters Inn, are traditionally and elegantly furnished but come with clean, modern and comfortable facilities. The suites have marvellous castle and garden views. **www.estalagemdoconvento.com**

ÓBIDOS Praia D'El Rey Marriot €€€€

Avenida Dona Inês de Castro 1, 2510-451 **Tel** *262 905 100* **Fax** *262 905 101* **Rooms** *179* **Road map** *B4*

The first 5-star luxury resort in western Portugal, this hotel overlooks a beautifully stark and unspoiled coastline and is equidistant between Óbidos and Peniche. Its 18-hole, par 72 championship golf course is considered one of the finest in Europe, and the acclaimed spa one of the best in the country. **www.marriottpraiadelrey.com**

ÓBIDOS Pousada do Castelo €€€€€

Paço Real, 2510-999 **Tel** *262 955 080* **Fax** *262 959 148* **Rooms** *9* **Road map** *B4*

The novelist Graham Greene stayed at this stunning *pousada*, converted from a 15th-century royal castle. Of striking architectural interest is the Noble's Gallery that overlooks the palace. It features two Manueline windows and a doorway with an ornate lintel moulded into intertwining tree trunks. Book early, as it is very popular. **www.pousadas.pt**

OURÉM Pousada Conde de Ourém

🏢 🏊 👥 🏢 P €€€€

Largo João Manso Castelos, 2490-481 **Tel** *249 540 920* **Fax** *249 542 955* **Rooms** *30* **Road map** *C4*

An unusual *pousada* set in a restored cluster of medieval houses within the walled town of Ourém, northeast of the sanctuary at Fátima. During excavations, builders discovered that two of the buildings were connected by an underground tunnel. The oldest part of the property used to be a small hospital. **www.pousadas.pt**

PENICHE Casa do Castelo

🏊 P €€

Estrada Nacional 114, No16, Atouguia da Baleia, 2525-025 **Tel** *262 750 647* **Fax** *262 750 937* **Rooms** *7* **Map** *B4*

Situated inland from Peniche and built on the ruins of a Moorish castle, the rooms of this extended 17th-century manor house are named after their decoration – the Red Room and the Green Room, whose windows open out into the garden, and Fleur, Boat and Star, all housed in the annexe. **www.solaresdeportugal.pt**

SANTARÉM Residencial Vitória

🖥 🏢 €

Rua 2° Visconde de Santarém 21, 2000-197 **Tel** *243 309 130* **Fax** *243 328 202* **Rooms** *20* **Road map** *C4*

A modest *pensão* whose façade is decorated in a smart combination of beige and white, Vitória is handy for Santarém's main sights and is open year round. The small, tidy rooms are spotless and welcoming and are equipped with satellite TV and telephone. A laundry service is provided by the owners.

SÃO MARTINHO DO PORTO Americana

🖥 🏢 €

Rua Dom José de Saldanha 2, 2460-645 **Tel** *262 989 1/0* **Fax** *262 989 349* **Rooms** *22* **Road map** *B4*

Conveniently located close to the sandy, sheltered beach popular with families, this friendly *pensão* offers pleasant rooms, six of which have air conditioning. A TV lounge provides the entertainment. There is a safe for depositing valuables. The waters off the coast are placid but can be chilly.

SÃO PEDRO DE MOEL Mar e Sol

🖥 🏢 🏢 P 🏢 €€

Avenida da Liberdade 1, 2430-501 **Tel** *244 590 000* **Fax** *244 590 019* **Rooms** *63* **Road map** *C4*

This neat and unpretentious hotel won't win any points for interior decor, but is a clear winner with its sea views. Set right beside the ocean and a spectacular beach, some of the rooms at Mar e Sol have private balconies. Friendly service makes this a very popular summer choice. **www.hotelmaresol.com**

TOMAR Hotel dos Templários

🖥 🏢 🏊 🏢 🏢 P 🏢 €€€

Largo Cândido dos Reis 1, 2304-909 **Tel** *249 310 100* **Fax** *249 322 191* **Rooms** *176* **Road map** *C4*

Surrounded by lush gardens and enjoying a privileged position in the city centre close to Tomar's historical zone, some of the rooms at this comfortable, four-star property look over the River Nabão. The hotel offers extensive sports and leisure facilities that include tennis courts, a gym and a health club. **www.hoteldostemplarios.com**

TOMAR Santa Iria

🏢 P €€€

Parque do Mouchão, 2300-536 **Tel** *249 313 326* **Fax** *249 321 238* **Rooms** *14* **Road map** *C4*

Wonderfully situated on an island park on the River Nabão, this discreetly elegant *estalagem* resembles a country hotel and yet is near many of the city's sights. With wood-panelled furniture, floors and ceilings, Santa Iria has an understated rural air about, though parts of the interior are Classical in style. **www.estalagemsantairia.com**

VILA FRANCA DE XIRA Lezíria Parque

🖥 🏢 🏢 P 🏢 €€

Estrada Nacional 1, Povos, 2600-246 **Tel** *263 276 670* **Fax** *263 276 990* **Rooms** *71* **Road map** *C5*

Despite its proximity to the busy A1 Lisbon-Oporto motorway, this modern, functional hotel offers quiet, tastefully decorated rooms and pleasant views over the River Tagus. The reception desk has information about jeep rides and boat cruises along the wetlands, as well as hikes and gastronomic and wine-tasting events. **www.leziriaparquehotel.pt**

THE BEIRAS

ALMEIDA Morgado

🖥 🏢 P €

Bairro de São Pedro, 6350-210 **Tel** *271 574 412* **Fax** *271 574 412* **Rooms** *12* **Road map** *E2*

Found just outside the walls of the fortress at Almeida, this modern *pensão* is clean and comfortable and offers very good value. The tidy, first floor rooms are well furnished and all have private bathroom facilities and TV installed, and the price includes a good breakfast. The friendly landlady doesn't speak English.

ALMEIDA Pousada da Senhora das Neves

🖥 🏢 🏢 P 🏢 €€€€

Rua da Muralha, 6350-112 **Tel** *271 574 283* **Fax** *271 574 320* **Rooms** *21* **Road map** *E2*

The clean, uninterrupted lines of this futuristic *pousada* contrast with the traditional terräced cottages that neighbour the property and the granite, star-shaped fortifications that enclose the town. Inside, the rooms are pleasantly furnished, some with four-poster beds. The lounge is warmed by an impressive open fireplace. **www.pousadas.pt**

AVEIRO Arcada

🖥 🏢 €€

Rua Viana do Castelo 4, 3800-275 **Tel** *234 421 885* **Fax** *234 421 886* **Rooms** *49* **Road map** *C3*

The city's landmark hotel property, Arcada is located in a Neo-Classical arcaded building overlooking the central canal and the quay, where the traditional seaweed-collecting *moliceiros* (boats) are moored. Full of character and elegance, with modern comforts, some rooms are especially attractive with ornate inlay headboards. **www.hotelarcada.com**

Key to Price Guide *see p382* **Key to Symbols** *see back cover flap*

AVEIRO Mercure Aveiro ⬚⬚⬚⬚ €€

Rua Luís Gomes Cravalho 23, 3800-211 **Tel** *234 404 400* **Fax** *234 404 401* **Rooms** *49* **Road map** *C3*

At first glance the exterior of this modern, centrally located hotel is reminiscent of a private mansion, replete with turret top, swaying palm tree and charming garden. Inside, the public areas are decorated in rich burgundy tones and the central staircase is lined with patterned *azulejo* tiles and stained-glass windows. **www.mercure.com**

AVEIRO Pousada da Ria ⬚⬚⬚⬚ €€€€

Bico do Muranzel, Torreira, 3870-301 **Tel** *234 860 180* **Fax** *234 838 333* **Rooms** *19* **Road map** *C3*

This modern *pousada* has an envious location on the banks of the River Aveiro. Most of the rooms have balconies overlooking the lagoon where the local painted boats *(moliceiros)* ply the peaceful waters. The interior is light and bright with floor-to-ceiling windows and a lot of pastel-hued wicker furniture. **www.pousadas.pt**

BUÇACO Palace Hotel Bussaco ⬚⬚⬚ €€€€

Buçaco, 3050-261 **Tel** *231 937 970* **Fax** *231 930 509* **Rooms** *64* **Road map** *C3*

This extraordinary late 19th-century neo-Manueline hotel, set in a luxuriant forest, was designed by Italian architect Luigi Manini and built as a hunting lodge for the last Portuguese kings. Its interior is richly decorated, with the palatial rooms featuring a range of period furniture, some with decorative *azulejo* tiles. **www.almeidahotels.com**

CARAMULO Estalagem do Caramulo ⬚⬚⬚⬚⬚ €€€

Avenida Dr Abel Lacerda, 3475-031 **Tel** *232 862 011* **Fax** *232 861 640* **Rooms** *12* **Road map** *C3*

This *estalagem* is set in the Serra do Caramulo and commands some stunning views of the surrounding countryside. The emphasis is on health and well-being and, apart from the fresh mountain air, guests can indulge in the hotel's modern spa facility where hot-stone massage is just one of the treatments available. **www.wrhotels.com**

CASTELO BRANCO Rainha Dona Amélia ⬚⬚⬚⬚⬚ €€

Rua de Santiago 15, 6000-179 **Tel** *272 348 800* **Fax** *272 348 808* **Rooms** *64* **Road map** *D4*

An excellent central location, close to the historical sights, makes this hotel an ideal choice for both tourists and business executives. The smart interior is styled in a functional manner and the rooms are spacious and well equipped with modern conveniences. Conferences and banquets are often hosted here. **www.hotelrainhadamelia.pt**

CASTRO D'AIRE Montemuro ⬚⬚⬚⬚⬚ €

Termas do Carvalhal, 3600-398 **Tel** *232 381 154* **Fax** *232 381 112* **Rooms** *80* **Road map** *D2*

Located in the mountains between Viseu and the Douro, Montemuro benefits from its privileged position in the heart of the Beira Alta. A modern property with well-appointed rooms and guest facilities, the hotel can arrange rafting and canoeing expeditions on the nearby River Paiva, as well as other outdoor activities. **www.montemuro.com**

CELORICO DA BEIRA Mira Serra ⬚⬚⬚⬚⬚⬚ €€

Bairro de Santa Eufémia, 6360-323 **Tel** *271 742 604* **Fax** *271 741 382* **Rooms** *42* **Road map** *D3*

As the name Mira Serra suggests, this smart, attractive hotel has stunning views of the Serra da Estrela mountain range – a rich cultural environment that contains historic castles, primitive chapels and ancient churches. Rooms are comfortable and guest facilities include a pleasant rear garden. Parking at a fee. **www.hmiraserra.com.pt**

COIMBRA Internacional ⬚⬚ €

Avenida Emidio Navarro 4, 3000-150 **Tel** *239 825 503* **Fax** *239 838 446* **Rooms** *27* **Road map** *C3*

Conveniently located close to the railway station, and overlooking the River Mondego, this welcoming but basic *pensão* occupies a once-grand 1840s building that became a hotel in 1945. The tiny rooms all have well-maintained bathrooms with showers. Service is functional but polite. **www.residencialinternacional.com**

COIMBRA Bragança ⬚⬚ €€

Largo das Ameias 10, 3000-024 **Tel** *239 822 171* **Fax** *239 836 135* **Rooms** *83* **Road map** *C3*

Don't be deterred by Bragança's office-block looks and old-fashioned character; the hotel boasts comfortable rooms and a great location in the heart of Coimbra. The polished marble in the lobby can also be found decorating the suites. The restaurant offers traditional Portuguese cuisine in pleasant surroundings. **www.hotel-braganca.com**

COIMBRA Astória ⬚⬚⬚⬚ €€€

Avenida Emidio Navarro 21, 3000-150 **Tel** *239 853 020* **Fax** *239 822 057* **Rooms** *62* **Road map** *C3*

One of Coimbra's best-known hotels, the Astória has preserved its Art Deco heritage and 1920s ambience while modernizing its extensive facilities. Stylish rooms offer fine views across the River Mondego, especially those in the turret façade. The first-class restaurant L'Amphitryon features the original orchestra gallery. **www.almeidahotels.com**

COIMBRA Quinta das Lágrimas ⬚⬚⬚⬚⬚ €€€€

Rua António Augusto Gonçalves, 3041-901 **Tel** *239 802 380* **Fax** *239 441 695* **Rooms** *52* **Road map** *C3*

The renowned Quinta das Lágrimas offers three accommodation options: the palace, the garden, and spa guest rooms. The beautiful 18th-century manor house, forever associated with lovers Pedro and Inês, is complemented by a modern hotel wing with guest rooms and a luxury spa. The restaurant is Michelin starred. **www.quintadaslagrimas.pt**

CONDEIXA-A-NOVA Pousada de Santa Cristina ⬚⬚⬚⬚⬚⬚ €€€€

Rua Francisco Lemos, 3150-142 **Tel** *239 944 025* **Fax** *239 943 097* **Rooms** *45* **Road map** *C3*

This modern but stately looking *pousada*, situated in its own gardens, began life as a 19th-century inn, and later operated as an orphanage and then a retirement home. Completely renovated and modernized, Santa Cristina is now a good base for visits to Coimbra and the impressive Roman ruins at Conímbriga. **www.pousadas.pt**

COVILHÃ Hotel Serra da Estrela

Penhas da Saúde, 6200-073 **Tel** *275 310 300* **Fax** *275 310 309* **Rooms** *51*   **Road map** *D3*

Set high in the Serra da Estrela, this modern hotel complex offers accommodation in the main building and in triangular bungalows. The standard of service is excellent and the hotel enjoys a high percentage of repeat custom. In December and January, if it snows, the winter sports programme is hugely popular. **www.turistrela.pt**

CURIA Curia Palace Hotel

Tamengos, 3780-541 **Tel** *231 510 300* **Fax** *231 515 531* **Rooms** *100*   **Road map** *C3*

The elegant Art Nouveau Curia Palace has numerous glamourous features that include a party and banqueting hall and an Art Deco swimming pool. The surrounding parkland has been reorganized, which means there is now direct access to the hotel's very own golf course. **www.almeidahotels.com**

FIGUEIRA DA FOZ Casa da Azenha Velha

Caceira de Cima, 3080-399 **Tel** *233 425 041* **Fax** *233 429 704* **Rooms** *6*   **Road map** *C3*

This Turismo Rural property used to be an old mill and is part of a large estate where horses, deer and wild boar are now reared. The large rooms are simply decorated and have decorative flourishes above the doors. The owners are always happy to impart the building's fascinating history.

FIGUEIRA DA FOZ Hotel Costa de Prata

Largo Coronel Galhardo 1, 3080-159 **Tel** *233 426 620* **Fax** *233 426 610* **Rooms** *68*   **Road map** *C3*

The modern façade of Costa de Prata looms large over the town's Esplanada Silva Guimarães and the beach and ocean beyond. The hotel is brightly decorated throughout and has a top-floor bar and breakfast room with a lofty panorama. Rooms at the rear enjoy town, river and hill views. **www.costadeprata.com**

GUARDA Solar de Alarcão

Rua Dom Miguel de Alarcão 25-27, 6300-684 **Tel** *271 211 275* **Fax** *271 214 392* **Rooms** *3*   **Road map** *D3*

This grand-looking *turismo de habitação* property occupies a weather-worn granite manor house built in 1686. The noble building has an upper colonnaded balcony and a private chapel with its own bell. The interior is crammed with antiques and the three double guest bedrooms all have private bathroom facilities.

LUSO Astória

Rua Emidio Navarro, 3050-224 **Tel** *231 939 182* **Rooms** *8*   **Road map** *C3*

This small *pensão* is a delight. Housed in a narrow, gabled-ended property on a main road, the rooms are furnished simply but exude their own charm and are comfortable, clean and safe. The bar has a friendly, down-to-earth atmosphere where, if it is busy, several languages can sometimes be heard at once.

LUSO Grande Hotel

Rua Dr Cid de Oliveira 86, 3050-210 **Tel** *231 937 937* **Fax** *231 937 930* **Rooms** *144*   **Road map** *C3*

Built on the slopes of the Buçaco hills and dominating the skyline of this attractive spa town, this large, elegant hotel welcomes families. A kid's club has been set up so parents can relax while their offspring explore. There is also a children's playground. The hotel has access to the spa. **www.hoteluso.com**

MANGUALDE Casa d'Azurara

Rua Nova 78, 3530-215 **Tel** *232 612 010* **Fax** *232 622 575* **Rooms** *15*   **Road map** *D3*

Originally built in the 18th century for the Dukes of Mangualde, this beautiful *estalagem* is a swish place to unwind and experience traditional Portuguese hospitality. Each room is individually decorated, with many original features. The building is set in attractive gardens. **www.azurara.com**

MANTEIGAS Pousada de São Lourenço

Penhas Douradas, 6260-200 **Tel** *275 980 050* **Fax** *275 982 453* **Rooms** *21*   **Road map** *D3*

A roaring log fire welcomes visitors to this traditional granite *pousada* set high in the Serra da Estrela. The well-appointed property enjoys a magnificent view over the River Zêzere valley and is ideal for hill walkers or hikers seeking a secluded retreat. The interior is replete in an attractive wood finish. **www.pousadas.pt**

MANTEIGAS Pousada do Convento de Belmonte

Belmonte, 6250-073 **Tel** *275 910 300* **Fax** *275 912 060* **Rooms** *24*   **Road map** *D3*

A property of great historical interest, this *pousada* was born out of the ruins of a 13th-century convent and has preserved the architectural features of the original building, including an amphitheatre in the woodlands. The modern, well-equipped rooms, some with four-poster beds, are positioned around the convent courtyard. **www.pousadas.pt**

MONSANTO Estalagem de Monsanto

Rua da Capela 3, 6060-091 **Tel** *277 314 471* **Fax** *277 314 481* **Rooms** *10*   **Road map** *D3*

Monsanto is one of Europe's oldest and most enchanting villages, where the tiny hillside houses are squeezed between giant granite boulders. This wonderful *estalagem* has successfully created a balance between traditional style and modern comfort. The attractive lobby features rotating exhibitions. **www.monsanto.homestead.com**

SABUGUEIRO Casas do Cruzeiro

Turismo de Aldeia, Seia, 6270-151 **Tel** *238 312 825* **Fax** *238 315 282* **Rooms** *32*   **Road map** *D3*

If getting away from it all is the idea, then the granite cottages of the Casas do Cruzeiro are perfect. Tucked away in Sabugeiro, the highest village in Portugal located in a Serra da Estrela valley, the houses offer simple apartments with kitchenette and fireplace. The rest is up to you. **www.quintadocrestelo.pt**

Key to Price Guide *see p382* **Key to Symbols** *see back cover flap*

VISEU Quinta de São Caetano   🏔️ 🅿️   €€

Rua da Poça das Feiticeiras 38, 3500-639 **Tel** *232 423 984* **Fax** *232 437 827* **Rooms** *6*   **Road map** *D3*

A distinguished 17th-century manor house set in quiet Viseu suburb, the ground-floor rooms of this venerable property have granite walls a meter thick. The philosophy here is that people arrive as guests and leave as friends, and the visitors' book reads of nothing but praise. The breakfast is colossal. **www.solaresdeportugal.pt**

VISEU Hotel Montebelo   🔳 🍴 🏔️ 📺 🗐 🅿️ ♿   €€€

Urbanização Quinta do Bosque, 3510-020 **Tel** *232 420 000* **Fax** *232 415 400* **Rooms** *172*   **Road map** *D3*

All steel and glass, this modern and well-equipped business hotel also has good facilities for tourists. It is particularly noted for its spa where guests can enjoy a number of treatments and therapies, including Turkish bath, sauna and massage. For those attracted to the outdoors, there's nearby horse-riding and golf. **www.hotelmontebelo.pt**

DOURO AND TRÁS-OS-MONTES

ALIJÓ Pousada de Barão do Forrester   🍴 🏔️ 🗐 🅿️   €€€€

Rua José Rufino, 5070-031 **Tel** *259 959 215* **Fax** *259 959 304* **Rooms** *21*   **Road map** *D2*

This grand, handsome-looking *pousada* is in the heart of port wine country and was named after the Englishman, James Forrester (1809–62), an advocate of pure wine *(see p252)*. The proximity of the Douro river is perfect for guests wanting to take a sightseeing cruise through one of the world's great wine-growing regions. **www.pousadas.pt**

AMARANTE Albergaria Dona Margaritta   🗐 🔳 🏔️ 🗐   €

Rua Cândido dos Reis 53, 4600-055 **Tel** *255 432 110* **Fax** *255 437 977* **Rooms** *22*   **Road map** *D2*

Advance booking is always necessary if you want to secure a riverside room at this splendid *albergaria*. Built in the early 20th century, the hotel is still family-run and has undergone extensive renovation. Its city-centre location makes it a perfect base to explore Amarante's wealth of attractions. **www.albergariadonamargaritta.pa-net.pt**

AMARANTE Pousada de São Gonçalo   🍴 🧍 🗐 🅿️ ♿   €€€

Serra do Marão-Ansiães, 4604-909, 2604-909 **Tel** *255 460 030* **Fax** *255 461 353* **Rooms** *15*   **Road map** *D2*

Embedded in the Marão mountain range and surrounded by tranquil pine forests, the unusual semi-circular shape of this friendly *pousada* affords a spectacular panorama of the Tâmega valley. Indeed, three of the rooms have balconies with views. Built in schist back in 1942, this was the second *pousada* to be opened. **www.pousadas.pt**

BRAGANÇA Classis   🔳 🗐 🅿️ ♿   €

Avenida João da Cruz 102, 5300-178 **Tel** *273 331 631* **Fax** *273 323 458* **Rooms** *20*   **Road map** *E1*

A pleasant, modern residential just a short walk from Bragança's historic city centre. The receptionist is friendly and helpful, happy to supply guests with a map highlighting the main tourist attractions. Rooms are comfortably furnished and the bathrooms well-maintained. The busy road is almost devoid of night time traffic.

BRAGANÇA Moinho do Caniço   🗐 🧍 🅿️   €€€

Ponte de Castrelos, 5340-219 **Tel & Fax** *273 323 577* **Rooms** *2*   **Road map** *E1*

This old water mill on the banks of the Baceiro offers the ultimate in tranquillity and solitude. Self-catering is the order of the day, though there is a restaurant just down the road. The living room has a fireplace and there is even a wine cellar. In summer, guests can make use of the outdoor barbecue area **www.montesinho.com/moinho**

BRAGANÇA Pousada de São Bartolomeu   🔳 🍴 🏔️ 🧍 🗐 🅿️   €€€€

Estrada do Turismo, 5300-271 **Tel** *273 331 493* **Fax** *273 323 453* **Rooms** *28*   **Road map** *E1*

Commanding a splendid panoramic view of the city of Bragança, from its location on top of a hill in the Nogueira mountain range, this *pousada's* interior features wooden furniture and stone walls, some of them incorporating abstract *azulejo* (tile) artwork. The rustic atmosphere is further enhanced by an inviting open fire. **www.pousadas.pt**

CHAVES Aquae Flaviae   🔳 🍴 🏔️ 🧍 📺 🗐 🅿️   €€

Praça do Brasil, 5400-123 **Tel** *276 309 000* **Fax** *276 309 010* **Rooms** *167*   **Road map** *D1*

An impressive hotel that dominates the skyline of Chaves, the modern and functional Aquae Flaviae is a favourite business meeting venue with its state-of-the art conference facilities. Tourists, though, are equally at home and can indulge in a comprehensive array of leisure options that include a health and beauty centre. **www.hoteis-arco.com**

CHAVES Hotel Forte de São Francisco   🔳 🍴 🏔️ 🗐 🅿️ ♿   €€€

Alto da Pedisqueira, 5400-435 **Tel** *276 333 700* **Fax** *276 333 701* **Rooms** *58*   **Road map** *D1*

Inaugurated in 1997 after a 10-year restoration project, this superb hotel is installed within the walls of a 17th-century fort and incorporates a convent from the same period, plus a 15th-century church. The blend of the historic with the contemporary is remarkable and makes a stay here truly memorable. **www.forte-s-francisco-hoteis.pt**

CINFÃES Casa de Rebolfe   🗐 🏔️ 🅿️   €€

Porto Antigo, 4690-423 **Tel** *228 313 482* **Fax** *255 562 334* **Rooms** *5*   **Road map** *D2*

Located east of Cinfães, near Porto Antigo, this 18th-century farmhouse, whose terraced hillsides extend to the banks of the River Douro, has been lovingly converted into a welcoming hotel. The interior reveals the property's noble origins in the carved stonework of the doorways, window frames and cornices. **www.casaderebolfe.com**

ESPINHO Praia Golfe

€€€€€

Rua 6, 4500-357 **Tel** *227 331 000* **Fax** *227 331 001* **Rooms** *133* **Road map** C2

With an appealing location right beside a wide, sandy beach, this modern and attractive hotel is a popular choice for summer stays, as well as a preferred conference venue during the off season. A year-round draw in the nearby casino; another is the hotel's restaurant with panoramic views. **www.praiagolfe.com**

LAMEGO Hotel Parque

€€

Parque Nossa Senhora dos Remédios, 5100-025 **Tel** *254 609 140* **Fax** *254 615 203* **Rooms** *60* **Road map** D2

Set in a grand whitewashed house next to the Santuário dos Remédios, this handsome property has a rather quaint interior and offers rustically decorated rooms overlooking a chestnut forest. The hotel is packed solid in the second week of September during the annual pilgrimage to the Baroque shrine, so book ahead. **www.hotel-parque.com**

LAMEGO Villa Hostilina

€€

Ortigosa, 5100-192 **Tel** *254 612 394* **Fax** *254 655 194* **Rooms** *7* **Road map** D2

Villa Hostilina is housed in a 19th-century farmhouse surrounded by grapevines and orchards. The charming, tranquil setting is reinforced by a pretty garden and a marvellous Douro valley landscape. Guests have the use of various sports and leisure facilities, including tennis courts and a well-equipped health club. **www.villahostilina.com**

MESÃO FRIO Casa d'Além

€€

Oliveira, Mesão Frio, 5040-204 **Tel** *254 321 991* **Fax** *254 321 991* **Rooms** *4* **Road map** D2

Originally a port wine-growing country estate dating from the 1920s, this family-run *quinta* is part of a rural canvas that includes terraced grapevines and a network of hiking trails that the owners can point out to visitors. The attractive interiors still retain their original decor, which lends the property a timeless air. **www.casadalem.pt**

MESÃO FRIO Pousada do Solar da Rede

€€€€€

Santa Cristina, Mesão Frio, 5040-336 **Tel** *254 890 130* **Fax** *254 890 139* **Rooms** *29* **Road map** D2

Set in an 18th-century manor house and furnished in sumptuous period style, the rooms of this noble *pousada* are individually decorated and contain beds that match the architectural grandeur of the property. The hall and staircase are fashioned out of grey-blue granite. Incorporated into the grounds are 25 hectares of vineyards. **www.pousadas.pt**

OPORTO Malaposta

€

Rua da Conceição 80, 4050-214 **Tel** *222 006 278* **Fax** *222 006 295* **Rooms** *37* **Road map** C2

Tucked away on a quiet side street, the attractive and modern Malaposta is a friendly, good-value hotel and benefits from its city-centre location. Within walking distance are some of Oporto's best-known historical monuments. Guests can use the nearby car park, free from 8pm–8am, and on weekends and bank holidays. **www.hotelmalaposta.com**

OPORTO Nave

€

Avenida Fernão de Magalhães 247, 4300-190 **Tel** *225 899 030* **Fax** *225 899 039* **Rooms** *81* **Road map** C2

Suitable either for business or pleasure, this excellent-value hotel is conveniently situated ten minutes walk from the centre of town. The modern facilities are what you would expect for a mid-range property, with comfortable and well-appointed rooms and a pleasant bar for an early evening drink. **www.hotelnave.com**

OPORTO Pensão Paris

€

Rua da Fábrica 27, 4050-247 **Tel** *222 073 140* **Fax** *222 073 149* **Rooms** *42* **Road map** C2

A characterful old-world hotel located in the Baixa area, whose atmosphere, location and price more than compensate for the fairly basic standard. Breakfast is taken in the drawing room, and guests can browse a small library or relax over a drink in the "Heritage Pub". There's even a small rear garden. **www.ghparis.pt**

OPORTO São José

€

Rua da Alegria 172, 4000-034 **Tel** *222 076 860* **Fax** *223 320 446* **Rooms** *43* **Road map** C3

This late 1960s establishment is one of several hotels in this bustling street. A polite and efficient service, together with a pleasant style and ambience, maintains its popularity among competitors. The rooms are comfortable, with satellite TV and direct dial telephone. There are also welcome parking facilities. **www.saojosehotelporto.com**

OPORTO Hotel da Bolsa

€€

Rua Ferreira Borges 101, 4050-253 **Tel** *222 026 768* **Fax** *222 058 888* **Rooms** *36* **Road map** C2

The "Stock Exchange" hotel has an interesting façade decorated with flourishing stonework above the upper-floor windows. The interior is not so unique, but rooms are nevertheless tidy and well appointed. The location is convenient for shopping and tourist sights. **www.hoteldabolsa.com**

OPORTO Internacional

€€

Rua do Almada 131, 4050-037 **Tel** *222 005 032* **Fax** *222 009 063* **Rooms** *35* **Road map** C3

This hotel fuses a curious but pleasing combination of Baroque and modern architecture in the reception rooms, a feature it has maintained despite a stylish makeover. The building is over 100 years old and is of considerable historical significance, situated as it is within the city's UNESCO World Heritage Site. **www.hi-porto.com**

OPORTO Pensão dos Aliados

€€

Rua Elísio de Melo 27, 4000-196 **Tel** *222 004 853* **Fax** *222 002 710* **Rooms** *38* **Road map** C3

Occupying the whole interior of an impressive building recognized as one of the city's great landmarks, this excellent *pensão* is a popular choice. Many of the rooms have private balconies that afford inspiring views of busy Avenida dos Aliados and Oporto's grandiose Câmara Municipal building. **www.residencialaliados.com**

Key to Price Guide *see p382* **Key to Symbols** *see back cover flap*

OPORTO Boa-Vista

🖼 🍴 🛏 🅿 €€€

Esplanada do Castelo 58, 4150-196 **Tel** *225 320 020* **Fax** *226 173 818* **Rooms** *71*   **Road map** *C2*

The attractive, fourth-floor terrace swimming pool is reason enough to stay at Boa-Vista, located on the right bank of the mouth of the Douro. The panorama back across the ocean is wonderful and the same view can be enjoyed from most of the rooms at this modern and comfortable hotel. **www.hotelboavista.com**

OPORTO Dom Henrique

🖼 🍴 🛏 €€€

Rua Guedes de Azevedo 179, 4049-009 **Tel** *223 401 616* **Fax** *223 401 666* **Rooms** *112*   **Road map** *C3*

A 1970s architectural icon, Dom Henrique is located right in the heart of the city and has 17 floors – two designated non-smoking – and a bar with a superb panoramic view. A metro station lies in the hotel's shadow and Oporto's main shopping area is within easy walking distance. **www.hoteldomhenrique.pt**

OPORTO Quinta da Granja

🛏 🅿 €€€

Rua Manuel Francisco Araújo 444, Maia, 4425-120 **Tel** *229 710 147* **Fax** *229 710 147* **Rooms** *5*   **Road map** *C3*

Five km (3 miles) from the city centre in the suburb of Maia, this quiet hotel is housed in a grand granite 18th-century manor house, blessed with a beautiful garden. The rooms are simple but elegant and decorated with antiques and high quality furnishings. Two night minimum stay; closed Nov–March.

OPORTO Infante de Sagres

🖼 🍴 🛏 €€€€

Praça D Filipa de Lencastre 62, 4050-259 **Tel** *223 398 500* **Fax** *223 398 599* **Rooms** *70*   **Road map** *C3*

This is a beautifully appointed city-centre hotel with public rooms full of rare antiques such as 17th-century Chinese porcelain and 19th-century French paintings. The refined and sophisticated atmosphere, together with bedrooms that offer everything for the discerning traveller, means reservations are essential. **www.hotelinfantesagres.pt**

OPORTO Pestana Porto

🖼 🍴 🛏 €€€€

Praça da Ribeira 1, 4050-513 **Tel** *223 402 300* **Fax** *223 402 400* **Rooms** *48*   **Road map** *C3*

One of the most desirable hotels in the city, this charming boutique property is located on the Praça da Ribeira, in a block of carefully restored riverfront buildings. The rooms are contemporary in style and fashionable in taste and offer gracious living and fabulous views. The romantic setting makes advance booking advisable. **www.pestana.com**

OPORTO Porto Palácio

🖼 🍴 ♨ 📺 🛏 🅿 ♿ €€€€

Avenida da Boavista 1269, 4100-130 **Tel** *226 086 600* **Fax** *226 091 467* **Rooms** *251*   **Road map** *C3*

This elegant hotel, situated in an affluent suburb of Oporto, is short drive away from the beach and the historical city centre. It offers an array of modern facilities, including a comprehensive health club and gymnasium and an "Executive Lounge", accessed by private elevator and reserved for business executives. **www.hotelportopalacio.com**

OPORTO Sheraton Porto Hotel & Spa

🖼 ♿ 🍴 ♨ 📺 🛏 🅿 €€€€

Rua Tenente Valadim 146, 4100-476 **Tel** *220 404 000* **Fax** *220 404 199* **Rooms** *266*   **Road map** *C3*

This modern hotel in the heart of the city uses materials such as marble, steel, wood and glass to create an elegant and comfortable ambience. Among its many amenities are a unique spa and wellness centre, pool, fitness room and cocktail lounge. The Porto Novo restaurant is considered one of the best in the city. **www.sheraton.com/porto**

PESO DA RÉGUA Hotel Régua Douro

🖼 🍴 ♨ 🛏 🅿 €€€

Largo da Estação da CP, 5050-237 **Tel** *254 320 700* **Fax** *254 320 709* **Rooms** *77*   **Road map** *D2*

An impressive, tiled mosaic depicting people working the land greets visitors at the entrance to Regua's largest hotel. Smart, functional and more geared towards business travellers than tourists, the hotel offers the city's best facilities plus a good view of the river. A good base for exploring the region. **www.hotelreguadouro.pt**

PINHÃO Quinta de la Rosa

🛏 🅿 €€

Pinhão, 5085-215 **Tel** *254 732 254* **Fax** *254 732 346* **Rooms** *7*   **Road map** *D2*

The portraits on the walls inside this delightful farmhouse trace the owners' family history back to 1715, when their ancestors first arrived in Portugal to take part in the port wine trade. Today, guests can sample first-class hospitality as well as fine vintages. There are rooms and cottages to rent. **www.quintadelarosa.com**

PINHÃO CS Vintage House Hotel

🍴 ♨ 🛏 🅿 €€€€

Lugar da Ponte, Pinhão, 5085-034 **Tel** *254 730 230* **Fax** *254 730 238* **Rooms** *43*   **Road map** *D2*

This elegant, luxurious hotel, located on the River Douro, is built on the site of an old port lodge and is surrounded by majestic vineyards. Rooms are individually decorated and each has a private balcony. The library bar serves some truly memorable wines and the restaurant some equally memorable cuisine. **www.cs-vintagehouse.com**

SABROSA Casa de Visconde de Chanceleiros

🍴 €€€

Largo da Fonte, 5085-201 **Tel** *254 730 190* **Fax** *254 730 199* **Rooms** *6*   **Road map** *D2*

Located 7 km (4 m) from Pinhão, this charming *Turismo de Habitação* occupies an 18th-century manor house and is imaginatively furnished to convey a rustic, homely flavour. Nowhere is this more evident than in the kitchen, where marvellous old copper utensils and ceramic pots and plates hang from stone walls. **www.chanceleiros.com**

TORRE DE MONCORVO Quinta das Aveleiras

♨ 🅿 €€€

Quinta das Aveleiras, 5160-206 **Tel & Fax** *279 258 280* **Rooms** *6*   **Road map** *E2*

Set amid woodland, terraced vines and olive groves, Quinta das Aveleiras is a sprawling estate on the edge of the Reboredo mountains. Accommodation is in carefully restored farm buildings; one of the suites is in a dovecote and another in an isolated schist house. Facilities include a tennis court and bicycle hire. **www.quintadasaveleiras.pt**

VIDAGO Vidago Palace Hotel
🔲 🍴 ♨ 🏋 🖥 🅿 €€€€€

Parque de Vidago, 5425-307 **Tel** *276 990 900* **Fax** *276 907 359* **Rooms** *83* **Road map** *D1*

This truly magnificent spa hotel impresses with its grandiose, neo-Romantic façade and stunning, charismatic interior décor – the inside staircase flanked by marble columns is beautiful and the bedrooms are simply charming. Due to reopen after renovation in 2010, phone to check. **www.vidagopalace.com**

VILA REAL Casa Agrícola da Levada
♨ 🏋 🅿 ⟁ €€

Timpeira, 5000-419 **Tel** *259 322 190* **Fax** *259 346 955* **Rooms** *9* **Road map** *D2*

Overlooking the River Corgo, this charming, 1920s family-run Art Deco house was designed by the Portuguese architect Raúl Lino, who also designed the chapel. Guests are really made to feel at home in the elegant rooms and can even take cookery lessons, or request a favourite dish from the kitchen. **www.casadelevada.com**

VILA REAL Mira Corgo
🔲 🍴 ♨ 🖥 🅿 ⟁ €€

Avenida 1° de Maio 78, 5000-651 **Tel** *259 325 001* **Fax** *259 325 006* **Rooms** *166* **Road map** *D2*

The modern Miracorgo's rather plain exterior is lifted considerably by the tastefully decorated interior with pleasant colour scheme. The public spaces are illustrated with the work of several well-known Portuguese artists. The hotel has superb views from the terrace of the deep ravine and river below. **www.hotelmiracorgo.com**

MINHO

BARCELOS Quinta de Santa Comba
📋 ♨ 🅿 €€

Lugar de Crujães, 4755-536 **Tel** *253 831 440* **Fax** *253 834 540* **Rooms** *6* **Road map** *C1*

This handsome and wonderfully atmospheric 18th-century residence once functioned as a country manor and the stone walls and wooden beams convey a rustic charm. Flourishing stonework characterizes much of the architecture, particularly on the neighbouring chapel's roof. Simply furnished, elegant rooms. **www.stacomba.com**

BOM JESUS DO MONTE Hotel do Elevador
🔲 🍴 🖥 🅿 €€€

Bom Jesus do Monte, 4710-455 **Tel** *253 603 400* **Fax** *253 603 409* **Rooms** *22* **Road map** *C1*

A luxurious and richly appointed hotel that derives its name from the 19th-century water-operated elevator that still takes visitors up to the Bom Jesus do Monte sanctuary. Comfortable rooms. The hotel fills quickly during Braga's Semana Santa (Holy Week) Easter celebrations so check ahead for availability. **www.hoteisbomjesus.pt**

BRAGA Comfort Inn Braga
🔲 🍴 🖥 🅿 ⟁ €

Estrada Nacional 14, Ferreiros, 4705-085 **Tel** *253 000 600* **Fax** *253 673 872* **Rooms** *70* **Road map** *C1*

Located a short distance from the city centre, and convenient for a quick stopover, this pleasant hotel offers all the usual amenities and every modern comfort and is idea for the tourist as well as the business traveller. Services include non-smoking rooms, a laundry service and a currency exchange facility. **www.choicehotelseurope.com**

BRAGA Dona Sofia
🔲 🖥 🅿 ⟁ €€

Largo São João do Souto 131, 4700-326 **Tel** *253 263 160* **Fax** *253 611 245* **Rooms** *34* **Road map** *C1*

Adjacent to a small square with a lovely fountain, the solid cream façade of this modern city-centre property is difficult to miss. It squats imposingly close to the landmark cathedral and the hotel is an ideal base from which to explore Braga's many churches, palaces, grand 18th-century houses and pretty gardens. **www.hoteldonasofia.com**

BRAGA Hotel Residencial da Estação
🔲 🍴 🖥 🅿 ⟁ €€

Largo da Estação 13, 4700-223 **Tel** *253 218 381* **Fax** *253 276 810* **Rooms** *51* **Road map** *C1*

A good economical standby, this modern 3-star hotel is located within a ten-minute walk of the town centre, opposite the railway station. The rooms are spacious and comfortably appointed, and some feature jacuzzi bathtubs. There is also one suite. The restaurant serves traditional Portuguese cuisine. **hoteldaestacao@htilthotels.com**

BRAGA Turismo de Braga
🔲 🍴 ♨ 🖥 🅿 €€

Praceta João XXI, 4715-036 **Tel** *253 206 000* **Fax** *253 206 010* **Rooms** *132* **Road map** *C1*

One of the region's largest hotels, the Turismo dominates a small square in the centre of town. The voluminous lobby is similar in size to the restaurant! The modern, comfortable rooms feature all the usual amenities and the 22 suites come with the added bonus of some splendid panoramic views. **www.hotelturismobraga.com**

CELORICO DE BASTO Casa do Campo
♨ 🅿 €€

Molares, 4890-414 **Tel & Fax** *255 361 231* **Rooms** *10* **Road map** *D1*

A granite gateway welcomes visitors to this early 18th-century country house, a greeting enriched by a pervading floral scent. Casa do Campo boasts a prize-winning garden, with immaculately trimmed camellias contoured into graceful designs. In fact, the grounds are said to contain Portugal's oldest camellia tree. **www.casadocampo.pt**

GUIMARÃES Casa de Sezim
♨ 🅿 €€

Santo Amaro, Nespereira, 4801-913 **Tel** *253 523 000* **Fax** *253 523 196* **Rooms** *6* **Road map** *C2*

The interior of this 18th-century manor house features a majestic ballroom, one wall of which is decorated by a detailed early 19th-century mural depicting country and coastal life. The property is built around an enclosed courtyard and furnished with fine antiques. The estate is a working vineyard and produces vinho verde. **www.sezim.pt**

GUIMARÃES Hotel de Guimarães 🔲🔢🏢🎦🗐🅿️ €€
Rua Eduardo Almeida, 4810-911 **Tel** *253 424 800* **Fax** *253 424 899* **Rooms** *116* **Road map** *C2*

A modern and stylish city-centre hotel decorated in purple, lilac and aquamarine hues was designed using a clever combination of wood and marble. The rooms are well equipped but pleasingly uncluttered. The hotel's draw is its spa, where guests can pamper themselves with a variety of therapies and treatments. **www.hotel-guimaraes.com**

GUIMARÃES Pousada de Nossa Senhora da Oliveira 🔲🗐🅿️ €€€€
Rua de Santa Maria, 4801-910 **Tel** *253 514 157* **Fax** *253 514 204* **Rooms** *16* **Road map** *C2*

This *pousada*, located in the old district of town, was once a distinguished aristocratic mansion and has been successfully transformed into an equally distinguished hotel. Inside, leather armchairs and antique paintings help preserve the original character of the house. The building overlooks a quiet square. **www.pousadas.pt**

GUIMARÃES Pousada de Santa Marinha 🔢🖾🛉🗐🅿️ €€€€€
Largo Domingos Leite Castro, 4810-011 **Tel** *253 511 249* **Fax** *253 514 459* **Rooms** *51* **Road map** *C2*

This marvellous building, once the 12th-century Santa Marinha da Costa monastery, has been carefully adapted to house this beautiful *pousada*. Original *azulejo* tiles adorn the sumptuous rooms. Dating from 1747, the tiles depict everyday life in Portugal. The gardens, too, are magnificent. **www.pousadas.pt**

PONTE DE LIMA Paço de Calheiros 🖾🅿️ €€€
Calheiros, 4990-575 **Tel** *258 947 164* **Fax** *258 947 294* **Rooms** *10* **Road map** *C1*

The flagship property in the *Turismo de Habitação* portfolio, this splendid Baroque manor house commands a scenic position on a hillside outside the town. Guests are made to feel welcome by the Count of Calheiros, who will proudly show you his 17th-century family home. Accommodation is in rooms or apartments. **www.solaresdeportugal.pt**

PÓVOA DE VARZIM Grande Hotel da Póvoa 🔲🔢🗐🅿️ €€
Largo Passeio Alegra 20, 4490-428 **Tel** *252 290 400* **Fax** *252 290 401* **Rooms** *86* **Road map** *C2*

Elegant in the contemporary sense of the word, this hotel is located in the centre of Póvoa de Varzim, right next to the casino and overlooking the beach. The interior is styled in soothing pastel hues, and a sense of calm pervades the building. The breakfast terrace provides an appetizing view. **www.grandehoteldapovoa.com**

VALENÇA DO MINHO Val Flores 🔲 €
Esplanade, 4930-768 **Tel** *251 824 106* **Fax** *251 824 129* **Rooms** *31* **Road map** *C1*

Located in the new part of town, outside the town's fortifications, this *residencial* is clean, functional and inexpensive. The rooms are sparsely furnished but comfortable and have TV. The bright interior is decorated in creams and blues and enriched by flourishing pot plants. Ideal for those travelling on a budget.

VALENÇA DO MINHO Albergaria Don Manuel 🔢🖾🗐🅿️ €€
Rua da Igreja 1, 4930-311 **Tel** *251 809 700* **Fax** *251 809 749* **Rooms** *32* **Road map** *C1*

Located on the edge of town, just 3 km (2 miles) from the Spanish border, this hotel is ideal for those touring the northern Minho region and neighbouring Galicia. The rooms are modern, and eight of the suites are equipped with hydro-massage bathtubs. There is also an outdoor pool and tennis court. **www.albergariadonmanuel.com**

VALENÇA DO MINHO Pousada de São Teotónio 🔢🖾🛉🗐 €€€€
Baluarte do Socorro, 4930-735 **Tel** *251 800 260* **Fax** *251 824 397* **Rooms** *18* **Road map** *C1*

The headboards of some of the beds in this small *pousada* are intricately carved and add character to the traditionally furnished rooms, 12 of which have enchanting views of the valley, across the peaceful River Minho to Tuy, in Spain. The hotel is set within weather-worn battlements of the town's fort. **www.pousadas.pt**

VIANA DO CASTELO Calatrava 🅿️ €
Rua Manuel Fiúza Júnior 157, 4900-458 **Tel** *258 828 911* **Fax** *258 828 637* **Rooms** *15* **Road map** *C1*

Located close to the old centre of Viana do Castelo, this friendly and welcoming *pensão* is neat and tidy and has old-fashioned decor. Copper plates decorate the wall over the lobby fireplace and the snug atmosphere extends to the comfortably furnished, spotless rooms. A good, economical choice. **calatrava_residencia@hotmail.com**

VIANA DO CASTELO Casa dos Costa Barros 🔲 €€
Rua de São Pedro 22-28, 4900-538 **Tel** *258 823 705* **Fax** *258 824 383* **Rooms** *8* **Road map** *C1*

This delightful house, which was constructed in the 16th century and has been owned by the same family since 1765, has handsome stone carvings over the outside windows that draw the eye into an elegant interior. The house is decorated with family heirlooms, period antiques and rare Ming dynasty vases. **www.casacostabarros.pt**

VIANA DO CASTELO Hotel Parque 🔲🖾🗐🅿️ €€€
Praça da Galiza, 4900-476 **Tel** *258 828 605* **Fax** *258 828 612* **Rooms** *124* **Road map** *C1*

Located just outside the old town near the River Lima, this welcoming hotel is set within attractive gardens and overlooks a large, inviting swimming pool. Most of the spacious, comfortable rooms have private balconies. The sixth-floor breakfast room has wonderful panoramic views. **www.hoteldoparque.com**

VIANA DO CASTELO Pousada Monte de Santa Luzia 🔲🔢🖾🛉🗐🅿️♿ €€€€
Monte de Santa Luzia, 4901-909 **Tel** *258 800 370* **Fax** *258 828 892* **Rooms** *51* **Road map** *C1*

This luxurious *pousada* began life in 1903, a gift to the town from Domingos José de Morais, a wealthy merchant who made his fortune in Brazil. Surrounded by eucalyptus and pines, it has a spectacular vantage point over Viana. Book well ahead if staying in August during the town's Romaria festivities. **www.pousadas.pt**

VIEIRA DO MINHO Pousada de São Bento   🍴🏊🚶📋🅿   €€€€

Caniçada, 4850-047 **Tel** *253 649 150* **Fax** *253 647 867* **Rooms** *29*   **Road map** *D1*

Set on the edge of the nature reserve of the Peneda-Gerês National Park, this comfortable, ivy-clad *pousada* has jaw-dropping views of the River Cávado valley. It was converted from a hunting lodge and is surrounded by a courtyard and a small garden. The modern interior retains a suitably rustic look. **www.pousadas.pt**

VILA DO CONDE Hotel Santana   📶🍴🏊📺📋🅿♿   €€€

Monte Santana, Azurara, 4480-160 **Tel** *252 640 460* **Fax** *252 642 693* **Rooms** *75*   **Road map** *C2*

This modern and comfortable hotel stands all on its own at a magnificent location overlooking the lush banks of the pretty River Ave. In fact, the view is a major selling point and can be admired from the many rooms with balconies. The hotel is within easy reach of Oporto airport. **www.santanahotel.net**

VILA NOVA DA CERVEIRA Pousada de Dom Dinis   🍴📋🅿   €€€€€

Largo do Terreiro, 4920-296 **Tel** *251 708 120* **Fax** *251 708 129* **Rooms** *29*   **Road map** *C1*

The rooms and suites at this historic *pousada* are situated in independent houses, some with small terraces, which are all part of the overall property. Built within the medieval castle at Vila Nova, the *pousada* blends in perfectly with the surrounding architecture. Wonderful views can be had from the castle walls. **www.pousadas.pt**

ALENTEJO

ALBERNÔA Herdade dos Grous   €€€

Albernôa, 7800-601 **Tel** *284 960 000* **Fax** *284 960 072* **Rooms** *24*   **Road map** *D6*

A splendid country estate located near Beja covering 1500 acres, the pretty rooms are surrounded by vineyards and afford wonderful views over a beautiful lake. The rustic flavour is carried through to the restaurant where food is prepared using organically grown ingredients. The wine is from the estate's own cellars. **www.herdadedosgrous.com**

ALVITO Pousada do Castelo de Alvito   🍴🏊📋♿   €€€€€

Castelo de Alvito, 7920-999 **Tel** *284 480 700* **Fax** *284 485 383* **Rooms** *20*   **Road map** *D6*

This elegant *pousada* is housed in a restored 15th-century, picture-postcard castle. The rooms are stylishly chic but retain their sense of history, and some of the beds are four-poster in design. The dining room features Gothic vaulting and there are Manueline details on the windows. Peacocks roam the tranquil gardens. **www.pousadas.pt**

BEJA Hotel Melius   📶🍴📺📋🅿♿   €€

Avenida Fialho de Almeida, 7800-053 **Tel** *284 313 080* **Fax** *284 321 825* **Rooms** *60*   **Road map** *D6*

The honeycombed façade of this large hotel, located at the southern edge of the medieval city of Beja, offers comfortable rooms with modern, 3-star facilities. Leisure options include a restaurant-bar, plus a modest gymnasium and sauna. Conference rooms are also available. For what it offers, Melius is exceptional value.

BEJA Pousada de São Francisco   📶🍴🏊📋🅿   €€€€€

Largo D Nuno Álvares Pereira, 7801-901 **Tel** *284 313 580* **Fax** *284 329 143* **Rooms** *35*   **Road map** *D6*

Housed in a former Franciscan convent founded in 1268, guests here are reminded of the building's humble origins when wandering through the lovingly restored cloister, Gothic chapel and chapter room, all adapted for modern use. Some bedrooms retain arched ceilings, installed during an 18th-century remodelling programme. **www.pousadas.pt**

CASTELO DE VIDE Casa do Parque   🏊📋   €

Avenida da Aramenha 37, 7320-101 **Tel** *245 901 250* **Fax** *245 901 228* **Rooms** *24*   **Road map** *D4*

The interior of this friendly *residencial* is as smart and tidy as its exterior. The spotless rooms all have views over a park with the distant mountains forming a pleasing backdrop. The restaurant serves traditional Portuguese cuisine. Guests have the use of a private swimming located 1 km (.6 mile) away. **www.rtsm.pt/pensao_casa_parque**

CRATO Pousada de Flor da Rosa   🍴🏊📋🅿   €€€€€

Mosteiro Flor da Rosa, 7430-999 **Tel** *245 997 210* **Fax** *245 997 212* **Rooms** *24*   **Road map** *D4*

An architecturally outstanding adaptation of the 14th-century Mosteiro de Santa Maria Flor da Rosa houses this enchanting *pousada*. The luxurious suites in the monastery's tower are breathtaking, and one has a beautiful, four-poster bed. Polished rosewood furniture adds a graceful touch. **www.pousadas.pt**

ELVAS Quinta de Santo António   🍴🏊🚶📋🅿♿   €€€

Estrada de Barbacena, 7350-903 **Tel** *268 636 460* **Fax** *268 625 050* **Rooms** *30*   **Road map** *D5*

This splendid *estalagem* is typical of the style of manor house found in the Alentejo. The long, low buildings are split into varying sized rooms that are cheerfully decorated and rustic in style. The lounge is particularly charming. The 18th-century gardens are elegant. The owners can arrange sporting activities. **www.qsa.com.pt**

ELVAS Pousada de Santa Luzia   🍴🏊🚶📋🅿   €€€€

Avenida de Badajoz, 7350-097 **Tel** *268 637 470* **Fax** *268 622 127* **Rooms** *25*   **Road map** *D5*

This venerable *pousada* was the first to open, in 1942, and is pleasantly decorated with printed fabrics. The overall interior design has changed little since its architect, Miguel Jacobetty Rosa, first put pen to paper. All rooms are located on the first floor. Guests have the use of a pool and tennis courts. **www.pousadas.pt**

ESTREMOZ Pousada da Rainha Santa Isabel 🏦🛏🖼📋 €€€€€

Largo Dom Dinis, 7100-509 **Tel** *268 332 075* **Fax** *268 332 079* **Rooms** *33* **Road map** *D5*

This grandiose *pousada* has been beautifully integrated into the 13th-century castle at Estremoz. The 17th- and 18th-century style furniture of the rooms includes four-poster beds and coats of arms. The inner courtyard is set with tables surrounding a small garden and lies in the shadow of the castle's majestic keep. **www.pousadas.pt**

ÉVORA IBIS Évora 🏊🏦📋🅿♿ €

Quinta da Tapada, Muralha, 7000-968 **Tel** *266 760 700* **Fax** *266 760 799* **Rooms** *87* **Road map** *D5*

Located just outside the walls that encircle the old town, this modern hotel is enormously popular due to its out-standing value. It is often full during festivals, special events and bank holidays. Accommodation is basic but has all the usual comforts of an IBIS property. Facilities include a good restaurant. **www.ibishotel.com**

ÉVORA Évorahotel 🏊🏦🏊🖼📋🅿 €€€

Avenida Túlio Espanca, N114, 7002-502 **Tel** *266 748 800* **Fax** *266 748 806* **Rooms** *170* **Road map** *D5*

Located on the outskirts of the old town, this is an impressive and inexpensive hotel popular with tourists and busi-ness travellers alike. In the evening, public spaces are enriched by the glow of Moorish-style lanterns and candlelight to create a soothing, relaxing ambience. The modern, well-equipped rooms have a balcony. **www.evorahotel.pt**

ÉVORA Solar Monfalim 📋🅿♿ €€€

Largo Misericórdia, 7000-646 **Tel** *266 750 000* **Fax** *266 742 367* **Rooms** *26* **Road map** *D5*

The colonnaded first-floor terrace of this Renaissance house is the perfect place to enjoy a cup of late afternoon tea. The building, located in the heart of the old town, used to belong to a nobleman and the first paying guest was received in 1892! The cosy interior is rustically decorated. **www.monfalimtur.pt**

ÉVORA Pousada dos Lóios 🏦🏊📋🅿 €€€€€

Largo Conde Vila Flor, 7000-804 **Tel** *266 730 070* **Fax** *266 707 248* **Rooms** *32* **Road map** *D5*

Originally a 15th-century monastery, the decorative public spaces in this elegant *pousada* contrast with the simple but characterful rooms that were converted from the monks' cells. An intricately embroidered carpet hangs from the wall skirting the marble staircase. The delightful swimming pool is sunk into an inner courtyard. **www.pousadas.pt**

MARVÃO Pousada de Santa Maria 🏦📋 €€€€

Rua 24 de Janeiro, 7330-122 **Tel** *245 993 201* **Fax** *245 993 440* **Rooms** *31* **Road map** *D4*

The colourful rooms in this handsome *pousada* offer two different visual experiences. Some look over a stunning mountain landscape while others face inwards into the lanes and alleyways of the old town. The *pousada* itself is set in a cosy, whitewashed townhouse with traditional painted furniture and friendly, attentive staff. **www.pousadas.pt**

MINAS DE SÃO DOMINGOS Estalagem São Domingos 🏦🏊🎿🖼📋🅿♿ €€€

Rua Dr Vargas, 7750-171 **Tel** *286 640 000* **Fax** *286 640 009* **Rooms** *31* **Road map** *D7*

Part of this wonderful *estalagem* occupies the former offices of British mining company Mason & Barry, who worked the nearby São Domingos copper mines. Rooms are located in the 19th-century manor house and a modern hotel wing. Guests may use the powerful telescope, housed in rooftop observatory. **www.hotelsaodomingos.com**

REDONDO Convento de São Paulo 🏦🏊📋🅿 €€€€

Aldeia da Serra, 7170-120 **Tel** *266 989 160* **Fax** *266 989 167* **Rooms** *40* **Road map** *D5*

Set in the remote Serra de Ossa mountain range, this beautiful and refined hotel is set in a former 12th-century monastery and is decorated with thousands of *azulejo* (tile) panels and frescoes in all the rooms. The bedrooms are converted from the original monks' cells. Fountains cool the various patios. **www.hotelconventospaulo.com**

SANTA CLARA-A-VELHA Pousada de Santa Clara 🏊🏦🏊🎿📋🅿♿ €€€€

Barragem de Santa Clara, 7665-879 **Tel** *283 882 250* **Fax** *283 882 402* **Rooms** *19* **Road map** *C7*

This unusually designed *pousada* enjoys a spectacularly peaceful setting overlooking the vast Santa-a-Clara reservoir. The hotel takes full advantage of its privileged location, with rooms that overlook the mountains or the dam. A range of activities such as hiking, fishing and watersports can be arranged by the staff. **www.pousadas.pt**

SANTIAGO DO CACÉM Caminhos de Santiago Hotel 🏊🏦🏊🎿📋🅿♿ €€€€

Rua Cidade de Beja, 7540-163 **Tel** *269 825 350* **Fax** *269 825 064* **Rooms** *35* **Road map** *C6*

Formerly a *pousada*, this four-star property is located on a hilltop within a short drive of the coast. The rooms are brightly decorated, and there's an outdoor pool and a bar with tables outside. The hotel's O Peregrino restaurant is renowned across the region for its fine Alentejan cuisine. Breakfast included. **www.hotelcaminhosdesantiago.pt**

SERPA Estalagem de São Gens 🏊🏦🏊📋🅿 €€

Alto de São Gens, 7830-099 **Tel** *284 540 420* **Fax** *284 544 337* **Rooms** *18* **Road map** *D6*

Located on a lofty elevation near the historic Nossa Senhora da Guadalupe chapel, this *estalagem* has spectacular views of the wide Alentejo plains: sunsets are especially dramatic. Rooms are comfortable, and the helpful staff can help organize jeep safaris, canoeing trips and hunting expeditions. **www.estalagemsgens.com**

SOUSEL Pousada de São Miguel 🏊🏦🏊📋🅿 €€€€

Serra de São Miguel, 7470-999 **Tel** *268 550 050* **Fax** *268 551 155* **Rooms** *32* **Road map** *D5*

This modern *pousada* is ideal for those in search of peace or outdoor pursuits – the surrounding countryside is per-fect for walking, mountain biking, horse riding and shooting. Alternatively, guests can relax by the pool. The rooms are comfortable and well appointed and a good restaurant and bar provide evening distraction. **www.pousadas.pt**

VILA NOVA DE MILFONTES Moinho da Asneira   🏊 🏃 🗏 🅿   €
Quinta do Rio Mira, 7645-014 **Tel** *283 996 182* **Fax** *283 997 138* **Rooms** *20*   **Road map** *C6*

Named after an old tidal mill, the comfortable rooms in the main house and hillside cottages of this country estate overlook the estuary of the River Mira and are close to the beach. The mill has its own private lagoon where guests can fish or indulge in a variety of watersports. **www.moinhodaasneira.com**

VILA VIÇOSA Pousada de Dom João IV   🍴 🏊 🗏 🅿   €€€€€
Convento das Chagas, Terreiro do Paço, 7160-251 **Tel** *268 980 742* **Fax** *268 980 747* **Rooms** *36*   **Road map** *D5*

Cloisters and a labyrinthine layout characterize this marvellous 17th-century royal convent, though the foundations may date from as early as 1514. The rooms are individually decorated, with the suites positively regal in appearance. The gardens are wonderfully serene, with trellised avenues that bloom with colour in spring. **www.pousadas.pt**

ALGARVE

ALBUFEIRA Alfagar   🍴 🏊 🏃 🅿   €€€
Aldeamento Turístico, Santa Eulália, 8200-912 **Tel** *289 540 220* **Fax** *289 542 770* **Rooms** *215*   **Road map** *C7*

This apartment complex commands a stunning cliff-top location overlooking the sea with direct access to Santa Eulália beach. The popular, self-contained tourist facility is set in 9 ha (22 acres) of gardens and incorporates three pools, tennis courts and a children's adventure playground. A restaurant and bar are also on hand. **www.alfagar.com**

ALBUFEIRA Falésia   📶 🍴 🏊 🏃 🗏 🅿 ♿   €€€
Praia da Falésia, 8200-911 **Tel** *289 501 237* **Fax** *289 501 270* **Rooms** *172*   **Road map** *C7*

Located near Falésia beach surrounded by umbrella pine, this smart hotel has brightly furnished and airy rooms that enjoy either pool or garden views. A huge, marble floor atrium decorated with hanging plants is a central feature. A piano bar provides nightly entertainment, and reception can arrange various outdoor activities. **www.falesia.com**

ALBUFEIRA Grande Real Santa Eulália Resort & Hotel Spa   📶 🍴 🏊 🏃 🖥 🗏 🅿 ♿   €€€€€
Praia Santa Eulália, 8200-916 **Tel** *289 598 000* **Fax** *289 598 001* **Rooms** *189*   **Road map** *C7*

One of the Algarve's 5-star hotels, this modern and attractive beachfront hotel has first-class facilities and every modern convenience. A major draw is the thalasso spa staffed by a fully qualified team of hydrotherapists and specialist fitness trainers. The hotel manages Le Club, a stylish restaurant and bar. **www.hoteisreal.com**

ALBUFEIRA Sheraton Algarve Hotel & Resort   📶 🍴 🏃 🖥 🗏 🅿 ♿   €€€€€
Praia da Falesia, 8200-909 **Tel** *289 500 100* **Fax** *289 501 960* **Rooms** *215*   **Road map** *C7*

One of southern Portugal's most emblematic properties, this luxury clifftop hotel offers deluxe rooms and palatial suites and an attention to detail that even the most discerning of clients would applaud. The 9-hole golf course requires a shot that must carry a deep chasm known as the Devil's Parlour. **www.starwoodhotels.com**

ALJEZUR O Palazim   🗏 🅿   €
Estrada Nacional 120, Aldeia Velha, 8670-113 **Tel & Fax** *282 998 249*   **Rooms** *15*   **Road map** *C7*

This welcoming and unpretentious boarding house is located in an attractive building and offers clean, comfortable double rooms with private bathroom and TV. The terrace affords a panoramic view of the old town and the surrounding countryside. The overall service is friendly and spirited and excellent value for money. **www.palazim.com**

ALMANCIL Quinta dos Rochas   🗏 🏊 🅿   €€
Fonte Coberta, 8135-019 **Tel** *289 393 165* **Fax** *289 399 198* **Rooms** *6*   **Road map** *D7*

This small *quinta* (country estate) is conveniently situated close to the beach and offers visitors the comforts of home, a friendly welcome and peaceful, rural surroundings. Decorative *azulejo* tiles brighten the halls, and polished dark-wood furniture characterizes the breakfast room. The rooms are spotless. **www.quintadosrochas.pt.vu**

ALMANCIL Hotel Quinta do Lago   📶 🍴 🏊 🏃 🗏 🅿 ♿   €€€€€
Quinta do Lago, 8135-024 **Tel** *289 350 350* **Fax** *289 396 393* **Rooms** *141*   **Road map** *D7*

Set amid 810 ha (2,000 acres) of rolling hills and pine woodland, this luxurious property is the Algarve's most famous hotel. The elegant rooms all have fabulous views over the Ria Formosa estuary and the nearby golf courses are some of the best in Europe. The modern spa offers the latest well-being treatments. **www.hotelquintadolago.com**

ALTE Alte Hotel   📶 🍴 🏊 🏃 🗏 🅿   €€
Estrada de Sta Margarida, Montinho, 8100-012 **Tel** *289 478 523* **Fax** *289 478 646* **Rooms** *30*   **Road map** *C7*

Alte has been voted Portugal's prettiest village and its rural setting makes it a favourite destination for tourists. The charming Alte Hotel is also in a peaceful location away from the teeming crowds on the coast and boasts excellent views and pleasant gardens. A shuttle bus transports residents to the beach. **www.altehotel.com**

ALVOR Pestana Alvor Praia   📶 🍴 🏊 🏃 🖥 🗏 🅿 ♿   €€€€€
Praia dos Três Irmãos, 8501-904 **Tel** *282 400 900* **Fax** *282 400 975* **Rooms** *195*   **Road map** *C7*

A large and superbly situated luxury hotel complex with gardens that lead directly down to the beach and a sea-water swimming pool. The hotel can arrange easy access to eight golf courses, two of which are owned by Pestana. A superb gymnasium and wellness centre provide alternative leisure pastimes. **www.pestana.com**

CALDAS DE MONCHIQUE Albergaria do Lageado   ▨▤ €

Caldas de Monchique, 8550-232 **Tel** *282 912 616* **Fax** *282 911 310* **Rooms** *19*   **Road map** C7

This spruce inn has a small pool surrounded by camellias and is situated in the centre of this delightful hamlet tucked away in the foothills of the Serra de Monchique. Surrounded by peaceful woodland and near a cluster of restaurants, the famed spa facility is across the road. Closed Dec–Jan. **www.albergariadolageado.com**

CARVOEIRO Colina Sol   ▨ ▥ ▨▤ P €€

Praia Vale Centeanes, 8400 517 **Tel** *282 350 820* **Fax** *282 358 651* **Rooms** *219*   **Road map** C7

Set in its own attractive grounds overlooking the sea, this large, neo-Moorish hotel complex offers fully self-contained one-, two- and three-bedroom apartments. The facility is ideal for those who prefer all modern conveniences under one roof. On site are tennis courts and a pool, plus bar and restaurant. **www.algarvesol.pt**

CARVOEIRO Tivoli Carvoeiro   ▨ ▥ ▨ ▦ ▤ P ♿ €€€

Vale do Covo, 8401-911 **Tel** *282 351 100* **Fax** *282 351 345* **Rooms** *293*   **Road map** C7

A plush hotel commanding a dramatic location perched above a small, picturesque cove. The spacious, well-appointed rooms all face the ocean. The secluded beach can be reached by stairway at low tide and the hotel runs its own professional dive centre. Leisure facilities include swimming pools and a putting green. **www.tivolihotels.com**

ESTÓI Monte do Casal   ▥ ▨▤ P €€€€€

Cerro do Lobo, 8005-436 **Tel** *289 991 503* **Fax** *289 991 341* **Rooms** *18*   **Road map** D7

A charming, luxury boutique hotel set in landscaped botanical gardens featuring lakes stocked with koi carp. Rooms feature mahogany furniture and white marble finishes. The Waterfall Suite is ideal for honeymooners. Michelin-recommended restaurant. Closed 2 weeks in Dec; Jan- mid Feb. **www.montedocasal.pt**

FARO Alnacir   ▨ P €

Estrada Senhor da Saúde 24, 8000-500 **Tel** *289 803 678* **Fax** *289 803 548* **Rooms** *53*   **Road map** D7

A tidy, modern hotel located on a quiet street close to the centre of the Algarve's regional capital. Pleasantly decorated throughout, two of the double rooms have a panoramic terrace overlooking the Ria Formosa Natural Park. Breakfast is served in a light, airy dining room. A laundry service is available. **www.alnacir.netfirms.com**

FARO Residencial Samé   ▨ €

Rua do Bocage 66, 8000-297 **Tel** *289 823 370* **Fax** *289 804 166* **Rooms** *36*   **Road map** D7

The blue and white façade is rather drab but this quiet hotel, a short walk east of the cathedral, offers clean modern rooms with television and well-maintained bathrooms. While the front rooms have small balconies, there's no view to speak of, and parking is difficult. Service is friendly and attentive. **residencialsame@gmail.com**

FARO Hotel Eva   ▨ ▥ ▨▤ ♿ €€€

Avenida da República 1, 8000-078 **Tel** *289 001 000* **Fax** *289 001 002* **Rooms** *134*   **Road map** D7

One of Faro's most popular hotels, Eva sits on the harbour front and is ideally situated for exploring the city. Modern and comfortable, many of the rooms look out over the marina and the ocean beyond. Guest services include a hairdresser and barber. The rooftop swimming pool is blissful in summer. **www.tdhotels.pt**

LAGOS Marina Rio   ▨ ▨▤ P ♿ €€

Avenida dos Descobrimentos, 8600-645 **Tel** *282 780 830* **Fax** *282 780 839* **Rooms** *36*   **Road map** C7

Located at the eastern end of Lagos, this modern and pleasant albergaria has attractive views over the marina and is just a short walk away from the town's historical centre. The front rooms all have balconies but most guests head for the rooftop sun terrace and the inviting swimming pool. **www.marinario.com**

LAGOS Quinta das Achadas   ▤ P €€

Estrada da Barragem, 8600-251 **Tel** *282 798 425* **Fax** *282 799 162* **Rooms** *6*   **Road map** C7

A family-run 19th-century farmhouse set in wonderful gardens well away from the bustle of the beaches. Accommodation features three individually decorated rooms and three self-catering apartments. Rich in character and rustic in style, this secluded location is perfect for families and those seeking peace and quiet. **www.algarveholiday.net**

LAGOS Belavista da Luz   ▨ ▥ ▤ P ♿ €€€

Praia da Luz, 8600-184 **Tel** *282 788 655* **Fax** *282 788 656* **Rooms** *39*   **Road map** C7

This attractive, horse-shoe shaped hotel encloses a large swimming pool and enjoys sweeping views of Praia da Luz bay. The comfortable rooms and modern facilities make it a favourite holiday option and is ideal for those with children. Closed four weeks during Nov–Dec and three weeks in Jan–Feb. **www.belavistadaluz.com**

LAGOS Hotel Tivoli Lagos   ▨ ▥ ▨ ▦ ▤ P ♿ €€€

Rua António Crisógono Santos, 8600-678 **Tel** *282 790 079* **Fax** *282 790 345* **Rooms** *323*   **Road map** C7

Built to exude the charm and character of a small village, this pleasant complex has five restaurants, a health club and swimming pool surrounded by trim gardens. The hotel operates its own beach club and barbeques are organized for hotel guests during the summer. A free shuttle service is also provided. **www.tivolihotels.com**

LOULÉ Loulé Jardim   ▨ ▨▤ P €€

Praça Manuel de Arriaga, 8100-665 **Tel** *289 413 094* **Fax** *289 463 177* **Rooms** *52*   **Road map** D7

This small hotel on a quiet garden square is an appealing conversion of a classic, early 20th-century town house. Some of the original architectural features have been retained. The rooms on the fourth floor all have balconies, and a modest swimming pool is cleverly incorporated into the third-floor terrace. **www.loulejardimhotel.com**

MONTE GORDO Vasco da Gama
€€€
Avenida Infante Dom Henrique, 8900-412 **Tel** *281 510 900* **Fax** *281 510 901* **Rooms** *171* **Road map** *D7*

Vasco da Gama's proximity to the border makes it a popular choice for Spanish holidaymakers. Set on the beach, the hotel has spacious rooms, each with its own balcony. Facilities are geared towards families and feature a children's pool and adventure playground. The nearby casino is a favourite evening diversion. **www.vascodagamahotel.com**

PORCHES Vila Vita Parc
€€€€
Alporchinhos, 8400-450 **Tel** *282 310 100* **Fax** *282 320 333* **Rooms** *182* **Road map** *C7*

Set along a beautiful stretch of coastline in its own immaculate gardens with tropical flowers, this large, luxurious hotel has deluxe double rooms, sumptuous suites and first-class apartments. A state-of-the-art health and beauty centre offers a wide range of therapies for prevention, revitalization and regeneration. **www.vilavitaparc.com**

PORTIMÃO Le Méridien Penina
€€€€
Penina, 8501-952 **Tel** *282 420 200* **Fax** *282 420 300* **Rooms** *196* **Road map** *C7*

Golf in the Algarve teed off here in 1966 with the masterpiece championship course designed by the late Sir Henry Cotton, who went to create a further two layouts. The luxurious Méridien also offers practice facilities and tuition. Non-golfers can use the tennis courts and a FIFA-sized football pitch. **www.starwoodhotels.com**

PORTIMÃO Tivoli Marina Portimão
€€€€€
Marina de Portimão, 8500-901 **Tel** *282 460 200* **Fax** *282 460 201* **Rooms** *196* **Road map** *C7*

Idyllically set alongside Portimão's modern marina, the Tivoli is very much at the heart of the action, surrounded by shops, restaurants, bars and, of course, the beach. With their stylish decor, the rooms offer every modern convenience and fine views of the marina and the ocean beyond. **www.tivolihotels.com**

PRAIA DA GALÉ Estalagem Vila Joya
€€€€€
Praia da Galé, Guia, 8201-902 **Tel** *289 591 795* **Fax** *289 591 201* **Rooms** *20* **Road map** *C7*

An award-winning boutique property set in beautiful grounds overlooking Praia de Galé. The understated luxury of the standard rooms complement the stylish and contemporary feel of the suites, and all enjoy splendid sea views. The spa facility is first class and the gourmet restaurant is Michelin starred. Reservations essential. **www.vilajoya.com**

SAGRES Navigator
€€
Rua Infante D Henrique, 8650-381 **Tel** *282 624 354* **Fax** *282 624 360* **Rooms** *55* **Road map** *C7*

The rooms at this popular hotel are individual apartments furnished to a good standard. The hotel sits on the Sagres promontory and affords some inspiring views. Guests can take advantage of the region's wealth of outdoor activity options including windsurfing, horse riding and hiking. **www.hotel-navigator.com**

SAGRES Pousada do Infante
€€€
Sagres, 8650-385 **Tel** *282 620 240* **Fax** *282 624 225* **Rooms** *52* **Road map** *C7*

Named after Henry the Navigator *(see p49)*, this purpose-built *pousada* has a superb location overlooking the ocean and the Sagres promontory. The comfortable and stylishly decorated rooms all have private balconies and sea views. An afternoon drink on the terrace is the best way to savour the historical atmosphere. **www.pousadas.pt**

SÃO BRÁS DE ALPORTEL Pousada de São Brás
€€€€
Poço dos Ferreiros, 8150-054 **Tel** *289 842 305* **Fax** *289 841 726* **Rooms** *33* **Road map** *D7*

This peaceful *pousada* is housed in a country manor deep in the Algarve hinterland and is designed to reflect an architectural style typical of the region. Set on top of a hill, the pleasant rooms afford some wonderful views of the surrounding hills, the town below and the distant ocean. **www.pousadas.pt**

SILVES Quinta do Rio
€
Sítio São Estevão **Tel** *282 445 528* **Fax** *282 445 528* **Rooms** *6* **Road map** *C7*

Only a few kilometers from the centre of Silves *(see pp332–3)*, this farmhouse, set in rolling countryside, is still home to the Italian family that grow fruit trees here. Visitors have access to the big garden and delicious dinners are available on request. The region's beaches are not far away. **www.quintariocountryinn.home.sapo.pt**

TAVIRA Convento de Santo António
€€
Rua de Santo António, 8800-373 **Tel** *281 325 632* **Fax** *281 325 632* **Rooms** *7* **Road map** *D7*

This charming whitewashed former convent offers elegant rooms around the shady patio, or pretty rooms converted from the monks' cells. The decoration is embellished with hand-crafted terracotta, rich *alcobaça* fabrics and beautiful *azulejo* tiles. The tiny cloisters are an architectural treasure. Breakfast is served to Gregorian chant. Closed Jan.

TAVIRA Quinta do Caracol
€€€
Rua São Pedro, 8800-405 **Tel** *281 322 475* **Fax** *281 323 175* **Rooms** *7* **Road map** *D7*

This 17th-century whitewashed country house is named *caracol* (snail in English) after the blue spirals that decorate the entrance to the *quinta* (estate). Surrounded by pretty gardens, the upscale bedrooms are all named after flowers. This is a quiet base from which to explore the coast and hilly interior. **www.quintadocaracol.com**

TAVIRA Pousada de Tavira Convento da Graça
€€€€€
Rua D Paio Peres Correia, 8800-407 **Tel** *281 329 040* **Fax** *281 381 741* **Rooms** *36* **Road map** *D7*

The only Algarve *pousada* classified as an historic property, the rooms are housed within the former Convento das Emitas de Santo Agostino, founded by D Sebastião in 1569. Traces of a Moorish street were unearthed during restoration and the foundations can be viewed through a glass panel near the bar area. **www.pousadas.pt**

Key to Price Guide *see p382* **Key to Symbols** *see back cover flap*

VILA REAL DE SANTO ANTÓNIO Guadiana

Avenida da República 94, 8900-206 **Tel** *281 511 482* **Fax** *281 511 478* **Rooms** *40*   **Road map** *D7*

A prettily refurbished and impressive 19th-century town house, this comfortable hotel stands across from the esplanade in the centre of town. The front facing rooms enjoy pleasant views across a small marina and the River Guadiana. A useful base from which to explore the eastern Algarve or neighbouring Spain. **www.hotelguadiana.com.pt**

VILAMOURA Tivoli Marina Marinotel

Marina de Vilamoura, 8125-901 **Tel** *289 303 303* **Fax** *289 303 345* **Rooms** *383*   **Road map** *D7*

Vilamoura's iconic hotel property. The privileged location overlooking the marina complex and a wide sweep of golden sand makes this a popular tourist and conference venue. The facilities are first-class and rooms enjoy every modern convenience. Leisure options include watersports, tennis, golf and horse riding. **www.tivolihotels.com**

VILAMOURA The Lake Resort

Praia da Falésia, 8126-910 **Tel** *289 320 700* **Fax** *289 320 701* **Rooms** *192*   **Road map** *D7*

So named because of the artificial lake that shimmers in front of the property, the luxury Lake Resort offers an interesting East meets West style concept, where guests are offered a choice of either Mediterranean or Oriental designed rooms. Complementing the theme is an Oriental tearoom and an Asian fusion restaurant. **www.thelakeresort.com**

MADEIRA

CANIÇO Roca Mar

Caminho Cais da Oilveira, 9125-028 **Tel** *291 934 334* **Fax** *291 934 044* **Rooms** *100*

Located on the south coast of the island, all rooms at the clifftop Roca Mar have large balconies from which to enjoy the wonderful ocean views and bracing sea air. The hotel offers a lively evening entertainments programme, as well as access to sports facilities and a free minibus to Funchal. **www.hotelrocamar.com**

CANIÇO Quinta Splendida

Estrada da Ponte Oliveira II, 9125-001 **Tel** *291 930 400* **Fax** *291 930 401* **Rooms** *141*

Accommodation at this half moon-shaped villa complex, set in the gardens of a 16th-century mansion, ranges from comfortable studio apartments to sumptuous suites. The grounds feature tropical trees and about 650 different species of flora. Dolphin and whale-watching excursions can be arranged. **www.quintasplendida.com**

FUNCHAL Residencial Vila Teresinha

Rua das Cruzes 21, 9000-025 **Tel** *291 741 723* **Fax** *291 744 515* **Rooms** *12*

Housed in a traditional Funchal townhouse, this lovely hotel is in a quiet residential area and has clean, pleasant rooms and a splendid top-floor terrace where breakfast can be taken. The restaurant serves delicious regional cuisine and the friendly bar has a good selection of fine Madeiras. **www.vilateresinha.com**

FUNCHAL Monte Carlo

Calçada da Saúde 10, 9001-801 **Tel** *291 226 131* **Fax** *291 226 134* **Rooms** *50*

This hotel is a steep walk uphill from the town centre but certainly worth the effort. Housed in a graciously ageing building that sports a resplendent, traditional façade, the rooms boast fine ocean and mountain views. The bar offers a selection of drinks and snacks in a relaxed and informal atmosphere. **www.hotelmontecarlomadeira.com**

FUNCHAL Pestana Casino Park

Rua Imperatriz Dona Amélia, 9000-513 **Tel** *291 209 100* **Fax** *291 232 076* **Rooms** *379*

Madeira's liveliest hotel, with a casino, cinema, cabaret and disco, has undergone extensive refurbishment. Designed by Oscar Niemeyer (architect of the Brazilian capital, Brasília), it is a masterpiece of modern architectural style. The upgraded facilities have consolidated the attractive, comfortable and stylish interior. **www.pestana.com**

FUNCHAL Quinta da Penha de França

Rua Imperatriz Dª Amélia, 9000-014 **Tel** *291 204 650* **Fax** *291 229 261* **Rooms** *109*

The family-run Penha de Franca comprises two different sections: the original complex built around a traditional clifftop mansion surrounded by subtropical gardens, and a modern, oceanfront hotel. A small footbridge and a lift connect the two properties and guests have access to both facilities, including restaurants and bars. **www.penhafranca.com**

FUNCHAL Quinta Perestrello

Rua Dr Pita 3, 9000-089 **Tel** *291 706 700* **Fax** *291 706 706* **Rooms** *36*

This mid- 19th-century mansion is beautifully decorated to the highest standards and filled with antique furniture. It offers luxurious accommodation in comfortable rooms that are divided into the original building and a new wing. The extensive grounds feature a swimming pool and guests have use of the Vistas spa. **www.charminghotelsmadeira.com**

FUNCHAL Pestana Miramar

Estrada Monumental 182-184, 9000-098 **Tel** *291 706 100* **Fax** *291 763 988* **Rooms** *58*

Sympathetically built around the old Miramar Hotel, the tastefully decorated apartments at this upscale holiday complex offer comfortable, modern conveniences and a wealth of leisure options including heated swimming pools, a health club and access to the sea. Guests can also choose from several restaurants. **www.pestana.com**

FUNCHAL Choupana Hills Resort
Travessa do Largo da Choupana, 9000-348 **Tel** *291 206 020* **Fax** *291 206 021* **Rooms** *62*

A luxurious tiered structure set high in the hills above the Atlantic, Choupana is constructed along Zen lines of symmetry and simplicity. The theme here is natural chic. The earthy interiors have Asian and African influences, and the spa includes *hammam* (Turkish bath) and yoga options. **www.choupanahills.com**

FUNCHAL Reid's Palace
Estrada Monumental 139, 9000-098 **Tel** *291 717 171* **Fax** *291 717 177* **Rooms** *163*

Founded in 1891, Madeira's most emblematic hotel is the haunt of wealthy and famous patrons – former guests Winston Churchill and George Bernard Shaw both have suites named after them. Furnished like a stately home, with chandeliers in the dining room, it enjoys primetime clifftop views and palm-fringed pools. **www.reidspalace.com**

PORTO MONIZ Pensão Salgueiro
Lugar do Tenente, 9270-095 **Tel** *291 724 280* **Fax** *291 762 171* **Rooms** *22*

This smart residencial has wonderful rooms and a suite that overlook Porto Moniz's natural rock pools and the crystalline ocean beyond. The hotel exudes a peaceful, family atmosphere, ideal for those wishing to explore Madeira's rugged north coast. Facilities include a solarium, a restaurant and private car park. **www.pensaosalgueiro.com**

PORTO SANTO Hotel Porto Santo
Campo de Baixo, 9400-015 **Tel** *291 980 140* **Fax** *291 980 149* **Rooms** *94*

Set right on the beach, this modern hotel has stylishly designed rooms with private balcony views. Facilities include a swimming pool, tennis courts, mini golf and a spacious lounge bar and restaurant. The Severiano Ballesteros designed 18-hole golf course is nearby, and there is also an easier 9-hole layout. **www.hotelportosanto.com**

PORTO SANTO Hotel Torre Praia
Rua Goulart Medeiros, 9400-164 **Tel** *291 980 450* **Fax** *291 982 487* **Rooms** *66*

A mid-sized hotel near all amenities, including the main attraction – the beach, to which it has direct access. The well-equipped rooms are comfortably furnished and the suites have spacious terraces with sun loungers and an ocean view. Sports and leisure facilities include a pool, squash court, gymnasium and sauna. **www.torrepraia.pt**

RIBEIRA BRAVA Bravamar
Rua Gago Coutinho e Sacadura Cabral 2A, 9350-209 **Tel** *291 952 220* **Fax** *291 951 122* **Rooms** *70*

A large, modern hotel located in the town centre just 25 minutes from Funchal, Bravamar has comfortably decorated rooms with all modern conveniences and either mountain or ocean views. Guests have access to a sun terrace and a swimming pool. The hotel's restaurant serves regional as well as international cuisine. **www.hotel-bravamar.com**

SERRA DE ÁGUA Pousada dos Vinháticos
Ribeira Brava, 9350-306 **Tel** *291 952 344* **Fax** *291 952 540* **Rooms** *21*

Uniquely situated in the Encumeada valley near the Laurissilva forest, a UNESCO World Heritage Site, this charming *pousada* is geared towards hill walkers and is suitably fashioned as a mountain lodge. The ensuite rooms are divided between a wooden building and one made of stone. Book a stay well in advance. **www.dorisol.com**

THE AZORES

CORVO Guest House Comodoro
Caminho do Areeiro, Ilha do Corvo, 9980-034 **Tel** *292 596 128* **Rooms** *7*

Apart from private houses, this is the only accommodation available on the tiny island of Corvo. Rooms at this cosy, family-run boarding house are comfortable and have private bathroom facilities and TV. Breakfast is served in a bright and airy dining room. It is wise to check availability ahead of a visit.

FAIAL Quinta das Buganvílias
Rua do Jogo 60, Castelo Branco, Horta, 9900-330 **Tel** *292 943 740* **Fax** *292 943 743* **Rooms** *8*

This idyllic, family-run *quinta* (estate) near the airport has a scent-filled rose garden, fruit orchard and commercial greenhouses filled with flowers. The homely feel extends to the rooms and self-contained apartments, set in an annexe next to the stone built manor house. The hospitality is friendly and the generous breakfast beautifully presented.

FAIAL Pousada Santa Cruz
Rua Vasco da Gama, Horta, 9900-017 **Tel** *292 202 200* **Fax** *292 392 836* **Rooms** *28*

This smart hotel is housed within the solid basalt walls of the 16th-century Santa Cruz fort, classified as a national monument. The stylish rooms have splendid balcony views over the swimming pool, the busy marina and Pico Island beyond. Leisure activity options include diving, fishing, whale watching and bicycle tours. **www.pousadas.pt**

FLORES Ocidental
Avenida dos Baleeiros, Santa Cruz das Flores, 9970-306 **Tel** *292 590 100* **Fax** *292 590 101* **Rooms** *36*

The main hotel on Flores is a functional block on the outskirts of Santa Cruz. The rooms are plain but tidy and comfortable and most have balconies facing the sea. The hotel's diving centre can arrange various expeditions and services include equipment hire, plus a shuttle to and from the quay. **www.hotelocidental.com**

GRACIOSA Santa Cruz

Largo Barão de Guadalupe 9, Santa Cruz da Graciosa, 9880-344 **Tel** *295 712 345* **Fax** *295 712 828* **Rooms** *18*

One of the few accommodation choices on Graciosa, Santa Cruz is a friendly *pensão* on a quiet square near the centre of town. The interior has a homely quality about it, and guests have the use of a TV lounge. Rooms are comfortable and simply furnished. Book well in advance.

PICO Aldeia da Fonte

Caminho da Fonte, Lajes do Pico, 9930-177 **Tel** *292 679 500* **Fax** *292 672 700* **Rooms** *32*

Described as an Atlantic charm hotel, Aldeia da Fonte is the ultimate romantic hideaway. With Pico mountain as a backdrop, the building blends in with the volcanic, subtropical landscape. Each of the rooms depicts a different aspect of the island's history and culture. The hotel's restaurant is highly recommended. **www.aldeiadafonte.com**

PICO Pico

Rua dos Biscoitos, Madalena, 9950-334 **Tel** *292 628 400* **Fax** *292 628 407* **Rooms** *69*

A modern establishment offering some rooms with balconies and views of the spectacular blackened peak of the island, or of Faial Island across the water. The rooms are decorated with pastel-hued flowered fabrics. Leisure options include a health club with gym, sauna and Turkish bath, plus an inviting kidney-shaped swimming pool. **www.picohotel.com**

SANTA MARIA Praia de Lobos

Rua Mercado, Vila do Porto, 9580-525 **Tel** *296 882 277* **Fax** *296 882 482* **Rooms** *34*

A smart, efficiently run hotel with an interesting façade, it lies in the centre of Vila do Porto and offers modern, comfortable facilities and a friendly welcome. The simply furnished ensuite rooms are complemented by a modest breakfast room, bar and sitting room. A laundry service is available. **www.hotelpraiadelobos.com**

SÃO JORGE Hotel São Jorge Garden

Rua Machado Pires, Velas, 9800-526 **Tel** *295 430 100* **Fax** *295 412 736* **Rooms** *58*

On the outskirts of Velas and 7 km (4 m) from the airport, this is the only modern hotel on the island and offers guests spacious rooms with sea or garden views. The poolside terrace enhances the panorama considerably. The friendly staff are happy to point out local beauty spots.

SÃO MIGUEL Casa Nossa Senhora do Carmo

Rua do Pópulo de Cima 220, Livramento, 9500-614 **Tel** *296 642 048* **Fax** *296 642 038* **Rooms** *5*

Located just east of Ponta Delgada near the island's best beach, Casa Nossa Senhora do Carmo is a lovingly restored and secluded 17th-century *quinta* (country estate) with a façade styled from local stone. The interior is full of antiques and family treasures and the rooms ooze warmth and character. Closed Dec. **carmo@virtualazores.com**

SÃO MIGUEL Bahia Palace

Praia de Baía D'Alto, 9680-365 **Tel** *296 539 130* **Fax** *296 539 138* **Rooms** *101*

This large, somewhat isolated complex on the south coast is popular with tourists seeking a self-contained hotel, and with business executives attracted by first-class conference rooms. Set in trim grounds and fanned by sea breezes, the hotel offers well-appointed rooms with modern facilities, and a bar with live music. **www.hotelbahaipalace.com**

SÃO MIGUEL São Pedro

Largo Almirante Dunn, Ponta Delgada, 9500-292 **Tel** *296 301 740* **Fax** *296 301 744* **Rooms** *16*

A charming mansion, built in 1812 for the Boston-born merchant Thomas Hickling – the first American counsel to the Azores – São Pedro is now a gracious harbourside hotel offering fine hospitality and lodging with a New England flair. The rooms are furnished with period antiques and the 19th-century atmosphere is tangible.

SÃO MIGUEL Solar de Lalém

Estrada de São Pedro, Maia, 9625-391 **Tel** *296 442 004* **Fax** *296 442 164* **Rooms** *10*

An elegant and historic 17th-century manor house on the north coast that has been decorated in a simple style by its easy-going German owners, Solar de Lalém was once the residence of a sea captain employed by the Portuguese royal court. Each room is individually styled and decorated with antiques. **www.solardelalem.com**

TERCEIRA Beira Mar

Largo Miguel Corte Real, Angra do Heroísmo, 9700-182 **Tel** *295 215 188* **Fax** *295 628 248* **Rooms** *23*

Overlooking the harbour, the black and white stone façade of this hotel is unmistakeable. The rooms are on the small side and are simply furnished but the location can't be beaten for exploring the old heart of the city. During the summer, meals can be enjoyed on the outside terrace. **www.hotelbeiramar.com**

TERCEIRA Quinta do Martelo

Canada do Martelo 24, Cantinho, São Francisco das Almas, 9700-576 **Tel** *295 642 842* **Fax** *295 642 841* **Rooms** *10*

The Quinta do Martelo is set in the grounds of Hammer's Farm, an idyllic rural estate set in verdant countryside. Guests are treated to a rustic welcome, with lodgings distributed throughout several traditional houses and rooms decorated with islands crafts. Superb, award-winning Azorean restaurant. **www.quintadomartelo.com**

TERCEIRA Quinta da Nasce-Água

Vinha Brava, 9700-236 **Tel** *295 628 500* **Fax** *295 628 502* **Rooms** *10*

Overlooking Angra do Heroísmo, this luxurious hotel is set in a restored 19th-century manor house. The property is surrounded by a lush, sub-tropical garden that features several rare species of flora. The rooms and public areas are furnished in a style that reflects the traditional heritage of this charming *quinta* (estate). **nasceagua@mail.telepac.pt**

WHERE TO EAT

Portugal is the country to feast on all kinds of fish and seafood, from clams, lobster and sardines to tuna, swordfish and *bacalhau* (salted cod), the national favourite. All along the coast are restaurants dedicated to cooking freshly caught fish. The Portuguese are great meat eaters too and justifiably proud of such dishes as roast kid and sucking pig. While meat may be

Sign for roast suckling pig at Mealhada

more common in inland regions, fresh fish is available throughout Portugal. Most restaurants are reasonably priced, and offer generous portions. Lisbon has plenty of cheap cafés and restaurants, as well as international ones, as does the Algarve. This introduction gives tips on types of eating places, menus, drinks and ordering to help you enjoy eating out in Portugal.

Drinks waiter at the Tivoli Palácio de Seteais, near Sintra *(see p414)*

TYPES OF RESTAURANTS

Eating venues come in all shapes and sizes and at all price levels. Among the most reasonable is the local *tasca* or tavern, often just a room with half-a-dozen tables presided over by a husband-and-wife team. These are often frequented by locals and professionals at lunch

time, which is a good lead to follow. The *casa de pasto* offers a budget three-course meal in a large dining room, while a *restaurante* is more formal and offers a wider choice of dishes. At a *marisqueira* (found all along the coast), the emphasis is on fresh fish and seafood. The *churrasqueira*, a very popular concept imported from Brazil, specializes in spit-roasted foods, while a *cervejaria* (beerhouse) is the ideal place to go for a beer and a snack. As a rule, restaurants in the better hotels are generally of good quality. *Pousadas (see pp380–81)*, found throughout the country, offer a network of high-quality restaurants featuring regional specialities.

Sign for Maria Rita's *(see p421)*

EATING HOURS

Lunch is usually served between 1 and 3 pm when many restaurants, especially in cities, get very crowded. Dinner is served from 7 to 10pm in most places, but can be later in restaurants and *cervejarias* in major cities and resort areas such as Lisbon, Oporto and the Algarve. Another choice for a very late dinner would be to combine a meal with a show at a *fado* house *(see pp64–5)*, open from about 9:30pm to 3 or 4am.

RESERVATIONS

It is a good idea to book ahead for expensive restaurants, and for those in popular locations in high season. Disabled people should certainly check in advance on facilities and access. Special facilities are generally lacking but most places will try to be helpful.

THE MENU

Some restaurants, especially in tourist areas, offer an *ementa turística*, a cheap, daily-changing three-course menu served with coffee and a drink (glass of wine, beer, water or soft drink). This provides a full meal at a good price with no hidden costs. Lunch, *almoço*, is often a two-course fixed menu, consisting of a fish or meat main course with potatoes or rice and either a starter or a

The impressive interior of the Cozinha Velha *(see p414)* at Queluz

Sharing the local veal speciality at Gabriela's, in Sendim (see p422)

pudding. To sample a local speciality, ask for the *prato do dia* – dish of the day.

Dinner *(jantar)* may be two or more courses, perhaps followed by ice cream, fruit, a simple dessert or cheese. Casserole-style dishes, such as fish or meat stews or *carne de porco à alentejana* (pork with clams), are brought to the table in a pot for people to share, as are large fish such as sea bass, which are sold by weight. One serving can easily be shared by two people and it is perfectly acceptable to ask for a *meia dose* or half-portion. Peculiar to Portugal is the plate of assorted appetizers – olives, cheese and sardine pâté – brought with bread at the start of a meal. These are not included in the menu price, and may add substantially to the bill.

VEGETARIANS

Vegetarians will not eat as well as fish lovers, although local cheeses and breads can be excellent. In Lisbon or along the Algarve, vegetarians will benefit from ethnic restaurants. Chefs will usually be happy to provide something meatless, though this will probably mean simply an omelette or a salad.

WINE AND DRINKS

It would be a shame to visit Portugal without sampling its two most famous fortified wines: port *(see pp254–5)* and Madeira *(see p351)*. Wherever you are, it is safe to order a bottle or jug of house wine to wash down your meal.

Otherwise, ask for the wine list, and choose one of Portugal's many native wines *(see pp28–9)*. Sagres and Super Bock are good beers and the bottled water is recommended. This comes either *com gás* (sparkling) or *sem gás* (still).

Relaxing at a seafront bar at Póvoa de Varzim in the Minho

CAFÉS AND CAKE SHOPS

Cafés are fundamental to Portuguese daily life and vary from modern white rooms to splendidly decorated, tiled and mirrored places where you can sit and talk or read the paper for hours. Many have tables outside. They make perfect meeting points and usually offer a range of snacks and sandwiches. At any time of the day a café is the obvious choice for a coffee break with a roll, croissant or cake. Do not miss the *pastelarias* (cake shops); the sweet-toothed Portuguese adore cakes, and the selections are excellent *(see p229)*.

PAYING THE BILL

It is common practice to add a 5–10 per cent tip to bills. Although service is not included, it provides a low wage which the tip is meant to supplement. Note that not all restaurants accept credit cards.

CHILDREN

In Portugal, children are seen as a blessing, so it is an ideal country for families to eat out together. Children's portions or half-portions at reduced prices are advertised or will be provided on request.

SMOKING

Smoking is permitted in many public places. If the extractor system is less than efficient, though, a smoking ban applies, and there will be a *proibido fumar* sign. No-smoking areas in restaurants are fairly rare.

COFFEE DRINKING IN PORTUGAL

Coffee is widely drunk in Portugal and served in many forms. The most popular is a small cup of strong black coffee like an espresso. In Lisbon and the South this is called *uma bica*; elsewhere ask for *um café*. A strong one is called *uma italiana*; for a weaker version, try *um carioca de café*. *Uma meia de leite* is half coffee, half milk. Strong coffee with a dash of milk is known as *um garoto escuro* (*um garoto claro* is quite milky). If you like your coffee with plenty of milk, ask for *um galão* (a gallon). This is served in a tall glass, and again you can order *um galão claro* (very milky) or *escuro* (strong).

Uma bica   Um galão

Choosing a Restaurant

The restaurants in this guide have been selected for their good value, exceptional food or interesting location. These listings highlight some of the factors that may influence your choice, such as whether you can opt to eat outdoors or if the venue offers live music. Entries are listed alphabetically within each price category.

PRICE DETAILS
Price categories are for a three-course meal for one with half a bottle of wine, including cover charge, service and VAT.
€ Under €20
€€ €20–€25
€€€ €25–€30
€€€€ €30–€35
€€€€€ Over €35

LISBON

ALCÂNTARA Alcântara Café

€€€€€

Rua Maria Luísa Holstein 15, 1300-388 **Tel** *213 637 176*   **Map** *3 A4*

Opened in the 1980s, this remains a classic Lisbon dining venue. The vast interior is styled on the Nautilus, the submarine from Jules Verne's *Twenty Thousand Leagues Under The Sea*. The menu reflects new Portuguese cuisine and is crammed with specialities like salmon escalopes. Impressive wine list. Reservations a must.

ALFAMA Hua-Ta-Li

€

Rua dos Bacalhoeiros 109-115, 1100-068 **Tel** *218 879 170*   **Map** *7 C4*

This large and popular Chinese restaurant is located in a semi-pedestrianized street close to the docks. A long list of great soups and all the regular rice and noodle dishes are available, plus one or two surprises such as prawn casserole and frogs' legs with chillis. Service is swift and somewhat hurried, but the portions are generous and well presented.

ALFAMA Lautasco

€

Beco do Azinhal 7a (off Rua de São Pedro), 1100-067 **Tel** *218 860 173*   **Map** *8 E4*

Rustically decorated with wooden panelling and wagon-wheel chandeliers, Lautasco specializes in typical Portuguese cuisine that can be enjoyed on the outside terrace. Decorative streamers and colourful spotlights enhance an already atmospheric setting and the restaurant is extremely popular in summer. Reservations recommended. Closed Sun.

ALFAMA Santo António de Alfama

€€€

Beco de São Miguel 7, 1100-538 **Tel** *218 881 328*   **Map** *8 E4*

No *fado* and sardines on the menu at this small restaurant in the Alfama – just good-quality modern Portuguese and international fare. The choice is impressive, with two dozen starters, plus the ever-popular *petiscos* (Portuguese-style tapas). The place prides itself on its *bacalhau* (cod) and *bife* (beef) dishes. Closed Tue.

AMOREIRAS Mezzaluna

€€€€€

Rua Artilharia Um 16, 1250-039 **Tel** *213 879 944*   **Map** *5 A4*

This attractive restaurant, in a quiet neighbourhood, is arguably one of the best Italian restaurants in the city. On the menu are classics like spaghetti alla carbonara, tagliatelle with shrimp and vodka sauce, and lemon *meccheroni*, an inspired combination of leek, salmon and capers with cognac cream sauce. Marvellous wine list. Closed Sat lunch & Sun.

AVENIDA Os Tibetanos

€

Rua do Salitre 117, 1250-198 **Tel** *213 142 038*   **Map** *4 F1*

Perfumed with incense and decorated with Tibetan prayer flags and images of the Dali Lama, this informal restaurant is an oasis for vegetarians. The imaginative and healthy menu is full of suggestions like *tofu com pesto e queijo de cabra* (tofu with pesto and goat's cheese). There's an open-air terrace at the rear of the building. Closed Sat & Sun.

AVENIDA Ribadouro

€€€

Rua do Salitre 2-12, 1250-200 **Tel** *213 549 411*   **Map** *4 F1*

On the corner of Avenida da Liberdade in a long, pointed building, Ribadouro is a great place to meet after a late film or show. Roomy, functional but with prompt service, the menu reads like a fisherman's wish list: oysters, buzios (whelks), crab, lobster and other seafood (all priced by the kilogram) stand alongside more conventional meat dishes.

BAIRRO ALTO Bota Alta

€

Travessa da Queimada 35-37, 1200-364 **Tel** *213 427 959*   **Map** *7 A3*

In the heart of Lisbon's bohemian quarter, the popular "High Boot" has an attractive interior, decorated with original paintings and ceramics, including an enormous clay boot placed on the bar. The menu is traditional Portuguese and includes *costeletas fumados à algarvia* (smoked ribs Algarve style) and *bacalhau real* (codfish). Closed Sat lunch & Sun.

BAIRRO ALTO Buenos Aires

€

Calçada Escadinhas do Duque 31b, 1200-155 **Tel** *213 420 739*   **Map** *7 A3*

The generous cuts of Argentine beef served with potatoes and a crispy green salad are the obvious choice at this decorative eatery that draws a young, attractive crowd. Cosy and intimate, the walls are festooned with colourful cards and posters. The menu features some truly memorable chocolate desserts. Reservations recommended. Closed Sun.

Key to Symbols *see back cover flap*

BAIRRO ALTO Casanostra

▤ €

Travessa do Poço da Cidade 60, 1200-334 **Tel** *213 425 931* **Map** *7 A3*

A favourite haunt of Lisbon's artistic and intellectual set, this Italian restaurant is renowned for its creative six-page menu. Popular choices include *penne all'arrabbiata* (pasta with bacon smothered in hot tomato and garlic sauce). The wine list has been carefully chosen to complement each dish. Closed Sat lunch.

BAIRRO ALTO A Charcutaria

▤ €€€

Rua do Alecrim 47a, 1200-015 **Tel** *213 423 845* **Map** *7 A4*

This is one of the best places in Lisbon to experience traditional Alentejo fare, and it's all about authentic cooking without the frills. Using fresh, seasonal produce, the kitchen conjures up regional delights such as *canja* (consommé) of partridge, sea bass with clams and dogfish soup. Closed Sat lunch & Sun.

BAIRRO ALTO Imperio dos Sentidos

▨▤ €€€

Rua da Atalaia 35-7, 1200-037 **Tel** *213 431 822* **Map** *4 F2*

Snuggling inside an early 20th-century building, this understated eatery, though not billed as a seafood restaurant, nonetheless entices clients with dishes such as pasta with creamed spinach sauce and shrimp, and salmon loin in red wine sauce. It's also well known for desserts, especially the hot chocolate *"petit gâteau"* with mint sauce. Closed Mon.

BAIRRO ALTO Bachus

▨▤▯ €€€€€

Largo da Trindade 9, 1200-466 **Tel** *210 961 909* **Map** *7 A3*

With its stylish Art Deco interior, Bachus specializes in both Portuguese and international cuisine, while providing a varied choice for vegetarians. Dishes range from the terrine of duck liver marinated in Muscatel to the monkfish medallions crusted with olives, sweet potato and fresh thyme. The pork loin is another highlight. Closed Sun & Mon.

BAIRRO ALTO Pap'Açorda

▤ €€€€€

Rua da Atalaia 57, 1200-037 **Tel** *213 464 811* **Map** *4 F2*

One of Lisbon's great gastronomic landmarks, this establishment was one of the first to modernize Portuguese food and remains one of the most successful restaurants in the city. Both Lisboetas and tourists come here for the delicious *açorda de mariscos* (bread stew and seafood). Comprehensive wine list. Reservations essential. Closed Sun & Mon.

BAIRRO ALTO Tavares Rico

▤ €€€€€

Rua da Misericórdia 35-37, 1200-270 **Tel** *213 421 112* **Map** *7 A4*

A revered institution with a more than 200-year-old history, this rich heritage makes Tavares a very special place to dine. Fashioned in gilt and walled with mirrors, the restored dining room exudes 18th-century charm and elegance. The menu is modern, international gourmet cuisine, with an outstanding wine list. Closed Sun & Mon.

BAIXA Muni

▧▨▤ €€€

Rua dos Correeiros 115-117, 1100-163 **Tel** *218 884 203* **Map** *7 B4*

Discreet and unassuming, this delightful restaurant does justice to traditional Portuguese fare. Taster dishes include an excellent octopus salad and *peixinhos da horta* (runner beans deep-fried in crispy batter). The *cabrito assado no forno* (oven-baked kid) is as succulent as you'll get anywhere. Wine stocked from every region in Portugal. Closed Sat & Sun.

BELÉM Rosa dos Mares

▨▤▯▣ €

Rua de Belém 2-4, 1300-085 **Tel** *213 621 811* **Map** *1 C4*

This attractive restaurant is named after a seafaring legend dating from the era of Discoveries. After months at sea, a crewmember spied roses floating in the water. The flowers heralded land. Overjoyed, the dockland collected the roses and upon return to Portugal presented them to the queen. Naturally, specialities here are fresh seafood. Closed Mon.

BELÉM No Solo Italia

▧▨▤▣ €€€

Avenida Brasilia 202, 1400-038 **Tel** *213 015 969* **Map** *1 B5*

This restaurant sits right at the edge of a small lake that's situated in front of the Monument to the Discoveries, with the river beyond. At night the monument is illuminated and the view from a waterside table is quite remarkable. So is the food, with a delicious range of Italian staples such as pasta dishes, pizzas and ice creams.

BELÉM BBC - Belém Bar Café

▧▩▰▤▯▣ €€€€€

Avenida de Brasilia - Pavilhão Poente, 1300-598 **Tel** *213 624 232* **Map** *2 E4*

Slick and sophisticated interior design at this riverside restaurant. The refined dining environment is further enhanced with one glance at the menu. Starters like tuna tartare with ginger and fresh herbs and main courses like one-sided salmon with plantain, lime chutney and cuttlefish ink gives some idea of the chef's ingenuity. Closed Sun & Mon.

BELÉM Vela Latina

▨▰▤▯▣ €€€€€

Doca do Bom Sucesso, 1400-038 **Tel** *213 017 118* **Map** *1 B5*

The relatively high prices here reflect Vela Latina's enviable waterfront location and its menu of classic, well-prepared Portuguese cuisine. Choices include lobster-filled crepes and fillet of hake with rice. There is a peaceful, unhurried air and of course, the view of the Tagus River and nearby Torre de Belém is priceless. Closed Sun.

CAMPO DE OURIQUE Tasquinha d'Adelaide

▨▤▣ €€€

Rua do Patrocínio 70-74, 1350-231 **Tel** *213 962 239* **Map** *3 C2*

The menu choice at this cosy restaurant has its origins in the Tras-os-Montes and as such diners can feast on regional dishes like *rojões à transmontana* (fried pork Tras-os-Montes) and *paletilha e sela de borrego no forno* (saddle of oven-racked lamb). A wide variety of wines are available to suit the palate. Arrive early to beat the locals. Closed Sun.

CAMPO PEQUENO Rodízio Grill €€

Campo Pequeno 79, 1000-082 **Tel** *217 939 760*   **Map** *5 C1*

Large, well-ordered restaurant built to serve a high turnaround of custom. The menu lists 40 starters alone! The theme is South American and dishes include the Brazilian BBQ – ribs of buffalo flavoured with spicy garlic and served with black beans and banana fritters. The buffet "pay as you weigh" price depends on how much you stack on your plate.

CAMPO PEQUENO Clube dos Empresários €€€€€

Avenida da República 38, 1050-194 **Tel** *217 994 280*   **Map** *5 C2*

This splendid restaurant is housed in a 1906 mansion. Originally founded as a place where politicians and businessmen could socialize, the dining experience is enhanced by original period furniture, antique artifacts and a French-influenced menu. It's a venue to dress for, but the owners insist that the casually attired are welcome for lunch. Closed Sun.

CAMPOLIDE Aya €€€

Galarias Twin Towers, Rua Campolide 531, 1060-034 **Tel** *217 271 115*   **Map** *5 A4*

Arguably the city's best Japanese restaurant, Aya's ambiance is one of low lights and hushed conversation, a relaxing way to enjoy the tempting selection of tempura, sushi and sashimi and some wonderful noodle dishes. Service here is polite and dignified, and worth the effort of heading off the beaten track to find. Reservations recommended.

CASTELO Restô do Chapitô €€€

Costa do Castelo 7, 1149-079 **Tel** *218 855 550*   **Map** *7 C3*

Chapitô is actually a school for performing arts and the cheerful ambience is carried through to the informal restaurant where you can enjoy dishes like steak with mustard sauce, trout with bacon and flame grilled sausages. Some tables offer incredible views of downtown Lisbon. Live jazz enlivens the weekends and the place can get very busy in summer.

CASTELO Casa do Leão €€€€€

Castelo de São Jorge, 1100-129 **Tel** *218 875 962*   **Map** *8 D3*

Chef's suggestions here include the excellent goat cheese terrine with cherry tomato confit followed by leg of duck with ratatouille. The restaurant is incorporated into the grounds of Castelo de São Jorge *(see pp76–7);* customers must book in advance to ensure the entrance fee is deducted from their bill. On warm days, tables are set outside.

CHIADO La Brasserie de l'Entrecôte €€€

Rua do Alecrim 117, 1200-016 **Tel** *213 473 616*   **Map** *7 A4*

There's only one fixed menu here, a crunchy green salad garnished with pine nuts and French dressing followed by prime cutlets of entrecôte steak, prepared as you wish, swamped in a cream and herb sauce and served with finger-thin French fries. There is a choice of 3 desserts. You can't book ahead, so arrive early for a table.

GRAÇA Via Graça €€€

Rua Damasceno Monteiro 9b, 1170-108 **Tel** *218 870 830*   **Map** *8 D1*

Via Graça is perched on the edge of a hill, serving a panorama that showcases the landmark Castelo de São Jorge. The late Hollywood actor Anthony Quinn used to come here when he was in town. The well-presented Portuguese cuisine includes dishes like *lombino de javali braseado* (wild boar). Excellent wine list. Closed Sat & Sun lunch.

LAPA Picanha €€

Rua das Janelas Verdes 96, 1200-692 **Tel** *213 975 401*   **Map** *4 D4*

For a set price you can eat all you want, but the meal is based around one ingredient: *picanha,* which is rump steak grilled on an open fire. Tread carefully and you'll have room for dessert, the choice of which includes cheesecake, chocolate mousse and tropical fruit. The interior is decorated with some beautiful *azulejo* tiles. Closed lunch.

LAPA Sua Excelência €€€

Rua do Conde 34, 1200-637 **Tel** *213 903 614*   **Map** *4 D3*

At "His Excellency", in Lisbon's diplomatic quarter, the proprietor can recite the menu in five languages. The food is classic Portuguese, with the *cogumelos salteados em manteiga com natas e vinho da Madeira* (fried mushrooms in a butter, cream and Madeira wine sauce) just one example of the chef's creativity. Booking advised. Closed Sat & Sun lunch.

LAPA A Confraria €€€€€

Pensão York House, Rua das Janelas Verdes 32, 1200-691 **Tel** *213 962 435*   **Map** *4 D3*

This charming hotel restaurant offers an eclectic menu and a delightful setting. Customers can sit inside and admire the tiled walls, or outside below a palm in the flower-laden garden. The cuisine is typically Portuguese and includes monkfish in a mustard sauce and partridge in a vinegar-flavoured marinade. The wine list features earthy Douro reds.

LAPA Restaurante Lapa €€€€€

Lapa Palace, Rua do Pau da Bandeira 4, 1249-021 **Tel** *213 949 494*   **Map** *3 C3*

Sumptuous gourmet dining in the luxury Lapa Palace Hotel. The seasonal menu places the emphasis firmly on Italian cooking of the highest order. Specialities include c*arpaccio clássico* (thinly sliced prime beef) and *tagliolini verdi gratinado com presunto* (home-made green thin noodles with ham *"au gratin"*). Top wine list.

MARQUÊS DE POMBAL Marisqueira Santa Marta €€€

Travessa do Enviado de Inglaterra 1d, 1150-139 **Tel** *213 525 638*   **Map** *5 C5*

At lunchtime, this place heaves with hungry mouths and it's often difficult to get a table. The restaurant is known for its wide range of fish and shellfish dishes, as well as for a good choice of traditional Portuguese fare. Value for money and a loyal clientele is another reason why you might have to wait before taking your seat.

MARQUÊS DE POMBAL Pabe ⬛☰🅿 €€€€
Rua Duque de Palmela 27a, 1250-097 **Tel** *213 537 484* **Map** *5 C5*

A city centre restaurant with a difference: the building is designed as a mock Tudor house, complete with stained-glass windows. The medieval atmosphere is further accentuated by wooden beams and copper tables. Try the charcoal grilled baby goat and the breaded squid in mayonnaise sauce, but not before a Bloody Mary apéritif, or a flute of champagne.

MARQUÊS DE POMBAL Eleven ☰🅿 €€€€€
Rua Marquês de Fronteira, Jardim Amália Rodrigues, 1070-310 **Tel** *213 862 211* **Map** *5 B4*

Named after 11 entrepreneurs who established Lisbon's first world-class design-driven restaurant, this is a Michelin-starred gastronomic *tour de force*. Contemporary interior and sophisticated ambience complemented by an international menu that pushes the boundaries of "concept cuisine" to new levels. Heady wine list. Book in advance. Closed Sun.

MARQUÊS DE POMBAL Restaurante 33A ☰🍽 €€€€€
Rua Alexandre Herculano 33a, 1250-008 **Tel** *213 546 079* **Map** *5 C5*

This restaurant has a small lounge space that resembles the interior of a hunting lodge, with stuffed deer and boar heads staring down impassively from the wall. In fact, the whole place has a rural ambience and a décor to match. The menu is traditional Portuguese and is more likely to be enjoyed by city types than country folk. Closed Sun & Sat lunch.

MOURARIA Tentações de Goa 👤☰ €
Rua S. Pedro Mártir 23, 1100-555 **Tel** *218 875 824* **Map** *7 C3*

A hidden little gem tucked away in a cobblestone backstreet, this modest restaurant is the recipient of a best ethnic food award for its exotic Goan menu. Dishes include lentils with lamb, fish massala and baby shark. The service is prompt and friendly and great value for money, considering this is slap bang in the city centre. Closed Sun.

PRAÇA ESPANHA O Polícia 👤☰🅿 €€
Rua Marquês Sá da Bandeira 112a, 1050-158 **Tel** *217 963 505* **Map** *5 B2*

So named because the owner's father was a policeman, the menu here changes daily but is based around seafood and shellfish. The *espetada de tamboril* (monkfish kebab) is particularly good. The restaurant has won numerous awards and attracts loyal patrons. Look out for the smiling policeman painted on the window. Closed Sun & Sat eve.

PRAÇA ESPANHA A Gôndola 👤🚠☰ €€€
Avenida de Berna 64, 1050-043 **Tel** *217 970 426* **Map** *5 B2*

Located opposite the Gulbenkian Centre, the daily specials here are great value. The menu, bursting with Portuguese and Italian dishes, features a vegetarian selection and some wicked desserts, including vodka sorbet. This is a charming place to unwind, especially during the summer when you can enjoy your meal in the pleasant gardens

PRAÇAO DO CHILE Cervejaria Portugalia ⬛👤☰🍽 €€
Avenida Almirante Reis 117, 1115-014 **Tel** *213 140 002* **Map** *6 E5*

This cavernous, atmospheric beer hall is the original of a national chain *(see p137)* and serves excellent seafood dishes like *açorda de camarão* (bread stew with prawns). The *presuntos* (cured hams) are also very good. A huge aquarium lines one side of the bar, where if you prefer you can just order a beer and soak in the atmosphere.

RATO Real Fábrica ⬛👤☰🍽 €€
Rua da Escola Politécnica 275, 1250-101 **Tel** *213 852 090* **Map** *4 E1*

Between 1735 and 1835, this was a silk-manufacturing factory under Royal patronage. Later abandoned, the building was refurbished in 1995. Roomy, with a wood and stone interior decor and an al fresco ambience, starters here include spicy Mozambique prawns. The signature dish is entrecote à Real Fábrica – steak fit for a king. Closed Sun.

RATO Casa da Comida 🚠☰🅿 €€€€€
Travessa das Amoreiras 1, 1250-025 **Tel** *213 885 376* **Map** *5 B5*

A refined restaurant with a charming patio overflowing with bouganvillia, this is a place to go for a romantic evening when good food is more important than price. The menu is haute cuisine in style and international in outlook, with caviar, frogs' legs, duck and pheasant. Naturally, the wine list is exceptional. Closed Sun and Mon & Sat lunch.

RESTAURADORES Casa do Alentejo 🎵☰ €
Rua das Portas de Santo Antão 58, 1150-268 **Tel** *213 405 140* **Map** *7 A2*

Visitors to this extraordinary 19th-century house are in for a surprise. Behind the unremarkable façade is a beautiful Moorish-style courtyard decorated with tiles inlaid with intricate Arabic calligraphy. Art exhibitions regularly take place here, as do choral recitals. The food is standard regional fare, but the exuberant surroundings more than compensate.

RESTAURADORES Solar dos Presuntos ☰ €€€
Rua das Portas de Santo Antão 150, 1150-269 **Tel** *213 424 253* **Map** *7 A2*

This restaurant is one of Lisbon's best places to sample *presunto* – leg of cured ham. The window display is devoted to hams and also allows passers-by to see cuts being prepared. Solar dos Presuntos is also well known for its fish and seafood dishes, and with a menu so rich in Portuguese culinary tradition reservations are advisable. Closed Sun.

RESTAURADORES Gambrinus ☰ €€€€€
Rua das Portas de Santo Antão 23, 1150-264 **Tel** *213 421 466* **Map** *7 B2*

One of the best seafood restaurants in the country, Gambrinus is exclusive and expensive. It is not only shellfish that attracts visitors, the menu lists Iranian Beluga caviar and truffle *foie gras*, among the starters. Fresh fish is the mainstay however, with a carefully selected choice available. The extensive wine list includes an array of vintage ports.

SALDANHA António   €

Rua Tomás Ribeiro 63, 1050-226 **Tel** *213 538 780*   **Map** *5 C3*

António's is a good stop for lunch. The cooking is straightforward and served up with a polite but no nonsense attitude. The portions are generous, with steak and fries or roast chicken a popular order. The dessert list leans heavily towards ice-cream. A handy take-away service is available and is considerably less than the sit-down price. Closed Sun.

SANTA APOLÓNIA Casanova   €

Avenida Infante Dom Henrique, at Cais da Pedra, 1900-264 **Tel** *218 877 532*   **Map** *8 F3*

This trendy Italian eatery has a prime position overlooking the river. A scribbled version of the menu is stencilled on the wall near the entrance and it's clear that pizzas are the speciality. They even offer an unusual but delicious chocolate-spread pizza as a dessert. Advance bookings are not accepted, so it's first come, first served.

SANTA APOLÓNIA Faz Figura   €€€€

Rua do Paraíso 15b, 1100-396 **Tel** *218 868 981*   **Map** *8 F2*

The tables on the covered terrace at this fashionable restaurant are hard to come by given the dizzy views of the Tagus river, but if you're prepared to wait you can linger over a drink in the bar. The menu is eclectic, with traditional Portuguese cuisine and dishes with an international twist. Children and vegetarians are catered for.

SANTA APOLÓNIA Bica do Sapato   €€€€€

Avenida Infante Dom Henrique, at Cais da Pedra, 1900-000 **Tel** *218 810 320*   **Map** *8 F3*

Part-owned by American actor John Malkovich, this trend-setting restaurant housed in a converted riverfront warehouse offers modern interpretations of Portuguese dishes in the gourmet area, bistro food in the café and a mix of Asian fusion and sushi specials upstairs. Minimalist decor and a soft jazz soundtrack. Booking advisable. Closed Sun & Mon lunch.

SANTOS Kais   €€€€€

Cais da Viscondessa, Rua da Cintura do Porto de Lisboa, 1200-109 **Tel** *213 932 930*   **Map** *4 D4*

Superb example of how an old warehouse can be transformed into a fashionable venue, Kais is two restaurants in one. Downstairs is "Adega" where typical Portuguese food is served. Upstairs, a refined international menu caters to discerning palates in an industrial chic setting. 200 wines from around the world. Reservations essential. Closed Sun.

SÃO BENTO Trivial   €€

Rua da Palmeira 44a, 1200-314 **Tel** *213 473 552*   **Map** *4 F2*

An informal atmosphere and discreet service has won this small and intimate restaurant a loyal patronage. Traditional Portuguese cuisine is the mainstay, with beefsteak the speciality. It's prepared either with mushrooms and pepper, Roquefort cheese or even vermouth! Parking in the vicinity is a real problem so avoid arriving by car. Closed Sun.

SÃO BENTO Conventual   €€€

Praça das Flores 45, 1200-192 **Tel** *213 909 246*   **Map** *4 E2*

Hugging one of Lisbon's most charming squares, this is a restaurant decorated with artifacts from convents. The menu reflects the Portuguese vernacular and offers some fine variations on regional cuisine. Specialities include duck and red pepper with a champagne sauce. The wine list suits all denominations. Closed Sun, and Mon & Sat lunch.

XABREGAS D'Avis   €€

Rua do Grilo 96-98, 1950-146 **Tel** *218 681 354*

Located east of the city centre near the former Convento dos Grilos and on the same side of the street as the Igreja de São Bartolomeu, this popular rustic-styled venue has a menu influenced by southern Portuguese cooking. Try the cod with coriander and *migas* (bread-based stew with spare ribs). The wine list features Alentejo labels. Closed Sun.

THE LISBON COAST

ALCÁCER DO SAL Dom Afonso II   €€€

Pousada de Alcácer do Sal, 7580-197 **Tel** *265 613 070*   **Road map** *C5*

Housed in the historic surrounds of the Pousada de Alcácer do Sal, the menu here is influenced by the ocean and the river, with Sado fish soup a typical starter. The river also provides the main ingredient for the unusual tomato rice with fried eel. Other more conventional though no less creative choices include lamb stew with a pennyroyal cream.

CASCAIS Casa Velha   €

Avenida Valbom 1, 2750-508 **Tel** *214 832 586*   **Road map** *B5*

In the heart of Cascais, the property resembles a traditional farmhouse with a maritime themed interior, complete with mock oil lanterns over the tables. The menu is predominantly seafood, with *caldeirada de peixe* (fish stew) and *cherne grelhado* (grilled halibut) among the favourites. The kitchen also rustles up delicious *paella*. Closed Wed.

CASCAIS Mayura   €

Rua Freitas Reis 15b, 2750-357 **Tel** *214 846 540*   **Road map** *B5*

Flavours from the sub-continent abound at this restaurant located in a quiet neighbourhood away from the beach. The menu is what you'd expect from any quality curry house but the presentation is first class. Besides the tandoori specialities, the kitchen serves a variety of spicy Goan dishes. The ceiling is decorated with colourful Indian shawls.

CASCAIS Eduardo's

Largo das Grutas 3, 2750-367 **Tel** *214 831 901*   **Road map** *B5*

With its wooden panels and squat appearance, this Belgian-run restaurant could be mistaken for a forester's lodge. Inside, an aquarium forms part of a dividing wall. The food slants towards French European, with options like *ragoût de borrego à flamenga* (Flemish style lamb ragoût) and delicious sweet crepes. Closed Sun.

CASCAIS Aromi– Some Place Else

Rua Frederico Arouca 32, 2750-343 **Tel** *214 862 191*   **Road map** *B5*

Located on the main pedestrian street in the old part of town, close to the beach and seaside promenade, this restaurant serves fine home-made Italian fare at reasonable prices. House specialities include vegetarian lasagne and a tasty tuna dish with asparagus. The mouthwatering millefeuille with strawberries rounds the meal off nicely.

CASCAIS O Pescador

Rua das Flores 10b, 2750-348 **Tel** *214 832 054*   **Road map** *B5*

This well-established seafood restaurant has lured Mick Jagger and Julio Iglesias, among many other famous personalities. It is decorated with quirky maritime artifacts. An ocean of choice leaps from the menu, with lobster soup, rose shrimp cocktail, spidercrab platter, swordfish steak and codfish *cataplana*. Closed Sun (winter); Mon lunch (summer).

CASCAIS Gourmet Hotel Miragem

Avenida Marginal 8554, 2775-536 **Tel** *210 060 600*   **Road map** *B5*

The Miragem's menu *table d'hôte* is a culinary roll call of some of the finest food on the coast, such as lobster cocotte with artichokes, truffles and *piquillo*, milk-fed veal medallions with citrus and pistachio pesto and asparagus risotto with wild mushrooms and parmesan cheese. The three restaurants here all offer international-influenced Portuguese cuisine.

CASCAIS The Mix

Avenida Rei Humberto de Itália 7, 2750-461 **Tel** *214 823 490*   **Road map** *B5*

Set in a remodelled 19th-century mansion but sporting a bright, airy modern look, The Mix offers sushi and Mediterranean fusion cuisine cooked in a way that preserves its flavour and structure. Choices include pigeon breast with beluga lentils and *foie gras* sauce. The floor-to-ceiling windows afford a full view of the deck and the rocky coast.

ERICEIRA Sall

Rua Capitão João Lopes 14, 2655-295 **Tel** *261 862 759*   **Road map** *B5*

Well situated on the seafront, Sall practically opens out into the ocean, and the menu is orientated in the same direction. The fish specialities include *feijoada de marisco* (seafood and bean stew) and seafood curry. The daily specials are another option. Surprisingly for such a modest eatery, the wine list is more than adequate. Closed Mon eve & Tue.

ESTORIL Pinto's

Arcadas do Parque 18b, 2765-087 **Tel** *214 687 247*   **Road map** *B5*

Close to the Palácio Hotel and with pleasant views across the esplanade gardens, Pinto's is a mix of bar, cafeteria and restaurant and is a great standby if you want a quick meal without breaking the bank. Pizzas, pastas, omelettes and burgers share the menu with a large selection of shellfish and some generous salads.

ESTORIL Estoril Mandarin

Casino Estoril, 2765-237 **Tel** *214 667 700*   **Road map** *B5*

This is the best place in Portugal to sample authentic Chinese cuisine. The Peking duck is sautéed, sliced and served wrapped in crisp lettuce leaves. Lunchtimes are a revelation, with delicious dim-sum a great choice. The menu also includes mini deep-fried spring rolls and shredded pork congee soup with egg. Closed Mon & Tue.

ESTORIL Four Seasons Grill

Hotel Palácio Estoril, Rua Particular, 2765-000 **Tel** *214 680 400*   **Road map** *B5*

Located in the Palácio Hotel, this is one of Estoril's most sophisticated fine dining venues. Set within a stylishly designed mezzanine and lower floor, the restaurant's decor changes according to each season of the year. The *à la carte* menu shines with superb Portuguese and international cuisine and is done justice by an inspired wine list and attentive service.

GUINCHO Estalagem Muchaxo

Praia do Guincho, 2750 642 **Tel** *214 870 221*   **Road map** *B5*

Housed in the *estalagem* of the same name, Muchaxo affords splendid views over Cabo da Roca, the most westerly point of the European mainland. The restaurant offers a good seafood menu, with the lobster in a tomato, cream and port sauce typical of the dishes on offer. The kitchen has its own shellfish beds, so fresh supply is constant.

GUINCHO Porto de Santa Maria

Estrada do Guincho, 2750-642 **Tel** *214 879 450*   **Road map** *B5*

With its stunning location overlooking Guincho beach and the Sintra Hills, this attractive restaurant is very popular. The menu pays tribute to the ocean with stuffed crab, rock lobster, oyster and shrimp just for starters. One of the house specialities is fish backed in crusty bread smothered with olive oil and garlic. The wine cellar is exemplary. Closed Mon.

MONTE ESTORIL O Sinaleiro

Avenida de Sabóia 595, 2765-278 **Tel** *214 685 439*   **Road map** *B5*

Unassuming but welcoming, O Sinaleiro divides itself between a bar and the restaurant proper. At first glance the menu appears to list fairly standard Portuguese fare, though the cooking is excellent. Look more closely though and you'll spy more unique fare like *espetada mista de caça* (barbecued wild boar and deer kebab). Closed Wed.

MONTE ESTORIL Com Sentido's 🖼️📖📶 ℗ €€€€

Avenida de Sabóia 515d, 2765-502 **Tel** *214 682 838*

Large, abstract canvasses adorn the walls of this fashionable restaurant and the care taken with the decor marries well with the time spent compiling the menu. Customers can opt for meals like the duck *magrêt* in orange sauce or milk-fed veal cutlet *confit* with sautéed Swiss chard. The dessert list is equally appealing. Closed Sun & Mon lunch.

PAÇO D'ARCOS Aquarela do Brasil 🎭🎵📖 ℗ €

Praça 5 de Outubro 12, 2770-029 **Tel** *214 415 412* **Road map** *B5*

This charming establishment resembles an art gallery more than a restaurant. *Aquarela* means watercolour, but the owners encourage artists to submit work for the walls in all mediums. The Brazilian food is wonderful, with generous portions offered in an easy-going manner. Expect some noisy banter. Closed Sun eve (winter); Tue lunch (summer).

PALMELA Pousada do Castelo de Palmela 🎭🖼️🎵📖 ℗ €€€€€

Pousada do Castelo de Palmela, 2950-317 **Tel** *212 351 226* **Road map** *C5*

The converted refectory of the 15th-century monastery provides a suitably romantic setting for a restaurant that offers discreet service in historic surroundings. The dining hall is part illuminated by chandelier that throws light across such delicacies as oyster soup or Dover sole in a beer marinade. The diverse cellar stocks several Muscatels.

PORTINHO DA ARRÁBIDA Beira-Mar ♿🎭🖼️📖📶 €€

Portinho da Arrábida, 2925-378 **Tel** *212 180 544* **Road map** *C5*

On warm days, the most sought-after tables are on the balcony overlooking the harbour. The stunning seaside setting helps whet the appetite for a robust selection of food and customers can enjoy specials such as *arroz de tamboril* (monkfish rice) and *arroz de marisco* (seafood rice). In summer, the sardines are a must! Closed Wed (in winter).

QUELUZ Cozinha Velha 🎵📖 ℗ €€

Largo Palácio Nacional de Queluz, 2745-191 **Tel** *214 356 158* **Road map** *B5*

Set in the old kitchens of the Queluz Royal Palace, this venerable restaurant draws on traditional Portuguese recipes. The building retains much of the 18th-century architecture, with the original stone chimney acting as a design centre-piece. The wealth of meat and fish dishes is complemented by excellent wines and a celebrated choice of desserts.

SESIMBRA Ribamar ♿🎭🖼️📖 ℗ €

Avenida dos Náufragos 29, 2970-637 **Tel** *212 234 853* **Road map** *C5*

Comfortable, cheerful and flooded with light, Ribamar sits right on the waterfront and is considered one of the best restaurants in the region. Along with the sea views, it serves up some wonderfully original concoctions, and there's always something new on the menu. Be daring and opt for the fish with seaweed, or cream of sea-urchin soup.

SETÚBAL Poço das Fontainhas 🎭🖼️📖📶 €€

Rua das Fontainhas 96, 2910-082 **Tel** *265 534 807* **Road map** *C5*

Tucked away near the Tróia ferry terminal, this popular restaurant is a bit tricky to find but well worth the effort. Atlantic-fresh fish and seafood dominate the menu, with *caldeirada à setubalense* (Setúbal-style fish and potato casserole) and *espetada de lulas* (squid kebab) among the highlights. Reservations recommended. Closed Mon.

SETÚBAL Pousada de São Filipe 🖼️📖 ℗ €€€€

Pousada de São Filipe, Castelo de São Filipe, 2900-300 **Tel** *265 550 070* **Road map** *C5*

The *pousada's* restaurant, Fortaleza, offers a jaw-dropping view of Setúbal and the Sado estuary and if it's warm, tables are set outside on the esplanade. The ambience is late 16th-century Portugal and the food reflects the country's centuries-old culinary tradition, with pumpkin cream soup, fried red mullet and grilled lamb with orange sauce.

SINTRA Monserrate ♿🎭📖📶 ℗ €

Hotel Tivoli Sintra, Praça de República, 2710-616 **Tel** *219 237 200* **Road map** *B5*

Housed in the Tivoli Hotel Sintra, this restaurant overlooks the lush, verdant Sintra valley, an inspiring view that is carried through to the Panorâmico bar. The international menu, which features dishes like *costeletas de borrego fritas com batata duchesse* (succulent fried lamb cutlets with duchess potatos) changes daily.

SINTRA Tulhas 🎭📖 €

Rua Gil Vicente 4-6, 2710-568 **Tel** *219 232 378* **Road map** *B5*

The mysterious hole near the entrance is the last vestige of a series of medieval granaries that once stood here (the Portuguese word for granary is *Tulhas*). Small and down-to-earth, the homemade food is wholesome and great value. The veal steak in Madeira wine is particularly flavoursome, but leave room for the cheesecake. Closed Wed.

SINTRA Lawrence's ♿🖼️📖 ℗ €€€€

Rua Consigliéri Pedroso 38-40, 2710-550 **Tel** *219 105 500* **Road map** *B5*

The owners describe Lawrence's as a restaurant with rooms rather than a hotel, such is the esteem in which they hold this gourmet venue. Indeed, Lord Byron and William Beckford are just two of the historical figures said to have eaten here. The *à la carte* cuisine is served with finesse, and there are over 200 wines to choose from.

SINTRA Restaurante Palácio de Seteais 🖼️📖 ℗ €€€€€

Avenida Earbosa du Bocage 8, Seteais, 2710-517 **Tel** *219 233 200* **Road map** *B5*

This former palace is a breathtaking example of 18th-century splendour, and is home to a splendid gourmet restaurant. The grand dining room, decorated with mythological motifs and frescos, affords outstanding views of the landscaped gardens and the coast. The menu is essentially Portuguese *haute cuisine*, with a wine list to match.

Key to Price Guide *see p408* **Key to Symbols** *see back cover flap*

ESTREMADURA AND RIBATEJO

ABRANTES Herdade de Cadouços
€
Água Travessa, Bemposta, 2205-163 **Tel** *241 760 000* **Road map** *C4*

Located in the hotel of the same name, on a large estate near Abrantes, this restaurant offers an intimate setting and fine views of the surrounding forest, lakes and hills. The menu features wild boar, hare and other locally caught game, as well as cod with cornbread and pork cutlets in breadcrumbs. Closed Sun eve & Mon (except Jul & Aug).

ABRANTES Santa Isabel
€
Rua Santa Isabel 12, 2200-393 **Tel** *967 893 970* **Road map** *C4*

A convenient city-centre choice, Santa Isabel offers cuisine influenced by the Ribatejo, the Beiras and the Alentejo regions of Portugal. One of the more unusual fish options is *sável com açorda* (shad with bread stew). Also on the menu is *arroz de lampreia* (lamprey with rice) and several pork dishes. Closed Sun & public holidays.

ABRANTES Cascata
€€
Rua Manuel Lopes Valente Júnior 19, 2200-260 **Tel** *241 361 011* **Road map** *C4*

Carefully presented regional cuisine served in an award-winning restaurant. The emphasis is on the traditional, and the menu heaves with a wealth of typical dishes like *feijoada de gambas com arroz crioulo* (prawn and bean rice). Desserts like the *delícia de noz com fios de ovos* (nut delicacy with egg strands) are delicious. Closed Mon.

ALCOBAÇA Trindade
€
Praça Dom Afonso Henriques 22, 2460-030 **Tel** *262 582 397* **Road map** *C4*

Located in a beautiful square next to the north wing of the imposing monastery, the specials here include regional favourites like *frango na púcara* (chicken stew) and *arroz de peixe com camarão* (fish and seafood rice). The house wine is very reasonable. The restaurant also houses a small café and a cake shop. Closed Wed; 2 weeks in May & Oct.

ALCOBAÇA Sentidos
€€
Rua Manuel Rodrigues Serrazina Fervença, 2460-743 **Tel** *262 505 370* **Road map** *C4*

Located in a hotel, Sentidos specializes in regional cuisine with French influences. The soft-brown colour scheme enhances the stylish interior to give a taste of what's to come. Delicious main courses include *tamboril com molho de vodka* (monkfish in vodka sauce) and *perca grelhada com molho de marisco* (grilled bass in seafood sauce).

ALMEIRIM Toucinho
€
Rua do Timor 72, 2080-103 **Tel** *243 592 237* **Road map** *C4*

Almeirim's most popular restaurant, this is a family-run establishment with fine country cooking. It is best known for its *sopa de pedra*, which is advertised in bold letters across the façade. The interior celebrates the bullfight, with colourful posters of tournament announcements decorating the walls. Reservations essential on Sundays. Closed Thu & Aug.

BATALHA Mestre Afonso Domingues
€€€
Largo Mestre Afonso Domingues, 2440-102 **Tel** *244 765 260* **Road map** *C4*

This centrally located restaurant, found in the *pousada* named after the architect of the nearby Santa Maria da Vitória monastery, serves such regional delights as fried pork with turnip tops and bream fillet with spinach. The terrace offers a superb view of the 14th-century monument and the whole experience is infused with a palatable sense of history.

CALDAS DA RAINHA A Lareira
€€
Rua da Lareira 35, Alto do Nobre, 2500-593 **Tel** *262 823 432* **Road map** *B4*

Nestling in a pinewood halfway between Caldas de Rainha and Foz de Arelho on the coast, A Lareira offers traditional Portuguese food as well as international dishes. Typical of the national dishes is *perdiz à Lareira* (partridge with chestnuts, fruits and vegetables) and *espetada de peru com ananás* (pork kebab with pineapple). Good wine list. Closed Tue.

CALDAS DA RAINHA Incógnito
€€€
Rua General Amílcar Mota, 2500-209 **Tel** *262 841 258* **Road map** *B4*

Incógnito offers fine Portuguese cuisine with a French twist in a chic, elegant interior. The dinner menu features a good choice of meat and fish dishes, with a leaner selection available at lunchtime. There are also a dozen different desserts to choose from. Closed Sun & Mon (but open Mon dinner in Jul & Aug).

FÁTIMA Dom Gonçalo Hotel & Spa
€€€
Rua Jacinto Marto 100, 2495-000 **Tel** *249 539 330* **Road map** *C4*

This is a welcoming and popular restaurant space set in the charming Dom Gonçalo Hotel. Tasty Portuguese fare like fillet of fish with prawn rice, or braised duck in orange sauce is served promptly and without fuss. The restaurant is very busy during Fátima's pilgrim dates, around the beginning of the second week in May and October.

FÁTIMA Tia Alice
€€€
Rua do Adro, 2495-557 **Tel** *249 531 737* **Road map** *C4*

Gastronomic tradition raised to a contemporary level makes this one of the hottest tables in town and a favourite culinary destination in May and October with Fátima's pilgrims. On the surface the food appears standard but the secret lies in the ingredients and preparation. House specialities include Trás-os-Montes-style rice. Closed Mon; Sun evening; Jul.

LEIRIA Tromba Riija   🧗📋   €€€

Rua Professores Portelas 22, 2400-406 **Tel** *244 855 072*   **Road map** C4

A positive feast awaits those brave enough to attempt to savour Tromba's entire buffet selection of *pesticos* (snacks). The table groans under the weight of breads, sausages, cheeses, fresh fish and seafood. Set meals include the belly-swelling pork and bean stew. Tue, Wed & Thu bookings only. Closed Mon; Sun evening; evening on public holidays.

NAZARÉ O Luis   📋   €

Sítio, 2450-065 **Tel** *262 551 826*   **Road map** C4

You have to take the funicular to Sítio to eat at this restaurant, located near the Nossa Senhora da Nazaré church. The interior is simple and discreet but has a homely feel missing from the better-known places in town. The speciality is *o barco* – a boat crammed with seafood of the day. The wine list includes refreshing vinho verde. Closed Thu.

NAZARÉ Mar Bravo   ♿🧗🛗📋   €€

Praça Sousa Oliveira 71, 2450-159 **Tel** *262 569 160*   **Road map** C4

Set in the hotel of the same name, Mar Bravo's best feature is a glass wall affording dramatic views over the ocean. The meat and fish menu choice includes starters like grilled prawns in garlic or *presunto Pata Negra* (cured black pig ham). The *chateaubriand à Mar Bravo* (tenderloin steak) is a favourite house speciality.

ÓBIDOS O Alcaide   🛗   €

Rua Direita, 2510-001 **Tel** *262 959 220*   **Road map** B4

Snuggled inside the castle walls on the picturesque Rua Direita, this rustic little jewel of a restaurant offers delicious food in a cosy atmosphere. Inventive Portuguese and international cuisine colour the menu, such as the cod fritters stuffed with Serra cheese served with chestnuts and baked apple. Closed Wed.

ÓBIDOS Castelo   📋   €€€€€

Pousada do Castelo, Paço Real, 2510-99 **Tel** *262 955 080*   **Road map** B4

Located in the *pousada*, which is part of the fairy-tale medieval castle, Castelo's unique location and stylish interior is mirrored in the food it serves, with *lombo de robalo selvagem com feijão-verde e bata suada à limão* (sea bass with green beans and puréed potato flavoured with lemon) just one of the well-presented gastronomic choices.

PENICHE Estelas   ♿📋P   €€

Rua Arquitecto Paulino Montês 21, 2520-294 **Tel** *262 782 435*   **Road map** B4

Estelas is situated in the town centre, next to the municipal market. The menu at the entrance lists just about every fish that can be caught in Portuguese waters including a local speciality, *robalo à ilha da Berlanga* (Berlanga sea bass) named after the nearby archipelago. The monkfish kebab, too, is a prize catch. Closed Wed & 2 weeks in Nov.

PENICHE Marisqueira Cortiçais   ♿🧗🛗   €€€€

Porto d'Areia Sul, 2520-000 **Tel** *262 787 262*   **Road map** B4

When Peniche lets its hair down and celebrates its festival of the sea *(see p31)* the first wave of revelry invariably takes place here. This may be because of its renowned *filet mignon com rabos de lagosta* (tender steak with broiled lobster tails) or the fact that it sits right on Cabo Carvoeiro beach. Closed Wed (Sep–Jul).

SANTARÉM Taberna do Quinzena   ♿🧗📋🍸   €

Rua Pedro de Santarém 93-95, 2000-223 **Tel** *243 322 804*   **Road map** C4

This bustling restaurant serving regional specialities has been in operation since the 19th century, originally as a simple tavern. The menu heaves with hearty Ribatejan fare, such as the enormous *pernil de porco no forno* (roast leg of pork) and the succulent *cabrito assado* (roast kid). A gastronomic landmark. Closed Sun; 15–31 Aug.

SANTARÉM Lugar da Frente   📋🍸P   €€€

Quinta do Gaio de Cima, EN3, Gaio, 2070-211 **Tel** *243 098 452*   **Road map** C4

Located in Cartaxo, south-west of Santarém, the interior of this smart, modern restaurant is washed is a sea of indigo. The constantly evolving menu leans towards traditional Portuguese cuisine. The chef's recommendations include *queijo de cabra com farinheira* (goat's cheese with spicy sausage) and the beef capacchio. Closed Mon; Sun evening.

TOMAR A Bela Vista   🍽🧗🛗   €

Rua Marquês Pombal 68, 2300-510 **Tel** *249 312 870*   **Road map** C4

This restaurant has beautiful views of the River Nabão and the castle, and is situated next to the old bridge. With all that for starters, main courses like *cabrito no forno* (roast kid) and *caldeirada* (fish stew) go down a treat. The flowered terrace is lovely during the summer months. Closed Mon evening & Tue; winter closure varies.

TOMAR Calça Perra Taj   🍽🛗📋🍸   €€

Rua Pedro Dias 59, 2300-589 **Tel** *249 346 723*   **Road map** C4

Located in the gardens of a 16th-century house, this is Tomar's first Indian restaurant. The proprietor hails from Kerala, in southern India, and has brought with him an exotic menu of spicy dishes that includes chicken and lamb vindaloo and biriani options. Be sure to try the *lassi de manga* (mango lassi) – mango milkshake Indian style. Closed Mon.

TOMAR Chico Elias   🍽📋P   €€

Rua Principal 70, Algarvias, 2300-302 **Tel** *249 311 067*   **Road map** C4

Family-run restaurant on the old road to Torres Novas, 2 km (1.2 miles) south of Tomar. The traditional recipes demand that much of the food be oven baked, and the chef is a dab hand at producing dishes like *coelho na abóbora* (rabbit with pumpkin). Book in advance – you can request a particular meal when doing so. Closed Sun eve, Tue; 1–15 Sep.

TORRES VEDRAS O Pátio do Faustino
♿ 🍴 🅿 €

Largo do Choupal, 2350-000 Tel 261 324 346 **Road map** B5

O Pátio is a large, rustic restaurant decorated in an eclectic style. Some rooms are adorned with antiques and Roman-style amphorae, others festooned with colourful football scarves. The restaurant caters for groups as well as individuals but all seek the delicious grilled fish dishes that are the speciality here, and the pleasant atmosphere. Closed Sun evening.

VILA FRANCA DE XIRA O Redondel
♿ 🚼 🍴 €€€

Arcadas da Praça de Touros, 2600-000 Tel 263 272 973 **Road map** C5

Housed under the elegant arches of the town's bullring, the restaurant's cuisine pays tribute to the *cavaleiro* (bullfighter) with such dishes as *costeleta de novilho à matador* (roasted ribs of prime beef). Other traditional Ribatejo dishes include *açorda de sável* (bread and shad fish stew). The wine list is a worthy match for the menu. Closed Mon.

THE BEIRAS

ALMEIDA Senhora das Neves
🍴 🅿 €€€

Pousada da Nossa Senhora das Neves, 6350-112 Tel 271 574 283 **Road map** E2

Set in the *pousada* inside Almeida's curious star-shaped fort, this bright and airy restaurant conveys a sense of history despite the hotel's modern look. The well-presented regional cuisine is extremely wholesome. A typical meal includes fish soup starter, codfish stuffed with smoked ham or grilled kid with creamed potatoes and almond pudding.

AVEIRO Cozinha do Rei
🚼 🔲 🍴 🅿 €€

Rua D Manuel Neves 66, 3800-101 Tel 234 483 710 **Road map** C3

The King's Kitchen serves the Hotel Dom Afonso V and is a large restaurant decorated in warm, inviting hues. The fish choice is exceptional, but it's the *espetada real e vitela assada* (royal veal kebab) that truly symbolizes the kitchen. The *ovos moles de Aveiro* (egg and sugar sweets) are a regional delicacy. Reservations recommended. Closed Wed.

AVEIRO Mercado do Peixe
🍴 €€

Largo do Mercado, Praça do Peixe, 3800-243 Tel 234 383 511 **Road map** C3

Situated above Aveiro's vibrant fish market and styled in a refreshingly modern, minimalist manner, this is a wonderful place at lunchtime to soak in the busy atmosphere of one of Portugal's busiest markets. The food is as fresh as it gets. Try the mussel soup as a starter. The *caldeiradas* (fish stews) are also excellent. Closed Sun evening & Mon.

AVEIRO O Mercantel
🚼 🍴 🅿 €€€

Rua António Santos Lé 16, 3800-105 Tel 234 428 057 **Road map** C3

This used to serve as a warehouse and would take delivery of fresh fish stocks from the canal barges lined up against the quay. Today, an eager clientele charts a course to this voluminous restaurant for its outstanding array of fresh fish and seafood. A good meat selection is also available. There's some romantic waterfront views. Closed Mon.

BELMONTE Pousada do Convento de Belmonte
♿ 🚼 🔲 🍴 🍷 🅿 €€€€€

Serra da Esperança, Belmonte, 6250-073 Tel 275 910 300 **Road map** D3

The restaurant, in line with the rest of the building, preserves the historical architecture of the former Nossa Senhora da Esperança convent and affords a dramatic panorama of the Cova da Beira. Ambitious regional Portuguese food is served alongside modern dishes such as duck breast with jasmine sauce and trout layered with *presunto* (cured ham).

BUÇACO Palace Hotel Bussaco
🔲 🍴 🍷 🅿 €€€€€

Palace Hotel do Buçaco, 3050-261 Tel 231 937 970 **Road map** C3

The dining room here is a Manueline fantasy, with an intricately carved balcony *(see p212)*. Palatial in dimensions and replete with paintings by João Vaz, the restaurant's cuisine is classical French and traditional Portuguese. Local dishes include fisherman's stew and roast suckling pig from Bairrada. Buçaco's acclaimed wines are bottled in the basement.

CARAMULO Restaurante Estalagem de Caramulo
🔲 🍴 🍷 🅿 €€€€

Avenida Dr Abel Lacerda, 3475-031 Tel 232 862 011 **Road map** C3

The panoramic restaurant at this *estalagem* really does live up to its name – the views of the rugged Serra do Caramulo are outstanding! The food is typically Portuguese made all the more appetizing after a walk in the mountains. Dishes include *arroz de pato á antiga* (traditional-style duck rice).

CASTELO BRANCO Praça Velha
🍴 €€

Praça Camões 17, 6000-000 Tel 272 328 640 **Road map** D4

Situated in an old granary transformed by visionary architects and interior designers, Praça Velha offers ambitious cuisine that combines traditional methods and modern creativity in dishes in like *paella D João V* and *lombo de porco com molho agridoce* (pork with corn). Wines from the Beira region figure prominently. Closed Sun evening & Mon.

COIMBRA Democratica
♿ 🍴 €

Travessa Rua Nova 7, 3000-000 Tel 239 823 784 **Road map** C3

This humble eatery is just two small rooms, the back one a favourite hangout for university students. A tasty snack is the *carapauzinhos* (fried mackerel). For something more substantial try the *prato do juiz* (judge's dish), a hearty pork casserole with potato and vegetables. The restaurant is signposted on Rua da Sofia. Closed Sun; public holidays.

COIMBRA O Trovador

Largo Sé Velha 15-17, 3000-383 **Tel** *239 825 475*   **Road map** *C3*

Positioned in front of Coimbra's Sé Velha and always a popular restaurant. The rustic decor adds to an already homely atmosphere and the food is typical of the region. Standard dishes abound, but for something more creative, go for the *chanfana* (kid stew in wine sauce). Weekend *fado* performances are not uncommon, so check for details. Closed Sun.

COIMBRA A Taberna

Rua dos Combatentes da Grande Guerra 86, 3030-181 **Tel** *239 716 265*   **Road map** *C3*

With its imposing stone arch and blazing wood oven, A Taberna offers a traditional Portuguese feast in a welcoming dining room. Try the *cogumelos selvagens com alho e salsa* (wild mushrooms with garlic and parsley) and the *polvo assado na brasa* (charcoal-grilled octopus). Reservations recommended. Closed Sun eve, Mon lunch & 1–15 Aug.

COIMBRA Arcadas da Capela

Quinta das Lágrimas, Rua António Augusto Gonçalves, 3041-901 **Tel** *239 802 380*   **Road map** *C3*

Dining at this luxury gourmet restaurant is a Michelin-starred treat. Executive chef Albano Lourenço changes the menu four times a year. One dish is themed around the doomed 14th-century affair between Pedro I and Inês de Castro. The kitchen celebrates the couple's lives with a four-course meal (available only at dinner).

CONDEIXA-A-NOVA Santa Cristina

Rua Francisco de Lemos, 3150-142 **Tel** *239 944 025*   **Road map** *C3*

A refined and contemporary styled restaurant aptly set in a modern *pousada* close to the famous ruins of Conimbriga. Regional favourites are listed together with several speciality dishes like roast kid with turnips tops and octopus rice and roast chicken with pepper sauce. The menu is supported by an interesting wine list.

GOUVEIA O Júlio

Rua do Loureiro 11, 6290-534 **Tel** *238 498 016*   **Road map** *D3*

The *arroz de carqueja com entrecosto* (steak rice) here is a classic example of Beira country cooking served in a rustic and unpretentious environment. In fact, the food is unashamedly traditional in orientation, with hearty dishes like *feijoca à pastor* (shepherd's bean stew) and *bacalhau à tia Arminda* (cod aunt Arminda) gracing the menu. Closed Tue.

GUARDA O Ferrinho

Rua Francisco de Passos 21, 6300-558 **Tel** *271 211 990*   **Road map** *D3*

With its solid 17th-century granite walls and noble appearance, this restaurant, next to the cathedral, blends well into Guarda's historical centre. The *ensopado de cabrito à Ferrinho* (kid broth) and *espetada mista de carnes* (mixed kebab) are two favourites, and game dishes like *guisado de javoli* (wild boar) are specialities when in season.

LUSO O Cesteiro

Rua Monsenhor Raúl Mira 76, 3050-235 **Tel** *231 939 360*   **Road map** *C3*

Located near the train station on the road leading out of town towards Mealhada, this unassuming but attractive eatery is a popular haunt with the locals. The hearty, unpretentious fare is fresh and wholesome and includes *chanfana* (kid stewed in wine), roast suckling pig with saffron sauce and various *bacalhau* (cod) dishes. Closed Wed.

MANTEIGAS São Lourenço

Penhas Douradas-Santa Maria, N232, 6260-200 **Tel** *275 980 050*   **Road map** *D3*

Set in a *pousada* high in the Serra da Estrela, north of Manteigas, the restaurant's decor matches the territory, all granite and wood. The red bean and cabbage soup is typical of the starters on offer. For the main course, try the *cabritinho no forno com arroz e esparregado* (oven baked kid with rice and asparagus seasoned with vinegar oil).

MEALHADA Pedro dos Leitões

Rua Álvaro Pedro 1, N1, Sernadelo, 3050-382 **Tel** *231 209 950*   **Road map** *C3*

Over 50 years in business, this is one of the region's best-known restaurants. A handy stop for travellers, the speciality is delicious *leitão* (suckling pig). The dish is served up in a manner of ways but is always accompanied by oven-roasted potatoes and onions. The menu also offers some fish options.

MONSANTO Estalagem de Monsanto

Rua da Capela 3, 6060-091 **Tel** *277 314 071*   **Road map** *E3*

The village of Monsanto sets the scene for this delightful restaurant set within the *estalagem*. National and regional cuisine is on offer but the local recipes really catch the eye. The soups are straight off the land: pumpkin, broad bean, turnip, chestnut and mushroom. Customers can select a four-course meal from the buffet. Closed Mon–Wed.

MONTEMOR-O-VELHO A Moagem

Largo Macedo Sotto Mayor, 3140-269 **Tel** *239 680 225*   **Road map** *C3*

Eel and lamprey dominate the menu at this charming riverside restaurant idyllically located on the edge of this hillside town. There is ample seating, and the classic interior exudes a formal ambience matched by the friendly, efficient service. The weekday lunchtime buffet is excellent value and full of choice. Closed Mon.

SORTELA Dom Sancho I

Largo do Corro, 6320-536 **Tel** *271 388 267*   **Road map** *D3*

Dom Sancho's weatherworn granite façade competes with the neighbouring Castelo da Sortelha for character, and the restaurant has a charming, medieval air. The cosy interior has a large open fireplace that helps fuel the appetite for dishes like *caldeirada de borrego* (lamb stew) and *feijoada de javoli* (wild boar with beans). Closed Sun evening & Mon.

Key to Price Guide *see p408* **Key to Symbols** *see back cover flap*

TRANCOSO O Museu

Largo de Santa Maria de Guimarães, 6420-101 **Tel** *271 811 810*　　　　　　　**Road map** D2

This restaurant is the former residence of the 15th-century priest Francisco da Costa, said to have fathered 224 children and narrowly escaped a death sentence imposed by King João II. The stonework walls enclose a rustic interior where smoked meats cooked with cabbage and potatoes are a speciality. Closed Sun eve & Mon (except Jul–Sep).

VISEU Casablanca

Avenida Emídio Navarro 70-72, 3500-124 **Tel** *232 422 239*　　　　　　　**Road map** D3

With a smart though modest interior decorated with pretty tiles, Casablanca's hallmark is an attentive attitude and quality cuisine. Fresh fish and seafood is the order of the day, with specialities like *arroz de polvo com gambas* (octopus rice with prawns). Meat dishes include *fondue de carne a Châteaubriant do lombinho* (fondue steak). Closed Mon.

VISEU Charrascaria Santa Eulália

Avenida Luís Martins, Repeses, 3500-227 **Tel** *232 436 283*　　　　　　　**Road map** D3

South of Viseu off the Estrada Nacional, Santa Eulália is a large spacious pit stop with a seafood-based menu. Salmon, bass, bream and perch are also on the menu, together with the usual variations of cod. Lamb, beef and pork dishes also hitch a ride. For those on the go, there's a handy take-away service available. Closed Thu.

VISEU O Cortiço

Rua Augusto Hilário 47, 3500-089 **Tel** *232 423 853*　　　　　　　**Road map** D3

This restaurant, located in the city's historical zone, comes highly recommended. The authentic regional cuisine leans towards meat dishes, some of which are christened with delightfully quirky names: the *coelho bêbado três dias em vida* (drunk rabbit with three days to live) is marinated in wine for several days before being cooked. Closed 24–25 Dec.

DOURO AND TRÁS-OS-MONTES

ALIJÓ Cêpa Torta

Rua Dr José Bulas Cruz, 5070-047 **Tel** *259 950 177*　　　　　　　**Road map** D2

Bright and modern, Cêpa Torta (twisted vine) is a classy fine-dining venue deep in the heart of port wine country. The menu sparkles with innovation, and the wine list is extensive. Husband-and-wife team Rui and Cristina keep an eye on things as guests tuck into port foie gras, partridge in chestnut purée and other such delicacies. Closed Tue.

ALIJÓ Barão de Forrester

Quinta Barão de Forrester, Rua José Ruffino, 5070-031 **Tel** *259 959 215*　　　　　　　**Road map** D2

Given its location deep in port country, it's no surprise that framed posters advertising several port wine houses decorate the walls of this tidy restaurant, which is housed in a *pousada*. A polished pine floor and printed fabric curtains also characterize the interior. Try the delicious roast kid transmontana-style or grilled octopus and pears with Muscatel wine.

AMARANTE São Gonçalo

Pousada de Marão-São Gonçalo, Ansiães, 4604-909 **Tel** *255 460 030*　　　　　　　**Road map** D2

Northeast of Amarante, São Gonçalo boasts a spectacular vista down a long, deep valley, especially at sunset. Housed in the *pousada* of the same name, the restaurant resembles a huge country kitchen with open fireplace and wrought-iron candelabras. The regional, rural menu features trout stuffed with ham, and pork with chestnuts.

AMARANTE Casa da Calçada

Largo do Paço 6, 4600-017 **Tel** *255 410 830*　　　　　　　**Road map** D2

This upscale, gourmet restaurant is housed in the Casa da Calçada, a splendid 16th-century former palace. The *menu degustion* perfectly complements the region's culinary heritage and the presentation, together with the wine choice, is what you'd expect from a Michelin-starred establishment. The interior conveys understated elegance.

BRAGANÇA Geadas

Rua do Loreto 32, 5300-184 **Tel** *273 324 413*　　　　　　　**Road map** E1

The window tables here command peaceful views of the River Fervença and the restaurant is very popular with Portuguese families at weekends. The large, comfortable exterior is styled in pinewood and local stone and the menu features typical regional cuisine like *perdiz estufada com castanhas* (partridge with chestnuts).

BRAGANÇA Solar Bragançano

Praça da Sé 34, 5300-271 **Tel** *273 323 875*　　　　　　　**Road map** E1

Housed on the first floor of an old mansion overlooking the main square, this restaurant has high ceilings that peer down on a dignified interior. It is the owners themselves who serve dishes like *faisão com castanhas* (pheasant with chestnuts). In summer, meals can be taken on the inner patio. Closed Mon in winter.

CHAVES Carvalho

Largo das Caldas, 5400-523 **Tel** *276 321 727*　　　　　　　**Road map** D1

There are fine views from this restaurant in Chaves's thermal spa complex. Starters include *melão ou manga com presunto* (sliced melon or mango with ham) and progress to main courses like *arroz de fumeiro* (rice with smoked meats). Be sure to try the heavenly *doce dos anjos à conventual* (convent angel's dessert). Closed Sun eve & Mon.

CHAVES Leonel   ♿ ⋔ 📋   €

Campo da Roda, 5400-007 **Tel** *276 323 188*   **Road map** *D1*

Located opposite the aerodome on the road southeast of Chaves towards São Julião de Montenegro, the menu here is small on quantity but big on quality. It includes *bacalhau au gratin* (baked codfish) and *açorda de marisco* (bread and shellfish stew) and the substantial portions make this place a popular dining spot. Closed Mon; 2 weeks in Nov.

ESPINHO Terraço Atlântico   ⋔ 📋 🍷 🅿   €€

Praia Golf Hotel, Rua 6, 4500-357 **Tel** *227 331 000*   **Road map** *C2*

Few restaurants have such a wonderful panoramic view as this one, though window tables are at a premium and reservations are recommended to secure one. Fish dishes are prominent on the menu, although the meat dishes are not forgotten, and both red and white wines from every region in Portugal are available.

GIMONDE Dom Roberto   ♿ ⋔ 🔲 📋 🅿   €€

EN 218, 5300-553 **Tel** *273 302 510*   **Road map** *D2*

The wooden balconies of this restaurant give it a somewhat Wild West look and the rustic, country theme is carried inside. The walls are decorated with antique farming implements, and painted over the fireplace is a wild boar in full flight. The restaurant is located on the riverside in the small town of Gimonde, 7 km (4 miles) east of Bragança.

LAMEGO Adega Matos   ⋔ 📋   €

Rua Trás da Sé 52, 5100-169 **Tel** *254 612 967*   **Road map** *D2*

Dishes like *enguias em molho de escabeche* (eels in pickle sauce) and *arroz de salpicão* (rice with pickled pork) spice up the traditional menu at this modest, town-centre restaurant located near the Sé (cathedral). The *frango no charraso* (grilled chicken) remains a firm favourite though, and is a popular take-away order. Closed Sun evening.

LAMEGO Restaurante Novo   ♿ ⋔ 🔲 📋   €

Largo da Sé 9, 5100-098 **Tel** *254 613 166*   **Road map** *D2*

This restaurant sits proudly in the town's main square, right in front of the cathedral. Its walls are adorned with mirrors and tiles, lending it a bright, airy feel. House specialities include *trutas grelhadas com presunto* (grilled trout stuffed with smoked ham) and *espetada de vitela com gambas* (veal and prawn kebabs). Closed Sat (Oct–Mar).

LEÇA DA PALMEIRA Casa da Chá Boa Nova   🔲 📋 🅿   €€€€€

Lugar da Boa Nova, Praia de Boa Nova, 4450-608 **Tel** *229 951 785*   **Road map** *C2*

The Tea House restaurant, set just above the shoreline on rocks overlooking the ocean, was designed by one of Portugal's eminent architects, Alvaro Siza Vieira. The menu is inspired by the vicinity and features dishes such as *feijoada de marisco* (bean and shellfish stew) and *robala assado no forno* (oven-baked sea bass). Closed Sun.

LEÇA DA PALMEIRA O Chanquinhas   🔲 📋 🅿   €€€€€

Rua de Santana 243, 4450-000 **Tel** *229 951 884*   **Road map** *C2*

O Chanquinhas occupies the elegant dining rooms of a large, aristocratic mansion. The cuisine is Portuguese and international in flavour and is served with a reserved grace. The menu lists specialities like *arroz de sarrabulho com rojões* (black pudding rice with fried pork) and fish dishes. The desserts are excellent. Closed Sun; 2 weeks in Aug.

MIRANDA DO DOURO A Balbina   ♿ ⋔   €

Rua Rainha Dona Catarina 1, 5210-228 **Tel** *273 432 394*   **Road map** *E1*

Well-known politicians sit with the locals and Spanish holidaymakers at this traditional restaurant situated just a short walk from Largo de Misericórdia. A popular order is the *bife à Balbina*, a steak of local Mirandesa beef. Another is *bacalhau à Balbina* (codfish). Game, such as pheasant and partridge, is available in season. Closed Easter, 25 Dec.

MIRANDA DO DOURO Buteko   ⋔ 📋   €

Largo Dom João III, 5210-000 **Tel** *273 431 231*   **Road map** *E1*

Set in the centre of town, and upstairs from its ice-cream parlour, Buteko's specialities include *posta Mirandesa* (beef), *bacalhau à Buteko* (cod in the house style) and *costeleta de vitela* (veal cutlets). An alternative choice is the lunch *ementa turística* (tourist menu) that includes a glass of house red wine. Closed Sun (winter); 2 weeks in Jan.

MIRANDELA Flor de Sal   🔲 📋 🍷 🅿   €€€

Parque Dr José Gama, 5370-000 **Tel** *278 203 063*   **Road map** *D1*

Perched over the banks of the River Tua, this contemporary restaurant features an elaborate set of themed menus. Specialities include *medalhão de vitela com redução de queijo terrincho* (veal medallions in a reduced cheese terrine sauce). The cellar stocks Portuguese reds and whites, champagnes and ports. Closed Sun evening & Mon lunch (winter).

MURÇA Miradouro   ⋔ 🔲 📋   €

Pensão Miradouro, Curves de Murça, 5090-136 **Tel** *259 512 461*   **Road map** *D2*

The small handwritten menu in this plain restaurant changes daily but the quality of the food remains constant. The list features national and regional favourites such as *cozido à Portuguesa* (boiled meat), *feijoada á transmontana* (bean and meat stew) and *cabrito assado no forno* (oven roast rabbit). The house wine washes it all down. Closed Tue; 8–15 Sep.

OPORTO Bule   ♿ ⋔ 🔲 📋   €

Rua de Timor 128, 4150-728 **Tel** *220 109 929*   **Road map** *C2*

This delightful restaurant near Castelo do Queijohas has charming views over a garden sloping down to the sea. The buffet has a sumptuous selection of *hors d'oeuvres* that include home-made pastries. Complementing this is an extensive choice of traditional Portuguese and international dishes.

Key to Price Guide *see p408* **Key to Symbols** *see back cover flap*

OPORTO Casa Aleixo €

Rua da Estação 216, 4300-171 **Tel** *225 370 462* **Road map** *C2*

Run by the same family since 1948, Casa Aleixo is located near Oporto's Campanhã railway station. The restaurant is known for its tripe dishes, but for those with less accustomed palates, the *filetes de polvo* (octopus) and the *cabrito assado* (roast kid) come highly recommended. Closed Sun & public holidays; 3 weeks in Aug.

OPORTO Mercearia €

Cais da Ribeira 32, 4050-510 **Tel** *222 004 389* **Road map** *C2*

With its low vaulted, granite stone ceiling and wooden beams, Mercearia exudes warmth and character, furnished with antique glass-fronted cabinets and walls decorated with old prints. The menu features traditional Portuguese cuisine with and emphasis on seafood and fish. Reservations recommended. Closed Tue in winter.

OPORTO Adega Vila Meà €€

Rua dos Caldeireiros 62, 4050-137 **Tel** *222 082 967* **Road map** *C2*

Lying in the shadow of the Torre dos Clérigos, this place is a busy, family-run restaurant known for its genuine northern cuisine. Each weekday features a "Special of the Day" that can range from cod pasties in bean rice to oven roast lamb. However, the waiters are quite happy to read aloud the chef's recommendations. Closed Sun.

OPORTO Peixes & Companhia €€

Rua do Ouro 133, 4150-000 **Tel** *226 185 655* **Road map** *C2*

A pleasant restaurant metaphorically filled to the gills with fish. The menu lists nothing else and meat is only available by prior arrangement. Fashioned throughout in an attractive wood finish, the windows open out to views across the river. The fish are prepared to your taste – either grilled, fried, boiled or baked. Closed Sun.

OPORTO Tripeiro €€

Rua Passos Manuel 195, 4000-385 **Tel** *222 005 886* **Road map** *C2*

Tripeiro – meaning tripe eater – is the name for a native of Oporto as well as this famous restaurant, which has been serving up tripe since 1942. Naturally, the house speciality reflects the restaurant's *raison d'être* but the menu also lists more conventional dishes, much of it seafood but all prepared in a traditional manner. Closed Sun evening.

OPORTO Restaurante Casa da Música €€€

Casa da Música, Avenida da Boavista, 4100-111 **Tel** *226 092 876* **Road map** *C2*

On the 7th floor of the city's Casa da Música building is this stark, angular restaurant. The menu is *haute cuisine* at accessible prices. Choices include poached eggs with warm Brie cheese, Savoy cabbage and bacon, and grilled lamb cutlets with country parsley sauce with baby potatoes. Closed Sun.

OPORTO Dom Tonho €€€€

Cais da Ribeira, 4050-509 **Tel** *222 004 307* **Road map** *C2*

Located in a refurbished 17th-century warehouse on the historic *ribeira* (quayside) in the shadow of the Dom Luís bridge, the menu here respects the culinary traditions of northern Portugal. Dishes like *arroz de pato à moda antiga* (duck rice-traditional style) are served in a contemporary space under soft spotlight. Good wine list. Closed 1 Jan, 25 Dec.

OPORTO Foz Velha €€€€

Esplanada do Castelo 141, Foz do Douro, 4150-196 **Tel** *226 154 178* **Road map** *C2*

Strawberry and red-rose hues paint this smart, fashionable restaurant with *joie de vivre*. The gourmet food is the chef's take on regional northern gastronomy, and the choice is extensive – the tasting menu alone offers 6 or 9 plates! The restaurant is located near Castelo da Foz and commands blissful ocean views. Closed Sun & Mon lunch.

OPORTO Bull and Bear €€€€

Avenida da Boavista 3431, 4149-017 **Tel** *226 107 669* **Road map** *C2*

One of Portugals's most highly regarded restaurants, with modern cuisine based on fresh, natural ingredients. The meals are refined, light and textured. The stylish interior, enriched by bold, abstract canvases, makes this one of Oporto's most fashionable fine dining venues. Weekend reservations obligatory.

OPORTO Dom Manuel €€€€€

Avenida Montevideu 384, 4150-516 **Tel** *226 170 179* **Road map** *C2*

Set in a late 19th-century mansion with marvellous Atlantic views, Dom Manuel's combination of impeccable service and choice cuisine is hard to beat. Specialities include *parrilhada mista* (fish and shellfish mixed grill) and *vitela assada com batatas e arroz parolo de legumes* (grilled veal with potatoes and vegetable rice). Closed Sun; last 2 weeks in Aug.

OPORTO Portucale €€€€€

Rua da Alegria 598, 4000-000 **Tel** *225 370 717* **Road map** *C2*

One of the finest restaurants in the country, on the upper floor of the Albergaria Miradouro hotel. The menu reflects the spirited partnership of traditional Portuguese and international cuisine, illustrated by the sole Walewski – fillets of sole with champagne, lobster, shellfish and grated cheese. Reservations required. Closed 24 Dec (evening), 25 Dec.

PESO DA RÉGUA Varanda da Régua €

Lugar da Boavista, Loureiro, 5050-000 **Tel** *254 336 949* **Road map** *D2*

Impressive panoramic views can be enjoyed, and equally agreeable dishes of Portuguese cuisine savoured at this friendly, family-run restaurant just north of Régua. Be sure to try the intriguingly named *febras de porco à Padre Piedade* (Father Pity's pork cutlets). Varanda da Régua is a popular venue for wedding parties so check ahead for availability.

ROMEU Maria Rita
Rua da Capela, 5370-620 **Tel** *278 939 134*   **Road map** *E1*

During the Middle Ages, pilgrims and journeymen would stop at a place near where this rustic townhouse restaurant now stands to rest and eat. Today, Maria Rita provides the sustenance. The spicy sausage soup or roast turkey is sure to put the bounce back in the boots of any weary traveller. Closed Sun evening & Mon.

SENDIM Gabriela
Largo da Igreja 27, 5225-106 **Tel** *273 739 180*   **Road map** *E2*

Six granite pillars prop up the balcony terrace of this attractive restaurant installed in a *pensão* of the same name. The cuisine is prepared to a high standard and includes regional favourites like *posta mirandesa com molho especial* (beef steak in a special sauce). The open fire is really appreciated during the winter months. Closed 24 Dec eve, 25 Dec.

TORRE DE MONCORVO O Artur
Lugar de Rentão, Carviçais, 5160-069 **Tel** *279 098 000*   **Road map** *E2*

Halfway between Torre de Moncorvo and Mogadouro, this country-style restaurant is richly decorated with ancient shotguns, farming tools and the frozen stares of several stuffed wild boar heads. The fare is similarly rustic in nature. The cheeses and desserts are worth trying, in particular the *bolo de castanha* (chestnut cake). Closed Sun evening.

VILA NOVA DE GAIA Presuntaria Transmontana
Avenida Diogo Leite 80, 4400-111 **Tel** *223 758 380*   **Road map** *C2*

This is one of two restaurants sharing the same name but both under the same management. A radiant panorama of Oporto looming over the River Douro is the perfect entrée for the nourishing Tras-os-Montes cuisine that flavours the menu. Only the cheeses represent another region in Portugal, that of the Alentejo.

VILA REAL O Espadeiro
Avenida Almeida Lucena, 5000-660 **Tel** *259 322 302*   **Road map** *D2*

This comfortable first-floor restaurant offers superbly prepared regional dishes accompanied by local wines. Standard fare includes *cabrito* (roast kid), *cod Espadeiro* and roast leg of pork. Specials include *arroz de feijocas com orelheira de porco* (pig's ears with beans and rice). The dish of the day is good value. Closed Tue.

VILA REAL Terra da Montanha
Rua 31 de Janeiro 16-18, 5000-603 **Tel** *259 372 075*   **Road map** *D1*

The tables at this place are located inside large wine vats, allowing for a rare form of privacy. On the menu is hearty local cuisine washed down with wines from the Douro and Trás-os-Montes regions. Try the *bacalhau com presunto e broa* (cod with smoked ham and corn bread) and the *arroz de pato* (duck risotto). Closed Sun eve, public holidays.

MINHO

ARCOS DE VALDEVEZ Costa do Vez
N121, Silvares, 4970-483 **Tel** *258 516 122*   **Road map** *C1*

In a pretty setting just north of Arcos, this attractive and comfortable restaurant maintains a regional cuisine with an emphasis on grills. The *espetada de lulas com gambas* (prawn and squid kebab) is a speciality. So, too, is the roast veal. A variety of wines are on offer, including vinho verdes. Closed Mon; last 2 weeks in Oct.

BARCELOS Bagoeira
Avenida Sidónio Pais 495, 4700-000 **Tel** *253 811 236*   **Road map** *C1*

Hotel Bagoeira's own enormous restaurant, divided into various rooms decorated in different styles. The gastronomy celebrates with gusto the Minho region and specialities like *rojões* (fried pork with potatoes) feature highly on the menu. The food is prepared with finesse and served in generous portions befitting the restaurant's gigantic dimensions.

BARCELOS Dom António
Rua Dom António Barroso 87, 4750-258 **Tel** *253 812 285*   **Road map** *C1*

Dom António is an attractive, stone-walled eatery whose rustic interior belies its city-centre location. The traditional Portuguese menu is supplemented by game in season. Typical choices include *vitela à moda de Barcelos* (veal Barcelos style) and the popular *arroz de frango* (chicken rice). Ask for for *laranjinhas doces* (orange pudding) for dessert.

BRAGA Expositor
Parque de Exposições, 4700-000 **Tel** *253 217 031*   **Road map** *C1*

Located in Braga's exhibitions park, this lively restaurant is one of the best places to observe Minhotos enjoying a family night out. Ingredients are often combined to create dishes like *arroz de cherne e de polvo* (stone bass and octopus rice). In winter, heartier meals like *cozida à Portuguesa* (meat stew) are served up. Closed Sun evening; Tue.

BRAGA Inácio
Campo das Hortas 4, 4700-000 **Tel** *253 613 235*   **Road map** *C1*

Located outside the city walls, the granite façade of the popular tasca-style Inácio is indicative of the architectural style associated with Braga's historical centre. Inside, the restaurant is decorated with unusual artifacts and rare antiques that can sometimes detract from the menu of first-rate Portuguese cuisine. Closed Tue; 2 weeks in April; 2 weeks in Sep.

BRAGA São Frutoso
Rua Costas Gomes 168, 4700-262 **Tel** *253 623 372* **Road map** *C1*

Located just north of Braga, near the São Frutuoso de Montélios chapel, dishes here include *vitela à São Frutuoso* (veal) and *pescada à São Frutuoso* (fish). More ambitious creations include *barriguinha de porco recheada e arroz de pato à moda de Braga* (pork belly stuffed with duck and rice). Closed Sun eve; Mon; 3 weeks in Aug; 24 & 25 Dec.

BRAGA Arcoense
Rua Eugenheiro José Justino Amorim 96, 4715-023 **Road map** *C1*

This is the perfect place to unwind after a hard day's sightseeing. The menu is simple but refined, featuring hearty regional versions of *assado misto* (mixed roast). The house speciality, *arroz de lavagante seco* (oven-baked rice with lobster), takes over an hour to prepare but is worth the wait. Reservations recommended. Closed Sun; 15 Aug–7 Sep.

CAMINHA Duque de Caminha
Rua Ricardo Joaquim de Sousa 111, 4910-155 **Tel** *258 722 046* **Road map** *C1*

With its prime location next to the parish church, Duque de Caminha prepares food that reflects the coastal and mountainous nature of the region. House specialities include lobster or sea bass with rice. Wild boar makes regular appearances on the menu during the winter months. Closed Sun evening & Mon (except Aug); 15–25 Dec.

GUIMARÃES El Rei D. Afonso
Praça de São Tiago 20, 4810-311 **Tel** *253 419 096* **Road map** *C1*

It's apt that a restaurant in Guimarães should be named after King Afonso, the first king of Portugal who chose the city as his capital. El Rei has chosen to offer its subjects an essentially regional menu but one that also mystifies. Ask for the *bacalhau mistério* (cod surprise) – a house-invented speciality. Closed Sun.

GUIMARÃES São Gião
Lugar de Vinhas, Moreira de Cónegos, 4810-000 **Tel** *253 561 853* **Road map** *C1*

Inspired by tradition but not afraid to be creative, São Gião's kitchen has become a byword for culinary excellence. The gourmet menu includes the imaginatively named *perdiz à Convento de Alcântara com cogumelos selvagens* (partridge with wild mushrooms) and *ovos mexidos com trufas* (scrambled egg with truffles). Closed Mon; Sun evening; Aug.

GUIMARÃES Solar do Arco
Rua de Santa Maria 48-50, 4810-443 **Tel** *253 513 072* **Road map** *C1*

Housed in an elegant mansion, Solar do Arco's entrance lies in the shadow of an arch joining one side of the street with the other. The restaurant interior has preserved the original granite walls to charming effect. The cuisine, including specialities like *arroz de tamboril* (monkfish with rice), is served with aplomb.

PONTE DA BARCA O Moinho
Campo Curro, 4980-614 **Tel** *258 452 035* **Road map** *C1*

A charming place with picture-postcard views of the River Lima, the spacious O Moinho is renowned across the region for its signature dish, *lampreia com arroz* (lamprey with rice). But that is not all the former mill is known for. The menu also lists old favourites like *cabrito da serra* (mountain kid). Closed Tue.

PONTE DE LIMA Encanada
Largo Doutor Rodrigues Alves, 4990-000 **Tel** *258 941 189* **Road map** *C1*

Incorporated into the façade of the municipal market building, this busy restaurant is well known for its desserts as well as its regional mainstays. The trout are plucked straight from the river and are a popular choice. Round a meal off with *leite crème queimado* (cream pudding with a singed top). Closed May; 25 Dec.

PONTE DE LIMA A Carvalheira
Antepaço, Arcozel, 4990-000 **Tel** *258 742 316* **Road map** *C1*

Nestling in a pleasant rural setting just northwest of Ponte de Lima, the country location is evident in the restaurant's rustic interior that uses natural stone and dark wood to great effect. The menu lists *chouriço* (spicy smoked sausage) among other starter options. The house special is cod with maize bread. Closed Mon; 25 Dec.

PÓVOA DE VARZIM O Marinheiro
Rua Gomes de Amorim, Estrada Fontes Novas, 4490-000 **Tel** *252 682 151* **Road map** *C2*

Designed in the shape of a fisherman's smack and decorated with fishing nets, lobster pots and buoys, there's really no mistaking what the menu favours at this busy restaurant. The *arroz de lagosta à Marinheiro* (sailor's lobster rice) is the signature dish and the ever-present codfish dishes always make a splash. Closed 25 Dec.

VALENÇA DO MINHO Mané
Avenida Miguel Dantas 5, 4930-678 **Tel** *251 823 402* **Road map** *C1*

The proprietors are from Moscow but the only concession to eastern European cuisine is the *bolo Húngaro* and *montanha Russa* sweet cake desserts. Otherwise, the menu is an amalgamation of Portuguese and Mediterranean cuisine, with fish and seafood. Pheasant and wild boar are available in season. Closed Sun evening; Mon (except Aug); Jan.

VALENÇA DO MINHO São Teotónio
Baluarte de Socorro, 4930-000 **Tel** *251 800 260* **Road map** *C1*

Every Wednesday this restaurant, located in a *pousada* within an old fort, offers a *buffet de bacalhau* (codfish buffet) comprising cod steak accompanied by tuna, red beans and cabbage, corn, lettuce, asparagus, tomato and onion. The rest of the week, hearty regional specialities suffice. Fantastic view across the Minho valley to Tuy in Spain.

VIANA DO CASTELO Cozinha das Malheiras   🗐   €€

Rua Gago Coutinho 19-21, 4900-510 **Tel** *258 823 680*   **Road map** *C1*

Making good use of the former manor house in which it is housed, the interior of this intimate, centrally located restaurant glows under candelabra suspended from an arched ceiling. The traditional cuisine is given an international twist with starters like smoked salmon with asparagus and Hollandaise sauce. Closed Tue; late Dec–early Jan.

VIANA DO CASTELO Camelo   🏃 🏠 🗐 🅿   €€€€

N202, Santa Marta de Portuzelo, 4925-090 **Tel** *258 839 090*   **Road map** *C1*

In a village 1 km (half a mile) from Viana do Castelo, this gem of a restaurant holds monthly festive banquets and has a capacity for around 850 people. Summer dining can be enjoyed under shady vines when specialities like *lampreia assada no forno* (oven baked lamprey) can be savoured. Closed Mon.

VIANA DO CASTELO Casa d'Armas   🗐   €€€€€

Largo 5 de Outubro, 4900-515 **Tel** *258 824 999*   **Road map** *C1*

Behind an imposing early 18th-century façade, the stone and wood-panelled interior of Casa d'Armas is enhanced by medieval decor and a tangible sense of history. The cuisine is equally noble, with dishes like *bifinhos de boi com cogumelos* (bull steak with mushrooms) and *polvinho ao alho* (baby octopus flavoured with garlic). Closed Wed.

VILA PRAIA DE ÂNCORA Tasquinha do Ibraim   🏃 🗐   €€

Rua dos Pescadores 11, 4910-000 **Tel** *258 911 689*   **Road map** *C1*

The entire contents of the sea appear to be listed on the menu of this well patronized restaurant that overlooks the harbour. The interior exudes a rustic atmosphere despite its proximity to the ocean, and there are tasty *costeletão* (T-bone steak) choices and other meat dishes available as an alternative to the fish and seafood. Closed Tue (Jan–Mar).

ALENTEJO

ALANDROAL A Maria   🏠 🗐 🅿   €€

Rua João de Deus 12, 7250-142 **Tel** *268 431 143*   **Road map** *D5*

A relaxed, easy-going ambience greets diners at this enchanting restaurant. Starters include *sopa de cacao* (dogfish soup) and main courses feature *pato em molho de vinho tinto* (duck in red wine sauce), among other plates. The outside terrace is perfect for warm evenings. Closed Mon evening; last 2 weeks Aug.

ALBERNÔA Herdade dos Grous   ♿ 🏃 🏠 🗐 🍷 🅿   €€€€

Herdade dos Grous, Albernôa, 7800-601 **Tel** *284 960 000*   **Road map** *D6*

A beautiful estate in the heart of the Alentejo countryside. Many of the ingredients used in the kitchen are organic and sourced from the surrounding farms. The outstanding gourmet menu has transformed countryside cooking into an art and is suitably complemented with wines from the estate's cellars. Closed Mon, Tue, Wed eve, Thu eve.

ALVITO Castelo de Alvito   ♿ 🏃 🗐 🅿   €€

Pousada do castelo de Alvito, 7920-999 **Tel** *284 480 700*   **Road map** *D6*

A 15th-century castle with beautiful gardens provides the setting for this splendid restaurant, with tables set under a low, vaulted ceiling; the look conjures up a medieval atmosphere. The *costeletas de borrego em molho de coentros* (lamb cutlets in coriander sauce) is delicious. The *bacalhau à Marquês de Alvito* (codfish) honours the castle's former owner.

BEJA Dom Dinis   🏃 🗐   €

Rua Dom Dinis, 7800-000 **Tel** *284 325 937*   **Road map** *D6*

The unassuming façade of this modest eatery stares directly at the castle and its landmark keep, built by the restaurant's namesake in the late 13th century. The food is nourishing rural fare, with dishes like *carne de porco à alentejana* (pork and shellfish) and *coelho com molho vilão* (rabbit in countryman sauce) on offer. Closed Wed.

BEJA Espelho d'Água   ♿ 🏠 🗐 🍷   €€

Rua de Lisboa, Parque da Cidade, 7800-292 **Tel** *284 325 103*   **Road map** *D6*

This restaurant's lakeside setting makes it a popular retreat during the summer months. Menu favourites include *carne de porco à alentejana* (Alentejo-style pork with clams) and the tasty beef and pineapple kebabs. With ample parking, boating and occasional concerts, the surrounding Parque da Cidade offers a pleasant day out. Closed Mon; 4–12 Jan.

CAMPO MAIOR O Faisão   🏃 🗐   €

Rua 1° de Maio 19, 7370-000 **Tel** *268 686 139*   **Road map** *E5*

Pictures of local life decorate the interior of this tidy restaurant and the effect is similar to that of being invited into someone's home. The menu is traditional in flavour, with a good selection of regional dishes such as *cozida de grão* (pork and chickpea stew). The house beef in mushroom sauce is very good.

CRATO Flor da Rosa   🏃 🗐 🅿   €€€

Pousada da Flor da Rosa, 7430-099 **Tel** *245 997 210*   **Road map** *D4*

The restaurant is located in the historic *pousada* adapted from the monastery which is thought to date from the mid-14th century. The restaurant's marvellous period interior is matched by the attractive menu. Specialities include *linguado recheado de camarão* (sole stuffed with shrimp) and *bife de vitela com queijo de Nisa* (veal with Nisa cheese).

ELVAS Pousada de Santa Luzia 🏛📖Ⓟ €€€€
Avenida de Badajoz, 7350-097 **Tel** *268 637 470* **Road map** *D4*

Not far from the Spanish border, the large restaurant of this *pousada* is popular with Portuguese and Spaniards alike, attracted by the gracious interior and the quality of the food on offer. The menu is national in outlook but includes regional favourites like *cabrito à lavrador* (roast kid, farmer's style). The wines, however, are all from the Alentejo.

ESTREMOZ Adega Típico do Isaías 📋🏛📖 €
Rua do Almeida 21, 7100-000 **Tel** *268 322 318* **Road map** *D5*

Set in an old wine cellar, this restaurant offers some wonderfully original rustic Alentejan cooking like *sopa de beldroegas* (purslane soup) and *migas de espargas bravos com carne de alguidar* (bread and meat stew with asparagus cooked in an earthenware pan). Good local wine by the jug. Closed Sun; first 3 weeks in Aug; public holidays.

ESTREMOZ São Rosas 📖 €€
Largo D.Dinis II, 7100-000 **Tel** *268 333 345* **Road map** *D5*

São Rosas sits in the town's main square. The cuisine features regional specialities like *tarte de perdiz* (partridge tart) but caters for more conservative tastes with dishes like *lombo assado com ameixas* (beef with prunes) and *migas de pão com carne de porco frita* (bread stew with fried pork). Closed Mon; 2 weeks in Jan; 2 weeks in July.

ÉVORA Cozinha de Santo Humberto 📖 €€
Rua da Moeda 39, 7000-513 **Tel** *266 704 251* **Road map** *D5*

Set in a narrow whitewashed cellar, St. Humberto's kitchen is adorned with antique cooking utensils, including heavy copper kettles suspended across the arched ceiling. The food is classic Alentejan, including *borrego assado no forno* (oven baked lamb) and *carne de porco com amêijoas* (pork with cockles). Closed Thu; first 3 weeks in Nov.

ÉVORA O Grémio 📖 €€€
Rua Alcárcova de Cima 10, 7000-842 **Tel** *266 742 931* **Road map** *D5*

Built into the city's Roman wall and overlooking a spot that was once a regular meeting point for farmers and herds-men, the starters here include grilled peppers and garlic prawns. The tasty hare stewed with beans is recommended, as is the steak Mestre d'Avis bathed in a red wine and honey sauce. Closed Wed.

ÉVORA Tasquinha do Oliveira ♿🏛📖 €€€
Rua Cândido dos Reis 45a, 7000-582 **Tel** *266 744 841* **Road map** *D5*

A small restaurant with a big reputation whose walls are decorated with brightly coloured ceramic bowls and old wooden utensils. The starters here alone number 20 plates, all composed of a delicious variety of *petiscos* (snacks). The *favas com chouriça* (broad beans with spicy sausage) is particularly appetizing. Closed Sun; first 2 weeks Aug.

ÉVORA Fialho 📖 €€€€
Travessa das Mascarenhas 16, 7000-557 **Tel** *266 703 079* **Road map** *D5*

Arguably the best restaurant in the Alentejo, and highly regarded throughout Portugal, Fialho has collected many awards for its inventive cuisine, such as *atum grelhado e amêijoas na cataplana* (grilled tuna and cockle cataplana) and *medalhões de porco preto* (medallions of black pork). Reservations essential. Closed Mon; 2 Jan; 1–24 Sep; 24 Dec.

MARVÃO O Sever 🏛🍴📖 €
Portagem, 7330-347 **Tel** *245 993 318* **Road map** *D4*

Located in Portagem, not far from Marvão, this pretty restaurant serves up wonderful views of the River Sever and is particularly inviting in summer, with dining on the terrace. The menu offers immaculately prepared regional specialities such as *perna de borrego assado no forno com castanhas* (oven roasted leg of lamb with chestnuts).

MÉRTOLA Alengarve 🏛🍴📖 €
Avenida Aureliano Mira Fernandes 20, 7750-320 **Tel** *286 612 210* **Road map** *D6*

This long-serving eatery, located near the roundabout at the entrance to the town, serves a wonderful *sopa de peixe do rio* (river fish soup). The good-value main dishes include *bife de atum de cebolada* (tuna steak with onions) and *migas com carne de porco à alentejana* (bread stew with pork and cockles). Closed Tue eve; Wed; 2 weeks in Oct.

MONSARAZ O Alcaide 🏛📖 €
Rua de Santiago 18, 7200-175 **Tel** *266 557 168* **Road map** *D5*

The views from the window tables are magnificent! The tiny interior is decorated with old farming tools and ceramic artifacts and oozes warmth and character. The menu is crammed with regional dishes that favour meat over fish but it's the wine list that really catches the eye, with some truly excellent labels. Reservations recommended. Closed Thu.

PORTALEGRE Tomba Lobos ♿🍴📖🍷 €€€
Bairro Pedra Basta, Lote 16, 7300-000 **Tel** *245 331 214* **Road map** *D5*

Set amid sprawling vineyards on the outskirts of Portalegre, Tomba Lobos is a first-rate fine-dining establishment led by a talented young chef. With its subtle blend of traditional flavours, the menu tantalizes the taste buds with offerings as varied and innovative as *bacalhau com espargos gratinado* (cod fishcakes with asparagus). Closed Sun eve & Mon.

REDONDO Convento de São Paulo ♿🏛📖Ⓟ €€€
Covento de São Paulo, Aldeia da Serra, 7170-120 **Tel** *266 989 160* **Road map** *D5*

Set in a beautiful hotel, the restaurant O Ermita offers traditional Alentejan cuisine, much of it using produce cultivated on the estate. Starters include *ervilhas com ovo e linguiça* (sweet peas with egg and thinly sliced sausage) and a variety of main dishes like *espadarte grelhado* (grilled swordfish) and *pato com molho de azeitonas* (duck with olive sauce).

SANTIAGO DO CACÉM A Deolinda   🚻 ♿ 🏠 📋   €

Cruz Alcaide, 7540-237 **Tel** *269 822 732*   **Road map** C6

Located in a modern building with a typically Alentejan decor, A Deolinda caters for a mostly local clientele with house specialities such as *perdiz à casa* (house-style partridge) and various grilled fish and roasted meat dishes. The atmosphere is warm and unpretentious, and the food is prepared by the restaurant's proprietor. Closed Mon.

SERPA Adega Molhóbico   📇 📋   €

Rua Quente 1, 7830-000 **Tel** *284 549 264*   **Road map** D6

Styled as an old wine cellar, all three rooms of this friendly restaurant are sometimes filled with partying locals, such is its popularity. The food is often outstanding and great value for money. Try the *cozida de grão* (pork and chickpea stew) or if you really want to blend in, the *pezinhos de Borrego guisados* (lamb's foot fricassee). Closed Wed.

TERRUGEM A Bolota   ♿ 🏠 📋   €€€€€

Quinta das Janelas Verdes, 7350-491 **Tel** *268 656 118*   **Road map** C6

This celebrated restaurant serves traditional gourmet cuisine. Starters such as *bolsitas de verdures com Vichyssoise de maçã* (leek and potato soup with apple and green vegetables) and main dishes like *pato estufado com framboesas* (stewed duck with raspberries) make reservations (minimum 6 people) essential. Closed Sun evening & Mon.

VIDIGUEIRA Vila Velha   🏠 📋   €€

Rua do Mal Anda 4, 7960-283 **Tel** *284 436 049*   **Road map** D5

The Old Villa is decorated with lovely regional costumes, rural artifacts and old photographs of farm folk and their families. Drawing on its rural heritage, the cuisine is traditional and full of flavour. Try the *borrego à pastora* (shepherd's lamb) or the *arroz de pato* (duck rice). Closed Mon.

VILA NOVA DE MILFONTES Marisqueira Dunas Mil   ♿ 🚻 📋 P   €€€

Off Avenida Marginal, 7645-000 **Tel** *283 996 420*   **Road map** C6

This well-regarded fish and seafood restaurant serves a delicious *arroz de marisco* (seafood rice) and *caldeirada de peixe* (fish stew). The dish of the day is always excellent value and the main ingredient guaranteed as locally caught. In summer, this place gets very busy with animated Portuguese families and holiday-makers from across Europe.

ALGARVE

ALBUFEIRA Evaristo   🚻 📋 P   €€

Praia do Evaristo, 8200-903 **Tel** *289 591 666*   **Road map** C7

This beachfront restaurant enjoys fabulous views over Praia do Evaristo, west of Albufeira. The fish and seafood are first class, and the menu features *lagosta na grelha* (broiled lobster), *lulas grelhadas em olho* (grilled squid with garlic) and an array of fresh fish. Meat choices include entrecote steak and fried chicken. Closed Jan & 1–14 Feb.

ALBUFEIRA Ruína   🚻 📋   €€

Rua Cais Herculano, 8200-000 **Tel** *289 512 094*   **Road map** C7

Set in a restored early 19th-century building with one of its walls containing vestiges of Roman fortifications, this is one of the best restaurants in town. Its privileged position affords great views over Fisherman's Beach and of course, the specialities of the house are fish and seafood. Rooms are set aside for coffee and for listening to *fado*.

ALBUFEIRA Le Club   🏠 🎵 📋 Y P   €€€€€

Praia de Santa Eulália, Santa Eulália, 8200-916 **Tel** *289 598 070*   **Road map** C7

Chic and sophisticated, Le Club boasts eye-catching decor by top interior designer Graça Viterbo and great ocean views. The *à la carte* menu looks to Italy for its inspiration and features dishes like *risotto de lagosta* (lobster risotto) and an excellent choice of Italian and Portuguese wines. Reservations recommended. Closed Tue–Sat (mid-Sep–Jun).

ALMANCIL A Quinta   📋 P   €€€€€

Rua Vale Formoso, 8100-267 **Tel** *289 393 357*   **Road map** D7

With an inspiring choice of *haute cuisine*, A Quinta's menu includes crisp confit of duck with plum tomato salsa and chive crème fraîche crushed new potatoes. Dessert choices feature *crème brûlée*, among other delights. The wine list is extensive. Reservations recommended. Closed Sun & Mon; mid-Dec–Jan.

ALMANCIL Gourmet Natural   ♿ 🚻 🏠 📋 Y   €€€€€

Estrada Vale do Lobo, 8135-018 **Tel** *289 355 271*   **Road map** D7

A slice of Uruguay tucked away in the countryside just north of Vale do Lobo. Located in an 18th-century farmhouse, the restaurant offers the best in Uruguayan cuisine, with the emphasis on steak. Other house specialities include mouthwatering *sashimi criollo*, sirloin pan-fried rare and coated with sesame, coriander and tare sauce. Dinner only.

ARMAÇÃO DE PÊRA Santola   🚻 🏠 📋   €€

Largo da Fortaleza, 8365-108 **Tel** *282 312 332*   **Road map** C7

With panoramic beach and ocean views, Santola has a pleasant, summer holiday atmosphere and is a reliable choice for seafood and shellfish dishes. Try the *camarão de falmejado* (flame-grilled prawns) or the *tamboril com alho francês* (monkfish with leek). The dessert list features regional delicacies like rich almond and fig cakes.

Key to Price Guide *see p408* **Key to Symbols** *see back cover flap*

CARVOEIRO Oasis €

Rua do Barranco 34, 8400-508 **Tel** *282 357 332* **Road map** *C7*

A popular restaurant with an inviting interior and a loyal clientele, starters here include sautéed prawns in garlic butter. The speciality is the rack of spare ribs, and the portions are enormous! Dessert options number ice-cream dishes and chocolate profiteroles. The outside terrace quickly fills up in summer. Dinner only. Closed Sun; 1 May; mid-Nov–Jan.

ESTOI Monte do Casal €€€€€

Cerro do Lobo, 8005-436 **Tel** *289 991 503* **Road map** *D7*

The *à la carte* and *menu degustation* choices at this idyllic country hotel offer French-based modern cuisine influenced by Portuguese and Thai recipes. Main courses include roast breast of duck with an oriental plum and ginger sauce, and prawns with garlic and coriander on Chinese noodles with creamed oyster sauce. Closed mid–Dec–mid-Feb.

ESTOMBAR O Charneco €

Rua Dom Sancho II, 8400-037 **Tel** *282 431 113* **Road map** *C7*

One of the best places in the region to sample authentic Algarve cooking. The tiny but industrious kitchen produces such regional delights as *pernil no forno* (roasted gammon) and *borrego guisado com feijão verde* (lamb fricassee with green beans) using traditional wood-burning ovens. The proprietors have won numerous culinary awards. Closed Sun.

FARO A Taska €

Rua do Alportel 38, 8000-239 **Tel** *289 824 739* **Road map** *D7*

Popular with locals, A Taska is a cosy restaurant spread out on different floors and decorated as an old tavern. The menu lists nourishing dishes like *arroz de lingueirão* (razor-clam with rice) and more exotic options such as *caril de gambas* (prawn curry). Delicious *mousse de amendoim* (peanut mousse) is among the desserts. Closed Sun; 1 Jan, 25 Dec.

FARO Dois Irmãos €

Praça Ferreira de Almeida 13, 8000-156 **Tel** *289 823 337* **Road map** *D7*

One of the most popular restaurants in Faro, the Two Brothers offers good quality cooking and friendly, efficient service. The menu is regional in taste but does feature some international dishes. Specialities include fish or meat *cataplana* and grilled cuttlefish. The siblings also do a very good paella.

FARO Mesa dos Mouros €

Largo Sé 10, 8000-138 **Tel** *966 784 536* **Road map** *D7*

The Moor's Table lies in the shadow of Faro's historic 13th-century cathedral on a corner of a large square lined by fragrant orange trees. The *javoli com molho frutos* (wild boar with rice, sultanas and mango sauce) is a speciality. Service is friendly and relaxed, and the outdoor terrace is a wonderful option in warm weather. Closed Sun.

FARO Camané €€€€€

Avenida da Nascente, Praia do Faro, 8005-520 **Tel** *289 817 539* **Road map** *D7*

Locals regard this place as one of the top five restaurants in the region, and with its privileged beachfront location on Ilha de Faro (Faro Island), snazzy design and excellent seafood, Camané is deserving of such praise. Specialities include monkfish and prawn fondue and stone bass with macaroni and clams. Closed Mon.

FERRAGUDO Sueste €€€

Rua da Ribeira 91, 8400-256 **Tel** *282 461 592* **Road map** *C7*

One of the south coast's finest seafood restaurants, with fish charcoal grilled to perfection on the quayside and brought to your table by smiling staff. The menu includes anchovies and unusual looking but great tasting emperor fish. The sunsets are breathtaking and boat taxis can be arranged to and from Portimão marina. Closed Mon & Jan–mid-Feb.

LAGOS Vista Alegra €€

Rua Ilha Terceira 19, 8600-000 **Tel** *282 792 151* **Road map** *C7*

This discreet French bistro seats just 20 persons but its diminutive interior belies its statue as one of the Algarve's *haute cuisine* hotspots. The food is prepared to exacting standards, and specialities include gratineed scallops, quail salad and ray in burnt butter sauce with capers. Open for dinner only, reservations essential. Closed Mon.

LAGOS No Pátio €€€

Rua Lançarote de Freitas 46, 8600-605 **Tel** *282 763 777* **Road map** *C7*

The British-run kitchen serves international cuisine exemplified by dishes like seared salmon with asparagus risotto, white wine and watercress cream. Good wine selection from Portuguese, Australian and US labels. There is a charming rear patio for secluded dining. Open for lunch Sun (except Jul & Aug) & dinner Thu–Sat (Tue–Sat Apr–Oct).

LOULÉ Casa dos Arcos €

Rua Sá de Miranda 23-25, 8100-000 **Tel** *289 416 713* **Road map** *D7*

Set in Loulé's historic centre, this unpretentious restaurant surprises with an impressive menu. It serves good-quality fish and seafood dishes, including swordfish steak, and the meat choices feature succulent filet mignon and the great standby, *bitoque* (beefsteak with egg, fried potatoes, salad and rice). Closed Mon (except Jul & Aug).

LOULÉ Bica Velha €€

Rua Martin Moniz 17-19, 8100-000 **Tel** *289 463 376* **Road map** *D7*

The oldest house in Loulé, dating from 1816, is the historic setting for this family-run restaurant. The rustic, timber and stone interior exudes a cosy intimacy which is at once appealing, as is the food. Specialities include *espetada de borrego* (lamb kebab), pork chop with apple sauce, and orange mousse dessert. Open daily for dinner only.

MEXILHOEIRA GRANDE Vila Lisa   🞠🞠🞠 €€€€

*Rua Francisco Bívar, 8500-000 **Tel** 282 968 478*   **Road map** C7

The colourful abstract canvasses lining the wall of this magical eatery are the work of the proprietor, a keen artist whose creativity in and out of the kitchen has made it the Algarve's most characterful restaurant, serving traditional Portuguese cuisine such as oven-roasted gammon. Reservations obligatory. Closed Oct–Jun: Sun–Thu.

ODIAXERE Cacto   🞠🞠🞠🞠 €€€

*Estrada Nacional 125, 8600-250 **Tel** 282 798 285*   **Road map** C7

A lively, colourful restaurant where customers have the option of enjoying their meal on an outside terrace shaded by leafy palmeiras. The beef salad starter or grilled garlic prawns are a perfect introduction to the speciality steaks and meat kebabs that are served with a choice of creamy pepper, garlic or blue cheese toppings. Closed Wed & Thu.

OLHÃO O Tamboril   🞠🞠🞠🞠 €€

*Avenida 5 de Outubro 174, 8700-304 **Tel** 289 714 625*   **Road map** D7

Olhão is the Algarve's principle fishing port and O Tamboril one of its finest fish restaurants. The catches here include *bife de atum* (tuna steak) and *tamboril* (monkfish), a house speciality. Also reeled in are some fine seafood dishes served grilled, with rice or in stews, and several variations of *bacalhau* (codfish). Closed Mon (except Jun–Aug).

PADERNE Veneza   🞠🞠🞠 €

*Mem Moniz, Paderne, 8200-000 **Tel** 289 367 129*   **Road map** C7

This unassuming roadside eatery, tucked away in the interior between Paderne and Albufeira, is well worth a diversion. The menu is typically Algarvean, featuring duck, lamb, grouse and partridge. The home-made country fare also includes cataplana choices and desserts of cheese, and fig, almond and apple-based tarts. Closed Tue, Wed lunch.

PORTIMÃO Titanic   🞠🞠🞠 €€€

*Rua Eng. Francisco Bívar, 8500-809 **Tel** 282 422 371*   **Road map** C7

This restaurant on Praia da Rocha has an elegant interior, an attractive bar and an air of sophistication. The food is equally agreeable, with prawn cocktail and fresh slices of melon and avocado just one of the many starters available. The lobster thermidor and lamb with mint sauce are two recommended house specialities. Closed lunch.

PORTIMÃO Buzio   🞠🞠🞠🞠🞠 €€€€€

*Aldeamento Prainha, Praia Três Irmaos, Alvor, 8501-904 **Tel** 282 458 772*   **Road map** C7

Boasting a prime location overlooking Alvor beach, just west of Portimão, Buzio is one of the more upmarket restaurants in the western Algarve. The menu offers modern Mediterranean cuisine enriched with regional influences. Highlights include sautéed scallops and mussels in a tomato sauce and octopus tentacles with garlic. Closed lunch; Sun.

PRAIA DA GALÉ Vila Joya   🞠🞠🞠🞠🞠 €€€€€

*Praia da Galé, near Guia, 8201-902 **Tel** 289 591 795*   **Road map** C7

Glowing with Michelin accolades, Estalagem Vila Joya's restaurant is directed by Austrian chef Dieter Koschina and is firmly established as a gourmet retreat. A few tables are available for non-residents but must be booked well in advance. Koschina personally visits markets across Europe in his quest for the finest ingredients. A memorable dining experience.

QUINTA DO LAGO 2 Passos   🞠🞠🞠🞠🞠 €€€€€

*Praia do Ancão, 8135-905 **Tel** 289 396 435*   **Road map** D7

This eye-catching, hexagonal restaurant stands on Praia do Ancão and commands a wonderful ocean view. A sea breeze ambience enhances the food on offer, especially the *lagosta no pote* (lobster in the pot). The diversity of the fish and seafood dishes makes this a popular summertime venue, especially at weekends. Closed Wed (Feb & Nov); Jan & Dec.

QUINTA DO LAGO Casa Velha   🞠🞠🞠🞠🞠 €€€€€

*Rotunda 6, Quinta do Lago, 8135-024 **Tel** 289 394 983*   **Road map** D7

Colour and flavour abound at this beautiful, highly regarded restaurant housed in a renovated 300-year-old farmhouse. The menu here is a fresh and original interpretation of modern French gourmet cuisine, with Mediterranean influences. The wine list is exemplary, as is the service and attention to detail. Reservations recommended. Closed Sun.

SAGRES O Telheiro do Infante   🞠🞠🞠🞠 €€

*Praia da Mareta, 8650-000 **Tel** 282 624 179*   **Road map** C7

With two floors, an esplanade and a terrace, this handy beachfront eatery packs a lot of space into its whitewashed and sometimes windswept walls. Right on the sand, with impressive views across the Sagres Peninsula, it is a magnet for beachgoers who come here to sample the excellent value fish and seafood dishes. Closed Tue & 24-25 Dec.

SAGRES Pousada do Infante   🞠🞠🞠 €€€€

*Pousada do Infante, 8135-905 **Tel** 282 620 240*   **Road map** C7

Housed in a *pousada*, the appropriately named "Sala Atlântico" restaurant's menu is inspired by the sea and the rugged Vicentina coastline. The cuisine is traditional Portuguese with interesting variations. Try the chicken with mussels and thyme or the carriage of lamb boiled in Muscatel wine. In summer, the sardines stuffed with tomato and herbs is a treat.

SILVES Marisqueira Rui   🞠🞠 €€€

*Rua Comendador Vilarinho 23, 8300-128 **Tel** 282 442 682*   **Road map** C7

Renowned across the Algarve for its outstanding choice of fish and seafood, Rui's is no place for a quiet dinner for two. This busy town-centre restaurant echoes the crunch of crab-cracking and gregarious laughter and is the perfect place to witness how the locals enjoy a good night out. Closed Tue.

TAVIRA A Ver Tavira
♿ 🛄 ♫ 📜 🍷 🅿 €€

Calçada da Galeria, 8800-000 **Tel** *281 381 363* **Road map** *D7*

The smooth stucco façade of this venue stands incongruous opposite the walls of Tavira's 13th-century Moorish castle. The restaurant is decorated in warm, rich tones and boasts a splendid veranda. The *menu degustation* allows diners to match wines with the cuisine, and there's also a tapas bar with live piano music. Open Jul–Sep for dinner only.

TAVIRA Quatro Águas
🚶 🛄 📜 🅿 €€

Quatro Águas, 8000-000 **Tel** *281 325 329* **Road map** *D7*

Located on the waterfront where the River Gilão meets the Ria Formosa estuary, Quatro Águas is famed for its views across the lagoon as much for its *camarão vermelho flamejado* (flambéed red shrimp) and *borrego com estragão* (lamb seasoned with tarragon). The restaurant is near the jumping-off point for the ferry to Ilha de Tavira.

VILAMOURA Pepper's Steakhouse
♿ 🚶 ♫ 📜 🍷 🅿 €€€€€

Tivoli Marina Vilamoura, 8125-901 **Tel** *289 303 303* **Road map** *D7*

Offering inspiring views of the marina – especially rewarding at night – the sophisticated Pepper's Steakhouse is housed in the plush Tivoli Marina Hotel. The *à la carte* menu features superbly cooked steaks and other meat dishes. The wine cellar is first-rate. Reservations advisable. Closed lunch.

MADEIRA

CÂMARA DE LOBOS Adega da Quinta
📜 🍷 €€€€

Quinta do Estreito, Rua José Joaquim da Costa, 9325-039 **Tel** *291 910 530*

This restaurant is situated in the gardens of the Quinta do Estreito where fine regional gastronomy is served together with beautiful views of the coast. The interior is rustic in style and features a low, wood beamed ceiling. The *quinta's* old wine cellar, stocked with vintage Madeiras, has been carefully preserved.

FUNCHAL O Jango
🚶 📜 🅿 €€

Rua de Santa Maria 166, 9050-040 **Tel** *291 221 280*

Squeezed into a converted fisherman's house in the old town, the decor here is an odd mix of local maritime tradition and African safari. The soups are marvellous and a perfect complement to dishes like *bouillabaisse* and *paella*. The *gambas à Indiana* (prawns) and the *bife à Jango* (beefsteak) are house specialities.

FUNCHAL O Tapassol
🛄 📜 €€

Rua Dom Carlos I, 62, 9000-000 **Tel** *291 225 023*

Booking is advised at this excellent small, upmarket restaurant in the old town. It's on the first floor of a traditional house and has a lovely roof patio with beautiful views across the district. The tomato and onion soup is a choice starter and you can dine on quail, mussels, limpets or rabbit. Wines are excellent and reasonably priced.

FUNCHAL Beerhouse
♿ 🚶 🛄 📜 €€€

Avenida Mar, Porto do Funchal, 9000-054 **Tel** *291 229 011*

Identified by its familiar white-coned roof, this harbour-front eatery is famed for its excellent golden rye beer brewed on the premises and served either by the glass or on tap with a 1-metre pipe placed on your table. Polished copper brew kettles decorate the restaurant's interior. Specialities include delicious *açorda de gambas* (prawn and bread stew).

FUNCHAL O Celeiro
🚶 🛄 📜 €€€

Rua Aranhas 22, 9000-044 **Tel** *291 230 622*

This appealing restaurant is situated on an old street and is identified by its English pub-style façade, complete with wooden window shutters, and an outside terrace. Its rustic interior offers candlelit dining and a fish-based menu featuring several dishes for two, such as shellfish and lobster *cataplana* and *bouillabaisse*. Closed Sat lunch & Sun.

FUNCHAL Riso
♿ 🛄 📜 🍷 €€€

Rua de Santa Maria 274, 9050-040 **Tel** *291 280 360*

Located in the heart of old Funchal, Riso is a modern restaurant entirely devoted to rice. Gaze out over the Atlantic from the clifftop terrace as you tuck into seafood risotto, *paella*, *risotto de cebola caramelizada com fillet de novilho grelhado* (caramelized onion risotto with grilled fillet steak) and other such delights. Reservations recommended.

FUNCHAL Barqueiro
🚶 📜 🅿 €€€€

Rua Ponta da Cruz, Centro Commercial Centromar 21, 9000-103 **Tel** *291 761 229*

One of Funchal's best fish and seafood venues, this relaxed and informal restaurant serves delicious local delicacies like *lapas* (limpets), *castanhitas* (winkles) and *ovas de espada* (scabbard fish roe). For something more substantial there's a wide choice of fresh fish dishes, including fresh lobster plucked straight from the aquarium.

FUNCHAL Dona Amélia
📜 🅿 €€€€

Rua Imperatriz d. Amélia 83, 9000-018 **Tel** *291 225 784*

Once a private residence, Mrs Amélia serves up some creative cuisine inspired by regional and international recipes. Flambé dishes and *espetadinhas* (small beef kebabs) on bay-wood skewers are the speciality. Alternatively, try the *três peixes na grelha com molho de abacate* (three fishes with avocado sauce). Dessert choice includes wonderful ice creams.

FUNCHAL Quinta da Palmeira
Avenida do Infante 17-19, 9000-015 **Tel** *291 221 814*

In this attractive, 19th-century town house traditional Portuguese dishes are prepared with flair and imagination. The *espada com salmão* (scabbard fish with salmon) is an inspired combination. The *gambas à moçambicana ou à Palmeira* (Mozambique prawns Palmeira style) is a house speciality. For dessert try the almond ice cream in hot chocolate sauce.

FUNCHAL Ristorante Villa Cipriani
Estrada Monumental 139, 9000-098 **Tel** *291 717 171*

Elegant but informal, Villa Cipriani enjoys a superb clifftop location alongside Reid's Palace Hotel. The menu is authentic gourmet Italian, with tagliatelle, spaghetti and linguini among the home-made pasta dishes and a rich variety of fish and meat dishes also available. The large outside terrace offers summer dining with ocean views. Closed lunch.

FUNCHAL Xôpana Restaurante
Travessa do Largo do Choupana, 9060-340 **Tel** *291 206 020*

First-class gourmet dining in a splendid location above Funchal harbour. The restaurant is in the Choupana Hills resort *(see p404)* and is renowned for French cuisine fused with exotic Asian influences, such as scallops with gomasio and crispy poppadum with piri-piri wok vegetables or veal filet mignon and crispy spring rolls in a sichuan pepper sauce.

PORTO MONIZ Orca
Rotunda da Piscina, Vila Porto Moniz, 9270-000 **Tel** *291 850 000*

Orca is fashioned entirely out of wood, apart from the large windows that enable diners to gaze out over the town's famous, natural rock pools and to the ocean beyond. The cuisine is regional, with dishes like *filete espada com banana* (scabbard fish with banana) and *bifes com tâmaras* (beefsteak with dates) flavouring the menu.

PORTO SANTO O Calhetas
Sítio de Calheta, Vila de Porto Santo, 9400-001 **Tel** *291 984 380*

Located on Porto Santo's southern tip, one of the most tranquil spots on the island, this restaurant serves a variety of fish and seafood dishes all freshly prepared and typical of the region. Specialities include *arroz de cherne* (stone bass rice). The sunsets over nearby Ilha do Cal are spectacular. A hotel pick-up and drop-off service is available.

PORTO SANTO Quinta do Serrado
Sítio do Pedregal, 9400-010 **Tel** *291 980 270*

The kitchen here focuses on home-style northern Portuguese gastronomy. Housed in a fabulously rustic *quinta*, the restaurant's menu lists *vitela com arroz de feijão* (veal with bean rice) and *cabrito assado no forno* (roast kid) among its specialities. Desserts include the unusual but delicious *pudim de maracujá* (sweet granadilla pudding).

RIBEIRA BRAVA D. Luís
Rua Cago Coutinho, Porto Vila., 9350-217 **Tel** *291 952 543*

Located in lower Ribeira Brava and fanned by salt-laced sea breezes, this informal restaurant is a favourite with locals and tourists alike, drawn to its good-value menu. The cuisine is Portuguese with an international twist and includes specials like *espetada mista de peixe* (mixed fish kebab) and the curiously named chicken dish, *frango Sophia Loren*.

RIBEIRA BRAVA Fajã dos Padres
Estrada Padre António Dinis Henriques I, 9300-261 **Tel** *291 944 538*

There are only two ways to reach Fajã dos Padres: by boat or a vertiginous elevator ride. Specialities pay homage to the sea and include *caldeirada de atum* (tuna stew) and *espada e lulas para grelhar* (grilled squid kebab). The fish options are impressive and include snapper, grouper and even parrotfish. Closed Tue; Dec 24, 25; second week Jan–1 Mar.

SANTANA Quinta do Furão
Achada do Gramacho, 9230-000 **Tel** *291 570 100*

Set in the *quinta* of the same name, this restaurant's brick stone and thatched wood interior is replete with a majestic fireplace that makes it a favourite on cold days. The inventive menu features dishes like *atum com molho de gengibre* (tuna in ginger sauce) and *bife em vinho tinto* (beefsteak in red wine). The terrace views are breathtaking.

SANTANA Cantinho da Serra
Estrada do Pico das Pedras, Pico António Fernandes, 9230-107 **Tel** *291 573 727*

Located near Pico das Pedras, this is one of the most picturesque of Madeira's restaurants. The cosy interior has windows framed by dappled flowered curtains and tables draped with crisp, blue check linen. The rustic charm is accentuated by a menu that features hearty, home-style regional cooking. Be sure to try the home-made liquor digestifs.

AZORES

CORVO Traineira
Rua Matriz, 9980-020 **Tel** *912 632 127*

One of only three restaurants on Corvo, at Traineira you can sample local delicacies like *linguiça* (sausage) and yam (sweet potato). Starters invariably include the famed *queijo da Ilha do Corvo* (Corvo cheese) and favourites like *enchidos das ilhas* (island pork stuffing). Azorean fishermen supply the restaurant with a fresh daily catch. Closed Sun.

FAIAL Capote 🍽 ℰ

Rua Conselheiro Miguel da Silveira 24, Horta, 9900-114 **Tel** *292 391 174*

A lively restaurant at the north end of the seafront facing the neighbouring island of Pico, Capote is popular with locals and yachties celebrating their return to dry land. An appetizing selection of grilled meat and fish dishes, plus house specialities like *feijoada à Capote* (bean-based stew), complements a more economical daily buffet.

FAIAL Sal e Pico 🛉🍽 P ℰℰℰℰℰ

Rua Vasco da Gama, Horta, 9900-017 **Tel** *292 202 200*

Housed in the *pousada* Santa Cruz, this is one of the best restaurants on the island. Its name plays on the fact that there are magnificent views of Pico to be enjoyed from the terrace. The high quality cooking produces dishes like fried pork with pineapple and roasted tuna. The passion fruit pie is a regional delicacy. Closed Jan & Dec.

FLORES Sereia 🛉🍽 ℰ

Rua Dr Amas da Silveira 30, Santa Cruz das Flores, 9970-331 **Tel** *292 542 229*

This long-established restaurant on a road leading down to the harbour in Santa Cruz serves reliably good food and is excellent value for money. House specialities are grilled catch of the day and the enormous *calderaida de peixe* (fish and potato casserole). The *linguiça* (thin smoked sausage) is also memorable. Closed Sun (except in summer).

PICO Ancoradouro 🛉🍴🍽 P ℰ

Areia Larga, Madalena, 9950-302 **Tel** *292 623 490*

Located just outside Pico's capital, Madalena, this modest restaurant has glorious views of neighbouring Faial island and is a favourite with the local population who come for *morcela com ananás* (black pudding with pineapple), grilled fish, mixed kebabs and seafood *cataplana* as well as *pudim de amêndoa* (almond pudding). Closed Wed.

PICO Hocus Pocus ♿🛉🍴🍽🍷 ℰℰ

Caminho da Fonte, Lajes do Pico, 9930-177 **Tel** *292 679 504*

With its old English-style wooden interior, Hocus Pocus is one of the Azores' more upmarket restaurants. An integral component of the Aldeia da Fonte hotel, it is a popular choice for vegetarians. The menu also features local meat and fish dishes, such as the succulent Sebastien steak in peppermint sauce and the delightful fish and seafood kebabs.

SANTA MARIA Candeia 🍴🛉 ℰℰ

Rosa Alta, São Pedro, 9580-000 **Tel** *296 884 804*

A popular restaurant that stands in the shadow of the local church, Candeia offers a varied fish-based menu that includes cod with béchamel sauce or baked in a terracotta terrine. It also does a very good fried octopus in garlic and red wine sauce. One of the house specialities is black scabbard fish grilled with banana and cheese. Closed Sat lunch & Sun.

SÃO JORGE Manezinho 🛉🍴 P ℰ

Furna das Pombras, Urzelina, 9800-429 **Tel** *295 414 404*

The draw at this simple seaside restaurant is the set-price seafood buffet. The famous *queijo de São Jorge* (cheese) is among the *petiscos* (snacks) available. Otherwise, the menu lists dishes like *ameijoas* (clams) from Fajã da Caldeira de Santo Cristo. The esplanade allows for al fresco dining during the summer, with impressive views of Pico. Closed Mon.

SÃO MIGUEL Monte Verde 🛉🍴🍽 ℰ

Rua da Areia 4, Ribeira Grande, 9600-000 **Tel** *296 472 975*

Monte Verde's interior comprises a first-floor dining room decorated with modern *azulejos* and a display balcony where diners can select their own fresh fish. A house speciality is the *tigelada de chicharro*, a stew made with thin, sardine-like fish. The *grelhados de carne à Monte Verde* (grilled meat) is another. Service is friendly and competent. Closed Mon.

SÃO MIGUEL Alcides 🍽 ℰℰ

Rua Hintze Ribeiro 67-77, Ponta Delgada, 9504-000 **Tel** *296 282 677*

An unpretentious but accomplished restaurant sporting a stylish interior situated in Ponta Delgado's historical zone close to the Igreja Matriz de São Sebastião. Besides the robust steak and chips fare, Alcides offers more emblematic dishes like *cavala assada* (grilled mackerel) and *lulas guisadas* (squid fricassee), with fresh fruit for dessert. Closed Sun.

SÃO MIGUEL O Miroma, Furnas ♿🍽🍷 P ℰℰ

Rua Dr Frederico Moniz Pereira 15, 9675-005 **Tel** *296 584 422*

One of several excellent restaurants in Furnas that serve up a unique and highly unusual *cozida* (stew) that is sealed in a huge pot and then buried underground and left to slowly cook for several hours in heat generated by subterranean volcanic springs. The meat, yam and vegetables simply melt in your mouth. Closed Wed.

TERCEIRA Casa do Peixe ℰ

Estrada Miguel Corte Real 30, Angra do Heroismo, 9701-000 **Tel** *295 217 678*

Overlooking the harbour, the city's former fish market has been turned into an atmospheric restaurant with a full menu that reads as if the market were still in operation. Choices listed as *peixe na telha* mean the fish dishes are served on tiles – a traditional way of presenting the meal. Closed Tue.

TERCEIRA Quinta do Martelo 🛉🍴🎵🍽 P ℰ

Canada do Martelo 24, Cantinho, São Mateus, 9700-576 **Tel** *295 642 842*

The restaurant at this cultural resort was once a humble grocer's store and is now the place to go to try genuine Azorean dishes like Holy Spirit soup (meat and vegetable in white wine) and *alcatra* (meat stew). The interior is faithfully reproduced as a country inn, complete with wooden furniture and hand-painted crockery. Closed Wed.

SHOPPING IN PORTUGAL

Portugal offers a wealth of tempting goods at reasonable prices for shoppers. The best buys include handmade leather goods and shoes, hand-crafted gold and silver jewellery, fine porcelain and crystal, glassware, and high-quality clothes ranging from hand-knitted sweaters to the latest fashion garments and designer labels. The appearance of shopping malls has brought a range of sophisti-cated consumer products onto the market. Fortunately, tradi-tional arts and crafts have not been lost as a result of this modernization. Pottery and ceramics, embroidery and lace, woodcarving and cork, copper artifacts, tapestries, carpets and fresh produce are of a high standard. The regional tourism office shops are some of the best places to buy genuine Portuguese handicrafts.

A beautiful Portuguese tile

Lisbon's enormous Centro Colombo shopping mall

OPENING HOURS

Normal shopping hours are 9am–1pm and 3–7pm Monday to Friday and 9 or 10am–1pm on Saturdays. However, many shops in the bigger towns and cities remain open during the lunch hour and on Saturday afternoons. The big shopping centres are open every day, including Sundays, from 10am to 11pm or midnight.

TAX-FREE GOODS

On most goods a 21 per cent value-added tax *(IVA – Imposto sobre o Valor Acrescentado)* is charged in mainland Portugal. In Madeira and the Azores, the tax is 20 per cent.

Portugal has more than 1,600 shops affiliated with the 'Tax Free for Tourists System', which can be identified by the logo of that name. Non-European Union visitors are exempt from IVA, provided that they stay in Portugal no longer than 180 days.

Obtaining a rebate in smaller shops may be complicated; it is simpler to buy in a shop with a 'tax free' sign outside. Ask the shop assistant for an *Isencão na Exportação* form, which must be presented to a customs official on your departure from Portugal.

HOW TO PAY

Most shops accept credit and visa cards, though you may need to pay with cash in some of the smaller shops outside the big cities. You may be asked to show a passport when purchasing expensive items by credit card.

Under EU regulations on consumer goods, you have a two-year guarantee on products. Faulty goods must be returned with the original receipt for exchange or repair.

SHOPPING MALLS

Springing up in ever increas-ing numbers, large shopping malls have exerted a big influence on shopping habits in Portugal. Lisbon's huge **Centro Colombo** boasts more than 420 stores. Opened in 1997, it is the Iberian Peninsula's largest shopping mall. It also houses a leisure complex, multiplex cinema, health club, driving range, chapel and bowling alley.

MARKETS

A social and commercial occasion, the street market is integral to Portuguese life. It is usually held in the town's main square; ask for the *mercado* or *feira* if in doubt. Most markets sell a wide range of goods from food to household items and clothes, but you will also see sites devoted to antiques and local crafts. Roadside stalls offer produce from smallholdings, including delicious home-made liqueurs, pastries and cakes. Most markets are held

Ceramics for sale at the open-air market in Barcelos

Colourful handmade ceramics from the Alentejo region

in the mornings only, but in tourist areas they may go on until late afternoon.

Portugal's most famous market is the one in Barcelos (see p275), held Thursday in the main square. Here you can buy a vast range of household goods and local produce, and handicrafts such as pottery, lace, rugs and clothes.

Lisbon's Feira da Ladra (Thieves' Market) (see p71) is probably the best-known flea market and attracts large crowds. The **Feira de Antiguidades** at Estação Oriente in the city is another good hunting ground, and the **Feira de Carcavelos, Feira de Cascais** and **Feira de São Pedro** in Sintra attract bargain hunters by the thousands.

CERAMICS

Antique hand-painted glazed tiles (azulejos) are highly sought-after and expensive (see p435), but excellent reproductions are available in museum shops such as Lisbon's Museu Nacional do Azulejos (see pp120–21). **Azulejos Sant' Ana** also produces excellent replicas of early tiles.

Portugal's oldest established ceramics company is **Vista Alegre**, which produces high-quality porcelain.

If you are visiting Viseu (see p215), look out for the beautiful black earthenware pottery made by a handful of master potters. Viseu is one of

the last few places where ceramics of this type are made.

Barcelos is renowned for its regional pottery, especially figures based on everyday rustic life and religious themes. The best can be seen in the local museum and **Centro de Artesanato** in the city, and finely made replicas are on sale in shops and markets. The village of São Pedro do Corval in the Alentejo region is known for its colourful hand-painted plates and pots depicting flower motifs or rural scenes, such as the harvest or the pig-slaughter. **Porches Pottery** in the Algarve is famous for its plates and pots decorated with revivalist designs of ancient Iberian forms and motifs.

A traditional clay boneco (doll)

HANDICRAFTS

Portugal is well known for its delicate embroidery and fine lace, and the best-known source is the island of Madeira. On the mainland, the best lace and embroidery comes from towns in the Minho such as Viana do Castelo, also famous for its brightly printed shawls. Embroidered bedspreads are sold in Castelo Branco in the Beira Baixa, and colourful carpets, such as those from Arraiolos, are sold throughout the Alentejo.

Popular regional items are embroidered lovers' handkerchiefs (lenços dos namorados) in the Minho region and the typical local costume which is

notable for its brilliant colours, rich ornaments and variety. The Minho is famous for its filigree gold and silver work, from traditional necklaces, heart-shaped pendants, earrings and rings to religious votives and trinkets.

Also unique to the Minho is the ancient floral art of palmito, a type of bouquet made with metallic coloured paper by young girls and women for religious ceremonies and as souvenirs for tourists. **Northern Crafts Minho** is a good source for these handicrafts.

Arraiolos in the Alentejo has been famous since the late 16th century for its hand-embroidered carpets, which are sewn in wool on a canvas frame. Originally, they followed traditional Persian and Indian designs, but from the 18th century, more modern designs became popular. Fine examples are on sale in many shops in the town, especially at **Tapetes de Arraiolos**, and elsewhere in Portugal.

The Alentejo is also the best region for buying hand-made rugs and bedspreads in brightly coloured materials. In the town of Estremoz you will find the unique traditional clay figures known as bonecos (dolls). The making of these gaily painted pieces depicting religious and rustic themes dates back more than two centuries.

Ornately embroidered clothing from Viana do Castelo in the Minho

Preparing to sample the wine at a stall in the Minho region

WINE AND SPIRITS

While it may be best known for fortified wines such as port and Madeira, Portugal also has a wide and varied range of excellent table wines *(see pp28-9)*, which are well represented in shops, supermarkets and wine merchants. Some of the most characterful wines, particularly reds, are made in the Douro region, where port is also made. More approachable reds (and inreasingly, whites) are made in the Alentejo, whose wines are much loved by the Portuguese themselves. Wines are widely available, but for a good selection try **Napoleão** in Baixa, or the **Coisas do Arco do Belém** or **Solar do Vinho do Porto** in Lisbon.

The wines in Portugal are inexpensive compared to other European countries, and include the whole range, from young green wines *(vinho verdes)* through popular rosés, fruity whites and robust reds to Madeira wine and ports. It is often cheaper to shop direct from the winemaking co-operatives.

Home distilling is also a favourite pastime in Portugal. Apart from distilled wine *(aguardente)* and a spirit made from grape skins *(bagaço)*, various liqueurs are made with cherries *(gingjinha)*, almonds, *(amêndoa)* and figs *(figo)*.

A speciality in the Algarve is *medronho*, a local firewater made from the fruit of the wild strawberry tree. Another Algarve regional product is

brandymel, a mixture of honey, herbs and *medronho* – once a traditional homemade remedy for coughs and influenza, but now produced commercially and much loved by the Portuguese.

CLOTHING AND SHOES

Portugal has a thriving textile industry, despite fierce competition from China and India, though much of the country's production in clothes and shoes goes to supply well-known designer brands abroad. With the advent of large clothing stores and shopping malls, however, there is no shortage of quality designer clothes. **Zara** is one of the popular clothing shops.

Some excellent-value seconds are on sale at local markets everywhere; a particularly well-known one is at Carcavelos between Lisbon and Estoril.

Shoe-making is a vital part of Portugal's economy. Hundreds of factories produce a range of different styles of shoes and sandals, which are exported all over the world. They also make good souvenirs.

Quality leather boots from Maderia – a popular gift

Leather goods, such as bags, purses, wallets, gloves and belts, are consistently good. Variations in price reflect the quality of the products.

Ornately embroidered women's linen blouses, fashioned in the regional style, are on sale in many craft shops. Prices are also reasonable for knitwear and woollen fishermen's sweaters from Nazaré *(see p182)*.

SIZE CHART

Women's dresses, coats and skirts

Portuguese	34	36	38	40	42	44	46
British	8	10	12	14	16	18	20
American	6	8	10	12	14	16	18

Women's shoes

Portuguese	36	37	38	39	40	41
British	3	4	5	6	7	8
American	5	6	7	8	9	10

Men's suits

Portuguese	44	46	48	50	52	54	56	58 (size)
British	34	36	38	40	42	44	46	48 (inches)
American	34	36	38	40	42	44	46	48 (inches)

Men's shirts

Portuguese	36	38	39	41	42	43	44	45 (size)
British	14	15	15½	16	16½	17	17½	18 (inches)
American	14	15	15½	16	16½	17	17½	18 (inches)

Men's shoes

Portuguese	39	40	41	42	43	44	45	46
British	6	7	7½	8	9	10	11	12
American	7	7½	8	8½	9½	10½	11	11½

ANTIQUES

Whether you are a connoisseur or casual collector, Portugal's antique shops and markets are bound to have something to catch your eye. Antique markets *(feiras de velharias)* take place in many regions, usually on Saturday or Sunday.

There is a steady demand for rare and unusual antiques, especially those connected with Portugal's trading links with the Orient over past centuries: Japanese lacquer work and mother of pearl, carvings in wood and ivory, and religious icons. Hand-painted tiles, introduced by the Moors in medieval times, now attract buyers from all over the world.

The best hunting grounds in Lisbon are in the Rua São Bento, Largo de S Martinho, Rua Augusto Rosa, and Rua D Pedro V. **Loja Azul** and **Antique Tiles** are two of the best shops for tiles.

Serra cheese from the Serra da Estrela

REGIONAL PRODUCE

Every region in Portugal offers its own specialities and it is best to buy fresh items in the region where they are made, though most of the better-known regional produce can be found throughout the country. Cured ham *(presunto)* from the north of Portugal is particularly good in Chaves *(see pp258–9)*. Monchique *(pp 320–21)* in the Algarve also has a reputation for cured ham. Spicy pork sausages *(linguiça)* are a speciality of Porto. The Minho region is known for its tasty garlic sausage made with turkey and chicken meat *(alheira de Mirandela)* and a sumptuous black sausage *(morcela)* made from pork.

A wide variety of cheese is made in Portugal. The best is reputed to be from the town of Serpa *(see pp217–20)* and the surrounding region of the lower Alentejo. Serpa cheese finds its way into many shops throughout the country. It is rivalled in taste and quality perhaps only by cheese made in the Serra da Estrela region *(see pp220–21)*.

An antique shop full of wares in Lisbon

DIRECTORY

SHOPPING MALLS

Centro Colombo
Avenida General Norton de Matos,
Benfica, Lisboa.

MARKETS

Feira de Antiguidades
Estação Oriente,
Lisboa.

Feira de Carcavelos
Largo Mercado,
Carcavelos.

Feira de Cascais
Placa Mercado Municipal,
Cascais.

Feira de São Pedro
São Pedro Sintra,
Sintra.

CERAMICS

Azulejos Sant'Ana
Rua do Alecrim 95,
Chiado, Lisboa.
Map 7 A5.
Tel 213 422 537.

Centro de Artesanato
Torre de Porta Nova,
Barcelos.

Porches Pottery
EN 125 Porches,
Algarve.

Vista Alegre
Largo do Chiado 22–23,
Chiado, Lisboa.
Map 7 A4.
Tel 213 461 401.
www.GiftCollectors.com

HANDICRAFTS

Northern Crafts Minho
www.artesminho.com

Tapetes de Arraiolos

Tapetes de Arraiolos
Rua Rombeiros Voluntários 7, Arraiolos.
Tel 266 429 057.
www.tapetesde arraiolos.net

CLOTHING AND SHOES

Zara
Rua Garrett 1,
Chiado, Lisboa.
Map 7 B4.
Tel 213 243 710.

WINE AND SPIRITS

Coisas do Arco do Vinho
Centro Cultural de Belém,
Lisboa. **Map** 1 B3.
Tel 213 642 031.

Napoleão

Napoleão
Rua dos Fanqueiros 72-6,
Baixa, Lisboa.
Map 7 A3.
Tel 218 872 042.

Solar do Vinho do Porto
Rua S Pedro de Alcântara,
45 Bairro Alto, Lisboa.
Map 7 A3.
Tel 213 475 707.
www.ivp.pt

ANTIQUES

Antique Tiles
Solar Rua D Pedro V 68-70, Bairro Alto, Lisboa.
Map 4 F2.

Loja Azul
Rua 9 Abril,
Solar dos Pinheiros 220b,
S Pedro de Estoril.
Tel 214 683 993.

ENTERTAINMENT IN PORTUGAL

The traditional love of music, dance and singing in Portugal is reflected in a vast range of cultural activities and entertainment. Theatre, classical and contemporary music, opera, dance, film festivals, pop, rock and jazz festivals and variety shows featuring internationally renowned performers can be enjoyed in many regions.

Portuguese drummer

The major venues and events are concentrated in Lisbon, Porto and other big cities, where there is abundant nightlife. Lisbon is considered one of the liveliest European capitals after dark. The colourful folklore festivals and carnivals that are rooted in Portuguese culture are celebrated in every corner of the country.

Lisbon's Teatro Nacional Dona Maria II

INFORMATION

The tourism boards issue a free monthly calendar of programmes, events and venues. The Portuguese newspapers all have a "what's on" section. The best weekly guides in English are in *The Resident* (www.portugal resident.com) and *Portugal News* (www.the-news.net), available in the Algarve with some outlets in Lisbon.

THEATRE AND DANCE

A wide range of professional and amateur productions can be seen in many cities and towns. Lisbon and Porto offer the widest choice, with many established theatres and cultural centres staging world-class productions.

Lisbon's Teatro Nacional Dona Maria II *(p127)* is the principal venue and Porto's **Teatro Rivoli** presents a prestigious two-week International Festival of Iberian theatre.

The Algarve is well served by municipal theatres. One of the biggest regional events is the **Algarve Folk Music and**

Contemporary Dance Festival that takes place at different venues with dancers from all over the world.

The Sintra Festival of classical music and dance is the pinnacle of cultural events in Portugal. It takes place in various stunning fairytale venues, including the romantic Palácio de Pena *(pp162–3)*, Palácio Nacional de Queluz *(pp166–7)* and Palácio de Seteais *(p157)*.

FILM

All of the latest releases, usually with subtitles, are screened in cinemas in shopping malls all over the country, while fringe cinema can be seen at a number of cultural centres and theatres.

The **Lisbon Film Festival** is the only festival dedicated exclusively to documentary films; it attracts entries from all over the world. The **Porto Film Festival** encompasses sci-fi, fantasy and thrillers.

The **Algarve International Film Festival** is the country's oldest film festival, catering for short films of up to 30 minutes' duration.

CLASSICAL MUSIC, OPERA AND BALLET

Some of the world's most famous orchestras and artists perform at the major venues. The most prestigious is the Funcação Calouste Gulbenkian *(p127)*, with its own orchestra and ballet company. The **Casa da Musica** in Porto has an extensive programme of dance and music.

ROCK AND JAZZ

The two biggest open-air rock festivals are **Rock in Rio Lisboa** and the **Super Bock Rock Festival**. Another big international event is the **Algarve Summer Festival** featuring some of the world's leading singers and groups.

Some of the biggest names in world jazz and blues appear at the major concert halls in the big cities and at the jazz festivals in Lisbon, Porto, Guimaraes, Viana do Castelo, and the Algarve.

Major venues in Lisbon for world class performances of jazz and other modern music include the Centro Cultural de

The Rock in Rio Lisboa festival attracts huge crowds

Trying to bring the bull to a standstill at the end of a bullfight

Belém *(p127)*, Praça Sony *(p127)*, **Culturgest**, and Pavilhão Atlântico *(p127)*.

One of the highlights of the year is the **Festival de Jazz do Porto**, with some of the legendary names in jazz and blues participating. The **Centro Cultural Vila Flor** in Guimarães hosts one Portugal's most important jazz festivals.

CARNIVALS

Celebrated mostly in honour of the Saints or Our Lady, Portuguese festivals and carnivals are colourful events with costumed dancers, decorated floats and papier maché models. The most famous is the **Loulé Carnival** in the Algarve. Thousands of visitors come to join in the three days of parades and merrymaking.

One of the most exuberant religious festivals is the Romaria de Nossa Senhora d'Agonia *(see p31)*.

The most extraordinary summer festival takes place in the small Alentejo village of **Flower Festival Campo Maior**, where the streets are decorated with thousands of paper flowers.

NIGHTLIFE

There is no shortage of places to enjoy a drink, listen to music and dance until the early hours of the morning in a club, disco or late-night bar. Irish bars are in vogue for a lively night out and gay bars have sprung up in many regions. For nightlife, Lisbon reigns supreme and the choice is

almost endless. The main districts are the riverside area that stretches along the dockland, and the Bairro Alto, known for its *(fado)* houses *(see pp64–5)*. The most sophisticated clubs are Lux *(see p127)* and Kapital *(see p127)*. The jet-set in Algarve flock to **T-Clube** in Quinta do Lago.

BULLFIGHTING

The Ribatejo region northeast of Lisbon is bullfighting country *(see pp146–7)* and the principal arena in this region is **Praça de Touros** in Santarem. Lisbon's major arena is the Campo Pequeno *(see p118)*.

The colourful Romaria de Nossa Senhora d'Agonia religious festival

DIRECTORY

THEATRE AND DANCE

Algarve Folk Music and Contemporary Dance Festival
www.allgarve.pt

Teatro Rivoli
Praça D João, Oporto.
Tel 222 071 260.
www.musica.iol.pt

FILM

Algarve International Film Festival
Tel 282 422 667.
www.algarvefilmfest.com

Lisbon Documentary Film Festival
Largo da Madalena 1–1º,
Lisbon. **Map** 7 C4.

Tel 218 883 093.
www.doclisboa.org

Porto Film Festival
Rua Aníbal Cunha 84,
Oporto. *Tel 222 058 819.*
www.fantasporto.com

CLASSICAL MUSIC, OPERA AND BALLET

Casa da Musica
Av de Boavista 604-610,
Oporto. *Tel 220 120 220.*
www.casadamusica.pt

ROCK AND JAZZ

Algarve Summer Festival
www.parquecidades-eim.pt

Centro Cultural Vila Flor
Avenida D Afonso Henrique Guimarães.
Tel 253 424 700.

Culturgest
Rua do Arco do Cego 1,
Lisbon. **Map** 6 D2.
Tel 217 905 155.
www.culturgest.pt

Festival de Jazz do Porto
www.portugaldiario.iol.pt

Rock in Rio Lisboa
www.rockinrio-lisboa.
sapo.pt

Super Bock Rock Festival
Lisbon and Oporto.
www.superbock.pt

CARNIVALS

Flower Festival Campo Maior
www.visitportugal.com

Loulé Carnival
Tel 289 800 400.
www.visitalgarve.pt

NIGHTLIFE

T-Clube
Quinta do Lago,
Almancil,
Algarve.
Tel 289 396 751.

BULLFIGHTING

Praça de Touros
Santarém.
Tel 243 324 358.

OUTDOOR ACTIVITIES AND SPECIALIST HOLIDAYS

Portugal offers an amazing variety of terrain with sports and leisure activities to match. The mild climate in the Algarve, Madeira and the Azores means that many outdoor leisure pursuits can be enjoyed throughout the year. Specialist holidays are available for a variety of activities, including microlight flying,

Visitors enjoying a sailing trip

whale watching, big game fishing, surfing and horse riding. Water skiing, jet skiing, canoeing and kayaking can also be enjoyed, as can mountaineering and rock-climbing. The unspoiled landscape invites leisurely walking. Golf *(see pp442–3)* and tennis facilities are well established.

INFORMATION

Regional tourist offices can provide information on sport and outdoor activities. In addition, the following English language/bi-lingual publications provide information: *Essential Algarve, Essential Lisboa, Essential Madeira, Goodlife Magazine* and the weekly newspapers *The Resident* and *Portugal News.*

WATER SPORTS

Surfing, windsurfing, diving, water skiing and jet skiing are popular along the coast and around the Atlantic islands. Vilamoura Lda and **Polvo Watersports**, operating out of **Vilamoura Marina**, are leading Algarve companies offering specialist holidays. Jet skis, water skis and wake boards (along with powerboats) can be hired with the services of expert instructors.

The best beaches for surfing are on the Lisbon coast at Guincho and Ericeira. In the Algarve the long sandy Praia de Vale Figueiras on the west coast is a major destination.

Equipment can be hired or bought from **Algarve Surf School Camp**, which offers lessons for beginners.

The Azores islands catch huge swells, though access can be difficult, and waves up to 1.8 m (6 ft) in summer and 4.5 m (15 ft) in winter are for professionals only. The most popular spots are Ribeira Grande and Rabo de Peixe on the north coast of São Miguel.

Madeira's coastline boasts exceptional conditions – expecially near the village of Jardim do Mar, Paul do Mar, the Ponta Pequena and the renowned Ponta do Jardim. Excellent but difficult surfing waters to access front the villages of Contreira, Ponta Delgada and São Vicente.

For windsurfers, Praia do Martinhal near Sagres in west Algarve is one of the most popular spots, with the **Surfcamp Algarve** on the beach.

Surfing – a popular pastime along the mainland coast and islands

Scuba divers are drawn to Portugal's clear, mild waters and wealth of marine life. The best diving is in the Algarve, the Berlengas Islands near Peniche on the Silver Coast, and Madeira and the Azores, where divers may see tropical species such as barracuda, monkfish, dolphins, rays and giant mantas. Diving centres include **Dive Time** in Lagos, **Tivoli Almansor Dive Centre** in Carvoeiro, **Torpedo Diving** in Vilamoura and **Espírito Azul Diving** on São Miguel, Azores.

SAILING AND CANOEING

The marinas at Lagos and Vilamoura in the Algarve are important sailing and yachting centres where international regattas are staged. The **Portimão Marina** and **Albufeira Marina** cater for the growing interest in yachting in southern Europe. The marina on the island of Faial in the Azores is a stopping-off point for trans-Atlantic yachtsmen. Madeira is an excellent destination for

Windsurfing near Martinhal in the Algarve

Walking along one of Madeira's *levadas* (irrigation channels)

boating and yachting, with many marinas.

Canoeing is popular on Portugal's rivers especially the Mondego, Zêzere, Arade, Cavado, Lima and Vez.

BOATING

Tour operators in the Algarve, Madeira and the Azores offer sightseeing cruises. Specialist holidays designed especially for wine buffs are offered by **Douro Azul** in the famous wine-growing region in northern Portugal. The itinerary combines river trips with journeys on the old steam engines along riverside routes that once transported the wines to the city of Porto, and include overnight stays at traditional wine-growing farms *(quintas)*.

WALKING AND CYCLING

Madeira is ideal as a walking destination, with picturesque villages, amazing mountain landscapes, rugged coastlines and golden beaches. The favourite routes follow the island's extensive network of irrigation channels *(levadas)*.

The Azores are a paradise for walkers and hikers, with flowered roads, volcanic mountainous terrain and verdant countryside. **Sherpa Expeditions** specializes in walking holidays here and in Madeira.

The Silver Coast (western central Portugal) has undulating terrain, forested hills and long sandy beaches, almost deserted for most of the year.

The Algarve offers exhilarating cliff-top walks, especially along the west coast. **Portugal Walks** specializes in walking holidays in this region. In the east Algarve the Ria Formosa Natural Park *(p331)* and the Sapal Nature Reserve near Castro Marim *(p333)* are popular locations for nature lovers and birdwatchers.

Inland, the hilly Serra de Calderão region provides walking terrain off the beaten track, with small villages providing welcome watering holes.

Verdant and more densely forested North Portugal is a joy to explore on foot. Here, you can follow the ancient paths of the pilgrims to the holy shrine of Santiago de Compostela in Spain.

Also well worth exploring are the Peneda-Gerês National Park *(pp272–3)* and further east Montesinho Natural Park *(p262)*, which offers scenic mountain routes.

The Alentejo has vast tracts of open plains, and near the bigger towns and cities, such as Évora, Elvas, and Serpa, the landscape and monuments are inspirational. The Lisbon coastline stretching north has enjoyable coastal and countryside routes. The areas around Cascais and Sintra, with its mountainous terrain and lush forestation, is pleasant for walks.

Mountain bikes can be hired in many areas of the country to search out the most scenic trails. **Mountain Bike Adventures** is a good source of information.

FLYING, PARAGLIDING AND SKYDIVING

Microlight flying is available at the **Algarve Sports Centre**. The center was established by ex-world champion Gerry Breen, who is the chief instructor here.

You can take lessons leading to a pilot's qualification recognized by the **Federação Portuguesa de Voo Livre** (National Association for Free Flight), or occasional pleasure flights along the rugged west Algarve coastline.

The weather conditions and terrain in parts of Portugal are also ideal for paragliding. Most students bring their own gear.

Adrenalin seekers can indulge in the exhilarating sport of skydiving at the **Aerodrome Municipal de Portimão** in the Algarve.

FISHING

The coastline, waterways and rivers of Portugal offer plenty of opportunities for fishing, from angling for trout in the

Microlight flying over Lagos Bay in the Algarve

Whale-watching expedition up close to a whale

rivers to big game fishing off the shores of the Algarve, the Lisbon Coast, the Silver Coast, Madeira and the Azores. Many of the rivers and lakes yield abundant trout, carp and eels.

A licence obtained locally from the **Instituto Florestal** is required to fish the rivers, but not for line fishing from the shore or from a boat at sea. Contact **Federação Portuguesa de Pesca Desportivo** for further information.

Among the companies offering big game fishing are **Big Game Fishing** and **Cruzeiros de Vilamoura** in the Algarve; **Madeira Game Fishing**, **Nautisantos Big Game Fishing**, **Turipesca** and **Katherine B Sportfishing** in Madeira; and **Big Game Fishing Azores** in the Azores.

Tennis player at the Vale de Lobo resort in the Algarve

TENNIS

Tennis courts are found almost everywhere in Portugal, and are an integral part of the facilities in most tourist resorts. Many resorts also have squash courts. The larger Algarve resorts, such as **Vale do Lobo**, offer tennis coaching holidays, or you can book a specialist tennis holiday through **Tennis Holidays in the Sun**.

WHALE WATCHING

The Azores is a prime spot to see whales and other cetaceans, such as dolphins, that are attracted to the warm waters and abundant food. In recent years as many as 20 different species have been seen. The whale-watching season lasts from May to October due to weather conditions, though whales inhabit the waters throughout the year.

Whale-watching holidays as well as daily expeditions are offered by **Whale Watch Azores**, **Futurismo Azores Whale Watching**, **Espaçotalassa** and **Pico Sport Lda**.

HORSE RIDING

Portugal's proud riding tradition stems mainly from the country's handsome Lusitano horses and the sturdy Garrano breed that roams free in the Peneda-Gêres National Park *(see pp272-3)*.

One of the most renowned equestrian centres for training Lusitano and Garrano horses is **Centro Equestre Vale do Lima**, where equestrian holidays with lessons and tuition in horse care, riding, and dressage are provided.

In the Algarve, **Quinta Martins**, **Pinetrees Riding Centre** and **Vale do Ferro** are well-known riding centres.

CAVING

The Algarve has more than 100 subterranean caves scattered across the central and eastern region, some dating from the Jurassic period. For more information, contact the **Centro de Estudos Espeleológicos e Arqueológicos do Algarve**.

Many of the caves have stalagmites and stalactites but visitors should explore only with a recommended guide.

On the Azores island of Terceira the Algar do Carvão is one of the volcanic wonders of the world. It is a giant cave that spirals downwards nearly 100 m (328 ft) from the opening of its conduit, ending at a crystal-clear lake. Milky white stalactites and stalagmites cover large areas of the roof and walls.

The smaller Gruta de Natal is safe and easy to explore with the help of an on-site guide.

CLIMBING AND MOUNTAINEERING

Madeira's volcanic origins and rugged mountain terrain, with cliff faces rising from the sea, offer exciting conquests for experienced climbers. The favourite areas are the central mountain range, the sea cliffs and some of the northern cliffs. The Azores offers a similar landscape, and the island of Pico provides the ultimate challenge to scale its 2,341-m (7,680 ft) mountain – the highest in Portugal.

Rock climbing in the rugged, volcanic terrain of Madeira

DIRECTORY

WATER SPORTS

Algarve Surf School Camp
Lagos, Algarve.
Tel 282 624 560.

Dive Time
Marina de Lagos,
Lagos, Algarve.
Tel 309 810 623.

Espírito Azul Diving
Rua do Pinedo 22,
Vila Franca do Campo,
São Miguel, Azores.
Tel 914 898 253.
www.espiritoazul.com

Polvo Watersports
Vilamoura Marina,
Algarve.
Tel 289 388 149.
www.polvowater
sports.com

Surfcamp Algarve
www.unitedsurf
camps.com

Tivoli Almansor Dive Centre
Hotel Tivoli, Carvoeiro,
Algarve.
Tel 282 351 194.

Torpedo Diving
Vilamoura, Algarve.
Tel 289 314 098.

Vilamoura Marina
8125-409 Quarteira.
Tel 289 310 560.
www.marinade
vilamoura.com

SAILING AND CANOEING

Albufeira Marina
Albufeira, Algarve.
www.marinade
albufeira.com.pt

Federação Portuguesa de Canoagem
Rua António Pinto
Machado 60, 3º,
4100-068 Oporto.
Tel 225 432 237.
www.fpcanoagem.pt

Portimão Marina
Edifício Admin Ponta
da Areia, Portimão.
Tel 282 400 680.
www.marinade
portimao.com.pt

BOATING

Douro Azul
Rua de São Francisco 4-2º
D, 4050-548, Oporto.
Tel 223 402 500.
www.douroazul.com

WALKING AND CYCLING

Mountain Bike Adventures
www.themountainbike
adventurecompany.com

Portugal Walks
37 Quinta do Montinho
Budens, 8650-060
Vila do Bispo, Algarve.
Tel 282 697 298.
www.portugalwalks.com

Sherpa Expeditions
www.sherpa-walking-
holidays.co.uk

FLYING, PARAGLIDING AND SKYDIVING

Aerodrome Municipal de Portimão
Montes de Alvor.
Tel 282 495 828.
www.skydive-algarve.com

Algarve Sports Centre
Torre de Controle,
Aerodróme de Lagos,
Lagos 8601-903, Algarve.
Tel 914 903 384.
www.gerrybreen.com

Federação Portuguesa de Voo Livre
Av Cidade de Lourenço
Marques, Modulo 2
Praceta B, Lisboa.
Tel 218 522 885.
www.fpvl.pt

FISHING

Big Game Fishing
P 8500-905, Portimão,
Algarve. www.
biggamefishing.info

Big Game Fishing Azores
Horta Marina,
Ilha de Faial, Azores.
Tel 292 392 375.
www.atlantic-
sportfisheries.com

Cruzeiros de Vilamoura
Cais Q Escritório no 8,
Marina de Vilamoura,
Algarve.
Tel 289 315 234.
www.cruzeiros-de-
vilamoura.com

Federação Portuguesa de Pesca Desportivo
Rua Eça de Queirós 3 1º,
1050-095 Lisbon.
Tel 213 140 177.

Instituto Florestal
Avenida de João
Crisóstomo 26-8º,
1069-040 Lisbon.
Tel 213 124 800.

Katherine B Sportfishing
Madeira.
www.fishmadeira.com

Madeira Game Fishing
Tel 291 227 169.
www.madeiragamefish.
com

Nautisantos Big Game Fishing
Funchal Marina,
Funchal, Madeira.
Tel 291 231 312.
www.nautisantos
fishing.com

Turipesca
Madeira.
Tel 291 231 063.
www.madeirafishing
centre.com

TENNIS

Tennis Holidays in the Sun
The Old Forge, High St,
Twyford, Winchester,
Hampshire SO21 1RT, UK.
Tel 01794 500 500.

Vale do Lobo
Estrada Vale do Lobo,
Almancil, Algarve.
Tel 289 353 333.
www.valedolobo.com

WHALE WATCHING

Espaçotalassa
Whale Watching and
Study Base, Rua do Saco,
9930 Laje do Pico.
Tel 292 672 010.
www.espacotalassa.com

Futurismo Azores Whale Watching
Estrada da Ribeira
Grande 1001 A,
Ponta Delgada, Azores.
Tel 296 628 522.
www.azoreswhales.com

Pico Sport Lda
Frank Wirth, 9950
Madalena, Pico Island,
Azores. *Tel 292 622 980.*
www.whales-dolphins.
net

Whale Watch Azores
1B Museum Square,
Keswick, Cumbria
CA12 5DZ, UK.
Tel 020 8144 2560.
www.whalewatchazores.
com

HORSE RIDING

Centro Equestre Vale do Lima
Quinta da Sobreira,
Ponte de Lima.
Tel 258 943 873.

Pinetrees Riding Centre
Estrada do Ançáo,
Almancil.
Tel 289 394 369.
www.pinetrees
ridingcentre.com

Quinta Martins
Algarve.
Tel 289 395 529.
algarvemartin@gmail.com

Vale do Ferro
Centro Hippico,
Mexilhoeira Grande,
8500 Portimão.
Tel 282 968 444.
www.valedeferro.com

CAVING

Centro de Estudos Espeleológicos e Arqueológicos do Algarve
Faro. *Tel 289 823 821.*

Golfing Holidays in Portugal

Portugal is well established as a golfing destination, and specialist golfing holidays have become a very popular way of visiting the country. The Algarve in particular has emerged as one of Europe's premier golfing regions. Its mild winters and large number of quality courses make it attractive to the serious as well as the recreational golfer. The other main golfing region is the area around Lisbon, but there are courses in central and northern Portugal as well. The Oporto Golf Club has the distinction of being one of the oldest courses in Europe. Madeira and the Azores also cater for the golfer.

The scenic Penha Longa Golf Club, Central Portugal

GENERAL INFORMATION

The majority of Portugal's nearly 60 golf courses are by the sea, with spectacular scenery. Along the mainland west coast, and in exposed areas of western Algarve, the wind increases as the day progresses, so golfers wishing to avoid it should opt for an early start. It is always best to book ahead. The main season runs from mid-autumn to late spring, but summer can also be busy. Rates vary from just over €30 to over €150 for a round of 18 holes, but there are many discounts available through tour operators, hotels and booking services.

MAJOR TOURNAMENTS

Portugal currently hosts three PGA tournaments: the Madeira Island Open, held in March at the Santo da Serra; the Open de Portugal, held in the Algarve or Lisbon area in

March or April; and the Portugal Masters, first held at Southern Portugal's Victoria Vilamoura in October 2007. Visit www.pga.com for further information on tournaments.

NORTHERN PORTUGAL

The north is the least developed in terms of golf, but it was here that golf began in Portugal when Scottish and English port shippers founded the **Oporto Golf Club** in 1890. The course, is the oldest in the Iberian peninsula. The par-71 circuit is laid out on sand dunes by the Atlantic. The **Amarante Golf Club** offers a varied par-68 mountain course.

LISBON AND CENTRAL PORTUGAL

Near the picturesque town of Óbidos, the **Praia d'El Rey Golf Club** is one of Portugal's

most highly regarded. Laid out by American golf architect Cabell Robinson, the long par-72 course is set in a coastal resort and extends across sand dunes, cliffs and pine woods. The course is accessible to players of all levels. **Oitavos Dunes** is part of the Quinta da Marinha resort near Cascais. The par-71 course, designed by Arthur Hills, offers great views of the Atlantic and the Sintra hills. It is set in the Sintra-Cascais Natural Park and runs in a loop among reforested sand dunes, pine woods and open coastal terrain. There is another 18-hole course within the resort, the **Quinta da Marinha Golf Club**. Nearby, is the **Penha Longa Golf Club** with a par-72 course in landscape similar to that of the Oitavos course. This is complemented by a 9-hole course. **Tróia Golf**, a challenging par-72 course of small greens and narrow fairways. Sections of the course run alongside Tróia beach, with a view of the Arrábida hills which protect the course and beach from northerly winds.

SOUTHERN PORTUGAL

Ammaia Golf Club, the only golf course in the large Alentejo region, is near Marvão, not far from the Spanish border. The wide fairways and large greens of this par-72 course make it amateur-friendly, but there are real challenges for proficient golfers, too. The course is currently closed for repairs.

Putting at historic Oporto Golf Club, Northern Portugal

Spectacular views of the Atlantic at Vale do Lobo, Southern Portugal

MADEIRA AND THE AZORES

Palheiro Golf is a beautiful mountain course. **Santo da Serra Golf** hosts the Madeira Island Open. **Porto Santo Golf** features two 18-hole courses, designed by Severiano Ballesteros. Dramatic clifftop ocean holes are combined with long holes along the island's famous beach. São Miguel, the main island in the Azores archipelago, has two golf courses: **Furnas** and **Batalha**. The former overlooks the stunning Furnas valley and the latter is by the ocean, on the island's north coast.

Porto Santo Golf on the island of Porto Santo, northeast of Madeira

The number and density of golf courses in the Algarve means that a visitor to any part of the region can reach a golf course in a couple of hours at most. The oldest course along this holiday coast is Penina, part of the Le Meridien Penina resort *(see p402)*. The par-73 parkland course is complemented by two 9-hole courses. Farther east, **Vale da Pinta** is a highly regarded par-71 course. The vast Vilamoura resort in central Algarve is home to no fewer than five golf courses, all of the highest standard. The **Victoria** Vilamoura course was acclaimed as one of the best in Europe within a year of opening. Slightly farther east is **Vale do Lobo**, the first golf resort in the Algarve, opened in 1962. Its Royal course is a demanding par-72 course with memorable scenery, overlooking the beach and the Atlantic. The resort's other course, Ocean, is regarded as equally challenging. Neighbouring **Quinta do Lago**, has two excellent golf courses, South and North. Also within the resort, but not owned by it, are two other top par-72 courses, **San Lorenzo** and **Pinheiros Altos**.

Winner at Santo da Serra, Madeira

DIRECTORY

NORTHERN PORTUGAL

Amarante Golf Club
Quinta da Deveza, Fregim.
Tel 255 446 060.

Oporto Golf Club
Paramos, Espinho.
Tel 227 342 008.

LISBON AND CENTRAL PORTUGAL

Oitavos Dunes
Quinta da Marinha.
Tel 214 860 600.
www.quintadamarinha-oitavosgolfe.pt

Penha Longa Golf Club
Caesar Park Penha Longa, Estrada da Lagoa Azul, Linhó. *Tel 219 249 031.*
www.penhalonga.com

Praia d'El Rey
Vale de Janelas, Amoreira.
Tel 262 905 005.
www.praia-del-rey.com

Quinta da Marinha Golf Club
Quinta da Marinha.
Tel 214 860 100.
www.quintadamarinha.com

Tróia Golf
Complexo Turístico de Tróia, Carvalhal.
Tel 265 494 024.
www.troiaresort.pt

SOUTHERN PORTUGAL

Ammaia Golf Club
Quinta do Prado, São Salvador da Aramenha, Marvão.
Tel 245 993 755.

Pinheiros Altos
Quinta do Lago, Almancil.
Tel 289 359 910.
www.pinheirosaltos.pt

Quinta do Lago
Almancil. *Tel 289 390 700.*
www.quintadolago.com

San Lorenzo
Quinta do Lago, Almancil.
Tel 289 396 522. www.sanlorenzogolfcourse.com

Vale do Lobo
Almancil. *Tel 289 353 465.*
www.valedolobo.com

Vale da Pinta
Carvoeiro, Lagoa.
Tel 282 340 900.
www.pestanagolf.com

Victoria Vilamoura
Vilamoura, E.N. 125.
Tel 289 310 188.
www.oceanicogolf.com

MADEIRA AND THE AZORES

Batalha
Fenais da Luz. *Tel 296 498 559.* www.azoresgolfislands.com

Furnas
Achada das Furnas. *Tel 296 584 651.* www.azoresgolfislands.com

Palheiro Golf
Sítio do Balançal, São Gonçalo. *Tel 291 790 120.*
www.palheirogolf.com

Porto Santo Golf
Sítio das Marinhas, Porto Santo. *Tel 291 983 778.*
www.portosantogolfe.com

Santo da Serra Golf
Santo da Serra, Machico.
Tel 291 550 100. www.santodaserragolf.com

SURVIVAL
GUIDE

PRACTICAL INFORMATION

Portugal is an easy country to visit. In the Algarve and the Lisbon area, where most tourists go, the choice of hotels, restaurants and entertainment is vast. English is widely spoken, and visitors are welcomed. But even in the

Sign for tourist information office

less developed parts of the country, visitors will find it easy to deal with friendly locals. Accommodation can be found virtually anywhere, children are always welcome, and food is good. Most towns also have helpful tourist offices.

WHEN TO GO

The country's long Atlantic coast is the single most important factor in Portugal's climate. Coastal regions can be very rainy in winter, and although temperatures don't drop that low, it often feels very cold. In the mountainous north it's not uncommon for snow to fall on higher ground. The exception is the Algarve, which despite also being on the Atlantic, faces south and is protected from northerly winds by inland hills.

The Algarve, then, is the only year-round destination, with hot summers and mild winters. Other coastal areas generally have warm to hot summers, with either balmy or windy evenings. Inland areas throughout the country are subject to more extreme conditions, with colder winters even in the Alentejo and hotter summers even in Trás-os-Montes. Madeira enjoys a more temperate climate, but the Azores are susceptible to winter storms. Spring and autumn are good times to visit because the weather is mild, but spring in particular may be wet *(see pp34–5)*.

VISAS AND PASSPORTS

EU nationals need only a valid passport to enter Portugal, which is a signatory to the Schengen Agreement. If they stay for more than six months, they should apply for a residence permit. There is currently no visa requirement for Americans, Canadians, New Zealanders or Australians entering Portugal. Nationals of those countries may stay for up to 90 days and then apply for an extension (usually another 90 days). However, travellers from outside the EU should check with the nearest Portuguese embassy or consulate before going, as visa regulations are subject to change.

Bottles of port

CUSTOMS INFORMATION

Restrictions apply to liquids carried on board aircraft. Consulates can generally provide up-to-date information on particular customs

regulations and prohibited goods. For more details on customs and other tax-related matters, see pages 432–3.

TOURIST INFORMATION

The Portuguese Ministry of Tourism divides the country into a number of touristic regions, which are separate from its administrative districts. All major cities or large towns within each touristic region have a municipal tourist office (*Posto de Turismo*), as do the larger towns on Madeira and the Azores. This guide gives details of the relevant tourist information office for each sight. Here, visitors can obtain information about the region, town plans, maps and details on regional events. In some cases they will also sell tickets for local shows and concerts. Information about local hotels will be available from the tourist office, though they will not usually book the accommodation.

Opening hours vary, but they generally follow the same opening hours as local shops. There are tourist offices at all the major airports, as well as in all cities and large towns. In more rural areas, offices are often closed at weekends, and may not offer the same services that can be found in larger towns. Visitors can also obtain information prior to travelling, from Portuguese tourist offices abroad. These offices will normally provide visitors planning a trip with a wide range of useful maps, fact sheets and tourist brochures.

High season on a beach in the resort of Albufeira, in the Algarve

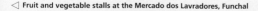

◁ **Fruit and vegetable stalls at the Mercado dos Lavradores, Funchal**

Signpost in the village of Marvão

ETIQUETTE

Although English is more widely spoken in Portugal than in neighbouring Spain, the Portuguese appreciate visitors' efforts, however small, to communicate in their language. A simple *bom dia* (good morning) or *boa tarde* (good afternoon) can work wonders. For any attempts at more advanced communication, be prepared to repeat yourself several times, allowing your listener to adjust to the peculiarities of your pronunciation. Portuguese retains some old-fashioned modes of address that are seen as polite rather than formal, including *o senhor* and *a senhora* where English uses "you". This contrasts with the informality of cheek kisses, used between men and women, as well as between women, in most situations except formal and business introductions. Men tend to shake hands.

Although dress is generally relaxed these days, arms should be covered up and shorts should not be worn when visiting churches.

LANGUAGE

Written Portuguese is fairly similar to Spanish, so if you know Spanish you should have little difficulty understanding Portuguese text. However, spoken Portuguese sounds nothing like spoken Spanish.

The Portuguese are proud of their language, which is widely spoken throughout the world as a result of former colonial ties with Brazil and a number of countries in Africa, and they may take offence at being addressed in Spanish. A phrase book containing the most useful words and phrases, along with their phonetic pronunciations, can be found on pages 495–6.

MUSEUMS AND ADMISSION PRICES

Most of Portugal's museums are run by the state, although there are also some private ones. In addition to the main national museums and galleries, there are many regional ones scattered around the country. These cover a range of topics, from the history of a region to the works of local artists. Most museums charge a small fee, which varies from €1 to €3. These charges are sometimes reduced or waived altogether on Sundays and public holidays.

Museum tickets

People under 14 and pensioners (with proof of age) may obtain a 40 per cent discount. Those under 26 with a *Cartão Jovem* (youth card) or ISIC card (International Student Identity Card) are entitled to half-price entrance *(see p448)*.

Tourists to Lisbon may also buy a Lisboa Card, available from the airport, tourist offices and travel agents. It allows free entry to 26 of the city's museums and reduced entry to many others, including a number of historic monuments, as well as free public transport for a fixed period. Lisboa Cards are valid for one, two or three days.

OPENING HOURS

Museums are usually open 10am–5pm from Tuesday to Sunday, with many closing for lunch either noon–2pm or 12:30–2:30pm. Smaller and private museums may have different opening times. Most museums and some sights close on Mondays and public holidays. Major churches are open during the day without a fixed timetable, although some may close between noon and 4pm. Smaller churches and those in rural areas may only be open for religious services, and in some cases you may need to find the keyholder for admittance.

PUBLIC CONVENIENCES

The Portuguese for toilets is *casa de banho*. If the usual figures of a man or woman are not shown, look for *homens, senhores* or *cavalheiros* (men), and *senhoras* or *damas* (ladies).

Toilet facilities are provided at motorway service areas approximately every 40 km (25 miles) and at coach and railway stations. They can also be found in shopping malls.

TRAVELLERS WITH SPECIAL NEEDS

Facilities for the disabled in Portugal have improved greatly, with wheelchairs and adapted toilets available at airports and the main stations, and reserved car parking increasingly evident. Ramps and lifts are installed in many public places. Some buses can accommodate wheelchair-bound passengers (identified

A dial-a-ride bus for the disabled *(transporte especial para deficientes)*

Family fun at the Slide and Splash park near Estombar, in the Algarve

by the blue-and-white wheelchair emblem at the front of the vehicle).

In addition, Lisbon and Oporto have a dial-a-ride bus service (see the Directory for more details). To book, phone and indicate when and where you would like to be picked up, and your destination. The operators speak only Portuguese, so you may need to ask your hotel for help. There is also a special taxi service in Lisbon, but it has to be booked well in advance.

Portugal-based specialist tour companies **Accessible Portugal** and **Wheeling Around the Algarve** design holidays for people who have reduced mobility or are in wheelchairs.

TRAVELLING WITH CHILDREN

Portugal is a family-friendly destination, and children from four to 12 years old enjoy a number of travel and sightseeing discounts, sometimes as much as 75 per cent; for those under four, it's very often free. Most restaurants have half-price kids' menus, and hotels and some guesthouses offer reduced tariffs for children under the age of eight if they share their parents' room. Many of the larger establishments provide a supervised crèche and playground facilities.

SENIOR TRAVELLERS

Travellers aged 60 and over can take advantage of a range of benefits – including discounted rail travel and reduced admission fees to many sightseeing attractions such as museums, national monuments and theatres – simply by showing some ID. Buses and metro trains have designated seating areas reserved for the elderly and the infirm, but you'll find that passengers are usually more than willing to give up their own seat if necessary.

STUDENT TRAVELLERS

Young people aged 12–25 may buy a *Cartão Jovem* (youth card), which costs about €8 and is valid for a year. It offers travel insurance and discounts for shops, restaurants, museums, travel and youth hostels *(see p.376)*. This card is supplied by the **Instituto Português da Juventude** (Portuguese Youth Institute). The International Student Identity Card (ISIC) provides the same benefits as the *Cartão Jovem* and can be bought in your own country. Backpackers have a

Student card

good choice of budget accommodation in Portugal, including several award-winning hostels in Lisbon.

WOMEN TRAVELLERS

Travelling alone in Portugal is fairly safe for women, although common principles, such as keeping to well-lit, public areas after dark, still apply. Some areas of Lisbon, such as the Baixa, Bairro Alto and Cais do Sodrá, and Oporto's Ribeira (riverfront) are best avoided at bar closing time. Resorts on the Algarve and Lisbon coasts tend to be the worst for unwanted attention. Hitching alone is not safe; use registered taxis or take public transport.

RELIGION

Roman Catholicism is the dominant religion in Portugal. Church services are held most evenings and every Sunday morning, as well as on religious holidays. Sightseeing in churches may sometimes be difficult (and is certainly not encouraged) while services are in progress.

Churches of other denominations, including Church of England, Baptist and Evangelical, can be found in larger towns and cities. **St Vincent's Anglican Church**, which travels from place to place, holds a number of religious services in the Algarve.

TIME

Portugal and Madeira follow Britain in adopting Greenwich Mean Time (GMT) in winter and moving the clocks forward one hour from March to September (as in British Summer Time). In the Azores, clocks are one hour behind GMT in winter and the same as GMT in summer. The 24-hour clock is more commonly used throughout Portugal.

ELECTRICITY

Voltage in Portugal is 220 volts, and plugs have two round pins. Most hotel bathrooms offer built-in adaptors for electric razors.

RESPONSIBLE TRAVEL

Portugal's green credentials are impressive, and they are exemplified by ecotourism organizations such as **Center**, which promotes cultural and environmental awareness through its partnership with Solares de Portugal, a nationwide network of historic private properties that are open to the public. At Zambujeira do Mar, in the Alentejo, is **Zmar**, the country's first sustainable and eco-friendly campsite, which harnesses solar energy to power its chalets.

Marina at Vilamoura resort, Algarve

Around 183 beaches and 16 marinas in Portugal have been honoured with a **Blue Flag** award, an initiative that works towards sustainable development through water quality, environmental education and safety. Many of these beaches are in the Algarve, where the Vilamoura resort has also won a Green Globe award, an accolade that recognizes businesses that strive to protect and conserve resources, reduce waste and prevent pollution.

Visitors to Portugal can make their own eco-friendly contribution by purchasing organic produce at local markets and opting for souvenirs made from cork, a totally sustainable product.

CONVERSION CHART

Imperial to Metric
1 inch = 2.54 centimetres
1 foot = 30 centimetres
1 mile = 1.6 kilometres
1 ounce = 28 grams
1 pound = 454 grams
1 pint = 0.6 litres
1 gallon = 4.6 litres

Metric to Imperial
1 millimetre = 0.04 inches
1 centimetre = 0.4 inches
1 metre = 3 feet 3 inches
1 kilometre = 0.6 miles
1 gram = 0.04 ounces
1 kilogram = 2.2 pounds
1 litre = 1.8 pints

DIRECTORY

EMBASSIES AND CONSULATES

United Kingdom
Rua de São Bernardo 33,
1249-082, Lisbon.
Map 4 D2.
Tel 213 924 000.

British Consulates
Azores *Tel 296 628 175.*
Funchal *Tel 291 212 860.*
Lisbon *Tel 213 924 000.*
Oporto *Tel 226 184 789.*
Portimão *Tel 282 490 750.*

Australia
Avenida da Liberdade
200, 2°, 1269-121,
Lisbon. **Map** 5 C5.
Tel 213 101 500.

Canada
Avenida da Liberdade
198–200, 3°, 1269-121,
Lisbon. **Map** 5 C5.
Tel 213 164 600.

Republic of Ireland
Rua da Imprensa à
Estrela 1, 4°,1200, Lisbon.
Map 4 E2.
Tel 213 929 440.

USA
Avenida das Forças
Armadas, 1600, Lisbon.
Tel 217 273 300.

TOURIST OFFICES

Coimbra
Largo da Portagem,
3000–337, Coimbra.
Tel 239 488 120.
www.turismo-centro.pt

Faro
Avenida 5 de Outubro
18–20, 8001–902, Faro.
Tel 289 800 400.
www.visitalgarve.pt

Lisbon
Lisboa Welcome Center,
Rua do Arsenal 15, 1100-
038, Lisbon. **Map** 7 A2.
Tel 210 312 700.
www.atl-turismolisboa.pt

Oporto
Rua Clube dos Fenianos
25, 4000–172, Oporto.
*Tel 223 393 470 or
223 393 472.*
www.portoturismo.pt

In the UK:
11 Belgrave Square,
London SW1X 8PP.
Tel 020 7201 6666.

In the USA:
Tel 800 767 8842.

In Canada:
Tel 416 921 7376.

DISABLED TRAVELLERS

Buses for the Disabled
Lisbon Carris.
Tel 213 613 141.
*(Bookings taken
9am–5pm Mon–Fri.)*

Oporto Portuguese
Red Cross.
Tel 226 006 353.
*(Buses for the Oporto
area must be booked
several days in advance.)*

Accessible Portugal
Tel 217 203 130.
www.accessibleportugal.
com

Wheeling Around the Algarve
www.apparelyzed.com/
support/holidays/world
wide/wheelchair-access-
portugal.html

STUDENT INFORMATION

Instituto Português da Juventude
Avenida da Liberdade 194,
1250 Lisbon.
Tel 213 179 200.
http://juventude.gov.pt/
portal

PLACES OF WORSHIP

St George's Church
Rua de São Jorge à Estrela
6, Lisbon.
Tel 214 692 303.

St James's Church
Largo da Maternidade de
Júlio Dinis, Oporto.
Tel 226 064 989.

Lisbon Synagogue
Rua A. Herculano 59,
Lisbon. *Tel 213 881 592.*

St Vincent's Anglican Church (Algarve)
Apartado 135, Boliqueime.
Tel 289 366 720.

RESPONSIBLE TRAVEL

Blue Flag
www.blueflag.org

Center
www.center.pt

Zmar Eco Camping Resort
www.zmar.eu

Personal Health and Security

Pharmacy sign

Portugal does not have a serious crime problem, but simple precautions should always be taken. Watch out for pickpockets in crowded areas and on public transport; avoid carrying large amounts of cash; and never leave valuables in parked cars. The police are helpful, but bureaucratic. Reporting a crime can be slow but is necessary. For minor health complaints, consult a pharmacy.

Police station at Bragança in the Trás-os-Montes region

PORTUGUESE POLICE

In all main cities and towns, the police force is the *Polícia de Segurança Pública* (PSP). A special unit patrols the rail and metro systems. Law and order in rural areas is kept by the *Guarda Nacional Republicana* (GNR). The *Brigada de Trânsito* (traffic police) division of the GNR, recognizable by its red armbands, is responsible for patrolling roads.

Motorway SOS telephone

REPORTING A CRIME

If you have any property stolen, contact the nearest police station immediately. Theft of documents, such as a passport, should also be reported to your consulate. Many insurance companies insist that policy holders report any theft within 24 hours. The police will file a report, which you will need in order to claim from your insurance company on your return home. Contact the PSP in towns or cities, or the GNR in rural areas. In all situations, keep calm and be polite to the authorities to avoid delays. The same applies should you be involved in a car accident. In rural areas you may be asked to accompany the other driver to the nearest police station to complete the necessary paperwork. Ask for an interpreter if no one there speaks English.

PERSONAL SECURITY

Violent crime is rare in Portugal; however, it is worth taking a few sensible precautions. In Lisbon, avoid quiet areas such as the Baixa after dark, and don't stroll alone through Bairro Alto, Alfama or around Cais do Sodré after bars' closing time. Always be aware of pickpockets and bag-snatchers. Similar precautions apply to some of the resorts in the Algarve and to the Ribeira district of Oporto.

It is a good idea to ignore any jeers and heckles – they are usually not as serious as they sound. Other precautions include not carrying large amounts of cash, and holding on to mobile phones and cameras. If you are robbed, do not try to resist.

WHAT TO DO IN AN EMERGENCY

The number to call in an emergency is 112. Dial the number and ask for the service you require – police (*polícia*), ambulance (*ambulância*) or fire brigade (*bombeiros*). If you need medical treatment, the casualty department (*serviço de urgência*) of the closest main hospital will treat you. On motorways and main roads, use the orange SOS telephone to call for help if you have a car accident. The service is in Portuguese; press the button and then wait for the operator, who will connect you.

HEALTH PRECAUTIONS

No vaccinations are needed for visitors, although doctors recommend being up-to-date with tetanus, diptheria and measles jabs. Tap water is safe to drink throughout the country. If you are visiting during the summer it is

Traffic policeman

PSP officer

GNR officer

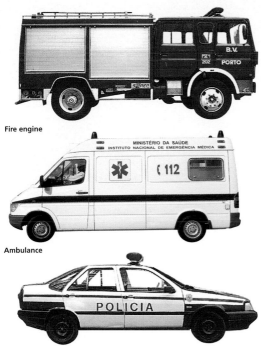

Fire engine

Ambulance

Police car

advisable to bring insect repellent, as mosquitoes, while they do not present any serious health problems, can be a nuisance.

MEDICAL TREATMENT

Social security coverage is available for all EU nationals, although you may have to pay first and reclaim later. To reclaim, you must obtain a European health insurance card (EHIC) before you travel. Apply for this at post offices throughout the UK or from the Department of Health; it comes with a booklet called *Health Advice for Travellers*, which explains entitlements and how to claim them. The card covers emergencies only, so medical insurance is strongly advised. Bear in mind that private health care is expensive in Portugal, and get an itemized bill for your insurance carrier. The **British Hospital** in Lisbon has English-speaking doctors, as do health centres on the Lisbon coast and throughout the Algarve. For details, look in the local English press.

PHARMACIES

In the event of minor ailments, head to the nearest pharmacy *(farmácia)*, where they can diagnose simple health problems and suggest treatment. Pharmacists can dispense a range of drugs that are available on prescription in many other countries. The sign for a *farmácia* is a green cross on a white background. They are open from 9am to 1pm and 3pm to 7pm on weekdays, and from 9am to 1pm on Saturdays. Each pharmacy displays a card showing the address of the nearest all-night pharmacy and a list of those with late closing (10pm).

TRAVEL AND HEALTH INSURANCE

While specific health risks are rare in Portugal, accidents can happen, so you should always take out comprehensive travel and health insurance before travelling. Make sure the policy covers you for

medical and health costs for an injury or sudden illness abroad, medical repatriation and personal liability. Always check any exclusions, and ensure your policy covers you for all the activities you wish to undertake. It's also a good idea to make several photocopies of the policy, leaving one copy at home for reference.

An insurance policy that covers the costs of legal advice, issued by companies such as Europ Assistance or Mondial Assistance, will help with the legal aspects of your insurance claim should you have an accident.

If you have not arranged this cover and need legal assistance, call your nearest consulate or the **Ordem dos Advogados** (lawyers' association), which can give you the names of English-speaking lawyers and help you with obtaining representation.

Lists of interpreters, if you require one, are given in the local Yellow Pages (*Páginas Amarelas*) under *Tradutores e Intérpretes*, or you can contact the **AP Portugal**, which is based in Lisbon.

Banking and Local Currency

BPI Bank logo

As a member state of the European Union, Portugal falls within the eurozone, and its unit of currency is the euro. Traveller's cheques are the safest way to carry money, but cashing them can be quite expensive and time-consuming, plus they are seldom accepted as payment. Credit and debit cards are often a more convenient option, and funds can be readily obtained from ATMs. Still, it is always a good idea to arrive with enough euros in cash to cover one or two days' expenditure. Bank exchange rates can vary and bureaux de change may be more convenient.

A *Multibanco* machine (ATM)

BANKS AND BUREAUX DE CHANGE

In Portugal, banks are open between 8:30am and 3pm, Monday to Friday. Some branches stay open for longer, usually until 6pm – enquire at individual banks to find out which these are, since they sometimes change. Banks are closed at week-ends and on public holidays.

Money can be changed at banks, bureaux de change (*agências de câmbios*) and at many hotels. Bank branches are everywhere, but be aware that their rates of exchange and commissions vary. Waiting times and bureaucratic practices can make banks a time-consuming option. Bureaux de change charge higher commissions than many banks but offer a more expedient service, as well as longer opening hours (including weekends). As a rule, hotels have the highest rates of exchange. At banks and bureaux de change you may be asked to show your passport or some other form of identification for exchange transactions. Alternatively, there are financial service companies, like Western Union, based in Portugal that can arrange person-to-person money transfers and money orders.

TRAVELLER'S CHEQUES AND CARDS

Traveller's cheques are a safe but not very convenient way of carrying money. It is rare for shops or hotels to accept them as payment, and cashing them may be quite expensive. In general, bureaux de change are better for this than banks, where commissions may be high.

Most visitors, however, find it most practical and convenient to withdraw cash from an automatic teller machine (*Multibanco*, or MB) using their credit/ debit card. *Multibanco* machines are typically found inside and outside bank branches, at public transport hubs and in shopping centres. Most accept Visa, MasterCard, American Express, Maestro and Cirrus cards. Bear in mind that transaction fees are always charged when withdrawing cash on a card, and that these are sometimes irrespective of the amount withdrawn. Fewer and larger withdrawals are therefore preferable to many small ones.

Larger denomination banknotes, such as the €200 and €500 notes, have a limited circulation in Portugal, and some establish-ments may refuse to accept them, preferring instead to work with smaller, more manageable denominations.

REGIONAL COST VARIATIONS

Costs in Portugal can vary considerably depending on which part of the country you are visiting. For example, hotel prices in Lisbon and Oporto and at some of the larger holiday resorts in the Algarve are generally higher than in similar establishments located inland and in the north of the country. Likewise, in these locations, you should expect to pay more for meals and drinks. In Madeira and the Azores, taxi hire is pricier than on the mainland.

DIRECTORY

MAJOR BANKS

Banco Bilbao Vizcaya Argentária
Avenida da Liberdade 222, Lisbon.
Tel 213 117 200.

Banco Português de Investimento (BPI)
Rua Tenente Valadim 284, Oporto.
Tel 226 073 100.

Banco Santander
Rua Dr. João Dias 16–18, Faro.
Tel 289 860 820.

Barclays Bank
Avenida da República 50, Lisbon.
Tel 217 911 285 or 707 50 50 50.

Caixa Geral de Depósitos
Rua do Ouro 49, Lisbon.
Tel 707 242 424.

LOST CARDS OR TRAVELLER'S CHEQUES

American Express
Tel 707 504 050.

MasterCard
Tel 020 7557 5000 (UK).

Travelex
Tel 01733 502 000 (UK).

Visa
Tel 0800 891 725 (UK) or 020 7937 8111 (general enquiries).

THE EURO

The euro (€) is the common currency of the European Union. It went into general circulation on 1 January 2002, initially for 12 countries. Portugal was one of those 12 countries, and its original currency, the escudo, was phased out by March 2002. EU members using the euro as sole currency are known as the eurozone. Several EU members have opted out of joining this common currency.

Euro notes are identical throughout the eurozone countries, each one including designs of fictional architectural structures. The coins, however, have one side identical (the value side), and one side with an image unique to each country. Both notes and coins are exchangeable in each of the eurozone countries.

Banknotes
Euro banknotes have seven denominations. The €5 note (grey in colour) is the smallest, followed by the €10 note (pink), €20 note (blue), €50 note (orange), €100 note (green), €200 note (yellow) and €500 note (purple). All notes show the stars of the European Union.

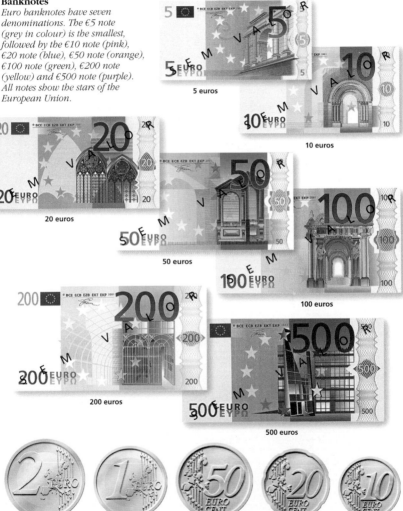

5 euros

10 euros

20 euros

50 euros

100 euros

200 euros

500 euros

2 euros

1 euro

50 cents

20 cents

10 cents

Coins
The euro has eight coin denominations: €1 and €2; 50 cents, 20 cents, 10 cents, 5 cents, 2 cents and 1 cent. The €1 and €2 coins are both silver and gold in colour. The 50-, 20- and 10-cent coins are gold. The 5-, 2- and 1-cent coins are bronze.

5 cents

2 cents

1 cent

Media and Communication

TMN mobile phone logo

Information and telecommunications technology in Portugal has advanced at a remarkable rate. Visitors should have few problems using public telephones, whether coin-operated or those that accept phone cards. The country's three main mobile phone operators, Vodafone, TMN and Optimus, all have roaming agreements and excellent coverage across the entire country, including Madeira and the Azores. Internet cafés can be found in all urban areas and some post offices also offer online facilities. English-language newspapers and magazines are readily available in major cities.

PUBLIC TELEPHONES

Public pay phones come in both the coin and the card variety, as well as in combinations of the two. They are found in booths in the streets as well as in bars, cafés and shopping centres. Card operated phones are more common and more convenient, accepting a variety of phone cards available from post offices, newsagents, tobacconists and Telecom company outlets. They also tend to be cheaper, with an average of about 3 cents for a local call. Some also accept credit cards, although that incurs a small extra charge.

International calls and calls to mobile phones are more expensive, but there are always special cards and deals to be had. An alternative is to make a call from a post office, if you have neither change or a card. You simply step into a free booth, make your call, and pay the cashier afterwards. The cost per unit is relatively low. Some cafés, restaurants and bars also have a units meter connected to their phone and calculate the cost of your call. They charge more than the post office but less than many of the hotels.

When making international calls and calls to mobile phones in particular, bear in mind that rates are lower off-peak between 9pm and 9am and at weekends and on public holidays.

A public phone booth

MOBILE PHONES

There are four main GSM frequencies (Global System for Mobile Communications) in use around the world, so if you want to guarantee that your phone will work, make sure you have a quad-band phone. Tri-band phones from outside the US are also usually compatible but, because the US uses two frequency bands itself, a US tri-band phone may only have limited global coverage. Contact your service provider for clarification.

To use your mobile phone abroad you may need to get "permission" from your network operator as often you have to pay a substantial premium for the international leg of the call.

Another popular option is to purchase a local SIM card – the electronic chip that links your phone to a particular network – that can be topped up with credit and uses the local mobile phone networks. You can only do this if your handset is "unlocked" – some operators lock their phones to specific networks. In Portugal hiring or even purchasing a mobile phone is a good idea if you intend to remain in the country for an extended period. The cost of calling both nationally and internationally will be significantly cheaper and you will not be charged for calls to a Portuguese phone unlike a phone from another country.

It is worth checking your insurance policy in case your phone gets stolen and keeping your network operator's helpline number handy for emergencies. Remember to bring an electrical adaptor for the charger if necessary.

INTERNET & EMAIL

Internet access is widely available in Portugal, with a plethora of Internet cafés found in all major cities and towns – especially at coastal resorts – and even some villages. Charges vary, but expect to pay between €1 to €3 per hour online. Facilities can also be found at some coach and rail terminals, large hotels, selected guesthouses, municipal libraries, local

MAKING A TELEPHONE CALL

- To make a call within a town or region, or from one town or region to another, dial the nine-digit number that you require.
- To phone Portugal from abroad dial the Portugal country code (+ 351), and then the nine-digit local number that you require.
- To call abroad from Portugal, dial 00 then the country code and local number. The country code for US and Canada is 1; Ireland is 353; UK is 44; Australia is 61; and New Zealand is 64.
- Portugal's directory enquiries number is 118. For international directory enquiries dial 177.

branches of the *Instituto Português da Juventude* (IPJ) and some youth hostels.

Post office customers can use NetPost, an Internet facility payable per hour using a special card. Wi-Fi hotspots, found in airports and some shopping malls, enable users to log in on the go, but this facility is not always free. Those using mobile phones or laptops should check with their Internet service provider (ISP) before departure.

POSTAL SERVICES

The postal service in Portugal is known as the *Correios*. It is reasonably efficient: a letter sent to a country within the EU should take five to seven

Internet cafés found all over Portugal

days, and a letter sent to the USA or further afield should take about seven to ten days. The *Correios* sign depicts a horse and rider in red.

Post offices are usually open from 9am until 6pm from Monday to Friday. Central post offices in major

cities have different opening times. These are 8am–10pm from Monday to Friday and 9am–6pm on Saturdays.

SENDING A LETTER

ctt correios

Correios (postal service) logo

First-class mail is known as *correio azul* and second-class mail is called *normal*. First-class letters are posted in blue postboxes and second-class post in red ones. At post offices there may be separate slots for national and international mail. There is also an express mail service called EMS, and for valuable letters, a recorded delivery service (*correio registado*) is available. Stamps (*selos*) can be bought from post offices or from any shop displaying the red and white *Correios* sign, and also from vending machines. These are found in airport terminals and in railway stations, as well as on the streets of large towns. If mailing larger items, using an international courier company such as FedEx or DHL may be a better option. Both have offices in Lisbon.

Portuguese newspapers

PORTUGUESE ADDRESSES

Portuguese addresses often include both the storey of a building and the location within that floor. The ground floor is the *rás-do-chão* (r/c), first

floor *primeiro andar* (1°), the second floor is expressed as 2°, and so on. Each floor is divided into left, *esquerdo* (E or Esq^{do}), right, *direito* (D or D^{to}).

NEWSPAPERS AND MAGAZINES

English-language newspapers printed in Europe are available at large newsagents on the day of publication, including the American *International Herald Tribune*. Various other European newspapers and periodicals are also generally on sale the same day of home publication, except following a bank holiday. UK papers and magazines purchased abroad are more expensive, and some sections, notably weekend supplements, are not included.

Portuguese daily newspapers include *Diário de Notícias* and *Público*. The weekly *Portugal News*, published on Friday, is the country's main English-language publication. Catering to the expat population, it provides a range of news and information about local events. Listings magazines available include the weekly *Time Out Lisbon*, published in Portuguese. A special edition, *Lisbon for Visitors*, is printed in English.

RADIO AND TELEVISION

Portugal has two state-owned television channels, RTP1 and RTP2, and two privately-owned channels, SIC and TVI. Most foreign-language programmes are broadcast in the original language, with Portuguese subtitles. Other European and international broadcasts are available via satellite and cable, and include the usual 24-hour news, music, sports and feature channels. The Algarve based Kiss FM is the only station that broadcasts year-round in the English language; RDP radio broadcasts in English in the summer only.

Information on collection times   First-class postbox

Portugal's Postboxes
First-class letters should be posted in blue (Correio Azul) boxes and second-class letters in red boxes.

Second-class postbox

TRAVEL INFORMATION

Portugal, Madeira and Porto Santo, as well as the major Azorean islands, have airports served by TAP, the national airline. European and other airlines fly to the international airports of Lisbon, Oporto, Faro and Funchal, which all get busier during the holiday season. Charter flights are often the cheapest alternative. Portugal's mainland rail network is fast and modern on busy lines such as Lisbon–Oporto and Lisbon–Faro, but slow on provincial lines.

Logo of TAP Air Portugal

Trains are inexpensive, especially if you are eligible for any of the discounts. Buses are sometimes faster and generally offer a wider choice of departures than the rail network. Car rental is not cheap (pre-arranged package deals are often the best value), but it does offer the greatest flexibility. Diesel costs less than petrol, while motorway tolls can be expensive. Road users should also be aware that Portugal has one of Europe's highest road-accident rates.

GREEN TRAVEL

Portugal's provincial rail system is not very extensive, and many railway stations are located some distance away from the towns and villages they serve. A private vehicle is therefore necessary to explore much of the country beyond major cities and main tourist zones. Likewise, without your own transport, it is difficult to travel around Madeira properly; in the Azores it is almost impossible. Buses and coaches are the alternatives, but off the beaten track they can be slow and infrequent.

Cycle tourism is gaining popularity. A designated cycle route, the 240-km (150-mile) **Ecovia** in the Algarve, connects Vila Real de Santo António in the east with Sagres in the west. Hikers fare better, since Portugal enjoys an extensive network of tracks, trails and footpaths. The **Instituto Português de Cartografia e Cadastro** sells good large-scale maps. The country's leading environ-

mental organization, **Quercus**, arranges guided walks in parts of the country and is involved in a number of ongoing eco projects.

Fuel-efficient houseboats can be hired to explore the Alqueva reservoir in the Alentejo, the largest man-made lake in Europe. This option does away with the need for a vehicle, and passengers can travel around the lake's 1,200-km (745-mile) shoreline with minimal disruption to the environment.

ARRIVING BY AIR

Lisbon and, to a lesser extent, Oporto have regular scheduled flights from European capitals and major cities, including London, Paris, Madrid, Rome, Munich, Frankfurt, Zurich and Milan. Most of these are daily, and in many cases there are several daily connections. **TAP**, Portugal's national carrier, currently operates about five daily flights from London (four from Heathrow

depending on your departure day and one from Gatwick) to Lisbon, and one to Oporto (from Heathrow and two from Gatwick), plus several weekly ones. Faro is the usual Portuguese destination for charter flights and low-cost airlines, particularly during the holiday season. Many companies also fly to Lisbon.

Madeira and Porto Santo are important package-holiday destinations, and charter flights are available to Funchal. The Azores are becoming a more accessible holiday destination, in terms of flights and prices *(see opposite)*.

Check-in at Lisbon Airport

AIRPORT	INFORMATION	DISTANCE TO CITY CENTRE	TAXI FARE TO CITY CENTRE	PUBLIC TRANSPORT TO CITY CENTRE
Lisbon	218 413 500	7 km (4 miles)	€10–15	🚌 20 minutes
Oporto	229 432 400	20 km (12 miles)	€15–20	🚌 30 minutes
Faro	289 800 800	6 km (4 miles)	€8	🚌 15 minutes
Funchal	291 520 700	18 km (11 miles)	€18–24	🚌 30 minutes
Ponta Delgada	296 205 400	3 km (2 miles)	€6	🚌 10 minutes
Horta	292 943 511	10 km (6 miles)	€7–8	🚌 15 minutes

AIR FARES

Charter flights are available to Lisbon and Faro, particularly during the summer months. Tickets have fixed outward and return dates, but as they are often cheaper than regular one-way tickets, many people only use the outward flight.

Major low-cost airlines also fly to Faro: **Ryanair** from Stansted, Liverpool, East Midlands, Glasgow, Dublin and Shannon; **easyJet** from Gatwick, Luton, Stansted, East Midlands, Bristol, Liverpool, Glasgow and Belfast; and **bmibaby** from East Midlands, Birmingham and Cardiff.

The best way to get a cheap ticket is to check websites such as www.cheapflights.com, which offer an overview of currently available deals.

LONG-HAUL FLIGHTS

Travellers from North America will usually have to change at a European hub. **Delta** flies to Lisbon via Paris (using a partner airline) daily. TAP's only direct flights from the US are out of Newark. South America is better served, thanks to Portugal's ties with Brazil: TAP has direct flights to and from several Brazilian destinations.

There are no direct flights to mainland Portugal from Canada, Australia or New Zealand; travellers from these countries usually change in London. North Americans wanting to visit the Azores will find a greater choice of direct connections, due to the large Azorean communities in the US and Canada. The same is true of Madeira.

TAP Air Portugal aircraft on the tarmac at Lisbon Airport

INTERNAL FLIGHTS

TAP also flies between major domestic destinations, including Lisbon, Oporto, Faro and Funchal. In partnership with **SATA**, TAP flies daily from Lisbon and Oporto to Funchal, and from Lisbon to São Miguel, Terceira and Faial in the Azores.

PACKAGE DEALS

Specialist holidays are a popular option in Portugal. These include stays in manor houses and *pousadas (see pp380–81)*, short breaks to Lisbon and Oporto, tennis and golfing holidays in the Algarve, and walking holidays in the Minho. These, together with package deals including hotel, villa or apartment accommodation, will often include bus transfer to your destination from the airport. Fly-drive deals are also available, to the Algarve especially, allowing you to spend less time at the airport dealing with paperwork. Car hire, when booked as part of a package deal, may be very reasonable. A list of companies specializing in these holidays is available from the **Portuguese National Tourist Office** (Turismo de Portugal).

Signs at the airport for visitors' facilities

(Carros de Aluguer / Rent a Car; Autocarros / Bus; Depósito de Bagagem / Left Luggage; Parque / Acesso do pobre)

DIRECTORY

GREEN TRAVEL

Ecovia (cycle routes)
www.ecoviasalgarve.org

Houseboats
www.amieiramarina.com

Instituto Português de Cartografia e Cadastro
Tel 213 819 600.

Quercus
www.quercus.pt

ARRIVING BY AIR

bmibaby
www.bmibaby.com

British Airways
London Tel 0870 850 9850.

easyJet
www.easyjet.com

Ryanair
www.ryanair.com

TAP Air Portugal
London Tel 0845 601 0932.
Dublin Tel 01 844 4300.
Lisbon Tel 707 205 700.

LONG-HAUL FLIGHTS

Delta
US Tel 800 221 1212.

INTERNAL FLIGHTS

SATA
Ponta Delgada.
Tel 707 227 282.

TAP
Lisbon Call Centre.
Tel 707 205 700.

PACKAGE DEALS

Portuguese National Tourist Office
11 Belgrave Square,
London SW1X 8PP.
Tel 020 7201 6666.

The spacious check-in area at Oporto Airport

Travelling by Rail

The Portuguese state railway, Comboios de Portugal (CP), provides an inexpensive, country-wide network. Quality of service can vary considerably, however, and while modernization to the system continues, progress is slow. The Alfa Pendular trains between Lisbon and Oporto, via Coimbra, and Lisbon and Faro, via Tunes, are fast and efficient, but for longer journeys, such as Lisbon to Évora, it may be quicker to take the bus.

High-speed Alfa Pendular train at Santa Apolónia station in Lisbon

Carved arch over entrance to Lisbon's Rossio station *(see p82)*

ARRIVING BY TRAIN

There are two main routes into Portugal by train. The first is to travel from Austerlitz station in Paris, changing at Irún on the French-Spanish border, then continuing on to the Portuguese border town of Vilar Formoso in the north. The train splits near Coimbra, heading north for Oporto and south for Lisbon, coming into Santa Apolónia station. The entire journey from London to Lisbon, using the Eurostar to reach Paris, takes 30 hours.

An alternative is to travel on the overnight train from Madrid, passing through Marvão and Santarám, then on to Lisbon. Travel from Madrid to Lisbon takes 10 hours. This train, called the "hotel-train", has luxurious carriages, some of which have showers.

TRAVELLING BY TRAIN

Most areas of Portugal are served by rail, although the more remote lines, such as Tua to Mirandela, have sadly been made obsolete, due to new road links. A bus service covers any gaps in the system, although it is wise to confirm that the service you require exists before setting off.

There are several categories of train in Portugal. The most comfortable and quickest is the modern Alfa Pendular, which travels between Lisbon, Coimbra and Oporto, and Lisbon, Tunes and Faro. The Rápido Inter-Cidades (IC) is only marginally slower, although less luxurious, and connects most important towns and cities. Most smaller towns and villages throughout the country are served by the Regional and the Inter-Regional lines. These local lines are slower than the Rápido and Alfa Pendular, with fewer facilities, but they stop at many more stations.

Logo for Comboios de Portugal

CITY STATIONS

Lisbon has four rail termini. **Santa Apolónia** station, on Avenida Infante Dom Henrique, serves the north and all international destinations. **Oriente**, by the Expo site Parque das Nações, is on the same line as Santa Apolónia and serves the south. **Entrecampos**, in the city centre, also serves the south. For more routes south and east, cross the river (using the Fertagus train service, which runs on the 25 de Abril bridge) to catch a train from **Barreiro** station. Trains for Estoril and Cascais (a 30-minute trip) leave from **Cais do Sodré** station.

Rossio station, near Praça dos Restauradores, serves Sintra and stations along the coast as far north as Figueira da Foz. Care should be taken on the Lisbon to Sintra line at night.

Coimbra has two mainline stations: trains from Lisbon and Oporto stop at **Coimbra B**, a five-minute shuttle ride from the central **Coimbra**.

Oporto has two mainline stations: international and long-distance trains come into **Campanhã**, to the east of the city; regional and suburban trains come into **São Bento** in the centre. From here there is a shuttle service to **Campanhã** station. The former rail station at Trindade is now a Metro station.

Exterior of station at Santiago do Cacém with *azujelo* decoration

Time Destination Platform Type of train Other remarks

Departures board in Santa Apolónia station, Lisbon

FARES

Fares within Portugal are fairly cheap in comparison with other European countries and there are numerous discounts available. Children under the age of four travel free, and those from four to twelve pay half-fare. There are also discounts for groups, students and pensioners.

Visitors are advised to check the CP website for changing information regarding fares and also for information on discounted tickets for selected groups. First-class travel on Portugal's trains is 40 per cent more expensive than second class, and second-class travel, while fairly basic on some lines, is usually sufficiently comfortable.

Families can save money by using the *cartão de família*, which gives good discounts, but only on journeys over 150 km (90 miles). It works as follows: one member of the family pays full fare, other members over 13 years of age pay half the full fare, and those under 13 pay a quarter of the fare.

An Interrail pass for young people under 26 gives unlimited travel on all European trains for a month, so will allow travel both to and within Portugal (if it is bought outside the country). The slightly more expensive Interrail 26-plus pass does not allow travel in Spain. For journeys within Portugal only, the Eurodomino pass offers unlimited travel for three, four, six or eight days, with a reduced rate offered to those younger than 26.

PORTUGAL'S PRINCIPAL RAILWAY LINES

BUYING TICKETS

Tickets for Alfa and Rápido (IC) trains can usually be booked up to 30 days ahead, although some services only offer 10-day advance bookings, so it is important to check first. Reservations can be made at stations or travel agents. If you want to buy a ticket the day you travel, arrive early as queues at the ticket office are normal, especially during peak hours and holiday periods. It is important that you buy a ticket before boarding, otherwise you are liable to be fined on the spot by the conductor. If buying your ticket online via CP's website (in English and Portuguese), note that you'll have to print out the ticket to present it with your passport.

Sign at ticket office showing where to buy advance tickets

Sign at ticket office showing where to buy tickets on day of travel

TIMETABLES

Main stations in Portugal provide a complete rail timetable, the Guia do Horário Oficial, which details all routes for Alfa Pendular, IC, Inter-Regional and Regional trains. A section in Portuguese only has details of the tickets and discounts that are available. The CP website displays all travel information including a countrywide timetable.

Driving in Portugal

Automóvel Clube de Portugal logo

Portugal's road network includes an expanding motorway system, but some older main roads may be in need of repair, while minor roads can be very rough and tortuous. Traffic jams are a problem in and near cities. Never attempt driving in the rush hour, and be wary of reckless Portuguese drivers.

Always carry your passport, licence, log book or rental contract, and car insurance. Failure to produce these *documentos* if the police stop you will incur a fine. It's obligatory for drivers and passengers to don green fluorescent vests following a breakdown or an accident. In addition, drivers must carry a collapsible warning triangle in the trunk to be used in the event of such an emergency.

A steep road near Gouveia in the Serra da Estrela *(see pp220–21)*

ARRIVING BY CAR

The quickest route is to cross the French–Spanish border at Irún and then take the E80 via Valladolid to Vilar Formoso in Portugal. To go to Lisbon or the Algarve, turn off at Burgos, head for Cáceres and then on to Badajoz.

Taking the car ferry to northern Spain from the UK reduces time on the road, but crossings are extremely long: 24 hours to Santander and 35 hours to Bilbao. **Brittany Ferries** travels to Santander leaving from Plymouth and Portsmouth (once a week, from April to December). **P&O**'s Portsmouth–Bilbao line runs twice-weekly services from February to December. A weekly car ferry operated by the Spanish company **Naviera Armas** *(see p463)* connects Portimão in the Algarve with Funchal in Madeira. There are no ferry services from the mainland to the Azores.

Driving time may also be reduced by using the Motorail link from Paris Gare d'Austerlitz to Lisbon, a twice-weekly service. Drivers load their cars one day, travel by passenger train the next, and pick up their cars on the third day. **French Railways** in the UK will supply information.

TRAVELLING AROUND BY CAR

Major roads include EN *(Estrada Nacional)* roads, many of which have been upgraded to either IP *(Itinerário Principal)* or IC *(Itinerário Complementar)* roads. IP roads are much used by heavy goods lorries avoiding motorway tolls, and they can be slow as a result.

Always fill up with petrol in town before setting off, as petrol stations can be scarce in remote areas. The best road maps are by Michelin or the Portuguese motoring organization, the **ACP** *(Automóvel Clube de Portugal)*.

RULES OF THE ROAD

Traffic drives on the right hand side, continental rules of the road apply and the international sign system is used. Unless there are signs to the contrary, traffic from the right has priority at squares, crossroads and junctions. Cars on round-abouts travel anticlockwise, and have priority over waiting traffic. There is very little advance warning of pedestrian crossings.

Seat belts must be used, and the alcohol limit is 0.05 per cent. Speed limits are 50 kph (31 mph) in towns and 90 kph (55 mph) on other roads and, and 120 kph (74 mph) on motorways. Breaking the speed limit incurs an on-the-spot fine, as does talking on a mobile phone while driving.

MOTORWAYS AND TOLLS

Portugal's expanding motor-way network *(see map on back endpaper)* links Lisbon with Braga and Guimarães in the north, and Oporto with Amarante and the Algarve in the south. Another section goes from Lisbon to Leiria, and a cross-country stretch runs east to the Spanish border at Elvas.

Traffic queueing to pass over the Ponte 25 de Abril, Lisbon

Apart from some sections near Lisbon and Oporto, all motorways have two lanes. Tolls are payable on motorways and on Lisbon's bridges – the Ponte 25 de Abril and the Ponte Vasco da Gama. Do not use the Via Verde (green lane) at tolls; this is only for the use of drivers who subscribe to an electronic system allowing them to pay automatically and avoid congestion.

PARKING

Finding a parking space in cities can be difficult. Most parking spaces in Lisbon and Oporto are now pay-and-display during the working week. A simpler and safer, if more expensive, alternative is one of the many new underground car parks. Follow the blue signs with a white P.

Signs in Lisbon for the coast, south via the Ponte 25 de Abril, and zoo

PETROL (GASOLINE)

Petrol is relatively expensive, and generally the same price countrywide. Diesel (*gasóleo*) is cheaper than petrol. Some pumps are self-service and colour-coded: green for un-leaded and black for diesel.

BREAKDOWN SERVICES

There is a reciprocal breakdown service between the ACP and other organiza-tions. To qualify, drivers should take out European cover with their own organization. On the motorway, use the SOS phones, and state that you are entitled to ACP cover. For drivers without cover, most towns have a garage with breakdown lorry.

A motorway toll – the left lane reserved for users of the Via Verde system

CAR HIRE

Car hire agencies may be found at Lisbon, Faro and Oporto airports and in main towns. Local firms usually offer better rates than international ones, but check the condition of the car and the insurance coverage carefully. You must have an international driving licence, be over the age of 23 and have held a licence for at least one year.

GREAT DRIVES

A particularly scenic drive is the EN1063 from Foz de Odeleite in the eastern Algarve, which hugs the banks of the River Guadiana all the way to the pretty riverside village of Alcoutim. The N255 from Reguengos de Monsaraz to Moura skirts the Alentejo's Barragem de Alqueva lake. To explore port wine country, take the N222 from Peso do Régua to Pinhão in the Douro.

For breathtaking mountain scenery in Madeira, head northwest out of Funchal, and follow the narrow hairpin ER107 to Curral das Freiras, in the heart of the island.

The R1-1 coastal road encircling Pico, in the Azores, allows you to take in both a stark, majestic landscape and the Atlantic Ocean.

DIRECTORY

ARRIVING BY CAR

Brittany Ferries
Tel 08709 076 103.

French Railways Motorail Department
Tel 0844 848 3339.

P&O
Tel 08716 64 64 64.

BREAKDOWN SERVICES

ACP
*Tel 213 180 100
or 707 509 510.*

CAR HIRE

A.A. Castanheira/ Budget, Lisbon
Tel 210 323 605.
www.budgetportugal.com

Auto Jardim, Faro
Tel 289 818 491.

Budget, Oporto
Tel 226 076 970.

Europcar, Faro
Tel 289 891 650 or 289 818 777.

Hertz, Lisbon
Tel 213 812 430.

Hertz, Oporto
Tel 223 395 300 or 229 437 690.

Sixt, Lisbon
Tel 218 407 927.

ROAD NUMBERS

Roads in Portugal may have up to three different numbers. Thanks to a building and upgrading pro-gramme, former EN or *Estrada Nacional* roads can also be IP (*Itinerário Principal*) roads. A road with an E (*Estrada Europeia*) number indicates that it is also a direct international route.

The Bragança-Oporto road is now the IP4, part motorway (A4) and part dual carriageway.

The road's original EN number (*Estrada Nacional*).

The E82 is an interna-tional route, ending in Spain near Valladolid.

Travelling by Coach

The logo of EVA, one of the country-wide coach companies

Since the privatization of Portugal's bus network, the Rodoviária Nacional (RN), coach companies have multiplied, and some routes are now even run by foreign companies. Regional operators compete with each other to offer better services to more destinations, and as a result, many coach journeys, such as Lisbon to the Algarve, are quicker and often more comfortable than the equivalent train journeys. Coaches also cover the increasing number of defunct sections of railway, such as Mirandela–Bragança and Beja–Moura.

A Rodonorte coach, which covers the far north of the country

GETTING TO PORTUGAL BY COACH

Travelling to Portugal by coach is cheap but very time-consuming. **Eurolines** runs a weekly summer service from Victoria Coach Station in London to Oporto. Passengers change in Area Suco in central Spain, and the journey takes 34 hours in total. The London-to-Lisbon service, which runs all year, takes even longer. Passengers change in Paris and spend two nights on the coach.

TRAVELLING AROUND BY COACH

Coach operators in Portugal include **Renex**, which links Faro, Lisbon, Oporto and Braga, and **EVA**, which focuses on the Algarve. **Rodoviária de Lisboa** connects Lisbon with Estremadura. In Vila Real, **Rodonorte** covers the extreme north, and **Rede Expressos**, based in Oporto, covers the inland areas of Portugal.

There is no central coach station in Lisbon and Oporto, as companies are private and operate separately, but the main coach terminus in Lisbon is on Avenida Casal Ribeiro. In Oporto, the main departure and arrival points are at Rua das Carmelitas and Praça

Dona Filipa de Lencastre. Information on routes and prices is available from tourist offices and travel agencies.

COACH TOURS

Bus and coach tours around Lisbon and Oporto are plentiful. **Cityrama** runs sightseeing tours of Lisbon and its coast, and daytrips to sights such as Batalha, Sintra and Mafra. It also offers a night-time tour of the city, taking in the Jerónimos monastery and then dinner with a *fado* show. From Oporto, it runs tours of the Minho and Douro valleys, and a six-day trip to Lisbon. **Gray Line**, part of Cityrama,

A Cityrama coach on an excursion along the Lisbon coast

also offers daytrips from Lisbon to Évora, a cruise on the Tagus and a trip lasting three days to the Algarve. Pick-up points are at the main hotels or central locations. It is also possible to arrange longer trips to areas of historical or scenic interest.

In the Algarve, there are frequent coach trips to places of interest such as Loulé, Silves and Monchique, the southwest and the River Guadiana, and further afield to Évora and Lisbon. Tourist offices, hotels and travel agencies can help with these, and pick-up points are the main coastal hotels.

DIRECTORY

LONDON

Eurolines
52 Grosvenor Gardens, London SW1W 0AU. *Tel 08717 81 81 77.* www.eurolines.com

NORTHERN PORTUGAL

Rede Expressos
Praça Marechal Humberto Delgado, Estrada das Laranjeiras, 1500-423 Lisbon. *Tel 213 581 472.* www.rede-expressos.pt

Renex
R Campo Mártires da Pátria 37, Oporto. *Tel 222 050 972.* www.renex.pt

Rodonorte
Rua D. Pedro de Castro, Vila Real. *Tel 259 340 710.* www.rodonorte.pt

LISBON

Cityrama/Gray Line
Avenida Duque d'Avila 116b, 1050-084 Lisbon. *Tel 213 191 090.* www.cityrama.pt

Renex
Gare do Oriente. *Tel 218 956 836.*

Rodoviária de Lisboa
Avenida do Brasil 45. *Tel 217 928 180.*

ALGARVE

EVA
Avenida da República 5, Faro. *Tel 289 899 700.* www.eva-bus.com

Travelling Around the Islands

On the rocky, mountainous islands of Madeira and the Azores, the pace of transport is necessarily slow, and some places are only accessible on foot. Driving needs care and patience, and you may find organized trips by coach or taxi are more relaxing and rewarding.

Inter-island aircraft on the runway on Pico

ISLAND HOPPING

TAP flies several times a day between Funchal and Porto Santo in the Madeira group; on the Azores, flights are operated by SATA *(see p457)*. Flights to Flores and Corvo are often disrupted by bad weather, so for extensive island hopping it is a good idea to insure against delays. SATA flights should be confirmed at least 72 hours before take-off.

A weekly car ferry service operated by Spanish company **Naviera Armas** connects Portimão, in the Algarve, with Funchal. The voyage takes 22 hours, and it's wise to book well ahead in the summer. **Porto Santo Line** runs a daily car ferry service between Madeira and Porto Santo. Regular car ferry services connect all the islands of the Azores except Corvo, which is served by passenger ferry, and are run by **Atlanticoline**.

AROUND MADEIRA

Companies such as **Intervisa** and **Blandy** organize coach trips. Taxis can be hired, but car rental is far more flexible *(see p461)*. Book ahead and allow plenty of time for travel: roads are steep and tortuous. Motorway extensions along the south coast have cut journey times considerably, but many places are still accessible only on foot.

AROUND THE AZORES

Cars can be hired on all the Azores except Corvo, from firms such as **Ilha Verde Rent-A-Car**. Charges are high, and the roads are precipitous, so it may be wise, at least on the smaller islands, to take a taxi tour. For day trips, agree a price, itinerary and return time before setting off. You should also pay for the driver's lunch. Check the weather first: if clouds conceal the mountains, there is no point setting out.

Tourist offices can supply information on coach trips by **Agência Açoreana de Viagens** and others, and on boat trips along the coast. Bicycles can be hired, but the mountainous terrain makes cycling difficult.

On the smaller islands it is usually easy to hitch a lift.

To enjoy the Azores on foot, ask your taxi driver to drop you off at the start of a route and pick you up further on. Try to obtain a detailed map of the Azores before arrival. Some routes are listed in specialist guidebooks sold locally.

DIRECTORY

MADEIRA

Blandy
Avenida Zarco 2,
Funchal. *Tel* 291 200 600.

Intervisa
Rua dos Aranhas 32, Funchal.
Tel 291 203 922.

AZORES

Agência Açoreana de Viagens
R. de Lisboa, Edifício
Varela 2º Andar,
Ponta Delgada, São Miguel.
Tel 296 301 880.

Ilha Verde Rent-A-Car
Praça 5 de Outubro 19,
Ponta Delgada.
Tel 296 304 890.

FERRY SERVICES

Naviera Armas
Tel (0034) 902 456 500.
www.navieraarmas.com

Porto Santo Line
Tel 291 210 300.
www.portosantoline.pt

Atlanticoline
Tel 296 282 092/93.
www.atlanticoline.pt

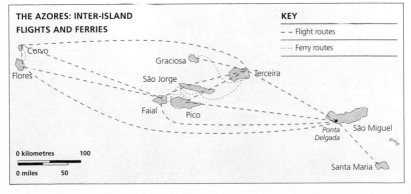

THE AZORES: INTER-ISLAND FLIGHTS AND FERRIES

KEY

– – Flight routes

---- Ferry routes

Corvo

Flores

Graciosa

São Jorge

Terceira

Faial

Pico

Ponta Delgada

São Miguel

Santa Maria

0 kilometres 100

0 miles 50

Travelling in Lisbon and Oporto

Sign for Metro in Lisbon

The interesting parts of most towns and cities in Portugal – generally the *centró histórico* – are small and eminently walkable, if you have both the time and inclination. In hilly cities such as Oporto and, particularly, Lisbon, the steep climbs can be avoided by using a choice of options such as centenarian tram, funicular or lift. Other cities are well served by buses, trolleybuses and taxis. Transport of any kind is best avoided during rush hour (8–10am and 5:30–7:30pm).

BUSES

Buses are a practical way to travel round and see the main cities, and Lisbon has an extensive network. When boarding the bus, enter at the front door and exit by the central door.

Tickets may be bought from the driver on boarding and must be clipped by the (*obliterador*) machine near the driver. However, it is much cheaper to buy tickets beforehand, usually for two journeys. Travelling without a valid ticket, if discovered by roaming inspectors, will incur a hefty fine.

Every bus (*autocarro*) must display its destination (*destino*) on a sign located at the front and most bus stops (*paragens*) have information for passengers about the route the bus will take.

BUS TOURS

In Oporto, **Cityrama** runs city tours at least twice a week, and more often in summer. They include a visit to a port lodge with tasting (*see p249*). Tickets are sold at the Cityrama office, and the tourist office in Praça Dom João I, where the buses depart. Cityrama also operates sightseeing tours in Lisbon, Madeira and the Azores, however, they have no office, but the tourist office can take bookings and enquiries.

TRAMS AND FUNICULARS

Fun ways of exploring Lisbon are by tram (*eléctrico*), funicular or lift (both *elevador*). Oporto has two short tram routes along and near the waterfront, and a funicular, the Elevador dos Guindais. In Lisbon, **Carris** runs a "hill tour" (*Linha das Colinas*) by antique tramcar.

A variety of funiculars offer wonderful views over Lisbon and ascend from river level up to the Bairro Alto: the Elevador da Bica starts near Cais do Sodré station and the Elevador da Glória goes from Praça dos Restauradores. The lifts in the Elevador de Santa Justa take visitors to a café at the top of the Bairro Alto (*see p84*). The Elevador da Lavra, can be taken from Praça dos Restauradores, which climbs to the Hospital São José.

LISBON METRO

Lisbon's Metro network has four lines, mainly on the north-south axis, and is divided into zones. It is the most efficient way to get around, especially during rush hour (8–10am and 5:30–7:30pm). The Metro operates between 6:30am and 1am.

Tickets are bought from machines or ticket offices at the station and are sold as reusable charge cards. The card will expire after one year

Viva Viagem card

TICKETS IN LISBON

Bus, tram, metro and funicular tickets are all the same and can be bought from any Carris kiosk. The basic multitrip Carris ticket is for two journeys and valid for an unlimited number of days. Other options are 1- and 3-day tickets. The Metro has its own system. Choose between a single-trip (€0.80) or a two-trip ticket (€1.60). There are also passes known as Viva Viagem cards; combined Carris/Metro 1-day tickets (€4.20); and 5-day Carris/Metro tickets (€21.00). Bring your ID to buy them.

Antique red tram operating the Linha do Tejo tour in Lisbon

No.15, Lisbon's long, streamlined tram

Lisbon's Elevador da Glória ascending to the Bairro Alto

and has an initial cost of €0.50. Cards must be validated on entering the platform area by passing them over an electronic scanner to open the gate, indicated by a green light. Exiting the station requires the same procedure.

When purchasing your cards you should always keep the receipt as you may need to present it when changing the card, or if it is damaged. Fines for travelling without a valid card are severe, so make sure it is in a safe and accessible place.

OPORTO METRO

Oporto's Metro network is in fact a light railway system with five lines that extend well beyond the city centre, through several zones. The hub is Trindade station, which is linked to the airport. The Metro operates between 6am and 1am.

Tickets (Andante Cards) can be bought from stations and at Andante shops and kiosks. Cards are reusable and holders need to know which zones they will cross to find out the cost.

Cards are validated by scanning machines. A single-trip ticket costs €0.95 across two zones and up to a maximum €3.45 for 12 zones. A one-day card (€5.00) permits travel across all zones. The Andante Inter-model card (€3.50) allows one-day travel on the Metro, buses, trams and the funicular.

TAXIS

Taxis are relatively inexpensive and if you share the cost it sometimes works out cheaper than a bus. Vacant taxis have their rooftop "taxi" signs switched on. From behind, they glow counter-intuitively red. The green lights indicate that the taxi is taken; two green lights mean that the higher rate is being charged (10pm–6am, weekends and public holidays), one that the normal rate applies. A flat rate of €1.60 is charged for any luggage placed in the trunk. The starting rate for a taxi

hailed in the street or at a taxi rank is €2.50. A telephone callout from a firm such as **Autocoope** costs an extra €0.80. The meter should always be used, although the driver might agree on a price beforehand for long trips.

DIRECTORY

BUS AND TRAM TOURS

Carris, Lisbon
Rua 1° de Maio 101,
1300 Lisbon.
Tel 213 613 000 or 213 613 354 (24 hrs).

Cityrama
Av. Duque D'Avila 116B,
1050-084 Lisbon.
Tel 213 191 090.

Coimbra Tourist Office
Largo da Portagem.
Tel 239 488 120.

RADIO TAXIS

Autocoope (Lisbon)
Tel 217 932 756.

Raditáxis (Oporto)
Tel 225 073 900.

METRO

Lisbon call centre
Tel 213 500 115 (Mon–Fri).
www.metrolisboa.pt

Oporto head office
Tel 225 081 000.
www.metrodoporto.pt

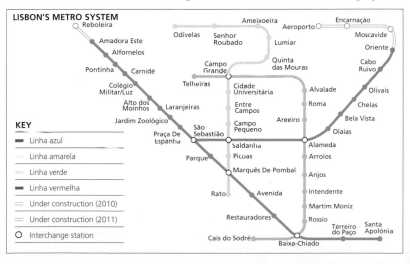

LISBON'S METRO SYSTEM

Reboleira
Ameixoeira
Encarnação
Aeroporto
Moscavide
Amadora Este
Odivelas
Senhor Roubado
Lumiar
Oriente
Alfornelos
Quinta das Mouras
Cabo Ruivo
Pontinha
Carnide
Campo Grande
Colégio Militar/Luz
Telheiras
Cidade Universitária
Alvalade
Olivais
Alto dos Moinhos
Laranjeiras
Entre Campos
Roma
Chelas
Jardim Zoológico
Campo Pequeno
Areeiro
Bela Vista
São Sebastião
Praça De Espanha
Olaias
Saldanha
Alameda
Parque
Picoas
Arroios
Marquês De Pombal
Anjos
Rato
Avenida
Intendente
Martim Moniz
Restauradores
Rossio
Santa Apolónia
Terreiro do Paço
Cais do Sodré
Baixa-Chiado

KEY

— Linha azul
— Linha amarela
— Linha verde
— Linha vermelha
= Under construction (2010)
= Under construction (2011)
○ Interchange station

General Index

Acknowledgments

Dorling Kindersley would like to thank the following people whose contributions and assistance have made the preparation of this book possible.

Consultant

Martin Symington was born and brought up in Portugal. A freelance travel writer, he is the author of *New Essential Portugal* (AA), and contributed to *Eyewitness Great Britain* and *Eyewitness Seville and Andalusia*. He writes extensively on Portugal and is a regular contributor to the *Daily Telegraph*, *Sunday Telegraph* and other British national newspapers.

Contributors

Susie Boulton studied history of art at Cambridge. She is a freelance travel writer and author of *Eyewitness Venice and the Veneto*.

Christopher Catling is a freelance travel writer and author of *Madeira* (AA) and *Eyewitness Florence & Tuscany*. He also contributed to *Eyewitness Italy* and *Eyewitness Great Britain*.

Marion Kaplan has written for a wide range of magazines and newspapers. She has lived in Portugal and wrote *The Portuguese* (Viking/Penguin 1992). She also contributed to the *Berlitz Travellers Guide to Portugal*.

Sarah Mcalister is a freelance editor and writer for *Time Out* guides and has spent much time in Lisbon and the surrounding area.

Alice Peebles is a freelance editor and writer and has worked on several *Eyewitness Travel Guides*.

Carol Rankin was born in Portugal. As an art historian, she has lectured extensively on most aspects of Portuguese art and architecture and has acted as consultant for various cultural projects.

Joe Staines is a freelance writer and co-author of *Exploring Rural Portugal* (Helm).

Robert Strauss is a travel writer and publisher. He worked for the Luso-British Institute in Oporto and has written several titles for Lonely Planet and Bradt Publications including the Portugal sections for *Western Europe* and *Mediterranean Europe* (Lonely Planet 1993).

Nigel Tisdall is a freelance journalist who has written many articles on the Azores. He also contributed to *France*, *Spain* and *California* in the Eyewitness Travel Guide series. Edite Vieira has written many books on Portuguese food including *The Taste of Portugal* (Grub Street). She is a member of the Guild of Food Writers and broadcasts regularly for the BBC World Service.

Additional Contributors

Dr Giray Ablay, Mihaela Rogalski, Gerry Stanbury, Paul Sterry, Paul Vernon.

Additional Illustrations

Richard Bonson, Chris Forsey, Chris Orr, Mel Pickering, Nicola Rodway.

Design and Editorial Assistance

Gillian Allan, Douglas Amrine, Emma Anacootee, Gillian Andrews, Paul Bernhardt, Uma Bhattacharya, Tessa Bindloss, Julie Bond, Vivien Crump, Joy FitzSimmons, Roger Green, Mark Harding, Vinod Harish, Mohammad Hassan, Paul Hines, Jasneet Kaur, Priya Kukadia, Vincent Kurien, Esther Labi, Kathryn Lane, Michelle de Larrabeiti, Felicity Laughton, Carly Madden, Nicola Malone, Helen Markham, Caroline Mead, Rebecca Mills, Robert Mitchell, Adam Moore, Helena Nogueira, David Noonan, Alice Peebles, Helen Peters, Marianne Petrou, Andrea Powell, Tom Prentice, Mani Ramaswamy, Andrew Ribeiro-Hargreave, Azeem Siddiqui, Sands Publishing Solutions, Sadie Smith, Alison Stace, Amanda Tomeh, Helen Townsend, Tomas Tranaeus, Fiona Wild.

Index

Hilary Bird.

Additional Photography

Steve Gorton/DK Studio, John Heseltine, Dave King, Martin Norris, Ian O' Leary, Jorge Morgado, Roger Phillips, Rough Guides/Eddie Gerald, Clive Streeter, Matthew Ward.

Photographic and Artwork Reference

Steven Evans, Nigel Tisdall.

Special Assistance

Emília Tavares, Arquivo Nacional de Fotografia, Lisboa; Luísa Cardia, Biblioteca Nacional e do Livro, Lisboa; Marina Gonçalves and Aida Pereira, Câmara Municipal de Lisboa; Caminhos de Ferro Portugueses; Carris, Lisboa; Enatur, Lisboa; Karen Ollier-Spry, John E. Fells and Sons Ltd; Maria Fátima Moreira, Fundação Bissaya-Barreto, Coimbra; Maria Helena Soares da Costa, Fundação Calouste Gulbenkian, Lisboa; João Campilho, Fundação da Casa de Bragança, Lisboa; Pilar Serras and José Aragão, ICEP, London; Instituto do Vinho do Porto, Porto; Simoneta Afonso, IPM, Lisboa; Mário Abreu, Dulce Ferraz, IPPAR, Lisboa; Pedro Moura Bessa and Eduardo Corte-Real, Livraria Civilização Editora, Porto; Metropolitano de Lisboa; Raquel Florentino and Cristina Leite, Museu da Cidade, Lisboa; João Castel Branco G. Pereira, Museu Nacional do Azulejo, Lisboa; TURIHAB, Ponte de Lima; Ilídio Barbosa, Universidade de Coimbra, Coimbra; Teresa Chicau at the tourist office in Évora, Conceição Estudante at the tourist office in Funchal and the staff at all the other tourist offices and town halls in Portugal.

Photography Permissions

Dorling Kindersley would like to thank the following for their assistance and kind permission to photograph at their establishments: Instituto Português do Património Arquitectónico e Arqueológico (IPPAR), Lisboa; Fundação da Casa de Alorna, Lisboa; Instituto Português dos Museus (IPM), Lisboa; Museu da Marinha, Lisboa; Museu do Mar, Cascais; Igreja de Santa Maria dos Olivais, Tomar and all the other churches, museums, hotels, restaurants, shops, galleries and sights too numerous to thank individually.

Picture Credits

t = top; tl = top left; tlc = top left centre; tc = top centre; tr = top right; cla = centre left above; ca = centre above; cra = centre right above; cl = centre left; c = centre; cr = centre right; clb = centre left below; cb = centre below; crb = centre right below; bl = bottom left; b = bottom; bc = bottom centre; blc = bottom left centre; brc = bottom right centre; bra = bottom right above; bla = bottom left above; br = bottom right; d = detail.

The work illustrated on page 119b, *Terreiro do Paço* by Dirk Stoop, is reproduced by kind permission of the Museu da Cidade, Lisboa.

The publisher would like to thank the following individuals, companies and picture libraries for permission to reproduce their photographs:

MAURÍCIO ABREU: 33t/cr, 147tr, 340bc/br, 360, 362t, 366b/c, 36/b, 368ca, 369c, 370tr/ca/cb, 372t, 373t, 399b; AISA: 38tr, 39tc, 39br, 56br, 104b; PUBLICICAÇÕES ALFA: 188b. ALAMY IMAGES: Jose Antunes 436tc, 437cr; Authors Image 10t; Buzz Pictures 438cra; Cephas Picture Library/Mick Rock 11br; Cephas Picture Library/Peter Stowell 434tl; Jean Dominique DALLET 435cla; Goncalo Diniz 124br; John Ferro Sims 124tc, 433c; Peter Forsberg 148cla; Terry Harris 13tc; Michael Howard 438bl; Iain Davidson Photographic 291tl; Iconotec 13br; Imagebroker/Günter Lenz 440tl; Imagebroker/Martin Moxter 457bl; Rainer Jahns 12br; John Warburton-Lee Photography/Ian Aitken 232cla; Marion Kaplan 433br; Craft Alan King 432tc; Yahdid Levy 149c; Cro Magnon 10br, 11clb, 290cla, 439tl; mediacolor's 291c; PCL 10cla; PhotoBliss 125tl; Les Polders 11tr, 233tl; H. Souto 433tl; Stockfolio/Gaboria 457bl; Stockfolio/Gaboria 434crb; Travelshots.com 149tl; Damien Tully 233c; Mikael Utterstrom 440br; Ken Walsh 105tl; ALGARVE TOURIST OFFICE: 288tr; ALLSPORT: Mike Powell 57crb; ARQUIVO NACIONAL DE FOTOGRAFIA-INSTITUTO PORTUGUÊS DE MUSEUS, Lisboa: Museu Nacional de Arte Antiga/Pedro Ferreira 96t, 97t; Francisco Matias 49tl; Carlos Monteiro 46cla; Luís Pavão 39tl, 52clb, 53c, 60t, 94bl/br, 95b, 97c; José Pessoa 24bl, 25tr, 45c, 49tr, 50tr, 51t/clb, 94tl/tr, 95t/cr, 96b, 97b; MUSEU NACIONAL DO AZULEJO: *Painel de azulejos Composição Geométrica*, 1970, Raul Lino-Fábrica Cerâmica Constância 27tr; Francisco Matias 26b; José Pessoa 26cra/27cb/bl; Colecções Arquivo Nacional de Fotografia/San Payo 39tr; Igreja de São Vicente de Fora/Carlos Monteiro 39bl; Museu Nacional dos Coches/José Pessoa 39bc, 101bl, 146br, 147b; Henrique Ruas 102b; Museu Nacional de Arqueologia/José Pessoa 40t, 41ca/cb, 103c; Museu Monográfico de Conimbriga 41tl; Museu de Mértola/Paulo Cintra 42cl; Igreja Matriz Santiago do Cacém/José Rubio 43tl; Museu Nacional Machado de Castro/Carlos Monteiro 44tl; José Pessoa 45tl; Biblioteca da Ajuda/José Pessoa 44cla; Museu de São Roque/Abreu Nunes 47tl; Museu Grão Vasco/José Pessoa 48bl; Universidade de Coimbra, Gabinete de Física/José Pessoa 52tr; Museu de Cerâmica das Caldas da Rainha/José Pessoa 54 cla; Museu do Chiado 55tl; Col. Jorge de Brito/José Pessoa 62/3tc; Col. António Chainho/José Pessoa 64b; Arnaldo Soares 64tr, 65tl; Museu Nacional do Teatro/Arnaldo Soares 64cl; Luisa Oliveira 65tr; Museu de Évora/José Pessoa 305 cra; TONY ARRUZA: 284–5, 38c, 44bl, *Portrait of Fernando Pessoa* by Almada Negreiros © DACS 2006: 56ca, 57br, 62/3c, 147ca.

JORGE BARROS S.P.A.: 228cr; INSTITUTO DA BIBLIOTECA NACIONAL E DO LIVRO, Lisboa: 37b, 46bca/b, 47crb, 50cb, 51br, 53br, 167bl, 185b; 285 (inset); GABRIELE BOISELLE: 146bl; BOUTINOT PRINCE WINE SHIPPERS, Stockport: 230br; THE BRIDGEMAN ART LIBRARY, with kind permission from Michael Chase: *Landscape near Lagos, Algarve, Portugal* by Sir Cedric Morris (1889–1982), BONHAMS, London: 8–9; By permission of THE BRITISH LIBRARY, London: *João I of Portugal being entertained by John of Gaunt* (d), from de Wavrin's *Chronicle d'Angleterre* (Roy 14E IV 244v) 46/7c; © Trustees of The British Museum, London: 43cla, 48br, 54bl.

CÂMARA MUNICIPAL DE LIEBOA: 51crb, António Rafael 62cl; CÂMARA MUNICIPAL DE OEIRAS: 52clb; CAMINHOS DE FERRO PORTUGUESES: 458c; CENTRO DE ARTE MODERNA: José Manuel Costa Alves 118tl; CENTRO EUROPEU JEAN MONNET: 57tl; CEPHAS: Mick Rock 28crb, 29c; CHAPITO: 126tr; COCKBURN SMITHES & CIA, S.A. (an Allied Domecq Company): 230crb; COMPANHIA CARRIS DE FERRO DE LISBOA: 447br, 464cr; CORBIS: Marco Cristofari 436cla; Reuters/Mike Finn-Kelcey 57tr; Peter Wilson 238br; CTT, CORREIOS: 455tc.

DIÁRIO DE NOTÍCIAS: 55cl; MICHAEL DIGGIN: 336t/b, 361t/b, 362b, 363t, 367t, 371t; Dow's Port 231cr.

EMPICS: Steve Etherington 32c; ESPAÇO TALASSA: Gerard Soury 370b; ET ARCHIVE: Naval Museum, Genoa 359b; Wellington Museum 195b; EUROPEAN COMMISSION: 453; GREG EVANS INTERNATIONAL: Greg Balfour Evans 289br; MARY EVANS PICTURE LIBRARY: 51bl, 63tr, 163b, 212b; EXPO '98: 57ca.

FOTOTECA INTERNACIONAL, Lisboa: Luís Elvas 33cl, 146tl/tr/cr; César Soares 27t, 38bl; LUÍZ O FRANQUINHO/ANTÓNIO DA COSTA: 339bla; FUNDAÇÃO DA CASA DE BRAGANÇA: 300t/c/b, 301bl; FUNDAÇÃO CALOUSTE GULBENKIAN: 126b; FUNDAÇÃO DA CASA DE MATEUS: Nicholas Sapieha 256b; Fundação Ricardo Do Espírito Santo Silva, Museu-Escola de Artes Decorativas Portuguesas 70c.

JORGE GALVÃO: 57clb; GERRY AND MANUELA BREEN'S ALGARVE AIRSPORTS CENTRE: 439br; GETTY

IMAGES: AFP/Francisco Leong 450bc; Richard Heathcote 443c; GIRAUDON: 48c; GUARDA NACIONAL REPUBLICANA: 450br.

ROBERT HARDING PICTURE LIBRARY: 17b; HEMISPHERES IMAGES: Laurent Giraudou 438tc; Philippe Renault 44ctl; KIT HOUGHTON: 32b; 147cb.

THE IMAGE BANK: Maurício Abreu 30bl; Moura Machado 23t, 363b, 373b; João Paulo 31cb, 229cl, 365t; IMAGES COLOUR LIBRARY: 228b; IMAGES OF PORTUGAL: 442cl.

MARION KAPLAN: 146cl, 229t/cr.

LUSA: António Cotrim 65c; André Kosters 91t; Manuel Moura 56bc, 359t; Luís Vasconcelos 90b.

JOSÉ MANUEL: 63br; ANTÓNIO MARQUES: 298c, 299b; Arxiu Mas: 50tl; METROPOLITANO DE LISBOA: 464cr; METROPOLITANO DE LISBOA, PAULO SINTRA: *Four Tiles from Lisbon Underground Station* (Cidade Universitária), Maria Helena Vieira da Silva © ADAGP, Paris and DACS, London 2006, 56tl; JOHN MILLER: 25b; MUSEU CERRALBO, Madrid: 42tl; MUSEU CALOUSTE GULBENKIAN, Lisboa: *Enamelled Silver Gilt Corsage Ornament, René Lalique* © ADAGP, Paris and DACS, London 2006, 114ca; 114t/ca/cb/b, 115t/ca/cb/b, 116c/b/t, 117b/t/c; MUSEU DA CIDADE, Lisboa: António Rafael 62tl/bl/br; 63c/bl; MUSEU DA MARINHA, Lisboa: 38br, 56cl, 106b.

NATIONAL MARITIME MUSEUM, London: 50ca; NATIONALMUSEET, Copenhagen: 48tr; NATURE PHOTOGRAPHERS: Brinsley Burbidge 338br, 339br; Andrew Cleave 338clb/bl, 339bl; Peter Craig-Cooper 331crb; Geoff du Feu 331b; Jean Hall 338bcr; Tony Schilling 338bcl; Paul Sterry 321c, 339bra/blc; NATUREPRESS: Juan Hidalgo-Candy Lopesino 32tl, 33br; NHPA: Michael Leach 371crb; Jean-Louis le Moigne 331cra.

OPORTO GOLF CLUB: 442br; ARCHIVO FOTOGRÁFICO ORONOZ: 38bc, 42/3c, 43b, 46lb, 181br.

PALACIO DE PENA: 118tl; Fotografia cedida y autorizada por el Patrimonio Nacional: 42cb;

PICTURES COLOUR LIBRARY: 432cl; PhotoLocation Ltd 12cl; THE PIERPONT MORGAN LIBRARY/ART RESOURCE, New York: 37t; POPPERFOTO: 55b; PORTO SANTO GOLFE: Filipe Pacheco 443cr; POUSADAS DE PORTUGAL: 380–81; POWERSTOCK PHOTOLIBRARY: 205t; PUNCHSTOCK: Digital Vision 12tr.

DIAS DOS REIS: 119tl; NORMAN RENOUF: 376b, 381b; REUTERS: Marcos Borga 436br; Nacho Doce 437tl; RCL, PAREDE: Rui Cunha 30t, 31cl, 32tr, 127t, 334–5, 338cra, 339cra, 341tr, 367c, 368t/b, 379; REX FEATURES: Sipa Press, Michel Ginies 57bl; MANUEL RIBEIRO: 26t; RADIO TELEVISÃO PORTUGUESA (RTP): 54t, 55clb, 56tr.

HARRY SMITH HORTICULTURAL PHOTOGRAPHIC COLLECTION: 339cla; SOLAR DO VINHO DO PORTO: 254b; SPECTRUM COLOUR LIBRARY: 238cl; TONY STONE IMAGES: Tony Arruza 30ca; Shaun Egan 288b; Graham Finlayson 41crb; Simeone Huber 286b; John Lawrence 31b; Ulli Seer 319t; SYMINGTON PORT AND MADEIRA SHIPPERS: Claudio Capone 29cl, 231t/cla/bc/br.

TAP AIR PORTUGAL: 457t, 456ca; Nigel Tisdall: 341tl, 364, 365b, 366t, 369t/b, 372c/b, 463t; TOPHAM PICTURE SOURCE: 56cra; ARQUIVOS NACIONAIS/TORRE DO TOMBO: 36, 44bla, 269b; TURIHAB: Roger Day 378tl; 378b.

NIK WHEELER: 316; PETER WILSON: 30br, 31tr, 56bl, 66, 82tl, 85br, 91b, 228tl/r/cl; WOODFALL WILD IMAGES: Mike Lane 171b; WORLD PICTURES: 289tc/bl; WYSE TRAVEL CONFEDERATION: 448cb.

Jacket
Front - DK IMAGES: Linda Whitwam clb; GETTY IMAGES; Stone/Stephen Johnson main image. Back - DK IMAGES: Joe Cornish cla, clb; Linda Whitwam bl, tl. Spine - DK IMAGES: Clive Streeter b; GETTY IMAGES: Stone/Stephen Johnson t.

Front Endpaper: All special photography except Maurício Abreu tl; Nik Wheeler br; Peter Wilson blc.

All other images © Dorling Kindersley. For further information see www.DKimages.com

---

SPECIAL EDITIONS OF DK TRAVEL GUIDES

DK Travel Guides can be purchased in bulk quantities at discounted prices for use in promotions or as premiums. We are also able to offer special editions and personalized jackets, corporate imprints, and excerpts from all of our books, tailored specifically to meet your own needs.

To find out more, please contact:
(in the United States) **SpecialSales@dk.com**
(in the UK) **TravelSpecialSales@uk.dk.com**
(in Canada) DK Special Sales at **general@ tourmaline.ca**
(in Australia)
business.development@pearson.com.au

Phrase Book

in Emergency

Help!	Socorro!	soo-**koh**-roo
Stop!	Páre!	**pahr'**
Call a doctor!	Chame um médico!	**shahm'** ooñ **meh**-dee-koo
Call an ambulance	Chame uma ambulância!	**shahm'** oo-muh añ-boo-lañ-see-uh
Call the police	Chame a polícia!	**shahm'** uh poo-**lee**-see-uh
Call the fire brigade	Chame os bombeiros!	**shahm'** oosh bom-**bay**-roosh
Where is the nearest telephone?	Há um telefone aqui perto?	ah ooñ te-le-**fon'** uh-**kee** pehr-too
Where is the nearest hospital?	Onde é o hospital mais próximo?	ond' eh oo ohsh-pee-**tahl' mysh** **pro**-see-moo

Communication Essentials

Yes	Sim	seeñ
No	Não	nowñ
Please	Por favor/ Faz favor	poor fuh-**vor** fash fuh-**vor**
Thank you	Obrigado/da	o-bree-**gah**-doo/duh
Excuse me	Desculpe	dish-**koolp'**
Hello	Olá oh-**lah**	
Goodbye	Adeus	a-**deh**-oosh
Good morning	Bom-dia	boñ **dee**-uh
Good afternoon	Boa-tarde	boh-uh **tard'**
Good night	Boa-noite	boh-uh **noyt'**
Yesterday	Ontem	oñ-**tayñ**
Today	Hoje	ohj'
Tomorrow	Amanhã	ah-mañ-**yañ**
Here	Aqui	uh-**kee**
There	Ali uh-**lee**	
What?	O quê?	oo keh
Which?	Qual?	**kwahl'**
When?	Quando?	**kwañ**-doo
Why?	Porquê?	poor-**keh**
Where?	Onde?	oñd'

Useful Phrases

How are you?	Como está?	**koh**-moo shtah
Very well, thank you.	Bem, obrigado/da.	bayñ o-bree-**gah**-doo/duh
Pleased to meet you.	Encantado/a.	eñ-kañ-**tah**-doo/duh
See you soon.	Até logo.	uh-**teh loh**-goo
That's fine.	Está bem.	shtah bayñ
Where is/are…?	Onde está/estão…?	ond' **shtah/shtowñ**
How far is it to…?	A que distância fica…?	uh kee dish-**tañ**-see-uh **fee**-kuh
Which way to…?	Como se vai para…?	**koh**-moo seh vy puh-ruh
Do you speak English?	Fala inglês?	**fah**-luh eeñ-**glehsh**
I don't understand.	Não compreendo.	nowñ kom-pree-**eñ**-doo
Could you speak more slowly please?	Pode falar mais devagar por favor?	**pohd'** fuh-**lar mysh** d'va-**gar** poor fuh-**vor**
I'm sorry.	Desculpe.	dish-**koolp'**

Useful Words

big	grande	**grañd'**
small	pequeno	pe-**keh**-noo
hot	quente	**keñt'**
cold	frio **free**-oo	
good	bom	boñ
bad	mau	**mah**-oo
quite a lot/enough	bastante	bash-**tañt'**
well	bem	bayñ
open	aberto	a-**behr**-too
closed	fechado	fe-**shah**-doo
left	esquerda	**shkehr**-duh
right	direita	dee-**ray**-tuh
straight on	em frente	ayñ **freñt'**
near	perto	**pehr**-too
far **loñj'**	longe	
up	para cima	pur-ruh **see**-muh
down	para baixo	pur-ruh **buy**-shoo
early	cedo	**seh**-doo
late	tarde	**tard'**
entrance	entrada	eñ-**trah**-duh
exit	saída	sa-**ee**-duh
toilets	casa de banho	**kah**-zuh d' **bañ**-yoo
more	mais	**mysh**
less	menos	**meh**-noosh

Making A Telephone Call

I'd like to place an international call.	Queria fazer uma chamada internacional.	kree-uh fuh-**zehr** oo-muh sha-**mah**-duh in-ter-na-see-oo-**nahl'**
a local call.	uma chamada local.	oo-muh sha-**mah**-duh loo-**kahl'**
Can I leave a message?	Posso deixar uma mensagem?	poh-soo day-**shar** oo-muh meñ-**sah**--jayñ

Shopping

How much does this cost?	Quanto custa isto?	**kwañ**-too **koosh**-tuh **eesh**-too
I would like…	Queria…	kree-uh
I'm just looking.	Estou só a ver obrigado/a.	shtoh soh uh vehr o-bree-**gah**-doo/uh
Do you take credit cards?	Aceita cartões de crédito?	uh-**say**-tuh kar-**toinsh** de **kreh**-dee-too
What time do you open?	A que horas abre?	uh kee oo-rash **ah**-bre
What time do you close?	A que horas fecha?	uh kee oo-rash **fay**-shuh
This one	Este	**ehst'**
That one	Esse	**ehss'**
expensive	caro	**kah**-roo
cheap	barato	buh-**rah**-too
size (clothes/shoes)	tamanho	ta-**man**-yoo
white	branco	**brañ**-koo
black	preto	**preh**-too
red	vermelho	ver-**melh**-yoo
yellow	amarelo	uh-muh-**reh**-loo
green	verde	**vehrd'**
blue	azul	uh-**zool'**

Types of Shop

antique shop	loja de antiguidades	**loh**-juh de añ-tee-gwee-**dahd'sh**
bakery	padaria	**pah**-duh-ree-uh
bank	banco	**bañ**-koo
bookshop	livraria	lee-vruh-**ree**-uh
butcher	talho	**tah**-lyoo
cake shop	pastelaria	**pash**-te-luh ree-uh
chemist	farmácia	far-**mah**-see-uh
fishmonger	peixaria	pay-shuh-**ree**-uh
hairdresser	cabeleireiro	kab'-lay-ray-roo
market	mercado	mehr-**kah**-doo
newsagent	quiosque	kee-**yohsk'**
post office	correios	koo-**ray**-oosh
shoe shop	sapataria	suh-puh-tuh-**ree**-uh
supermarket	supermercado	soo-**pehr**-mer-**kah**-doo
tobacconist	tabacaria	tuh-buh-kuh-**ree**-uh
travel agency	agência de viagens	uh-**jen**-see-uh de vee-**ah**-jayñsh

Sightseeing

cathedral	sé seh	
church	igreja	ee-**gray**-juh
garden	jardim	jar-**deeñ**
library	biblioteca	bee-blee-oo-**teh**-kuh
museum	museu	moo-**zeh**-oo
tourist information office	posto de turismo	**posh**-too d' too-**reesh**-moo
closed for holidays	fechado para férias	fe-**sha**-doo puh-ruh **feh**-ree-ash
bus station	estação de autocarros	shta-**sowñ** d' oh-too-kah-**roosh**
railway station	estação de comboios	shta-**sowñ** d' koñ-**boy**-oosh

Staying in a Hotel

Do you have a vacant room?	Tem um quarto livre?	tayñ ooñ **kwar**-too **leevr'**
room with a bath	um quarto com casa de banho	ooñ **kwar**-too koñ **kah**-zuh d' **bañ**-yoo
shower	duche	**doosh**
single room	quarto individual	**kwar**-too een-dee-vee-doo-**ahl'**
double room	quarto de casal	**kwar**-too d' kuh-**zahl'**
twin room	quarto com duas camas	**kwar**-too koñ **doo**-ash **kah**-mash
porter	porteiro	poor-**tay**-roo
key	chave	**shahv'**
I have a reservation.	Tenho um quarto reservado.	**tayñ**-yoo ooñ **kwar**-too re-ser-**vah**-doo

Eating Out

English	Portuguese	Pronunciation
Have you got a table for...?	Tem uma mesa para...?	tayñ oo-muh meh-zuh puh-ruh
I want to reserve a table.	Quero reservar uma mesa.	keh-roo re-zehr-var oo-muh meh-zuh
The bill please.	A conta por favor/faz favor.	uh kohn-tuh poor fuh-vor/fash fuh-vor
I am a vegetarian.	Sou vegetariano/a.	Soh ve-je-tuh-ree-ah-noo/uh
Waiter	Por favor!/Faz favor!	poor fuh-vor fash fuh-vor
the menu	a lista	uh leesh-tuh
fixed-price menu	a ementa turística	uh ee-mehñ-tuh too-reesh-tee-kuh
wine list	a lista de vinhos	uh leesh-tuh de veeñ-yoosh
glass	um copo	ooñ koh-poo
bottle	uma garrafa	oo-muh guh-rah-fuh
half bottle	meia-garrafa	may-uh guh-rah-fuh
knife	uma faca	oo-muh fah-kuh
fork	um garfo	ooñ gar-foo
spoon	uma colher	oo-muh kool-yair
plate	um prato	ooñ prah-too
napkin	um guardanapo	ooñ goo-ar-duh-nah-poo
breakfast	pequeno-almoço	pe-keh-noo-ahl-moh-soo
lunch	almoço	ahl-moh-soo
dinner	jantar	jan-tar
cover	couvert	koo-vehr
starter	entrada	eñ-trah-duh
main course	prato principal	prah-too prin-see-pahl
dish of the day	prato do dia	prah-too doo dee-uh
set dish	combinado	koñ-bee-nah-doo
half portion	meia-dose	may-uh doh-se
dessert	sobremesa	soh-bre-meh-zuh
rare	mal passado	mahl puh-sah-doo
medium	médio	meh-dee-oo
well done	bem passado	bayñ puh-sah-doo

Menu Decoder

Word	Pronunciation	Meaning
abacate	uh-buh-kaht'	avocado
açorda	uh-sor-duh	bread-based stew (often seafood)
açúcar	uh-soo-kar	sugar
água mineral	ah-gwuh mee-ne-rahl'	mineral water
(com gás)	koñ gas	sparkling
(sem gás)	sayñ gas	still
alho	al-yoo	garlic
alperce	ahl'-pehrce	apricot
amêijoas	uh-may-joo-ash	clams
ananás	uh-nuh-nahsh	pineapple
arroz	uh-rohsh	rice
assado	uh-sah-doo	baked
atum	uh-tooñ	tuna
aves	ah-vesh	poultry
azeite	uh-zayt'	olive oil
azeitonas	uh-zay-toh-nash	olives
bacalhau	buh-kuh-lyow	dried, salted cod
banana	buh-nah-nuh	banana
batatas	buh-tah-tash	potatoes
batatas fritas	buh-tah-tash free-tash	french fries
batido	buh-tee-doo	milk-shake
bica	bee-kuh	espresso
bife	beef	steak
bolacha	boo-lah-shuh	biscuit
bolo	boh-loo	cake
borrego	boo-reh-goo	lamb
caça	kah-ssuh	game
café	kuh-feh	coffee
camarões	kuh-muh-roysh	large prawns
caracóis	kuh-ruh-koysh	snails
caranguejo	kuh-rañ-gay-joo	crab
carne	karn'	meat
cataplana	kuh-tuh-plah-nuh	sealed wok used to steam dishes
cebola	se-boh-luh	onion
cerveja	sehr-vay-juh	beer
chá	shah	tea
cherne	shern'	stone bass
chocolate	shoh-koh-laht'	chocolate
chocos	shoh-koosh	cuttlefish
chouriço	shoh-ree-soo	red, spicy sausage
churrasco	shoo-rash-coo	on the spit
cogumelos	koo-goo-meh-loosh	mushrooms
cozido	koo-zee-doo	boiled
enguias	eñ-gee-ash	eels
fiambre	fee-añbr'	ham
fígado	fee-guh-doo	liver
frango	frañ-goo	chicken
frito	free-too	fried
fruta	froo-tuh	fruit
gambas	gam-bash	prawns
gelado	je-lah-doo	ice cream
gelo	jeh-loo	ice
goraz	goo-rash	bream
grelhado	grel-yah-doo	grilled
iscas	eesh-kash	marinated liver
lagosta	luh-gohsh-tuh	lobster
laranja	luh-rañ-juh	orange
leite	layt'	milk
limão	lee-mowñ	lemon
limonada	lee-moo-nah-duh	lemonade
linguado	leeñ-gwah-doo	sole
lulas	loo-lash	squid
maçã	muh-sañ	apple
manteiga	mañ-tay-guh	butter
mariscos	muh-reesh-koosh	seafood
meia-de-leite	may-uh-d' layt'	white coffee
ostras	osh-trash	oysters
ovos	oh-voosh	eggs
pão	powñ	bread
pastel	pash-tehl'	cake
pato	pah-too	duck
peixe	paysh'	fish
peixe-espada	paysh'-shpah-duh	scabbard fish
pimenta	pee-meñ-tuh	pepper
polvo	pohl'-voo	octopus
porco	por-coo	pork
queijo	kay-joo	cheese
sal	sahl'	salt
salada	suh-lah-duh	salad
salsichas	sahl-see-shash	sausages
sandes	sañ-desh	sandwich
santola	sañ-toh-luh	spider crab
sopa	soh-puh	soup
sumo	soo-moo	juice
tamboril	tañ-boo-ril'	monkfish
tarte	tart'	pie/cake
tomate	too-maht'	tomato
torrada	too-rah-duh	toast
tosta	tohsh-tuh	toasted sandwich
vinagre	vee-nah-gre	vinegar
vinho branco	veeñ-yoo brañ-koo	white wine
vinho tinto	veeñ-yoo teeñ-too	red wine
vitela	vee-teh-luh	veal

Numbers

0	zero	zeh-roo
1	um	ooñ
2	dois	doysh
3	três	tresh
4	quatro	kwa-troo
5	cinco	seeñ-koo
6	seis	saysh
7	sete	set'
8	oito	oy-too
9	nove	nov'
10	dez	desh
11	onze	oñz'
12	doze	doz'
13	treze	trez'
14	catorze	ka-torz'
15	quinze	keeñz'
16	dezasseis	de-zuh-saysh
17	dezassete	de-zuh-set'
18	dezoito	de-zoy-too
19	dezanove	de-zuh-nov'
20	vinte	veent'
21	vinte e um	veen-tee-ooñ
30	trinta	treeñ-tuh
40	quarenta	kwa-reñ-tuh
50	cinquenta	seen-kweñ-tuh
60	sessenta	se-señ-tuh
70	setenta	se-teñ-tuh
80	oitenta	oy-teñ-tuh
90	noventa	noo-veñ-tuh
100	cem	sayñ
101	cento e um	señ-too-ee-ooñ
102	cento e dois	señ-too ee doysh
200	duzentos	doo-zeñ-toosh
300	trezentos	tre-zeñ-toosh
400	quatrocentos	kwa-troo-señ-toosh
500	quinhentos	kee-nyeñ-toosh
700	setecentos	set'-señ-toosh
900	novecentos	nov'-señ-toosh
1,000	mil	meel'

Time

English	Portuguese	Pronunciation
one minute	um minuto	ooñ mee-noo-too
one hour	uma hora	oo-muh oh-ruh
half an hour	meia-hora	may-uh-oh-ruh
Monday	segunda-feira	se-goon-duh-fay-ruh
Tuesday	terça-feira	ter-sa-fay-ruh
Wednesday	quarta-feira	kwar-ta-fay-ruh
Thursday	quinta-feira	keeñ-ta-fay-ruh
Friday	sexta-feira	say-shta-fay-ruh
Saturday	sábado	sah-ba-doo
Sunday	domingo	doo-meen-goo

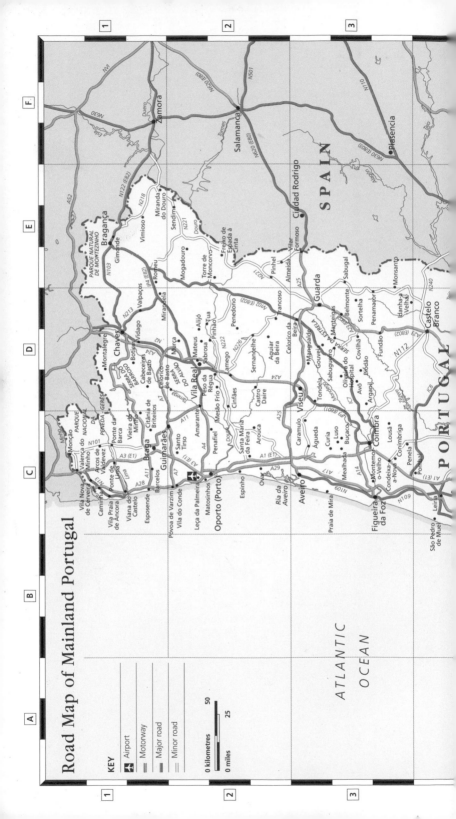

Road Map of Mainland Portugal

KEY

✈ Airport
━━━ Motorway
━━━ Major road
─── Minor road

0 kilometres   50
0 miles   25

ATLANTIC

OCEAN

SPAIN

PORTUGAL

Zamora
Salamanca
Plasencia
Ciudad Rodrigo
Guarda
Bragança
Chaves
Vila Real
Vila Nova de Cerveira
Caminha
Vila Praia de Âncora
Viana do Castelo
Esposende
Póvoa de Varzim
Vila do Conde
Leça da Palmeira
Matosinhos
Oporto (Porto)
Espinho
Ovar
Aveiro
Ria de Aveiro
Praia de Mira
Figueira da Foz
São Pedro de Muel
Leiria
Coimbra
Condeixa-a-Nova
Conímbriga
Penela
Lousã
Pombal
Montemor-o-Velho
Mealhada
Bucaco
Luso
Curia
Águeda
Caramulo
Viseu
Tondela
Oliveira do Hospital
Gouveia
Covilhã
Fundão
Castelo Branco
Idanha-a-Velha
Monsanto
Penamacor
Sabugal
Belmonte
Sortelha
Guarda
Almeida
Vilar Formoso
Pinhel
Freixo de Espada à Cinta
Torre de Moncorvo
Mogadouro
Miranda do Douro
Sendim
Vimioso
Gimonde
Valpaços
Mirandela
Murça
Alijó
Pinhão
Tua
Mateus
Sabrosa
Peso da Régua
Lamego
Mesão Frio
Cinfães
Castro Daire
Arouca
Santa Maria da Feira
Penafiel
Amarante
Santo Tirso
Guimarães
Braga
Barcelos
Citânia de Briteiros
Vieira do Minho
Ponte da Barca
Arcos de Valdevez
Ponte de Lima
Valença do Minho
Monção
Melgaço
Montalegre
Cabeceiras de Basto
Celorico de Basto
Vidago
Boticas
Korneu
Penedono
Trancoso
Celorico da Beira
Sernancelhe
Aguiar da Beira
Mangualde
Argamil
Bôdão
Avô
Sabugueiro
Arganil
Agueda
Oliveira do Hospital

PARQUE NACIONAL DA PENEDA-GERÊS
PARQUE NATURAL DE MONTEZINHO
SERRA DO BARROSO
SERRA DO MARÃO
SERRA DA ESTRELA

Douro
Minho
Lima
Duero
Tormes

N630
N501
N620 (E80)
N122 (E82)
N218
N103
N213
N221
N231
N226
N222
N2
N224
A24
A7
A11
A4
A3 (E1)
A28
A17
A29
A1 (E1)
A14
A25
IP2 (E802)
IP5 (E801)
N110
N240
N112
N109
N101
IC9
N240
A23
A52

1 2 3

A B C D E F